JAVASCRIPT®
THE NEW TOYS

T0179594

JavaScript®
The New Toys

JavaScript®

THE NEW TOYS

T.J. Crowder

wrox™

A Wiley Brand

JavaScript®: The New Toys

Copyright © 2020 by Thomas Scott "T.J." Crowder

Published simultaneously in Canada

ISBN: 978-1-119-36797-6
ISBN: 978-1-119-36797-0 (ebk)
ISBN: 978-1-119-36796-3 (ebk)

Manufactured in the United States of America

V152594_062220

For general information on our other products and services please contact our Customer Care Department within the United States at (877) 762-2974, outside the United States at (317) 572-3993 or fax (317) 572-4002.

Wiley publishes in a variety of print and electronic formats and by print-on-demand. Some material included with standard print versions of this book may not be included in e-books or in print-on-demand. If this book refers to media such as a CD or DVD that is not included in the version you purchased, you may download this material at http://booksupport.wiley.com. For more information about Wiley products, visit www.wiley.com.

Library of Congress Control Number: 2018965303

To Wendy and James, who've met late nights and working weekends with unstinting support and loving encouragement.

ABOUT THE AUTHOR

T.J. CROWDER is a software engineer with 30 years of professional experience, at least half that time working with JavaScript. He runs Farsight Software, a UK software consulting and product company. As one of the top 10 contributors on Stack Overflow and *the* top contributor in the JavaScript tag, he likes to use what he's learned to help others with the technical challenges they're facing, with an emphasis not just on imparting knowledge, but on helping with the process of solving problems.

T.J. started programming in his early teens in California, playing around with the Apple II and Sinclair ZX-80 and -81 using BASIC and assembly language. He got his first proper job with computers many years later, working a technical support position for a company with a PC (DOS) product for court reporters. While working support, he taught himself C from the TurboC manuals in the office, reverse-engineered the company's undocumented, compressed binary file format, and used that knowledge to create a much-requested feature for the product in his spare time (one the company soon started shipping). Before long the development department took him in and over the next several years gave him the opportunity, resources, and responsibility to grow into a programmer and, eventually, into their lead engineer, creating various products including their first Windows product.

At his next company he took on a professional services and developer education role that saw him customizing the company's enterprise product on-site for clients (using VB6, JavaScript, and HTML) and teaching training classes to the clients' developers; eventually he was writing the training classes. A move from the U.S. to London put him back in a straight development role where he was able to increase his software design, SQL, Java, and JavaScript skills before branching out into independent contracting.

Since then through circumstance he's been doing primarily closed-source remote development work for a variety of companies and organizations (a NATO agency, a UK local government authority, and various private firms) working primarily in JavaScript, SQL, C#, and (recently) TypeScript. The desire for community led him first to the PrototypeJS mailing list back in the day, then to Stack Overflow, and now to various platforms.

English and American by birth, American by upbringing, T.J. lives in a village in central England with his wife and son.

ABOUT THE TECHNICAL EDITOR

CHAIM KRAUSE is an expert computer programmer with over thirty years of experience to prove it. He has worked as a lead tech support engineer for ISPs as early as 1995, as a senior developer support engineer with Borland for Delphi, and has worked in Silicon Valley for over a decade in various roles, including technical support engineer and developer support engineer. He is currently a military simulation specialist for the US Army's Command and General Staff College, working on projects such as developing serious games for use in training exercises. He has also authored several video training courses on Linux topics, and has been a technical reviewer for over two dozen books.

ABOUT THE TECHNICAL PROOFREADER

MARCIA K. WILBUR is a technical communicator consulting in the semiconductor field, focusing on Industrial IoT (IIoT) and AI. Marcia holds degrees in computer science, technical communication, and information technology. As Copper Linux User Group president, she is heavily involved with the maker community leading West Side Linux + Pi and the East Valley leading regular Raspberry Pi, Beaglebone, Banana Pi/Pro, and ESP8266 Projects including home automation, gaming consoles, surveillance, network, multimedia, and other "pi fun".

ACKNOWLEDGMENTS

"I wrote a book" is almost never an accurate statement.

Sure, all the unquoted words in the book are mine. But none of them would be here if it weren't for others—others offering support, offering perspective, offering encouragement; others reviewing drafts to help cut the chaff and reveal the nugget of usefulness buried within; others asking questions in a variety of forums over the years, giving me the opportunity to practice the art and craft of explaining what meager knowledge I've been able to pick up; others answering *my* questions, directly and by pointing to resources; others helping hone my language and improve my wordcraft.

All of which waffle means: I owe thanks to a lot of people. This is my first proper book, and I made just about every mistake there is to make. The people below caught and corrected as many of them as they could. Any that remain are mine.

Primarily, thanks to my wife Wendy for her amazing support, for being an endless and willing source of strength and font of encouragement, for bringing me back when (as James Taylor puts it) I find myself careening in places where I should not let me go.

Thanks to my son James for putting up with Dad being squirrelled away in the office so much.

Thanks to my mother Virginia and father Norman for instilling in me a love of language, learning, reading, and writing. These are gifts that last a lifetime.

Thanks to my best friend Jock for being an ever-patient sounding board and source of encouragement—and, for that matter, for having been instrumental in getting me interested in programming in the first place.

Thanks to all of my editors and reviewers at Wiley & Sons: Jim Minatel and Pete Gaughan for supporting and maintaining the project even in the face of a frustrating author; David Clark and Chaim Krause for editorial and technical review; Kim Cofer for her excellent copyediting and help with grammar, syntax, and clarity; to Nancy Bell for her proofreading; to the artists and compositors in the production department; and to all the others I've failed to mention by name for supporting all aspects of the project.

Thanks to Andreas Bergmaier for helping me keep my technical T's crossed and I's dotted—Andreas' keen eye and deep understanding were a huge help throughout the book.

Thanks to TC39 member Daniel Ehrenberg of Igalia for helping me better understand how TC39 works, and for kindly reviewing and helping me refine Chapter 1. His gentle corrections, input, and insight dramatically improved that chapter.

Thanks to TC39 member Lars T. Hansen of Mozilla (co-author of the shared memory and atomics JavaScript proposal) for his kind and invaluable help with getting the details and scope right in Chapter 16. His deep knowledge and perspective made all the difference there.

And finally, thanks to you, dear reader, for giving your time and attention to my efforts here. I hope it serves you well.

CONTENTS

CHAPTER 15: REGULAR EXPRESSION UPDATES 397

INTRODUCTION

THIS BOOK IS FOR ANY JAVASCRIPT (OR TYPESCRIPT) programmer who wants to get up to speed on the latest features added to JavaScript in the last few years, and who wants to know how to stay informed as the language continues to evolve and grow. You can find nearly all of the information in this book *somewhere* on the web if you look hard enough and you're cautious about what sites you trust; this book provides all of the technical details in one place, along with showing you how to keep track of the changes as they continue to be made. You can continue to stay up-to-date via the book's website at `https://thenewtoys.dev`, where I continue covering new features as they're added.

WHAT DOES THIS BOOK COVER?

Here's a glance at what's in each chapter:

Chapter 1: The New Toys in ES2015–ES2020, and Beyond — begins with introducing various players in the JavaScript world and some important terminology. Then it describes the definition of "The New Toys" for the purposes of the book; covers the way new features are added to JavaScript, how that process is managed, and by whom; and explains how to follow and participate in that process. It finishes by introducing some tools for using the new toys in older environments (or using the very newest toys in current environments).

Chapter 2: Block-Scoped Declarations: let and const — covers the new declaration keywords `let` and `const` and the new scoping concepts they support, including in-depth coverage of scoping in loops, particularly the new handling in `for` loops.

Chapter 3: New Function Features — covers the variety of new features related to functions: arrow functions, default parameter values, rest parameters, the `name` property, and various syntax improvements.

Chapter 4: Classes — covers the new `class` feature: the basics, what it is and what it isn't, subclassing, `super`, subclassing built-ins like `Array` and `Error`, and the `new.target` feature. Chapter 4 leaves coverage of private fields and other features making their way through the proposals process to Chapter 18.

Chapter 5: New Object Features — covers computed property names, shorthand properties, getting and setting an object's prototype, the new Symbol type and how it relates to objects, method syntax, property order, property spread syntax, and a host of new object functions.

Chapter 6: Iterables, Iterators, for-of, Iterable Spread, Generators — covers iteration, a powerful new tool for collections and lists, and generators, a powerful new way to interact with functions.

Chapter 7: Destructuring — covers this important new syntax and how to use it to extract data from objects and from arrays and other iterables, with defaults, deep picking, and more.

Chapter 8: Promises — dives deep into this important new tool for coping with asynchronous processes.

Chapter 9: Asynchronous Functions, Iterators, and Generators — goes into detail about the new async/await syntax that lets you use familiar logical flow structures with asynchronous code, as well as how asynchronous iterators and generators work and the new for-await-of loop.

Chapter 10: Templates, Tag Functions, and New String Features — describes template literal syntax, tag functions, and lots of new string features like better Unicode support, updates to familiar methods, and lots of new methods.

Chapter 11: New Array Features, Typed Arrays — covers the wide range of new array methods, various other array updates, typed arrays such as Int32Array, and advanced features for interacting with typed array data.

Chapter 12: Maps and Sets — teaches you all about the new keyed collections Map and Set, and also their "weak" cousins WeakMap and WeakSet.

Chapter 13: Modules — is a deep dive into this exciting and powerful way to organize your code.

Chapter 14: Reflection—Reflect and Proxy — covers the powerful new dynamic metaprogramming features of the Reflect and Proxy objects and how they relate to one another.

Chapter 15: Regular Expression Updates — describes all of the updates to regular expressions that have been done the past several years such as new flags, named capture groups, lookbehind assertions, and new Unicode features.

Chapter 16: Shared Memory — covers the complex and potentially difficult area of sharing memory across threads in a JavaScript program, including covering SharedArrayBuffer and the Atomics object as well as fundamental concepts and notes on pitfalls.

Chapter 17: Miscellany — covers a wide range of things that didn't quite fit in elsewhere: BigInt, the new integer literal syntaxes (binary, new octal), optional catch bindings, new math methods, the exponentiation operator, various additions to the Math object (no pun!), tail call optimization, nullish coalescing, optional chaining, and "Annex B" (browser-only) features defined for compatibility reasons.

Chapter 18: Upcoming Class Features — takes us a bit into the future, describing enhancements to classes that haven't quite been finished yet but which are far along in the process: public field declarations, private fields, and private methods.

Chapter 19: A Look Ahead . . . — winds up with looking forward to some further enhancements currently in the pipeline: top-level await, WeakRefs and cleanup callbacks, RegExp match indices, Atomics.asyncWait, a couple of new syntax features, legacy RegExp features, and various upcoming standard library additions.

Appendix: Fantastic Features and Where to Find Them — *(with apologies to J.K. Rowling)* provides lists of the new toys and tells you which chapter covers each of them. The lists are: Features in Alphabetical Order; New Fundamentals; New Syntax, Keywords, Operators, Loops, and Similar; New Literal Forms; Standard Library Additions and Changes; and Miscellaneous.

WHO SHOULD READ THIS BOOK

You should read this book if:

➤ You have at least a basic understanding of JavaScript, and

➤ You want to learn the new features added in the last several years.

This isn't an academic book just for experts. It's a pragmatic book for everyday JavaScript programmers.

Almost anyone picking up this book is already going to know *some* of what's in it, and almost no one picking up this book will already know *all* of it. Maybe you're already clear on the basics of `let` and `const`, but you don't quite get `async` functions yet. Maybe promises are old hat to you, but you saw some syntax you didn't recognize in some modern code you ran across. You'll find all of it from ES2015 through ES2020 (and beyond) covered here.

HOW TO USE THIS BOOK

Read Chapter 1. Chapter 1 defines a lot of terms I use throughout the rest of the book. Skipping Chapter 1 will likely trip you up.

After that, you have a choice to make: read the chapters in order, or jump around?

I've laid out the chapters in the order I have for a reason; and I build on the content of earlier chapters in later chapters. For instance, you'll learn about promises in Chapter 8, which is important to understanding `async` functions in Chapter 9. Naturally, I suggest reading them in the order I've arranged them. But I bet you're a smart person who knows their own mind; if you jump around instead, you'll be just fine.

I do suggest that you read—or at least skim—all of the chapters (with the possible exception of Chapter 16; more on that in a minute). Even if you think you know a feature, there's probably something here that you don't know, or only think you know. For instance: maybe you're planning to skip Chapter 2 because you already know all there is to know about `let` and `const`. Maybe you even know why

```
for (let i = 0; i < 10; ++i) { /*...*/
    setTimeout(() => console.log(i));
}
```

creates ten *different* variables called `i`, and why using

```
let a = "ay";
var b = "bee";
```

at global scope creates a `window.b` property but doesn't create a `window.a` property. Even if you do, I'd skim Chapter 2 just to be sure there aren't other wrinkles you haven't picked up.

Chapter 16 is a bit of a special case: it's about sharing memory between threads. Most JavaScript programmers don't need to share memory between threads. *Some* of you will, and that's why Chapter 16 is there, but most won't and if you're in that category, just tuck away the fact that *if* you think you need shared memory at some point in the future you can come back and learn about it in Chapter 16. That's just fine.

Beyond all that: run the examples, experiment with them, and above all enjoy yourself.

HOW TO CONTACT THE AUTHOR

I'd love to hear your feedback. Please feel free to reach out:

- ➤ If you think you've found an error, please write to `errata@wiley.com`.
- ➤ You can download the examples and listings at `https://thenewtoys.dev/bookcode` or `https://www.wiley.com/go/javascript-newtoys`.
- ➤ You can ask me questions and/or talk with other readers on `https://thenewtoys.dev`.
- ➤ You can reach me on Twitter at `@tjcrowder`.
- ➤ I'm usually hanging out in the JavaScript tag on `https://stackoverflow.com/`.

Enjoy!

JavaScript®
The New Toys

1

The New Toys in ES2015–ES2020, and Beyond

WHAT'S IN THIS CHAPTER?

➤ Definitions, who's who, and terminology

➤ Explanation of JavaScript versions (ES6? ES2020?)

➤ What are the "new toys"?

➤ The process driving new JavaScript features

➤ Tools for using next-generation JavaScript

CODE DOWNLOADS FOR THIS CHAPTER

You can download the code for this chapter at `https://thenewtoys.dev/bookcode` or `https://www.wiley.com/go/javascript-newtoys`.

JavaScript has changed a lot in the last few years.

If you were an active JavaScript developer in the 2000s, for a while there you could be forgiven for thinking JavaScript was standing still. After the 3rd Edition specification in December 1999, developers were waiting fully 10 years for the next edition of the specification. From the outside, it seemed like nothing was happening. In fact, lots of work was being done; it just wasn't finding its way into the official specification and multiple JavaScript engines. We could (but won't) spend an entire chapter—if not a book—on what various different groups in important positions vis-à-vis JavaScript were doing and how they couldn't agree on a common path forward for some time. The key thing is that they ultimately *did* agree on a way forward, at a fateful meeting in Oslo in July 2008 after much advance negotiation. That common ground, which Brendan Eich (creator of JavaScript) later called Harmony, paved the way for the 5th Edition specification in December 2009 (the 4th Edition was never completed), and laid the basis for ongoing progress.

And my, how things have progressed.

In this chapter, you'll get an overview of the new features since 2009 (which the rest of the book covers in detail). You'll learn who's in charge of moving JavaScript forward, what process is now used to do so, and how you can keep track of what's coming and get involved if you like. You'll learn about tools you can use to write modern JavaScript today, even if you have to target environments that haven't kept up.

DEFINITIONS, WHO'S WHO, AND TERMINOLOGY

To talk about what's going on with JavaScript, we need to define some names and common terminology.

Ecma? ECMAScript? TC39?

What we think of as "JavaScript" is standardized as "ECMAScript" by Ecma International,[1] a standards organization responsible for multiple computing standards. The ECMAScript standard is ECMA-262. The people in charge of the standard are members of Ecma International Technical Committee 39 ("TC39"), charged with "Standardization of the general purpose, cross platform, vendor-neutral programming language ECMAScript. This includes the language syntax, semantics, and libraries and complementary technologies that support the language."[2] They manage other standards as well, such as the JSON Syntax Specification (ECMA-404), and notably the ECMAScript Internationalization API Specification (ECMA-402).

In this book and in common usage, JavaScript is ECMAScript and vice versa. Sometimes, particularly during the decade of different groups doing different things, "JavaScript" was used to specifically mean the language Mozilla was developing (which had several features that either never made it into ECMAScript, or changed markedly before they did), but since Harmony that usage is increasingly outdated.

ES6? ES7? ES2015? ES2020?

Having all these various abbreviations can be confusing, not least because some have edition numbers but others have years. This section explains what they are and why there are two kinds of them.

Up through the 5th Edition, TC39 referred to versions of the specification via their edition number. The full title of the 5th Edition spec is:

> Standard ECMA-262
>
> 5th Edition / December 2009
>
> ECMAScript Language Specification

---

[1] Formerly known as the European Computer Manufacturer's Association (ECMA), but now only the E in Ecma is capitalized in the organization's name.
[2] http://www.ecma-international.org/memento/TC39.htm

Since "ECMAScript 5th Edition" is a bit of a mouthful, saying "ES5" was the natural thing to do.

Starting with the 6th Edition in 2015, TC39 adopted a continual improvement process where the specification is a living editor's draft[3] with annual snapshots. (More about that later in this chapter.) When they did that, they added the year to the language name:

> Standard ECMA-262
>
> 6th Edition / June 2015
>
> ECMAScript® **2015** Language Specification

So the ECMAScript 6th Edition standard ("ES6") defines ECMAScript 2015, or "ES2015" for short. Prior to publication, "ES6" became a buzzword of its own and is still in common usage. (Unfortunately, it's often used inaccurately, referring not just to features from ES2015, but also to features that came afterward in ES2016, ES2017, and so on.)

That's why there are two styles, the style using the edition (ES6, ES7, . . .) and the style using the year (ES2015, ES2016, . . .). Which you use is up to you. ES6 is ES2015 (or sometimes, incorrectly, ES2015+), ES7 is ES2016, ES8 is ES2017, and so on through (as of this book's release) ES11, which is ES2020. You'll also see "ESnext" or "ES.next," which are sometimes used to refer to upcoming changes.

In this book, I use what I see as the emerging consensus: the old style for ES5 and earlier, and the new style for ES2015 and later.

All of that said, although I will usually call out the specific edition where a feature was introduced, the fact that `Array.prototype.includes` is from ES2016 and `Object.values` is from ES2017 doesn't really matter very much. What matters more is what's actually supported in your target environments and whether you need to either refrain from using a specific feature, or transpile and/or polyfill it. (More on transpiling and polyfilling later in the "Using Today's Toys in Yesterday's Environments, and Tomorrow's Toys Today" section.)

JavaScript "Engines," Browsers, and Others

In this book I'll use the term "JavaScript engine" to refer to the software component that runs JavaScript code. A JavaScript engine must know how to:

➤ Parse JavaScript,

➤ Either interpret it or compile it to machine code (or both), and

➤ Run the result within an environment that works as described by the specification.

JavaScript engines are also sometimes called virtual machines, or VMs for short.

One usual place you find JavaScript engines is in web browsers, of course:

➤ Google's Chrome browser uses their V8 engine (also used in Chromium, Opera, and Microsoft Edge v79 and later), except on iOS (more on that in a bit).

➤ Apple's Safari browser (for Mac OS and for iOS) uses their JavaScriptCore engine.

---

[3] `https://tc39.es/ecma262/`

➤ Mozilla's Firefox uses their SpiderMonkey engine, except on iOS.

➤ Microsoft's Internet Explorer uses their JScript engine, which is increasingly out of date as it only gets security fixes.

➤ Microsoft Edge v44 and earlier ("Legacy Edge") uses Microsoft's Chakra engine. In January 2020, Edge v79 was released, which is based on the Chromium project and uses the V8 engine, except on iOS. (The version number jumped from 44 to 79 to align with Chromium.) Chakra is still used in various products that use the Microsoft WebView control, such as Microsoft Office JavaScript add-ins, though it may be replaced at some stage. (WebView2, using Chromium Edge, is in developer preview as of early 2020.)

Chrome, Firefox, Edge, and other browsers running on Apple's iOS operating system for iPad and iPhone can't currently use their own JavaScript engines, because to compile and run JavaScript (rather than just interpreting it), they have to allocate executable memory, and only Apple's own iOS apps are allowed to do that, not ones from other vendors. So Chrome and Firefox (and others) have to use Apple's JavaScriptCore instead on iOS even though they use their own engine on desktop and Android. (At least, that's true for now; the V8 team added an "interpreter only" mode to V8 in 2019, which means Chrome and others using V8 could use that mode on iOS, since it doesn't have to use executable memory.) In this book, if I say something is "supported by Chrome" or "supported by Firefox," I'm referring to the non-iOS versions using V8 or SpiderMonkey, respectively.

JavaScript engines are also used in desktop applications (Electron,[4] React Native,[5] and others), web servers and other kinds of servers (often using Node.js[6]), non-web applications, embedded apps—just about everywhere.

WHAT ARE THE "NEW TOYS"?

For this book, the "new toys" are the new features added to JavaScript in ES2015 through ES2020 (and previewing some that are coming soon). The language has come a *long* way in those six updates. The following is a general overview. (Appendix A has a more complete list of changes.) Some of the terms on the list may be unfamiliar; don't worry about that, you'll learn them across the course of the book.

➤ *Opt-in block scope* (`let`, `const`): Narrower scoping for variables, clever handling of `for` loop body scope, "variables" whose value cannot change (`const`)

➤ *"Arrow" functions*: Lightweight, concise functions that are particularly useful for callbacks since they close over `this` rather than having their own `this` value that's set when they're called

➤ *Improvements to function parameters*: Default values; parameter destructuring, "rest" parameters, trailing commas

➤ *Iterable objects*: Well-defined semantics for creating and consuming iterable objects (such as arrays and strings), in-language iteration constructs (`for-of`, `for-await-of`); generator functions for generating sequences that can be iterated (including asynchronous sequences)

---

[4] https://www.electronjs.org/
[5] https://reactnative.dev/
[6] https://nodejs.org/

➤ *"Spread" syntax*: Spreading out array (or other iterable) entries into new arrays, spreading out object properties into new objects, and spreading out iterable entries into discrete function arguments; particularly useful for functional programming, or anywhere immutable structures are used

➤ *"Rest" syntax*: Gathering together the "rest" of an object's properties, an iterable's values, or a function's arguments into an object or array

➤ *Other syntax improvements*: Allowing a trailing comma in the argument list when calling a function; omitting unused identifiers in `catch` clauses; new-style octal literals; binary literals; separator characters in numeric literals; and more

➤ *Destructuring*: Picking out the values from arrays/objects in a concise way that mirrors object and array literal syntax

➤ `class`: Markedly simpler, declarative syntax for creating constructor functions and associated prototype objects, while preserving JavaScript's inherent prototypical nature

➤ *Asynchronous programming improvements*: Promises, `async` functions and `await`; these markedly decrease "callback hell"

➤ *Object literal improvements*: Computed property names, shorthand properties, method syntax, trailing commas after property definitions

➤ *Template literals*: A simple, declarative way to create strings with dynamic content, and go beyond strings with tagged template functions

➤ *Typed arrays*: Low-level true arrays for using native APIs (and more)

➤ *Shared memory*: The ability to genuinely share memory between JavaScript threads (including inter-thread coordination primitives)

➤ *Unicode string improvements*: Unicode code point escape sequences; support for accessing code points instead of code units

➤ *Regular Expression improvements*: Lookbehind assertions; named capture groups; capture indices; Unicode property escapes; Unicode case insensitivity

➤ *Maps*: Key/value collections where the keys don't have to be strings

➤ *Sets*: Collections of unique values with well-defined semantics

➤ *WeakMap, WeakSet, and WeakRef*: Built-ins for holding only weak references to objects (allowing them to be garbage collected)

➤ *Standard library additions*: New methods on `Object`, `Array`, `Array.prototype`, `String`, `String.prototype`, `Math`, and others

➤ *Support for dynamic metaprogramming*: `Proxy` and `Reflect`

➤ *Symbols*: Guaranteed-unique values (particularly useful for unique property names)

➤ *BigInt*: Arbitrary precision integers

➤ Many, many others

All these new features, in particular the new syntax, could be overwhelming. Don't be concerned! There's no need to adopt new features until/unless you're ready to and have need of them. One of the key principles TC39 adheres to is "Don't break the web." That means that JavaScript must remain "web compatible"—that is, compatible with the huge body of code that already exists in the world today.[7] If you don't need a new feature, or you don't like a new feature, you don't have to use it. Your old way of doing whatever that feature does will always continue to work. But in many cases, you're likely to find there's a compelling reason for the new feature, in particular new syntax features: they make something simpler and less error-prone to write and understand, or—in the case of `Proxy` and `WeakMap`/`WeakSet`, shared memory, and others—they enable things that mostly couldn't be done without them.

For space reasons, this book only covers the new toys in the JavaScript specification itself, ECMA-262. But there are some exciting new toys in the ECMAScript Internationalization API Specification[8] as well, ECMA-402, which is well worth reading. You can find coverage of ECMA-402 on this book's website at `https://thenewtoys.dev/internationalization`.

HOW DO NEW TOYS GET CREATED?

In this section you'll learn who's in charge of moving JavaScript forward, what process they use to do so, and how to follow and participate in that process.

Who's in Charge

You learned earlier that Ecma International's Technical Committee 39 (TC39) is in charge of creating and releasing updated specifications for the ECMAScript standard. The committee is made up of JavaScript developers, framework authors, large website authors/maintainers, programming language researchers, representatives from all the major JavaScript engines, influential JavaScripters, and other stakeholders in JavaScript's success and future. They have regular meetings, historically six per year for three days. To participate in meetings as a member, your organization can join Ecma.[9] TC39 navigates the difficult waters of developers' desires, implementation complexity, security concerns, backward compatibility, and many other design inputs to bring new and useful features to the JavaScript community.

To ensure that the committee works as part of the community rather than separate from it, TC39 maintains the ecma262 GitHub repository[10] with the up-to-date specification (browsable at `https://tc39.es/ecma262/`) and a proposals repository[11] for proposals going through the TC39 process described in the next section. Some members are also active on the TC39 Discourse group.[12] Notes of the TC39 meetings and associated materials (slides, etc.) are posted to `https://github.com/tc39/notes`.

---

[7] The committee also cares about significant JavaScript code that isn't directly related to the web, too.
[8] `https://tc39.es/ecma402/`
[9] `https://ecma-international.org/memento/join.htm`
[10] `https://github.com/tc39/ecma262`
[11] `https://github.com/tc39/proposals`
[12] `https://es.discourse.group/`

You can learn more about TC39, and how to get involved, at `https://tc39.es/`. You can also learn more about how TC39 works at `https://github.com/tc39/how-we-work`.

The Process

TC39 adopted a well-defined process in November 2013 and first published it in January 2014. The process has multiple stages that TC39 moves proposals through (Stage 0 through Stage 4), with clear expectations at each stage, and clear criteria for moving from one stage to the next. Once a proposal meets the criteria to move to the next stage, the committee decides by consensus whether to move it forward.

It's worth reading the process document itself,[13] but in brief, the stages are:

➤ *Stage 0 – Strawperson*: Someone's had an idea they think is worth considering so they've thought about it, written it up a bit, and put it forward. (This stage almost isn't a stage, and the term has been applied to different things at different times.) If the person putting it forward isn't a TC39 member, they need to register as a non-member contributor[14] (which anyone can do). Some Stage 0 proposals end up being listed in the TC39 proposals repository, but others don't; typically it's just ones that have gained a potential champion who is a committee member. If a Stage 0 proposal gains enough interest, a TC39 member may get it added to the agenda for a TC39 meeting to be discussed and considered for Stage 1.

➤ *Stage 1 – Proposal*: Once a proposal has been put to the committee and there's consensus to investigate it further, the committee moves it to Stage 1 with a champion to guide it through the process. If there isn't already a GitHub repo for it, the originator or champion or another interested party creates one. Then members of the community (whether on the committee or not) discuss it, develop it further, research similar technology in other languages or environments, refine the scope, figure out the general form of a solution, and generally flesh out the idea. As a result of this work, it might turn out that the benefits aren't worth the costs, or it could be that the idea needs to be broken up and added to other proposals, etc. But if the proposal has legs, the people involved (who may have changed over time) will put together some initial draft specification language, API, and semantics and put it forward to TC39 to be considered for Stage 2.

➤ *Stage 2 – Draft*: When it's ready, a Stage 1 proposal can be presented at a TC39 meeting to be considered for Stage 2. This means seeking consensus that the proposal should go ahead, with the expectation it will likely go through the entire process. Stage 2 is the stage where the community refines the precise syntax, semantics, API, and so on and describes the solution in detail using formal specification language. Often, polyfills and/or Babel plugins get created at this stage to enable experimentation with real use. Depending on its scope, a proposal may stay at Stage 2 for some time as the details are worked out.

---

[13] `https://tc39.es/process-document/`
[14] `https://tc39.es/agreements/contributor/`

➤ *Stage 3 – Candidate*: Once the team has matured a proposal to a final draft form and created formal specification language for it, the champion can put it forward for Stage 3. This means seeking consensus that the proposal is ready to be implemented in JavaScript engines. At Stage 3, the proposal itself is nearly stable. Changes at this point are expected to be limited to implementation-driven feedback, such as corner cases discovered during implementation, web-compatibility issues, or difficulty of implementation.

➤ *Stage 4 – Finished*: At this point, the feature is complete and is ready to be added to the editor's draft at `https://tc39.es/ecma262/`. To reach this final stage, the feature must have acceptance tests in TC39's test262 test suite;[15] at least two distinct compatible implementations that pass the tests (for instance, shipping in V8 in Chrome Canary and SpiderMonkey in Firefox Nightly, or SpiderMonkey in Firefox and JavaScriptCore in Safari Tech Preview, etc.). Once those criteria are met, the final step to reach Stage 4 is for the team working on the feature to send a pull request to the ecma262 repository to incorporate the specification changes into the editor's draft , and the ECMAScript editor group to accept that PR.

That's the process *proposals* go through to become part of JavaScript. But not every change is a proposal. Smaller changes can be made through consensus at TC39 meetings based on a pull request to the specification. For instance, the output of `Date.prototype.toString` changed between ES2017 and ES2018 (see Chapter 17) as the result of consensus on a pull request, not a staged proposal. Often, these are editorial changes, or changes reflecting the reality of what JavaScript engines already do but which isn't in the specification, or changes to what the specification says to do that have been agreed on because TC39 believes they're both desirable and "web compatible" (won't break a large amount of existing code), such as the change in ES2019 making `Array.prototype.sort` a stable sort (see Chapter 11). If you want to know what changes are being considered or made in this way, watch the "needs consensus" label in the `https://github.com/tc39/ecma262` repo (and similarly the `https://github.com/tc39/ecma402` repo for ECMA-402 changes). To find ones that have been completed, look in the "has consensus," "editorial change," and/or "normative change" labels. At some point there may be a more formal process for these "needs consensus" changes, but for now this is how you watch for them.

Getting Involved

If you see a proposal that interests you and you want to get involved, when should you do that? What should that involvement look like?

One key thing is: get involved early. Once a proposal has reached Stage 3, only critical changes based on implementation experience are typically considered. The best times to get involved are at Stages 0, 1, and 2. That's when you can provide insight based on your experience, help define semantics, try out what's being proposed using tools like Babel (which you'll learn about in a later section), etc. It's not that you can't find a useful role in a Stage 3 proposal (there are sometimes tasks to be done in terms of firming up specification text or helping write developer documentation), just be aware that suggesting changes at Stage 3 usually isn't useful unless you're one of the people implementing it in a JavaScript engine and you run into a problem.

---

[15] `https://github.com/tc39/test262`

So: you've found a proposal you want to get involved in; what now? It's up to you, but here are some suggestions:

➤ *Do your research.* Read the proposal's explainer (the README.md that's linked from the TC39 list of proposals) and other documents closely and carefully. If they refer to prior art (such as a similar feature in another language), it's useful to read up on that prior art. If there's initial specification text, read it. (This guide may be helpful there: https://timothygu.me/es-howto/.) You want to be sure that the input you provide is well-informed.

➤ *Try the feature out!* Even if you can't use it yet, you can write speculative code (code you can't run, but can think about) to consider how well the proposal is solving the problem it sets out to solve. If there's a Babel plugin for it, try writing and running code. See how the feature works for you and provide feedback on it.

➤ *Look for ways you can help.* Aside from suggestions and feedback, there are lots of ways to help with a proposal. For instance, you can look for issues where a consensus has been reached about what to do, but no one's had the time to do it (researching prior art, updating the explainer, updating spec text). You could do those updates, if it's something you're comfortable doing. You can coordinate with the proposal authors by discussing contributions in GitHub issues.

When getting involved, remember to treat everyone with respect and to be friendly, patient, inclusive, and considerate. Be careful with the words you choose. You're more likely to have influence by treating people well and demonstrating a collaborative spirit than by seeming cross, dismissive, or obstructive. Note that TC39's meetings and online spaces used to develop proposals are governed by a Code of Conduct.[16] Please refer improper conduct to TC39's Code of Conduct committee (see the linked document).

KEEPING UP WITH THE NEW TOYS

You don't *have* to keep up with the new toys. As I've mentioned, your old way of doing things isn't going away. But if you're reading this book, I suspect you want to.

As you were reading through the process earlier, one thing that may have stricken you is that the process guarantees that new features make it into the real world *before* they are added to the specification. In contrast, when ES5 came out in 2009 and ES2015 came out in 2015, most of the features they described didn't exist (in the form described) in any JavaScript engine then shipping. If the spec follows the new features rather than the other way around, how do you keep up with what features are coming next? Here are some ways:

➤ Watch the proposals repository on GitHub (https://github.com/tc39/proposals). If something gets to Stage 3, it's probably going to get added within a year or two. Even Stage 2 features are at least likely to get added eventually, though any feature can be rejected by TC39 at nearly any stage.

---

[16] https://tc39.es/code-of-conduct/

➤   Read the meeting notes of TC39 meetings posted at `https://github.com/tc39/notes`.

➤   Participate in the TC39 Discourse group (`https://es.discourse.group/`).[17]

➤   Pay attention to what's going on with the tools discussed in the next section.

You can also follow along at `https://thenewtoys.dev`, where I continue coverage of what's coming next.

USING TODAY'S TOYS IN YESTERDAY'S ENVIRONMENTS, AND TOMORROW'S TOYS TODAY

In terms of just learning the features covered in this book, you don't need to worry about dealing with environments that don't support them; nearly everything covered (other than Chapters 18 and 19) is supported by current versions of the Chrome, Firefox, Safari, and Edge desktop browsers and Node.js at least. Simply use one of those to run the code.

USING NODE.JS TO RUN EXAMPLES

By default, when you run a script with Node.js, like this:

```
node script.js
```

it runs it at *module scope*, not global scope. A few examples in this book demonstrate things that only happen at global scope, so they won't work when you run the code that way.

For those examples, either use a browser to run the code, or use Node.js's read/evaluate/print loop (REPL) instead. To use the REPL, you don't specify the script file to run as an argument to the `node` command. Instead, you redirect the script into it using the < operator (this works both on Unix/Linux/Mac OS systems and on Windows):

```
node < script.js
```

I'll remind you to do this when an example needs to be run at global scope.

At some stage, though, you're likely to want to use new features in an environment that doesn't support them. For instance, most JavaScript development still targets web browsers, and the JavaScript engines in different browsers get new features at different times (if at all—Internet Explorer doesn't support any of the new features discussed in this book,[18] but still has some global market share as of this writing, particularly in government and large company intranets).

---

[17] The Discourse instance largely replaces the informal discussion es-discuss mailing list. The list still exists, but many TC39 representatives recommend avoiding its use.
[18] At least not properly; it has an incomplete version of let and const.

This was an issue when ES5 was released, since very little of it was implemented in any shipping JavaScript engine at the time. But most of ES5 was new standard library features, rather than significant syntax changes, so those could be "polyfilled" (added by including an extra script that provided the missing objects/functions) using various projects like es5-shim.js,[19] core-js,[20] es-shims,[21] or similar. During the development of ES2015 in 2010 through 2015, though, it was clear that real-world experience of new syntax was required to do a good job of developing that syntax, but JavaScript implementations didn't have the new syntax yet—an apparent catch-22.

Tool builders to the rescue! They created tools like Traceur[22] and Babel[23] (formerly 6to5), which take source code using the new syntax as input, convert it to use older syntax, and output that older-style code (along, optionally, with polyfills and other runtime support functions). Similarly, TypeScript[24] supported major parts of what would become ES2015 well before the specification was completed. These tools let you write new-style code, but convert it to old-style code before delivering it to old environments. This conversion process is variously called "compiling" or "transpiling." This was initially handy for feedback on the JavaScript improvements being planned for ES2015, but even when ES2015 came out it was a useful way to write new-style code if you were planning to run it in an environment without the new features.

As of this writing, Traceur has gone quiet, but Babel is in use by a large fraction of JavaScript developers worldwide. Babel has transforms for nearly all features that are in the process, even ones at Stage 1, which may change markedly before progressing. (So use those at your own risk. Stage 3 onward are fairly safe to use.) You select the transform plugins you want to use, write your code using those features, and Babel produces code you can use in environments without those features.

Transpiling an Example with Babel

In this section, we'll take a quick look at using Babel to transpile code using an ES2015 feature, called an *arrow function*, into ES5-compatible code that works on IE11. But this is just an example; you could just as easily use Babel to transform code using a Stage 3 feature not yet present in any shipping JavaScript engine into ES2020-compatible code. Babel also supports some transforms that aren't in the process at all, such as JSX[25] (used in some JavaScript frameworks, notably React[26]). The truly adventurous can write their own transform plugins just for use on their projects!

To install Babel, you'll want Node.js and npm (Node Package Manager). If you don't already have those installed on your system, either:

➤ Go to `https://nodejs.org/` and use the appropriate installer/package for your system to install it; or

➤ Use the Node Version Manager, which provides a handy way to install Node versions and to switch between them: `https://github.com/nvm-sh/nvm`

npm comes bundled with Node.js, so you don't have to install it separately.

---

[19] `https://github.com/es-shims/es5-shim`
[20] `https://github.com/zloirock/core-js`
[21] `https://github.com/es-shims/`
[22] `https://github.com/google/traceur-compiler`
[23] `http://babeljs.io/`
[24] `http://typescriptlang.org/`
[25] `https://facebook.github.io/jsx/`
[26] `https://reactjs.org/`

Once you have them installed:

1. Create a directory for this example (for instance, `example` in your home directory).

2. Open a command prompt/terminal window and change to the directory you just created.

3. Use `npm` to create a `package.json` file: Type

    npm init

    and press Enter. `npm` will ask a series of questions; answer the questions as you like (or just press Enter in response to all of them). When done, it will write out `package.json` to your example directory.

4. Next, install Babel. (The following steps are from going to `https://babeljs.io/docs/setup/#installation` and then clicking the CLI button; you might want to check there for updates.) Type

    npm install --save-dev @babel/core @babel/cli

    and press Enter. `npm` will download and install Babel, its command-line interface, and all of its dependencies into your example project. (You may get a warning related to a module called `fsevents` and/or some deprecation warnings; that's okay.)

5. At this point, you could start using Babel by calling it directly, but let's make it easier by adding an `npm` script entry to `package.json`. Open `package.json` in your favorite editor. If there isn't a top-level `scripts` entry, create one (but current versions of `npm` will have included one with a `test` script that shows an error). Within the `scripts` entry, add this setting:

    `"build": "babel src -d lib"`

    Now your `package.json` should look something like Listing 1-1. (Yours may still have `test` entry in `scripts`; that's fine. It also may have a different license, I always change the default to MIT.) Make sure to save the file.

LISTING 1-1: Example package.json—package.json

```
{
  "name": "example",
  "version": "1.0.0",
  "description": "",
  "main": "index.js",
  "scripts": {
    "build": "babel src -d lib"
  },
  "author": "",
  "license": "MIT",
  "devDependencies": {
    "@babel/cli": "^7.2.3",
    "@babel/core": "^7.2.2"
  }
}
```

6. Babel is highly modular. Although we've installed it, we haven't told it to do anything yet. For this example, we'll use one of its presets to tell it to transform ES2015 code to ES5 code, by installing and then configuring the preset. To install the preset, type

```
npm install --save-dev babel-preset-env
```

and press Enter. In the next step we'll configure it.

7. Now we need to create a configuration file for Babel, `.babelrc` (note the leading dot). Create the file with these contents (or use the one from the chapter downloads):

```
{
  "presets": [
    [
      "env",
      {
        "targets": {
          "ie": "11"
        }
      }
    ]
  ]
}
```

That configuration tells Babel to use its env preset, which the Babel documentation describes as ". . . a smart preset that allows you to use the latest JavaScript without needing to micromanage which syntax transforms . . . are needed by your target environment(s)." In this configuration, setting the target `"ie": "11"` tells the env preset that you're targeting IE11, which is appropriate for the following example. For your real use, you'll want to look at the documentation for the env preset[27] and/or other presets or plugins you may want to use instead.

That's it for the Babel setup for this example. Now let's create some code for it to transpile. Create a subdirectory of your example directory called src, and create a file in it called index.js with the contents of Listing 1-2. (At the end of the process, I'll show you a list of what files should be where, so don't worry too much if you're slightly unsure; just create the file and you can move it if it ends up in the wrong place.)

LISTING 1-2: ES2015 transpiling example input—index.js

```
var obj = {
    rex: /\d/,
    checkArray: function(array) {
        return array.some(entry => this.rex.test(entry));
    }
};
console.log(obj.checkArray(["no", "digits", "in", "this", "array"])); // false
console.log(obj.checkArray(["this", "array", "has", "1", "digit"]));  // true
```

---

[27] https://babeljs.io/docs/en/babel-preset-env#docsNav

The code in Listing 1-2 uses just one ES2015+ feature: an *arrow function*, the `entry =>` `this.rex.test(entry)` within the call to `some`, which I've highlighted in the code. (Yes, that's really a function.) You'll learn about arrow functions in Chapter 3. The brief, incomplete version is that they offer a concise way to define a function (as you can see) and that they close over `this` just like closing over a variable (rather than having `this` set by how they're called). When `obj.checkArray(...)` is called, `this` within the call refers to `obj` *even within the* `some` *callback*, so `this.rex` refers to the `rex` property on `obj`. That wouldn't be true if the callback were a traditional function.

At this point, your example directory should have these contents:

```
example/
+-- node_modules/
|   +-- (various directories and files)
+-- src/
|   +-- index.js
+-- .babelrc
+-- package.json
+-- package-lock.json
```

You're ready to transpile! Type

npm run build

and press Enter. Babel will do its thing, create the `lib` output directory for you, and write the ES5 version of `index.js` to it. The result in `lib/index.js` will look something like Listing 1-3.

LISTING 1-3: ES2015 transpiling example output—index-transpiled-to-es5.js

```
"use strict";

var obj = {
  rex: /\d/,
  checkArray: function checkArray(array) {
    var _this = this;

    return array.some(function (entry) {
      return _this.rex.test(entry);
    });
  }
};
console.log(obj.checkArray(["no", "digits", "in", "this", "array"])); // false

console.log(obj.checkArray(["this", "array", "has", "1", "digit"])); // true
```

If you compare `src/index.js` (Listing 1-2) to `lib/index.js` (Listing 1-3), you'll see only a couple of changes (other than whitespace). First, Babel added a `"use strict";` directive to the top of the transpiled file (recall that strict mode is a feature added in ES5 that modifies the behavior of a couple of things that were problematic for various reasons). This is Babel's default, but it can be turned off if you have code that relies on loose mode.

The interesting thing, though, is how it rewrote the arrow function. It created a variable within `checkArray` called `_this`, set its value to `this`, and then used a traditional function as the `some` callback; within the function, it used `_this` instead of `this`. That fits with my earlier description of arrow functions—that they close over `this` just like closing over a variable. Babel just made that happen in a way an ES5 environment can understand.

This is obviously just a very small example, but it illustrates the point and gives you a taste of one tool you might use if you need to do this in your projects. Babel can be integrated into your build system, whether you use Gulp,[28] Grunt,[29] Webpack,[30] Browserify,[31] Rollup,[32] or just about any other; the installation page at `https://babeljs.io/docs/setup/#installation` has instructions for all the major ones.

REVIEW

JavaScript has changed enormously over the past several years, particularly 2015 onward. It will continue to change in the future. But there's no need to be concerned about getting overloaded with all the new features; JavaScript will always be backward-compatible, so there's no need to adopt a new feature until/unless you're ready to do so and have need of it.

The new features run the gamut from small tweaks like allowing a trailing comma in a function call arguments list and new convenience methods in the standard library, to major improvements like declarative `class` syntax (Chapter 4), `async` functions (Chapter 9), and modules (Chapter 13).

The people ultimately in charge of moving JavaScript forward are the members of TC39 (Technical Committee 39 of Ecma International), which is made up of JavaScript developers, programming language researchers, library and large website authors, representatives from major JavaScript engines, and other stakeholders in JavaScript's success and future. But anyone can get involved.

The process for new features is public and open. You can follow progress and stay up to date via various GitHub repositories, published meeting notes, and the TC39 Discourse group. Also, I continue coverage where this book leaves off on the book's site at `https://thenewtoys.dev`.

Most of the features covered in this book are supported by the JavaScript engines in cutting-edge browsers like Chrome, Firefox, Safari, and Edge, and by recent releases of engines in non-browser environments like Node.js, Electron, React Native, etc.

Older environments like Internet Explorer can be supported via JavaScript-to-JavaScript compilation (aka "transpilation"), converting old-style code into new-style code, with tools (like Babel) that can be integrated into your build system. Some features (like the Proxy objects you'll learn about in Chapter 14) can't be fully supported in this way, but many can.

Okay. The stage is set . . .

On to the new toys!

---

[28] `https://gulpjs.com/`
[29] `https://gruntjs.com/`
[30] `https://webpack.js.org/`
[31] `http://browserify.org/`
[32] `https://rollupjs.org/`

2

Block-Scoped Declarations: let and const

WHAT'S IN THIS CHAPTER?

- ➤ An introduction to `let` and `const`
- ➤ Definition of "block scope" with examples
- ➤ Shadowing and hoisting: the Temporal Dead Zone
- ➤ Using `const` for variables that shouldn't change
- ➤ Creating global variables that aren't on the global object
- ➤ Using block scope in loops

CODE DOWNLOADS FOR THIS CHAPTER

You can download the code for this chapter at `https://thenewtoys.dev/bookcode` or `https://www.wiley.com/go/javascript-newtoys`.

In this chapter you'll learn how the new `let` and `const` declarations work and what problems they solve. Throughout the chapter, you'll see some behaviors of `var` that have proved problematic, and you'll learn how `let` and `const` solve those problems. You'll see how `let` and `const` provide true block scope and prevent confusion caused by repeated declarations or by using a variable before you initialize it. You'll discover how block scope means you can use `let` to avoid the traditional "closures in loop" problem, and how `const` lets you create *constants*: "variables" whose values cannot change. You'll learn how `let` and `const` avoid creating even more properties on the already-overburdened global object. In short, you'll learn why `let` and `const` are the new `var`, and why `var` no longer has a place in modern JavaScript programming.

AN INTRODUCTION TO LET AND CONST

Like `var`, `let` declares variables:

```
let x = 2;
x += 40;
console.log(x); // 42
```

You can use `let` anywhere you can use `var`. Just as with `var`, you don't have to use an initializer with `let`; if you don't, the variable's value defaults to `undefined`:

```
let a;
console.log(a); // undefined
```

That's about where the similarities between `let` and `var` end. As you'll learn throughout this chapter, other than those basic similarities, `var` and `let` behave quite differently. More on that later; let's look at `const`.

`const` declares constants:

```
const value = Math.random();
console.log(value < 0.5 ? "Heads" : "Tails");
```

Constants are just like variables, except their values can't change. Because of that, you do need to supply an initializer; constants have no default value. Other than creating constants instead of variables and requiring an initializer, `const` is just like `let`. It's also much more useful than you probably expect, as you'll see across the course of this chapter.

TRUE BLOCK SCOPE

`var` jumps out of blocks. If you declare a variable within a block using `var`, it's not just in scope within that block, but outside it as well:

```
function jumpOut() {
    var a = [1, 2, 3];
    for (var i = 0; i < a.length; ++i) {
        var value = a[i];
        console.log(value);
    }
    console.log("Outside loop " + value);  // Why can we use 'value' here?
}
jumpOut();
```

The author of `jumpOut` probably didn't mean for `value` to be accessible outside the loop, but it is. (So is `i`.) Why is this a problem? There are a couple of reasons. First, variables should be scoped as narrowly as possible for maintainability reasons; they should only be around as long as you need them, and no longer. Second, any time the apparent intent of code and its actual effect differ, you're asking for bugs and maintenance issues.

let and const solve this by having true *block scope*: they exist only within the block they're declared in. Here's an example with *let*:

```
function stayContained() {
    var a = [1, 2, 3];
    for (var i = 0; i < a.length; ++i) {
        let value = a[i];
        console.log(value);
    }
    console.log("Outside loop" + value); // ReferenceError: 'value' is not defined
}
stayContained();
```

Now, value is scoped to the block in which it appears. It doesn't exist in the rest of the function. It's only around for as long as it's needed, and the apparent intent matches the actual effect.

(In stayContained, I didn't change the other variables from var to *let*. That was just to highlight the fact that what mattered was changing the declaration of value. Naturally, you can change the others as well.)

REPEATED DECLARATIONS ARE AN ERROR

var is happy to let you repeat yourself. You can declare the same variable with var as many times as you like. For example:

```
function redundantRepetition() {
    var x = "alpha";
    console.log(x);
    // ...lots of code here...
    var x = "bravo";
    console.log(x);
    // ...lots of code here...
    return x;
}
redundantRepetition();
```

That code is perfectly correct syntactically. The fact that it declares x more than once is completely ignored by the JavaScript engine; it creates a single x variable that's used throughout the function. As with the var in a block earlier, though, the apparent intent of the code and its actual effect are at odds with one another. Redeclaring a variable you've already declared is probably a mistake. In this case, it's likely that the original author of redundantRepetition didn't have the middle bit there and it was supposed to return "alpha"; but then someone else came along later and added a bit in the middle, not realizing x was already in use.

Like many things, good programming practice (keeping functions short) and/or lint tools and/or a good IDE can help here, which is great, but now so can JavaScript itself—*let* and const make repeated declarations in the same scope an error:

```
function redundantRepetition() {
    let x = "alpha";
    console.log(x);
    // ...lots of code here...
    let x = "bravo";          // SyntaxError: Identifier 'x' has already been declared
```

```
    console.log(x);
    // ...lots of code here...
    return x;
}
redundantRepetition();
```

It's the best kind of error, too: a proactive one. The error is raised when the code is *parsed*; it doesn't wait until later when you call `redundantRepetition` before telling you about the problem.

HOISTING AND THE TEMPORAL DEAD ZONE

`var` declarations are famously *hoisted*. With `var`, you can use a variable before you declare it:

```
function example() {
    console.log(answer);
    answer = 42;
    console.log(answer);
    var answer = 67;
}
example();
```

When you run `example`, it outputs the following:

```
undefined
42
```

We've cheerfully used the variable before it was declared, but the `var` declaration was seemingly moved to the top of the function. And *only* the declaration moved, not the initializer attached to it (the `= 67` part of `var answer = 67`).

This happens because when entering the `example` function, the JavaScript engine scans through the function handling `var` declarations and creating the necessary variables before it starts running any of the step-by-step code; it "hoists" (lifts) the declarations to the top of the function. When it does that, it initializes the variables they declare with a default value of `undefined`. But again, the apparent intent of the code and its actual effect are out of sync, which probably means there's a bug here. It looks like that first line is trying to assign to an `answer` variable that is in a containing scope (perhaps even a global), but instead it uses a local. It also looks like the author intended that when `answer` was created, it would start out with the value `67`.

With `let` and `const`, you can't use a variable until its declaration is processed in the step-by-step execution of the code:

```
function boringOldLinearTime() {
    answer = 42;            // ReferenceError: 'answer' is not defined
    console.log(answer);
    let answer;
}
boringOldLinearTime();
```

Seemingly, the `let` declaration isn't hoisted up to the top of the function like a `var` declaration is. But that's a popular misconception: `let` and `const` are hoisted, too. They're just hoisted *differently*.

Consider the observation earlier that the code may have been trying to assign to an answer in a containing scope. Let's look at that scenario:

```
let answer;                  // The outer 'answer'
function hoisting() {
    answer = 42;             // ReferenceError: 'answer' is not defined
    console.log(answer);
    let answer;              // The inner 'answer'
}
hoisting();
```

If the inner answer doesn't exist until the let answer; statement at the end, then at the beginning of the function where answer = 42; is, shouldn't that line assign to the outer answer?

It could have been designed that way, yes; but how confusing would that be? Using an identifier for one thing early in the scope but for something else later in the scope is asking for bugs.

Instead, let and const use a concept called the *Temporal Dead Zone* (TDZ), a period of time within the code execution where the identifier can't be used at all, not even to refer to something in a containing scope. Just like with var, the JavaScript engine looks through the code for let and const declarations and processes them before starting the step-by-step execution of the code. But instead of making answer accessible and giving it the value undefined, the engine marks answer as "not yet initialized":

```
let answer;                  // The outer 'answer'
function notInitializedYet() {
                             // Reserve 'answer' here
    answer = 42;             // ReferenceError: 'answer' is not defined
    console.log(answer);
    let answer;              // The inner 'answer'
}
notInitializedYet();
```

The TDZ starts when code execution enters the scope where the declaration appears and continues until the declaration is run (along with any initializer attached to it). In this example, the inner answer is reserved at the beginning of notInitializedYet (that's where the TDZ starts) and initialized where the declaration is (that's where the TDZ ends). So let and const are still hoisted, they're just hoisted differently than var is.

It's important to understand that the TDZ is *temporal* (related to time), not *spatial* (related to space/location). It's not a section at the top of the scope where the identifier can't be used. It's a *period of time* during which the identifier can't be used. Run the code in Listing 2-1.

LISTING 2-1: Example of the temporal nature of the TDZ—tdz-is-temporal.js

```
function temporalExample() {
    const f = () => {
        console.log(value);
    };
    let value = 42;
    f();
}
temporalExample();
```

If the TDZ were *spatial*, if it were a block of code at the top of temporalExample where value couldn't be used, that code wouldn't work. But the TDZ is *temporal*, and by the time f uses value, the declaration has been run, so there's no problem. If you swapped the last two lines of that function, moving the f(); line above the let value = 42; line, then it would fail because f would try to use value before it was initialized. (Try it!)

The TDZ applies to blocks just as much as it applies to functions:

```
function blockExample(str) {
    let p = "prefix";                    // The outer 'p' declaration
    if (str) {
        p = p.toUpperCase();             // ReferenceError: 'p' is not defined
        str = str.toUpperCase();
        let p = str.indexOf("X");        // The inner 'p' declaration
        if (p != -1) {
            str = str.substring(0, p);
        }
    }
    return p + str;
}
```

You can't use p in that first line inside the block, because even though it's declared in the function, there's a *shadowing* declaration inside the block taking ownership of the p identifier. So the identifier can only refer to the new inner p, and only after the let declaration has been run. This prevents confusion about which p the code is using.

A NEW KIND OF GLOBAL

When you use var at global scope, it creates a global variable. In ES5 and earlier, all global variables were also properties of the global object. But that changed with ES2015: now JavaScript has traditional globals created with var (which are also properties of the global object) and also new-style globals (which are not properties of the global object). let and const at global scope create this new kind of global.

> ## ACCESSING THE GLOBAL OBJECT
>
> You'll recall that there's one global object, and you can get access to it via this at global scope, or by using a global that the environment defines for it (if any) such as window or self on browsers or global on Node.js. (In some environments, such as browsers, it's not really the global object, it's a facade on the global object, but that's close enough.)

Here's an example of using var to create a global that is also a property of the global object; note that you must run this at global scope (if you're using Node.js or jsFiddle.net, remember to make sure you're working at global scope, not module or function scope, as described in Chapter 1).

```
var answer = 42;
console.log("answer == " + answer);
console.log("this.answer == " + this.answer);
console.log("has property? " + ("answer" in this));
```

When you run that, you'll see:

```
answer == 42
this.answer == 42
has property? true
```

Now try it with `let` (in a fresh window):

```
let answer = 42;
console.log("answer == " + answer);
console.log("this.answer == " + this.answer);
console.log("has property? " + ("answer" in this));
```

This time, you get:

```
answer == 42
this.answer == undefined
has property? false
```

Notice that `answer` isn't a property on the global object anymore.

It's the same with `const`: it creates a global, but the global isn't a property of the global object.

These globals are still accessible anywhere, even if they aren't properties of the global object, so this doesn't mean you should stop avoiding globals. Given that, can you think of some reasons that having them not be properties of the global object is useful?

There are at least a couple of reasons:

➤ The global object is already dramatically overburdened with properties in the most common environment: a web browser. Not only do all `var`-declared globals end up on it, but it also gets properties for all elements with an `id`, most elements with a `name`, and many other "automatic globals." It's just overcrowded. Stemming the tide is a good thing.

➤ It makes them harder to discover from other code. To use a `let` or `const` global, you have to know its name; you can't discover it by looking at the names of the properties in the global object. This isn't all that useful—if you want privacy, don't create a global—but it's slightly less of an information leak.

➤ It may make it possible for the JavaScript engine to optimize access to them (particularly `const`s) in ways that can't be applied to properties of the global object.

Speaking of automatic globals, a global declared with `let` or `const` (or `class`) shadows an automatic global (that is, it hides it; the `let` or `const` declaration "wins"); a global declared with `var` doesn't in all cases. The classic example is trying to use a global called `name` on a web browser. On a browser, the global object is the Window object for the page, which has a property called `name`, which cannot be shadowed with a `var` global and whose value is always a string:

```
// On a browser at global scope
var name = 42;
console.log(typeof name); // "string"
```

A `let` or `const` global will successfully shadow it, though, or any other automatic global/window property:

```
// On a browser at global scope
let name = 42;
console.log(typeof name); // "number"
```

Principally, though, decoupling `let` and `const` from the global object is just part and parcel of the direction of the language as it moves away from relying on the global object—something you'll learn more about in subsequent chapters, particularly Chapter 13 (Modules).

CONST: CONSTANTS FOR JAVASCRIPT

We've already covered several things about `const` that it shares with `let`; this section covers `const` in depth.

const Basics

As you know, `const` creates a constant:

```
const answer = 42;
console.log(answer); // 42
```

It's exactly like creating a variable with `let`, with all the same scope rules, the Temporal Dead Zone, etc., except that you cannot assign a new value to a constant, whereas of course you can assign a new value to a variable.

What do you think happens when you try to assign a new value to a constant? What would be the most useful thing?

Right—you get an error:

```
const answer = 42;
console.log(answer); // 42
answer = 67;         // TypeError: invalid assignment to const 'answer'
```

> **NOTE** *The text of the error message varies from implementation to implementation, but it will be a* `TypeError`*. As of this writing, at least one implementation amusingly and oxymoronically says "TypeError: Assignment to constant variable".*

At first glance, it may seem that you'd only want to use `const` for things like avoiding having "magic numbers" in code, such as a standard delay you might use in code before showing a busy message when you're doing something the user initiated:

```
const BUSY_DISPLAY_DELAY = 300; // milliseconds
```

But `const` is useful for far more than that. Although we frequently do change the values of variables, we just as frequently don't change their values; we just use them to hold unchanging information.

Let's look at a real-world example: Listing 2-2 has a simple loop for appending text to divs depending on whether they have a particular class. It seems to make fairly straightforward use of variables.

LISTING 2-2: ES5 Version of div update loop—element-loop-es5.js

```
var list, n, element, text;
list = document.querySelectorAll("div.foo");
for (n = 0; n < list.length; ++n) {
    element = list[n];
    text = element.classList.contains("bar") ? " [bar]" : "[not bar]";
    element.appendChild(document.createTextNode(text));
}
```

There are four variables in that code. If you look closely, you'll see that one of them isn't like the other three. Can you spot what's different?

One of them has a value that never changes: list. The others (n, element, and text) are actually variables, but list is a constant.

We'll come back to that code in a later section after covering a couple more aspects of const, but in the back of your mind in the meantime, consider how you might apply let and const to that code (without removing any of the identifiers) based on what you know so far.

Objects Referenced by a const Are Still Mutable

It's important to remember what it is that can't be changed with a constant: the value of the *constant*. If that value is an object reference, it doesn't in any way mean that the object is *immutable* (that its state can't be changed); the object is still *mutable* (it can still be changed). It just means you can't make the constant point to a *different* object (because that would change the value of the constant). Let's explore that:

```
const obj = {
    value: "before"
};
console.log(obj.value);        // "before"
```

So far, you have a reference to an object in a constant. In memory, you have something like Figure 2-1.

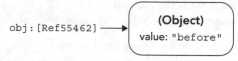

FIGURE 2-1

The obj constant doesn't directly contain the object, it contains a reference to the object (shown in Figure 2-1 as "Ref55462" but of course that's just conceptual; you never see the real value of object references). So if you change the object's state:

```
obj.value = "after";
console.log(obj.value);        // "after"
```

you're not changing the value of the obj constant; it's still a reference to the same object ("Ref55462"). It's just that the object's state has been updated so it stores a different value for its value property; see Figure 2-2.

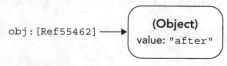

FIGURE 2-2

What `const` does is prevent you changing the actual value of `obj`, either to make it refer to a different object, or to set it to `null`, or something else entirely:

```
obj = {}; // TypeError: invalid assignment to const 'obj'
```

Here's a practical example, a function that adds a paragraph with the given HTML to a parent element:

```
function addParagraph(parent, html) {
    const p = document.createElement("p");
    p.innerHTML = html;
    parent.appendChild(p);
    return p;
}
```

Since the code only changes the state of the paragraph (by setting its `innerHTML` property), not which paragraph `p` refers to, you can make `p` constant.

BLOCK SCOPE IN LOOPS

You saw block scope earlier in this chapter. On the face of it, it's quite simple—a variable declared with `let` or `const` inside a block is only accessible within the block:

```
function anotherBlockExample(str) {
    if (str) {
        let index = str.indexOf("X");    // 'index' only exists within the block
        if (index != -1) {
            str = str.substring(0, index);
        }
    }
    // Can't use 'index' here, it's out of scope
    return str;
}
anotherBlockExample();
```

But what if the block is attached to a loop? Do all loop iterations use the same variable? Or are there separate variables created for each iteration? How do closures created within the loop behave?

The people designing block scope for JavaScript did the clever thing: each loop iteration gets its own block variables, in almost exactly the same way that different calls to a function each get their own local variables. This means you can use block scope to solve the classic "closures in loops" problem.

The "Closures in Loops" Problem

You're probably familiar with the "closures in loops" problem, though perhaps not by that name; run the code in Listing 2-3 to see the problem in action.

LISTING 2-3: Closures in loops problem—closures-in-loops-problem.js

```
function closuresInLoopsProblem() {
    for (var counter = 1; counter <= 3; ++counter) {
        setTimeout(function() {
            console.log(counter);
        }, 10);
    }
}
closuresInLoopsProblem();
```

(Ignore any features `setTimeout` may have to help us with this problem; it's just a placeholder for any asynchronous operation.)

You might expect that code to output 1, then 2, then 3, but instead it outputs 4, 4, 4. The reason is that each timer doesn't run its callback until after the loop finishes. By the time they call the callbacks, `counter`'s value is 4, and because it's declared with `var`, `counter` is defined throughout the `closuresInLoopsProblem` function. All three timer callbacks close over the same `counter` variable, so they all see the value 4.

In ES5 and earlier, the usual way to solve that is by introducing another function and passing `counter` into it as an argument, then using that argument instead of `counter` in the `console.log`. Coders frequently do it with an inline anonymous function they call immediately, such as in Listing 2-4.

LISTING 2-4: Closures in loops, standard ES5 solution—closures-in-loops-es5.js

```
function closuresInLoopsES5() {
    for (var counter = 1; counter <= 3; ++counter) {
        (function(value) {        // The beginning of the anonymous function
            setTimeout(function() {
                console.log(value);
            }, 10);
        })(counter);              // The end of it, and the call to it
    }
}
closuresInLoopsES5();
```

When you run that, it outputs the expected 1, 2, 3, because the timer functions are using `value`, not `counter`, and each call to the anonymous wrapper function gets its own `value` parameter for the timer function to close over. Nothing changes any of those `value` parameters, so the callbacks log the expected values (1, 2, and 3).

Thanks to ES2015's `let`, though, you can solve it much more simply: by just changing `var` to `let`. Run the code in Listing 2-5.

LISTING 2-5: Closures in loops, solved with let—closures-in-loops-with-let.js

```
function closuresInLoopsWithLet() {
    for (let counter = 1; counter <= 3; ++counter) {
        setTimeout(function() {
            console.log(counter);
        }, 10);
    }
}
closuresInLoopsWithLet();
```

Running that also gives you the expected 1, 2, 3. One small change, one massive impact. But how does it work? Surely the functions still close over `counter`? How can they all see different values?

Just like the calls to the anonymous function created multiple `value` parameters for the timer functions to close over, the loop above in Listing 2-5 creates multiple `counter` variables for the timer functions created in the loop to close over, one for each loop iteration. So each iteration gets its own `counter` variable.

To understand how, we need to look more closely at how variables (and constants) work in JavaScript. This will also help you with some later chapters.

Bindings: How Variables, Constants, and Other Identifiers Work

Earlier in this chapter you learned that `const`'s constants work just like `let`'s variables in terms of scope, the kinds of values they can hold, etc. There's a good reason for that. Under the covers, variables and constants are the same thing, which the specification calls *bindings* (specifically in this case, *identifier bindings*): a link between an identifier and the storage for its value. When you create a variable, for instance with

```
let x = 42;
```

you're creating a binding for the identifier named x and storing the value 42 in that binding's storage slot. In that case, it's a *mutable* binding (a binding whose value can change). When you create a constant, you create an *immutable* binding (a binding whose value cannot change).

Identifier bindings have names and values. Sound like anything you know? They're a bit like object properties aren't they? And like object properties, they're in a container, which I'm going to call an *environment object*.[1] For instance, the environment object for the context where this code runs:

```
let a = 1;
const b = 2;
```

would look something like Figure 2-3.

To handle nested scopes, environment objects are linked together in a chain: each has a link to the one "outside" it.

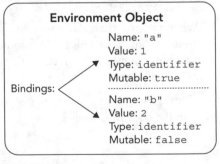

FIGURE 2-3

---

[1] What I'm calling an "environment object" is divided in the specification into a *Lexical Environment* and the *Environment Record* it contains. The division isn't important here.

If code needs an identifier that isn't in the current environment object, it follows the link to the outer environment object to find it (repeating as necessary, up through the global environment—which is how global variables work).

The outer environment is set in various ways. For instance, when code execution enters a block with block-scoped identifiers in it, the environment object for the block gets the environment object for the code containing the block as its outer environment. When a function is called, the environment object for the call gets the environment where the function was created (which is saved on the function; the spec calls it the [[Environment]] internal slot of the function) as its outer environment. That's how closures work.

For instance, consider this code (assume it's at global scope):

```
let x = 1;
function example() {
    const y = 2;
    return function() {
        let z = 3;
        console.log(z, y, x);
    };
}
const f = example();
f();
```

Within the f() call, when code execution gets to the console.log line, the environment object chain looks something like Figure 2-4 (overleaf).

Let's follow that through:

➤ The JavaScript engine creates the global environment (EnvObject1) and adds the bindings x, f, and example to it.

➤ It creates the example function, setting example's saved environment link to the current environment (the global one, EnvObject1), and setting the example binding's value to the function.

➤ It runs the let x = 1; line, setting x to 1.

➤ It runs the const f = example(); line:

   ➤ It creates a new environment object for the call (EnvObject2), setting its outer environment to example's saved environment (EnvObject1).

   ➤ It creates a binding called y in that environment object.

   ➤ It runs the const y = 2; line, setting y to 2.

   ➤ It creates the function, setting the current environment (EnvObject2, the one for the call to example) as its saved environment.

   ➤ It returns the function from the call.

   ➤ It assigns the function to f.

➤ Finally, the engine runs the `f();` line, calling the function f refers to:

    ➤ It creates a new environment object for the call (`EnvObject3`), setting its outer environment to the function's saved environment (`EnvObject2`, the one from the call to `example` earlier), and creating the z binding on it.

    ➤ It sets z to 3.

    ➤ It runs the `console.log` line.

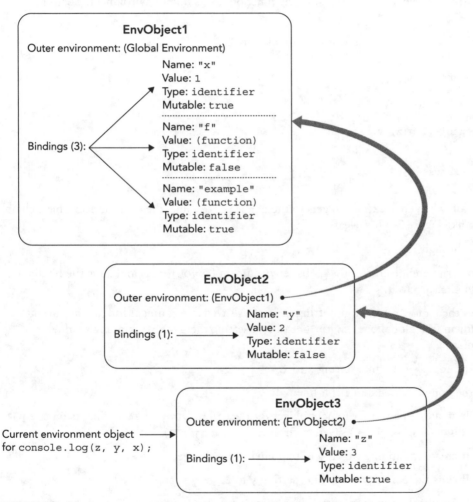

FIGURE 2-4

In the `console.log` line, the engine finds z in the current environment, but has to go to the outer environment (the one for the call to `example`) to find y, and has to go two levels out to find x.

How does all this help us understand `closuresInLoopsWithLet`? Let's look at that function again; see Listing 2-6.

LISTING 2-6: Closures in loops, solved with let (again)—closures-in-loops-with-let.js

```javascript
function closuresInLoopsWithLet() {
    for (let counter = 1; counter <= 3; ++counter) {
        setTimeout(function() {
            console.log(counter);
        }, 10);
    }
}
closuresInLoopsWithLet();
```

When executing the `for` loop, the JavaScript engine creates a new environment object for each loop iteration, each with its own, separate `counter` variable, so each timer callback closes over a different `counter` variable. Here's what the JavaScript engine does with that loop:

1. It creates an environment object for the call; let's call it `CallEnvObject`.

2. It sets `CallEnvObject`'s outer environment reference to the saved environment on the `closuresInLoopsWithLet` function (the one where it was created; in this case, the global environment).

3. It begins processing the `for` by remembering the list of variables declared with `let` in the initialization part of the `for`; in this case, there's just one, `counter`, though you could have more.

4. It creates a new environment object for the initialization part of the loop, using `CallEnv-Object` as its outer environment, and creates a binding on it for `counter` with the value 1.

5. It creates a new environment object (`LoopEnvObject1`) for the first iteration, using `Call-EnvObject` as its outer environment object.

6. Referring to its list from Step 3, it creates a binding for `counter` on `LoopEnvObject1`, setting its value to 1 (the value from the initialization environment object).

7. It sets `LoopEnvObject1` as the current environment object.

8. Because the test `counter <= 3` is true, it executes the body of the `for` by creating the first timer function (let's call it `timerFunction1`), giving it a reference to `LoopEnvObject1` as its saved environment object.

9. It calls `setTimeout` passing a reference to `timerFunction1` into it.

At this point, you have something like Figure 2-5 in memory.

FIGURE 2-5

Now the JavaScript engine is ready for the next loop iteration:

10. It creates a new environment object (`LoopEnvObject2`) using `CallEnvObject` as its outer environment.

11. Using its list of bindings from Step 3, it creates a binding for `counter` on `LoopEnvObject2` and sets its value to the current value of `counter` on `LoopEnvObject1` (1, in this case).

12. It sets `LoopEnvObject2` as the current environment object.

13. It does the "increment" part of the `for` loop: `++counter`. The `counter` it increments is the one in the current environment object, `LoopEnvObject2`. Since its value is 1, it becomes 2.

14. It continues with the `for` loop: since the condition is true, it executes the loop body by creating the second timer function (`timerFunction2`), giving it a reference to `LoopEnvObject2` so it closes over the information in it.

15. It calls `setTimeout` passing in a reference to `timerFunction2`.

As you can see, the two timer functions close over different environment objects with different copies of `counter`. The first one still has `counter = 1`; the second one has `counter = 2`. At this point, you have something like Figure 2-6 in memory.

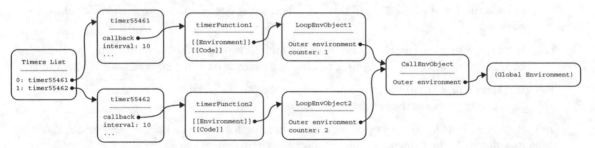

FIGURE 2-6

The whole thing happens for the third and last loop iteration and you end up with something like Figure 2-7 (see page opposite) in memory.

When the timer functions are called by the timers, since they each use a separate environment object, each with its own copy of `counter`, you see 1, 2, 3 instead of the 4, 4, 4 you saw with `var` where all were sharing the same environment object and variable.

In short, the mechanics of block scope in the loop did exactly what our ES5 solution's anonymous function did: gave each timer function a different environment object to close over with its own copy of the binding (`counter` in the `let` solution, `value` in the ES5 solution). But it did it more efficiently, without requiring a separate function and function call.

Sometimes, of course, you want the old behavior. In that case, just declare the variable before the loop (which is, of course, what `var` did).

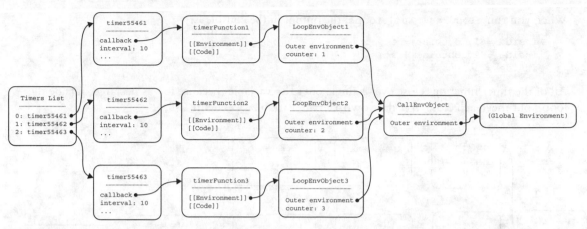

FIGURE 2-7

The only part of the behavior you've just learned about that's specific to `for` loops is the part where it keeps track of what `let` variables were created in the initializer part of the `for` and copies the value of those bindings from one environment object to the next. But the fact a block gets its own environment object isn't at all limited to `for` loops, and among other things that means `while` and `do-while` loops also benefit from blocks getting their own environment objects. Let's look at how.

while and do-while Loops

`while` and `do-while` also benefit from the fact blocks get their own environment objects. Since they don't have `for`'s initialization expression, they don't do the thing where they copy forward the values of the bindings declared there, but the block associated with each loop iteration still gets its own environment. Let's see that in action. Run Listing 2-7.

LISTING 2-7: Closures in while loops—closures-in-while-loops.js

```
function closuresInWhileLoops() {
    let outside = 1;
    while (outside <= 3) {
        let inside = outside;
        setTimeout(function() {
            console.log("inside = " + inside + ", outside = " + outside);
        }, 10);
        ++outside;
    }
}
closuresInWhileLoops();
```

When you run `closuresInWhileLoops`, the output in the console is:

```
inside = 1, outside = 4
inside = 2, outside = 4
inside = 3, outside = 4
```

All of the timer functions close over a single `outside` variable (because it was declared outside the loop), but they each close over their own `inside` variable. See Figure 2-8.

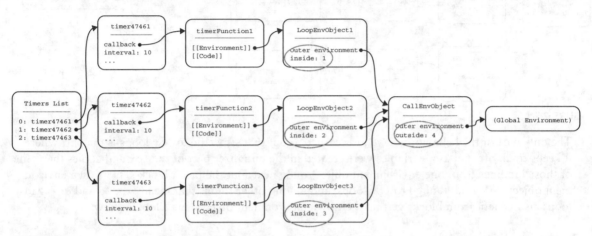

FIGURE 2-8

Performance Implications

Thinking about how block scope in loops works, you might be thinking: "Wait, if I use block variables in the loop and it has to create a new environment object to hold them and set up a chain, and (for `for` loops) copy the iteration binding value from one to the next, won't that slow down my loops?"

There are two answers to that:

1. You probably don't care. Remember that premature optimization is just that: premature. Worry about it if and when you have a real performance problem you're solving.

2. Yes and no. It is definitely more overhead if the JavaScript engine hasn't optimized the difference away, and there are times (including our closures in loops example) where it can't optimize the difference away. Other times, if we're not creating closures or the engine can determine that the closures don't use the per-loop-iteration variables, it may well be able to optimize the difference away. Modern engines do a lot of optimization. When ES2015's `let` was newish, Chrome's V8 engine ran `for` loops markedly slower if you used `let` for the loop variable than if you used `var`. That speed difference disappeared (for cases where closures weren't being created and such) as V8's engineers found ways to optimize it.

If you run into an actual problem with a loop, and it's not important that you have separate copies of the variables, just move them into the enclosing scope:

```
let n;
for (n = 0; n < aReallyReallyBigNumber; ++n) {
    // ...
}
```

or if you don't want it in that scope, wrap the entire loop in an anonymous block and declare the variable in that block:

```
function wrappingInAnonymousBlock() {
    // ...some unrelated code...

    // Now we've identified a performance/memory problem with the per-iteration
    // initialization of 'n', so we use an anonymous block to have just one 'n'
    {
        let n;
        for (n = 0; n < aReallyReallyBigNumber; ++n) {
            // ...
        }
    }

    // ...more unrelated code...
}
wrappingInAnonymousBlock();
```

const in Loop Blocks

In the earlier section on `const`, you saw a simple `div` update loop (repeated in Listing 2-8) where one of the variables (`list`) actually never changed, and I asked you to think about how you'd apply `let` and `const` to the code (without removing any identifiers).

LISTING 2-8: ES5 version of div update loop—element-loop-es5.js

```
var list, n, element, text;
list = document.querySelectorAll("div.foo");
for (n = 0; n < list.length; ++n) {
    element = list[n];
    text = element.classList.contains("bar") ? " [bar]" : "[not bar]";
    element.appendChild(document.createTextNode(text));
}
```

Did you come up with something like Listing 2-9?

LISTING 2-9: ES2015 version of div update loop—element-loop-es2015.js

```
const list = document.querySelectorAll("div.foo");
for (let n = 0; n < list.length; ++n) {
    const element = list[n];
    const text = element.classList.contains("bar") ? " [bar]" : "[not bar]";
    element.appendChild(document.createTextNode(text));
}
```

At the time, you may not have thought to move `element` and `text` into the `for` loop's block, or if you did you may have left them as `let` rather than `const` declarations. But their values within the block never change, and of course each block gets its own copy of them, so they're constants within its scope and we can mark our intent just to use them, not modify them, by declaring them `const`.

You don't have to declare something `const` just because you don't change it. Whether you do is a matter of style and something your team should discuss and come to agreement on (do use `const`, don't use `const`, or leave it up to individual style). There are pragmatic benefits to using it during development (you get an early error if you try to change something a teammate declared `const`; you then either purposefully change the declaration or don't change the value of that constant), but your team may be using full test suites that will also find the error (albeit somewhat later).

const in for-in Loops

In addition to the usual `for` loop with the four parts (initialization, test, increment, body), JavaScript has other types of `for` loop: `for-in`, `for-of`, and `for-await-of`. (You'll learn about `for-of` in Chapter 6; `for-await-of` in Chapter 9.) Let's take a quick look at a typical `for-in`:

```
var obj = {a: 1, b: 2};
for (var key in obj) {
    console.log(key + ": " + obj[key]);
}
```

If you were going to write that in ES2015+, would you use `let` or `const` for `key`?

You can use either. `for-in` loops with lexical declarations get a separate environment object for each loop iteration just like `while` does. Since the code in the loop body doesn't change `key`, it can be `const` if you like:

```
const obj = {a: 1, b: 2};
for (const key in obj) {
    console.log(key + ": " + obj[key]);
}
```

OLD HABITS TO NEW

Here are some old habits that you may want to replace with new habits.

Use const or let Instead of var

Old habit: Using `var`.

New habit: Use `const` or `let` instead. The only remaining use cases for `var` are legacy code, for instance having a top-level

```
var MyApp = MyApp || {};
```

in several scripts that may be loaded on a page and all write to different parts of the `MyApp` object, and doing that is superseded by modules (see Chapter 13).

If you adopt const for "variables" you don't intend to change, you'll probably find that you use const much more than you originally thought you would, especially since with object references it doesn't mean you can't change the state of the object, it just means you can't change what object the constant refers to. If you're writing object-heavy code (which is almost inevitable with JavaScript), it's surprising how few actual *variables* you end up with.

Keep Variables Narrowly Scoped

Old habit: Listing vars at the top of the function, since that's where var was hoisted to anyway.

New habit: Use let and const in the narrowest appropriate scope, where reasonable. This improves the maintainability of the code.

Use Block Scope Instead of Inline Anonymous Functions

Old habit: Using inline anonymous functions to solve the closures-with-loops problem:

```
for (var n = 0; n < 3; ++n) {
    (function(value) {
        setTimeout(function() {
            console.log(value);
        }, 10);
    })(n);
}
```

New habit: Use block scope instead:

```
for (let n = 0; n < 3; ++n) {
    setTimeout(function() {
        console.log(n);
    }, 10);
}
```

Much cleaner and easier to read.

That said, don't replace perfectly good named, reusable functions with block scope without good reason:

```
// If it's already like this, with a reusable named function, no need
// to move the function code into the loop
function delayedLog(msg, delay) {
    setTimeout(function() {
        console.log(msg);
    }, delay);
}
// ...later...
for (let n = 0; n < 3; ++n) {
    delayedLog(n, 10);
}
```

Block scope isn't a substitute for rightsizing functions, but it is a useful tool for eliminating confusing inline anonymous ones.

If you use scoping functions at global scope to avoid creating global variables, you can even replace those with a block (or a module, as you'll learn in Chapter 13). Blocks don't have to be attached to a flow-control statement like `if` or `for`; they can be free-standing. So your scoping function can just be a scoping block:

```
{                          // Scoping block
    let answer = 42;       // 'answer' is local to the block, not global
    console.log(answer);
}
```

3

New Function Features

WHAT'S IN THIS CHAPTER?

➤ Arrow functions and lexical `this`, `super`, etc.

➤ Default parameter values

➤ "Rest" parameters

➤ Trailing commas in parameter lists and function calls

➤ The function `name` property

➤ Function declarations inside blocks

CODE DOWNLOADS FOR THIS CHAPTER

You can download the code for this chapter at `https://thenewtoys.dev/bookcode` or `https://www.wiley.com/go/javascript-newtoys`.

In this chapter you'll learn about many of the exciting new features of functions in modern JavaScript, such as *arrow functions*, a lightweight, concise new form of function that solves an entire class of issues with callbacks; *default parameter values* for simplifying function code and improving support for tools; *rest parameters* providing true arrays of the "rest" of the arguments to a function after the named ones; the newly official `name` property on functions and the many and varied ways it gets set; and how function declarations within flow-control blocks work.

There are three function-related things we defer to later chapters:

➤ *Destructured parameters* are covered in Chapter 7.

➤ *Generator functions* are covered in Chapter 6.

➤ `async` *functions* are covered in Chapter 9.

> ### PARAMETER VS. ARGUMENT
>
> In programming, we have two closely related terms that are frequently used inter-changeably: *parameter* and *argument*. A function declares and uses *parameters*. You call that function with specific values for those parameters called *arguments*. Let's do a quick example:
>
> ```
> function foo(bar) {
>     console.log(bar * 6);
> }
> foo(7);
> ```
>
> The function foo declares and uses a *parameter* named bar. The code calls foo with the *argument* 7.

ARROW FUNCTIONS AND LEXICAL THIS, SUPER, ETC.

ES2015 added *arrow functions* to JavaScript. Arrow functions solve a whole class of problems, particularly with callbacks: making sure that this inside the function is the same as this outside it. They're also lighter-weight and more concise than traditional functions created using the function keyword (sometimes much more concise).

Let's start with the syntax and then we'll look more closely at this and the other things arrow functions handle differently from traditional functions.

Arrow Function Syntax

Arrow functions come in two forms: ones with a *concise body* (often called *concise arrow functions*) and ones with a standard *function body* (I call them *verbose arrow functions*, though they're still not as verbose as traditional functions). We'll look at the concise form first.

Suppose you want to filter an array, keeping only the entries whose value is less than 30. You'd probably do it by using Array.prototype.filter and passing in a callback function. In ES5, that would look like this:

```
var array = [42, 67, 3, 23, 14];
var filtered = array.filter(function(entry) {
    return entry < 30;
});
console.log(filtered); // [3, 23, 14]
```

This is a common use case for callbacks: a callback that needs to do something simple and return a value. Arrow functions provide a very concise way to do it:

```
const array = [42, 67, 3, 23, 14];
const filtered = array.filter(entry => entry < 30);
console.log(filtered); // [3, 23, 14]
```

When you compare it to the traditional function you're used to, it almost doesn't look like a function at all! Don't worry, you'll soon get used to it.

As you can see, the concise form of an arrow function is literally just the name of the parameter(s) it accepts, then an arrow (=>) to tell the parser this is an arrow function, and then an expression defining the value it returns. That's it. No `function` keyword, no curly braces to define a function body, no `return` keyword; just the parameters, the arrow, and the body expression.

When you want an arrow function to accept multiple parameters, you need to wrap its parameter list in parentheses to make it clear that they're all parameters for the arrow function. For instance, if you wanted to sort the array rather than filtering it, you'd do this:

```
const array = [42, 67, 3, 23, 14];
array.sort((a, b) => a - b);
console.log(array); // [3, 14, 23, 42, 67]
```

Notice the parentheses around the parameters. Why do you think the syntax had to require them?

Consider how it would look if they weren't there:

```
array.sort(a, b => a - b);
```

See the problem? Right! It looks like we're passing two arguments to the `sort` method: a variable called a, and the arrow function b => a - b. So the parentheses are necessary if you have multiple parameters. (You can always include them, even if there's only one parameter, if you like to be consistent.)

You also use parentheses when you don't need to accept any parameters, such as in a timer callback—just leave them empty:

```
setTimeout(() => console.log("timer fired"), 200);
```

Although concise arrow functions are frequently written without line breaks, that's not at all a requirement of the concise syntax; if you had a complex calculation to do in the `array.sort` callback, you could put it on its own line:

```
const array = [42, 67, 3, 23, 14];
array.sort((a, b) =>
    a % 2 ? b % 2 ? a - b : -1 : b % 2 ? 1 : a - b
);
console.log(array); // [3, 23, 67, 14, 42]
```

That code sorts the array in two groups: first the odd numbers and then the even ones. The body of the function is still a single (complicated) expression, which is important for the concise arrow form.

But what if your arrow function needs to have multiple statements rather than just a single expression? Maybe you think the `sort` call would be clearer if you broke up that complicated expression (I certainly think it would be). For that, you can use the *function body* form (or as I call it, *verbose* form) by providing a function body using curly braces after the arrow:

```
const array = [42, 67, 3, 23, 14];
array.sort((a, b) => {
    const aIsOdd = a % 2;
    const bIsOdd = b % 2;
    if (aIsOdd) {
        return bIsOdd ? a - b : -1;
    }
    return bIsOdd ? 1 : a - b;
});
console.log(array); // [3, 23, 67, 14, 42]
```

That callback does exactly what the earlier one did, using multiple simple statements rather than a single complex expression.

Two things to notice about the verbose form:

➤ There's an opening curly brace immediately after the arrow. That's what tells the parser that you're using the verbose form, where the function body is inside curly braces just like with traditional functions.

➤ You use `return` to return a value, just like with a traditional function. If you didn't use `return`, then just like a traditional function, the arrow function wouldn't explicitly provide a return value and calling it would result in the value `undefined`.

Just as a concise arrow function doesn't have to be on one line, a verbose one doesn't have to be on multiple lines. As is usually the case, where you do line breaks is up to you.

WARNING: THE COMMA OPERATOR AND ARROW FUNCTIONS

Because the concise form of an arrow function takes an expression after the `=>`, some programmers have taken to using the comma operator to avoid using the verbose form if they have just two or three things to do in the function. Recall that the comma operator is one of JavaScript's odder operators: it evaluates its left-hand operand, throws away the resulting value, and then evaluates its right-hand operand and takes that value as its result. Example:

```
function returnSecond(a, b) {
    return a, b;
}
console.log(returnSecond(1, 2)); // 2
```

The result of `return a, b;` is the value of `b`.

How does this relate to arrow functions? It lets you do more than one thing in the expression used by the concise form, by using an expression in the left-hand operand that has a side effect. Let's say you have an array of "handlers" wrapped around "items," and you want to transform each entry by passing the handler into an `unregister` function, and then pass its item into a `register` function and remember the result. With a traditional function you'd do this:

```
handlers = handlers.map(function(handler) {
    unregister(handler);
```

```
            return register(handler.item);
    });
```

You can make that shorter by using a verbose arrow function:

```
    handlers = handlers.map(handler => {
        unregister(handler);
        return register(handler.item);
    });
```

But some programmers will use a *concise* arrow function instead, using (or perhaps *ab*using) the comma operator:

```
    handlers = handlers.map(handler =>
        (unregister(handler), register(handler.item))
    );
```

(But usually all on one line.) You have to put parentheses around the comma expression (otherwise the parser would think you were passing two arguments to `handlers.map` instead of one), so the only reason it's shorter than the verbose form is it avoids writing the `return` keyword.

Whether you consider this to be a handy use of the comma operator or an abuse of it, just be aware that you are likely to see it used this way in the wild.

There's one "gotcha" to be aware of with the concise form of arrow functions: a concise arrow function returning an object created with an object literal.

Suppose you have an array of strings and you want to convert it into an array of objects using the string as their name property. That sounds like a job for `Array`'s map method and a concise arrow function:

```
    const a = ["Joe", "Mohammed", "María"];
    const b = a.map(name => {name: name});        // Doesn't work
    console.log(b);
```

But when you try to run that, you get an array with a bunch of `undefined`s in it instead of objects. (Or depending on the object you create, a syntax error.) What happened?

The issue is that the opening curly brace tells the JavaScript parser that you're using the verbose form, not the concise form, so it uses that brace to start the body and then uses the contents (`name: name`) as the body of the verbose arrow function, like this traditional function:

```
    const a = ["Joe", "Mohammed", "María"];
    const b = a.map(function(name) {              // Doesn't work
        name: name
    });
    console.log(b);
```

Since the function doesn't return anything (because the parser thinks you're using the verbose form), the result of calling it is the value `undefined`, and you end up with an array filled with `undefined`. The body of the function isn't a syntax error (in this example) because it looks like a label (you remember labels, the things you can use with nested loops to break the outer loop) followed by a free-standing reference to a variable. That's valid syntax, although it doesn't do anything.

The answer is to wrap the object literal in parentheses so that the parser doesn't see a curly brace just after the arrow, and knows you're using the concise form:

```
const a = ["Joe", "Mohammed", "María"];
const b = a.map(name => ({name: name}));          // Works
console.log(b);
```

Or, of course, use the verbose form and `return`. Whatever seems clearest to you when writing it.

Brief tangent: the object literal in that call to `map` could be even shorter thanks to *shorthand properties*, which you'll learn about in Chapter 5.

Arrow Functions and Lexical this

So far, you've seen that arrow functions can make your code more concise. That's useful just on its own, but it's not their main trick. Their main trick is that unlike traditional functions, they don't have their own version of `this`. Instead, they close over the `this` of the context where they're created, just like closing over a variable.

Why is that useful? Let's take a familiar problem: you're writing code in an object method, and you want to use a callback, but you want `this` within the callback to refer to your object. With a traditional function, it wouldn't, because traditional functions have their own `this` that's set by how they're called. Because of that, it's common to use a variable the callback can close over as a workaround, as in this ES5 code:

```
Thingy.prototype.delayedPrepAndShow = function() {
    var self = this;
    this.showTimer = setTimeout(function() {
        self.prep();
        self.show();
    }, this.showDelay);
};
```

Now you're using the variable `self` instead of `this` inside the callback, so it doesn't matter that the callback has its own version of `this` with a different value.

Since arrow functions don't have their own `this`, they close over `this` just like the ES5 example closes over the variable `self`. So you can rewrite that callback as an arrow function without any need for the `self` variable:

```
Thingy.prototype.delayedPrepAndShow = function() {
    this.showTimer = setTimeout(() => {
        this.prep();
        this.show();
    }, this.showDelay);
};
```

Much simpler. (In Chapter 4 you'll learn a new way to create that method, instead of assigning to a `Thingy.prototype` property.)

`this` isn't the only thing that arrow functions close over. They also close over `arguments` (the automatic pseudo-array of all of the arguments the function received), and two other things you'll learn about in Chapter 4 (`super` and `new.target`).

Arrow Functions Cannot Be Constructors

Since they don't have their own `this`, it stands to reason that arrow functions can't be constructor functions. That is, you can't use them with `new`:

```
const Doomed = () => { };
const d = new Doomed(); // TypeError: Doomed is not a constructor
```

After all, the primary purpose of a constructor function is to fill in the newly constructed object, which is passed to the function as `this`. If the function doesn't have its own `this`, it can't set properties on the new object, and it doesn't make sense for it to be a constructor. Using them as constructors is explicitly disallowed.

Explicitly disallowing it made it possible for arrow functions to be lighter-weight than traditional functions, because they don't have to have a `prototype` property on them with an object attached to it. You'll recall that when you use a function as a constructor, the prototype of the new object that's created is assigned from the function's `prototype`:

```
function Thingy() {
}
var t = new Thingy();
console.log(Object.getPrototypeOf(t) === Thingy.prototype); // true
```

Since the JavaScript engine can't know in advance whether you're going to use a traditional function as a constructor, it has to put the `prototype` property and an object for it to refer to on every traditional function you create. (Subject to optimization, of course.)

But since arrow functions can't be constructors, they don't get a `prototype` property:

```
function traditional() {
}
const arrow = () => {
};
console.log("prototype" in traditional); // true
console.log("prototype" in arrow);       // false
```

Arrow functions aren't the only new things about functions in modern JavaScript, though, not at all.

DEFAULT PARAMETER VALUES

As of ES2015, you can supply default values for parameters. In ES5 and earlier, you'd have to do it with code, like this:

```
function animate(type, duration) {
    if (duration === undefined) { // (Or any of several similar checks)
        duration = 300;
    }
    // ...do the work...
}
```

Now you can do it declaratively:

```
function animate(type, duration = 300) {
    // ...do the work...
}
```

This is more concise and easier for tools to support.

The default kicks in if the value of the parameter is `undefined` when the function is called. If you leave the argument off entirely when calling the function, the parameter's value is `undefined`. If you supply `undefined` as the value, its value is also `undefined` (of course). Either way, the function uses the default value instead.

Let's see it in action: run the code in Listing 3-1.

LISTING 3-1: Basic default parameters—basic-default-parameters.js

```
function animate(type, duration = 300) {
    console.log(type + ", " + duration);
}
animate("fadeout");              // "fadeout, 300"
animate("fadeout", undefined); // "fadeout, 300" (again)
animate("fadeout", 200);       // "fadeout, 200"
```

The code to handle default values is effectively inserted at the beginning of the function by the JavaScript engine; however, that code is in its own scope as you'll see later.

In that example, you could provide defaults for both `type` and `duration` if you liked:

```
function animate(type = "fadeout", duration = 300) {
    // ...do the work...
}
```

And unlike some other languages, you can also provide a default for `type` but not for `duration`:

```
function animate(type = "fadeout", duration) {
    // ...do the work...
}
```

That may seem a bit odd (arguably, it *is* a bit odd), but it goes back to the fact that the default is applied if the value is `undefined`. That's frequently because the argument wasn't given, but it can also be because `undefined` was given explicitly. Run the code in Listing 3-2.

LISTING 3-2: Defaulting the first parameter—default-first-parameter.js

```
function animate(type = "fadeout", duration) {
    console.log(type + ", " + duration);
}
animate("fadeout", 300);    // "fadeout, 300"
animate(undefined, 300);    // "fadeout, 300" (again)
animate("fadein",  300);    // "fadein, 300"
animate();                  // "fadeout, undefined"
```

Defaults Are Expressions

A parameter default is an expression; it doesn't have to be just a literal value. The default can even call a function. The default expression is evaluated when the function is called, not when the function is defined, and *only* if the default is needed for that particular call to the function.

For instance, suppose you wanted to use a different duration for each type of animation, and you had a function that gave you the default duration for a given type. You could write the `animate` function like this:

```
function animate(type, duration = getDefaultDuration(type)) {
    // ...do the work...
}
```

`getDefaultDuration` isn't called unless needed. That's treated almost exactly like this:

```
function animate(type, duration) {
    if (duration === undefined) {
        duration = getDefaultDuration(type);
    }
    // ...do the work...
}
```

The main difference relates to scope, which we'll come to in a moment.

In that example, the default for `duration` uses the `type` parameter. That's fine, because `type` comes before `duration`. If `type` came after `duration`, it would be a `ReferenceError` if `duration`'s default were needed for a particular call:

```
function animate(duration = getDefaultDuration(type), type) {
    // ...do the work...
}
animate(undefined, "dissolve"); // ReferenceError: type is not defined
```

This is just as though you'd tried to access the value of a variable declared with `let` before the `let` declaration, as you saw in Chapter 2. From the JavaScript engine's perspective, that function looks a lot like this (again, other than scope):

```
function animate() {
    let duration = /*...get the value of argument 0...*/;
    if (duration === undefined) {
        duration = getDefaultDuration(type);
    }
    let type = /*...get the value of argument 1...*/;
    // ...do the work...
}
```

If you call it without a `duration`, the code filling in the default tries to use `type` when it's in the Temporal Dead Zone, so you get an error.

The rule is simple: a default can use parameters listed before it, but not parameters listed after it.

Defaults Are Evaluated in Their Own Scope

As you've learned, defaults can refer to other parameters as long as they're before the default in the list, and they can refer to things that are part of the outer scope (like the `getDefaultDuration` function in the earlier example). But they can't refer to anything defined *within* the function body, not even things that are hoisted. Run Listing 3-3.

LISTING 3-3: Defaults can't refer to things in the function body—default-access-body.js

```
function example(value = x) {
    var x = 42;
    console.log(value);
}
example(); // ReferenceError: x is not defined
```

I've used `var` there because it doesn't have the Temporal Dead Zone; it's hoisted to the top of the scope where it's declared. But the default value expression still couldn't use it. The reason is that defaults are evaluated in their own scope, which exists between the scope containing the function and the scope inside the function (see Figure 3-1). It's as though the function were wrapped in another function that handled doing the defaults, a bit like this:

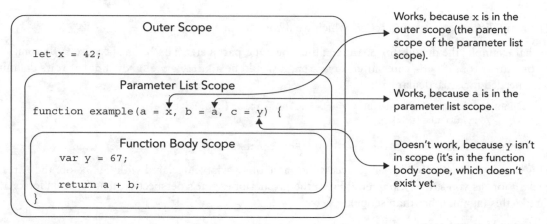

FIGURE 3-1

```
function example(value) {
    if (value === undefined) {
        value = x;
    }
    const exampleImplementation = () => {
        var x = 42;
        console.log(value);
    };
    return exampleImplementation();
}
example(); // ReferenceError: x is not defined
```

That's not literally how it's done, of course, but conceptually it's very close.

Fortunately, just looking at a function with its parameter list, the pieces are visually distinct (the parameter list is set apart from the function body), so it's easy to understand the parameter list having its own scope.

NON-SIMPLE PARAMETER LISTS AND CHANGING STRICT MODE

A parameter list that's just a bare list of parameters, without defaults or any of the other ES2015+ parameter features you'll learn about, is called a "simple" parameter list. If a parameter list uses any of the new features, it's called a "non-simple" parameter list (creative, eh?).

Perhaps surprisingly, a function with a non-simple parameter list can't have a `"use strict"` directive:

```
function example(answer = 42) {
    "use strict";          // SyntaxError: Illegal 'use strict' directive
                           // in function with non-simple parameter list
    console.log(answer);
}
```

Why is that an error? Because if that function is defined in loose mode code, the directive would enable strict mode within the function. The problem with *that* is that a non-simple parameter list effectively involves automatic processing (such a applying defaults) that occurs *within* the parameter list. If a function definition appears in loose mode but the function starts with `"use strict"`, should the code in the parameter list be in strict mode or loose mode? Consider this example:

```
function example(callback = o => { with (o) { return answer; } }) {
    "use strict";
    console.log(callback({answer: 42}));
}
```

Should that be a syntax error (since `with` isn't allowed in strict mode), or not? Is the parameter list strict, or loose?

To avoid the confusion that question raises, the function isn't allowed do that. Moreover, to avoid parsing complexity, even if the function definition appears in an already-strict context, it still can't have a `"use strict"` directive if it has a non-simple parameter list. It can only inherit the strictness of the context in which it's defined.

Defaults Don't Add to the Arity of the Function

The *arity* of a function is typically defined as the number of formal declared parameters it has, which in JavaScript you can get from the `length` property of the function:

```
function none() {
}
console.log(none.length); // 0
function one(a) {
}
```

```
    console.log(one.length);   // 1
    function two(a, b) {
    }
    console.log(two.length);   // 2
```

In JavaScript, parameters with default values don't get counted when calculating the arity, and in fact they prevent any subsequent parameters from being counted as well:

```
    function stillOne(a, b = 42) {
    }
    console.log(stillOne.length);     // 1
    function oneYetAgain(a, b = 42, c) {
    }
    console.log(oneYetAgain.length); // 1
```

The result for the `stillOne` function is simple enough: it has one parameter without a default and one with, so its arity is 1. The result for the `oneYetAgain` function is more interesting in that its `c` parameter doesn't have an explicit default, but because the parameter in front of it does, it isn't counted toward the arity.

"REST" PARAMETERS

Normally, when you write a function you know what parameters it will need and it will need the same number of parameters on each call. But some functions need to accept a varying number of parameters. For instance, before `Object.assign` was added in ES2015, many a JavaScript programmer's toolkit included an `extend` function accepting a target object and one or more source objects; the function copies the properties from the source objects onto the target. In ES5 and earlier, you'd use the `arguments` pseudo-array to access those arguments, like this:

```
    function extend(target) {
        var n, source;
        for (n = 1; n < arguments.length; ++n) {
            source = arguments[n];
            Object.keys(source).forEach(function(key) {
                target[key] = source[key];
            });
        }
        return target;
    }
    var obj = extend({}, {a: 1}, {b: 2});
    console.log(obj); // {a: 1, b: 2}
```

But `arguments` has some issues:

➤ In loose mode, it has performance problems caused by how it's linked to the formal parameters (but that can be addressed by using strict mode).

➤ It has *all* of the arguments, meaning you have to index beyond the ones that are the same as your formal parameters (which is why the `extend` example starts its `for` loop with `n = 1` instead of `n = 0`; we want to skip the argument for the `target` parameter).

➤ It's array-like, but not an array, so it doesn't have array features like `forEach` or `map`.

➤ Arrow functions don't have their own `arguments` object.

➤ Subjectively speaking, it has a clunky name that doesn't capture the function-specific meaning of those arguments.

ES2015 added a solution to those problems: the "rest" parameter. If you declare the last parameter with an ellipsis (`...`) in front of it, that tells the JavaScript engine to gather up all of the actual arguments from that point forward (the "rest" of the arguments) and put them in that parameter as a genuine array.

If you update the earlier `extend` function to use a rest parameter, because that rest parameter's value is an actual array, you can use `forEach` (or `for-of`, which you'll learn about in Chapter 6) instead of `for`:

```
function extend(target, ...sources) {
    sources.forEach(source => {
        Object.keys(source).forEach(key => {
            target[key] = source[key];
        });
    });
    return target;
}
const obj = extend({}, {a: 1}, {b: 2});
console.log(obj); // {a: 1, b: 2}
```

Taking it further, `extend` itself could be an arrow function, since it doesn't need its own `arguments` pseudo-array anymore:

```
const extend = (target, ...sources) => {
    sources.forEach(source => {
        Object.keys(source).forEach(key => {
            target[key] = source[key];
        });
    });
    return target;
};
const obj = extend({}, {a: 1}, {b: 2});
console.log(obj); // {a: 1, b: 2}
```

But what happens if there are no arguments supplied for the rest parameter at all? That is, what if we call our `extend` function with just one argument, a target object, and no source objects at all? (Odd as that would be to do.) What do you think the value of `sources` is then?

You probably inferred the answer from the implementation of the `extends` function: you get an empty array, which is why that code didn't need to check `sources` to be sure it had an array. (The designers of this feature could have gone with having `sources` contain `undefined` in this case, but they went with the empty array for consistency.)

Note that `...` is not an operator, although you'll hear people calling it "the rest operator." It's just "syntax" or "notation" (in this case, rest parameter syntax/notation). You'll learn more about `...` and why it isn't an operator (and can't be one) in Chapter 5.

TRAILING COMMAS IN PARAMETER LISTS AND FUNCTION CALLS

Some coding styles list the parameters to the function on separate lines, perhaps to accommodate line comments describing them or similar:

```
function example(
    question,   // (string) The question, must end with a question mark
    answer      // (string) The answer, must end with appropriate punctuation
) {
    // ...
}
```

Similarly, when calling functions, it's sometimes useful to put each argument on its own line, particularly if the argument is a long expression:

```
example(
    "Do you like building software?",
    "Big time!"
);
```

In both cases, as the codebase evolves and you need to add a third parameter to the function, you have to add a comma to the previous line when adding the new line with the new parameter/argument:

```
function example(
    question,   // (string) The question, must end with a question mark
    answer,     // (string) The answer, must end with appropriate punctuation
    required    // (boolean) Coerced if necessary (so default is false)
) {
    // ...
}
example(
    "Do you like building software?",
    "Big time!",
    true
);
```

Forgetting to do that is a common error, and needing to do it makes a code change unrelated to those lines appear to involve those lines (for instance, in commit diffs), just because you added a comma.

ES2017 makes it possible to have a *trailing comma* at the end of parameter lists and argument lists. As of ES2017, you can write the original two-parameter version of the function like this:

```
function example(
    question,   // (string) The question, must end with a question mark
    answer,     // (string) The answer, must end with appropriate punctuation
) {
    // ...
}
```

and call it like this:

```
example(
    "Do you like building software?",
    "Big time!",
);
```

This is purely a syntax change, it doesn't change anything else. There isn't some third unnamed parameter or anything like that. The function with just `question` and `answer` still has just two parameters; its arity, as reflected in its `length` property, is still 2.

Later when adding the third parameter, you just add the new lines; you don't have to change the existing ones:

```
function example(
    question,    // (string) The question, must end with a question mark
    answer,      // (string) The answer, must end with appropriate punctuation
    required,    // (boolean) Coerced if necessary (so default is false)
) {
    // ...
}
example(
    "Do you like building software?",
    "Big time!",
    true,
);
```

THE FUNCTION NAME PROPERTY

ES2015 finally standardized the function `name` property (it was a nonstandard extension in some JavaScript engines for years) and did so in a very interesting and powerful way that, among other things, makes many functions that used to be anonymous no longer anonymous.

The obvious way that a function gets a name is through a function declaration or named function expression:

```
// Declaration
function foo() {
}
console.log(foo.name); // "foo"
// Named function expression
const f = function bar() {
};
console.log(f.name);   // "bar"
```

Names are handy for reporting purposes, and particularly useful in call stacks on errors.

Interestingly, you can give a name to a function even if you use an *anonymous* function expression. For instance, if you assign the result of the expression to a constant or variable:

```
let foo = function() {
};
console.log(foo.name); // "foo"
```

This is not magic guesswork by the JavaScript engine. It's clearly and carefully defined in the specification exactly when and where the names are set.

It doesn't matter if you're declaring the variable when you assign the function or if you assign the function later; what matters is when you *create* the function:

```
let foo;
foo = function() {
};
console.log(foo.name); // "foo"
```

Arrow function expressions work just like anonymous function expressions:

```
let foo = () => {
};
console.log(foo.name); // "foo"
```

It's not just variable/constant assignments, though; there are lots more places the name is derived from context.

For example, in an object literal, if you assign an anonymous function expression's result to a property, the function gets the name of the property:

```
const obj = {
    foo: function() {
    }
};
console.log(obj.foo.name); // "foo"
```

(It also works if you use the *method* syntax you'll learn about in Chapter 5.)

It even works when using a function as a default parameter value:

```
(function(callback = function() { }) {
    console.log(callback.name); // "callback"
})();
```

However, there is one operation that, perhaps surprisingly, does *not* set the function's name—assigning to an object property on an existing object. For example:

```
const obj = {};
obj.foo = function() {
};
console.log(obj.foo.name); // "" - there's no name
```

Why not? TC39 considered this specific usage to be too much of an information leak. Suppose an app has a cache of handlers keyed by some secret information related to a user and needs to pass the handler to some external code. If it created the handler like this:

```
cache[getUserSecret(user)] = function() {};
```

and the function name was set by that operation, giving out the handler function to third-party code would give out the value from getUserSecret(user). So the committee intentionally omitted that particular operation from setting the function name.

FUNCTION DECLARATIONS IN BLOCKS

For years, putting a function declaration inside a block wasn't covered by the specification, but it wasn't disallowed, either. JavaScript engines could handle them as an "allowable extension." As of ES2015, function declarations in blocks are part of the specification. There are standard rules for them, and also "legacy web semantics" that only apply in loose mode on web browsers.

First, let's look at what a function declaration in a block is:

```
function simple() {
    if (someCondition) {
        function doSomething() {
        }
        setInterval(doSomething, 1000);
    }
}
simple();
```

That has a function declaration (not a function expression) inside a block. But function declarations are hoisted, processed prior to any step-by-step code. So what would a function declaration inside a block even mean?

Since the syntax wasn't specified but wasn't disallowed, the makers of JavaScript engines were free to define their own meaning for that syntax in their engines. Naturally, this led to problems, since different engines did different things. The `simple` function earlier wasn't particularly troublesome, but consider this:

```
function branching(num) {
    console.log(num);
    if (num < 0.5) {
        function doSomething() {
            console.log("true");
        }
    } else {
        function doSomething() {
            console.log("false");
        }
    }
    doSomething();
}
branching(Math.random());
```

In an ES5 world, there are at least three ways to handle that.

The first and most obvious option is: make it a syntax error.

The second option is to treat it as though the declarations were really function expressions, like this:

```
function branching(num) {
    console.log(num);
    var doSomething;
    if (num < 0.5) {
```

```
            doSomething = function doSomething() {
                console.log("true");
            };
        } else {
            doSomething = function doSomething() {
                console.log("false");
            };
        }
        doSomething();
    }
    branching(Math.random());
```

That ends up logging either "true" or "false" depending on the random number, which is likely what the author intended.

The third option is to treat it like multiple hoisted declarations in the same scope:

```
    function branching(num) {
        function doSomething() {
            console.log("true");
        }
        function doSomething() {
            console.log("false");
        }
        console.log(num);
        if (Math.random() < 0.5) {
        } else {
        }
        doSomething();
    }
    branching(Math.random());
```

That always logs "false" (because when you have repeated declarations in the same scope—which you're allowed to do—the last one wins). That probably isn't what the author intended (in this specific case), but is more in keeping with the fact that function declarations are hoisted rather than being processed as part of the step-by-step code.

So what did JavaScript engine makers do?

All three.

Some engines (though—with a brief exception—mostly minor ones) went with option 1, others with option 2, others with option 3. It was a mess.

When TC39 went to define semantics for function declarations in blocks, they had the very difficult task of specifying something reasonable and consistent without invalidating significant code out in the world. So they did two things:

➤ They defined standard semantics that are in keeping with the rest of ES2015.

➤ They defined "legacy web semantics" for loose-mode code in web browsers only.

Function Declarations in Blocks: Standard Semantics

The simplest handling is the standard semantics, which are always in effect in strict mode (even on web browsers). I suggest you use strict mode in order to avoid accidentally writing code relying on legacy semantics. With standard semantics, function declarations are effectively converted into function expressions assigned to `let` variables (so they're scoped to the block they're in), hoisted to the top of the block. Let's take the earlier `branching` function and add a bit more logging to see the hoisting:

```
"use strict";
function branching(num) {
    console.log(num);
    if (num < 0.5) {
        console.log("true branch, typeof doSomething = " + typeof doSomething);
        function doSomething() {
            console.log("true");
        }
    } else {
        console.log("false branch, typeof doSomething = " + typeof doSomething);
        function doSomething() {
            console.log("false");
        }
    }
    doSomething();
}
branching(Math.random());
```

In strict mode, the JavaScript engine treats that code as though it were like this:

```
"use strict";
function branching(num) {
    console.log(num);
    if (num < 0.5) {
        let doSomething = function doSomething() {
            console.log("true");
        };
        console.log("true branch, typeof doSomething = " + typeof doSomething);
    } else {
        let doSomething = function doSomething() {
            console.log("false");
        };
        console.log("false branch, typeof doSomething = " + typeof doSomething);
    }
    doSomething();
}
branching(Math.random());
```

Notice how each declaration was effectively hoisted within its block, up above the `console.log` call.

Naturally, if you run that, it fails, because the `doSomething` at the very end is not a declared identifier in the function's top level scope, since the `doSomething` in each block is block-scoped. So let's change our example to something that will run, and run it; see Listing 3-4.

LISTING 3-4: Function declaration in block: strict mode—func-decl-block-strict.js

```
"use strict";
function branching(num) {
    let f;
    console.log(num);
    if (num < 0.5) {
        console.log("true branch, typeof doSomething = " + typeof doSomething);
        f = doSomething;
        function doSomething() {
            console.log("true");
        }
    } else {
        console.log("false branch, typeof doSomething = " + typeof doSomething);
        f = doSomething;
        function doSomething() {
            console.log("false");
        }
    }
    f();
}
branching(Math.random());
```

Now, when you run it, f ends up referring to one function or the other, and either logs "true" or "false." Because of hoisting, doSomething refers to the function when it's assigned to f, even though that assignment is above the declaration.

Function Declarations in Blocks: Legacy Web Semantics

In loose mode on web browsers, legacy web semantics defined by Annex B of the specification apply. (Some engines apply them even outside web browsers.) The specification notes that, when not treating function declarations in blocks as syntax errors, the different ways engines handled them meant that only scenarios that were handled the same way by an intersection of those JavaScript engines could be relied upon. Those three scenarios are:

1. A function is declared and only referenced within a single block.

2. A function is declared and possibly used within a single block but also referenced by an inner function definition that is not contained within that same block.

3. A function is declared and possibly used within a single block but also referenced within subsequent blocks.

The example branching function we've used in this chapter doesn't fit any of those three scenarios, because it has two function declarations using the same name in two different blocks, and then references that name in code following those blocks. But if you have legacy loose-mode code matching one of these three scenarios, you can expect it to work cross-browser. That doesn't mean you should write *new* code that relies on legacy web semantics. Instead, write code relying only on the standard semantics (perhaps using strict mode to ensure that).

The legacy semantics are much the same as standard semantics, but in addition to the `let` variable within the block for the function declared in the block, there's also a `var` variable for it in the containing function's scope (or global scope, if all of this isn't inside a function). Unlike the `let` in the block, the `var`'s assignment isn't hoisted to the top of the block, it's done when the function declaration is reached in the code. (This seems odd, but it's to support case #2 of the intersection of behaviors across major engines prior to standardization.)

Again, the `branching` example doesn't fit the list of common handling that legacy semantics are meant to address, but legacy semantics do say how it's meant to be handled now (whereas in older engines it may not be handled this way): because there's a `doSomething` var-style variable at function scope, the `doSomething` call at the end works. Let's look at the example again, without the `"use strict";`, and with logging both before and after the function declarations. Load and run Listing 3-5.

LISTING 3-5: Function declaration in block: web compatibility—func-decl-block-web-compat.js

```
function branching(num) {
    console.log("num = " + num + ", typeof doSomething = " + typeof doSomething);
    if (num < 0.5) {
        console.log("true branch, typeof doSomething = " + typeof doSomething);
        function doSomething() {
            console.log("true");
        }
        console.log("end of true block");
    } else {
        console.log("false branch, typeof doSomething = " + typeof doSomething);
        function doSomething() {
            console.log("false");
        }
        console.log("end of false block");
    }
    doSomething();
}
branching(Math.random());
```

As you can see, this time the `doSomething` at the end isn't out of scope. In loose mode, the JavaScript engine treats that effectively like the following (except, of course, both `varDoSomething` and `letDoSomething` are simply `doSomething`):

```
function branching(num) {
    var varDoSomething;
    console.log("num = " + num + ", typeof doSomething = " + typeof varDoSomething);
    if (num < 0.5) {
        let letDoSomething = function doSomething() {
            console.log("true");
        };
        console.log("true branch, typeof doSomething = " + typeof letDoSomething);
        varDoSomething = letDoSomething; // where the declaration was
        console.log("end of true block");
    } else {
```

```
        let letDoSomething = function doSomething() {
            console.log("false");
        };
        console.log("false branch, typeof doSomething = " + typeof letDoSomething);
        varDoSomething = letDoSomething; // where the declaration was
        console.log("end of false block");
    }
    varDoSomething();
}
branching(Math.random());
```

Since the functions are assigned to a function-scope `var` variable, it's accessible outside the blocks. But the declarations are still hoisted within their blocks.

But again, it's best not to write new code relying on these legacy semantics. Instead, the consistency of strict mode is the way to go.

OLD HABITS TO NEW

With all of these new function features, there are a lot of old habits we can update.

Use Arrow Functions Instead of Various this Value Workarounds

Old habit: Various workarounds for having access to the calling context's `this` in a callback, such as:

➤ Using a variable, e.g. `var self = this;`

➤ Using `Function.prototype.bind`

➤ Using the `thisArg` parameter of functions that support it

Examples:

```
// Using a variable
var self = this;
this.entries.forEach(function(entry) {
    if (entry.matches(str)) {
        self.appendEntry(entry);
    }
});

// Using Function.prototype.bind
this.entries.forEach(function(entry) {
    if (entry.matches(str)) {
        this.appendEntry(entry);
    }
}.bind(this));

// Using 'thisArg'
this.entries.forEach(function(entry) {
```

```
        if (entry.matches(str)) {
            this.appendEntry(entry);
        }
    }, this);
```

New habit: Use an arrow function:

```
this.entries.forEach(entry => {
    if (entry.matches(str)) {
        this.appendEntry(entry);
    }
});
```

Use Arrow Functions for Callbacks When Not Using this or arguments

Old habit: Using traditional functions for callbacks that don't use `this` or `arguments` (because you didn't have a choice):

```
someArray.sort(function(a, b) {
    return a - b;
});
```

New habit: If the callback doesn't use `this` or `arguments`, use an arrow function. Arrow functions are lighter-weight and more concise:

```
someArray.sort((a, b) => a - b);
```

The majority of array callbacks (such as on `sort`, `forEach`, `map`, `reduce`, . . .), callbacks on string `replace` calls, promise creation and resolution callbacks (you'll learn about promises in Chapter 8), and many others can all usually be arrow functions.

Consider Arrow Functions Elsewhere As Well

Old habit: Using traditional functions for everything, because (again) you didn't have a choice.

New habit: Consider whether using an arrow function makes sense even if it's not a callback. This will be primarily a matter of style. For example, look at this function, which produces an initial-capped string from an input string:

```
function initialCap(str) {
    return str.charAt(0).toUpperCase() + str.substring(1);
}
```

Compared with the arrow function version:

```
const initialCap = str =>
    str.charAt(0).toUpperCase() + str.substring(1);
```

In theory, the arrow function doesn't have the cruft associated with the traditional function. Also, you can use `const` as in that example to avoid the identifier being reassigned (or use `let` if you don't want to prevent that).

Traditional functions aren't going anywhere, of course. Hoisting is sometimes useful, some prefer having the `function` keyword flag up functions, and if brevity is your thing it's worth noting that even

```
let x = () => { /*...*/ };
```

is ever-so-slightly longer than

```
function x() { /*...*/ }
```

although granted

```
let x=()=>{ /*...*/ };
```

is ever-so-slightly shorter.

It largely comes down to your style preference (and your team's).

Don't Use Arrow Functions When the Caller Needs to Control the Value of this

Old habit: Using a traditional function as a callback where it's important that the caller controls what `this` is.

New habit: Um...keep doing that.

Sometimes, it's important that the caller sets what `this` is. For instance, in browser code using jQuery, you frequently want jQuery to control what `this` is in a callback. Or when responding to DOM events that you've hooked up with `addEventListener`, because it will set `this` to refer to the element when calling your callback (although you can use the event object's `currentTarget` property instead). Or when defining object methods that are shared between objects (for instance, because they're on the prototype), because it's important to allow `this` to be set when they're called.

So while switching to arrow functions is useful in some cases, sometimes an old traditional function (or the method syntax you'll learn about in Chapters 4 and 5) is what you want.

Use Default Parameter Values Rather Than Code Providing Defaults

Old habit: Using code inside the function to provide a default for a parameter:

```
function doSomething(delay) {
    if (delay === undefined) {
        delay = 300;
    }
    // ...
}
```

New habit: Where possible, use default parameter values instead:

```
function doSomething(delay = 300) {
    // ...
}
```

Use a Rest Parameter Instead of the arguments Keyword

Old habit: Using the `arguments` pseudo-array in functions accepting varying numbers of arguments.

New habit: Use a rest parameter.

Consider Trailing Commas if Warranted

Old habit: Not including a trailing comma in parameter lists and function calls (because they weren't allowed):

```
function example(
    question,   // (string) The question, must end with a question mark
    answer      // (string) The answer, must end with appropriate punctuation
) {
    // ...
}
// ...
example(
    "Do you like building software?",
    "Big time!"
);
```

New habit: Depending on your style/your team's style, you could consider using trailing commas so adding further parameters/arguments as the code evolves doesn't require changing the lines defining what used to be the last parameter or argument:

```
function example(
    question,   // (string) The question, must end with a question mark
    answer,     // (string) The answer, must end with appropriate punctuation
) {
    // ...
}
// ...
example(
    "Do you like building software?",
    "Big time!",
);
```

However, this is a matter of style.

Classes

CODE DOWNLOADS FOR THIS CHAPTER

You can download the code for this chapter at `https://thenewtoys.dev/bookcode` or `https://www.wiley.com/go/javascript-newtoys`.

In this chapter you'll learn how `class` syntax works for creating JavaScript constructors and associated prototype objects. We'll compare and contrast the new syntax with the old, highlight that it's still the same prototypical inheritance JavaScript is famous for, and explore how powerful and simple the new syntax is. You'll see how to create subclasses, including subclasses of built-ins (even ones that can't be subclassed in ES5 and earlier like `Array` and `Error`), how `super` works, and what `new.target` is for and how to use it.

This chapter doesn't cover features that are coming in ES2020 or ES2021 like public class fields, private class fields, and private methods. See Chapter 18 for coverage of those.

WHAT IS A CLASS?

Before looking at the new syntax, let's address the elephant in the room: JavaScript doesn't really have classes, does it? It just emulates them with prototypes, right?

That's a popular perspective, because people confuse the kind of class provided by class-based languages like Java or C# with the general concept of a class in computer science terms. But classes are more than just the largely static constructs those sorts of languages provide. In the more general sense, for a language to have *classes* it has to provide two things: encapsulation (bundling data and methods together[1]) and inheritance. Having classes isn't the same as being class-based, it's just that the language supports encapsulation and inheritance. Prototypical languages can (and do) have classes and have since before JavaScript was invented; the mechanism they use to provide the second requirement (inheritance) is prototype objects.

JavaScript has always been one of the most object-oriented languages you'll find. It's certainly been able to do things in a class-like way since at least ECMAScript 1. Some might pedantically argue it didn't have classes in a computer science sense until ES5 added `Object.create` to directly support inheritance (even though you could emulate `Object.create` with a helper function). Others might argue even ES5 doesn't qualify because it lacks declarative constructs and a simple way to refer to superclass methods.

But the pedants can stop arguing. As of ES2015, even those objections are laid to rest: JavaScript has classes.

Let's see how they work in modern JavaScript. Along the way, we'll compare the new syntax with the old ES5 and earlier syntax.

INTRODUCING THE NEW CLASS SYNTAX

Listing 4-1 shows a basic example of `class`: a class whose instances are colors expressed in RGB. (The listing has some method body code omitted, because the goal here is just to show the overall syntax. The method code is in the file in the downloads, which you can run, and it will be shown later.)

---

[1] The term *encapsulation* can also refer to data hiding (private properties and such), but that isn't necessary for a language to have "classes." (However, JavaScript *does* provide data hiding, via closures and via WeakMap, which you'll learn about in Chapter 12, and soon via private fields, which you'll learn about in Chapter 18.)

LISTING 4-1: Basic class with class syntax—basic-class.js

```
class Color {
    constructor(r = 0, g = 0, b = 0) {
        this.r = r;
        this.g = g;
        this.b = b;
    }

    get rgb() {
        return "rgb(" + this.r + ", " + this.g + ", " + this.b + ")";
    }

    set rgb(value) {
        // ...code shown later...
    }

    toString() {
        return this.rgb;
    }

    static fromCSS(css) {
        // ...code shown later...
    }
}

let c = new Color(30, 144, 255);
console.log(String(c));          // "rgb(30, 144, 255)"
c = Color.fromCSS("00A");
console.log(String(c));          // "rgb(0, 0, 170)"
```

That defines a class with:

➤ A *constructor*

➤ Three *data properties* (r, g, and b)

➤ An *accessor property* (rgb)

➤ A *prototype method* (toString) (these are also sometimes called *instance methods* since you usually access them through instances, but *prototype method* is more accurate; an actual *instance method* would exist only on the instance rather than being inherited from the prototype)

➤ A *static method* (fromCSS) (these are also sometimes called *class methods*)

Let's build that up in parts.

The first thing to write is the class definition itself, which as you can see is a new structure. As with functions, you define classes with either declarations or expressions:

```
// Class declaration
class Color {
}
```

```
// Anonymous class expression
let Color = class {
};

// Named class expression
let C = class Color {
};
```

We'll stick with declarations for now and come back to expressions later.

Class declarations are not hoisted the way function declarations are; instead, they're hoisted (or half-hoisted) the way `let` and `const` declarations are, complete with the Temporal Dead Zone you learned about in Chapter 2: only the identifier is hoisted, not the initialization of it. Also like `let` and `const`, if you declare the class at global scope, the class's identifier is a global but not a property of the global object.

Adding a Constructor

Even with just what we have so far, the class has a default constructor, since we haven't provided an explicit one; more about that in a moment. For now, let's add a constructor to the class that actually does something. You define code for the constructor in a `constructor` definition, like this:

```
class Color {
    constructor(r = 0, g = 0, b = 0) {
        this.r = r;
        this.g = g;
        this.b = b;
    }
}
```

This defines the function that will be associated with the class's identifier, `Color`. Notice the syntax: you don't use the keyword `function` anywhere, just the name `constructor`, an opening parenthesis, the parameter list if any (in this case, r, g, and b), a closing parenthesis, the curly braces to define the constructor body, and the code for the constructor within those braces. (In real-world code, you might validate the r, g, and b values; I've left that out of the example to keep it short.)

> **NOTE** *There's no semicolon after the closing curly brace of the* `constructor` *definition. Constructor and method definitions in a class body are like declarations, which don't have semicolons after them. (A semicolon is tolerated if present, though; the grammar makes specific allowance for them to avoid making this easy mistake a syntax error.)*

In ES5 and earlier, you probably would have defined that constructor like this:

```
// Older (~ES5) near-equivalent
function Color(r, g, b) {
    // ...
}
```

but since `class` declarations aren't hoisted like `function` declarations, those aren't exactly equivalent; it's more like a function expression assigned to a variable:

```
// Older (~ES5) near-equivalent
var Color = function Color(r, g, b) {
    // ...
};
```

One thing to note here is how with `class` syntax, you write a structure for the class as a whole and write the constructor definition separately within it, whereas with the old syntax you just defined a function (and it was down to how you used that function whether it was just a function or the constructor for a class). The new syntax is like that so you can define other aspects of the class *declaratively*, within the same container: the `class` construct.

As noted earlier, providing an explicit constructor is optional; the `Color` class would be perfectly valid without one (other than not setting up its x, y, and z properties). If you don't provide a constructor, the JavaScript engine creates one for you that does nothing, exactly as though you had this in the class:

```
constructor() {
}
```

(In subclasses it does something, as you'll learn later.)

The constructor is a function, but you can only call it as part of the object creation process: running the constructor function must be the result of using `new` (either directly or indirectly by using `new` on a subclass) or the result of calling `Reflect.construct` (which you'll learn about in Chapter 14). If you try to call it when not creating an object, it throws an error:

```
Color();        // TypeError: Class constructor Color cannot
                // be invoked without 'new'
```

This addresses a whole range of bugs the old syntax didn't, where a function meant to be a constructor could also be called without `new`, leading to extremely confusing results (or bloated code to prevent it).

Let's add that "bloated code" to the ES5 `Color` example to make it (somewhat) disallow calls except through `new`:

```
// Older (~ES5) near-equivalent
var Color = function Color(r, g, b) {
    if (!(this instanceof Color)) {
        throw new TypeError(
            "Class constructor Color cannot be invoked without 'new'"
        );
    }
    // ...
};
```

That doesn't actually force it to be called as part of the object construction process (you could just call it via `Color.call` or `Color.apply` with a preexisting object), but it at least makes an attempt to.

You can see that already, even in a minimal class, you're getting real advantages in terms of robustness from using the new syntax, while cutting down boilerplate code.

Code inside a `class` is always in strict mode, even if the surrounding code is not. So to be really thorough with the ES5 example, we'd have to wrap all that in a scoping function and use strict mode within it. But let's just assume our code is already in strict mode rather than further complicating our ES5 example.

Adding Instance Properties

At least for now, the standard way to set up properties on new instances of a class is to assign to them in the constructor just like you do in ES5:

```
class Color {
    constructor(r = 0, g = 0, b = 0) {
        this.r = r;
        this.g = g;
        this.b = b;
    }
}
```

Because those properties are created through basic assignment, they're configurable, writable, and enumerable.

Naturally, in addition to (or instead of) properties you get from parameters, you could set up a property that doesn't come from a constructor argument, just using a literal or a value that comes from somewhere else. If you wanted all `Color` instances to start out black, for instance, you could leave off the r, g, and b parameters and just make the r, g, and b properties all start out with the value zero:

```
class Color {
    constructor() {
        this.r = 0;
        this.g = 0;
        this.b = 0;
    }
}
```

> **NOTE** *In Chapter 18 you'll learn about a feature that is likely to be in ES2020 or ES2021 but which is already widely used via transpilation: public class field (property) declarations.*

Adding a Prototype Method

Now let's add a method that will be put on the class's `prototype` object so all instances have access to it:

```
class Color {
    constructor(r = 0, g = 0, b = 0) {
        this.r = r;
        this.g = g;
        this.b = b;
    }
```

```
    toString() {
        return "rgb(" + this.r + ", " + this.g + ", " + this.b + ")";
    }
}
```

Note that there's no comma between the constructor definition and the `toString` definition, as there would be if they were in an object literal. A class definition isn't like an object literal; you don't separate things with commas. (If you do, you'll get a syntax error.)

The method syntax shown earlier puts the method on the `Color.prototype` object, so instances of the class inherit that method from their prototype:

```
const c = new Color(30, 144, 255);
console.log(c.toString());              // "rgb(30, 144, 255)"
```

Contrast the new syntax with how prototype functions are typically added in ES5:

```
// Older (~ES5) near-equivalent
Color.prototype.toString = function toString() {
    return "rgb(" + this.r + ", " + this.g + ", " + this.b + ")";
};
```

The new syntax, ES2015's *method syntax*, is more declarative and concise. It also marks the function specifically as a method, which gives it access to features it wouldn't have as a simple function (such as `super`; you'll learn about that later). The new syntax also makes the method non-enumerable, a reasonable default for methods on prototypes, which the ES5 version shown earlier doesn't. (To make it non-enumerable in the ES5 code, you'd have to define it with `Object.defineProperty` instead of using assignment.)

A method is also, by definition, not a constructor function, and so the JavaScript engine doesn't put a `prototype` property and associated object on it:

```
class Color {
    // ...
    toString() {
        // ...
    }
}
const c = new Color(30, 144, 255);
console.log(typeof c.toString.prototype); // "undefined"
```

Since methods aren't constructors, trying to call them via `new` results in an error.

In contrast, in ES5, all functions might be used as constructors as far as the engine knows, and so it has to give them a `prototype` property with an object attached:

```
// Older (~ES5) near-equivalent
var Color = function Color(r, g, b) {
    // ...
};
Color.prototype.toString = function toString() {
    // ...
};
var c = new Color(30, 144, 255);
console.log(typeof c.toString.prototype); // "object"
```

In theory, then, method syntax is more memory-efficient than the older function syntax. In practice, it wouldn't be surprising if JavaScript engines were already able to optimize away unneeded `prototype` properties even on ES5 methods.

Adding a Static Method

In building up the example `Color` class, so far you've seen a constructor, a couple of instance properties, and a prototype method. Let's add a *static method*, which is a method attached to `Color` itself instead of to the prototype:

```
class Color {
    // ...

    static fromCSS(css) {
        const match = /^#?([0-9a-f]{3}|[0-9a-f]{6});?$/i.exec(css);
        if (!match) {
            throw new Error("Invalid CSS code: " + css);
        }
        let vals = match[1];
        if (vals.length === 3) {
            vals = vals[0] + vals[0] + vals[1] + vals[1] + vals[2] + vals[2];
        }
        return new this(
            parseInt(vals.substring(0, 2), 16),
            parseInt(vals.substring(2, 4), 16),
            parseInt(vals.substring(4, 6), 16)
        );
    }
}
```

> **NOTE** *This particular static method,* `fromCSS`, *creates and returns a new instance of the class. Obviously, not all static methods do that, but this one does. The way it does so in this example is by calling* `new this(/*...*/)`, *which works because when you call* `Color.fromCSS(/*...*/)`, *as usual* `this` *within the call is set to the object the property was accessed on (*`Color` *in this case), so* `new this(/*...*/)` *is the same as* `new Color(/*...*/)`. *Later, in the section on subclassing, you'll learn about an alternative you could use there if appropriate.*

The `static` keyword tells the JavaScript engine to put that method on `Color` itself, not on `Color.prototype`. You call it on `Color` directly:

```
const c = Color.fromCSS("#1E90FF");
console.log(c.toString());          // "rgb(30, 144, 255)"
```

Previously in ES5 you would have done this by assigning to a property on the `Color` function:

```
Color.fromCSS = function fromCSS(css) {
    // ...
};
```

As with prototype methods, using method syntax means that `fromCSS` doesn't have a `prototype` property with an object assigned to it, which that ES5 version would, and can't be called as a constructor.

Adding an Accessor Property

Let's add an *accessor property* to the `Color` class. An accessor property is a property with a getter method, setter method, or both. For `Color`, let's provide an `rgb` property that gets the color as a standard `rgb(r,g,b)` string, and update the `toString` method to use that property instead of creating the string itself:

```
class Color {
    // ...

    get rgb() {
        return "rgb(" + this.r + ", " + this.g + ", " + this.b + ")";
    }

    toString() {
        return this.rgb;
    }
}
let c = new Color(30, 144, 255);
console.log(c.rgb);              // "rgb(30, 144, 255)"
```

As you can see, this is just like defining an accessor in an object literal in ES5. There's one small difference in the result: accessor properties in `class` constructs are non-enumerable, which again makes sense for something defined on a prototype, whereas accessor properties defined in object literals are enumerable.

So far, `Color`'s `rgb` accessor is read-only (a getter with no setter). If you wanted to add a setter, you'd define a `set` method as well:

```
class Color {
    // ...

    get rgb() {
        return "rgb(" + this.r + ", " + this.g + ", " + this.b + ")";
    }

    set rgb(value) {
        let s = String(value);
        let match = /^rgb\(((\d{1,3}),(\d{1,3}),(\d{1,3}))\)$/i.exec(
            s.replace(/\s/g, "")
        );
```

```
            if (!match) {
                throw new Error("Invalid rgb color string '" + s + "'");
            }
            this.r = parseInt(match[1], 10);
            this.g = parseInt(match[2], 10);
            this.b = parseInt(match[3], 10);
        }

        // ...
    }
```

Now you can set `rgb` as well as getting it:

```
let c = new Color();
console.log(c.rgb);              // "rgb(0, 0, 0)"
c.rgb = "rgb(30, 144, 255)";
console.log(c.r);               // 30
console.log(c.g);               // 144
console.log(c.b);               // 255
console.log(c.rgb);             // "rgb(30, 144, 255)"
```

Defining an accessor in ES5 is a bit painful if you want to add it to the existing object on the `prototype` property (rather than replacing that object with a new one):

```
// Older (~ES5) near-equivalent
Object.defineProperty(Color.prototype, "rgb", {
    get: function() {
        return "rgb(" + this.r + ", " + this.g + ", " + this.b + ")";
    },
    set: function(value) {
        // ...
    },
    configurable: true
});
```

You can also define static accessor properties, though that's likely to be a rare use case. Simply define an accessor with `static` before it:

```
class StaticAccessorExample {
    static get cappedClassName() {
        return this.name.toUpperCase();
    }
}
console.log(StaticAccessorExample.cappedClassName); // STATICACCESSOREXAMPLE
```

Computed Method Names

Sometimes, you want to create methods with names that are determined at runtime rather than literally provided in the code. This is particularly important when using *Symbols*, which you'll learn about in Chapter 5. In ES5 it was easy enough to do that with brackets property accessor syntax:

```
// Older (~ES5) example
var name = "foo" + Math.floor(Math.random() * 1000);
SomeClass.prototype[name] = function() {
    // ...
};
```

In ES2015, you can do much the same with method syntax:

```
let name = "foo" + Math.floor(Math.random() * 1000);
class SomeClass {
    [name]() {
        // ...
    }
}
```

Note the square brackets around the method name. They work exactly the same way they do in a property accessor:

➤ You can put any expression inside them.

➤ The expression is evaluated when the class definition is evaluated.

➤ If the result isn't a string or a Symbol (Chapter 5), it's converted to a string.

➤ The result is used as the method name.

Static methods and accessor property methods can have computed names as well. Here's an example of a static method that gets its name from the result of a multiplication expression:

```
class Guide {
    static [6 * 7]() {
        console.log("Life, the Universe, and Everything");
    }
}
Guide["42"](); // "Life, the Universe, and Everything"
```

COMPARING WITH THE OLDER SYNTAX

Although you've already seen comparisons between the new syntax with the old along the way in this chapter, let's compare a complete `Color` class definition in ES2015 syntax with its near-equivalent ES5 version. Compare Listing 4-2 with Listing 4-3.

LISTING 4-2: Full basic class with class syntax—full-basic-class.js

```
class Color {
    constructor(r = 0, g = 0, b = 0) {
        this.r = r;
        this.g = g;
        this.b = b;
    }

    get rgb() {
        return "rgb(" + this.r + ", " + this.g + ", " + this.b + ")";
    }

    set rgb(value) {
        let s = String(value);
        let match = /^rgb\(((\d{1,3}),(\d{1,3}),(\d{1,3})\)$/i.exec(
```

```
                s.replace(/\s/g, "")
            );
            if (!match) {
                throw new Error("Invalid rgb color string '" + s + "'");
            }
            this.r = parseInt(match[1], 10);
            this.g = parseInt(match[2], 10);
            this.b = parseInt(match[3], 10);
        }

    toString() {
        return this.rgb;
    }

    static fromCSS(css) {
        const match = /^#?([0-9a-f]{3}|[0-9a-f]{6});?$/i.exec(css);
        if (!match) {
            throw new Error("Invalid CSS code: " + css);
        }
        let vals = match[1];
        if (vals.length === 3) {
            vals = vals[0] + vals[0] + vals[1] + vals[1] + vals[2] + vals[2];
        }
        return new this(
            parseInt(vals.substring(0, 2), 16),
            parseInt(vals.substring(2, 4), 16),
            parseInt(vals.substring(4, 6), 16)
        );
    }
}

// Usage
let c = new Color(30, 144, 255);
console.log(String(c));              // "rgb(30, 144, 255)"
c = Color.fromCSS("00A");
console.log(String(c));              // "rgb(0, 0, 170)"
```

LISTING 4-3: Basic class with old-style syntax—full-basic-class-old-style.js

```
"use strict";
var Color = function Color(r, g, b) {
    if (!(this instanceof Color)) {
        throw new TypeError(
            "Class constructor Color cannot be invoked without 'new'"
        );
    }
    this.r = r || 0;
    this.g = g || 0;
    this.b = b || 0;
};
```

```
Object.defineProperty(Color.prototype, "rgb", {
    get: function() {
        return "rgb(" + this.r + ", " + this.g + ", " + this.b + ")";
    },
    set: function(value) {
        var s = String(value);
        var match = /^rgb\((\d{1,3}),(\d{1,3}),(\d{1,3})\)$/i.exec(
            s.replace(/\s/g, "")
        );
        if (!match) {
            throw new Error("Invalid rgb color string '" + s + "'");
        }
        this.r = parseInt(match[1], 10);
        this.g = parseInt(match[2], 10);
        this.b = parseInt(match[3], 10);
    },
    configurable: true
});

Color.prototype.toString = function() {
    return this.rgb;
};
Color.fromCSS = function(css) {
    var match = /^#?([0-9a-f]{3}|[0-9a-f]{6});?$/i.exec(css);
    if (!match) {
        throw new Error("Invalid CSS code: " + css);
    }
    var vals = match[1];
    if (vals.length === 3) {
        vals = vals[0] + vals[0] + vals[1] + vals[1] + vals[2] + vals[2];
    }
    return new this(
        parseInt(vals.substring(0, 2), 16),
        parseInt(vals.substring(2, 4), 16),
        parseInt(vals.substring(4, 6), 16)
    );
};

// Usage
var c = new Color(30, 144, 255);
console.log(String(c));             // "rgb(30, 144, 255)"
c = Color.fromCSS("00A");
console.log(String(c));             // "rgb(0, 0, 170)"
```

CREATING SUBCLASSES

The new syntax is useful even for base classes, but it really comes into its own with subclasses. Just setting up inheritance of constructors in ES5 is fairly complex and error-prone; using the "super" version of a method in a subclass is even more so. With the class syntax, all of that difficulty is swept away.

Let's create a subclass of `Color` called `ColorWithAlpha`,[2] with an opacity property:

```
class ColorWithAlpha extends Color {
}
```

Yes, that's really all that you have to do to create a subclass. There's more you *can* do and presumably *will* do, but that's all you *have* to do. That does the following things:

➤ Creates the `ColorWithAlpha` subclass constructor.

➤ Makes `Color` (the superclass constructor function) `ColorWithAlpha`'s prototype so any static properties/methods on `Color` are accessible from `ColorWithAlpha`. (We'll come back to this; the idea of a function having a prototype other than `Function.prototype` is new and may seem a bit surprising.)

➤ Creates the subclass prototype object, `ColorWithAlpha.prototype`.

➤ Makes `Color.prototype` that object's prototype, so that objects created with `new ColorWithAlpha` inherit the superclass properties and methods.

Figure 4-1 gives a picture of the `Color`/`ColorWithAlpha` relationship. Note the two parallel lines of inheritance: one line of inheritance for the constructor functions (`ColorWithAlpha` to `Color` to `Function.prototype` to `Object.prototype`) and a parallel one for objects created with those constructors (`ColorWithAlpha.prototype` to `Color.prototype` to `Object.prototype`).

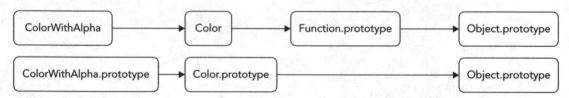

FIGURE 4-1

Run Listing 4-4 to see that the basics of the subclass are set up just by that simple declaration.

LISTING 4-4: Class with basic subclass—class-and-basic-subclass.js

```
class Color {
    constructor(r = 0, g = 0, b = 0) {
        this.r = r;
        this.g = g;
        this.b = b;
    }

    get rgb() {
        return "rgb(" + this.r + ", " + this.g + ", " + this.b + ")";
    }
```

---

[2] Why "alpha"? `ColorWithAlpha` will use RGBA. In RGBA, the A is for "alpha," referring to the "alpha channel" that transparency information is stored/transmitted in.

```
    set rgb(value) {
        let s = String(value);
        let match = /^rgb\(((\d{1,3}),(\d{1,3}),(\d{1,3})\)$/i.exec(
            s.replace(/\s/g, "")
        );
        if (!match) {
            throw new Error("Invalid rgb color string '" + s + "'");
        }
        this.r = parseInt(match[1], 10);
        this.g = parseInt(match[2], 10);
        this.b = parseInt(match[3], 10);
    }

    toString() {
        return this.rgb;
    }

    static fromCSS(css) {
        const match = /^#?([0-9a-f]{3}|[0-9a-f]{6});?$/i.exec(css);
        if (!match) {
            throw new Error("Invalid CSS code: " + css);
        }
        let vals = match[1];
        if (vals.length === 3) {
            vals = vals[0] + vals[0] + vals[1] + vals[1] + vals[2] + vals[2];
        }
        return new this(
            parseInt(vals.substring(0, 2), 16),
            parseInt(vals.substring(2, 4), 16),
            parseInt(vals.substring(4, 6), 16)
        );
    }
}

class ColorWithAlpha extends Color {
}

// Usage:
const c = new ColorWithAlpha(30, 144, 255);
console.log(String(c)); // "rgb(30, 144, 255)"
```

Note that even though there's no explicitly defined constructor in `ColorWithAlpha`, using it to construct a color worked just fine. That's because the JavaScript engine provided a default constructor. Instead of the "do nothing" default the engine provides for base classes, the default for subclasses calls the superclass's constructor, passing along all of the arguments it receives. (You may hear people say that the subclass *inherits* the constructor, but it doesn't; the engine creates a separate function that calls the superclass constructor.) This is a very powerful default, meaning that in many cases, there's no need to supply an explicit constructor in subclasses.

> **NOTE** *If you've worked in Java or C# or similar, there's a big difference between JavaScript's default constructor and the one that the Java or C# compiler would supply for you. In Java and C# (and many related languages), the default constructor accepts no parameters and calls the superclass constructor with no arguments:*
>
> ```
> // Java
> Subclass() {
>     super();
> }
> // C#
> Subclass() : base() {
> }
> ```
>
> *But in JavaScript, the default constructor for a subclass accepts any number of arguments and passes all of them into the superclass constructor:*
>
> ```
> // JavaScript
> constructor(/*...any number of parameters here...*/) {
>     super(/*...all are passed to super here...*/);
> }
> ```
>
> *(You'll learn about* super *in the next section.)*
>
> *This is a natural outgrowth of the fact that JavaScript doesn't use function overloading and function signatures the way Java and C# do. In Java or C#, you could have multiple "overloaded" constructors, each accepting a different number or types of parameters. In JavaScript, you have only one constructor, and any variations in the parameter lists are handled within the constructor. It simply makes more sense to have the default call the superclass with all arguments it received rather than none, so that a subclass that doesn't need to change what the constructor expects can just leave the constructor off entirely.*

To illustrate how the new syntax works, let's take the subclass definition:

```
class ColorWithAlpha extends Color {
}
```

and compare it with the near-equivalent in ES5 syntax:

```
// Older (~ES5) near-equivalent
var ColorWithAlpha = function ColorWithAlpha() {
    Color.apply(this, arguments);
};
ColorWithAlpha.prototype = Object.create(Color.prototype);
ColorWithAlpha.prototype.constructor = ColorWithAlpha;
```

That's a fair bit of boilerplate code, with a lot of opportunity for error, just to set up a subclass, and it doesn't make Color's static properties and methods available on ColorWithAlpha. It's not terrible, but it's non-obvious and easy to get wrong. The new syntax is clearer, more declarative, offers more functionality, and is easier to use.

There's not much point in creating a subclass, though, if we're not going to make it do something different from the superclass. Let's add some features to ColorWithAlpha, for which you'll need to know about super.

The super Keyword

To add features to ColorWithAlpha, in many cases you'll need to know about a new keyword: super. You use super in constructors and methods to refer to aspects of the superclass. There are two ways you can use it:

➤ super(): In a subclass constructor, you call super as though it were a function to create the object and have the superclass do its initialization of the object.

➤ super.property and super.method(): You refer to properties and methods of the superclass prototype by accessing them on super rather than on this. (Of course, you can use either dot notation, super.property, or brackets notation, super["property"].)

The next two sections go into the details of using super.

> **NOTE** super *isn't just for use in classes. In Chapter 5 you'll see how* super *works in methods on objects created with object literals instead of* new.

Writing Subclass Constructors

ColorWithAlpha will need a property that Color doesn't have: the opacity. Let's give it a property called a ("alpha") to store it in. The a property will have values in the range 0 to 1 (inclusive); for instance, the value 0.7 means the color is 70% opaque (30% transparent).

Since ColorWithAlpha needs to accept a fourth construction parameter, it can't just use the default constructor anymore. It needs its own:

```
class ColorWithAlpha extends Color {
    constructor(r = 0, g = 0, b = 0, a = 1) {
        super(r, g, b);
        this.a = a;
    }
}
```

The first thing ColorWithAlpha does is call super, passing in the r, g, and b parameters. This creates the object and lets Color do its initialization of the object. In ES5, the constructor might look like this:

```
// Older (~ES5) near-equivalent
var ColorWithAlpha = function ColorWithAlpha(r, g, b, a) {
    Color.call(this, r, g, b);
    this.a = a;
};
```

The `Color.call(this, r, g, b)` is the near-equivalent of `super(r, g, b)`. But there's a significant difference: in ES5, the object was created before the first line of `ColorWithAlpha` ran. You could reverse the two lines in it if you wanted to (though it would be poor practice):

```
var ColorWithAlpha = function ColorWithAlpha(r, g, b, a) {
    this.a = a;                    // Works even though it's before the call to Color
    Color.call(this, r, g, b);
};
```

That isn't true with `class`. At the beginning of `ColorWithAlpha`'s code, the object hasn't been created yet. If you try to use `this`, you'll get an error. You can only use `this` once the object has been created, and it isn't created until you call `super`. Try running the code in Listing 4-5.

LISTING 4-5: Accessing this before super—accessing-this-before-super.js

```
class Color {
    constructor(r = 0, g = 0, b = 0) {
        this.r = r;
        this.g = g;
        this.b = b;
    }
}

class ColorWithAlpha extends Color {
    constructor(r = 0, g = 0, b = 0, a = 1) {
        this.a = a;                    // ERROR HERE
        super(r, g, b);
    }
}

// Usage:
const c = new ColorWithAlpha(30, 144, 255, 0.5);
```

The exact error you get will vary from JavaScript engine to JavaScript engine. Here are some examples:

➤ `ReferenceError: Must call super constructor in derived class before accessing 'this' or returning from derived constructor`

➤ `ReferenceError: must call super constructor before using |this| in ColorWithAlpha class constructor`

➤ `ReferenceError: this is not defined`

This requirement is there to ensure that the initialization of the object being constructed is done from the base upward. You can have code in your constructor prior to calling `super`, but it cannot use `this` or anything else instance-specific until after the object has been created and the superclass has had its chance to initialize the instance.

Not only is `this` off-limits until you call `super`, but you *must* call `super` at some point in a subclass constructor. If you don't, an error occurs when the constructor returns. Finally, unsurprisingly, trying to call `super` twice is an error: you can't create the object when it already exists!

Inheriting and Accessing Superclass Prototype Properties and Methods

Sometimes, a subclass overrides the definition of a method, providing its own instead of using the one inherited from the superclass. For instance, `ColorWithAlpha` should have its own `toString` that uses `rgba` notation and includes the a property:

```
class ColorWithAlpha extends Color {
    // ...

    toString() {
        return "rgba(" + this.r + ", " +
                         this.g + ", " +
                         this.b + ", " +
                         this.a + ")";
    }
}
```

With that in place, calling `toString` on a `ColorWithAlpha` instance will use that definition instead of the one from `Color`.

Sometimes, though, the subclass method needs to call the superclass method as part of its implementation. Obviously `this.methodName()` wouldn't work, because it would just be calling itself; you need to go up a level. To do that, you call the superclass method via `super.methodName()`.

Let's look at that by adding a `brightness` method to `Color` that calculates the brightness (luminance) of the color:

```
class Color {
    // ...

    brightness() {
        return Math.sqrt(
            (this.r * this.r * 0.299) +
            (this.g * this.g * 0.587) +
            (this.b * this.b * 0.114)
        );
    }
}
```

Without getting into the math (and this is just one definition of luminance; there are others), those constants adjust the colors to allow for the fact that human eyes perceive the brightness of red, green, and blue differently.

That definition of `brightness` works for `Color`, but not `ColorWithAlpha`, which needs to take its opacity into account: at a minimum it needs to dim its brightness based on its transparency, and ideally it wants to know what background color will be behind it so it can account for the brightness of that color, since the background color will partially show through. So `ColorWithAlpha` needs its own version of `brightness`, like this:

```
class ColorWithAlpha extends Color {
    // ...
```

```
        brightness(bgColor) {
            let result = super.brightness() * this.a;
            if (bgColor && this.a !== 1) {
                result = (result + (bgColor.brightness() * (1 - this.a))) / 2;
            }
            return result;
        }
    }
```

It uses `Color`'s `brightness` to get the basic brightness of its color (`super.brightness()`), then applies the opacity. If it was given a background color and the current color isn't fully opaque, it takes the background color's brightness into account. Listing 4-6 has the full code of `Color` and `ColorWithAlpha` so far, and some examples using `brightness`. Run it, perhaps stepping through it in the debugger, to see all this in action.

LISTING 4-6: Using superclass method via super—using-superclass-method.js

```
class Color {
    constructor(r = 0, g = 0, b = 0) {
        this.r = r;
        this.g = g;
        this.b = b;
    }

    get rgb() {
        return "rgb(" + this.r + ", " + this.g + ", " + this.b + ")";
    }

    set rgb(value) {
        let s = String(value);
        let match = /^rgb\(((\d{1,3}),(\d{1,3}),(\d{1,3})\)$/i.exec(
            s.replace(/\s/g, "")
        );
        if (!match) {
            throw new Error("Invalid rgb color string '" + s + "'");
        }
        this.r = parseInt(match[1], 10);
        this.g = parseInt(match[2], 10);
        this.b = parseInt(match[3], 10);
    }

    toString() {
        return this.rgb;
    }

    brightness() {
        return Math.sqrt(
            (this.r * this.r * 0.299) +
            (this.g * this.g * 0.587) +
            (this.b * this.b * 0.114)
        );
    }
```

```
    static fromCSS(css) {
        const match = /^#?([0-9a-f]{3}|[0-9a-f]{6});?$/i.exec(css);
        if (!match) {
            throw new Error("Invalid CSS code: " + css);
        }
        let vals = match[1];
        if (vals.length === 3) {
            vals = vals[0] + vals[0] + vals[1] + vals[1] + vals[2] + vals[2];
        }
        return new this(
            parseInt(vals.substring(0, 2), 16),
            parseInt(vals.substring(2, 4), 16),
            parseInt(vals.substring(4, 6), 16)
        );
    }
}

class ColorWithAlpha extends Color {
    constructor(r = 0, g = 0, b = 0, a = 1) {
        super(r, g, b);
        this.a = a;
    }

    brightness(bgColor) {
        let result = super.brightness() * this.a;
        if (bgColor && this.a !== 1) {
            result = (result + (bgColor.brightness() * (1 - this.a))) / 2;
        }
        return result;
    }

    toString() {
        return "rgba(" + this.r + ", " +
                         this.g + ", " +
                         this.b + ", " +
                         this.a + ")";
    }
}

// Start with dark gray, full opacity
const ca = new ColorWithAlpha(169, 169, 169);
console.log(String(ca));                    // "rgba(169, 169, 169, 1)"
console.log(ca.brightness());               // 169
// Make it half-transparent
ca.a = 0.5;
console.log(String(ca));                    // "rgba(169, 169, 169, 0.5)"
console.log(ca.brightness());               // 84.5
// Brightness when over a blue background
const blue = new ColorWithAlpha(0, 0, 255);
console.log(ca.brightness(blue));           // 63.774477345571015
```

Let's look at how you might define that `brightness` method in ES5:

```
// Older (~ES5) near-equivalent
ColorWithAlpha.prototype.brightness = function brightness(bgColor) {
    var result = Color.prototype.brightness.call(this) * this.a;
    if (bgColor && this.a !== 1) {
        result = (result + (bgColor.brightness() * (1 - this.a))) / 2;
    }
    return result;
};
```

The highlighted line with the superclass `brightness` call can be written several ways. This way explicitly refers to `Color` (the superclass), which isn't ideal since you might change the parent class when refactoring. Another option is to use `Object.getPrototypeOf` on `ColorWithAlpha.prototype`:

```
var superproto = Object.getPrototypeOf(ColorWithAlpha.prototype);
var result = superproto.brightness.call(this) * this.a;
```

Or use `Object.getPrototypeOf` twice:

```
var superproto = Object.getPrototypeOf(Object.getPrototypeOf(this));
var result = superproto.brightness.call(this) * this.a;
```

They're all awkward, and they all have to manage `this` by using `call`. In ES2015+, `super` just handles it for you.

This syntax isn't just for methods, you can use it to access non-method properties on the prototype as well. But it's rare to have non-method properties on class prototype objects, and rarer still to want to access them directly rather than through the instance.

Inheriting Static Methods

Earlier you learned how to create a static method in a class. In JavaScript, static methods are inherited by subclasses. Run Listing 4-7, which shows using `fromCSS` (which is defined on `Color`) on `ColorWithAlpha`.

LISTING 4-7: Accessing static methods through subclass—accessing-static-method-through-subclass.js

```
class Color {
    // ...same as Listing 4-6...
}

class ColorWithAlpha extends Color {
    // ...same as Listing 4-6...
}

const ca = ColorWithAlpha.fromCSS("#1E90FF");
console.log(String(ca));                   // "rgba(30, 144, 255, 1)"
console.log(ca.constructor.name);          // "ColorWithAlpha"
console.log(ca instanceof ColorWithAlpha); // true
```

Note how you can call `fromCSS` on `ColorWithAlpha`, and note that the result is a `ColorWithAlpha` instance, not a `Color` instance. Let's look at why that works.

At the beginning of this section on subclassing, you learned that using the `extends` clause creates two inheritance chains: one on the constructor itself, and one on the constructor's `prototype` object; see Figure 4-2, which is a copy of the earlier Figure 4-1.

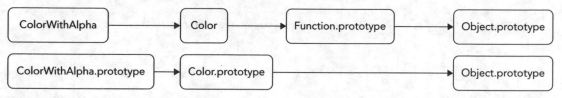

FIGURE 4-2

The constructor inheritance chain is a new thing in ES2015. Up through ES5, there was no standard way to have a true JavaScript function whose prototype was anything but `Function.prototype`. But it makes perfect sense for a subclass's constructor to use the superclass constructor as its prototype, and consequently to inherit its properties and methods.

But why did `fromCSS` create a `ColorWithAlpha` object instead of a `Color` object, if it's defined on `Color`? We touched on that very briefly earlier in this chapter. Let's look again at how `Color` defines `fromCSS`:

```
class Color {
    // ...

    static fromCSS(css) {
        const match = /^#?([0-9a-f]{3}|[0-9a-f]{6});?$/i.exec(css);
        if (!match) {
            throw new Error("Invalid CSS code: " + css);
        }
        let vals = match[1];
        if (vals.length === 3) {
            vals = vals[0] + vals[0] + vals[1] + vals[1] + vals[2] + vals[2];
        }
        return new this(
            parseInt(vals.substring(0, 2), 16),
            parseInt(vals.substring(2, 4), 16),
            parseInt(vals.substring(4, 6), 16)
        );
    }
}
```

The key thing there is that it creates the object using `new this`, rather than `new Color`. If you call `fromCSS` on `Color`, `this` within the call is `Color`; but if you call it on `ColorWithAlpha`, `this` within the call is `ColorWithAlpha`, so that's the constructor that gets called by `new this`. Try copying the `accessing-static-method-through-subclass.js` file from the downloads and changing it to `new Color` instead.

super in Static Methods

Since the subclass constructor truly inherits from the superclass constructor, you can use super within a static subclass method to refer to the superclass version. Suppose you wanted to allow a second argument to fromCSS for opacity in ColorWithAlpha; see Listing 4-8. The implementation just calls super.fromCSS and then adds the opacity to the resulting object.

LISTING 4-8: Using super in a static method—super-in-static-method.js

```
class Color {
    // ...same as Listing 4-6...
}

class ColorWithAlpha extends Color {
    constructor(r = 0, g = 0, b = 0, a = 1) {
        super(r, g, b);
        this.a = a;
    }

    brightness(bgColor) {
        let result = super.brightness() * this.a;
        if (bgColor && this.a !== 1) {
            result = (result + (bgColor.brightness() * (1 - this.a))) / 2;
        }
        return result;
    }

    toString() {
        return "rgba(" + this.r + ", " +
                         this.g + ", " +
                         this.b + ", " +
                         this.a + ")";
    }

    static fromCSS(css, a = 1) {
        const result = super.fromCSS(css);
        result.a = a;
        return result;
    }
}

const ca = ColorWithAlpha.fromCSS("#1E90FF", 0.5);
console.log(String(ca));                    // "rgba(30, 144, 255, 0.5)"
```

Methods Returning New Instances

In this section you'll learn about patterns for creating new instances of a class from its methods, both static methods like Color.fromCSS and instance methods like slice and map on arrays.

You've already seen a static method using one pattern to create an instance of the class: `Color.fromCSS`, which uses `new this(/*...*/)` to create the new instance. It works pretty well. When you call `Color.fromCSS`, you get a `Color` instance. When you call `ColorWithAlpha.fromCSS`, you get a `ColorWithAlpha` instance. That's the behavior you usually want. In an instance method, you'd use `this.constructor` rather than `this`, because `this.constructor` usually refers to the constructor of the object. For instance, here's a method for `Color` that returns a color that's half the brightness of the original:

```
halfBright() {
    const ctor = this.constructor || Color;
    return new ctor(
        Math.round(this.r / 2),
        Math.round(this.g / 2),
        Math.round(this.b / 2)
    );
}
```

But suppose you wanted to create a `Color` subclass in which `fromCSS` and `halfBright` returned an instance of `Color` instead? (That's a slightly odd thing to have `fromCSS` do, but let's ignore that for the moment.) With the current implementations of `fromCSS` and `halfBright`, you'd have to override them and use `Color` explicitly, along these lines:

```
class ColorSubclass extends Color {
    static fromCSS(css) {
        return Color.fromCSS(css);
    }
    halfBright() {
        return new Color(
            Math.round(this.r / 2),
            Math.round(this.g / 2),
            Math.round(this.b / 2)
        );
    }
}
```

That's okay for just one method or maybe even two. But what if `Color` had several other operations that created new instances and you wanted those to create `Color` rather than `ColorSubclass` instances? You'd have to override all of them, too. That could start to get messy. (Think about all of the array methods like `slice` and `map` that create new arrays, and the hassle it would be to override all of them in an array subclass if you didn't want the default behavior.)

If you want most methods that create new instances to use the same constructor in a way that's easy for subclasses to override, there's a better alternative: `Symbol.species`.

Symbols are something we haven't covered yet. You'll learn about them in Chapter 5. For the moment, all you need to know is that they're a new kind of primitive, they can be used as a property key (like a string, but they're not strings), and that there are "well known" ones available as properties on the `Symbol` function, including the one we'll use here: `Symbol.species`.

`Symbol.species` is part of a pattern designed specifically to allow subclasses to control what happens in methods that need to create new instances of "the" class. In the base class (`Color` in this example), instead of using the constructor the method has from `this` or `this.constructor` as we've done so far, methods using the species pattern determine the constructor to use by looking up the `Symbol.species` property on `this` / `this.constructor`. If the result is `null` or `undefined`, the class defines a default that it uses instead. In `fromCSS` that would look like this:

```
static fromCSS(css) {
    // ...
    let ctor = this[Symbol.species];
    if (ctor === null || ctor === undefined) {
        ctor = Color;
    }
    return new ctor(/*...*/);
}
```

Since `null` and `undefined` are both falsy, and a constructor function by definition is never falsy, you could simplify that a bit:

```
static fromCSS(css) {
    // ...
    const ctor = this && this[Symbol.species] || Color;
    return new ctor(/*...*/);
}
```

(Later you'll learn why we're using an explicit fallback there, `Color`, rather than using `this`.)

Note that the code is a bit defensive, checking that `this` is truthy (since class code is in strict mode and `this` can be any value, including `undefined`).

Again, though, it may be a bit odd for a static method to do that (depending on your use case). Let's look at doing it in the prototype method `halfBright`:

```
halfBright() {
    const ctor = this && this.constructor &&
                 this.constructor[Symbol.species] || Color;
    return new Color(
        Math.round(this.r / 2),
        Math.round(this.g / 2),
        Math.round(this.b / 2)
    );
}
```

(In Chapter 19 you'll learn about optional chaining, which would make the first statement in `halfBright` simpler: `const ctor = this?.constructor?.[Symbol.species] || Color;`)

When using the `Symbol.species` pattern, the base class defines that property in a clever way—as an accessor returning `this`:

```
class Color {
    static get [Symbol.species]() {
        return this;
    }
    // ...
}
```

That way, if the subclass doesn't override the `Symbol.species` property, it'll be just as though the class used `new this(/*...*/)`: the constructor the method was called on will be used (`Color` or `ColorWithAlpha`, depending). But if the subclass overrides the `Symbol.species` property, the constructor from that override gets used instead.

Putting all those pieces together:

```
class Color {
    static get [Symbol.species]() {
        return this;
    }

    static fromCSS(css) {
        const ctor = this && this[Symbol.species] || Color;
        return new ctor(/*...*/);
    }

    halfBright() {
        const ctor = this && this.constructor &&
                     this.constructor[Symbol.species] || Color;
        return new ctor(/*...*/);
    }

    // ...
}
```

The standard library objects that use this pattern only use it for prototype and instance methods, not static methods. That's because there was no strong reason for using it in static methods, and doing so you end up with odd or even misleading code like `ColorWithAlpha.fromCSS` returning a `Color` instance instead of a `ColorWithAlpha` instance. See Listing 4-9 for a simple synthetic example more along the lines of how the standard library uses the species pattern.

LISTING 4-9: Using Symbol.species—using-Symbol-species.js

```
class Base {
    constructor(data) {
        this.data = data;
    }

    static get [Symbol.species]() {
        return this;
    }

    static create(data) {
        // Doesn't use `Symbol.species`
        const ctor = this || Base;
        return new ctor(data);
    }

    clone() {
        // Uses `Symbol.species`
        const ctor = this && this.constructor &&
                     this.constructor[Symbol.species] || Base;
        return new ctor(this.data);
    }
}
// Sub1 uses the default behavior, which is often what you want
class Sub1 extends Base {
}
```

```
    // Sub2 makes any method that respects the pattern use Base instead of Sub2
    class Sub2 extends Base {
        static get [Symbol.species]() {
            return Base;
        }
    }

    const a = Base.create(1);
    console.log(a.constructor.name);          // "Base"
    const aclone = a.clone();
    console.log(aclone.constructor.name);     // "Base"

    const b = Sub1.create(2);
    console.log(b.constructor.name);          // "Sub1"
    const bclone = b.clone();
    console.log(bclone.constructor.name);     // "Sub1"

    const c = Sub2.create(3);
    console.log(c.constructor.name);          // "Sub2"
    const d = new Sub2(4);
    console.log(d.constructor.name);          // "Sub2"
    console.log(d.data);                      // 4
    const dclone = d.clone();
    console.log(dclone.constructor.name);     // "Base"
    console.log(dclone.data);                 // 4
```

Notice how calling `create` on `Sub1` created a `Sub1` instance, and calling `clone` on that instance also created a `Sub1` instance; calling `create` on `Sub2` created a `Sub2` instance, but calling `clone` on a `Sub2` instance created a `Base` instance.

Earlier I said I'd tell you why we're using an explicit default in that example (`Base`; and `Color` in the earlier examples) if the value of the `Symbol.species` property is `null` or `undefined`. That's what the built-in classes like `Array` do. They could have used `this` (in static methods) or `this.constructor` (in prototype methods) as the default instead, but by using an explicit default, they give subclasses of subclasses a way to ask for the *original* default rather than the current subclass constructor. So with the `Base` from the previous example, in this code:

```
    class Sub extends Base {
    }

    class SubSub1 extends Sub {
    }

    class SubSub2 extends Sub {
        static get [Symbol.species]() {
            return null;
        }
    }

    const x = new SubSub1(1).clone();
    console.log(x.constructor.name); // "SubSub1"

    const y = new SubSub2(2).clone();
    console.log(y.constructor.name); // "Base", not "SubSub2" or "Sub"
```

the default from `Base` is applied in `SubSub2`'s `clone` method, rather than something from a subclass. (Try it using `explicit-constructor-default.js` from the downloads.)

Subclassing Built-ins

In ES5, some of the built-in constructors such as `Error` and `Array` were notoriously impossible to properly subclass; that's been fixed in ES2015. Subclassing a built-in with `class` is just like subclassing anything else. (You can also subclass them without `class` syntax via `Reflect.construct`; more on that in Chapter 14.) Let's look at an array example. Listing 4-10 shows a very simple `Elements` class that extends `Array` with a `style` method that sets style information on the DOM elements in the array. Try running it in a page with at least three `div` elements in it (there's a `subclassing-array.html` file in the downloads you can use).

LISTING 4-10: Subclassing Array—subclassing-array.js

```
class Elements extends Array {
    select(source) {
        if (source) {
            if (typeof source === "string") {
                const list = document.querySelectorAll(source);
                list.forEach(element => this.push(element));
            } else {
                this.push(source);
            }
        }
        return this;
    }

    style(props) {
        this.forEach(element => {
            for (const name in props) {
                element.style[name] = props[name];
            }
        });
        return this;
    }
}

// Usage
new Elements()
    .select("div")
    .style({color: "green"})
    .slice(1)
    .style({border: "1px solid red"});
```

The "Usage" code at the end:

➤ Creates an instance of `Elements`, which is a subclass of `Array`

➤ Uses its `select` method to add all `div` elements on the page to the instance (using the array method `push` to add them)

➤ Styles those elements with green text

➤ Creates a new `Elements` instance using the array method `slice` to take just the second and third `div` elements

➤ Adds a red border around those `div` elements with the `style` method

(Note how using `slice` created a new `Elements` instance, not just a new `Array`. That's because `Array` uses the `Symbol.species` pattern you learned about in the last section, and `Elements` doesn't override the default.)

`Elements` is just an example, of course. In a real implementation, you'd probably pass the selector into the `Elements` constructor rather than using a separate `select` call afterward to populate the instance. Doing that in a robust way requires using a feature you haven't learned about yet (iterable spread, in Chapter 6). If you want to see what it would look like (also using `for-of` [Chapter 6], `Object.entries` [Chapter 5], and destructuring [Chapter 7]), refer to `subclassing-array-using-later-chapter-features.js` in the downloads.

Where super Is Available

Before ES2015, we used the term *method* loosely in JavaScript to refer to any function assigned to an object property (or perhaps only the ones that use `this`). As of ES2015, while that's still common informally, there is now a distinction between true methods and functions assigned to properties: code inside a true method has access to `super`; code in a traditional `function` assigned to a property does not. Let's prove that to ourselves with Listing 4-11: read through and try to run it.

LISTING 4-11: Method vs. function—method-vs-function.js

```
class SuperClass {
    test() {
        return "SuperClass's test";
    }
}
class SubClass extends SuperClass {
    test1() {
        return "SubClass's test1: " + super.test();
    }
}
SubClass.prototype.test2 = function() {
    return "SubClass's test2: " + super.test();      // ERROR HERE
};

const obj = new SubClass();
obj.test1();
obj.test2();
```

The JavaScript engine will refuse to parse that code, complaining that `super` wasn't expected on the line marked in the listing. But why not?

Because methods have a link to the object on which they're created, but traditional functions assigned to properties don't. When used in a property lookup operation like super.foo, super relies on an internal field of the containing function called [[HomeObject]]. The JavaScript engine gets the object from the [[HomeObject]] field of the method, gets its prototype, and then looks for the method property on that object, like this pseudocode:

```
// Pseudocode
let method = (the running method);
let homeObject = method.[[HomeObject]];
let proto = Object.getPrototypeOf(homeObject);
let value = proto.foo;
```

"But wait," you say. "Why would super care where the method was defined? It just goes to this's prototype, right? Or this's prototype's prototype?"

No, it can't work that way. To see why, consider the three-layer hierarchy in Listing 4-12.

LISTING 4-12: Three-layer hierarchy—three-layer-hierarchy.js

```
class Base {
    test() {
        return "Base test";
    }
}
class Sub extends Base {
    test() {
        return "Sub test > " + super.test();
    }
}
class SubSub extends Sub {
    test() {
        return "SubSub test > " + super.test();
    }
}

// Usage:
const obj = new SubSub();
console.log(obj.test()); // SubSub test > Sub test > Base test
```

When you create that obj instance, its prototype chain looks like Figure 4-3.

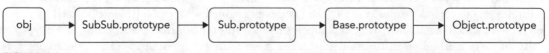

FIGURE 4-3

Let's suppose super worked from this, knowing that it needed to go to this's prototype's prototype because it's being used in a prototype method. When you call obj.test, this equals obj. When it uses super.test(), getting the prototype of the prototype works: the prototype of obj is `SubSub.prototype`, and the prototype of `SubSub.prototype` is `Sub.prototype`, so it gets `test` from `Sub.prototype`; all is good so far. Then, it calls `Sub.prototype`'s `test` with `this` set to obj. As part of its code, `Sub.prototype.test` *also* calls `super.test()`. Now the JavaScript engine is stuck. It can't do the same thing it did to get from `SubSub` to `Sub` because `this` is still obj, so `this`'s prototype's prototype is still `Sub.prototype`, and it would just end up in the same place. Look through the code in Listing 4-13 and run it; eventually it raises a stack overflow error because `Sub.prototype.test` keeps calling itself.

LISTING 4-13: Broken three-layer hierarchy—broken-three-layer-hierarchy.js

```javascript
function getFakeSuper(o) {
    return Object.getPrototypeOf(Object.getPrototypeOf(o));
}
class Base {
    test() {
        console.log("Base's test");
        return "Base test";
    }
}
class Sub extends Base {
    test() {
        console.log("Sub's test");
        return "Sub test > " + getFakeSuper(this).test.call(this);
    }
}
class SubSub extends Sub {
    test() {
        console.log("SubSub's test");
        return "SubSub test > " + getFakeSuper(this).test.call(this);
    }
}

// Usage:
const obj = new SubSub();
console.log(obj.test()); // "SubSub's test", then "Sub's test" repeatedly
                         // until a stack overflow error occurs
```

That's why the methods need to have a field saying what object they're defined on (their [[HomeObject]]), so the JavaScript engine can get that object and then get its prototype to access the super's version of `test`. Refer to Figure 4-4 to follow through the following explanation: within `obj.test`, to do `super.test()` the JavaScript engine looks at the [[HomeObject]] on `obj.test`, which is `SubSub.prototype`, then gets the prototype of that object (`Sub.prototype`) and calls the `test` method on it. To handle the `super.test()` in `Sub.prototype.test`, the engine gets [[HomeObject]] from `Sub.prototype.test` and gets *its* prototype, which is `Base.prototype`, and then calls the `test` method on it.

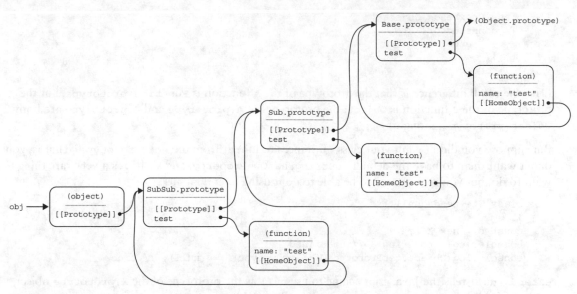

FIGURE 4-4

There is an important consequence of this: copying methods from object to object (a familiar pattern with "mixins"—objects with utility functions you copy into multiple prototypes) doesn't change the method's [[HomeObject]]. If you use super in a mixin method, it continues to use the prototype of its *original* home object, not the prototype of the object it's been copied to. This can create subtle crosstalk between the method's original home and the object you copied it to. If you do that on purpose (using a feature of the mixin's original parent), that's fine; but if you use super in a mixin method expecting it to work within the hierarchy of its new home, it'll be a bug.

At one stage when ES2015 was being developed, there was a function you could use to change the [[HomeObject]] of a method (specifically to enable mixins), but it was dropped before the spec was completed and hasn't been added back (yet). So for the moment at least, define mixins with traditional functions, or don't use super in them, or if you do, do it because you intend it to continue to work within its original hierarchy, not its new one.

LEAVING OFF OBJECT.PROTOTYPE

By default, even a base class is effectively a subclass of Object: instances of it inherit from Object.prototype. That's where they get their default toString, hasOwnProperty, and other such methods. That is, the following two classes are effectively the same:

```
class A {
    constructor() {
    }
}
```

```
class B extends Object {
    constructor() {
        super();
    }
}
```

(The one small difference is that the prototype of the A function is `Function.prototype`, but the prototype of the B function is `Object`; the prototypes of `A.prototype` and `B.prototype` are both `Object.prototype`, though.)

But suppose you didn't want your class's instances to inherit from `Object.prototype`? That is, you didn't want them to have the default `toString`, `hasOwnProperty`, and such? It's a very rare thing to want to do, but you're supposed to be able to do it using `extends null`:

```
class X extends null {
}
const o = new X();
console.log(o.toString); // undefined
console.log(Object.getPrototypeOf(X.prototype) === null); // true
```

`extends null` tells the JavaScript engine to use `null` as the prototype of the `X.prototype` object, instead of using `Object.prototype` as it normally would.

However, while the intention of the feature was always clear, there were minor issues with the precise technical details with regard to `extends null` in the ES2015 and subsequent specifications, which caused problems for implementations. As a result, `extends null` doesn't work yet in most major JavaScript engines as of this writing. (It fails when doing `new X`.) If you have a use case requiring `extends null`, be sure to test in your target environments. (But you always do that anyway, right?)

NEW.TARGET

Functions and constructors can be called in two ways:

➤ Directly (although constructors created via `class` syntax disallow it)

➤ As part of creating an object (via `new`, `super`, or `Reflect.construct` [discussed in Chapter 14])

Sometimes, it's important to know how your function was called. Perhaps you want to make a class abstract (only allow instances to be created as part of a subclass), or final (don't allow subclasses). Perhaps you want a function that changes what it does depending on whether it was called via `new` or directly.

In those cases, you can use `new.target` to find out how the function was called. If the function was called directly (not via `new`), `new.target` will have the value `undefined`:

```
function example() {
    console.log(new.target);
}
example(); // undefined
```

If the current function was the direct target of the new operator, new.target refers to the current function:

```
class Base {
    constructor() {
        console.log(new.target.name);
    }
}
new Base(); // "Base"
```

If the current function was called via super, new.target refers to the subclass constructor that was the target of new:

```
class Base {
    constructor() {
        console.log(new.target.name);
    }
}

class Sub extends Base {
    // (This is exactly what the default constructor would be, but I've included
    // it for clarity, to explicitly show the `super()` call.)
    constructor() {
        super();
    }
}

new Sub();  // "Sub"
```

(Other ways using Reflect.construct are covered in Chapter 14.)

With that in mind, let's use it for all three of the scenarios mentioned in the section introduction: an abstract class, a final class, and a function that does different things depending on whether it was called as a constructor or as a function.

Listing 4-14 defines an abstract class called Shape and two subclasses, Triangle and Rectangle. An abstract class is a class that cannot be directly instantiated; it can only be instantiated via a subclass. Shape is made abstract by throwing an error if new.target === Shape is true in the constructor, since that would mean it was being created via new Shape (or an equivalent). When instantiating Triangle (for instance), new.target is Triangle, not Shape, so the constructor doesn't throw an error.

LISTING 4-14: Abstract class—abstract-class.js

```
class Shape {
    constructor(color) {
        if (new.target === Shape) {
            throw new Error("Shape can't be directly instantiated");
        }
        this.color = color;
    }
```

```
    toString() {
        return "[" + this.constructor.name + ", sides = " +
                this.sides + ", color = " + this.color + "]";
    }
}
class Triangle extends Shape {
    get sides() {
        return 3;
    }
}
class Rectangle extends Shape {
    get sides() {
        return 4;
    }
}
const t = new Triangle("orange");
console.log(String(t));      // "[Triangle, sides = 3, color = orange]"

const r = new Rectangle("blue");
console.log(String(r));      // "[Rectangle, sides = 4, color = blue]"

const s = new Shape("red"); // Error: "Shape can't be directly instantiated"
```

(Even with the check, it's possible to create an object that directly uses Shape.prototype as its prototype, since you don't have to call Shape to do that [you can use Object.create]. But that presupposes someone actively working around the way Shape is defined to be used.)

A final class is the converse of that; it *disallows* subclass instances. Listing 4-15 does that by doing the reverse of the Shape check: it throws an error if new.target isn't equal to the class's own constructor. When you try to create an instance of InvalidThingy, you get an error. (Unfortunately, it's not currently possible to make that error more proactive, throwing it when the InvalidThingy class definition is evaluated instead of later when new InvalidThingy is used.)

LISTING 4-15: Final class—final-class.js

```
class Thingy {
    constructor() {
        if (new.target !== Thingy) {
            throw new Error("Thingy subclasses aren't supported.");
        }
    }
}
class InvalidThingy extends Thingy {
}

console.log("Creating Thingy...");
const t = new Thingy();          // works
console.log("Creating InvalidThingy...");
const i = new InvalidThingy();  // Error: "Thingy subclasses aren't supported."
```

(As with the Shape example, with Object.create it's still possible to create objects with a prototype that inherits from Thingy.prototype, and so which are in some way subclass objects, but again that presupposes actively working around Thingy.)

Finally, Listing 4-16 defines a function that does different things depending on whether it was called as a function or via new; note that you can only do this with a traditional function, because constructors defined via class cannot be called except as part of object construction. This example detects it hasn't been called via new (or an equivalent) and converts that into a call with new.

LISTING 4-16: Function that changes based on how it's called—function-or-constructor.js

```
const TwoWays = function TwoWays() {
    if (!new.target) {
        console.log("Called directly; using 'new' instead");
        return new TwoWays();
    }
    console.log("Called via 'new'");
};
console.log("With new:");
let t1 = new TwoWays();
// "Called via 'new'"

console.log("Without new:");
let t2 = TwoWays();
// "Called directly; using 'new' instead"
// "Called via 'new'"
```

CLASS DECLARATIONS VS. CLASS EXPRESSIONS

Like function, class can be used as a declaration or as an expression. And like function, it depends on the context where it appears: if it appears where either a statement or an expression is valid, it's a declaration; if it appears where only an expression is valid, it's an expression.

```
// Declaration
class Class1 {
}

// Anonymous class expression
let Color = class {
};

// Named class expression
let C = class Color {
};
```

class Declarations

class declarations work very similarly to function declarations, although with an important difference.

Like function declarations, class declarations:

➤   Add the class's name to the current scope, and

➤   Don't need a semicolon after the closing curly brace. (You can put one there, because Java-Script ignores unnecessary semicolons, but it's not needed by the declaration.)

Unlike function declarations, `class` declarations:

➤ Are not hoisted, they're half-hoisted: the identifier is reserved throughout the scope, but not initialized until the declaration is reached in the step-by-step execution of the code.

➤ Participate in the Temporal Dead Zone.

➤ Do not create a property on the global object for the class name if used at global scope; instead, they create globals that aren't properties of the global object.

Those last bits probably seem familiar. That's because they're the same as the rules you learned in Chapter 2 for `let` and `const`. Those rules apply to `class` declarations, too.

Listing 4-17 demonstrates the various aspects of a `class` declaration. (The code in Listing 4-17 must be run at global scope to demonstrate what happens with `class` declarations at global scope. Remember that you can't run this in Node.js in the usual way; you have to either use a browser or run it in Node.js's REPL environment. See Chapter 1.)

LISTING 4-17: class declarations—class-declarations.js

```
// Trying to use `TheClass` here would result in a ReferenceError
// because of the Temporal Dead Zone

let name = "foo" + Math.floor(Math.random() * 1000);

// The declaration
class TheClass {
    // Since the declaration is processed as part of the
    // step-by-step code, we can use `name` here and know that
    // it will have the value we assigned it above
    [name]() {
        console.log("This is the method " + name);
    }
} // <== No semicolon expected here

// A global was created
console.log(typeof TheClass);      // "function"

// But no property on the global object
console.log(typeof this.TheClass); // "undefined"
```

class Expressions

`class` expressions work very similarly to `function` expressions:

➤ They have both named and anonymous forms.

➤ They do not add the class's name to the scope in which they appear, but do make the class's name available within the class definition itself (if it has a name).

➤ They result in a value (the class's constructor) that can be assigned to a variable or a constant, passed into a function, or ignored.

➤ The JavaScript engine will infer the value of the `name` property for a class created with an anonymous class expression from context, using the same rules you learned in Chapter 3 for anonymous function expressions.

➤ When used as the right-hand side of an assignment, they do not terminate the assignment expression; if the class expression is the last thing in the assignment expression, it should be followed by a semicolon. (In many cases, Automatic Semicolon Insertion [ASI] can correct a missing semicolon, but not always.)

Listing 4-18 demonstrates aspects of the `class` expression.

LISTING 4-18: class expressions—class-expressions.js

```
let name = "foo" + Math.floor(Math.random() * 1000);

// The expression
const C = class TheClass {
    [name]() {
        console.log("This is the method " + name +
                    " in the class " + TheClass.name);
        // The class name is in-scope -^
        // within the definition
    }
}; // <== Semicolon needed here (although ASI will supply it
   //      if possible)

// The class's name was not added to this scope
console.log(typeof TheClass);       // "undefined"

// The value of the expression is the class
console.log(typeof C);              // "function"
```

MORE TO COME

There are several more features coming soon to `class` definitions (likely in ES2021), such as public class field (property) declarations, private fields, private methods, public and private static fields, and private static methods. You can use many of these today with transpilation. These are all covered in Chapter 18.

OLD HABITS TO NEW

Just the one "old habit to new" for this chapter.

Use class When Creating Constructor Functions

Old habit: Using traditional function syntax to create constructor functions (because you had no choice!):

```
var Color = function Color(r, g, b) {
    this.r = r;
    this.g = g;
    this.b = b;
};
Color.prototype.toString = function toString() {
    return "rgb(" + this.r + ", " + this.g + ", " + this.b + ")";
};
console.log(String(new Color(30, 144, 255)));
```

New habit: Use class instead:

```
class Color  {
    constructor(r, g, b) {
        this.r = r;
        this.g = g;
        this.b = b;
    }
    toString() {
        return "rgb(" + this.r + ", " + this.g + ", " + this.b + ")";
    }
};
console.log(String(new Color(30, 144, 255)));
```

This doesn't mean you should start using class if you *don't* use constructor functions; constructor functions and their prototype property (in both ES5 and ES2015+) are just one way of using Java-Script's prototypical inheritance. But if you do use constructor functions, then given all the benefits of conciseness, expressiveness, and functionality, using class instead is clearly beneficial.

5

New Object Features

WHAT'S IN THIS CHAPTER?

- ➤ Computed property names
- ➤ Shorthand properties
- ➤ Getting and setting an object's prototype
- ➤ `__proto__` on browsers
- ➤ Method syntax, and `super` outside classes
- ➤ Symbol
- ➤ Various new object utility functions
- ➤ `Symbol.toPrimitive`
- ➤ Property order
- ➤ Property spread syntax

CODE DOWNLOADS FOR THIS CHAPTER

You can download the code for this chapter at `https://thenewtoys.dev/bookcode` or `https://www.wiley.com/go/javascript-newtoys`.

In this chapter you'll learn about the new object features in ES2015+, from features that help you write less repetitive or more concise code to ones that let you do things you couldn't do before.

COMPUTED PROPERTY NAMES

In ES5, if you wanted to create an object with a property whose name came from a variable, you had to first create the object, then add the property to it as a separate operation, like this:

```
var name = "answer";
var obj = {};
obj[name] = 42;
console.log(obj); // {answer: 42}
```

That's a bit awkward, so ES2015 added *computed property names*, which use square brackets ([]), just like the square brackets used in the preceding code, in the property definition itself:

```
var name = "answer";
var obj = {
    [name]: 42
};
console.log(obj); // {answer: 42}
```

(I've used var there to emphasize this isn't related to let, but I'll go back to using let and const now.)

The brackets in the property definition work just like the brackets you've always used when getting/setting property values. That means you can use any expression within the square brackets, and the result of the expression will be used as the name:

```
let prefix = "ans";
let obj = {
    [prefix + "wer"]: 42
};
console.log(obj); // {answer: 42}
```

The expression is evaluated immediately, as part of evaluating the object literal, as each property definition is evaluated (in source code order). To illustrate that, the following example does exactly what the previous one does other than having the extra temporary variables temp and name:

```
let prefix = "ans";
let temp = {};
let name = prefix + "wer";
temp[name] = 42;
let obj = temp;
console.log(obj); // {answer: 42}
```

You can see the order in action here:

```
let counter = 0;
let obj = {
    [counter++]: counter++,
    [counter++]: counter++
};
console.log(obj);          // {"0": 1, "2": 3}
```

Note the order in which `counter` was used and incremented: first to get the name for the first property (`0`, which is converted to `"0"` when used as a property name), then to get that property's value (`1`), then to get the name for the second property (`2`, which is converted to `"2"`), and finally to get that property's value (`3`).

SHORTHAND PROPERTIES

It's fairly common to want to create an object with properties whose values come from variables (or other in-scope identifiers, like parameters) of the same name. For instance, suppose you have a `getMinMax` function that finds the minimum and maximum numbers in an array and returns an object with `min` and `max` properties. The ES5 version would typically look like this:

```
function getMinMax(nums) {
    var min, max;
    // (omitted - find `min` and `max` by looping through `nums`)
    return {min: min, max: max};
}
```

Notice the repetition when creating the object at the end, having to specify `min` and `max` twice (once for the name of the property, again for the value for that property).

As of ES2015, you can use *shorthand properties*. You just give the identifier once, and it's used both to name the property and to identify where to get the property value from:

```
function getMinMax(nums) {
    let min, max;
    // (omitted - find `min` and `max` by looping through `nums`)
    return {min, max};
}
```

Naturally, you can only do this when the value is coming from a simple in-scope identifier (variable, parameter, etc.); if the value comes from the result of any other expression, you still need to use the `name: expression` form.

GETTING AND SETTING AN OBJECT'S PROTOTYPE

It's always been possible to create an object inheriting from a specific prototype object via a constructor function. ES5 added the ability to do it directly via `Object.create`, and to get the prototype of an object via `Object.getPrototypeOf`. ES2015 adds the ability to *set* the prototype of an existing object. It's a very unusual thing to want to do, but it's now possible.

Object.setPrototypeOf

The primary way to do it is via `Object.setPrototypeOf`, which accepts the object to change and the prototype to give it. Here's an example:

```
const p1 = {
    greet: function() {
        console.log("p1 greet, name = " + this.name);
    }
```

```
};
const p2 = {
    greet: function() {
        console.log("p2 greet, name = " + this.name);
    }
};
const obj = Object.create(p1);
obj.name = "Joe";
obj.greet(); // p1 greet, name = Joe
Object.setPrototypeOf(obj, p2);
obj.greet(); // p2 greet, name = Joe
```

In that code, `obj` starts out using `p1` as its prototype, so the first call to `obj.greet()` uses `p1`'s `greet` and shows `"p1 greet, name = Joe"`. Then the code changes the prototype of `obj` to use `p2`, so the second call to `greet` uses `p2`'s `greet` and shows `"p2 greet, name = Joe"` instead.

Again, changing the prototype of an object after you've created it is unusual, and doing so may well de-optimize the object, making property lookup on it much slower. But if you absolutely have to do it, now you can via a standard mechanism.

The __proto__ Property on Browsers

In the browser environment, you can use an accessor property called __proto__ to get and set the prototype of an object, but don't do so in new code. Officially, it's not defined for JavaScript engines that aren't in a browser (although the engine may provide it anyway).

> **NOTE** __proto__ *is a legacy feature that's been standardized only to officially describe the behavior it had as a non-standard extension. In new code, you shouldn't use it; use* getPrototypeOf *and* setPrototypeOf *instead.*

Here's an example of using __proto__; this is the same code as an example from the last section using `Object.setPrototypeOf`, the only change is the second-to-last line:

```
const p1 = {
    greet: function() {
        console.log("p1 greet, name = " + this.name);
    }
};
const p2 = {
    greet: function() {
        console.log("p2 greet, name = " + this.name);
    }
};
const obj = Object.create(p1);
obj.name = "Joe";
obj.greet(); // p1 greet, name = Joe
obj.__proto__ = p2;
obj.greet(); // p2 greet, name = Joe
```

__proto__ is an accessor property defined by Object.prototype, so the object you use it on has to inherit from Object.prototype (directly or indirectly) for you to use it. An object created via Object.create(null), for instance, doesn't have __proto__, and neither would any object that used that object as its prototype.

The __proto__ Literal Property Name on Browsers

__proto__ can also be used in an object literal to set the prototype of the resulting object:

```
const p = {
    hi() {
        console.log("hi");
    }
};
const obj = {
    __proto__: p
};
obj.hi(); // "hi"
```

This is explicit syntax, *not* a by-product of the __proto__ accessor property, and it only works when specified literally. For instance, you can't use a computed property name to do it:

```
const p = {
    hi() {
        console.log("hi");
    }
};
const name = "__proto__";
const obj = {
    [name]: p
};
obj.hi(); // TypeError: obj.hi is not a function
```

Again, don't use __proto__ in new code; use Object.create to create an object with the correct prototype in the first place, and use Object.getPrototypeOf and Object.setPrototypeOf if necessary to get or set the prototype afterward. That way, you don't have to worry about whether the code is running in a browser or not, and (in the case of the accessor property) whether the object inherits from Object.prototype or not.

METHOD SYNTAX, AND SUPER OUTSIDE CLASSES

In Chapter 4 you learned about method definitions within class constructs. ES2015 adds method syntax to object literals, too. Where previously you would have written something verbose with the function keyword like this:

```
var obj1 = {
    name: "Joe",
    say: function() {
        console.log(this.name);
    }
};
obj1.say(); // "Joe"
```

the new method syntax lets you write this:

```
const obj2 = {
    name: "Joe",
    say() {
        console.log(this.name);
    }
};
obj2.say(); // "Joe"
```

That is, you leave out the colon and the `function` keyword entirely.

Method syntax is not just a shorthand syntax for defining functions in object literals, although in most cases it's fine to act as though it were. As it does in classes, method syntax does both more and less than a property initialized with a traditional function:

➤ The method doesn't have a `prototype` property with an object on it, and can't be used as a constructor.

➤ The method gets a link to the object it's defined on, its *home object*. The example using the traditional function (`obj1`) only created a link from the object to the function, via the object's `say` property; see Figure 5-1. The method syntax example creates a link both ways: from the object (`obj2`) to the function (via the `say` property), and from the function to its home object (`obj2`) via [[HomeObject]] field you learned about in Chapter 4; see Figure 5-2.

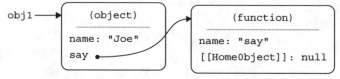

FIGURE 5-1

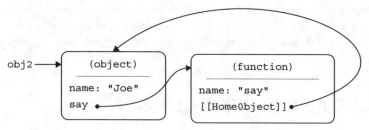

FIGURE 5-2

The purpose of the link from the method back to the object is to support using `super` within the method. Suppose, for instance, you wanted to create an object whose `toString` function used its prototype's `toString`, but then made it all caps. In ES5, you would have had to call the prototype's function explicitly, like this:

```
var obj = {
    toString: function() {
```

```
            return Object.prototype.toString.call(this).toUpperCase();
        }
    };
    console.log(obj.toString()); // "[OBJECT OBJECT]"
```

With ES2015+, you can use method syntax and `super` instead:

```
    const obj = {
        toString() {
            return super.toString().toUpperCase();
        }
    };
    console.log(obj.toString()); // "[OBJECT OBJECT]"
```

The method name doesn't have to be a literal identifier; as with property keys it can be a string (using either double or single quotes), or a computed name:

```
    const s = "ple";
    const obj = {
        "biz-baz"() {          // String literal method name
            console.log("Ran biz-baz");
        },
        ["exam" + s]() {    // Computed method name
            console.log("Ran example");
        }
    };
    obj["biz-baz"](); // "Ran biz-baz"
    obj.example();    // "Ran example"
```

At first, `super` in methods in object literals seems fairly limited, since the object's prototype is going to be `Object.prototype`, because it's created by an object literal. But as you learned earlier, in ES2015+ you can change the prototype of an object after it's created, and on browsers you can use `__proto__` in the literal to set the prototype to something other than `Object.prototype` to start with (though it's best not to do that in new code). The way `super` is implemented ensures that if you do that, it works as expected:

```
    const obj = {
        toString() {
            return super.toString().toUpperCase();
        }
    };
    Object.setPrototypeOf(obj, {
        toString() {
            return "a different string";
        }
    });
    console.log(obj.toString()); // "A DIFFERENT STRING"
```

This is where [[HomeObject]] comes in. The way the JavaScript engine handles a property reference on `super` (such as `super.toString`), with some details skipped for clarity, is this:

1. It gets the value of the current function's [[HomeObject]] internal slot. In this example, that's the object `obj` refers to.

2. It gets the *current* prototype of that object (as of when the `super.toString` code is run, not when the function was created).

3. It looks up the property on that prototype object, and uses it.

By the time the example calls `obj.toString()`, the code has already changed the prototype of the object `obj` refers to, so the new prototype's `toString` is used instead of the original prototype's `toString`.

In theory, the [[HomeObject]] link is there whether the method uses `super` or not. In practice, JavaScript engines are likely to optimize the link away if you don't use `super` (and also don't use things like `eval` that limit their ability to optimize in the method).

SYMBOL

Up through ES5, property names ("keys") were always strings (even the ones frequently written as numbers, such as array indexes). As of ES2015, that changed: property keys can now be strings or Symbols.

A *Symbol* is a unique primitive value. Being unique is its primary purpose and feature. Although the use of Symbols goes beyond object properties, I've included them in this chapter because that's where you'll normally use them.

"NAME" OR "KEY"?

Is it a property "name," or a property "key"? The answer is: yes. The specification has this to say:

"Properties are identified using key values. A property key value is either an ECMAScript String value or a Symbol value. All String and Symbol values, including the empty string, are valid as property keys. A *property name* is a property key that is a String value."

So in theory it's a property "key" if it could be a string or a Symbol, a property "name" if it's a string. But it's still common (including in the specification text itself) to refer to "a property named P" where P could be a string or a Symbol, and as you'll learn later the ES5 function `Object.keys` includes strings but doesn't include Symbols (if it had been added in ES2015, perhaps it would have been called `Object.names`—or perhaps it would have included Symbols). So don't read too much into "key" vs. "name"; people will often say "name" when they should, by the specification's definition at least, say "key."

Why Symbols?

We'll look at how you create and use Symbols in a moment, but first let's ask the question: Why is it so important to have guaranteed-unique values you can use as property keys?

Guaranteed-unique values are just generally useful (as the popularity of GUIDs demonstrates), but one key motivator for Symbols in JavaScript was that they made it possible to add several things to ES2015 that couldn't have been added otherwise. Several of the new features require looking for new properties on objects and using them if they exist. That wouldn't be backward-compatible if the keys were strings.

For example, the `toString` function on `Object.prototype` creates a string in the form `"[object XYZ]"`. For objects created by the built-in constructors like `Date`, the XYZ will be the name of the constructor (`"[object Date]"`, `"[object Array]"`, etc.). But before ES2015, for instances created by your own constructors (or just plain objects), the string would just be `"[object Object]"`.

In ES2015, TC39 wanted to be able to let the programmer decide what the XYZ should be with the default `toString`, by specifying an object property with the name that should be used. The problem is, there's no safe string name they could have picked for that property, because any string name they picked may have been used in the wild for a different purpose, so using it might break existing code. But they couldn't just start using the name of the constructor, either, because that would also break existing code that relied on seeing `"[object Object]"` for those objects. The new feature had to be opt-in.

Symbols to the rescue! `Object.toString` looks for a property identified by a Symbol, not a string. That means it can't conflict with any other property that may exist on objects defined before ES2015 (since Symbols didn't exist yet). Here's that property in action:

```
class Example1 {
}
class Example2 {
    get [Symbol.toStringTag]() {
        return "Example2";
    }
}
console.log(new Example1().toString()); // "[object Object]"
console.log(new Example2().toString()); // "[object Example2]"
```

The value of `Symbol.toStringTag` is a predefined *well-known Symbol*[1] that the `Object.prototype.toString` method looks for: when it would have returned `"[object Object]"` in ES5, in ES2015+ it looks for the `Symbol.toStringTag` property and if its value is a string, `toString` uses its value for the XYZ part of the resulting `"[object XYZ]"` string; if not, it uses `Object` as it used to. In the example, `new Example1().toString()` returned `"[object Object]"` because there was no property on the object with the appropriate Symbol name. But the call to `new Example2().toString()` returned `"[object Example2]"` because the property was there (inherited from `Example.prototype`) and had the value `"Example2"`.

The common use case for `toStringTag` is classes as in the preceding example, but it works just as well for plain objects, which is useful if you prefer other types of object factories rather than constructor functions:

```
// Direct usage
const obj1 = {
    [Symbol.toStringTag]: "Nifty"
};
console.log(obj1.toString()); // "[object Nifty]"
```

---

[1] You'll learn more about well-known Symbols later in this chapter.

```
// Via a prototype
const p = {
    [Symbol.toStringTag]: "Spiffy"
};
const obj2 = Object.create(p);
console.log(obj2.toString()); // "[object Spiffy]"
```

Enough of the *why* of Symbols, let's look at the *how*.

Creating and Using Symbols

You get a new, unique Symbol by calling the `Symbol` function. It's not a constructor—remember, Symbols are primitives—so you don't use `new`. Once you have your Symbol, you can add it to an object using computed property name notation during creation, or using brackets notation after creation:

```
const mySymbol = Symbol();
const obj = {
    [mySymbol]: 6                     // Computed property name
};
const anotherSymbol = Symbol();
obj[anotherSymbol] = 7;              // Brackets notation
console.log(obj[mySymbol]);         // 6
console.log(obj[anotherSymbol]);    // 7
```

As an aid to debugging, you can give a Symbol a description when creating it, by passing a string into `Symbol`:

```
const mySymbol = Symbol("my symbol");
console.log(mySymbol); // Symbol(my symbol)
```

In an environment where `console.log` shows a representation of the Symbol, the `console.log` of `mySymbol` in that code might show `"Symbol(my symbol)"`, which is the string returned by `toString` on Symbols.

As of ES2019, a Symbol's description is available as a `description` property on the Symbol:

```
const mySymbol = Symbol("my symbol");
console.log(mySymbol.description); // "my symbol"
```

The description is purely a description, it has no other meaning. (Later, you'll see `Symbol.for`, in which the description is also used for another purpose.) The description is not the value of the Symbol, and two different Symbols can have the same description but still be different Symbols:

```
const a = Symbol("my symbol");
console.log(a);          // Symbol(my symbol)
const b = Symbol("my symbol");
console.log(b);          // Symbol(my symbol)
console.log(a === b); // false
const obj = {
    [a]: 6,
    [b]: 7
};
console.log(obj[a]);    // 6
console.log(obj[b]);    // 7
```

Properties keyed by Symbols rather than strings are not included in `for-in` loops or the array returned by `Object.keys`, even when they're enumerable properties (and own[2] properties, in the case of `Object.keys`).

Symbols Are Not for Privacy

One common misconception about Symbols is that they're for private properties. For instance, consider this code:

```
const everUpward = (() => {
    const count = Symbol("count");
    return {
        [count]: 0,
        increment() {
            return ++this[count];
        },
        get() {
            return this[count];
        }
    };
})();
console.log(everUpward.get());              // 0
everUpward.increment();
console.log(everUpward.get());              // 1
console.log(everUpward["count"]);           // undefined
console.log(everUpward[Symbol("count")]);   // undefined
```

If you don't have access to the Symbol stored in `count`, you can't get the property, right? It's not the `"count"` property, after all, and the `count` constant is private to the function in which it's declared.

No, the Symbol stored in `count` isn't private (even though the constant referring to it is) because Symbols are *discoverable*. For instance, you can get the Symbols an object uses via the aptly named `Object.getOwnPropertySymbols`. Since they're discoverable, Symbols don't provide any privacy for properties. A bit of obscurity, perhaps, particularly if you don't give them descriptions; but no privacy. Truly private properties will be introduced in ES2020 or later via an entirely different mechanism (see Chapter 18), or you can use a WeakMap (Chapter 12) to hold truly private information for an object.

So why the misconception? Partially because of the path Symbols took on their way to being added to JavaScript: they started life as "private Name objects" and were indeed originally expected to be used as a mechanism for creating private properties on objects. Over time, their name changed, they became primitives, and using them for private properties didn't pan out, but having a guaranteed-unique identifier turned out to be quite useful, so Symbols were kept.

Global Symbols

When you call `Symbol` to create your Symbol, only your code knows about it unless you make it accessible to other code somehow (for instance, by making it the key of a property on an object).

---

[2] Remember that objects can inherit properties, and they can have their *own* properties. An "own" property is a property that exists directly on the object, rather than being inherited.

Normally that's what you want. But a complication can arise, particularly for library authors, especially when you need to use Symbols across *realms*.

A *realm* is the overall container in which a bit of code lives, consisting of a global environment, the intrinsics for that environment (Array, Object, Date, etc.), all the code loaded into that environment, and other bits of state and such. If you think of a browser, the realm your code lives in is the window for the page you've included it in and all of that window's associated stuff (pardon the technical jargon).

Your code doesn't only have access to its own realm, though, it can also get access to things in other realms: a child window has a different realm from its parent window, a web worker has its own realm distinct from the realm that created it, etc. But in many cases, code in those realms can pass objects between the realms. That's not a problem, but if code in two different realms needs to share access to a property identified by a Symbol, then the Symbol needs to be shared as well. This is where *global Symbols* come in.

For instance, suppose you're writing a class called `BarkCounter`, and `BarkCounter` stores information on objects using a Symbol. See the fairly silly example in Listing 5-1.

LISTING 5-1: A silly BarkCounter class, version 1—barkcounter-version-1.js

```
const BarkCounter = (() => {
    const barks = Symbol("nifty-barks");

    return class BarkCounter {
        constructor(other = null) {
            this[barks] = other && barks in other ? other[barks] : 0;
        }

        bark() {
            return ++this[barks];
        }

        showBarks(label) {
            console.log(label + ": Barks = " + this[barks]);
        }
    };
})();
```

Instances of the `BarkCounter` class count the number of times you call `bark` on them (I told you it was silly). They respond to a `bark` call by incrementing the count and returning the new value. They store the count of `bark` calls in a property keyed with the Symbol stored in the `barks` constant. If you pass an object into the `BarkCounter` constructor that has a property keyed with that Symbol, it copies the count of `barks` from that instance; otherwise, it starts at 0. You can ask it to show the number of `barks` in the console, but you can't ask it to give you the number of `barks`.

Here's `BarkCounter` in action:

```
const b1 = new BarkCounter();
b1.bark();
b1.bark();
b1.showBarks("b1");              // b1: Barks = 2
```

```
    const b2 = new BarkCounter(b1);
    b2.showBarks("b2");              // b2: Barks = 2
```

Notice that that code successfully copied the barks count from b1 to b2. That's because the code creating b2 passes b1 into the same BarkCounter constructor that created it, so the same Symbol is used when looking up the number of barks on b1.

Let's look at a cross-realm example by using BarkCounter in a main window and in an iframe, passing an instance of BarkCounter from the main window to the iframe. See Listings 5-2 and 5-3.

LISTING 5-2: Using BarkCounter cross-realm: Main, version 1—barkcounter-main-1.html

```html
<!doctype html>
<html>
<head>
<meta charset="UTF-8">
<title>BarkCounter Across Realms - Main - Version 1</title>
</head>
<body>
<script src="barkcounter-version-1.js"></script>
<script>
var barkCounterFrame = document.createElement("iframe");
barkCounterFrame.addEventListener("load", function() {
    const b1 = new BarkCounter();
    b1.bark();
    b1.bark();
    b1.showBarks("main");            // main: Barks = 2
    barkCounterFrame.contentWindow.useBarkCounter(b1);
});
barkCounterFrame.src = "barkcounter-frame-1.html";
document.body.appendChild(barkCounterFrame);
</script>
</body>
</html>
```

LISTING 5-3: Using BarkCounter cross-realm: Frame, version 1—barkcounter-frame-1.html

```html
<!doctype html>
<html>
<head>
<meta charset="UTF-8">
<title>BarkCounter Across Realms - Frame - Version 1</title>
</head>
<body>
<script src="barkcounter-version-1.js"></script>
<script>
function useBarkCounter(b1) {
    b1.showBarks("frame-b1");
    const b2 = new BarkCounter(b1);
    b2.showBarks("frame-b2");
}
</script>
</body>
</html>
```

`barkcounter-main-1.html` loads an iframe, and once it's loaded creates an instance of `BarkCounter` (b1) and passes it to a global function in the iframe called `useBarkCounter`. The main window and the iframe are different realms.

`barkcounter-frame-1.html`'s `useBarkCounter` receives the `BarkCounter` instance and, like the code shown earlier, passes it into the `BarkCounter` constructor, which tries to copy the number of barks from `b1` into the new instance.

Copy those files along with `barkcounter-version-1.js` to your local web server, then in your browser open the developer tools console and load `barkcounter-main-1.html`. The output is:

```
main: Barks = 2
frame-b1: Barks = 2
frame-b2: Barks = 0
```

The `barks` property didn't get copied. (If it had, that last line would show 2, not 0.) Why not?

The problem is that the copy of `BarkCounter` loaded into the main window is separate from the copy of `BarkCounter` loaded in the iframe window, and they both create their own `barks` Symbol. Those Symbols are, by definition, not equal, so when the `BarkCounter` constructor tried to get the number of barks from `b1`, it didn't see any and used 0 as its starting point.

Ideally, all loaded copies of `BarkCounter` should share the same Symbol for barks. You *could* do that by passing the Symbol from the main window to the iframe along with `b1`, but that gets complicated quickly. In this particular case you could also loop through the properties of `b1` and see if any were named with a Symbol that had the appropriate description, but that doesn't work in all situations (not least if the Symbol doesn't have a description, or a different Symbol has the same description).

Instead, you can do it by publishing the Symbol to the *global Symbol registry* associated with a string key by using the `Symbol.for` function instead of the `Symbol` function. It's a small modification to the `BarkCounter` code, changing this line:

```
const barks = Symbol("nifty-barks");
```

to this:

```
const barks = Symbol.for("nifty-barks");
```

`Symbol.for` checks to see if there's a Symbol in the global registry for the key you provide and returns it if there is; if not, it creates a new Symbol (using the key as the description), adds it to the registry, and returns that new Symbol.

That change is in the "–2" versions of the files (`barkcounter-version-2.js`, `barkcounter-main-2.html`, and `barkcounter-frame-2.html`). Load those onto your local server and run them in the browser, and you'll see:

```
main: Barks = 2
frame-b1: Barks = 2
frame-b2: Barks = 2
```

Both copies of `BarkCounter` use the same global Symbol: the main file's call to `Symbol.for` created and registered it, then the frame file's `Symbol.for` call retrieved the registered Symbol. So copying the number of barks from b1 to b2 works, because both BarkCounter constructors use the same Symbol for the property.

As with global variables, avoid global Symbols when you have other alternatives, but use them when they're the right thing. If you do use them, be sure to use a sufficiently unique name to avoid conflicts with other uses, or with ones that may be defined in future versions of the specification.

You'll see a particularly handy use of global Symbols in Chapter 6 when learning about *iterators* and *iterables*.

One final thing about global Symbols: if you need to know if a Symbol is in the global Symbol registry, and if so what key it's assigned to, you can use Symbol.keyFor:

```
const s = Symbol.for("my-nifty-symbol");
const key = Symbol.keyFor(s);
console.log(key); // "my-nifty-symbol"
```

Symbol.keyFor returns undefined if the Symbol you pass to it isn't in the global registry.

Well-Known Symbols

The specification defines several *well-known Symbols* that get used by various operations in the language. These Symbols are accessible via properties on the Symbol function. You saw one of these in Chapter 4 (Symbol.species) and another earlier in this chapter (Symbol.toStringTag). Here's a list of all of the well-known Symbols in ES2015–ES2018 (ES2019 didn't add any and it doesn't look like ES2020 will) and the chapter they're covered in:

➤ Symbol.asyncIterator (Chapter 9)

➤ Symbol.hasInstance (Chapter 17)

➤ Symbol.isConcatSpreadable (Chapter 17)

➤ Symbol.iterator (Chapter 6)

➤ Symbol.match (Chapter 10)

➤ Symbol.replace (Chapter 10)

➤ Symbol.search (Chapter 10)

➤ Symbol.species (Chapter 4)

➤ Symbol.split (Chapter 10)

➤ Symbol.toPrimitive (Chapter 5)

➤ Symbol.toStringTag (Chapter 5)

➤ Symbol.unscopables (Chapter 17)

All currently defined well-known Symbols are also global (so they're shared across realms), although the spec leaves the door open to having some that aren't global in the future.

NEW OBJECT FUNCTIONS

ES2015 and ES2017 added a few new functions to the `Object` constructor. Let's run through them.

Object.assign

`Object.assign` is JavaScript's version of the common "extend" function that copies properties from one or more source objects into a target object. Suppose you have a function that presents a message box to a user that supports the options `title`, `text`, `icon`, `className`, and `buttons`, where all of them (and even the options object itself) are optional.[3] That's a fair number of options. You could accept them as parameters to the function, but doing that raises some issues:

➤ You have to remember the order when writing calls to the function (though your IDE may be able to help).

➤ If most of them are optional, the code in the function that figures out which options the caller has supplied and which they omitted can quickly become quite complex.

➤ If several have the same type (most of the options in this example are strings), it can be not just complex, but *impossible* for the function code to determine which ones the caller supplied.

Although you could use the default parameter values feature you learned about in Chapter 3 and pass `undefined` for the ones you want defaults for, that's quite awkward.

In this situation, it's common to use an object with properties for the options, instead of discrete parameters. To make some of those properties optional, the usual approach is to copy the passed-in object and mix in defaults from a defaults object. In ES5 without any helper functions, it looks something like this, which is fairly cumbersome:

```
function showDialog(opts) {
    var options = {};
    var optionName;
    var hasOwn = Object.prototype.hasOwnProperty;
    for (optionName in defaultOptions) {
        if (hasOwn.call(defaultOptions, optionName)) {
            options[optionName] = defaultOptions[optionName];
        }
    }
    if (opts) { // remember that `opts` is optional
        for (optionName in opts) {
            if (hasOwn.call(opts, optionName)) {
                options[optionName] = opts[optionName];
            }
        }
    }
    // (Use `options.title`, `options.text`, etc.)
}
```

---

[3] Okay, granted, `text` would probably be required in the real world. But let's say it's optional here.

This is so common and so cumbersome that the "extend" function became common in many tool-kits (jQuery, Underscore/Lodash, etc.) and became an idiom in JavaScript. The traditional "extend" accepts a target object and then any number of source objects, copying own, enumerable properties from the source objects to the target object, and then returning the target object as its return value.

Which is what `Object.assign` does. Here's that `showDialog` function using `Object.assign` rather than using inline code (and switching to `const`, although it's not necessary):

```javascript
function showDialog(opts) {
    const options = Object.assign({}, defaultOptions, opts);
    // (Use `options.title`, `options.text`, etc.)
}
```

Much cleaner! That creates an object and passes it as the first argument (the "target" object), followed by the source objects to copy, then remembers that object (which is the return value) in `options`.

`Object.assign` works through the source objects (`defaultOptions` and `opts` in the example) in order left-to-right, so the last one "wins" when more than one of them has a value for the same property (since its value overwrites any previous ones).That means the final `options` object will have options from `opts` for the options `opts` has, or defaults from `defaultOptions` for the ones `opts` doesn't have.

`Object.assign` skips arguments that are `null` or `undefined`, so the `showDialog` code doesn't have to do anything to handle the case where `opts` wasn't provided by the caller at all.

Like the "extend" functions that inspired it, `Object.assign` only copies own, enumerable properties from the source objects, not inherited ones, and not ones marked non-enumerable, just like the loops in the cumbersome version did. It returns the target object. However, it copies properties keyed by Symbols as well as those keyed by strings, which the `for-in` example earlier would not (`for-in` only loops through the string-named properties of an object).

In Chapter 7 you'll learn a different way you can solve this specific problem using *destructuring parameters*, and later in this chapter you'll learn about ES2018's *property spread*, which works a lot like `Object.assign` but doesn't quite replace it (as you'll learn later).

Object.is

ES2015's `Object.is` compares two values according to the specification's SameValue abstract operation. The SameValue operation is like `===` (strict equality) except:

➤ `NaN` is equal to itself (whereas `NaN === NaN` is false)

➤ Positive zero (`+0`) and negative zero (`-0`) are *not* equal to each other (whereas `+0 === -0` is true)

So:

```javascript
console.log(Object.is(+0, -0));   // false
console.log(Object.is(NaN, NaN)); // true
```

and for everything else, it's just like `===`.

Object.values

ES5 added `Object.keys`, which gives you an array of the names of the object's own, enumerable properties whose keys are strings (not Symbols). `Object.values`, added in ES2017, is the logical counterpart: it provides an array of the *values* of those same properties.

```
const obj = {
    a: 1,
    b: 2,
    c: 3
};
console.log(Object.values(obj)); // [1, 2, 3]
```

The values of inherited properties, non-enumerable properties, and properties keyed by Symbols are not included.

Object.entries

Rounding out the list of ways of accessing the own, enumerable string-keyed properties, ES2017 also added `Object.entries`, which gives you an array of `[name, value]` arrays:

```
const obj = {
    a: 1,
    b: 2,
    c: 3
};
console.log(Object.entries(obj)); // [["a", 1], ["b", 2], ["c", 3]]
```

`Object.entries` makes for quite a powerful tool, particularly in combination with the `for-of` loop you'll learn about in Chapter 6; *destructuring*, which you'll learn about in Chapter 7; and `Object.fromEntries`, which you'll learn about . . . now!

Object.fromEntries

`Object.fromEntries` is a utility function added in ES2019 that accepts a list (any iterable) of key/value pairs and creates an object from them:

```
const obj = Object.fromEntries([
    ["a", 1],
    ["b", 2],
    ["c", 3]
]);
console.log(obj);
// => {a: 1, b: 2, c: 3}
```

`fromEntries` is the converse of `Object.entries`. It's also handy for turning a Map (Chapter 12) into an object, since `Map.prototype.entries` returns the exact type of list `Object.fromEntries` expects.

Object.getOwnPropertySymbols

ES2015's `Object.getOwnPropertySymbols` is the counterpoint to the ES5 method `Object.getOwnPropertyNames` but, as the method name suggests, it returns an array of Symbols for the object's own Symbol-named properties (whereas `Object.getOwnPropertyNames` returns an array of strings for the string-named ones).

Object.getOwnPropertyDescriptors

ES2017's `Object.getOwnPropertyDescriptors` returns an object with property descriptors for all of the object's own properties (including non-enumerable ones and ones keyed with Symbols rather than strings).

One use for it is passing the object it returns into `Object.defineProperties` on another object, to copy the definitions to that object:

```
const s = Symbol("example");
const o1 = {
    // A property named with a Symbol
    [s]: "one",
    // An accessor property
    get example() {
        return this[s];
    },
    set example(value) {
        this[s] = value;
    },
    // A data property
    data: "value"
};
// A non-enumerable property
Object.defineProperty(o1, "nonEnum", {
    value: 42,
    writable: true,
    configurable: true
});
// Copy those properties to a new object
const descriptors = Object.getOwnPropertyDescriptors(o1);
const o2 = Object.defineProperties({}, descriptors);
console.log(o2.example); // "one"
o2.example = "updated";
console.log(o2[s]);       // "updated", the accessor property wrote to the [s] prop
console.log(o2.nonEnum); // 42
console.log(o2.data);    // "value"
```

Contrast this with using `Object.assign` in that same situation, which wouldn't copy the accessor property as an accessor property; instead, it would copy the *value* returned by the accessor property as of when `Object.assign` was called. It also wouldn't copy the non-enumerable property.

SYMBOL.TOPRIMITIVE

`Symbol.toPrimitive` provides a new, more powerful way to hook into the conversion of your objects to primitive values.

First, a bit of background. Famously, JavaScript coerces/converts values in various contexts, including coercing/converting objects to primitive values. The operation being done may prefer the result to be a number or a string (or may have no preference). For instance, in `n - obj` (where `obj` is an object), the preference is to convert `obj` to a number so the subtraction can be carried out. But in `n + obj`, there's no preference for number vs. string. Other times, such as `String(obj)` or `someString.indexOf(obj)`, the preference is for a string. In specification terms, there's a "hint" to the ToPrimitive operation which is either Number, String, or absent (meaning no preference).

For your own objects, traditionally you've hooked into this conversion process by implementing `toString` (which is used by operations preferring a string) and/or `valueOf` (which is used by all others, so both those that prefer a number and those that have no preference). That works fairly well, but it does mean that your object can't do different things when the preference is for a number or there's no preference at all; those two things are lumped together into `valueOf`.

`Symbol.toPrimitive` solves that problem. If your object has a method keyed by `Symbol.toPrimitive` (either an "own" method or an inherited one), that method gets used rather than `valueOf` or `toString`. Even better, it receives the preferred type (the *type hint*) as an argument: `"number"`, `"string"`, or `"default"` if the operation has no preference. Suppose you have this object:

```
const obj = {
    [Symbol.toPrimitive](hint) {
        const result = hint === "string" ? "str" : 42;
        console.log("hint = " + hint + ", returning " + JSON.stringify(result));
        return result;
    }
};
```

If you use the addition operator (+) on that, since there's no preference, your `Symbol.toPrimitive` method is called with the hint `"default"`:

```
console.log("foo" + obj);
// hint = default, returning 42
// foo42
```

It's `"default"` whether the other operand is a string, number, or something else:

```
console.log(2 + obj);
// hint = default, returning 42
// 44
```

But with the subtraction operator (-), the hint is `"number"`:

```
console.log(2 - obj);
// hint = number, returning 42
// -40
```

When a string is desired, unsurprisingly the hint is `"string"`:

```
console.log(String(obj));
// hint = string, returning "str"
// str
console.log("this is a string".indexOf(obj));
// hint = string, returning "str"
// 10 (the index of "str" in "this is a string")
```

Your method must return a primitive value or a TypeError occurs. The value does *not* have to match the hint. The hint is just a hint, you can still return (for instance) a number even if the hint is for a string, or a boolean even if the hint is for a number.

`Symbol.toPrimitive` takes some magic out of the specification that was there for the Date object. Until ES2015, the internal operation ToPrimitive uses that decides whether to call `valueOf` or `toString` (called [[DefaultValue]]) had a special case for Date objects: if there was no type hint, the default was to act as though the hint were Number *except* for Date objects, which defaulted to String instead. That's why Date objects get converted to string when you use + on them, even though they get converted to numbers when you use - on them. Without `Symbol.toPrimitive`, it was impossible to do that in your own objects.

For completeness, if your object doesn't have a `Symbol.toPrimitive` method, the specification defines that, effectively, the following is done:

```
[Symbol.toPrimitive](hint) {
    let methods = hint === "string"
            ? ["toString", "valueOf"]
            : ["valueOf", "toString"];
    for (const methodName of methods) {
        const method = this[methodName];
        if (typeof method === "function") {
            const result = method.call(this);
            if (result === null || typeof result !== "object") {
                return result;
            }
        }
    }
    throw new TypeError();
}
```

PROPERTY ORDER

It used to be one of those shout-it-from-the-rooftops things: "Object properties have no order!" But . . . people kept expecting object properties to have order, particularly properties with names like `1`, `7`, and `10`, such as those in arrays (those names are *strings*, remember; see the "A Myth of Arrays" inset), which people overwhelmingly expect to be visited in numeric order even when using object (not array) iteration mechanisms like `for-in`. And early JavaScript engines gave properties an apparent order, which later engines copied (though often with slight differences), and people relied on.

A MYTH OF ARRAYS

Standard arrays in JavaScript are a bit of a myth: as defined in the specification, they aren't arrays in the classic computing sense of being a contiguous block of memory divided into equally sized slots. (JavaScript does have those now in the form of typed arrays, as you'll learn in Chapter 11.) They're just objects that inherit from `Array.prototype`, have special behavior associated with their `length` property, and have properties whose names, although strings, are *array indexes* by the specification's definition. (An *array index*[4] is a property name consisting entirely of digits which, when converted to a number, is a whole number whose value is $0 \leq value < 2^{32}-1$.) Other than that, arrays are just objects like any other. Of course, JavaScript engines heavily optimize arrays where possible, in many cases making them actual arrays, but they're defined as objects, which has ramifications such as the fact that the keys you get if you apply `for-in` to an array are strings.

---

[4] `https://tc39.github.io/ecma262/#sec-object-type`

Because people kept wanting or even relying on property order, and JavaScript engines had settled on two similar (but different) orders, to make things predictable the order was standardized in ES2015, but only for certain operations, and only for "own" properties (not inherited properties). The order is:

➤ First, properties whose keys are strings that are *integer indexes*, in numeric order. An *integer index* is a string that is all digits and that, when converted to a number, is in the range $0 \le value < 2^{53}-1$. (This is slightly different from an *array index* [see "A Myth of Arrays" earlier], which has a lower upper bound.)

➤ Then, other properties whose keys are strings, in the order the property was *created* on the object.

➤ Then, properties whose keys are Symbols, in the order the property was created on the object.

In ES2015-ES2019, that order did not apply to the `for-in` loop (not even just the order of "own" properties) or the arrays returned by `Object.keys`, `Object.values`, or `Object.entries`. That way, JavaScript engines didn't have to change the order of those existing operations if their implementers didn't want to risk impacting existing code. The new order *was* specified for many other methods, such as `Object.getOwnPropertyNames` and `JSON.stringify` from ES5 and `Object.getOwnPropertySymbols` and `Reflect.ownKeys` from ES2015. But ES2020 updates even `for-in` and the methods listed above and such, provided that neither the object nor any of its prototypes is a Proxy (Chapter 14), a typed array or similar (Chapter 11), a module namespace object (Chapter 13), or an "exotic" host-provided object (like a DOM element).

In the general case, despite there being a defined order now, it's rarely if ever a good idea to rely on the order of properties in an object. Doing so is brittle. For instance, suppose you have a function that adds two properties to an object:

```
function example(obj) {
    obj.answer = 42;
    obj.question = "Life, the Universe, and Everything";
    return obj;
}
```

If you call it with an object with no `answer` or `question` property, like this:

```
const obj = example({});
```

then the order will reliably be `answer`, then `question`, because that's the order in which the code adds the properties.

But suppose you pass it an object with a question property on it already:

```
const obj = example({question: "What's the meaning of life?"});
```

Now, the order is `question`, then `answer`, because `question` was added to the object first (example just updated the value of the property instead of creating it).

PROPERTY SPREAD SYNTAX

Sometimes, you want to create an object with all of the properties of another object, perhaps updating a couple of their values. This is particularly prevalent when programming with the "immutable" approach where you never modify an object; instead, you create a new replacement object incorporating the modifications.

Before ES2018, doing that required explicitly specifying the properties to copy, or writing a `for-in` loop or similar, or using a helper function such as the common `extend` idiom mentioned earlier in this chapter, perhaps even JavaScript's own `Object.assign`. In ES2018+, you can use *property spread syntax* instead.

Let's look again at that example usage of `Object.assign` from earlier in this chapter:

```
function showDialog(opts) {
    const options = Object.assign({}, defaultOptions, opts);
    // (Use `options.title`, `options.text`, etc.)
}
```

ES2018 provides a way to do it with syntax instead of a function call: within an object literal, you can use an ellipsis (`...`) in front of any expression to "spread out" the own, enumerable properties of the expression's result.[5] Here's that `showDialog` example using property spread:

```
function showDialog(opts) {
    const options = {...defaultOptions, ...opts};
    // (Use `options.title`, `options.text`, etc.)
}
```

That creates a new object, filling it in with properties from `defaultOptions`, and then with properties from `opts`. As always in object literals, properties are processed in source code order (top down, left to right) so if `defaultOptions` and `opts` both have a property with the same name, the value from `opts` "wins."

Property spread is only valid within an object literal. It works almost exactly like `Object.assign`: if the source of the property spread (the result of the expression that follows the ellipsis) is `null` or `undefined`, the property spread does nothing (it's *not* an error); and property spread only uses the object's own, enumerable properties, not ones inherited from its prototype or non-enumerable properties.

At first glance, it seems like you could use property spread instead of `Object.assign` everywhere, but `Object.assign` still has a role: it can assign to an *existing* object, whereas property spread can only be used when creating a *new* object.

---

[5] If the expression results in a primitive, that primitive is coerced to object before the spread operation begins. For instance, a primitive string is coerced to a String object.

> **NOTE** *It's tempting to think of ... as an operator, but it isn't one, and can't be. An operator is like a function: it has operands (like a function's arguments) and produces a single result value (like a function's return value). But no "result value" can say "create these properties in the object." So the ellipsis is primary syntax/notation; not an operator. It's like the parentheses around a* while *loop's condition: in that case,* () *aren't the grouping operator, they're just part of the syntax of a* while *loop. The distinction matters, because an operator can be used anywhere an expression is expected; ... can only be used in certain specific places (for property spread, only inside an object literal).*

OLD HABITS TO NEW

All these new syntax features and helpers give us a few habits we can update:

Use Computed Syntax When Creating Properties with Dynamic Names

Old habit: Creating properties whose names are determined at runtime as a second step after creating the object:

```
let name = "answer";
let obj = {};
obj[name] = 42;
console.log(obj[name]); // 42
```

New habit: Use computed property names instead:

```
let name = "answer";
let obj = {
    [name]: 42
};
console.log(obj[name]); // 42
```

Use Shorthand Syntax When Initializing a Property from a Variable with the Same Name

Old habit: Providing the name of a property even when the property's value is coming from an in-scope identifier (for instance, a variable) with the same name:

```
function getMinMax() {
    let min, max;
    // ...
    return {min: min, max: max};
}
```

New habit: Use shorthand property syntax instead:

```
function getMinMax() {
    let min, max;
    // ...
    return {min, max};
}
```

Use Object.assign instead of Custom "Extend" Functions or Copying All Properties Explicitly

Old habit: Using a custom `extend` (or similar) function or laboriously copying all of the (own, enumerable) properties from one object to another **existing** object with a loop.

New habit: Use `Object.assign` instead.

Use Spread Syntax When Creating a New Object Based on an Existing Object's Properties

Old habit: Using a custom `extend` or `Object.assign` to create a **new** object based on an existing object's properties:

```
const s1 = {a: 1, b: 2};
const s2 = {a: "updated", c: 3};
const dest = Object.assign({}, s1, s2);
console.log(dest); // {"a": "updated", "b": 2, "c": 3}
```

New habit: Use property spread syntax:

```
const s1 = {a: 1, b: 2};
const s2 = {a: "updated", c: 3};
const dest = {...s1, ...s2};
console.log(dest); // {"a": "updated", "b": 2, "c": 3}
```

Use Symbol to Avoid Name Collision

Old habit: Using obscure string names for properties in an attempt to avoid colliding with names outside your control.

New habit: Use Symbols for those instead.

Use Object.getPrototypeOf/setPrototypeOf Instead of __proto__

Old habit: Getting or setting the prototype of an object via the previously non-standard extension `__proto__`.

New habit: Use the standard `Object.getPrototypeOf` and `Object.setPrototypeOf` instead (even though `__proto__` is now standardized on web browsers).

Use Method Syntax for Methods

Old habit: Using a property initializer for functions that you intend to be methods of the object:

```
const obj = {
    example: function() {
        // ...
    }
};
```

New habit: Use method syntax instead:

```
const obj = {
    example() {
        // ...
    }
};
```

Just remember that if you use `super`, the method will have a link to its original object, so if you copy it to another object, it will continue to use the prototype of its original object, not the new one. If you *don't* use `super` (and don't use `eval`), a good JavaScript engine will optimize that link away.

Iterables, Iterators, for-of, Iterable Spread, Generators

WHAT'S IN THIS CHAPTER?

➤ Iterators and Iterables

➤ `for-of` loops

➤ Iterable spread syntax

➤ Generators and generator functions

CODE DOWNLOADS FOR THIS CHAPTER

You can download the code for this chapter at `https://thenewtoys.dev/bookcode` or `https://www.wiley.com/go/javascript-newtoys`.

JavaScript got a new feature in ES2015: generalized iteration, the classic "for each" idiom popular in many languages. In this chapter you'll learn about the new feature's *iterators* and *iterables* and how you create and use them. You'll also learn about JavaScript's powerful new *generators* that make creating iterators easy, and also take the concept further, making communication two-way.

ITERATORS, ITERABLES, THE FOR-OF LOOP, AND ITERABLE SPREAD SYNTAX

In this section, you'll learn about JavaScript's new iterators and iterables, the `for-of` loop that makes using iterators easy, and the handy spread syntax (`...`) for iterables.

Iterators and Iterables

Many languages have some kind of "for each" construct for looping through the entries of an array or list or other collection object. For years, JavaScript only had the `for-in` loop, which isn't a general-purpose tool (it's just for looping through the properties of an object). The new *Iterator* and *Iterable* "interfaces" (see note) and new language constructs that use them change that.

> **NOTE** *Starting with ES2015, the specification mentions "interfaces" (in the sense of code interfaces) for the first time. Since JavaScript isn't strongly typed, an "interface" is purely a convention. The specification's description is that an interface ". . . is a set of property keys whose associated values match a specific specification. Any object that provides all the properties as described by an interface's specification* conforms *to that interface. An interface is not represented by a distinct object. There may be many separately implemented objects that conform to any interface. An individual object may conform to multiple interfaces."*

An *iterator* is an object with a `next` method; each time you call `next`, it returns the next value (if any) in the sequence it represents, and a flag saying whether it's done.

An *iterable* is an object with a standard method for getting an iterator for its contents. All list- or collection-style objects in the JavaScript standard library are iterable—arrays, strings, typed arrays (Chapter 11), Maps (Chapter 12), and Sets (Chapter 12). Plain objects are *not* iterable by default.

Let's examine the basics.

The for-of Loop: Using an Iterator Implicitly

You can get and use the iterator directly, but it's more common to use it indirectly, for instance by using the new `for-of` loop. `for-of` gets an iterator from the iterable and uses it to loop through the iterable's contents.

> **NOTE** `for-of` *isn't the only language feature that you can use to implicitly use iterators. There are several new features that use iterables under the covers, including: iterable spread syntax (later in this chapter); destructuring (Chapter 7);* `Promise.all` *(Chapter 8);* `Array.from` *(Chapter 11), and Maps and Sets (Chapter 12).*

Arrays are iterable, so let's look at looping through an array with `for-of`:

```
const a = ["a", "b", "c"];
for (const value of a) {
    console.log(value);
}
// =>
// "a"
```

```
// "b"
// "c"
```

Running that code shows `"a"`, then `"b"`, then `"c"`: the `for-of` statement gets an iterator from the array behind the scenes, then uses it to loop through the values, making each value available as `value` within the loop body.

Note that `for-of` is different from `for-in`. If you use `for-in` on that array, you get `"0"`, then `"1"`, then `"2"`—the names of the properties for the array's entries. `for-of` provides the *values* of the entries, as defined by the array's iterator. This also means that `for-of` will *only* give you values of the array's *entries*, not the values of any other properties you may have added to it (since arrays are objects). Compare:

```
const a = ["a", "b", "c"];
a.extra = "extra property";
for (const value of a) {
    console.log(value);
}
// The above produces "a", "b", and "c"

for (const key in a) {
    console.log(key);
}
// The above produces "0", "1", "2", and "extra"
```

Did you notice the `const value` in the examples so far? You'll remember from Chapter 2 that when you declare a variable in a `for` loop with `let`, a *new* variable is created for each iteration of the loop. That's true in a `for-of` or `for-in` loop as well. But in `for-of`/`for-in`, since the variable's value is never modified by the loop statement,[1] you can declare it with `const` if you like. (`let` or `var` would also be fine, with the usual caveats on the scope of `var`. If you want to change the value in the loop body, use `let`.)

`for-of` is very convenient and you'll use it a lot. But because it does everything for you, it doesn't help you understand the details of iterators much. How does it get the iterator? How does it use it? Let's look more closely. . .

Using an Iterator Explicitly

Suppose you wanted to use the iterator explicitly. You'd do that like this:

```
const a = ["a", "b", "c"];
const it = a[Symbol.iterator](); // Step 1
let result = it.next();          // Step 2
while (!result.done) {           // Step 3.a
    console.log(result.value);   // Step 3.b
    result = it.next();          // Step 3.c
}
```

---

[1] Whereas in a `for` loop, you may recall that the control variable is modified during a loop iteration: specifically, at the beginning of the second iteration onward. See "Block Scope in Loops" in Chapter 2, specifically the detailed series of steps in the "Bindings: How Variables, Constants, and Other Identifiers Work" subsection.

Let's look at each step of that.

Step 1 gets an iterator from the array. Iterables provide a method for this whose name is the *well-known Symbol* `Symbol.iterator` (you learned about well-known Symbols in Chapter 5). You call that method to get the iterator:

```
const it = a[Symbol.iterator]();
```

Step 2 calls the iterator's `next` function to get a *result object*. A result object is an object conforming to the *IteratorResult* interface, which essentially means it has a `done` property indicating whether the iterator is done iterating, and a `value` property containing the value for the current iteration:

```
let result = it.next();
```

Step 3 performs the loop, using a series of sub-steps. (a) while the `done` property on the result object is false (or at least falsy[2]), it (b) uses the `value`, then (c) calls `next` again:

```
while (!result.done) {           // Step 3.a
    console.log(result.value);   // Step 3.b
    result = it.next();          // Step 3.c
}
```

> **NOTE** *The symbols used for iteration (*`Symbol.iterator` *and another you'll learn about in Chapter 9) are* global Symbols *(see Chapter 5), so iteration works across realms.*

You've probably noted that coding the `result = it.next()` call in two places introduces a minor code maintenance hazard. That's one reason to use `for-of` or other automatic constructs where possible. But you could also do the call in the `while` loop's condition expression:

```
const a = ["a", "b", "c"];
const it = a[Symbol.iterator]();
let result;
while (!(result = it.next()).done) {
    console.log(result.value);
}
```

Now it's in just one place.

Although a result object is defined as having a `done` property and a `value` property, `done` is optional if its value would be `false`, and `value` is optional if its value would be `undefined`.

Those are the basic steps of using an iterator.

---

[2] Recall that *falsy* values are considered `false` when used as booleans. The falsy values are 0, NaN, "", `undefined`, `null`, and of course, `false`; all other values are truthy. (Well...on browsers there's also `document.all`; you'll learn about its odd falsiness in Chapter 17.)

Stopping Iteration Early

When you're using an iterator, you may have reason to stop early. For instance, if you're searching through an iterator's sequence for something, you'd probably stop when you found it. But if you just stop calling `next`, the iterator doesn't know you're done with it. It may well be holding onto resources it could let go of if you're done with it. It will let go of them eventually anyway when it gets garbage collected (unless they're something that garbage collection doesn't handle), but iterators have a way to be more proactive: an optional method called `return`. It tells the iterator you're done with it, and that it should clean up any resources it would normally clean up once it had reached the end of the sequence.

Since it's optional, you need to test for it before you call it. Here's an example:

```
const a = ["a", "b", "c", "d"];
const it = a[Symbol.iterator]();
let result;
while (!(result = it.next()).done) {
    if (result.value === "c") {
        if (it.return) {
            it.return();
        }
        break;
    }
}
```

(In Chapter 19 you'll learn about *optional chaining*, which would let you write that more concisely. Instead of the `if`, you could just write `it.return?.()`; See that chapter for details.)

The specification says that `return` must return a result object (like `next` does) which "typically" has `done` set to `true`, and that if you pass an argument into `return`, the result object's `value` should "typically" be that argument's value, but it also says that requirement is not enforced (and later you'll see ways to break it). Consequently, you probably don't want to count on either behavior. Iterators provided by the JavaScript runtime itself will behave that way if they have a `return`, but you can't count on iterators from third-party libraries doing so.

You may be wondering how you call `return` on the iterator if you're using `for-of`, since you don't have an explicit reference to the iterator:

```
const a = ["a", "b", "c", "d"];
for (const value of a) {
    if (value === "c") {
        if (???.return) {
            ???.return();
        }
        break;
    }
}
```

The answer is: you don't have to, because `for-of` does it for you when you exit the loop without completing it (that is, by using `break`, or by returning, or throwing an error). So you don't have to worry about it at all:

```
const a = ["a", "b", "c", "d"];
for (const value of a) {
```

```
        if (value === "c") {
            break; // This is just fine, it calls the iterator's `return`
        }
    }
```

There's a second optional method: `throw`. You won't normally use it with simple iterators, and `for-of` never calls it (even if you throw an error from the body of the `for-of`). You'll learn about `throw` later in this chapter where you learn about *generator functions*.

Iterator Prototype Objects

All iterator objects provided by the JavaScript runtime inherit from a prototype object providing the appropriate `next` method for the iterable you got it from. For instance, array iterators inherit from an array iterator prototype object, which provides the appropriate `next` method for arrays. That array iterator prototype is known in the specification as `%ArrayIteratorPrototype%`. String iterators inherit from `%StringIteratorPrototype%`, Map (Chapter 12) iterators inherit from `%MapIteratorPrototype%`, etc.

> **NOTE** *There are no publicly defined globals or properties that provide direct references to these in the standard runtime, but you can easily get a reference to one by using* `Object.getPrototypeOf` *on an iterator of the type you want, such as an array iterator.*

All of these iterator prototypes have an underlying prototype, which the spec creatively calls `%IteratorPrototype%`. It defines just one property, and the property it defines may seem a bit odd, since it isn't part of the Iterator interface. It defines a `Symbol.iterator` method that returns `this`; effectively:

```
const iteratorPrototype = { // (This name is conceptual, not actual)
    [Symbol.iterator]() {
        return this;
    }
};
```

You're probably thinking, "But wait, isn't that for *iterables*? Why would you have it on an *iterator* instead?!"

The answers are: "Yes," and, "So that they're also iterable." Making an iterator iterable makes it possible to pass the iterator to `for-of` or other constructs expecting an iterable. For instance, if you wanted to loop over all entries but the first in an array without using `slice` to get a subset of the array:

```
const a = ["one", "two", "three", "four"];
const it = a[Symbol.iterator]();
it.next();
for (const value of it) {
    console.log(value);
}
```

```
// =>
// "two"
// "three"
// "four"
```

You'll learn more about that in the "Iterable Iterators" section later in this chapter, but I wanted to explain the seemingly odd method provided by `%IteratorPrototype%`.

Mostly, you won't need to care about these prototype objects. However, there are at least two situations where you might want to access these prototypes:

1. If you want to add functionality to the iterators

2. If you were implementing an iterator manually (see the next section), which you typically won't do

You'll see #2 in the next section. Let's look at #1: adding functionality.

Before we do, note that all the usual caveats about modifying the prototypes of built-in objects apply:

A. Ensure that any properties/methods you add are non-enumerable.

B. Ensure that they have names that are unlikely to conflict with features that may be added in the future. You might consider using Symbols.

C. In the vast majority of cases, library code (rather than application or page-specific code) should avoid prototype modifications entirely.

With all of that said, let's add a method to all iterators (or at least, ones inheriting from `%IteratorPrototype%`): finding the first entry that matches a condition, like the `find` method on arrays. We won't call it `find`, because that would violate caveat (B), so we'll call it `myFind`. Just like the `find` on arrays, it'll accept a callback and optional argument to use as `this` when calling the callback, and return the first result object for which the callback returns a truthy value, or the last result object (which will have `done = true`) if it never does.

To add a method to `%IteratorPrototype%`, first we have to get a reference to it. There's no public global or property that refers directly to it, but we know from the specification that the prototype of an array iterator is `%ArrayIteratorPrototype%`, and we know (also from the spec) that *its* prototype is `%IteratorPrototype%`. So we can get `%IteratorPrototype%` by creating an array, getting an iterator for it, and getting its prototype's prototype:

```
const iteratorPrototype = Object.getPrototypeOf(
    Object.getPrototypeOf([][Symbol.iterator]())
);
```

The specification even has a note saying exactly that.

Now that we have a reference to it, we can add our method to it. Normally, methods on prototypes are non-enumerable, but are writable and configurable, so we'll use `Object.defineProperty`. The method itself is quite simple: call `next` until the callback returns a truthy value, or we run out of values.

```
Object.defineProperty(iteratorPrototype, "myFind", {
    value(callback, thisArg) {
```

```
            let result;
            while (!(result = this.next()).done) {
                if (callback.call(thisArg, result.value)) {
                    break;
                }
            }
            return result;
        },
        writable: true,
        configurable: true
});
```

Run the code in Listing 6-1 to see it in action. Once the new method is defined, the example uses it to find entries in an array of strings that have the letter "e" in them.

LISTING 6-1: Adding myFind to Iterators—adding-myFind.js

```
// Adding it
const iteratorPrototype = Object.getPrototypeOf(
    Object.getPrototypeOf([][Symbol.iterator]())
);
Object.defineProperty(iteratorPrototype, "myFind", {
    value(callback, thisArg) {
        let result;
        while (!(result = this.next()).done) {
            if (callback.call(thisArg, result.value)) {
                break;
            }
        }
        return result;
    },
    writable: true,
    configurable: true
});

// Using it
const a = ["one", "two", "three", "four", "five", "six"];
const it = a[Symbol.iterator]();
let result;
while (!(result = it.myFind(v => v.includes("e"))).done) {
    console.log("Found: " + result.value);
}
console.log("Done");
```

An extension like this is only useful when the iterator is being used explicitly, though. Later when you learn about *generator functions*, you'll learn a simpler way to do this.

Making Something Iterable

You've seen that you get an iterator by calling an iterable's `Symbol.iterator` method. And you've seen that an iterator is an object with, at minimum, a `next` method that returns the "next" result object with `value` and `done`. To make something iterable, you simply provide that `Symbol.iterator` method.

Let's create a pseudo-array with just a plain object:

```
const a = {
    0: "a",
    1: "b",
    2: "c",
    length: 3
};
```

That object is not iterable, because plain objects by default are not iterable:

```
for (const value of a) { // TypeError: a is not iterable
    console.log(value);
}
```

To make it iterable, you need to add a function as its `Symbol.iterator` property:

```
a[Symbol.iterator] = /* function goes here */;
```

ERRORS WHEN THINGS AREN'T ITERABLE

On most JavaScript engines now, when you try to use an object that isn't iterable where an iterable object is expected, you get a fairly clear error, "`x is not iterable`" or similar. But on some engines, it may not be quite so clear: "`undefined is not a function`." This happens when the JavaScript engine doesn't have special handling for this situation, because it looks up `Symbol.iterator` on the object and tries to call the resulting value; if the object doesn't have a `Symbol.iterator` property, the result of looking it up is `undefined`, and when you try to call `undefined` as a function, you get that error. Thankfully, most engines add special handling to make it clearer now.

The next step is to write the function, having it return an iterator object. Later in this chapter you'll learn about *generator functions*, which you'll probably use most of the time to implement iterators. But since generator functions do most of the work for you, they hide some of the details, so let's do it manually first.

As a first approach, you'd probably implement the iterator for this pseudo-array object something like this:

```
// Take 1
a[Symbol.iterator] = function() {
    let index = 0;
    return {
        next: () => {
            if (index < this.length) {
                return {value: this[index++], done: false};
            }
            return {value: undefined, done: true};
        }
    };
};
```

(Note that `next` is an arrow function. It's important that it uses the `this` that the `Symbol.iterator` method was called with, regardless of how it's called, so that `this` refers to the pseudo-array. Alternatively, you could use method syntax and use a rather than `this` in both places it's used, since `next` closes over a in this example. But if you were doing this on a class and needed to access instance information like `length`, you wouldn't usually have anything but `this` to close over, so an arrow function makes sense.)

That version is okay, but it doesn't make the iterator inherit from `%IteratorPrototype%`, like all iterators you get from the JavaScript runtime do. So if you add to `%IteratorPrototype%` as we did earlier with `myFind`, this iterator won't have the addition. It also doesn't inherit the prototype property that makes iterators iterable. Let's make it inherit from `%IteratorPrototype%`:

```
// Take 2
a[Symbol.iterator] = function() {
    let index = 0;
    const itPrototype = Object.getPrototypeOf(
        Object.getPrototypeOf([][Symbol.iterator]())
    );
    const it = Object.assign(Object.create(itPrototype), {
        next: () => {
            if (index < this.length) {
                return {value: this[index++], done: false};
            }
            return {value: undefined, done: true};
        }
    });
    return it;
};
```

If you write these manual iterators a lot, you'll probably want a reusable function to do most of that for you which you just pass your `next` implementation into. But again, you'll probably use generator functions instead. (We'll get to that section soon, really.)

Try running the code in Listing 6-2.

LISTING 6-2: Basic iterable example—basic-iterable-example.js

```
// Basic iterator example when not using a generator function
const a = {
    0: "a",
    1: "b",
    2: "c",
    length: 3,
    [Symbol.iterator]() {
        let index = 0;
        const itPrototype = Object.getPrototypeOf(
            Object.getPrototypeOf([][Symbol.iterator]())
        );
        const it = Object.assign(Object.create(itPrototype), {
            next: () => {
                if (index < this.length) {
                    return {value: this[index++], done: false};
                }
```

```
                    return {value: undefined, done: true};
                }
            });
            return it;
        }
    };
    for (const value of a) {
        console.log(value);
    }
```

That example is just for a single object, but often you'll want to define a class of objects that are all iterable. The typical way to do that is by putting the `Symbol.iterator` function on a prototype object that the class of objects uses. Let's look at an example using the `class` syntax you learned in Chapter 4: a very simple `LinkedList` class that's iterable. See Listing 6-3.

LISTING 6-3: Iterator on a class—iterator-on-class.js

```javascript
// Basic iterator example on a class when not using a generator function
class LinkedList {
    constructor() {
        this.head = this.tail = null;
    }

    add(value) {
        const entry = {value, next: null};
        if (!this.tail) {
            this.head = this.tail = entry;
        } else {
            this.tail = this.tail.next = entry;
        }
    }

    [Symbol.iterator]() {
        let current = this.head;
        const itPrototype = Object.getPrototypeOf(
            Object.getPrototypeOf([][Symbol.iterator]())
        );
        const it = Object.assign(Object.create(itPrototype), {
            next() {
                if (current) {
                    const value = current.value;
                    current = current.next;
                    return {value, done: false};
                }
                return {value: undefined, done: true};
            }
        });
        return it;
    }
}

const list = new LinkedList();
list.add("one");
```

continues

LISTING 6-3 *(continued)*

```
list.add("two");
list.add("three");

for (const value of list) {
    console.log(value);
}
```

It's fundamentally the same as the previous iterator implementation; it's just defined on the prototype rather than directly on the object. Also, since `next` doesn't use `this` (unlike the pseudo-array example, this doesn't need any instance-specific information; each node links to the next), it can be defined using method syntax rather than as a property referring to an arrow function.

Iterable Iterators

Earlier you learned that all iterators inheriting from `%IteratorPrototype%` are also *iterable*, because `%IteratorPrototype%` provides a `Symbol.iterator` method that does `return this`—simply returning the iterator it was called on. There are various reasons to make iterators iterable:

As described earlier, you might want to skip or specially handle an entry or some entries, then process the rest with a `for-of` loop or other mechanism that consumes an iterable (rather than an iterator).

Or suppose you want to provide an iterator without any iterable object, for instance as the return value of a function. The caller may want to use `for-of` or similar on it. Making it iterable lets them do that.

Here's an example of a function returning an iterator that's also iterable. The iterator provides the parent of the DOM element we pass it (and then that parent's parent, etc., until it runs out of parents):

```
// Example that doesn't inherit from %IteratorPrototype% (if it did,
// we wouldn't need to implement the [Symbol.iterator] function)
function parents(element) {
    return {
        next() {
            element = element && element.parentNode;
            if (element && element.nodeType === Node.ELEMENT_NODE) {
                return {value: element};
            }
            return {done: true};
        },
        // Makes this iterator an iterable
        [Symbol.iterator]() {
            return this;
        }
    };
}
```

You wouldn't really write the function like that, of course, because firstly, you'd probably write a generator function instead (we'll get there, I promise!), and secondly, even if you didn't, you'd have the iterator inherit from `%IteratorPrototype%` instead of implementing `Symbol.iterator` yourself. But try it out with the page in Listing 6-4. Then, try modifying it to make the iterator inherit from `%IteratorPrototype%` instead of implementing the `Symbol.iterator` method yourself.

LISTING 6-4: Iterable iterator example—iterable-iterator-example.html

```html
<!doctype html>
<html>
<head>
<meta charset="UTF-8">
<title>Iterable Iterator Example</title>
</head>
<body>
<div>
    <span>
        <em id="target">Look in the console for the output</em>
    </span>
</div>
<script>

// Not really how you'd write this, but shows how implementing the Symbol.iterator
// method makes it possible to use an iterator with `for-of`
function parents(element) {
    return {
        next() {
            element = element && element.parentNode;
            if (element && element.nodeType === Node.ELEMENT_NODE) {
                return {value: element};
            }
            return {done: true};
        },
        // Makes this iterator an iterable
        [Symbol.iterator]() {
            return this;
        }
    };
}
for (const parent of parents(document.getElementById("target"))) {
    console.log(parent.tagName);
}
</script>
</body>
</html>
```

Iterable Spread Syntax

Iterable spread syntax provides a way to consume an iterable by spreading out its result values as discrete values when calling a function or creating an array. (In Chapter 5 you learned about another kind of spread, *property spread syntax*, which is similar but different, and only used in object literals.)

Spread syntax for arrays and other iterables was introduced in ES2015. Let's look at an example: finding the lowest number in an array of numbers. You could write a loop to do it, but you know that `Math.min` accepts a variable number of arguments and returns the lowest of them. For example:

```
console.log(Math.min(27, 14, 12, 64)); // 12
```

So you could use that if you had discrete numbers to pass in. But if you have an *array* of numbers:

```
// ES5
var a = [27, 14, 12, 64];
```

then how do you supply them to `Math.min` as discrete arguments? The old pre-ES2015 way was to use `Function.prototype.apply`. It was long-winded and odd-looking:

```
// ES5
var a = [27, 14, 12, 64];
console.log(Math.min.apply(Math, a)); // 12
```

With spread syntax, though, you can spread out the array as discrete arguments instead:

```
const a = [27, 14, 12, 64];
console.log(Math.min(...a)); // 12
```

As you can see, spread uses the ellipsis (three dots in a row, like the *rest* parameter you learned about in Chapter 3 and property spread you learned about in Chapter 5).

You can use spread syntax anywhere in the argument list. For instance, if you had two numbers in individual variables as well as the list of numbers in the array:

```
const num1 = 16;
const num2 = 50;
const a = [27, 14, 12, 64];
```

and you wanted to get the minimum value of all of them, you could do any of these:

```
console.log(Math.min(num1, num2, ...a)); // Math.min(16, 50, 27, 14, 12, 64) == 12
console.log(Math.min(num1, ...a, num2)); // Math.min(16, 27, 14, 12, 64, 50) == 12
console.log(Math.min(...a, num1, num2)); // Math.min(27, 14, 12, 64, 16, 50) == 12
```

Where you put the spread changes the order of the arguments passed to `Math.max`. It happens that `Math.max` doesn't care about the order, but other functions that accept variable parameter lists may well care (for instance, the `push` method of arrays pushes the arguments you give it into the array in the order you give them).

The other use of iterable spread syntax is expanding an array (or other iterable) inside an array literal:

```
const defaultItems = ["a", "b", "c"];
function example(items) {
    const allItems = [...items, ...defaultItems];
    console.log(allItems);
}
example([1, 2, 3]); // 1, 2, 3, "a", "b", "c"
```

Note that, again, order matters. If you put `defaultItems` first, then `items`, you'd get a different result:

```
const defaultItems = ["a", "b", "c"];
function example(items) {
    const allItems = [...defaultItems, ...items];
    console.log(allItems);
}
example([1, 2, 3]); // "a", "b", "c", 1, 2, 3
```

Iterators, for-of, and the DOM

The majority use of JavaScript is, of course, on web browsers or applications built with web technologies. The DOM has various collection objects, such as the `NodeList` returned by `querySelectorAll` or the older `HTMLCollection` returned by `getElementsByTagName` and other older methods. You're probably wondering, "Can I use `for-of` on those? Are they iterable?"

`NodeList` is on modern, cutting-edge browsers (up-to-date Chrome, Firefox, Edge, and Safari), and `HTMLCollection` is too on all of those except the pre-Chromium version of Edge. The WHAT-WG DOM specification marks `NodeList` as iterable, but not `HTMLCollection`, so the old version of Edge is in line with the specification while the others add this feature to `HTMLCollection` despite it not being specified.

Listing 6-5 shows a (silly) example iterating through a `NodeList` from `querySelectorAll`.

LISTING 6-5: Looping through DOM collection—looping-dom-collections.html

```html
<!doctype html>
<html>
<head>
<meta charset="UTF-8">
<title>Looping DOM Collections</title>
</head>
<body>
<p>
    Lorem <span class="cap">ipsum</span> dolor sit amet, consectetur adipiscing
    elit, sed do eiusmod <span class="cap">tempor</span> incididunt ut
    <span>labore</span> et dolore <span class="cap">magna</span>
    <span class="other">aliqua</span>.
</p>
<script>
for (const span of document.querySelectorAll("span.cap")) {
    span.textContent = span.textContent.toUpperCase();
}
</script>
</body>
</html>
```

You probably don't need to convert DOM collections to arrays nearly as much now as you had to in the past. For instance, you used to have to convert a DOM collection to an array to use `forEach` on it; on modern browsers, that's no longer necessary, because the collections have `forEach` now. But if you have a specific need for an array (perhaps you want to use some advanced array methods), you can use iterable spread to convert the DOM collection to one. This converts a `NodeList` into an array, for instance:

```
const niftyLinkArray = [...document.querySelectorAll("div.nifty > a")];
```

If you're transpiling for use on older browsers, you'll probably need a polyfill to make iteration work for arrays, and that's true for DOM collections as well. Typically, the transpiler you're using will offer polyfills for iteration for `Array.prototype` at least, and possibly `NodeList.prototype` as well. They may be optional ones you need to specifically enable. If your preferred polyfill only handles `Array.prototype` and not the DOM collections, you can apply the `Array.prototype` one to the DOM collections. (The same with `Array.prototype.forEach`.) See Listing 6-6. (It's written in ES5 so it can be used directly even in older environments. You'd include it in your bundle after any polyfills you're using.) But double-check first that the tool you're using doesn't handle these for you; it's generally better to use curated polyfills rather than rolling your own.

LISTING 6-6: Applying Array.prototype iterator to DOM collections—
polyfill-dom-collections.js

```
;(function() {
    if (Object.defineProperty) {
        var iterator = typeof Symbol !== "undefined" &&
                    Symbol.iterator &&
                    Array.prototype[Symbol.iterator];
        var forEach = Array.prototype.forEach;
        var update = function(collection) {
            var proto = collection && collection.prototype;
            if (proto) {
                if (iterator && !proto[Symbol.iterator]) {
                    Object.defineProperty(proto, Symbol.iterator, {
                        value: iterator,
                        writable: true,
                        configurable: true
                    });
                }
                if (forEach && !proto.forEach) {
                    Object.defineProperty(proto, "forEach", {
                        value: forEach,
                        writable: true,
                        configurable: true
                    });
                }
            }
        };

        if (typeof NodeList !== "undefined") {
            update(NodeList);
        }
        if (typeof HTMLCollection !== "undefined") {
            update(HTMLCollection);
        }
    }
})();
```

GENERATOR FUNCTIONS

Generator functions are, at heart, functions that can seemingly pause in the middle of what they're doing, produce a value, optionally accept a new value, and then keep going—repeatedly, as often as necessary (forever, if you like). This makes them very powerful, and seemingly complex at first, but in fact they're quite simple.

They don't really pause in the middle. Under the covers, generator functions create and return *generator objects*. Generator objects are iterators but with a two-way information flow. Where iterators only *produce* values, generators can both *produce* and *consume* values.

You could create a generator object manually, but generator functions provide syntax to markedly simplify the process (just like for-of simplifies the process of using an iterator).

A Basic Generator Function Just Producing Values

We'll start with a very basic generator function with only a one-way flow of information: producing values. See Listing 6-7.

LISTING 6-7: Basic generator example—basic-generator-example.js

```
function* simple() {
    for (let n = 1; n <= 3; ++n) {
        yield n;
    }
}
for (const value of simple()) {
    console.log(value);
}
```

When you run Listing 6-7, it shows the numbers 1 through 3 in the console:

1. The code calls `simple`, getting a generator object, then gives that object to `for-of`.

2. `for-of` asks the generator object for an iterator. The generator object returns *itself* as the iterator (generator objects inherit indirectly from `%IteratorPrototype%` and so they have the "`return this`" `Symbol.iterator` method it provides).

3. `for-of` uses the generator object's `next` method to get the values in the loop and pass each of them to `console.log`.

There are some new things in that code.

First, note the `*` after the `function` keyword. That's what makes it a generator function. You can have whitespace after `function` and before the `*` if you like, it's purely a matter of style.

Second, note the new keyword `yield`. It marks where a generator function seemingly pauses and then resumes. The value you put after it (if any) is the value the generator produces at that point. So in Listing 6-7, the `yield n;` produces 1, then 2, then 3, and then it's done. The code using the generator sees those via the `for-of` (because generators are also iterators).

CONTEXT-SENSITIVE KEYWORDS

Several of the new features being added to JavaScript involve new keywords, like `yield`. But like `yield`, many of these new keywords haven't always been reserved words in JavaScript and may have been used as identifiers (variable names and such) in existing code. So how can they suddenly become keywords without breaking that existing code?

This is done in a couple of different ways, but what they have in common is that the new keyword is only a keyword in contexts where it couldn't have appeared before; in contexts where it could have appeared before, it isn't a keyword and code can use it as an identifier.

continues

continued

One way this is done is by defining the new keyword only in a location where an identifier would be a syntax error; by definition, that means there's no existing, working code that would be broken by the change. (You'll see an example of this in Chapter 9: `async` is a keyword when it's just before `function`; before it was added, `async function` was a syntax error just like `foo function` still is.)

Another way this is done is by defining the new keyword only within a structure that didn't exist before. Since it didn't exist before, there can't be any existing code using an identifier there. That's how `yield` works: it's only a keyword within a generator function, and generator functions are new; before generator functions were added, `function*` was a syntax error. Outside of a generator function, `yield` can be used as an identifier.

Using Generator Functions to Create Iterators

Since generator functions create generators, and generators are a form of iterator, you can use generator function syntax to write your own iterator—and doing so is *much* simpler and more concise than all of that code you saw earlier creating the iterator object with the right prototype and implementing the `next` method. Let's look again at the earlier implementation of an example iterator; see Listing 6-8 (which repeats Listing 6-2 from earlier).

LISTING 6-8: Basic iterable example (again)—basic-iterable-example.js

```javascript
// Basic iterator example when not using a generator function
const a = {
    0: "a",
    1: "b",
    2: "c",
    length: 3,
    [Symbol.iterator]() {
        let index = 0;
        const itPrototype = Object.getPrototypeOf(
            Object.getPrototypeOf([][Symbol.iterator]())
        );
        const it = Object.assign(Object.create(itPrototype), {
            next: () => {
                if (index < this.length) {
                    return {value: this[index++], done: false};
                }
                return {value: undefined, done: true};
            }
        });
        return it;
    }
};
for (const value of a) {
    console.log(value);
}
```

Compare that to Listing 6-9, which does the same thing with a generator function.

LISTING 6-9: Basic iterable example using generator—iterable-using-generator-example.js

```javascript
const a = {
    0: "a",
    1: "b",
    2: "c",
    length: 3,
    // The next example shows a simpler way to write the next line
    [Symbol.iterator]: function*() {
        for (let index = 0; index < this.length; ++index) {
            yield this[index];
        }
    }
};
for (const value of a) {
    console.log(value);
}
```

Much simpler, much clearer (once you know what `yield` means). The generator function does all the heavy lifting for you. You write the *logic* rather than worrying about the plumbing details.

That example uses property definition syntax:

```javascript
[Symbol.iterator]: function*() {
```

but it could have used method syntax as well, since generator functions can be methods. Let's look at that . . .

Generator Functions As Methods

Generator functions can be methods, with all the features of methods (such as being able to use `super`). Earlier you saw an example of a very simple iterable `LinkedList` class, with a manually implemented iterator. Let's revisit that class implementing the iterator with a generator function instead, using method syntax. See Listing 6-10.

LISTING 6-10: Class with generator method for iterator—generator-method-example.js

```javascript
class LinkedList {
    constructor() {
        this.head = this.tail = null;
    }

    add(value) {
        const entry = {value, next: null};
        if (!this.tail) {
            this.head = this.tail = entry;
        } else {
            this.tail = this.tail.next = entry;
        }
    }
```

continues

LISTING 6-10 *(continued)*

```
    *[Symbol.iterator]() {
        for (let current = this.head; current; current = current.next) {
            yield current.value;
        }
    }
}

const list = new LinkedList();
list.add("one");
list.add("two");
list.add("three");

for (const value of list) {
    console.log(value);
}
```

Notice how the generator method is declared: you put an asterisk (*) in front of the method name, just like the asterisk in front of the function name after the keyword `function`. (In this example the method name is using the computed name syntax you learned about in Chapter 4, but it could be a simple name if we weren't defining a Symbol-named method.) This mirrors the syntax of getter and setter method declarations, using * where `get` or `set` would be. Also notice how much simpler, clearer, and more concise the generator version is than the manually coded one.

Using a Generator Directly

So far you've seen consuming the values from generators via `for-of`, as though they were just iterators. Like iterators, you can use the generator directly as well; see Listing 6-11.

LISTING 6-11: Basic generator used directly—basic-generator-used-directly.js

```
function* simple() {
    for (let n = 1; n <= 3; ++n) {
        yield n;
    }
}
const g = simple();
let result;
while (!(result = g.next()).done) {
    console.log(result.value);
}
```

That code gets the generator object (`g`) from the generator function (`simple`), then uses it exactly the way you saw iterators used before (since generators are iterators). That isn't very exciting, but it becomes much more interesting when you start passing values *to* the generator rather than just taking values *from* it, as you'll learn in the next section.

Consuming Values with Generators

Up until now, all of the generators you've seen in this chapter only *produced* values, by providing an operand to `yield`. This is really useful for writing iterators and never-ending sequences like Fibonacci numbers and such, but generators have another trick up their sleeve: they can *consume* values, too. The *result* of the `yield` operator is the value pushed to the generator, the value it can *consume*.

You can't push values to generators via `for-of`, so instead you have to use them directly and pass the value you want to push to the generator into `next` when calling it.

Here's a really simple example: a generator that sums two numbers pushed to it. See Listing 6-12.

LISTING 6-12: Basic two-way generator—basic-two-way-generator-example.js

```
function* add() {
    console.log("starting");
    const value1 = yield "Please provide value 1";
    console.log("value1 is " + value1);
    const value2 = yield "Please provide value 2";
    console.log("value2 is " + value2);
    return value1 + value2;
}

let result;
const gen = add();
result = gen.next();      // "starting"
console.log(result);      // {value: "Please provide value 1", done: false}
result = gen.next(35);    // "value1 is 35"
console.log(result);      // {value: "Please provide value 2", done: false}
result = gen.next(7);     // "value2 is 7"
console.log(result);      // {value: 42, done: true}
```

Let's follow Listing 6-12 through in detail:

1. `const gen = add()` calls the generator function and stores the generator object it returns in the `gen` constant. None of the logic inside the generator function has run yet—the "starting" line does not appear in the log.

2. `gen.next()` runs the generator code up until the first `yield`. The "starting" line is output, then the operand of the first `yield`, `"Please provide value 1"`, is evaluated and provided by the generator to the caller.

3. That value is received by the calling code in the first result object, which is stored in `result`.

4. `console.log(result)` shows the first result: {value: "Please provide value 1", done: false}.

5. `gen.next(35)` sends the value 35 to the generator.

6. The generator code continues: that value (35) becomes the result of the `yield`. (That's the generator *consuming* the value passed to it.) The code assigns that value to `value1`, logs it, and produces (yields) the value `"Please provide value 2"`.

7. The calling code receives that value on the next result object, and logs that new result object: `{value: "Please provide value 2", done: false}`.

8. `gen.next(7)` sends the value 7 to the generator.

9. The generator code continues: that value (7) becomes the result of `yield`. The code assigns it to `value2`, logs the value, and returns the sum of `value1` and `value2`.

10. The calling code receives the result object, saves it in `result`, and logs it. Note that this time, `value` is the sum (42), and `done` is `true`. It's `true` because the generator *returned* that value, rather than *yielding* it.

This example is obviously extremely basic, but it demonstrates how the logic in the generator function seemingly pauses, waiting for the next input from the code using the generator.

Notice that in that example, the first call to `gen.next()` doesn't have any argument. In fact, if you put an argument there, the generator never sees it. That first call to `next` advances the generator from the beginning of the function to the first `yield`, then returns a result object with the value that the first `yield` produces. Since generator function code receives values from `next` as the *result* of `yield`, there's no way for them to receive a value passed in that first call to `next`. To provide initial input to the generator, pass an argument in the generator function's arguments list, rather than to the first call to `next`. (In the example, to give `add` a value right at the outset, you'd pass it into `add` rather than passing it to the first call to `next`.)

The very basic example you've seen so far doesn't have the generator's logic depend on the values pushed to it, but often those values will be used for branching within the generator. Listing 6-13 shows an example of that; run it in a browser.

LISTING 6-13: A very simple guessing page—guesser.html

```
<!doctype html>
<html>
<head>
<meta charset="UTF-8">
<title>Guesser</title>
<style>
.done .hide-when-done {
    display: none;
}

.running .hide-when-running {
    display: none;
}
</style>
</head>
<body>
<p id="text"> </p>
```

```
<input class="hide-when-done" type="button" id="btn-yes" value="Yes">
<input class="hide-when-done" type="button" id="btn-no" value="No">
<input class="hide-when-running" type="button" id="btn-again" value="Go Again">
<script>
function* guesser() {
    if (yield "Are you employed / self-employed at the moment?") {
        if (yield "Do you work full-time?") {
            return "You're in full-time employment.";
        } else {
            return "You're in part-time employment.";
        }
    } else {
        if (yield "Do you spend time taking care of someone instead of working?") {
            if (yield "Are you a stay-at-home parent?") {
                return "You're a parent.";
            } else {
                return "You must be a caregiver.";
            }
        } else {
            if (yield "Are you at school / studying?") {
                return "You're a student.";
            } else {
                if (yield "Are you retired?") {
                    return "You're a retiree.";
                }
                else {
                    return "You're a layabout! ;-)";
                }
            }
        }
    }
}

function init() {
    const text     = document.getElementById("text");
    const btnYes    = document.getElementById("btn-yes");
    const btnNo     = document.getElementById("btn-no");
    const btnAgain = document.getElementById("btn-again");

    let gen;

    function start() {
        gen = guesser();
        update(gen.next());
        showRunning(true);
    }

    function update(result) {
        text.textContent = result.value;
        if (result.done) {
            showRunning(false);
        }
    }
```

continues

LISTING 6-13 *(continued)*

```
    function showRunning(running) {
        const {classList} = document.body;
        classList.remove(running ? "done" : "running");
        classList.add(running ? "running" : "done");
    }

    btnYes.addEventListener("click", () => {
        update(gen.next(true));
    });
    btnNo.addEventListener("click", () => {
        update(gen.next(false));
    });
    btnAgain.addEventListener("click", start);

    start();
}

init();
</script>
</body>
</html>
```

As you can see from the listing, that generator branches a fair bit based on the values it consumes. It's a state machine, but it's written using the same logical flow syntax you use in other JavaScript code.

It's common for generators to involve loops, sometimes endless loops. See Listing 6-14, which shows a "keep a running sum of the last three inputs" generator.

LISTING 6-14: "Sum of last three" generator—sum-of-last-three-generator.js

```
function* sumThree() {
    const lastThree = [];
    let sum = 0;
    while (true) {
        const value = yield sum;
        lastThree.push(value);
        sum += value;
        if (lastThree.length > 3) {
            sum -= lastThree.shift();
        }
    }
}

const it = sumThree();
console.log(it.next().value);  // 0  (there haven't been any values passed in yet)
console.log(it.next(1).value); // 1  (1)
console.log(it.next(7).value); // 8  (1 + 7)
console.log(it.next(4).value); // 12 (1 + 7 + 4)
console.log(it.next(2).value); // 13 (7 + 4 + 2; 1 "fell off")
console.log(it.next(3).value); // 9  (4 + 2 + 3; 7 "fell off")
```

The generator in Listing 6-14 keeps track of the last three values you feed it, returning an updated sum of those last three each time you call it. When you're using it, you don't have to keep track of the values yourself or worry about the logic of maintaining the running sum, including subtracting values from it when they drop off; you just push values to it and use the sum it produces.

Using return in a Generator Function

As you saw briefly earlier, the generator created by a generator function does an interesting thing when you use the return statement with a return value: it produces a result object that has the return value and done = true. Here's an example:

```
function* usingReturn() {
    yield 1;
    yield 2;
    return 3;
}
console.log("Using for-of:");
for (const value of usingReturn()) {
    console.log(value);
}
// =>
// 1
// 2
console.log("Using the generator directly:");
const g = usingReturn();
let result;
while (!(result = g.next()).done) {
    console.log(result);
}
// =>
// {value: 1, done: false}
// {value: 2, done: false}
console.log(result);
// =>
// {value: 3, done: true}
```

There are a couple of things to notice there:

➤ for-of doesn't see the value on the done = true result object, because like the while loops you've seen, it checks done and exits without looking at value.

➤ The final console.log(result); shows the return value along with done = true.

The generator only provides the return value once. If you keep calling next even after getting a result object with done = true, you'll get result objects with done = true and value = undefined.

Precedence of the yield Operator

The yield operator has very low precedence. That means that as much of the expression following it as possible is grouped together before yield is done. It's important to be aware of that, because otherwise reasonable-looking code can trip you up. For example, suppose you were consuming a value in a generator and wanted to use the value in a calculation. This seems okay at first glance:

```
let a = yield + 2 + 30; // WRONG
```

It does run, but the results are odd:

```
function* example() {
    let a = yield + 2 + 30; // WRONG
    return a;
}
const gen = example();
console.log(gen.next());    // {value: 32, done: false}
console.log(gen.next(10)); // {value: 10, done: true}
```

The first call just primes the generator (remember that code in generator functions doesn't see a value passed to the first call to `next`). The result of the second call is just the value passed in; it doesn't get 2 and 30 added to it. Why? A clue to the answer can be found in the first call's result, which has `value = 32`.

Remember that the expression to the right of `yield` is its operand, which is evaluated and becomes the value from `next`. That line is really doing this:

```
let a = yield (+ 2 + 30);
```

which is really just:

```
let a = yield 2 + 30;
```

because the unary + that was in front of the 2 doesn't do anything to the 2 (it's already a number).

If you tried to use multiplication rather than addition or subtraction there, you'd get a syntax error:

```
let a = yield * 2 + 30; // ERROR
```

That happens because there's no unary * operator.

You might think you'd just move `yield` to the end:

```
let a = 2 + 30 + yield; // ERROR
```

but the JavaScript grammar doesn't allow that (largely for historical and parsing-complexity reasons). Instead, the clearest way is just to put it in its own statement:

```
function* example() {
    let x = yield;
    let a = x + 2 + 30;
    return a;
}
const gen = example();
console.log(gen.next());    // {value: undefined, done: false}
console.log(gen.next(10)); // {value: 42, done: true}
```

However, if you prefer you can use parentheses around the `yield` instead, and then use it anywhere in the expression that makes sense:

```
function* example() {
    let a = (yield) + 2 + 30;
```

```
        return a;
    }
    const gen = example();
    console.log(gen.next());   // {value: undefined, done: false}
    console.log(gen.next(10)); // {value: 42, done: true}
```

The return and throw Methods: Terminating a Generator

Generators created by generator functions implement both of the optional methods of the Iterator interface, return and throw. Using them, code using the generator can, in effect, inject a return statement or throw statement into the generator function's logic where the current yield is.

You'll remember from slightly earlier in this chapter that when a generator issues a return statement, the calling code sees a result object with both a meaningful value and done = true:

```
    function* example() {
        yield 1;
        yield 2;
        return 3;
    }
    const gen = example();
    console.log(gen.next()); // {value: 1, done: false}
    console.log(gen.next()); // {value: 2, done: false}
    console.log(gen.next()); // {value: 3, done: true}
```

By using the generator's return method, the calling code can issue a return that isn't actually in the generator function's code; run Listing 6-15.

LISTING 6-15: Forced return in a generator—generator-forced-return.js

```
    function* example() {
        yield 1;
        yield 2;
        yield 3;
    }
    const gen = example();
    console.log(gen.next());     // {value: 1, done: false}
    console.log(gen.return(42)); // {value: 42, done: true}
    console.log(gen.next());     // {value: undefined, done: true}
```

The first call to gen.next() advances the generator to the first yield and produces the value 1. The gen.return(42) call then forces the generator to return 42, exactly as though it had return 42 in its code where that first yield is (the one where it's suspended when return is called). And just as if it had return 42 in its code, the function terminates, so the yield 2 and yield 3 statements are both skipped. Since the generator has completed, all following calls to next just return a result object with done = true and value = undefined, as you can see in the last call in Listing 6-15.

The throw method works the same way, injecting a throw instead of a return. Run Listing 6-16.

LISTING 6-16: Forced throw in a generator—generator-forced-throw.js

```
function* example() {
    yield 1;
    yield 2;
    yield 3;
}
const gen = example();
console.log(gen.next());                     // {value: 1, done: false}
console.log(gen.throw(new Error("boom"))); // Uncaught Error: boom
console.log(gen.next());                     // (never executed)
```

This is exactly as though the generator had `throw new Error("boom");` in its logic where the current `yield` is.

Just as with the `return` and `throw` statements, a generator can use `try`/`catch`/`finally` to interact with injected returns and throws. Run Listing 6-17.

LISTING 6-17: Catching forced throw in a generator—generator-catch-forced-throw.js

```
function* example() {
    let n = 0;
    try {
        while (true) {
            yield n++;
        }
    } catch (e) {
        while (n >= 0) {
            yield n--;
        }
    }
}
const gen = example();
console.log(gen.next());               // {value: 0, done: false}
console.log(gen.next());               // {value: 1, done: false}
console.log(gen.throw(new Error())); // {value: 2, done: false}
console.log(gen.next());               // {value: 1, done: false}
console.log(gen.next());               // {value: 0, done: false}
console.log(gen.next());               // {value: undefined, done: true}
```

Notice how the `throw` was handled by the generator: it responded by switching from counting up (in the `try` block) to counting down (in the `catch` block). This isn't particularly useful on its own and isn't something you'd want to do without a *very* strong reason (you'd be better off writing the generator so you could pass it a value via `gen.next()` that told the generator to change direction), but can be useful when a generator chains to another generator, in the usual way that using `try`/`catch` can be useful when calling one function from another. More on generators chaining to each other in the next section.

Yielding a Generator or Iterable: yield*

A generator can pass control to another generator (or any iterable) and then pick up again when that generator (or iterable) is done by using `yield*`. Run Listing 6-18.

LISTING 6-18: yield* example—yield-star-example.js

```javascript
function* collect(count) {
    const data = [];
    if (count < 1 || Math.floor(count) !== count) {
        throw new Error("count must be an integer >= 1");
    }
    do {
        let msg = "values needed: " + count;
        data.push(yield msg);
    } while (--count > 0);
    return data;
}

function* outer() {
    // Have `collect` collect two values:
    let data1 = yield* collect(2);
    console.log("data collected by collect(2) =", data1);
    // Have `collect` collect three values:
    let data2 = yield* collect(3);
    console.log("data collected by collect(3) =", data2);
    // Return an array of results
    return [data1, data2];
}

let g = outer();
let result;
console.log("next got:", g.next());
console.log("next got:", g.next("a"));
console.log("next got:", g.next("b"));
console.log("next got:", g.next("c"));
console.log("next got:", g.next("d"));
console.log("next got:", g.next("e"));
```

Running Listing 6-18 produces the following output:

```
next got: { value: "values needed: 2", done: false }
next got: { value: "values needed: 1", done: false }
data collected by collect(2) = [ "a", "b" ]
next got: { value: "values needed: 3", done: false }
next got: { value: "values needed: 2", done: false }
next got: { value: "values needed: 1", done: false }
data collected by collect(3) = [ "c", "d", "e" ]
next got: { value: [ [ "a", "b" ], [ "c", "d", "e" ] ], done: true }
```

When `outer` yields to `collect` with `yield*`, calls you make to the `next` method of `outer`'s generator call `next` on the generator from `collect`, producing those values and passing in the ones it consumes. For instance, this line in `outer`:

```javascript
let data1 = yield* collect(2);
```

translates roughly (but only roughly) to this:

```javascript
// Indicative, but not exactly correct
let gen1 = collect(2);
let result, input;
```

```
    while (!(result = gen1.next(input)).done) {
        input = yield result.value;
    }
    let data1 = result.value;
```

However, in addition to that, the JavaScript runtime ensures that calls to throw and return when a generator is doing yield* propagate down through the pipeline to the deepest generator/iterator and take effect from there upward. (Whereas with the "indicative" code shown earlier, calling throw or return on that generator wouldn't get passed on; it would just take effect in the generator you called it on.)

Listing 6-19 shows an example of using return to terminate an inner generator along with its outer generator.

LISTING 6-19: Forwarded return—forwarded-return.js

```
function* inner() {
    try {
        let n = 0;
        while (true) {
            yield "inner " + n++;
        }
    } finally {
        console.log("inner terminated");
    }
}
function* outer() {
    try {
        yield "outer before";
        yield* inner();
        yield "outer after";
    } finally {
        console.log("outer terminated");
    }
}

const gen = outer();
let result = gen.next();
console.log(result);       // {value: "outer before", done: false}
result = gen.next();
console.log(result);       // {value: "inner 0", done: false}
result = gen.next();
console.log(result);       // {value: "inner 1", done: false}
result = gen.return(42);   // "inner terminated"
                           // "outer terminated"
console.log(result);       // {value: 42, done: true}
result = gen.next();
console.log(result);       // {value: undefined, done: true}
```

Running that, notice how when the generator from outer is using yield* to pass control to the generator from inner, the call to return on the generator from outer is forwarded to the inner generator and takes effect there, as you can see by the console.log in its finally block. But it didn't just cause a return there, it also caused one in the `outer` generator as well. It's as though there were a `return 42` in the inner generator, and the outer generator returned the inner's return value, where the `yield`s each generator was suspended at were.

The outer generator doesn't have to stop producing values just because you terminated the inner one. In the downloads, the file `forwarded-return-with-yield.js` is just like `forwarded-return.js` with this line just above the `console.log("outer terminated");` line:

```
yield "outer finally";
```

Run `forwarded-return-with-yield.js`. It produces slightly different output:

```
const gen = outer();
let result = gen.next();
console.log(result);      // {value: "outer before", done: false}
result = gen.next();
console.log(result);      // {value: "inner 0", done: false}
result = gen.next();
console.log(result);      // {value: "inner 1", done: false}
result = gen.return(42); // "inner terminated"
console.log(result);      // {value: "outer finally", done: false}
result = gen.next();      // "outer terminated"
console.log(result);      // {value: 42, done: true}
```

Notice that the `gen.return` call *didn't* return the value that you passed into it (42). Instead, it returned the value `"outer finally"` produced in the outer generator by the new `yield` and still has `done = false`. But later, after the final `next` call, when the generator is finished it returns a result object with `value = 42` and `done = true`. It may seem odd that the 42 was retained and then returned later, but that's how `finally` blocks work outside generator functions, too. For example:

```
function example() {
    try {
        console.log("a");
        return 42;
    } finally {
        console.log("b");
    }
}
const result = example(); // "a"
                          // "b"
console.log(result);      // 42
```

It's possible for the generator to return a different value than the one you give in the `return` method call. This is, again, like having a `return` statement. What does this non-generator function return?

```
function foo() {
    try {
        return "a";
    } finally {
        return "b";
    }
}
console.log(foo());
```

Right! It returns "b", because it overrides the first return with the one in the finally block. This is generally poor practice, but it *is* possible. Generator functions can do that too, including overriding an injected return:

```
function* foo(n) {
    try {
        while (true) {
            n = yield n * 2;
        }
    } finally {
        return "override";  // (Generally poor practice)
    }
}
const gen = foo(2);
console.log(gen.next());    // { value: 4, done: false }
console.log(gen.next(3));   // { value: 6, done: false }
console.log(gen.return(4)); // { value: "override", done: true }
```

Notice that the result object returned from the return had value = "override", not value = 4.

Since yield* forwards these calls to the innermost generator, the inner in Listing 6-19 could do the same thing. Here's a pared-down example of that:

```
function* inner() {
    try {
        yield "something";
    } finally {
        return "override"; // (Generally poor practice)
    }
}
function* outer() {
    yield* inner();
}
const gen = outer();
let result = gen.next();
console.log(gen.return(42)); // {value: "override", done: true}
```

Notice how the call to return got forwarded from outer's generator to inner's. That made inner effectively issue a return on the yield line, but then that return was overridden by the one in the finally block. Then, the call to return also made outer return inner's return value, even though there's no code in outer that does that.

Using the throw method in this situation is simpler to understand: it behaves exactly as though the innermost active generator/iterator had used the throw statement. So naturally it propagates up through the (effective) call stack until/unless it's caught via try/catch (or overridden with a return in a finally block as in the previous example):

```
function* inner() {
    try {
        yield "something";
        console.log("inner - done");
    } finally {
        console.log("inner - finally");
    }
}
function* outer() {
    try {
```

```
            yield* inner();
            console.log("outer - done");
        } finally {
            console.log("outer - finally");
        }
    }
    const gen = outer();
    let result = gen.next();
    result = gen.throw(new Error("boom")); // inner - finally
                                           // outer - finally
                                           // Uncaught Error: "boom"
```

OLD HABITS TO NEW

Here are some changes to consider making in your coding, subject to your style choices of course.

Use Constructs That Consume Iterables

Old habit: Using a `for` loop or `forEach` to loop through arrays:

```
for (let n = 0; n < array.length; ++n) {
    console.log(array[n]);
}
// or
array.forEach(entry => console.log(entry));
```

New habit: When you don't need the index in the body of the loop, use `for-of` instead:

```
for (const entry of array) {
    console.log(entry);
}
```

However, there are still use cases for `for` and `forEach`:

➤ If you need the index variable in the body of the loop[3]

➤ If you're passing a preexisting function to `forEach` instead of creating a new one

Use DOM Collection Iteration Features

Old habit: Converting a DOM collection to an array just to loop through it, or using `Array.prototype.forEach.call` on a DOM collection:

```
Array.prototype.slice.call(document.querySelectorAll("div")).forEach(div => {
    // ...
});
// or
Array.prototype.forEach.call(document.querySelectorAll("div"), div => {
    // ...
});
```

---

[3] In Chapter 11 you'll learn about the new `entries` method on arrays, which combined with *iterable destructuring* that you'll learn about in Chapter 7 would also let you use `for-of` even when you do want the index, if you like.

New habit: Ensure DOM collections are iterable in your environment (perhaps by polyfilling) and use that iterability directly:

```
for (const div of document.querySelectorAll("div")) {
    // ...
}
```

Use the Iterable and Iterator Interfaces

Old habit: Defining custom iteration techniques on your own collection types.

New habit: Make the collection types iterable instead by implementing the Symbol.iterator function and an iterator (perhaps written using a generator function).

Use Iterable Spread Syntax in Most Places You Used to Use Function.prototype.apply

Old habit: Using Function.prototype.apply when using an array to provide discrete arguments to a function:

```
const array = [23, 42, 17, 27];
console.log(Math.min.apply(Math, array)); // 17
```

New habit: Use spread syntax:

```
const array = [23, 42, 17, 27];
console.log(Math.min(...array)); // 17
```

Use Generators

Old habit: Writing highly complex state machines that can be better modeled with code-flow syntax.

New habit: Define the logic in a generator function instead and use the resulting generator object. For state machines that *aren't* better modeled with code-flow syntax, though, a generator function may not be the right choice.

7

Destructuring

➤ Object destructuring

➤ Array/iterable destructuring

➤ Destructuring default values

➤ Parameter destructuring

CODE DOWNLOADS FOR THIS CHAPTER

You can download the code for this chapter at https://thenewtoys.dev/bookcode or https://www.wiley.com/go/javascript-newtoys.

In this chapter you'll learn about *destructuring*, which provides powerful syntax for extracting values from objects and arrays into variables. You'll learn how the new syntax helps you access object and array contents more concisely and/or expressively.

OVERVIEW

Destructuring is *extracting* things from the structure they're in, in this case with syntax. You've been doing a kind of manual destructuring as long as you've been programming (probably without calling it that!), for instance by taking the value of an object property and putting it in a variable:

```
var first = obj.first; // Manual destructuring
```

That code *destructures* first by copying it from obj (extracting it from the object structure).

Destructuring syntax, added in ES2015 and extended in ES2018, gives you a new way to do that, which can be more concise (though isn't necessarily) and quite powerful, providing default values, renaming, nesting, and rest syntax. It also provides clarity and expressiveness, particularly when applied to function parameters.

BASIC OBJECT DESTRUCTURING

The new syntax gives you a new way to destructure things, usually with less repetition and fewer unnecessary variables. (It might seem more verbose initially, but bear with me.) Instead of writing:

```
let obj = {first: 1, second: 2};
let a = obj.first;          // Old, manual destructuring
console.log(a);             // 1
```

you can write:

```
let obj = {first: 1, second: 2};
let {first: a} = obj;       // New destructuring syntax
console.log(a);             // 1
```

That destructuring tells the JavaScript engine to put the value of the `first` property into the variable a. Again, for the moment, that's both longer and more awkward than the manual form, but you'll see how it gets more concise and expressive in a moment.

Notice how the destructuring pattern `{first: a}` looks exactly like an object literal. That's intentional: the syntax for them is *exactly the same*, even though they serve converse purposes. An object literal puts a structure together, while an object destructuring pattern takes it apart—in exactly the same way. In the object literal `{first: a}`, `first` is the name of the property to create, and a is the *source* of the property's value. In the object destructuring pattern `{first: a}`, it's the converse: `first` is the name of the property to read, and a is the *target* to put the value into. The JavaScript engine knows whether you're writing an object literal or object destructuring pattern from context: an object literal can't be on the left-hand side of an assignment (for instance), and a destructuring pattern can't be used where a value is expected, such as on the right-hand side of an assignment.

The fact that object literals and object destructuring patterns are effectively mirror images of each other is even clearer if you do something like this:

```
let {first: a} = {first: 42};
console.log(a); // 42
```

See Figure 7-1 for a visualization of that first line. First the object literal is evaluated, creating a new object and putting the value 42 into its `first` property, then when doing the assignment to the right-hand side, the destructuring pattern takes the value of the `first` property and puts it in the variable a.

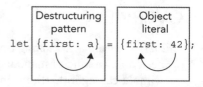

FIGURE 7-1

The *target* in the preceding example is a variable being declared with `let`, the variable `a`. But the target of a destructuring pattern can be anything you can assign to: a variable, an object property, an array entry, etc. —if it can be on the left-hand side of an assignment, you can assign to it with destructuring. (That also means you can make the target another destructuring pattern. You'll learn about that later in the "Nested Destructuring" section.)

Let's continue with the initial example in this section. Just like manual destructuring, if the object doesn't have the property you're trying to read, the variable will get the value `undefined`:

```
let obj = {first: 1, second: 2};
let {third: c} = obj;
console.log(c);         // undefined, obj doesn't have a property called 'third'
```

That destructuring is exactly the same as `let c = obj.third;`, so it does the same thing.

It's very common to want to use the name of the property as the name of the variable as well, so rather than repeating it like this:

```
let obj = {first: 1, second: 2};
let {first: first} = obj;
console.log(first);         // 1
```

you can just leave the colon and name after it off:

```
let obj = {first: 1, second: 2};
let {first} = obj;
console.log(first);         // 1
```

Now it's more concise than the equivalent, since the old equivalent repeats the name:

```
let first = obj.first;
```

If `{first}` looks familiar, it's because it's the converse of the shorthand properties you learned about in Chapter 5: if that were an object literal, it would create a property called `first` and get the initial value for the property from an in-scope identifier called `first`. Again, object destructuring syntax is exactly the same as object literal syntax; it's just what the JavaScript engine does with it that's different between the two.

Since using the same name like that is so common, for now I'm going to do that in the examples; later in this chapter I'll come back to using a different name for the variable and the reasons you might want to do that.

> **NOTE** *I use* `let` *in various examples, but destructuring is not a feature of* `let` *(or* `const`*, or* `var`*). How (and where) you declare the variables doesn't matter; destructuring isn't linked to variable declaration. More on that in a moment.*

Destructuring starts to be really powerful when you're picking out more than one property:

```
const obj = {first: 1, second: 2};
let {first, second} = obj;
console.log(first, second); // 1 2
```

That's equivalent to:

```
const obj = {first: 1, second: 2};
let first = obj.first, second = obj.second;
console.log(first, second); // 1 2
```

This is where the expressiveness comes in. By putting the {first, second} on the left-hand side and just having the object on the right, it's quite clear (once you're used to it!) what you're taking from the object. In contrast, in the longer form second is buried in the middle of the statement and easily overlooked. It also saves a fair bit of typing/reading in that example: instead of having to write first, second, and obj twice (or read them twice if reading code), you only have to type/read them once.

It's not just about being concise and expressive, though, it also helps you avoid unnecessary temporary variables. Suppose you need to call a function that returns an object, and you just want two properties from that object. Instead of:

```
const obj = getSomeObject();
let first = obj.first;
let second = obj.second;
```

you can do this:

```
let {first, second} = getSomeObject();
```

No need for the obj variable at all!

Destructuring isn't limited to variable/constant initializers; you can use it in any assignment (and in parameter lists, as you'll see in a later section). There's one small "gotcha": if you're doing the assignment where the JavaScript parser is expecting a statement (not an expression), you need to wrap the assignment expression in parentheses since otherwise the parser treats the initial curly brace ({) as the beginning of a block.

```
let first, second;
// ...
{first, second} = getSomeObject();   // SyntaxError: Unexpected token =
({first, second} = getSomeObject()); // Works
```

Using the parentheses tells the parser it's dealing with an expression, and so the leading { can't be the beginning of a block.

Destructuring is just syntactic sugar for picking out the properties with the old-style equivalent code. Knowing that, what do you think would happen with the following code?

```
let {first, second} = undefined;
```

It helps to consider what the de-sugared version would look like:

```
const temp = undefined;
let first = temp.first, second = temp.second;
```

If you're thinking it's an error, you're spot on: that's exactly right. As always, it's a TypeError to try to read a property from undefined (or null).

Similarly, what's the result here?

```
let {first, second} = 42;
```

No, not an error, bit of a trick question there. Remember the de-sugared version:

```
const temp = 42;
let first = temp.first, second = temp.second;
```

Just like any other time you treat a number like an object, the primitive number is coerced to a Number object and, in that example, the properties `first` and `second` are read from that object. They don't exist, of course (unless someone's been modifying `Number.prototype`!), so `first` and `second` get the value `undefined`. (Try it with `toString` instead of `first`, though, and log the type of what you get.)

BASIC ARRAY (AND ITERABLE) DESTRUCTURING

You can destructure arrays and other iterables, too. Unsurprisingly, the syntax uses square brackets (`[]`) instead of the curly braces (`{}`) used by object destructuring:

```
const arr = [1, 2];
const [first, second] = arr;
console.log(first, second); // 1 2
```

In fact, just as object destructuring uses the exact same syntax as an object literal, array destructuring uses the exact same syntax as an array literal. The value each target receives depends on where it is in the pattern. So with `[first, second]`, `first` gets the value from `arr[0]` because it's in the 0th position, and `second` gets the value from `arr[1]` because it's in the 1st position. It's just like you'd written:

```
const arr = [1, 2];
const first = arr[0], second = arr[1];
console.log(first, second); // 1 2
```

It's valid to leave out elements you don't want. Notice that the following code has no variable in the 0th position:

```
const arr = [1, 2];
const [, second] = arr;
console.log(second); // 2
```

You can leave gaps in the middle, too:

```
const arr = [1, 2, 3, 4, 5];
const [, b, , , e] = arr;
console.log(b, e); // 2 5
```

Of course, just like with the array literals they mirror, readability suffers if you're leaving out more than a couple of elements. (See "Using Different Names" later in this chapter for an alternative.)

Unlike object destructuring, you don't need to wrap the expression in parentheses when you're doing assignment rather than initialization where a statement is expected; the initial square bracket (`[`) isn't ambiguous the way the initial curly brace (`{`) is, at least not in the normal case:

```
const arr = [1, 2];
let first, second;
[first, second] = arr;
console.log(first, second); // 1 2
```

However, if you're in the habit of relying on automatic semicolon insertion (ASI) rather than writing explicit semicolons, as always beware of starting a statement with a square bracket, since ASI will often assume it's part of the expression at the end of the previous line if there's no semicolon to tell it otherwise. The code in the previous example would be fine without semicolons, but it wouldn't be if you had (for instance) a function call prior to the destructuring:

```
const arr = [1, 2]
let first, second
console.log("ASI hazard")
[first, second] = arr  // TypeError: Cannot set property 'undefined' of undefined
console.log(first, second)
```

That fails because the parser treats the `[first, second]` as a property accessor (with a comma expression inside) that's setting a property on whatever `console.log` returns, as though you'd written

```
console.log("ASI hazard")[first, second] = arr
```

Through a series of steps that ends up trying to set the value of a property on the result of `console.log`. Since `console.log` returns `undefined`, that fails; you can't set properties on `undefined`. (ASI hazards like this don't always result in error messages, sometimes you just get odd bugs. But this one would.)

If you rely on ASI, you probably already know about that hazard and are in the habit of putting a semicolon at the beginning of a line that would otherwise start with an opening square bracket, which solves the problem:

```
const arr = [1, 2]
let first, second
console.log("ASI hazard")
;[first, second] = arr
console.log(first, second) // 1, 2
```

Using destructuring just means you may have more lines that start with square brackets.

DEFAULTS

As you learned in the last section, if the object doesn't have the property you've specified in your destructuring pattern, the target will get the value `undefined` (just like when when you destructure manually):

```
const obj = {first: 1, second: 2};
const {third} = obj;
console.log(third); // undefined
```

With destructuring, you can specify a default that will *only* be applied if the property is missing or has the value `undefined`:

```
const obj = {first: 1, second: 2};
const {third = 3} = obj;
console.log(third); // 3
```

This is exactly like the default function parameters you saw in Chapter 3: the default is only evaluated, and only used, if the result of retrieving the property is the value `undefined` (either because the object didn't have the property, or the property had the value `undefined`). And like function parameter defaults, while it's similar to the `third = obj.third || 3` trick, it's less problematic, because the default only kicks in if the effective value is `undefined`, *not* if it's any other falsy value:[1]

```
const obj = {first: 1, second: 2, third: 0};
const {third = 3} = obj;
console.log(third); // 0, not 3
```

"FALSY" AND "TRUTHY"

A *falsy* value is any value that coerces to `false` when used as a boolean, such as in an `if` condition. The falsy values are 0, "", NaN, null, undefined, and of course, `false`. (The DOM's `document.all` is also falsy, you'll learn about that in Chapter 17.) All other values are *truthy*.

Let's look closer at default destructuring values; run the code in Listing 7-1.

LISTING 7-1: Default destructuring values—default-destructuring-value.js

```
function getDefault(val) {
    console.log("defaulted to " + val);
    return val;
}
const obj = {first: 1, second: 2, third: 3, fourth: undefined};
const {
    third = getDefault("three"),
    fourth = getDefault("four"),
    fifth = getDefault("five")
} = obj;
// "defaulted to four"
// "defaulted to five"
console.log(third);  // 3
console.log(fourth); // "four"
console.log(fifth);  // "five"
```

Notice that `getDefault` isn't called for `third`, because `obj` has a property called `third` with a non-`undefined` value. But it's called for `fourth`, because although `obj` has a property called `fourth`, its value is `undefined`. And `getDefault` is called for `fifth`, because `obj` doesn't have a `fifth` property at all, so its effective value is `undefined`. Also notice that the calls to `getDefault` were in order, first the one for `fourth` and then the one for `fifth`. Destructuring is done in source code order.

---

[1] The *nullish coalescing operator* you'll learn about in Chapter 17 gets you even closer: the statement `const third = obj.third ?? 3;` will only use the right-hand operand if the left-hand operand's value is `undefined` or `null`. See Chapter 17 for details. So that's similar, but both parameter and destructuring defaults only kick in for `undefined`.

Because destructuring is done in source code order, later targets can refer to the value of earlier targets in their defaults (like defaults in parameter lists). So, for instance, if you're destructuring a, b, and c from an object and want the default for c to be a * 3, you can do that declaratively:

```
const obj = {a: 10, b: 20};
const {a, b, c = a * 3} = obj;
console.log(c);   // 30
```

You can only refer to targets defined *earlier* in the pattern; this doesn't work, for instance:

```
const obj = {a: 10, b: 20};
const {c = a * 3, b, a} = obj; // ReferenceError: a is not defined
console.log(c);
```

That makes sense if you consider the de-sugared version; a hasn't been declared yet:

```
const obj = {a: 10, b: 20};
const c = typeof obj.a === "undefined"
          ? a * 3        // ReferenceError: a is not defined
          : obj.c;
const b = obj.b;
const a = obj.a;
console.log(c);
```

If the variables were already declared, you could use them though. What do you think the result of running this code is?

```
let a, b, c;
const obj = {a: 10, b: 20};
({c = a * 3, b, a} = obj);
console.log(c);
```

Did you say it outputs NaN? Right! Because when c's default is calculated, a has the value undefined, and undefined * 3 is NaN.

REST SYNTAX IN DESTRUCTURING PATTERNS

You saw rest syntax in Chapter 3 when learning about using a rest parameter in a function's parameter list. You can also use rest syntax when destructuring, and it works the same way:

```
const a = [1, 2, 3, 4, 5];
const [first, second, ...rest] = a;
console.log(first);     // 1
console.log(second);    // 2
console.log(rest);      // [3, 4, 5]
```

In that code, first gets the value of the first array entry, second gets the value of the second entry, and rest gets a new array containing the rest of the values. The rest entry in the pattern must be at the end (just like the rest *parameter* needed to be at the end of the function parameter list).

Rest syntax for array destructuring was in ES2015; ES2018 added rest syntax for object destructuring as well, which is the converse of object property spread (Chapter 5):

```
const obj = {a: 1, b: 2, c: 3, d: 4, e: 5};
const {a, d, ...rest} = obj;
console.log(a);      // 1
```

```
console.log(d);      // 4
console.log(rest);   // {b: 2, c: 3, e: 5}
```

The rest entry gets a new object with the properties from the original object that weren't consumed by other entries in the destructuring pattern. In that example, the object got the b, c, and e properties but not a and d because a and d were consumed by an earlier part of the pattern. Just like the rest entry of iterable destructuring, it has to be the last thing in the pattern.

USING DIFFERENT NAMES

Other than early in this chapter, all of the object destructuring you've seen so far has used the name of the source property as the name of the target variable/constant. Let's look again at a slightly updated example from earlier:

```
const obj = {first: 1, second: 2};
let {first} = obj;
console.log(first);      // 1
```

Suppose you had a good reason for not using that property name as the variable name? For instance, suppose the property name isn't a valid identifier:

```
const obj = {"my-name": 1};
let {my-name} = obj;      // SyntaxError: Unexpected token -
let {"my-name"} = obj;    // SyntaxError: Unexpected token }
```

Property names can contain just about anything, but an identifier name has fairly strict rules (no dashes, for instance) and unlike property names, there's no quoted format for identifiers.

If you were doing it manually, you'd just use a different name:

```
const obj = {"my-name": 1};
const myName = obj["my-name"];
console.log(myName);      // 1
```

You can do that with destructuring, too, by including an explicit variable name instead of using short-hand syntax:

```
const obj = {"my-name": 1};
const {"my-name": myName} = obj;
console.log(myName);      // 1
```

That's the equivalent of the manual version earlier. Remember that the syntax is identical to object initializer syntax. That includes the fact that the property name can be quoted.

If the property name is a valid identifier name but you just don't want to use that name for some reason, you don't need the quotes:

```
const obj = {first: 1};
const {first: myName} = obj;
console.log(myName);      // 1
```

This is also handy when you're picking out a set of specific indexes from an array. Recall the earlier example leaving gaps in the pattern:

```
const arr = [1, 2, 3, 4, 5];
const [, b, , , e] = arr;
console.log(b, e); // 2, 5
```

That works, but keeping track of the number of gaps there (particularly before e) makes reading it difficult. Since arrays are objects, you can perhaps make that clearer by using object destructuring rather than array destructuring:

```
const arr = [1, 2, 3, 4, 5];
const {1: b, 4: e} = arr;
console.log(b, e); // 2 5
```

Since numeric constants are valid property names, but not valid identifiers (you can't have variables called 1 and 4), you don't need quotes, but you do need to rename them (to b and e in this case).

This index trick works because array indexes are property names, so this trick doesn't work on iterables in general, just arrays. (If the iterable is finite, you can use `Array.from` to get an array for it and then apply this trick, though that may be overkill.)

When specifying the target explicitly, the target of destructuring can be anything you can assign to. It could be an object property, for instance:

```
const source = {example: 42};
const dest = {};
({example: dest.result} = source);
console.log(dest.result); // 42
```

COMPUTED PROPERTY NAMES

In Chapter 5 you learned about computed property names in object literals. Since object destructuring uses the exact same syntax as object literals, you can use computed property names when destructuring, too:

```
let source = {a: "ayy", b: "bee"};
let name = Math.random() < 0.5 ? "a" : "b";
let {[name]: dest} = source;
console.log(dest); // "ayy" half the time, "bee" the other half
```

In that code, half the time the name variable gets the value "a" and half the time it gets the value "b", so the dest variable gets its value from the a property half the time and gets its value from the b property the other half.

NESTED DESTRUCTURING

So far you've seen taking array entry and object property values from just the top level of the array/object, but destructuring syntax can go deeper by using *nesting* in the pattern. You'll never guess, but you do it the same way you create nested objects/arrays in object and array literals! Who would have thought. Let's look at that.

Recall that in the following, array is the target for the value of the a property:

```
const obj = {a: [1, 2, 3], b: [4, 5, 6]};
let {a: array} = obj;
console.log(array); // [1, 2, 3]
```

In that case, the target (the part to the right of the :) is the variable or constant, etc., that the destructured value should go into. That's been true in all of the examples you've seen so far. But if you just want the first two entries in that array, as discrete variables, you can make the target an array destructuring pattern instead, with target variables inside it:

```
const obj = {a: [1, 2, 3], b: [4, 5, 6]};
let {a: [first, second]} = obj;
console.log(first, second); // 1 2
```

Notice again how this exactly mirrors creating an object with a property initialized with a new array built using the values from `first` and `second`. We're just using it on the other side of the equals sign, because we're taking the structure apart rather than putting it together.

Naturally it works just as well for objects:

```
const arr = {first: {a: 1, b: 2}, second: {a: 3, b: 4}};
const {first: {a}, second: {b}} = arr;
console.log(a, b); // 1 4
```

That code picked out the `a` property from the object referenced by the `first` property, and the `b` property from the object referenced by the `second` property.

The outer structure could be an array instead of an object as well:

```
const arr = [{a: 1, b: 2}, {a: 3, b: 4}];
const [{a}, {b}] = arr;
console.log(a, b); // 1 4
```

That code picked out the `a` property from the object in the first array entry, and the `b` property from the object in the second array entry.

As with object and array literals, the amount of nesting you can use is essentially unlimited.

PARAMETER DESTRUCTURING

Destructuring isn't just for assignments. You can destructure function parameters, too:

```
function example({a, b}) {
    console.log(a, b);
}
const o = {a: "ayy", b: "bee", c: "see", d: "dee"};
example(o);              // "ayy" "bee"
example({a: 1, b: 2});  // 1 2
```

Note the object destructuring (`{a, b}`) used in the parameter list. That `example` accepts a single parameter and destructures it into two local bindings, almost as though you'd written:

```
function example(obj) {
    let {a, b} = obj;
    console.log(a, b);
}
```

(It's "almost" because of the temporary parameter `obj` and because, if the parameter list includes any default parameter values, it occurs in a scope specific to the parameter list rather than within the function body. Also, parameters are more like variables declared with var than variables declared with let, for historic reasons.)

The parameter being destructured doesn't have to be the first one, or the only one; it can be anywhere in the parameter list:

```
function example(first, {a, b}, last) {
    console.log(first, a, b, last);
}
const o = {a: "ayy", b: "bee", c: "see", d: "dee"};
example("alpha", o, "omega");                    // "alpha" "ayy" "bee" "omega"
example("primero", {a: 1, b: 2}, "ultimo"); // "primero" 1 2 "ultimo"
```

Conceptually, you can imagine it as one big nested array destructuring pattern, where the parameter list is enclosed in square brackets to form an array destructuring pattern, and then the equals sign and an array of the arguments go on the right. See Figure 7-2.

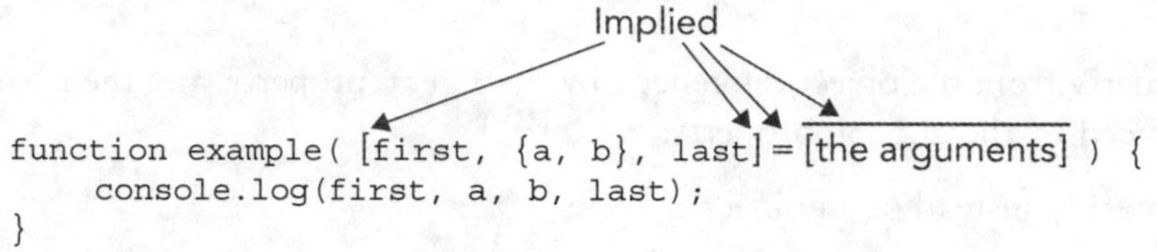

```
function example( [first, {a, b}, last] = [the arguments] ) {
    console.log(first, a, b, last);
}
```

FIGURE 7-2

So this function and call:

```
function example(first, {a, b}, last) {
    console.log(first, a, b, last);
}
example(1, {a: 2, b: 3}, 4); // 1 2 3 4
```

work exactly the way this assignment does with those arguments as an array:

```
let [first, {a, b}, last] = [1, {a: 2, b: 3}, 4];
console.log(first, a, b, last); // 1 2 3 4
```

Naturally you can use iterable destructuring as well:

```
function example([a, b]) {
    console.log(a, b);
}
const arr = [1, 2, 3, 4];
example(arr);                  // 1, 2
example(["ayy", "bee"]);       // "ayy", "bee"
```

And similarly, destructuring default values:

```
function example({a, b = 2}) {
    console.log(a, b);
}
const o = {a: 1};
example(o);                    // 1 2
```

There, b was defaulted because o didn't have it. It would also have been defaulted if o had had it, but its value had been undefined.

In that example, although `b` didn't exist on the object that was passed in, an object *was* passed in. But what about the case where no object is passed in at all? Given that same `example` function, what do you think happens with the following call?

```
example();
```

If you said it would be an error, spot on. It's just like doing this:

```
let {a, b = 2} = undefined;
```

or, if you consider the entire parameter list, doing this:

```
let [{a, b = 2}] = [];
```

You can't read properties from `undefined`; trying to is a `TypeError`.

Thinking back to what you learned in Chapter 3, is there something you could use to handle the case where no object is passed in at all?

Yes! A default parameter value. Hang onto your hats:

```
function example({a, b = "prop b def"} = {a: "param def a", b: "param def b"}) {
    console.log(a, b);
}
example();                    // "param def a" "param def b"
example({a: "ayy"});          // "ayy" "prop b def"
```

That could be a bit confusing, so let's diagram it (see Figure 7-3):

➤ `{a, b = "prop b def"}` is the parameter destructuring pattern.

➤ The `= "prop b def"` part of the pattern is the default for the destructured `b` property (if it's not in the object passed in, or has the value `undefined`).

➤ `= {a: "param def a", b: "param def b"}` is the default parameter value (if no argument is passed for this parameter, or the argument's value is `undefined`).

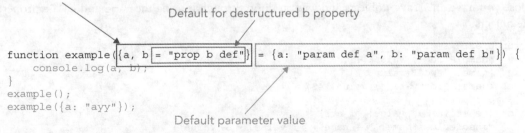

FIGURE 7-3

Using that knowledge, let's look at the two calls. The first call:

```
example();
```

didn't pass anything in for the parameter, so the default parameter value `{a: "param def a", b: "param def b"}` was used. That has a value for `b`, so the destructured `b` got the value `"param def b"`.

The second call:

```
example({a: "ayy"});
```

passed in an object with no b, so the default parameter value didn't apply (we have an argument for the parameter, and its value isn't undefined), but the destructuring default value for b did apply since the object doesn't have a b property. So b got the value "b def".

As you were working through that example, a thought may have occurred to you about default function parameters. If it didn't, stop for a moment and think about the various things you've learned in this section. (Hint: it has to do with parameter lists being implicit destructuring patterns, think of Figure 7-3 . . .)

Got it? This one's a bit tricky, if you aren't seeing it yet, don't worry! It's this: default function parameters are effectively just default destructuring values. That example function parameter list is equivalent to this destructuring when you call example with no parameters:

```
let [{a, b = "b def"} = {a: "param def a", b: "param def b"}] = [];
console.log(a, b); // "param def a", "param def b"
```

One final note about destructuring in parameter lists: using destructuring in a parameter list makes it *non-simple*. As you learned in Chapter 3, a function with a non-simple parameter list can't contain a "use strict" directive; if you want it to be in strict mode, it has to appear in a context that's *already* in strict mode.

DESTRUCTURING IN LOOPS

In JavaScript, there are some assignments that don't look a lot like assignments. In particular, the for-in and for-of[2] loops assign to the loop variable at the beginning of each loop iteration. You can use destructuring in them, too. It's not a lot of use in a for-in loop (the keys a for-in provides are always strings, and it's rare you want to destructure a string—although you can, since strings are iterable), but it can be very handy when using for-of.

Suppose you have an array of objects and want to loop through it using the name and value property of the objects:

```
const arr = [
    {name: "one", value: 1},
    {name: "two", value: 2},
    {name: "forty-two", value: 42}
];
for (const {name, value} of arr) {
    console.log("Name: " + name + ", value: " + value);
}
```

Or suppose you have an object and you want to loop over its "own" (not inherited) property names and values. You might use a for-in loop:

```
const obj = {a: 1, b: 2, c: 3};
for (const name in obj) {
```

---

[2] And for-await-of, which you'll learn about in Chapter 9.

```
            if (obj.hasOwnProperty(name)) {
                const value = obj[name];
                console.log(name + " = " + value);
            }
        }
```

Or you could get rid of that hasOwnPropertyCheck by using a for-of loop and the Object.entries function you learned about in Chapter 5:

```
        const obj = {a: 1, b: 2, c: 3};
        for (const entry of Object.entries(obj)) {
            console.log(entry[0] + " = " + entry[1]);
        }
```

but entry[0] and entry[1] aren't very meaningful names. With destructuring, you can make that code much clearer with iterable destructuring:

```
        const obj = {a: 1, b: 2, c: 3};
        for (const [name, value] of Object.entries(obj)) {
            console.log(name + " = " + value);
        }
```

OLD HABITS TO NEW

Effectively, this section could be just "use destructuring wherever it makes sense." But here are some specific examples where it may make sense.

Use Destructuring When Getting Only Some Properties from an Object

Old habit: Getting an object from a function and remembering it in a variable, only to then use only a small number of its properties:

```
        const person = getThePerson();
        console.log("The person is " + person.firstName + " " + person.lastName);
```

New habit: Use destructuring instead in situations where you don't need the object itself for anything later:

```
        const {firstName, lastName} = getThePerson();
        console.log("The person is " + firstName + " " + lastName);
```

Use Destructuring for Options Objects

Old habit: Using options objects for functions with lots of options.

New habit: Consider using destructuring.

Before destructuring, a function accepting five options, where the five option's default is based on the one option's value, might look like this:

```
        function doSomethingNifty(options) {
            options = Object.assign({}, options, {
                // The default options
```

```
            one: 1,
            two: 2,
            three: 3,
            four: 4

        });
        if (options.five === undefined) {
            options.five = options.one * 5;
        }
        console.log("The 'five' option is: " + options.five);
        // ...
    }
    doSomethingNifty(); // The 'five' option is: 5
```

That hides the defaults inside the function's code, meaning that any complicated default value has to be special-cased, and meaning you have to do a property access on your options object each time you use an option.

Instead, you can define your default options as destructuring defaults, handle the defaulting of five within the destructuring default, provide an overall blank object for the parameter default value, and the use the resulting bindings directly:

```
    function doSomethingNifty({
            one = 1,
            two = 2,
            three = 3,
            four = 4,
            five = one * 5
    } = {}) {
        console.log("The 'five' option is: " + five);
        // ...
    }
    doSomethingNifty(); // The 'five' option is: 5
```

8

Promises

WHAT'S IN THIS CHAPTER?

➤ Creating and using promises

➤ "Promises" and "thenables"

➤ Promise patterns

➤ Promise anti-patterns

In this chapter you'll learn about ES2015's *promises*, which simplify and standardize the handling of one-off asynchronous operations, reducing "callback hell" (and paving the way for ES2018's *async functions*, covered in Chapter 9). A promise is an object representing an asynchronous result (like an HTTP request completing or a one-off timer firing). You use a promise to observe the result of an asynchronous process, and/or give the promise to other code so that other code can observe that result. Promises are JavaScript's version of a pattern variously called *promises*, *futures*, or *deferreds*. They draw heavily on prior art, in particular the Promises/A+ specification[1] and the work leading up to it.

Before we get started: You may have heard that promises are obsolete, because ES2018 added `async` functions (Chapter 9). That's mostly incorrect. It's true that you'll interact with promises *differently* when using `async` functions, but you'll still be interacting with them, and you'll still need to have a solid idea how they work. Also, there are times you'll use promises directly, even in an `async` function.

---

[1] `https://promisesaplus.com/`

WHY PROMISES?

A promise doesn't do anything of its own, it's just a way to observe the result of something asynchronous. Promises don't make operations asynchronous. They just provide a means of *observing* the completion of operations that are *already* asynchronous. So what good are they?

Before promises, simple callbacks were commonly used for this, but they have some issues:

➤ Combining multiple async operations (in series or in parallel) quickly leads to deeply nested callbacks ("callback hell").

➤ Callbacks have no standard way of indicating an error occurred; instead, each function or API you use has to define how it reports an error. There are several common ways, which are different from one another, making it difficult when combining multiple libraries or modules, or moving from project to project.

➤ Not having a standard way of indicating success/failure means you can't use common tools to manage complexity.

➤ Adding a callback to a process that has already completed is also not standardized. In some cases, it means the callback is never called; in others, it gets called synchronously; and in others, it will get called asynchronously. Checking the details for each API you use each time you need to handle this is time-consuming and easy to forget. The bugs you get when you assume or misremember are often subtle and hard to find.

➤ Adding multiple callbacks to an operation is either impossible or not standardized.

Promises deal with all of that by providing simple, standard semantics addressing all of those issues. You'll see how as you learn those semantics throughout this chapter. Along the way, you'll see examples of using promises vs. bare callbacks that illustrate the preceding issues.

PROMISE FUNDAMENTALS

In this section, first you'll learn the very basics of promises; then in subsequent sections you'll learn more detail of the various aspects of creating and using them. There's a fair bit of terminology up front.

Overview

A promise is an object with three possible states:

➤ *Pending*: The promise is pending/outstanding/not yet settled.

➤ *Fulfilled*: The promise has been settled with a value. This usually means success.

➤ *Rejected*: The promise has been settled with a rejection reason. This usually means failure.

A promise starts out pending and then can only be *settled* (fulfilled or rejected) once. A settled promise can't go back to being pending. A fulfilled promise can't change to a rejected one or vice versa. Once settled, the promise's state never changes.

A fulfilled promise has a *fulfillment value* (usually simply *value*); a rejected promise has a *rejection reason* (sometimes simply *reason*, though *error* is common as well).

When you *resolve* a promise, you're either fulfilling it with a value or you're making it dependent on another promise.[2] When you make it dependent on another promise, you "*resolve* it *to*" the other promise. That means ultimately it might be fulfilled or rejected, depending on what happens to the other promise.

When you *reject* a promise, you're making it rejected with a rejection reason.

> ### ERRORS AS REJECTION REASONS
>
> In the code in this chapter, you'll notice that all of the examples of rejection reasons are `Error` instances. I do that because rejecting a promise is like using `throw`. In both cases, having the stack information `Error` provides is useful. Doing that is a matter of style and best practices, though; you can use any value you want as a rejection reason, just like you can use any value you want with `throw` and `try/catch`.

You can't directly observe a promise's state and value/rejection reason (if any); you can only get them by adding handler functions that the promise calls. A JavaScript promise has three methods for registering handlers:

➤ `then`: Adds a *fulfillment handler* to call if/when the promise gets fulfilled[3]

➤ `catch`: Adds a *rejection handler* to call if/when the promise gets rejected

➤ `finally`: Adds a *finally handler* to call if/when the promise gets settled, regardless of how (added in ES2018)

One of the key aspects of promises is that `then`, `catch`, and `finally` *return a new promise*. The new promise is connected to the promise you called the method on: it will get fulfilled or rejected depending on what happens to that original promise and what your handler function(s) do. We'll come back to this key point throughout this chapter.

---

[2] Or a "thenable." You'll learn about thenables a little further along in this chapter.
[3] That's what the single-argument version does. You can also call it with two arguments, which you'll learn about in "The `then` Method with Two Arguments" later in this chapter.

Example

Listing 8-1 has a simple example of creating and using a promise, using `setTimeout` for the asynchronous operation being observed. Run the example repeatedly. Half the time, the promise it creates gets fulfilled; the other half, it gets rejected.

LISTING 8-1: Simple promise example—simple-promise-example.js

```javascript
function example() {
    return new Promise((resolve, reject) => {
        setTimeout(() => {
            try {
                const succeed = Math.random() < 0.5;
                if (succeed) {
                    console.log("resolving with 42 (will fulfill the promise)");
                    resolve(42);
                } else {
                    console.log("rejecting with new Error('failed')");
                    throw new Error("failed");
                }
            } catch (e) {
                reject(e);
            }
        }, 100);
    });
}

example()
.then(value => {  // fulfillment handler
    console.log("fulfilled with", value);
})
.catch(error => { // rejection handler
    console.error("rejected with", error);
})
.finally(() => {  // finally handler
    console.log("finally");
});
```

There are three parts to that:

1. Creating the promise: done by the `example` function, which creates and returns it

2. Resolving or rejecting the promise: done by the `example` function's timer callback

3. Using the promise: done by the code calling `example`

`example` uses the `Promise` constructor to create the promise, passing in a function. The function you give the `Promise` constructor has a fancy name: *executor function*. The `Promise` constructor calls the executor function (synchronously) passing two functions to it as arguments: `resolve` and `reject`. (Those are the conventional names. But of course, you can use whatever names you want for the parameters in your executor function. Sometimes you see `fulfill` instead of `resolve`, although that's not quite correct as you'll see in a moment.) You use the `resolve` and `reject` functions to determine what happens to the promise:

➤ If you call `resolve` with another promise,[4] the promise gets *resolved to* that other promise (it will get fulfilled or rejected depending on what happens to that other promise). This is why `fulfill` isn't an accurate name for the first function; when you call it with another promise, it doesn't fulfill the promise you created, it just resolves it to that other promise, which might reject.

➤ If you call `resolve` with any other value, the promise gets fulfilled with that value.

➤ If you call `reject`, the promise gets rejected using the reason you pass into `reject` (usually an `Error`, but that's a matter of style). Unlike `resolve`, `reject` doesn't do something different if you give it a promise. It always uses what you give it as the rejection reason.

The promise can *only* be resolved or rejected using those functions. Nothing can resolve or reject it without them. They aren't available as methods on the promise object itself, so you can give the promise object to other code knowing that the code receiving it can only consume the promise, not resolve or reject it.

In `example`'s case, it calls `setTimeout` to start an asynchronous operation. It has to use `setTimeout` or similar because, again, promises are just a way of *observing* the completion of asynchronous operations, not *creating* asynchronous operations.[5] When the timer expires, `example`'s timer callback either calls `resolve` or `reject` depending on the random result.

Turning to how the promise is used: The code using `example` uses a chain of calls, in this case `then` followed by `catch` followed by `finally`, to hook up a fulfillment handler, a rejection handler, and a `finally` handler, respectively. Chaining is quite common with promise methods, for reasons you'll learn as you progress through the chapter.

Run the code in Listing 8-1 enough times to see both a fulfillment and a rejection. When the promise gets fulfilled, the chain calls the fulfillment handler with the fulfillment value, then the `finally` handler (which doesn't receive any value). When the promise gets rejected, the chain calls the rejection handler with the rejection reason, then the `finally` handler (which, again, doesn't receive any value). It would also call the rejection handler (and then the `finally` handler) if the original promise was fulfilled but the fulfillment handler threw an error; more on that in a bit.

The fulfillment, rejection, and `finally` handlers serve the same purpose as the blocks in a `try`/`catch`/`finally` statement:

```
try {
    // do something
    // fulfillment handler
} catch (error) {
    // rejection handler
} finally {
    // finally handler
}
```

There are slight differences you'll learn later, particularly around `finally`, but that's fundamentally a good way to think about fulfillment, rejection, and `finally` handlers.

---

[4] Or, again, any "thenable." You'll learn about thenables in the next section.
[5] There's a small caveat here that we'll come to later.

Using `new Promise` is fairly rare compared with using a promise from an API function or the ones you get from `then`, `catch`, and `finally`, so we'll focus initially on using promises, then come back to the details of creating them.

Promises and "Thenables"

JavaScript's promises follow rules defined by the ECMAScript specification, which draw heavily on prior art, in particular the Promises/A+ specification and the work leading up to it. JavaScript's promises are fully compliant with the Promises/A+ specification, and have some additional features intentionally not covered by that specification, such as `catch` and `finally`. (The Promises/A+ specification is intentionally minimalist and defines only `then`, because what `catch` and `finally` do can be done with the two-argument version of `then` that you'll learn about in a later section.)

One aspect of the Promises/A+ specification is the concept of "thenables" as distinct from "promises." Here's how that specification defines them:

➤ A "promise" is an object or function with a `then` method whose behavior conforms to [the Promises/A+ specification].

➤ A "thenable" is an object or function that defines a `then` method.

So all promises are thenables, but not all thenables are promises. An object might define a method called `then` that doesn't work as defined for promises; that object would be a thenable, but not a promise.

Why is this important? Interoperability.

Sometimes, a promise implementation needs to know whether a value is a simple value it can use to fulfill the promise, or a thenable it should resolve the promise to. It does that by checking if the value is an object with a `then` method: if so, the object is assumed to be a thenable and the promise implementation uses its `then` method to resolve the promise to the thenable. This is imperfect, since an object can have a `then` method that means something completely unrelated to promises, but it was the best solution at the time promises were being added to JavaScript because it allowed the multiple promise libraries that existed at the time (and still exist) to interoperate without every implementation having to be updated to add some other feature to mark its promises as being promises. (It would have been a great use case for a Symbol [Chapter 5], for instance, if it had been possible to update every library to add it.)

Up to this point, I've used "promise" with a footnote in a couple of places where "thenable" would be more accurate. Now that you know what a thenable is, I'll start using it where appropriate.

USING AN EXISTING PROMISE

As you've seen, you hook into the fulfillment, rejection, or completion of a promise using handlers registered with `then`, `catch`, and `finally`. In this section, you'll learn about that in more detail, learn some of the general patterns for using promises, and also learn how promises solve some of the issues mentioned earlier in "Why Promises?"

The then Method

You've already briefly seen the then method in action, hooking into a promise's fulfillment.[6] Let's look at then in a bit more detail. Consider this very basic call to then:

```
p2 = p1.then(result => doSomethingWith(result.toUpperCase()));
```

As you've already learned, it registers a fulfillment handler, creating and returning a new promise (p2) that will get fulfilled or rejected depending on what happens to the original promise (p1) and what you do in your handler. If p1 gets rejected, the handler isn't called and p2 is rejected with p1's rejection reason. If p1 gets fulfilled, the handler gets called. Here's what happens to p2 depending on what your handler does:

➤ If you return a thenable, p2 gets resolved to that thenable (it will get fulfilled or rejected depending on what happens to that thenable).

➤ If you return any other value, p2 gets fulfilled with that value.

➤ If you use throw (or call a function that throws), p2 gets rejected using what you threw (usually an Error) as the rejection reason.

Those three bullet points probably seem familiar. That's because they're nearly identical to the bullet points you saw earlier saying what you can do with the resolve and reject functions you get in a promise executor function. Returning something from your then handler is just like calling resolve. Using throw in your handler is just like calling reject.

This ability to return a thenable is one of the keys of promises, so let's look at it more closely.

Chaining Promises

The fact that you can return a promise (or any thenable) from a then/catch/finally handler to resolve the promise they create means that if you need to do a series of asynchronous operations that provide promises/thenables, you can use then on the first operation and have the handler return the thenable for the second operation, repeated as many times as you need. Here's a chain with three operations returning promises:

```
firstOperation()
.then(firstResult => secondOperation(firstResult)) // or: .then(secondOperation)
.then(secondResult => thirdOperation(secondResult * 2))
.then(thirdResult => { /* Use `thirdResult` */ })
.catch(error => { console.error(error); });
```

When that code runs, firstOperation starts the first operation and returns a promise. Calls to then and catch set up handlers for what happens next (see Figure 8-1, overleaf). Later, when the first operation completes, what happens next depends on what happened to the first operation: if it fulfills its promise, the first fulfillment handler gets run and starts the second operation, returning the promise secondOperation provides. See Figure 8-2 (overleaf).

---

[6] Later you'll learn about the two-argument version that can also hook into rejection.

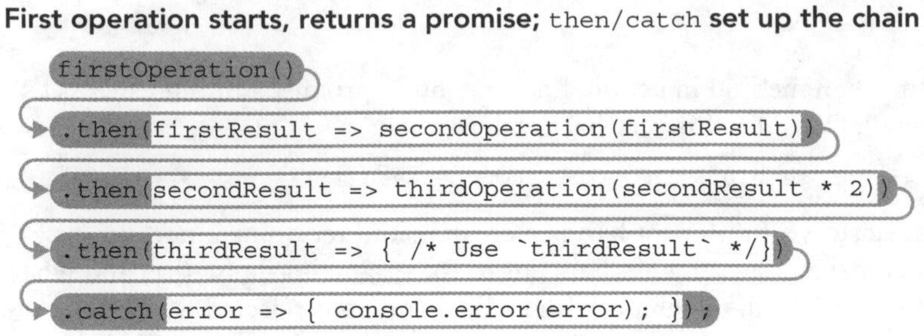

First operation starts, returns a promise; then/catch set up the chain

```
firstOperation()
.then(firstResult => secondOperation(firstResult))
.then(secondResult => thirdOperation(secondResult * 2))
.then(thirdResult => { /* Use `thirdResult` */})
.catch(error => { console.error(error); });
```

FIGURE 8-1

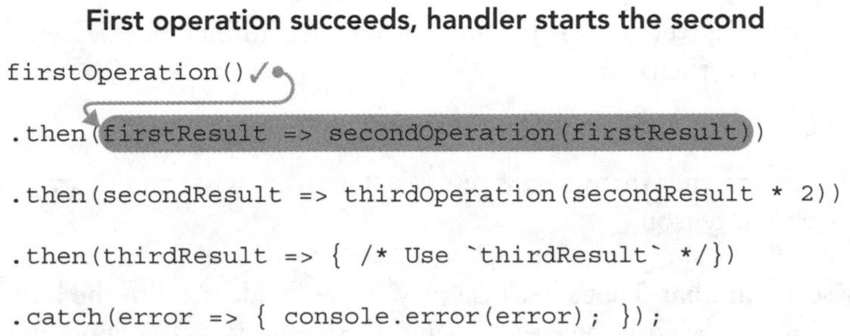

First operation succeeds, handler starts the second

```
firstOperation()✓
.then(firstResult => secondOperation(firstResult))
.then(secondResult => thirdOperation(secondResult * 2))
.then(thirdResult => { /* Use `thirdResult` */})
.catch(error => { console.error(error); });
```

FIGURE 8-2

If the second operation fulfills its promise, that fulfills the promise the first then returned, and the next fulfillment handler gets run (Figure 8-3): it starts the third operation and returns the promise of its result.

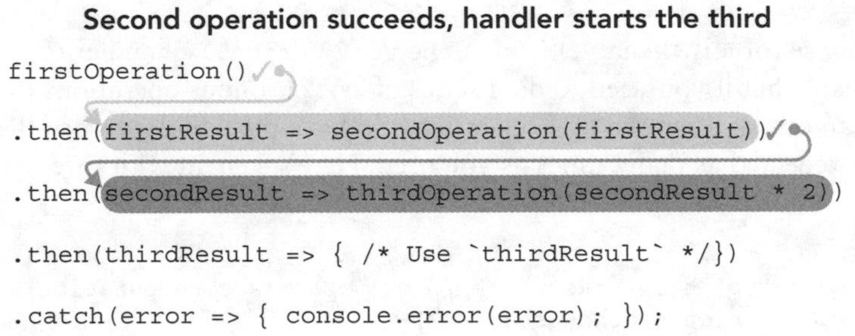

Second operation succeeds, handler starts the third

```
firstOperation()✓
.then(firstResult => secondOperation(firstResult))✓
.then(secondResult => thirdOperation(secondResult * 2))
.then(thirdResult => { /* Use `thirdResult` */})
.catch(error => { console.error(error); });
```

FIGURE 8-3

If the third operation fulfills its promise, that fulfills the promise from the second then. That calls the code that uses the third result. Provided that code doesn't throw or return a rejected promise, the chain completes (Figure 8-4, opposite). The rejection handler doesn't get run at all in that case, since there were no rejections.

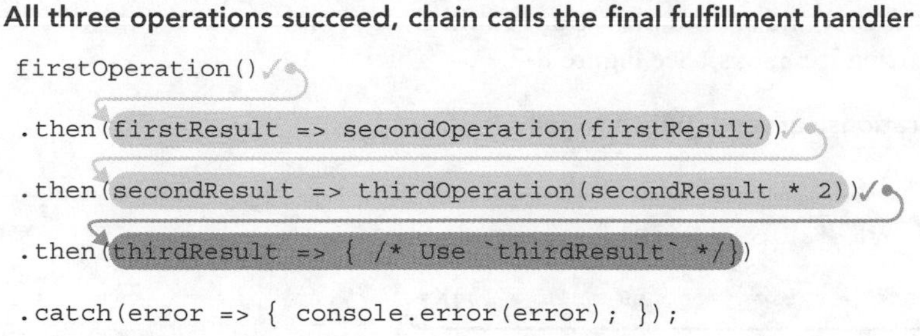

All three operations succeed, chain calls the final fulfillment handler

```
firstOperation()
.then(firstResult => secondOperation(firstResult))
.then(secondResult => thirdOperation(secondResult * 2))
.then(thirdResult => { /* Use `thirdResult` */})
.catch(error => { console.error(error); });
```

FIGURE 8-4

If the first operation rejects its promise, though, that rejects the promise from the first `then`, which rejects the promise from the second `then`, which rejects the promise from the *third* `then`, which calls the rejection handler at the end. None of the `then` callbacks get called, because they were for fulfillment, not rejection. See Figure 8-5.

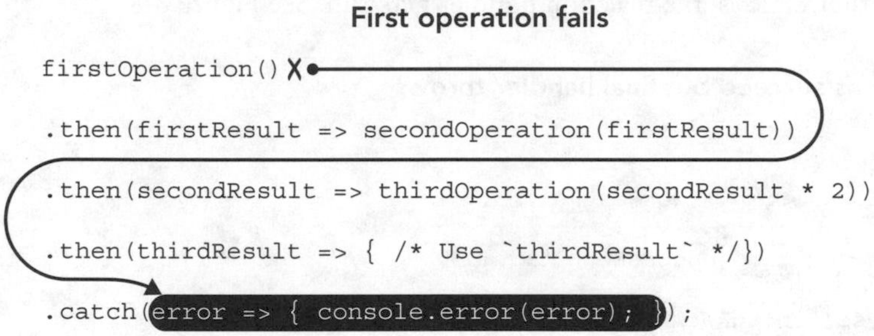

First operation fails

```
firstOperation()
.then(firstResult => secondOperation(firstResult))
.then(secondResult => thirdOperation(secondResult * 2))
.then(thirdResult => { /* Use `thirdResult` */})
.catch(error => { console.error(error); });
```

FIGURE 8-5

If the first operation succeeds and its fulfillment handler starts the second operation and returns its promise, but the second operation fails and rejects its promise, that rejects the promise from the first `then`, which rejects the promise from the second `then`, which rejects the promise from the third `then`, which calls the rejection handler. See Figure 8-6. (Similarly, if the first operation succeeds but the fulfillment handler `throws`, the same thing happens: the remaining fulfillment handlers are skipped, and the rejection handler runs.)

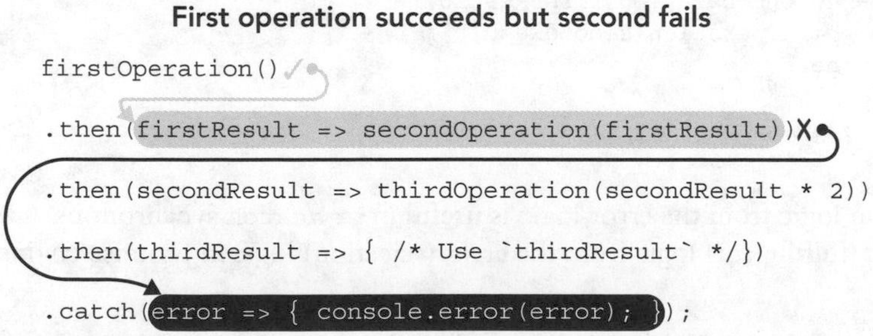

First operation succeeds but second fails

```
firstOperation()
.then(firstResult => secondOperation(firstResult))
.then(secondResult => thirdOperation(secondResult * 2))
.then(thirdResult => { /* Use `thirdResult` */})
.catch(error => { console.error(error); });
```

FIGURE 8-6

Naturally, the same is true if the first and second operations fulfill their promises but the third rejects its promise (or the handler starting it `throws`). See Figure 8-7.

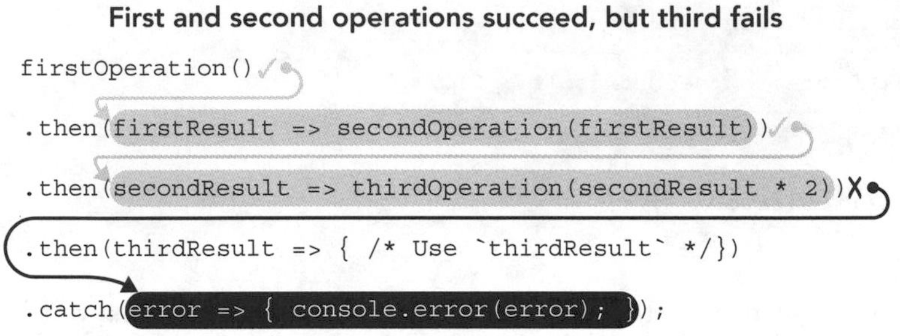

First and second operations succeed, but third fails

```
firstOperation()
 .then(firstResult => secondOperation(firstResult))
 .then(secondResult => thirdOperation(secondResult * 2))
 .then(thirdResult => { /* Use `thirdResult` */})
 .catch(error => { console.error(error); });
```

FIGURE 8-7

If all three operations succeed, the final fulfillment handler is run. If that handler `throws`, either directly or by calling a function that `throws`, the rejection handler gets run. See Figure 8-8.

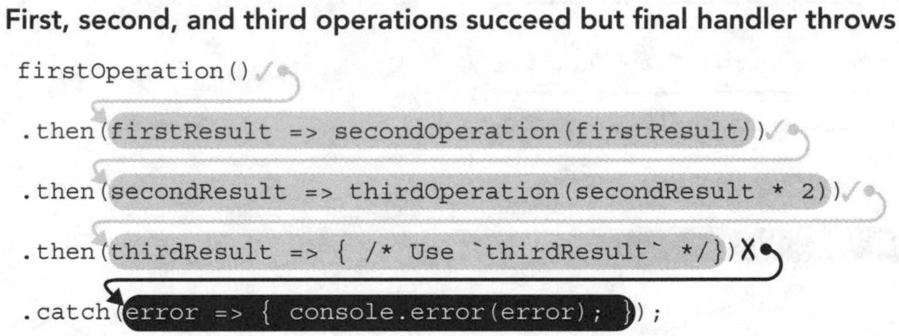

First, second, and third operations succeed but final handler throws

```
firstOperation()
 .then(firstResult => secondOperation(firstResult))
 .then(secondResult => thirdOperation(secondResult * 2))
 .then(thirdResult => { /* Use `thirdResult` */})
 .catch(error => { console.error(error); });
```

FIGURE 8-8

As you can see, a promise chain of this kind is very much like a `try`/`catch` block around three synchronous operations (and some final code), like this:

```
// The same logic with synchronous operations
try {
    const firstResult = firstOperation();
    const secondResult = secondOperation(firstResult);
    const thirdResult = thirdOperation(secondResult * 2);
    // Use `thirdResult` here
} catch (error) {
    console.error(error);
}
```

Just as the separation of the main logic from the error logic is useful in `try`/`catch` synchronous code, the separation of the main (fulfillment) logic from the error (rejection) logic in promise chains is useful.

You can see these various scenarios play out by repeatedly running the `basic-promise-chain.js` file from the downloads. That file uses `Math.random` to give each operation (first, second, and third) a 20% chance of failing, and to give the final fulfillment handler a 20% chance of `throwing`.

HANDLERS ARE JUST FUNCTIONS

Handler functions are just functions; there's nothing special about them. In the example in this section, I've used an arrow function where I didn't really need to:

```
firstOperation()
.then(firstResult => secondOperation(firstResult))
.then(secondResult => thirdOperation(secondResult * 2))
.then(thirdResult => { /* Use `thirdResult` */ })
.catch(error => { console.error(error); });
```

That code could be written like this instead:

```
firstOperation()
.then(secondOperation)
.then(secondResult => thirdOperation(secondResult * 2))
.then(thirdResult => { /* Use `thirdResult` */ })
.catch(error => { console.error(error); });
```

There's no need to wrap `secondOperation` in an arrow function if you're just passing the value from the first operation into it; just pass the function reference into `then` instead.

Doing that is safe even in the case of a function that accepts optional second, third, etc. arguments, because promise handler functions always receive exactly one argument: the value (`then`) or rejection reason (`catch`). That means you don't have the problem that you have with, say, the array `map` function and `parseInt` where `a = a.map(parseInt)` doesn't work correctly because `map` calls its callback with three arguments, not just one, and `parseInt` accepts an optional second argument.

Comparison with Callbacks

Let's compare the promise chain from the previous section with using bare callbacks. For this comparison, let's assume that the functions starting the asynchronous operations accept a callback: if the operation succeeds, they call the callback with `null` as the first argument and the result value as the second; if the operation fails, they call the callback with an error as the first argument. (This is one of the more common patterns for callbacks, popularized by Node.js among others.) Here's how the previous sequence would look using that convention:

```
firstOperation((error, firstResult) => {
    if (error) {
        console.error(error);
        // (Perhaps you'd use `return;` here to avoid the `else`)
    } else {
        secondOperation(firstResult, (error, secondResult) => {
            if (error) {
                console.error(error);
                // Perhaps: `return;`
```

```
            } else {
                thirdOperation(secondResult * 2, (error, thirdResult) => {
                    if (error) {
                        console.error(error);
                        // Perhaps: `return;`
                    } else {
                        try {
                            /* Use `thirdResult` */
                        } catch (error) {
                            console.error(error);
                        }
                    }
                });
            }
        });
    }
});
```

You can run this using `basic-callback-chain.js` from the downloads.

Notice how each step has to be nested in the callback of the previous step. This is the famous "callback hell," and part of the reason some programmers use just a two-character indentation—despite how hard it is to read—so their deeply nested callbacks don't go off the right of the screen. It's *possible* to write that code without having the callbacks nested within one another, but it's awkward and verbose.

Really, to be more accurate there would need to be a `try`/`catch` block around the call to `secondOperation` and another one around the call to `thirdOperation`, but I didn't want to overcomplicate the example—which underscores the point about how promises make this simpler.

The catch Method

You've already learned that the `catch` method registers a handler that gets called when the promise gets rejected. Other than that the handler you give it gets called on rejection rather than fulfillment, `catch` is *exactly* like `then`. With this:

```
p2 = p1.catch(error => doSomethingWith(error))
```

`catch` registers a rejection handler on `p1`, creating and returning a new promise (`p2`) that will get fulfilled or rejected depending on what happens to the original promise (`p1`) and what you do in your handler. If `p1` gets fulfilled, the handler isn't called and `p2` is fulfilled with `p1`'s fulfillment value. If `p1` gets rejected, the handler gets called. Here's what happens to `p2` depending on what your handler does:

➤   If you return a thenable, `p2` gets resolved to that thenable.

➤   If you return any other value, `p2` gets fulfilled with that value.

➤   If you use `throw`, `p2` gets rejected using what you threw as the rejection reason.

Sound familiar? Right! That's exactly what `then` does with its handler, which is, in turn, exactly what the `resolve` function you get in a promise executor function does. The consistency is useful, you don't have to remember different rules for different resolution mechanisms.

One thing to notice in particular is that if you return a non-thenable from the `catch` handler, the promise from `catch` gets *fulfilled*. That converts the rejection from `p1` into a fulfillment of `p2`. If you think about it, that's just like the `catch` in a `try`/`catch`: unless you re-throw the error in your `catch` block, the `catch` block stops the error from propagating. The `catch` method on promises works the same way.

There's a slight downside to that: it means you can inadvertently mask errors by putting a `catch` handler in the wrong place. Consider:

```
someOperation()
    .catch(error => {
        reportError(error);
    })
    .then(result => {
        console.log(result.someProperty);
    });
```

With that code, if the operation started by `someOperation` fails, `reportError` gets called with the error (so far, so good), but you'll get an error in the console that looks something like this:

```
Uncaught (in promise) TypeError: Cannot read property 'someProperty' of undefined
```

Why is it trying to read `someProperty` of `undefined`? The promise rejected, so why is the `then` handler being called?

Let's go back to our `try`/`catch`/`finally` analogue. That code is the logical (not literal) equivalent of this:

```
let result;
try {
    result = someOperation();
} catch (error) {
    reportError(error);
    result = undefined;
}
console.log(result.someProperty);
```

The `catch` caught the error and output it, but didn't do anything to propagate the error. So the code after the `try`/`catch` still runs and tries to use `result.someProperty`, which fails because `result` is `undefined`.

The promise version is doing the same thing, because the rejection handler caught the error, handled it, and then didn't return anything, which is like returning `undefined`. That fulfilled the promise from `catch` with `undefined`. So that promise called its fulfillment handler, passed in `undefined` as `result`, and when the handler tried to use `result.someProperty`, it caused a new error.

"But what's with this 'unhandled rejection' thing?" you may be asking. If a promise gets rejected and no code is in place to handle the rejection, JavaScript engines report an "unhandled rejection" since that's usually a bug. The code in that example doesn't handle errors from the final fulfillment handler (the one with `result.someProperty` in it), so when the error trying to use `result.someProperty` makes the promise from `then` reject, it's an "Unhandled rejection," since there's nothing to handle it.

Sometimes, of course, you might want to put a `catch` in the middle specifically to do exactly that: handle an error and allow the chain to continue with some substitute value or similar. It's absolutely fine if you're doing it on purpose.

DETECTING UNHANDLED REJECTIONS

The process of determining whether a rejection is handled is fairly complex since it has to take into account the fact that a rejection handler can be added *after* the promise is already rejected. For example, suppose you're calling an API function that returns a promise, and it might reject synchronously (during the call to the API function) because you've given it bad argument values, or it might reject asynchronously later (because the asynchronous process it starts fails). Your call to it might look like this:

```
apiFunction(/*...arguments...*/)
.then(result => {
    // ...use the result...
})
.catch(error => {
    // ...handle/report the error...
});
```

If the rejection is caused synchronously, by a bad argument value, the promise is *already rejected* before your code gets a chance to attach a rejection handler to it. But you wouldn't want the JavaScript engine to complain about it being an unhandled rejection, because your code *does* handle it. The rejection will trigger the code in your rejection handler that handles/reports the error. So it's not as simple as "It's time to reject this promise. Does it have any rejection handlers attached to it?" It's more complex than that.

Modern engines do it in a fairly sophisticated way, but may still have the odd false positive or false negative.

The finally Method

The `finally` method is, as you've learned, very much like the `finally` block of a try/catch/ finally. It adds a handler that gets called whether the promise gets fulfilled or rejected (like a `finally` block). Like `then` and `catch`, it returns a new promise that gets fulfilled or rejected based on what happens to the original promise and what the `finally` handler does. But *unlike* then and catch, its handler is always called, and the things its handler can do to what's passing through it are limited.

Here's a simple example:

```
function doStuff() {
    spinner.start();
```

```
        return getSomething()
            .then(result => render(result.stuff))
            .finally(() => spinner.stop());
    }
```

This function starts a spinner spinning to show the user it's doing something, uses `getSomething`—a function that returns a promise—to start an asynchronous operation, then shows the result if the promise gets fulfilled, and stops the spinner no matter what happens to the promise.

Note that this function doesn't attempt to handle errors; instead, it returns the final promise in the chain. That's fairly normal; it allows the calling code to know whether the operation succeeded and allows error handling to happen at the highest level (often an event handler or similar, e.g., the entry point into the JavaScript code). By using `finally`, this code can defer error handling to the caller while being sure to stop the spinner even when an error occurs.

In the normal case, a `finally` handler has no effect on the fulfillment or rejection passing through it (again, like a `finally` block): any value it returns other than a thenable that is/gets rejected is ignored. But if it throws an error or returns a thenable that rejects, that error/rejection supersedes any fulfillment or rejection passing through it (just like `throw` in a `finally` block). So it can't change a fulfillment value—not even if it returns a different value—but it can change a rejection reason into a different rejection reason, it can change a fulfillment into a rejection, and it can *delay* a fulfillment (by returning a thenable that is ultimately fulfilled; you'll see an example in a moment).

Or to put it another way: it's like a `finally` block that can't contain a `return` statement.[7] It might have a `throw` or might call a function that throws, but it can't return a new value.

Run the code in Listing 8-2 to see an example.

LISTING 8-2: finally returning value—finally-returning-value.js

```
// Function returning promise that gets fulfilled after the given
// delay with the given value
function returnWithDelay(value, delay = 10) {
    return new Promise(resolve => setTimeout(resolve, delay, value));
}

// The function doing the work
function doSomething() {
    return returnWithDelay("original value")
        .finally(() => {
            return "value from finally";
        });
}

doSomething()
    .then(value => {
        console.log("value = " + value); // "value = original value"
    });
```

---

[7] Having a `return` in a `finally` block is usually poor practice anyway.

In that example, doSomething calls returnWithDelay and has a finally handler (in the real world, it would be for some kind of cleanup). doSomething returns the promise created by calling finally. The code calls doSomething and uses the promise it returns (the one from finally). Note that the finally handler returns a value, but the promise from finally *doesn't* use that as its fulfillment value. It uses the value it received from the promise it was called on instead. The return value from the finally handler wasn't a thenable, so it was completely ignored.

The reason for preventing a finally handler from changing fulfillments is twofold:

➤ The primary use case of finally is to clean up when you're done with something, but without affecting that thing's result.

➤ Pragmatically, the promise mechanism can't tell the difference between a function that doesn't use return at all (code execution just "falls off the end" of the function), a function that uses return with no operand, and a function that uses return undefined, because the result of calling all three of those functions is the same: the value undefined. For example:

```
function a() {
}
function b() {
    return;
}
function c() {
    return undefined;
}
console.log(a()); // undefined
console.log(b()); // undefined
console.log(c()); // undefined
```

In contrast, in a try/catch/finally structure, the JavaScript engine *can* tell the difference between a finally block where code execution just falls off the end (not affecting the return value of the function it's in) and one that issues a return statement. Since the promise mechanism can't tell that difference, though, and since the primary purpose of a finally handler is to do cleanup without changing anything, it makes sense to ignore the return value of the finally handler.

Just because the handler can't affect the chain's fulfillment value doesn't mean it can't return a promise or thenable, however. And if it does, the chain waits for that promise/thenable to settle, just like when then and catch handlers return thenables, since the promise/thenable may reject. Run the code in Listing 8-3 for an example.

LISTING 8-3: finally returning promise that gets fulfilled—finally-returning-promise.js

```
// Function returning promise that gets fulfilled after the given
// delay with the given value
function returnWithDelay(value, delay = 100) {
    return new Promise(resolve => setTimeout(resolve, delay, value));
}

// The function doing the work
function doSomething() {
```

```
            return returnWithDelay("original value")
                .finally(() => {
                    return returnWithDelay("unused value from finally", 1000);
                })
        }

        console.time("example");
        doSomething()
            .then(value => {
                console.log("value = " + value); // "value = original value"
                console.timeEnd("example");      // example: 1100ms (or similar)
            });
```

Notice that although the value wasn't changed by the fact the `finally` handler returned a promise that was fulfilled later, the chain *did* wait for that promise to get fulfilled before continuing. It took roughly 1110ms to complete instead of just 100ms, because of the 1000ms delay from the `returnWithDelay` inside the `finally` handler.

If the thenable the `finally` handler returns *rejects*, however, that supersedes the fulfillment; see Listing 8-4.

LISTING 8-4: finally causing rejection—finally-causing-rejection.js

```
// Function returning promise that gets fulfilled after the given
// delay with the given value
function returnWithDelay(value, delay = 100) {
    return new Promise(resolve => setTimeout(resolve, delay, value));
}

// Function returning promise that is *rejected* after the given
// delay with the given error
function rejectWithDelay(error, delay = 100) {
    return new Promise((resolve, reject) => setTimeout(reject, delay, error));
}

console.time("example");
returnWithDelay("original value")
    .finally(() => {
        return rejectWithDelay(new Error("error from finally"), 1000);
    })
    .then(value => {
        // Not called
        console.log("value = " + value);
    })
    .catch(error => {
        console.error("error = ", error);   // "error =  Error: error from finally"
    })
    .finally(() => {
        console.timeEnd("example");          // example: 1100ms (or similar)
    });
```

throw in then, catch, and finally Handlers

You've heard a couple of times in this chapter that if you `throw` in a `then`, `catch`, or `finally` handler, it makes the promise created by `then`/`catch`/`finally` reject with the value you throw. Let's look at an example of that from real-world web programming.

On modern browsers, the old `XMLHttpRequest` object is superseded by the new `fetch` function, which returns a promise and is generally simpler to use. In essence, you do `fetch(url)` and it returns a promise, which gets fulfilled or rejected depending on the success/failure of the network operation. On success, the fulfillment value is a `Response` object with various properties, as well as methods (which also return promises) for reading the body of the response as text, as an `ArrayBuffer` (see Chapter 11), as text but then parsing it as JSON, as a blob, etc. So naïve use of `fetch` to, say, retrieve some data in JSON format tends to look like this:

```
// WRONG
fetch("/some/url")
    .then(response => response.json())
    .then(data => {
        // Do something with the data...
    })
    .catch(error => {
        // Do something with the error
    });
```

That's missing an important step, though. Just as one had to check the result of the `status` property when using `XMLHttpRequest`, one has to check the response status (directly or indirectly) with `fetch` as well, because the promise from `fetch` only rejects when there's a *network error*. Anything else—a 404, a 500 server error, etc.—is a fulfillment with that status code, not a rejection, because the network operation succeeded even though the HTTP operation failed.

Easily 99.99% of the time you use `fetch`, though, you don't care why you didn't get what you asked for (whether it was a network error or an HTTP error); you just care that you didn't get it. The easiest way to handle that is to throw an error from the first `then` handler:

```
fetch("/some/url")
    .then(response => {
        if (!response.ok) {
            throw new Error("HTTP error " + response.status);
        }
        return response.json();
    });
    .then(data => {
        // Do something with the data...
    })
    .catch(error => {
        // Do something with the error
    });
```

That `then` handler converts the fulfillment with an HTTP error into a rejection by checking the `response.ok` convenience property (it's `true` if the HTTP response status code is a success code, `false` otherwise) and using `throw` if it's `false` to do the rejection. Since you almost always want that check, you'd probably give yourself a utility function that did it. And since error handlers may need access to the response, you might give yourself a custom `Error` subclass to provide that, since `Error`'s `message` is a string, something like Listing 8-5 (opposite).

LISTING 8-5: fetch wrapper converting HTTP errors to rejections—fetch-converting-http-errors.js

```
class FetchError extends Error {
    constructor(response, message = "HTTP error " + response.status) {
        super(message);
        this.response = response;
    }
}
const myFetch = (...args) => {
    return fetch(...args).then(response => {
        if (!response.ok) {
            throw new FetchError(response);
        }
        return response;
    });
};
```

With that, you could write the earlier example the obvious way:

```
myFetch("/some/url")
    .then(response => response.json())
    .then(data => {
        // Do something with the data...
    })
    .catch(error => {
        // Do something with the error
    });
```

The then handler in myFetch converts fulfillment-with-an-HTTP-error to rejection, by using throw in its handler.

The then Method with Two Arguments

All of the examples of then you've seen so far only pass it a single handler. But then can accept *two* handlers: one for fulfillment, and another for rejection.

```
doSomething()
    .then(
        /*f1*/ value => {
            // Do something with `value`
        },
        /*f2*/ error => {
            // Do something with `error`
        }
    );
```

In that example, if the promise from doSomething gets fulfilled, the first handler is called; if it's rejected, the second handler is called.

Using p.then(f1, f2) is *not* the same as using p.then(f1).catch(f2). There's a big difference: the two-argument version of then attaches both handlers to the promise you call it on, but using catch after then attaches the rejection handler to the promise then returns instead. That means that with p.then(f1, f2), f2 is only called if p rejects, not if f1 throws an error or returns a promise that rejects. With p.then(f1).catch(f2), f2 is called if p rejects *or* if f1 throws an error or returns a promise that rejects.

BOTH OF THEN'S ARGUMENTS ARE OPTIONAL

If you want to hook up a rejection handler and not hook up a fulfillment handler, you can do that by passing undefined as the first argument: `.then(undefined, rejectionHandler)`.

"Wait," you say, "isn't that what catch is for?" Yes it is. catch is literally just a wrapper around then, effectively defined like this example using method syntax:

```
catch(onRejected) {
    return this.then(undefined, onRejected);
}
```

finally is also just a wrapper around then, but it has logic in the handlers it passes to then rather than just passing through the handler it receives like catch does.

The fact that catch and finally are built purely in terms of calls to then (literally, not just conceptually) will come up again later in this chapter.

Normally, you want just the single-argument version of then, and to chain any rejection handler onto the promise it returns via catch. But if you only want to handle errors from the original promise and not from the fulfillment handler, you'd use the two-argument version. For instance, suppose you have myFetch from the previous section and you want to retrieve some JSON data from the server, supplying a default if the server responds with an error, but you don't want to handle an error (if there is one) from reading and parsing the JSON (the response.json() call). Using the two-argument then would make sense for that:

```
myFetch("/get-message")
    .then(
        response => response.json(),
        error => ({message: "default data"})
    )
    .then(data => {
        doSomethingWith(data.message);
    })
    .catch(error => {
        // Handle overall error
    });
```

Doing that with the single-argument version of then is more awkward. You either end up with your handler getting called for errors in the call to json by doing a .then(...).catch(...), or you have to wrap your default in an object with a json function so you can put your catch first:

```
// Awkward version avoiding using the two-argument `then`
// Not best practice
```

```
myFetch("/get-message")
    .catch(() => {
        return {json() { return {message: "default data"}; };
    })
    .then(response => response.json())
    .then(data => {
        doSomethingWith(data.message);
    })
    .catch(error => {
        // Handle overall error
    });
```

In practice, you usually want the `.then(f1).catch(f2)` structure, but in those relatively rare cases where you want to handle errors from the `then` handler *differently* from a rejection of the original promise (as in this example), the two-argument version of `then` is there for you to use.

ADDING HANDLERS TO ALREADY SETTLED PROMISES

In the "Why Promises?" section at the beginning of this chapter, two of the issues with bare callbacks were:

➤ Adding a callback to a process that has already completed is also not standardized. In some cases, it means the callback is never called; in others, it gets called synchronously; and in others, it will get called asynchronously. Checking the details for each API you use each time you need to handle this is time-consuming and easy to forget. The bugs you get when you assume or misremember are often subtle and hard to find.

➤ Adding multiple callbacks to an operation is either impossible or not standardized.

Promises deal with those by providing standard semantics for adding completion handlers (including multiple ones), and by guaranteeing two things:

➤ The handler will get called (provided it's for the appropriate kind of settlement, fulfillment or rejection).

➤ The call will be asynchronous.

That means that if you have code that receives a promise from somewhere, and does this:

```
console.log("before");
thePromise.then(() => {
    console.log("within");
});
console.log("after");
```

the code is guaranteed by the specification to output `"before"`, then `"after"`, and then later (if the promise gets fulfilled *or it's already fulfilled*) `"within"`. If the promise gets fulfilled later, the call to the fulfillment handler is scheduled later. If the promise is already fulfilled, it's scheduled (but not executed) during the call to `then`. A call to a fulfillment or rejection handler is scheduled by adding a job for it to the promise job queue; see the "Script Jobs and Promise Jobs" inset for more about job queues. Run `then-on-fulfilled-promise.js` from the downloads to see this in action.

Ensuring that handlers are only ever called asynchronously, even on already settled promises, is the only way promises themselves make something asynchronous that isn't already asynchronous.

SCRIPT JOBS AND PROMISE JOBS

Each JavaScript thread in a JavaScript engine runs a loop that services job queues. A job is a unit of work that the thread will run from beginning to end without running anything else. There are two standard job queues: script jobs and promise jobs. (Or as the HTML specification calls them, tasks and microtasks.) Script evaluation, module evaluation (Chapter 13), DOM event callbacks, and timer callbacks are examples of script jobs / tasks (aka "*macro*tasks"). Promise reactions (calling promise fulfillment or rejection handlers) are promise jobs / *micro*tasks: when scheduling a call to a fulfillment or rejection handler, the engine puts a job for that call in the promise job queue. All of the jobs in the promise job queue are executed at the end of a script job, before the next script job is run (even if that script job was added to the script job queue long before the promise job was added to the promise job queue). That includes promise jobs added by a promise job. For instance, if the first promise job in the promise jobs queue schedules another promise reaction, that reaction happens after the promise job that scheduled it, but before the next script job runs. Conceptually, it looks like this:

```
// Just conceptual, not literal!
while (running) {
    if (scriptJobs.isEmpty()) {
        sleepUntilScriptJobIsAdded();
    }
    assert(promiseJobs.isEmpty());
    const scriptJob = scriptJobs.pop();
    scriptJob.run(); // May add jobs to promiseJobs and/or scriptJobs
    while (!promiseJobs.isEmpty()) {
        const promiseJob = promiseJobs.pop();
        promiseJob.run(); // May add jobs to promiseJobs and/or scriptJobs
    }
}
```

In effect, promise reactions are higher priority than other jobs.

(Host environments may have other kinds of jobs as well. For instance, Node.js has setImmediate, which schedules work in a way that isn't the same as either a script job or a promise job.)

CREATING PROMISES

There are several ways to create promises. The primary way you create promises is the way you've already learned: using then, catch, or finally on an existing promise. To create a promise when you don't already have one, you can use the `Promise` constructor or one of a couple of utility functions.

The Promise Constructor

The `Promise` constructor creates a promise. There's a frequent misconception that `new Promise` turns a synchronous operation into an asynchronous one. It doesn't. Promises don't make operations asynchronous; they just provide a consistent means of reporting the result of something that's *already* asynchronous.

It's rare to need to use `new Promise`. That may seem surprising, but most of the time, you'll get a promise some other way:

➤ You're calling something (an API function, etc.) that returns one.

➤ You get one from `then`, `catch`, or `finally` on an existing promise.

➤ You get one from a utility function that knows how to convert a particular style of callback API from that callback style to a promise (which is really just a specific example of the first bullet point in this list).

➤ You get one from one of the `Promise` static methods such as `Promise.resolve` or `Promise.reject`, described later in this section.

Any time you already have a promise or a thenable, you don't need `new Promise`. Either use `then` to chain onto it or, if it's a thenable and you want a promise, use `Promise.resolve` (which you'll learn about in the next section).

But sometimes you do need to create a promise from scratch. For instance, looking at the third bullet point in the preceding list, perhaps you're the one writing a utility function that converts a callback API to a promise API. Let's look at that.

Suppose you have some promise-based code, and you need to work with an API function that doesn't provide a promise; instead, it accepts an object containing options, and two of those options are callbacks for success and failure:

```
const noop = () => {}; // A function that does nothing
/* Does something.
 * @param    data        The data to do something with
 * @param    time        The time to take
 * @param    onSuccess   Callback for success, called with two arguments:
 *                        the result, and a status code
 * @param    onError     Callback for failure, called with one argument
 *                        (an error message as a string).
 */
function doSomething({ data, time = 10, onSuccess = noop, onError = noop} = {}) {
    // ...
}
```

Since your code is promise-based it would be useful to have a promise-based version of `doSomething`. You might write a wrapper for it that looks like `promiseSomething` in Listing 8-6. (Hopefully you'd give it a better name than that, though.)

LISTING 8-6: Wrapper for mock API function—mock-api-function-wrapper.js

```javascript
function promiseSomething(options = {}) {
    return new Promise((resolve, reject) => {
        doSomething({
            ...options,
            // Since `doSomething` calls `onSuccess` with two
            // arguments, we need to wrap them up in an object
            // to pass to `resolve`
            onSuccess(result, status) {
                resolve({result, status});
            },
            // `doSomething` calls `onError` with a string error,
            // wrap it in an Error instance
            onError(message) {
                reject(new Error(message));
            }
        });
    });
}
```

You may recall from the beginning of the chapter that the function you pass into the `Promise` constructor is called an *executor function*. It's responsible for starting the process for which the `Promise` will report success or failure. The `Promise` constructor calls the executor synchronously, meaning that the code in the executor function runs before `promiseSomething` returns the promise.

You saw an executor function early on in this chapter, and of course just now in Listing 8-6. To recap, an executor function receives two arguments: the function to call to resolve the promise (typically given the name `resolve`, but you can call it anything you want), and the function to call to reject the promise (typically given the name `reject`). Nothing can settle the promise unless it has access to one of those two functions. Each accepts a single parameter: `resolve` accepts a thenable (in which case it resolves the promise to that thenable) or a non-thenable value (in which case it fulfills the promise); `reject` accepts the rejection reason (error). If you call either of them with no arguments, `undefined` is used for the value or rejection reason. If you call either of them with more than one argument, only the first argument is used; any others are ignored. Finally, after you've called `resolve` or `reject` the first time, calling either of them again does nothing. It doesn't raise an error, but the call is completely ignored. That's because once a promise is resolved (fulfilled or resolved to a thenable) or rejected, you can't change that. The resolution or rejection is set in stone.

Let's look at what the executor function in Listing 8-6 does:

➤ It creates a new options object and uses property spread (which you learned about in Chapter 5) to give it the properties from the options object passed in, adding its own `onSuccess` and `onError` functions.

➤ For `onSuccess`, the code uses a function that takes the two arguments it's given and creates an object with `result` and `status` properties, then calls `resolve` with that object to fulfill the promise and set the object as the fulfillment value.

➤ For `onError`, the code uses a function that takes the string error message from `doSomething`, wraps it in an `Error` instance, and calls `reject` with that error.

Now, you can use `promiseSomething` in your promise-based code:

```
promiseSomething({data: "example"})
    .then(({result, status}) => {
        console.log("Got:", result, status);
    })
    .catch(error => {
        console.error(error);
    });
```

For a full runnable example, run `full-mock-api-function-example.js` from the downloads.

Note that unlike `resolve`, `reject` doesn't work differently if you give it a thenable. It *always* takes what you give it and makes it the rejection reason. It always makes the promise reject; it doesn't resolve the promise to what you pass it like `resolve` does. Even if you pass it a thenable, it doesn't wait for that thenable to settle; it uses the thenable itself as the rejection reason. For example, this code:

```
new Promise((resolve, reject) => {
    const willReject = new Promise((resolve2, reject2) => {
        setTimeout(() => {
            reject2(new Error("rejected"));
        }, 100);
    });
    reject(willReject);
})
.catch(error => {
    console.error(error);
});
```

passes the `willReject` promise to the `catch` handler *immediately*, without waiting for it to settle. (Then, 100ms later, it causes an unhandled rejection error because nothing handles the fact that `willReject` rejected.)

That's a big difference between `resolve` and `reject`. While `resolve` resolves the promise, including possibly resolving it to another promise or thenable (which may involve waiting for that other promise/thenable to settle), `reject` will only ever reject the promise immediately.

Promise.resolve

`Promise.resolve(x)` is effectively shorthand for:

```
x instanceof Promise ? x : new Promise(resolve => resolve(x))
```

except that in `Promise.resolve(x)`, x is only evaluated once. It returns its argument directly if that argument is an instance of `Promise` (not just a thenable); otherwise, it creates a new promise and resolves that promise to the value you gave it—meaning that if the value is a thenable, the promise is resolved to that thenable, and if the value isn't a thenable the promise is fulfilled with that value.

`Promise.resolve` is quite handy for converting a thenable into a native promise, since the promise it returns settles depending on how the thenable gets settled. It's also useful if you're accepting something, let's call it x, that could be a promise, a thenable, or a plain value: you pass it through `Promise.resolve`:

```
x = Promise.resolve(x);
```

and then it's always a promise. For example, suppose you want a utility function that logs a value, either the value itself or, if it's a thenable, its fulfillment value or rejection reason. You'd run the parameter through `Promise.resolve`:

```
function pLog(x) {
    Promise.resolve(x)
    .then(value => {
        console.log(value);
    })
    .catch(error => {
        console.error(error);
    });
}
```

Then you can call it either with a simple value:

```
pLog(42);
// => 42 (after a "tick" because it's guaranteed to be asynchronous)
```

or with a promise or other thenable:

```
pLog(new Promise(resolve => setTimeout(resolve, 1000, 42)));
// => 42 (after ~1000ms)
```

Since the promise/thenable may reject, the promise from `Promise.resolve` may also reject:

```
pLog(new Promise((resolve, reject) => {
    setTimeout(reject, 1000, new Error("failed"));
));
// => error: failed (after ~1000ms)
```

Another use case is priming a series of promise-enabled asynchronous operations, where each chains on the fulfillment of the previous one. You'll learn more about that in the section "Promises in Series," later in this chapter).

Promise.reject

`Promise.reject(x)` is shorthand for:

```
new Promise((resolve, reject) => reject(x))
```

That is, it creates a promise rejected with the rejection reason you give it.

`Promise.reject` isn't as general-purpose as `Promise.resolve`, but one common use case for it is in a `then` handler when you want to convert fulfillment to rejection. Some programmers prefer to return a rejected promise, like this:

```
.then(value => {
    if (value == null) {
        return Promise.reject(new Error());
    }
    return value;
}
```

rather than using `throw`, like this:

```
.then(value => {
    if (value == null) {
        throw new Error();
    }
    return value;
}
```

They both end up doing the same thing, but for reasons of personal style, you may see `Promise.reject` used for this, particularly when it means a concise arrow function can be used instead of a verbose one. For instance, the example earlier could be written with a concise arrow function:

```
.then(value => value == null ? Promise.reject(new Error()) : value);
```

You can't use `throw` in a concise arrow function (yet), because `throw` is a statement, and the body of a concise arrow function is a single expression. (`throw` expressions[8] are an active proposal, though, so that may change.)

OTHER PROMISE UTILITY METHODS

`Promise.resolve` and `Promise.reject` aren't the only promise utility functions available; there are several more that we'll look at in this section.

Promise.all

Suppose you have three asynchronous operations you need to perform that don't rely on each other, so it's fine if they overlap with one another, and you only want to use the results when you have the results from all three. If you used a promise chain, they'd run sequentially. So how to wait for them? You could start each of them, remember its promise, and then call `then` on them sequentially, but it gets pretty ugly:

```
let p1 = firstOperation();
let p2 = secondOperation();
let p3 = thirdOperation();
p1.then(firstResult => {
    return p2.then(secondResult => {
        return p3.then(thirdResult => {
            // Use `firstResult`, `secondResult`, and `thirdResult` here
        });
    });
})
.catch(error) {
    // Handle error
});
```

`Promise.all` to the rescue! `Promise.all` accepts an iterable (such as an array) and waits for any thenables in it to settle, returning a promise that either A) gets fulfilled when *all* of the thenables in the iterable are fulfilled, or B) gets rejected as soon as *any* of them gets rejected. When it gets

---

[8] https://github.com/tc39/proposal-throw-expressions

fulfilled, the fulfillment value is an array that has the fulfillment values of the thenables along with any non-thenable values from the original iterable, in the same order as the iterable it was called with. When it gets rejected, it uses the rejection reason of the thenable that got rejected (which, remember, is the *first* thenable that rejected).

You can wait for those three operations that can run in parallel with `Promise.all` like this:

```
Promise.all([firstOperation(), secondOperation(), thirdOperation()])
    .then(([firstResult, secondResult, thirdResult]) => {
        // Use `firstResult`, `secondResult`, and `thirdResult` here
    })
    .catch(error => {
        // Handle error
    });
```

It doesn't matter if `secondOperation` completes before `firstOperation`. `Promise.all` ensures the fulfillment values are in the same order as the thenables it receives; the result of the first thenable is always the first in the array, the result of the second is always the second, etc. Similarly, any non-thenable values in the original iterable are in the same place in the result array. See Figure 8-9.

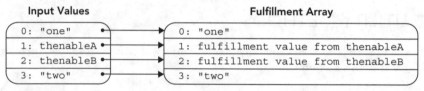

FIGURE 8-9

Notice the use of destructuring in the `then` handler in the example earlier. If you're working with a known number of entries in the iterable you pass to `Promise.all`, as opposed to something you create dynamically with an unknown number of entries, using destructuring in the `then` handler can improve the clarity of the code. But it's entirely optional.

If you call `Promise.all` with an empty iterable, its promise gets fulfilled immediately with an empty array.

If *any* of the thenables rejects, the promise from `Promise.all` rejects with just that rejection reason, without waiting for the other thenables to settle. It doesn't give you access to any fulfillments that may have occurred prior to the rejection nor, of course, any fulfillments or rejections that happen afterward. It does, however, silently "handle" rejections after the first, so they don't cause unhandled rejection errors.

Remember that any non-thenable values just get passed through. That's because `Promise.all` passes all of the values from the iterable through `Promise.resolve` when it receives them, then uses the resulting promises. For example, if you had just two operations to run and a third value you wanted to pass with them, you could do that like this:

```
Promise.all([firstOperation(), secondOperation(), 42])
    .then(([a, b, c]) => {
        // Use `a`, `b`, and `c` here
        // `c` will be 42 in this example
```

```
    })
    .catch(error => {
        // Handle error
    });
```

The value doesn't have to be at the end; it can be anywhere:

```
Promise.all([firstOperation(), 42, secondOperation()])
    .then(([a, b, c]) => {
        // Use `a`, `b`, and `c` here
        // `b` will be 42 in this example
    })
    .catch(error => {
        // Handle error
    });
```

Promise.race

`Promise.race` accepts an iterable of values (usually thenables) and watches them race, providing a promise for the result of the race. The promise gets fulfilled as soon as the first thenable gets fulfilled, or rejected as soon as the first thenable gets rejected, using the fulfillment value or rejection reason from that "winning" promise. Like `Promise.all`, it passes the values from the iterator through `Promise.resolve`, so non-thenables work as well.

Timeouts are one use case for `Promise.race`. Suppose you need to fetch something with a timeout, but the fetch mechanism you're using doesn't provide a timeout feature. You can run a race between the fetch and a timer:

```
// (Assume timeoutAfter returns a promise that gets rejected with a
// timeout error after the given number of milliseconds)
Promise.race([fetchSomething(), timeoutAfter(1000)])
    .then(data => {
        // Do something with the data
    })
    .catch(error => {
        // Handle the error or timeout
    });
```

When the timeout wins the race, that doesn't stop the fetch operation, but it ignores it when the fetch operation eventually finishes (either way) later. Of course, if the fetch mechanism you're using supports a timeout, or a way to cancel it, you'll want to use that instead.

Promise.allSettled

`Promise.allSettled` passes all of the values from the iterable you give it through `Promise.resolve` and waits for all of them to settle, whether getting fulfilled or rejected, and returns an array of objects with a `status` property and either a `value` or `reason` property. If the `status` property is `"fulfilled"`, the promise was fulfilled, and the object's `value` has the fulfillment value. If the `status` is `"rejected"`, the promise was rejected, and `reason` has the rejection reason. (If you check `status`, ensure you spell `"fulfilled"` correctly; it's easy to mistakenly include a second "l" on "ful".)

As with `Promise.all`, the array will be in the same order as the iterable that was provided, even if the thenables settle out of order.

Here's an example:

```
Promise.allSettled([Promise.resolve("v"), Promise.reject(new Error("e"))])
.then(results => {
    console.log(results);
});
// Outputs something similar to:
// [
//      {status: "fulfilled", value: "v"},
//      {status: "rejected", reason: Error("e")}
// ]
```

Promise.any

`Promise.any`,[9] Stage 3 as of this writing, is the converse of `Promise.all`. Like `Promise.all`, it accepts an iterable of values it passes through `Promise.resolve` and returns a promise. But while `Promise.all` defines success (fulfillment) as "*all* the thenables got fulfilled," `Promise.any` defines success as "*any* of the thenables got fulfilled." It fulfills its promise with the fulfillment value of the first thenable that got fulfilled. If all of the thenables get rejected, it rejects its promise with an `AggregateError` whose `errors` property is an array of rejection reasons. Like `Promise.all`'s array of fulfillment values, the array of rejection reasons is always in the same order as the values from the iterable it received.

PROMISE PATTERNS

In this section, you'll learn some patterns that are helpful when working with promises.

Handle Errors or Return the Promise

One fundamental rule of promises is: Either handle errors, or propagate the promise chain (e.g., by returning the latest result of `then`, `catch`, or `finally`) to your caller. Breaking this rule is likely the largest source of program incorrectness when using promises.

Suppose you have a function that fetches and shows an updated score when called:

```
function showUpdatedScore(id) {
    myFetch("getscore?id=" + id).then(displayScore);
}
```

What if `myFetch` runs into a problem? Nothing handles that promise rejection. In a browser, that unhandled rejection will be reported in the console. On Node.js it's reported in the console, and may

---

[9] `https://github.com/tc39/proposal-promise-any`

terminate the program entirely.[10] Moreover, whatever called `showUpdatedScore` doesn't know it didn't work. Instead, `showUpdatedScore` should return the promise from `then`:

```
function showUpdatedScore(id) {
    return myFetch("getscore?id=" + id).then(displayScore);
}
```

Then, whatever is calling it can handle errors or pass on the chain as necessary (perhaps in combination with other asynchronous operations it's doing). For instance:

```
function showUpdates(scoreId, nameId) {
    return Promise.all([showUpdatedScore(scoreId), showUpdatedName(nameId)]);
}
```

Every layer needs to either handle rejections or return a promise to its caller, expecting the caller to handle rejections. The top level has to do the rejection handling, since it has nothing it can pass the chain onto:

```
button.addEventListener("click", () => {
    const {scoreId, nameId} = this.dataset;
    showUpdatedScore(scoreId, nameId).catch(reportError);
}
```

With synchronous exceptions, the propagation is built into the mechanism. With promises, you need to ensure that the propagation happens by returning the last promise in the chain. But don't despair! In Chapter 9, you'll see how it becomes automatic again in an `async` function.

Promises in Series

If you have a series of operations that need to happen one after another, and want to either collect all their results or just feed each result into the next operation, there's a handy way to do that: construct a chain of promises using a loop. You start with an array (or any iterable) of the functions you want to call (or if you're calling the same function in every case, an array/iterable of arguments you want to call it with), and loop through the array to create a promise chain, chaining each operation on the fulfillment of the previous one via `then`. You start out with a call to `Promise.resolve` passing in the initial value.

A lot of people do this using the `reduce` function on arrays, so let's quickly recap the concept of `reduce`: it takes a callback and a seed value (the way we're using it here) and calls the callback with the seed value and the first entry in the array, then calls the callback again with the return value from the first call and the next entry in the array, repeatedly until it finishes the array, returning the final result from the callback. So this `reduce` call:

```
console.log(["a", "b", "c"].reduce((acc, entry) => acc + " " + entry, "String:"));
console.log(value); // "String: a b c"
```

---

[10] That's the plan as of this writing, anyway. For the moment, Node.js v13 still just shows a warning when the unhandled rejection is detected saying that in some future version, unhandled rejections will terminate the process.

calls the callback with `"String:"` (the seed value) and `"a"` (the first array entry), then calls it again with `"String: a"` (the result of the previous call) and `"b"` (the next array entry), then calls it again with `"String: a b"` (the result of the previous call) and `"c"` (the last array entry), then returns the final result: `"String: a b c"`. It does the same thing this code does:

```
const callback = (acc, entry) => acc + " " + entry;
callback(callback(callback("String:", "a"), "b"), "c")
console.log(value); // "String: a b c"
```

but more flexibly, because it can handle however many entries there are in the array.

Let's apply that to promises. Suppose you have a function that passes a value through a series of configurable transformation functions (like middleware in a web server process, or a series of image data filters):

```
function handleTransforms(value, transforms) {
    // ...
}
```

Since the list of transforms varies from call to call, it's provided as an array of transform functions. Each function accepts a value to transform and produces the transformed value, either synchronously or asynchronously. If it's asynchronous, it returns a promise. Creating a promise chain in a loop works well for this task: you use the initial value as the seed value for the `reduce` accumulator, and loop through the functions, chaining the promises together. Something like this:

```
function handleTransforms(value, transforms) {
    return transforms.reduce(
        (p, transform) => p.then(v => transform(v)), // The callback
        Promise.resolve(value)                       // The seed value
    );
}
```

Code using `reduce` can be a bit tricky to read, though; let's look at a version that does the same thing using a `for-of` loop:

```
function handleTransforms(value, transforms) {
    let chain = Promise.resolve(value);
    for (const transform of transforms) {
        chain = chain.then(v => transform(v));
    }
    return chain;
}
```

(The arrow functions in the two preceding examples could be removed, instead of `.then(v => transform(v))` you could just write `.then(transform)`.)

Let's assume we call `handleTransforms` with the transform functions a, b, and c. Whether you're using the reduce code or the `for-of` code, `handleTransforms` sets up the chain and then returns before any of the callbacks runs (because the `then` on the promise from `Promise.resolve` has the guarantee that it will only run its callback asynchronously). Then, this happens:

➤   Almost immediately, the first callback gets run. It passes the initial value into a, which returns either a value or a promise. That resolves the promise from the first call to `then`.

➤ That fulfillment calls the callback to the second `then`, passing the value that `a` returned into `b` and returning `b`'s result. That resolves the promise from the second call to `then`.

➤ That fulfillment calls the callback to the third `then`, passing the value that `b` returned into `c` and returning `c`'s result. That resolves the promise from the third call to `then`.

The caller sees the final promise, which will either get fulfilled with the final value from `c` or rejected with a rejection reason supplied by either `a`, `b`, or `c`.

In Chapter 9 you'll learn about the `async` functions added in ES2018. With `async` functions, the loop is even clearer (once you know what that `await` thing is). Here's a sneak peak:

```
// `async` functions are covered in Chapter 9
async function handleTransforms(value, transforms) {
    let result = value;
    for (const transform of transforms) {
        result = await transform(result);
    }
    return result;
}
```

Promises in Parallel

To run a group of operations in parallel, start them one at a time building up an array (or other iterable) of the promises each returns, and use `Promise.all` to wait for them all to complete. (See the earlier section on `Promise.all`.)

For instance, if you had an array of URLs, all of which you wanted to fetch, and you were happy to fetch them all in parallel, you might use `map` to start the fetch operations and get promises for them, then `Promise.all` to wait for the results:

```
Promise.all(arrayOfURLs.map(
    url => myFetch(url).then(response => response.json())
))
.then(results => {
    // Use the array of results
    console.log(results);
})
.catch(error => {
    // Handle the error
    console.error(error);
});
```

Given the note at the end of the "Promises in Series" section earlier, you're probably wondering whether `async` functions make this a lot simpler, too. The answer is: somewhat, but you still use `Promise.all`. Here's a sneak peak:

```
// this code must be in an `async` function (Chapter 9)
try {
    const results = await Promise.all(arrayOfURLs.map(
        url => myFetch(url).then(response => response.json())
    ));
```

```
        // Use the array of results
        console.log(results);
    } catch (error) {
        // Handle/report the error
        console.error(error);
    }
```

PROMISE ANTI-PATTERNS

In this section, you'll learn about some common promise-related anti-patterns to avoid.

Unnecessary new Promise(/*...*/)

Programmers who are new to promises frequently write code like this:

```
// INCORRECT
function getData(id) {
    return new Promise((resolve, reject) => {
        myFetch("/url/for/data?id=" + id)
            .then(response => response.json())
            .then(data => resolve(data))
            .catch(error => reject(error));
    });
}
```

or various permutations of it. As you know, though, then and catch *already* return promises, so there's no need for the new Promise there at all. The preceding should just be written like this:

```
function getData(id) {
    return myFetch("/url/for/data?id=" + id)
        .then(response => response.json());
}
```

Not Handling Errors (or Not Properly)

Not handling errors, or not handling errors properly, is hardly unique to using promises. But whereas exceptions automatically propagate through the call stack until/unless handled by a catch block, promise rejections don't, leading to hidden errors. (Or they *were* hidden errors, until JavaScript environments started reporting unhandled rejections.)

Remember the rule from the earlier section on promise patterns: the fundamental rule of promises is either handle errors, or propagate the promise chain to the caller so the caller can handle them.

Letting Errors Go Unnoticed When Converting a Callback API

When wrapping a callback API in a promise wrapper, it's easy to accidentally allow errors to go unhandled. For instance, consider this hypothetical wrapper for an API returning rows from a database:

```
// INCORRECT
function getAllRows(query) {
    return new Promise((resolve, reject) => {
```

```
            query.execute((err, resultSet) => {
                if (err) {
                    reject(err); // or `reject(new Error(err))` or similar
                } else {
                    const results = [];
                    while (resultSet.next()) {
                        data.push(resultSet.getRow());
                    }
                    resolve(results);
                }
            });
        });
    }
```

At first glance that looks reasonable. It does the query, and if the query returns an error it uses it to reject; if not, it builds an array of results and fulfills its promise with them.

But what if `resultSet.next()` throws an error? Perhaps the underlying database connection died. That would terminate the callback, meaning *neither* `resolve` *nor* `reject` is ever called, most likely failing silently, and leaving the promise unsettled forever.

Instead, ensure errors in the callback are caught and turned into a rejection:

```
function getAllRows(query) {
    return new Promise((resolve, reject) => {
        query.execute((err, resultSet) => {
            try {
                if (err) {
                    throw err; // or `throw new Error(err)` or similar
                }
                const results = [];
                while (resultSet.next()) {
                    data.push(resultSet.getRow());
                }
                resolve(results);
            } catch (error) {
                reject(error);
            }
        });
    });
}
```

You don't need the `try`/`catch` around the call to `query.execute` because if an error is thrown by the promise executor function itself (rather than a callback later), the `Promise` constructor uses that error to reject the promise automatically.

Implicitly Converting Rejection to Fulfillment

Programmers new to promises who've heard the fundamental rule (handle errors or return the promise chain) sometimes mishear it as "... *and* return the promise chain" and end up writing code like this:

```
function getData(id) {
    return myFetch("/url/for/data?id=" + id)
```

```
        .then(response => response.json())
        .catch(error => {
            reportError(error);
        });
    }
```

Do you see the problem with that code? (It's a bit subtle.)

The problem is that if an error occurs, getData's promise will be *fulfilled* with the value undefined, never rejected. The catch handler has no return value, so calling it results in the value undefined, and that means the promise catch created gets fulfilled with the value undefined, not rejected. That makes getData quite awkward to use: any then handler on it has to check whether it got undefined or the data it asked for.

The rule is "... *or* return the promise chain," and that's what getData should do:

```
function getData(id) {
    return myFetch("/url/for/data?id=" + id)
        .then(response => response.json());
}
```

That allows the caller to use then and catch on the result, knowing that the then handler will receive the data and the catch handler will receive rejections.

Trying to Use Results Outside the Chain

Programmers new to asynchronous programming frequently write code like this:

```
let result;
startSomething()
.then(response => {
    result = response.result;
});
doSomethingWith(result);
```

The problem here is that result will be undefined when doSomethingWith(result); runs, because the callback to then is asynchronous. Instead, the call to doSomethingWith should be *inside* the then callback (and of course, the code needs to either handle rejection or return the promise chain to something that will):

```
startSomething()
.then(response => {
    doSomethingWith(response.result);
})
.catch(reportError);
```

Using Do-Nothing Handlers

When first using promises, some programmers write do-nothing handlers, like this:

```
// INCORRECT
startSomething()
.then(value => value)
```

```
.then(response => {
    doSomethingWith(response.data);
})
.catch(error => { throw error; });
```

Two out of three of those handlers are pointless (and there's another problem with that code as shown). Which are they?

Right! If you're not changing the value in some way or using it for something, you don't need a `then` handler; and throwing an error from a `catch` handler just rejects the promise `catch` created. So the first `then` call and the `catch` call don't do anything. The code could be just this (which still has a problem):

```
startSomething()
.then(response => {
    doSomethingWith(response.data);
});
```

As an aside, have you spotted the remaining problem? It's a bit tricky to see it without more context, but the problem is that it needs to handle errors, or return the chain to something that will.

Branching the Chain Incorrectly

Another common problem when starting out is branching the chain incorrectly, like this:

```
// INCORRECT
const p = startSomething();
p.then(response => {
    doSomethingWith(response.result);
});
p.catch(handleError);
```

The problem here is that errors from the `then` handler aren't handled, because `catch` is called on the *original* promise, not the promise from `then`. If `handleError` should be called both for errors from the original promise and also errors from the `then` handler, that should be written just as a chain:

```
startSomething()
.then(response => {
    doSomethingWith(response.result);
})
.catch(handleError);
```

If the reason the author wrote it the other way is that they want to handle errors from the fulfillment handler differently than errors from the original promise, there are a couple of ways to do it. There's the two-argument version of `then`:

```
startSomething()
.then(
    response => {
        doSomethingWith(response.result);
    },
    handleErrorFromOriginalPromise
)
.catch(handleErrorFromThenHandler);
```

That assumes `handleErrorFromOriginalPromise` never throws and doesn't return a promise that gets rejected).

Or, you can add a rejection handler to the original structure, perhaps reordered a bit:

```
const p = startSomething();
p.catch(handleErrorFromOriginalPromise);
p.then(response => {
    doSomethingWith(response.result);
})
.catch(handleErrorFromThenHandler);
```

PROMISE SUBCLASSES

You can create your own subclasses of `Promise` in the usual ways. For instance, by using the `class` syntax you learned about in Chapter 4:

```
class MyPromise extends Promise {
    // ...custom functionality here...
}
```

When doing so, it's important not to break the various fundamental guarantees that promises provide. For instance, don't override the `then` method and have it call the handler synchronously when the promise is already fulfilled; that breaks the guarantee that the handler will always be called asynchronously. If you did that, your subclass would be a valid *thenable*, but it wouldn't be a *promise*, which breaks the "is a" rule of subclassing.

> **NOTE** *Creating a promise subclass isn't something you're likely to want to do, not least because it's so easy to accidentally end up dealing with a native promise instead of your subclass. For instance, if dealing with an API that provides promises, to use your promise subclass you have to wrap the promise from that API in your subclass (typically by using* `YourPromiseSubclass.resolve(theNativePromise)`*). That said, provided you subclass* `Promise` *correctly, you can trust that the promises you get from its own methods will be instances of your subclass.*

Since `then`, `catch`, `finally`, `Promise.resolve`, `Promise.reject`, `Promise.all`, and so on all return promises, you may be concerned that if you create a subclass, you'll need to override *all* of the `Promise` methods. Good news! The implementations of `Promise`'s methods are smart: they make sure that they create their new promise using the subclass. In fact, the empty `MyPromise` shell shown at the beginning of this section is fully functional, and calling `then` (or `catch` or `finally`) on instances of `MyPromise` (or using `MyPromise.resolve`, `MyPromise.reject`, etc.) returns a new instance of `MyPromise` that behaves correctly. You don't have to explicitly implement anything:

```
class MyPromise extends Promise {
}
const p1 = MyPromise.resolve(42);
```

```
const p2 = p1.then(() => { /*...*/});
console.log(p1 instanceof MyPromise); // true
console.log(p2 instanceof MyPromise); // true
```

If you decide to subclass `Promise`, here are some things to keep in mind:

➤ There shouldn't be any need to define your own constructor, the default one is sufficient. But if you define the constructor:

 ➤ Make sure you pass the first argument (the executor function) to `super()`.

 ➤ Make sure you don't expect to receive any other arguments (because you won't receive any from the implementations of `Promise` methods that use the constructor, such as `then`).

➤ If you override `then`, `catch`, or `finally`, make sure you don't break the fundamental guarantees they provide (for instance, don't execute the handler synchronously).

➤ Remember that `then` is the central method of promise instances. `catch` and `finally` call `then` to do their work (literally, not just conceptually). If you need to hook into the process of hooking up handlers to the promise, you only need to override `then`.

➤ If you override `then`, remember that it has *two* parameters (conventionally called `onFulfilled` and `onRejected`), and *both* of them are optional.

➤ If you create new methods that create promises, don't call your own constructor directly (e.g., `new MyPromise()`); that's unfriendly to subclasses. Instead, either use the `Symbol.species` pattern you learned about in Chapter 4 (use `new this.constructor[Symbol.species](/*...*/)` in an instance method or `new this[Symbol.species](/*...*/)` in a static method) or just directly use `new this.constructor(/*...*/)` in an instance method and `new this(/*...*/)` in a static method. The native `Promise` class does the latter, it doesn't use the species pattern.

➤ Similarly, if you want to use `MyPromise.resolve` or `MyPromise.reject` in a `MyPromise` method's code, don't use them directly, use `this.constructor.resolve/reject` in an instance method or `this.resolve/reject` in a static method.

Again, though, it's unlikely that you'll really need to subclass `Promise`.

OLD HABITS TO NEW

There's really just the one "Old Habit" to consider changing here.

Use Promises Instead of Success/Failure Callbacks

Old habit: Having a function that starts a one-off asynchronous process accept a callback (or two, or three) to report success, failure, and completion.

New habit: Return a promise instead, explicitly or implicitly via an `async` function (which you'll learn about in Chapter 9).

Asynchronous Functions, Iterators, and Generators

WHAT'S IN THIS CHAPTER?

➤ `async` functions

➤ `await` operator

➤ `async` iterators and generators

➤ `for-await-of` statement

CODE DOWNLOADS FOR THIS CHAPTER

You can download the code for this chapter at `https://thenewtoys.dev/bookcode` or `https://www.wiley.com/go/javascript-newtoys`.

In this chapter you'll learn about ES2018's `async` functions and the `await` operator, which provide syntax for writing asynchronous code using the same familiar flow control structures you use when writing synchronous code (`for` loops, `if` statements, `try`/`catch`/`finally`, calling functions and waiting for their results, etc.). You'll also learn about `async` iterators, `async` generators, and the `for-await-of` statement.

Because `async` functions build on promises, if you haven't already read Chapter 8, you'll want to do that now before moving on to this chapter.

ASYNC FUNCTIONS

In some sense, `async`/`await` syntax is "just" syntactic sugar for creating and consuming promises, and yet it completely transforms how you write your asynchronous code, letting you write the logical flow rather than writing only the synchronous flow and using callbacks for the asynchronous parts. `async`/`await` fundamentally changes, and simplifies, writing asynchronous code.

In a non-`async` function, you're writing a series of operations that the JavaScript engine will carry out, in order, without allowing anything else to happen while it's doing so (see the "Single Thread Per Realm" inset). That code might pass a callback to something that will call it asynchronously later, but the code doing that is just passing in the function to call later, the call isn't done right away.

For example, consider this code (assume all of these functions are synchronous):

```
function example() {
    let result = getSomething();
    if (result.flag) {
        doSomethingWith(result);
    } else {
        reportAnError();
    }
}
```

In `example`, the code calls `getSomething`, checks a flag on the object it got back, and then either calls `doSomethingWith` passing in the object, or calls `reportAnError`. All of that happens one thing after the last , with nothing else happening in the meantime.[1]

SINGLE THREAD PER REALM

Earlier when I said the engine carries out the steps of a non-`async` function " . . . without allowing anything else to happen while it's doing so . . . " there's an implicit " . . . on that thread . . . " qualifier. JavaScript defines semantics for only a single thread per *realm* (such as a browser tab), sometimes sharing that one thread across multiple realms (such as multiple tabs in a browser from the same origin that can directly call each other's code). That means that only a single thread has direct access to the variables and such being used by your code. (Chapter 16 explains how `SharedArrayBuffer` lets you share *data* across threads, but not *variables*.) While there are some JavaScript environments that allow multiple threads in the same realm (the Java Virtual Machine is one example, running JavaScript via scripting support), they're very rare and there are no standard semantics for them in JavaScript. For this chapter, please assume the standard type of environment such as you'd find in Node.js or a browser where there's only a single thread in the realm.

---

[1] Other than that, any thread can be suspended (paused) by the environment. What can't happen is that the thread then does *other* work in this same JavaScript realm.

Before `async` functions, doing similar things with asynchronous operations involved passing around callbacks, perhaps promise callbacks. For example, using `fetch` (the `XMLHttpRequest` replacement on modern browsers), in a non-`async` function you might have this code:

```
function getTheData(spinner) {
    spinner.start();
    return fetch("/some/resource")
        .then(response => {
            if (!response.ok) {
                throw new Error("HTTP status " + response.status);
            }
            return response.json();
        })
        .then(data => {
            useData();
            return data;
        })
        .finally(() => {
            spinner.stop();
        });
}
```

That will call `spinner.start`, then call `fetch`, then call `then` on the promise it returns, then call `then` on the promise *that* returns, then call `finally` on the promise *that* returns, and return the promise from `finally`. All of that happens in an unbroken series with nothing else happening in between. Later, when the request completes, those callbacks get run, but that's after `getTheData` has returned. After `getTheData` returns and before those operations complete, the thread can do other things.

Here's that same code in an `async` function:

```
async function getTheData(spinner) {
    spinner.start();
    try {
        let response = await fetch("/some/resource");
        if (!response.ok) {
            throw new Error("HTTP status " + response.status);
        }
        let data = await response.json();
        useData(data);
        return data;
    } finally {
        spinner.stop();
    }
}
```

The code looks synchronous, doesn't it? But it isn't. It has places where it pauses and waits for an asynchronous process to complete. While it's waiting, the thread can do other things. Those places are marked by the `await` keyword.

The four key features of `async` functions are:

➤ `async` functions implicitly create and return promises.

➤ In an `async` function, `await` consumes promises, marking a point where the code will wait asynchronously for the promise to settle.

➤ While the function is waiting for the promise to settle, the thread can run other code.

➤ In an `async` function, code you've traditionally seen as synchronous (`for` loops, `a + b`, `try`/`catch`/`finally`, etc.) is asynchronous if it contains `await`. The logic is the same, but the timing is different: there can be execution pauses to allow the awaited promise to settle.

➤ Exceptions are rejections, and rejections are exceptions; `return`s are resolutions, and fulfillments are results (that is, if you `await` a promise, you see the promise's fulfillment value as the result of the `await` expression).

Let's look at each of those in more detail.

async Functions Create Promises

An `async` function creates and returns a promise under the covers, resolving or rejecting that promise based on the code within the function. The following is an *indicative* translation of how the `getTheData` async function shown earlier is handled conceptually by the JavaScript engine. It's not literally correct, but it's close enough to get an idea of how the engine handles it.

```
// NOT how you would write this yourself
function getTheData(spinner) {
    return new Promise((resolve, reject) => {
        spinner.start();
        // This inner promise's executor function is the `try` block
        new Promise(tryResolve => {
            tryResolve(
                Promise.resolve(fetch("/some/resource"))
                .then(response => {
                    if (!response.ok) {
                        throw new Error("HTTP status " + response.status);
                    }
                    return Promise.resolve(response.json())
                        .then(data => {
                            useData(data);
                            return data;
                        });
                })
            );
        })
        .finally(() => {
            spinner.stop();
        })
        .then(resolve, reject);
    });
}
```

That's not how you'd write it if you were writing it with promises directly, not least because—as you learned in Chapter 8—you don't need `new Promise` when you already have the promise from `fetch`. But it's a reasonable indication of how an `async` function works under the covers.

Notice that the part of that `async` function prior to the first `await` (the call to `spinner.start` and the call to `fetch`) is *synchronous*: in the translated version, it's been relocated into promise executor functions, which are called synchronously. This is an important part of how an `async` function works: it creates its promise and runs its code synchronously until the first `await` or `return` (or the logic falls off the end of the function). If that synchronous code throws, the `async` function rejects its promise. Once the synchronous code has completed (normally or with an error), the `async` function returns its promise to the caller. That's so it can synchronously start a process that will complete asynchronously, just like a promise executor function does.

Your first reaction to the "translated" code, having read Chapter 8 and in particular its section on anti-patterns, might well be "But that uses `new Promise` (twice!). It should just chain off the promise from `fetch`." That's true, but the way `async` functions work has to be generic enough to allow for the possibility your code never uses `await` and so there's no promise to chain from, although there's little reason to use an `async` function that never `await`s. This example also has to ensure that the `finally` handler runs if there's an exception calling `fetch`, which it wouldn't if the function just chained off the `fetch` promise. You'd write the function differently if you were doing it manually, but `async` functions have a couple of things they need to ensure:

➤ That the promise they return is a *native* promise. Just returning the result of `then` would mean the result could be a third-party promise—or possibly not even a promise, if the object it's calling `then` on is *thenable* but not a promise. (Though it could do that by using `Promise.resolve`.)

➤ That any error thrown, even during the synchronous part of the code, is turned into a rejection, not a synchronous exception.

Using `new Promise`, despite being an anti-pattern in most cases for manually written code when you have a promise to chain from, addresses both of those requirements. Both of them could have been solved in other ways, but this simple way is how the spec is written.

await Consumes Promises

The other thing you can see in the "translated" version of `getTheData` is that `await` consumes promises. If the operand of `await` isn't a native promise, the JavaScript engine creates a native promise and uses the operand's value to resolve it. Then, the JavaScript engine waits for that promise to settle before proceeding with the following code in the function, as though it used `then` and passed in both fulfillment and rejection handlers. Remember that resolving the promise doesn't necessarily mean fulfilling it; if the operand to `await` is a thenable, the native promise is resolved to that thenable and will get rejected if the thenable gets rejected. If the value isn't a thenable, the native promise is fulfilled with the value. The `await` operator does that by effectively using `Promise.resolve` on the operand's value, everywhere `await` is used. (Not `Promise.resolve` literally, but the underlying operation it does, creating a promise and resolving it to the value.)

Standard Logic Is Asynchronous When await Is Used

In an `async` function, code that's traditionally synchronous is asynchronous if there's an `await` involved. For instance, consider this asynchronous function:

```
async function fetchInSeries(urls) {
    const results = [];
    for (const url of urls) {
        const response = await fetch(url);
```

```
                    if (!response.ok) {
                        throw new Error("HTTP error " + response.status);
                    }
                    results.push(await response.json());
                }
            return results;
        }
```

To run this, use `async-fetchInSeries.html`, `async-fetchInSeries.js`, `1.json`, `2.json`, and `3.json` in the downloads. You'll need to serve them through a web server to run this with most browsers, since doing ajax requests from pages loaded from `file://` URLs is often disallowed.

If that were a non-async function (or it didn't use `await`), those `fetch` calls would be in parallel (all running at once), not in series (running one after another). But because this is an `async` function and `await` is used within the `for-of` loop the loop runs asynchronously. The version of that using promises directly might look something like this instead:

```
function fetchInSeries(urls) {
    let chain = Promise.resolve([]);
    for (const url of urls) {
        chain = chain.then(results => {
            return fetch(url)
                .then(response => {
                    if (!response.ok) {
                        throw new Error("HTTP error " + response.status);
                    }
                    return response.json();
                })
                .then(result => {
                    results.push(result);
                    return results;
                });
        });
    }
    return chain;
}
```

To run this, use `promise-fetchInSeries.html`, `promise-fetchInSeries.js`, `1.json`, `2.json`, and `3.json` in the downloads. Again, you'll need to serve them through a web server rather than just opening the HTML locally.

Notice how the `for-of` loop just sets up the promise chain (as you saw in Chapter 8), completing before any of the asynchronous work is done. Also notice how much more complicated and difficult to follow the code is.

This is a major part of the power of `async` functions: you write the *logic* in the old familiar way, using `await` to handle waiting for asynchronous results rather than having to break up your logical flow with callback functions.

Rejections Are Exceptions, Exceptions Are Rejections; Fulfillments Are Results, Returns Are Resolutions

Similarly to how `for-of` and `while` and other control-flow statements are adapted to handle asynchronous work inside `async` functions, `try/catch/finally`, `throw`, and `return` are all adapted as well:

➤ Rejections are exceptions. When you `await` a promise, and the promise rejects, that is turned into an exception and can be caught by using `try/catch/finally`.

➤ Exceptions are rejections. If you `throw` in an `async` function (and don't `catch` it), that's converted into a rejection of the function's promise.

➤ `returns` are resolutions. If you `return` from an `async` function, that resolves its promise with the value of the operand you provided `return` (either fulfilling it if you provide a non-thenable value, or resolving it to the thenable if you provide one).

You saw this in the `getTheData` example earlier, which used `try/finally` to ensure that `spinner.stop` was called when the operation completed. Let's look more closely. Run the code in Listing 9-1.

LISTING 9-1: try/catch in an async function—async-try-catch.js

```
function delayedFailure() {
    return new Promise((resolve, reject) => {
        setTimeout(() => {
            reject(new Error("failed"));
        }, 800);
    });
}
async function example() {
    try {
        await delayedFailure();
        console.log("Done"); // (Execution doesn't get here)
    } catch (error) {
        console.error("Caught:", error);
    }
}
example();
```

`delayedFailure` returns a promise that it later rejects, but when using `await`, an `async` function like `example` sees that as an exception and lets you use `try/catch/finally` to handle it.

ASYNC FUNCTION CALLS AT THE TOP LEVEL

Listing 9-1 calls an `async` function at the top level of the script. When doing that, it's essential that either you know the `async` function will never throw an error (that is, the promise it returns will never be rejected), or that you add a `catch` handler to the promise it returns. That's true of Listing 9-1's `example` because the entire function body is in a `try` block with a `catch` attached to it (at least, it's true unless for some reason `console.error` throws an exception). In the general case where the `async` function may well fail, ensure errors are handled:

```
example().catch(error => {
    // Handle/report the error here
});
```

Let's look at the other side of it: `throw`. Run the code in Listing 9-2.

LISTING 9-2: throw in an async function—async-throw.js

```
function delay(ms, value) {
    return new Promise(resolve => setTimeout(resolve, ms, value));
}
async function delayedFailure() {
    await delay(800);
    throw new Error("failed");
}
function example() {
    delayedFailure()
        .then(() => {
            console.log("Done"); // (Execution doesn't get here)
        })
        .catch(error => {
            console.error("Caught:", error);
        });
}
example();
```

This version of `delayedFailure` is an `async` function that waits 800ms and then uses `throw` to throw an exception. This non-`async` version of `example` uses the promise's methods rather than `await`, and sees that exception as a promise rejection, catching it via a rejection handler.

Although the code in Listings 9-1 and 9-2 uses `new Error`, that's just convention (and arguably best practice); since JavaScript allows you to throw any value, and to use any value as a rejection reason, you don't have to use `Error`. See Listing 9-3, for instance, which uses strings instead. But as you learned in Chapter 8, using `Error` instances has debugging advantages thanks to the call stack information they have.

```
// `reject` using just a string
function delayedFailure1() {
    return new Promise((resolve, reject) => {
        setTimeout(() => {
            reject("failed 1"); // Rejecting with a value that isn't an
Error instance
        }, 800);
    });
}
async function example1() {
    try {
        await delayedFailure1();
        console.log("Done"); // (Execution doesn't get here)
    } catch (error) {
        console.error("Caught:", error); // Caught: "failed 1"
    }
}
example1();

// `throw` using just a string
function delay(ms, value) {
    return new Promise(resolve => setTimeout(resolve, ms, value));
}
async function delayedFailure2() {
    await delay(800);
    throw "failed 2"; // Throwing a value that isn't an Error instance
}
function example2() {
    delayedFailure2()
        .then(() => {
            console.log("Done"); // (Execution doesn't get here)
        })
        .catch(error => {
            console.error("Caught:", error); // Caught: "failed 2"
        });
}
example2();
```

Parallel Operations in async Functions

Using await in an async function suspends the function until the promise you're awaiting settles. But suppose you want to do a series of operations that can run in parallel in an async function?

This is one of the situations where you find yourself using promises (or at least promise methods) directly again, even in an async function. Suppose you have a fetchJSON function like this:

```
async function fetchJSON(url) {
    const response = await fetch(url);
```

```
        if (!response.ok) {
            throw new Error("HTTP error " + response.status);
        }
        return response.json();
    }
```

Now suppose you have three resources you want to fetch, and it's fine to do them in parallel. You *don't* want to do this:

```
// Don't do this if you want them done in parallel
const data = [
    await fetchJSON("1.json"),
    await fetchJSON("2.json"),
    await fetchJSON("3.json")
];
```

The reason is that they'll be done in series (one after another), not in parallel. Remember that Java-Script engine evaluates the expressions making up the array's contents before it creates the array and assigns it to the `data` variable, so the function is suspended at `await fetchJSON("1.json")` until that promise settles, then at `await fetchJSON("2.json")`, etc.

Thinking back to Chapter 8, you'll probably remember that there *is* something specifically designed to handle parallel operations with promises: `Promise.all`. Even though you're using an `async` function, there's no reason you can't use it:

```
const data = await Promise.all([
    fetchJSON("1.json"),
    fetchJSON("2.json"),
    fetchJSON("3.json")
]);
```

You `await` the promise from `Promise.all`, not the individual promises from the `fetchJSON` calls. You let those promises populate the array you pass to `Promise.all`.

You can use `Promise.race` and the various others in the same way.

You Don't Need return await

You may have noticed that the `fetchJSON` function in this section ends with

```
    return response.json();
```

not

```
    return await response.json();
```

There's no need for `await` there. An `async` function uses the value you return to resolve the promise the function created, so if the return value is a thenable, it's already effectively `awaited`. Writing `return await` is a bit like writing `await await`. You may see `return await` occasionally, and it seems to behave the same way, but it doesn't, quite. If the operand is a thenable, not a native promise, it adds an extra layer of promise resolution, which holds things up by one asynchronous cycle (or "tick"). That is, the version with `await` settles slightly later than it would have without `await`. You can see it action by running the following (`return-await-thenable.js` in the downloads):

```
function thenableResolve(value) {
    return {
        then(onFulfilled) {
```

```
                    // A thenable may call its callback synchronously like this; a native
                    // promise never will. This example uses a synchronous callback to
                    // avoid giving the impression that the mechanism used to make it
                    // asynchronous is the cause of the extra tick.
                    onFulfilled(value);
            }
        };
    }
    async function a() {
        return await thenableResolve("a");
    }
    async function b() {
        return thenableResolve("b");
    }
    a().then(value => console.log(value));
    b().then(value => console.log(value));
    // b
    // a
```

Note how b's callback runs before a's, even though a was called first. a's callback has to wait for one extra asynchronous cycle because of the await.

This also used to be true if you awaited a native promise, but ES2020 includes a specification change allowing `return await nativePromise` to be optimized to remove the extra asynchronous tick, and that optimization is already finding its way into JavaScript engines. If you're using Node.js v13 or later,[2] or an up-to-date version of Chrome, Chromium, or Brave, they all have a version of V8 that has the optimization. If you use Node.js v12 or earlier (with no flags) or Chrome v72 or earlier, they use a version of V8 without the optimization. Run the following (`return-await-native.js`) on something modern to see the optimization at work:

```
    async function a() {
        return await Promise.resolve("a");
    }
    async function b() {
        return Promise.resolve("b");
    }
    a().then(value => console.log(value));
    b().then(value => console.log(value));
```

With an engine that has the optimization, you see a first, then b. In an engine without it, you see b first, then a.

Bottom-line: you don't need `return await`, just use return.

Pitfall: Using an async Function in an Unexpected Place

Suppose you're doing a `filter` operation on an array:

```
    filteredArray = theArray.filter((entry) => {
        // ...
    });
```

---

[2] Node.js v11 and v12 also have it, behind a `--harmony-await-optimization` flag.

and you want to use data from an asynchronous operation in the `filter` callback. Perhaps you throw an `await fetch(entry.url)` in:

```
// Fails
filteredArray = theArray.filter((entry) => {
    const response = await fetch(entry.url);
    const keep = response.ok ? (await response.json()).keep : false;
    return keep;
});
```

But you get an error complaining about the `await` keyword, because you're trying to use it outside an `async` function. The temptation is to slap an `async` on the `filter` callback:

```
// WRONG
filteredArray = theArray.filter(async (entry) => {
    const response = await fetch(entry.url);
    const keep = response.ok ? (await response.json()).keep : false;
    return keep;
});
```

Now you don't get errors . . . but your `filteredArray` still has all the values the original array had! And it doesn't wait for the `fetch` operations to finish. Why do you think that is? (Hint: what does an `async` function return, and what is `filter` expecting?)

Right! The problem is that an `async` function always returns a promise, and `filter` doesn't expect a promise, it expects a keep/don't keep flag. Promises are objects, and objects are truthy, so `filter` sees each returned promise as a flag saying to keep the entry.

This comes up a lot when people first start using `async`/`await`. It's a powerful tool, but it's important to remember that when the function you're writing is a callback, you need to consider how that callback's return value will be used. Only use an `async` function as a callback if what's calling it (`filter` in this example) expects to get a promise back from it.

There are a couple of places where it's perfectly valid to use an `async` function as a callback to a non–promise-specific API. One good example is using `map` on an array to build an array of promises to pass to `Promise.all` or similar. But the majority of the time, if you find yourself writing an `async` function as a callback to something that isn't expressly promise-related, double-check that you're not falling into this pit.

ASYNC ITERATORS, ITERABLES, AND GENERATORS

In Chapter 6 you learned about iterators, iterables, and generators. As of ES2018, there are asynchronous versions of all of those. If you haven't read Chapter 6 yet, you'll want to do that before continuing with this section.

You'll recall that an iterator is an object with a `next` method that returns a result object with `done` and `value` properties. An *asynchronous* iterator is an iterator that returns a *promise* of a result object rather than returning a result object directly.

You'll also recall that an *iterable* is an object that has a `Symbol.iterator` method that returns an iterator. *Asynchronous* iterables have an analogous method, `Symbol.asyncIterator`, that returns an asynchronous iterator.

Finally, you'll remember that a generator function provides syntax for creating generator objects, which are objects that produce and consume values and have `next`, `throw`, and `return` methods. An *asynchronous* generator function creates an asynchronous generator, which produces *promises* of values rather than values themselves.

In the next two sections we'll look at asynchronous iterators and asynchronous generators in more detail.

Asynchronous Iterators

An asynchronous iterator is, again, simply an iterator whose `next` method provides a promise of a result object rather than the result object itself. As with an iterator, you can write it manually (either making `next` an async method or returning a promise manually), or use an asynchronous generator function (since asynchronous generators are also asynchronous iterators). Or you could even write it entirely manually using `new Promise` as necessary.

The vast majority of the time, you're best off writing an async generator function when you want an async iterator. As with iterators, though, it's useful to understand the underlying mechanics. You'll learn about asynchronous generators in a later section; in this section, let's implement an asynchronous iterator manually so you get a good look at the mechanics of it.

You may recall from Chapter 6 that all of the iterators you get from JavaScript itself inherit from a prototype object the spec calls `%IteratorPrototype%`. `%IteratorPrototype%` provides a default `Symbol.iterator` method that returns the iterator itself so that iterators are iterable, which is handy for `for-of` statements and such. It also provides a place to add features to iterators. Asynchronous iterators work the same way: any asynchronous iterator you get from JavaScript itself (as opposed to third-party code) inherits from an object the spec calls `%AsyncIteratorPrototype%`. It provides a default `Symbol.asyncIterator` method that returns the iterator itself, so that asynchronous iterators are also asynchronous iterables, which will be useful when you learn about `for-await-of` later in this chapter.

As with `%IteratorPrototype%`, there's no publicly accessible global or property referring to `%AsyncIteratorPrototype%`, and it's a bit more awkward to get to than `%IteratorPrototype%`. Here's how:

```
const asyncIteratorPrototype =
    Object.getPrototypeOf(
        Object.getPrototypeOf(
            (async function *(){}).prototype
        )
    );
```

Perhaps it's just as well you won't normally implement asynchronous iterators manually. If you want the gory details behind that, see the "How to Get %AsyncIteratorPrototype%" inset.

Now that you know how to get the prototype for your asynchronous iterator, it's time to create it. Earlier in this chapter you saw a `fetchInSeries` function that fetched several URLs one after another via `fetch` and provided an array with all of the results. Suppose you wanted a function to fetch them individually and provide that result before moving on to the next. That's a use case for an asynchronous iterator; see Listing 9-4.

HOW TO GET %AsyncIteratorPrototype%

Since there's no publicly accessible global or property that directly refers to `%AsyncIteratorPrototype%`, if you need to get it, you have to do so indirectly. The concise code for doing that is shown in the main text. Here's a version split into its individual steps to make it simpler to understand:

```js
let a = (async function *(){}).prototype;  // Get the prototype this async generator
                                            // function would assign to instances
let b = Object.getPrototypeOf(a);          // Its prototype is %AsyncGeneratorPrototype%
let asyncIteratorPrototype =
        Object.getPrototypeOf(b);          // Its prototype is %AsyncIteratorPrototype%
```

You create an asynchronous generator function (a function that, when called, will create an asynchronous generator) using the `async` generator syntax you'll learn about in a later section. Then you get its `prototype` property (the prototype it will assign to the generators it creates). Then you get its prototype, which is the prototype of asynchronous generator objects (which the spec calls `%AsyncGeneratorPrototype%`). Then you get *its* prototype, which is the prototype for asynchronous iterators, `%AsyncIteratorPrototype%`.

Again, perhaps it's good that you normally won't want to create asynchronous iterators manually. Instead, just use an asynchronous generator function.

LISTING 9-4: Using an async function to create an asynchronous iterator—async-iterator-fetchInSeries.js

```js
function fetchInSeries([...urls]) {
    const asyncIteratorPrototype =
        Object.getPrototypeOf(
            Object.getPrototypeOf(
                async function*(){}
            ).prototype
        );
    let index = 0;
    return Object.assign(
        Object.create(asyncIteratorPrototype),
        {
            async next() {
                if (index >= urls.length) {
                    return {done: true};
                }
                const url = urls[index++];
                const response = await fetch(url);
```

```
            if (!response.ok) {
                throw new Error("Error getting URL: " + url);
            }
            return {value: await response.json(), done: false};
        }
    }
);
}
```

This implementation of `fetchInSeries` returns an asynchronous iterator, which is implemented as an `async` function. Since it's an `async` function, it returns a promise each time it's called, which is fulfilled via a `return` statement or rejected via a `throw` statement.

You may be wondering about the destructuring in the parameter list. Why (`[...urls]`) rather than just (`urls`)? By using destructuring, the code makes a defensive copy of the array that was passed in since, of course, the calling code could modify the original array. It's nothing to do with asynchronous iterators per se, just fairly standard practice for a function that works with a received array asynchronously.

Here's one way you could use `fetchInSeries` by getting the iterator manually and calling `next`:

```
// In an async function
const it = fetchInSeries(["1.json", "2.json", "3.json"]);
let result;
while (!(result = await it.next()).done) {
    console.log(result.value);
}
```

Notice that the code uses `await it.next()` to get the next result object, since `next` returns a promise.

You can see that in action by taking the `async-iterator-fetchInSeries.html`, `async-iterator-fetchInSeries.js`, `1.json`, `2.json`, and `3.json` files from the downloads and putting them in a directory on your local web server, then opening them via HTTP. Again, just opening the HTML directly from the file system won't work, because of the ajax.

Again, in real code you'd probably just write an `async` generator function to make an asynchronous iterator. If you do write one manually, beware that since `next` starts an asynchronous operation and returns a promise for it, you can get the next call to `next` before the previous call's operation completes. The code in the example in this section is fine with that, but it wouldn't be if it used this version of `next` instead:

```
// WRONG
async next() {
    if (index >= urls.length) {
        return {done: true};
    }
    const url = urls[index];
    const response = await fetch(url);
```

```
        ++index;
        if (!response.ok) {
            throw new Error("Error getting URL: " + url);
        }
        return {value: await response.json()};
    }
```

Because there's an `await` between the `index` check against `urls.length` and the `++index` that increments it, two calls to `next` that overlap would both fetch the same URL (and the second would be skipped)—a difficult-to-diagnose bug.

Let's look at how you write an asynchronous generator.

Asynchronous Generators

An asynchronous generator function is, unsurprisingly, a combination of an `async` function and a generator function. You create one by using both the `async` keyword and the `*` indicating a generator function. When called, it creates an asynchronous generator. Inside an asynchronous generator function you can use `await` to wait for an asynchronous operation to complete, and `yield` to yield a value (and consume a value, as with non-`async` generator functions).

See Listing 9-5 for the asynchronous generator version of `fetchInSeries`. (You can run it via `async-generator-fetchInSeries.html` in the downloads.)

LISTING 9-5: Using an async generator function—async-generator-fetchInSeries.js

```
async function* fetchInSeries([...urls]) {
    for (const url of urls) {
        const response = await fetch(url);
        if (!response.ok) {
            throw new Error("HTTP error " + response.status);
        }
        yield response.json();
    }
}
```

That's so much simpler than writing it manually! The basic logic is still the same, but instead of having to use a closure over the `index` variable, you can just use a `for-of` loop with `await` inside it to loop through the URLs, and `yield` each result. Also, the generator automatically gets an appropriate prototype: `fetchInSeries.prototype`, which inherits from `%AsyncGeneratorPrototype%`, which inherits from `%AsyncIteratorPrototype%`.

The code to use it (manually for now, you'll learn about a simpler way using `for-await-of` in the next section) is the same as before:

```
// In an async function
const g = fetchInSeries(["1.json", "2.json", "3.json"]);
let result;
while (!(result = await g.next()).done) {
    console.log(result.value);
}
```

Look again at this line in the code in the preceding asynchronous generator function:

```
yield response.json();
```

It directly yields a promise. You may see that line written like this instead:

```
yield await response.json(); // Not best practice
```

and they both *seem* to do the same thing. Why is `await` optional there? Because in an asynchronous generator function, `yield` automatically applies `await` to any operand you give it, so it's not necessary there. It's like `return await` in an `async` function: it just adds another layer of promise resolution, potentially delaying it another "tick" (see "You Don't Need `return await`" earlier in this chapter for details).

So far, we've only used an asynchronous generator to *produce* values, but generators can *consume* values as well: you can pass values into `next` that the generator will see as the result of the `yield` operator. Since a non-`async` generator produces and consumes values, and an `async` generator wraps the values you `yield` in promises automatically, you might wonder if it will automatically `await` a promise if you pass one into `next`. No, it doesn't. If you pass a promise into `next`, the `async` generator code sees that promise as the result of the `yield` operator and has to `await` it explicitly (or use `then`, etc.). Although this is asymmetrical with what happens when you yield a promise, it means you have control over what you do with a promise if one is provided to your asynchronous generator code. Perhaps you want to gather several up into an array and then `await` `Promise.all` on it. Not automatically awaiting the value received from `yield` gives you that flexibility.

Let's modify `fetchInSeries` so you can pass a flag into `next` saying you want to skip the next entry; see Listing 9-6.

LISTING 9-6: async generator consuming values—async-generator-fetchInSeries-with-skip.js

```
async function* fetchInSeries([...urls]) {
    let skipNext = false;
    for (const url of urls) {
        if (skipNext) {
            skipNext = false;
        } else {
            const response = await fetch(url);
            if (!response.ok) {
                throw new Error("HTTP error " + response.status);
            }
            skipNext = yield response.json();
        }
    }
}
```

To see this in action, copy the files `async-generator-fetchInSeries-with-skip.html`, `async-generator-fetchInSeries-with-skip.js`, `1.json`, `2.json`, and `3.json` to your local web server and open the HTML file from there (via HTTP).

One final note about async generators: once the generator pauses and returns a promise from `next`, the generator's code doesn't continue until that promise is settled, even if you call `next` again. The second call to `next` returns a second promise as usual but doesn't advance the generator. When the first promise settles, then the generator advances and (eventually) settles the second promise. This is true of calls to the generator's `return` and `throw` methods as well.

for-await-of

So far you've only seen examples using an asynchronous iterator explicitly, getting the iterator object and calling its `next` method:

```
// In an async function
const it = fetchInSeries(["1.json", "2.json", "3.json"]);
let result;
while (!(result = await it.next()).done) {
    console.log(result.value);
}
```

But just as there's a `for-of` loop for using a synchronous iterator more conveniently (Chapter 6), there's a `for-await-of` loop for using an asynchronous iterator more conveniently:

```
for await (const value of fetchInSeries(["1.json", "2.json", "3.json"])) {
    console.log(value);
}
```

`for-await-of` gets an iterator from what you pass it by calling its `Symbol.asyncIterator` method[3] and then automatically `awaits` the result of calling `next` for you.

To see that in action, copy the files `for-await-of.html`, `async-generator-fetchInSeries-with-skip.js`, `1.json`, `2.json`, and `3.json` to your local web server and open the HTML file from there (via HTTP).

OLD HABITS TO NEW

Here are some old habits you might consider updating to use the new toys you learned about in this chapter.

Use async Functions and await Instead of Explicit Promises and then/catch

Old habit: Using explicit promise syntax:

```
function fetchJSON(url) {
    return fetch(url)
        .then(response => {
```

---

[3] Remember that if you pass it an asynchronous *iterator* rather than an asynchronous *iterable*, that's fine provided the iterator has been created correctly (that is, has the `Symbol.asyncIterator` method that returns `this`).

```
                if (!response.ok) {
                    throw new Error("HTTP error " + response.status);
                }
                return response.json();
            });
        }
```

New habit: Use async/await instead, so you can write the logic of your code without having to use callbacks for the asynchronous parts:

```
async function fetchJSON(url) {
    const response = await fetch(url);
    if (!response.ok) {
        throw new Error("HTTP error " + response.status);
    }
    return response.json();
}
```

10

Templates, Tag Functions, and New String Features

WROX.COM CODE DOWNLOADS FOR THIS CHAPTER

You can download the code for this chapter at `https://thenewtoys.dev/bookcode` or `https://www.wiley.com/go/javascript-newtoys`.

In this chapter, you'll learn about ES2015's new template literals and template tag functions, plus new string features such as improved Unicode support, iteration, and added methods.

TEMPLATE LITERALS

ES2015's *template literals* provide a way to create strings (and other things) using a literal syntax combining text and embedded substitutions. You're familiar with other kinds of literals, such as string literals delimited with quotes (`"hi"`) and regular expression literals delimited with slashes (/\s/). Template literals are delimited with backticks (`` ` ``), also called *grave accents*. This character is in various places on various different language keyboard layouts; on English-language keyboards it tends to be in the top left near Esc, but again, the location varies.

Template literals come in two varieties: untagged and tagged. We'll look at untagged (standalone) template literals first, then tagged literals.

Basic Functionality (Untagged Template Literals)

An untagged template literal creates a string. Here's a simple example:

```
console.log(`This is a template literal`);
```

So far, that doesn't seem to offer anything that a string literal doesn't, but template literals have several handy features. Within a template literal, you can use *substitutions* to fill in content from any expression. A substitution starts with a dollar sign ($) immediately followed by an opening curly brace ({), and ends with a closing curly brace (}); everything between the curly braces is the body of the substitution: a JavaScript expression. The expression is evaluated when the template literal is evaluated. Its result is used in place of the substitution. Here's an example:

```
const name = "Fred";
console.log(`My name is ${name}`);              // My name is Fred
console.log(`Say it loud! ${name.toUpperCase()}!`); // Say it loud! FRED!
```

In an untagged template literal, if the expression's result isn't a string, it's converted to one.

If you need to have an actual dollar sign followed by a curly brace in your text, escape the dollar sign:

```
console.log(`Not a substitution: \${foo}`); // Not a substitution: ${foo}
```

You don't need to escape dollar signs unless they're followed by an opening curly brace.

Another handy feature is that unlike string literals, template literals can contain unescaped newlines, which are retained in the template. This code:

```
console.log(`Line 1
Line 2`);
```

outputs

```
Line 1
Line 2
```

Note that any leading whitespace on the line following the newline *is* included in the template. So this:

```
for (const n of [1, 2, 3]) {
    console.log(`Line ${n}-1
    Line ${n}-2`);
}
```

outputs

```
Line 1-1
    Line 1-2
```

```
    Line 2-1
        Line 2-2
    Line 3-1
        Line 3-2
```

Since the content of the substitution is any JavaScript expression, you can have newlines and indentation if your substitution body is complex. That's just whitespace in the expression, so it isn't included in the string:

```
const a = ["one", "two", "three"];
console.log(`Complex: ${
    a.reverse()
     .join()
     .toUpperCase()
}`);                      // "Complex: THREE,TWO,ONE"
```

The expression in the substitution body isn't limited in any way; it's a full expression. Among other things, that means you can put a template literal within a template literal, though it can quickly become difficult to read and maintain:

```
const a = ["text", "from", "users"];
const lbl = "Label from user";
show(`<div>${escapeHTML(`${lbl}: ${a.join()}`)}</div>`);
```

That works just fine. But as a matter of style, it's probably better to move that inner template literal out of the outer one for simplicity:

```
const a = ["text", "from", "users"];
const lbl = "Label from user";
const userContent = `${lbl}: ${a.join()}`;
show(`<div>${escapeHTML(userContent)}</div>`);
```

Within a template literal, all the standard escape sequences work just like they do in string literals: \n creates a newline, \u2122 is the ™ character, and so on. That means that to put an actual backslash in the template, you need to escape it just like in a string literal: \\.

Template Tag Functions (Tagged Template Literals)

In addition to their untagged use to create strings, template literals combined with *tag functions* are useful for other purposes.

A *tag function* is a function designed to be called using tagged function call syntax, which doesn't use parentheses (()) like normal calls do; instead, you write the function name followed by a template literal (optionally with whitespace in between):

```
example`This is the template to pass to the function`;
// or
example `This is the template to pass to the function`;
```

This *calls* the example function. It's a new style of function call for JavaScript (as of ES2015). When called this way, the example function receives the *template* from the template literal (an array of the literal's hardcoded text segments) as its first argument followed by discrete arguments for the values resulting from evaluating the substitution expressions. For an example, run the code from Listing 10-1.

LISTING 10-1: Basic tag function example—tag-function-example.js

```
function example(template, value0, value1, value2) {
    console.log(template);
    console.log(value0, value1, value2);
}
const a = 1, b = 2, c = 3;
example`Testing ${a} ${b} ${c}.`;
```

That code outputs the following:

```
["testing ", " ", " ", "."]
1 2 3
```

Note that the template array contains the initial word `"testing "` including the trailing space, the whitespace between the three substitutions, and the text after the last substitution at the end of the template (the period). The arguments following that have the substitution values (`value0` contains the result of `${a}`, `value1` contains the result of `${b}`, and so on).

Unless your function expects a fixed number of substitutions, it's common to use a rest parameter for the values of the substitutions, like this:

```
function example(template, ...values) {
    console.log(template);
    console.log(values);
}
const a = 1, b = 2, c = 3;
example`Testing ${a} ${b} ${c}.`;
```

That outputs much the same thing as before, except the values are in an array (`values`) now:

```
["testing ", " ", " ", "."]
[1, 2, 3]
```

The evaluated substitution values are not converted to strings; your tag function gets the *actual* value. That value may be a primitive like the numbers in the `values` array in the preceding example, or an object reference, or a function reference—any value at all. Listing 10-2 has an example just to emphasize that point, since for most of the rest of this section, it happens that we'll be using substitutions that result in strings.

LISTING 10-2: Tag function getting non-string value—non-string-value-example.js

```
const logJSON = (template, ...values) => {
    let result = template[0];
    for (let index = 1; index < template.length; ++index) {
        result += JSON.stringify(values[index - 1]) + template[index];
    }
    console.log(result);
};

const a = [1, 2, 3];
const o = {"answer": 42};
const s = "foo";
logJSON`Logging: a = ${a} and o = ${o} and s = ${s}`;
```

Running this shows:

```
Logging: a = [1,2,3] and o = {"answer":42} and s = "foo"
```

As you can see, `logJSON` received the array and object, not versions of them converted to string.

`Array.prototype.reduce` is handy for when you're interspersing entries from the `template` and the `values` array, as `logJSON` does. `template` is guaranteed to have at least one entry,[1] and to be one entry longer than `values`, so `reduce` without a seed works well for zipping them together. See Listing 10-3 for a version of `logJSON` using `reduce` instead of a loop.

LISTING 10-3: Tag function getting non-string value (reduce)—non-string-value-example-reduce.js

```javascript
const logJSON = (template, ...values) => {
    const result = template.reduce((acc, str, index) =>
        acc + JSON.stringify(values[index - 1]) + str
    );
    console.log(result);
};

const a = [1, 2, 3];
const o = {"answer": 42};
const s = "foo";
logJSON`Logging: a = ${a} and o = ${o} and s = ${s}`;
```

This idiom works well for tag functions. For instance, if you wanted to emulate the string creation behavior of untagged template literals, you could do it like this:

```javascript
function emulateUntagged(template, ...values) {
    return template.reduce((acc, str, index) => acc + values[index - 1] + str);
}
const a = 1, b = 2, c = 3;
console.log(emulateUntagged`Testing ${a} ${b} ${c}.`);
```

(You probably wouldn't use `reduce` to do exactly what it's doing there, though; later you'll learn about a simpler option for this specific example. But `reduce` is useful if you may be performing some operation on the values in the process of building the result.)

Creating strings from templates is a very powerful use case, but there are plenty of non-string use cases as well. Tag functions and template literals allow you to create nearly any domain-specific language (DSL) you may need.

Regular expressions make a good example.

It's awkward to use the `RegExp` constructor because it accepts a string, and so any backslashes meant for the regular expression have to be escaped (and any backslashes meant to be used literally have to be *double*-escaped: once for the string literal, and once for regex; four backslashes in total). This is one of the reasons we have regular expression literals in JavaScript.

---

[1] You may remember that calling `reduce` on an empty array raises an error if you don't provide a seed value, but since `template` is guaranteed never to be empty, we don't have that problem with `logJSON` (provided it's called as a tag function).

But if you want to use a variable's value in a regular expression, you have to use the regular expression constructor and fight with the backslashes and the lack of clarity; you can't use a literal. Tag functions to the rescue!

"But wait," you ask, "aren't the strings in the `template` parameter . . . just strings? Haven't the escape sequences created by the backslashes, if any, already been processed?"

Good point! They have, yes; which is why the `template` array has an extra property called `raw`. (This takes advantage of the fact that arrays are objects, so they can have properties that aren't array entries.) The `raw` property contains an array of *the raw text* of the text segments of the template. Run the code from Listing 10-4.

Listing 10-4: Tag function showing raw string segments—tag-function-raw-strings.js

```
function example(template) {
    const first = template.raw[0];
    console.log(first);
    console.log(first.length);
    console.log(first[0]);
}
example`\u000A\x0a\n`;
```

This code takes the raw version of the first text segment you pass in (the only one, in the example) and outputs it, its length, and just its first character. It outputs the following:

```
\u000A\x0a\n
12
\
```

Notice that the backslashes are actually backslashes; the escape sequences have not been interpreted. Also note that they haven't been turned into some canonical form; they are *as written in the template literal*. You know that because `\u000A`, `\x0a`, and `\n` all encode the exact same character (U+000A, a newline). But the raw version is just that: raw. It's the raw content of that text segment in the template literal.

Using that `raw` array, you can build a tag function to create a regular expression where the text of the template literal is used, er, literally:

```
const createRegex = (template, ...values) => {
    // Build the source from the raw text segments and values
    // (in a later section, you'll see something that can replace
    // this reduce call)
    const source = template.raw.reduce(
        (acc, str, index) => acc + values[index - 1] + str
    );
    // Check it's in /expr/flags form
    const match = /^\/(.+)\/([a-z]*)$/.exec(source);
    if (!match) {
        throw new Error("Invalid regular expression");
    }
    // Get the expression and flags, create
    const [, expr, flags = ""] = match;
    return new RegExp(expr, flags);
};
```

INVALID ESCAPE SEQUENCES IN TEMPLATE LITERALS

In ES2015 through ES2017, the escape sequences in template literals were restricted to valid JavaScript escape sequences. So for instance, \ufoo would cause a syntax error, because a Unicode escape sequence must have digits, not foo, after the \u. That was limiting for DSLs, though, so ES2018 lifted that restriction. If a text segment contains an invalid escape sequence, its entry in the template has the value undefined, and the raw text is in template.raw:

```
const show = (template) => {
    console.log("template:");
    console.log(template);
    console.log("template.raw:");
    console.log(template.raw);
};
show`Has invalid escape: \ufoo${","}Has only valid escapes: \n`;
```

This outputs

```
template:
[undefined, "Has only valid escapes: \n"]
template.raw:
["Has invalid escape: \\ufoo", "Has only valid escapes: \\n"]
```

With that tag function, you can write regular expressions with embedded variables without having to double-escape things:

```
const alternatives = ["this", "that", "the other"];
const rex = createRegex`/\b(?:${alternatives.map(escapeRegExp).join("|")})\b/i`;
```

This code assumes an escapeRegExp function that isn't part of the standard JavaScript library, but is in many a programmer's toolkit. Run Listing 10-5 for a complete example (including the escapeRegExp function).

LISTING 10-5: createRegex complete example—createRegex-example.js

```
const createRegex = (template, ...values) => {
    // Build the source from the raw text segments and values
    // (in a later section, you'll see something that can replace
    // this reduce call)
    const source = template.raw.reduce(
        (acc, str, index) => acc + values[index - 1] + str
    );
    // Check it's in /expr/flags form
    const match = /^\/(.+)\/([a-z]*)$/.exec(source);
    if (!match) {
        throw new Error("Invalid regular expression");
    }
    // Get the expression and flags, create
    const [, expr, flags = ""] = match;
    return new RegExp(expr, flags);
```

```
};
// From the TC39 proposal: https://github.com/benjamingr/RegExp.escape
const escapeRegExp = s => String(s).replace(/[\\^$*+?.()|[\]{}]/g, "\\$&");

const alternatives = ["this", "that", "the other"];
const rex = createRegex`/\b(?:${alternatives.map(escapeRegExp).join("|")})\b/i`;

const test = (str, expect) => {
    const result = rex.test(str);
    console.log(str + ":", result, "=>", !result == !expect ? "Good" : "ERROR");
};
test("doesn't have either", false);
test("has_this_but_not_delimited", false);
test("has this ", true);
test("has the other ", true);
```

Regular expressions are just one example of a DSL, though. You might create a tag function to use human-like logic expressions to query a JavaScript object tree, using substitutions for both the values and the tree (or trees) to search:

```
// Hypothetical example
const data = [
    {type: "widget", price: 40.0},
    {type: "gadget", price: 30.0},
    {type: "thingy", price: 10.0},
    // ...
];

//...called in response to user input...
function searchClick(event) {
    const types = getSelectedTypes();        // Perhaps `["widget", "gadget"]`
    const priceLimit = getSelectedPriceLimit(); // Perhaps `35`
    const results = search`${data} for type in ${types} and price < ${priceLimit}`;
    for (const result of results) {
        // ...show result...
    }
}
```

String.raw

When used as a tag function, `String.raw` returns a string with the *raw* text segments from the template combined with any evaluated substitution values. For example:

```
const answer = 42;
console.log(String.raw`Answer:\t${answer}`); // Answer:\t42
```

Notice that the escape sequence `\t` has not been interpreted; the resulting string literally has a backslash followed by the letter `t`. What could this possibly be useful for?

It's useful any time you want to create a string without having escape sequences in the string interpreted. For instance:

➤ Specifying a hardcoded path in a utility script on a Windows computer:

```
fs.open(String.raw`C:\nifty\stuff.json`)
```

➤ Creating a regular expression containing backslashes and a variable portion (an alternative to the `createRegex` function you saw earlier):

```
new RegExp(String.raw`^\d+${separator}\d+$`)
```

➤ Outputting LaTeX or PDF sequences (which can also contain backslashes)

Basically, `String.raw` is useful any time you want the raw string you typed (possibly with substitutions), not an interpreted string.

It's also really useful when used by *other* tag functions. For example, in the `createRegex` tag function earlier, to create the raw source of our DSL (in our case, a regular expression), we needed to put back together the `raw` array of text segments and the values passed to the tag function via substitutions, like this:

```
const source = template.raw.reduce(
    (acc, str, index) => acc + values[index - 1] + str
);
```

For a certain class of tag functions (ones gathering the template and values—perhaps pre-processed values—into a string), this is a common requirement, and it's exactly what `String.raw` does. So we can call it to do that part for us, replacing the `reduce` call. Since we're calling it without a template literal, we use normal `()` notation, not tag notation, for the call:

```
const source = String.raw(template, ...values);
```

That makes the `createRegex` function simpler:

```
const createRegex = (template, ...values) => {
    // Build the source from the raw text segments and values
    const source = String.raw(template, ...values);
    // Check it's in /expr/flags form
    const match = /^\/(.+)\/([a-z]*)$/.exec(source);
    if (!match) {
        throw new Error("Invalid regular expression");
    }
    // Get the expression and flags, create
    const [, expr, flags = ""] = match;
    return new RegExp(expr, flags);
};
```

Run the `simpler-createRegex.js` file from the downloads to see this in action.

Reusing Template Literals

One often-asked question about template literals is: how do you reuse them? After all, the result of an untagged template literal isn't a template object, it's a string. What if you want a template you're going to reuse? For instance, suppose you often want to output a first name, last name, and then a nickname or "handle" in parentheses. You might use a template literal like `` `${firstName} ${lastName} (${handle})` ``, but that's immediately evaluated and turned into a string. How do you reuse it?

This is a classic case of overthinking something, but it comes up again and again.

As is often the case when the question is "How do I reuse this?" the answer is to wrap it in a function:

```
const formatUser = (firstName, lastName, handle) =>
    `${firstName} ${lastName} (${handle})`;
console.log(formatUser("Joe", "Bloggs", "@joebloggs"));
```

Template Literals and Automatic Semicolon Insertion

If you prefer to write your code without semicolons (relying on Automatic Semicolon Insertion), you're probably used to avoiding starting a line with an opening parenthesis or square bracket ((or [), because it can get combined with the end of the previous line. This can cause behavior you didn't intend, such as an errant function call or a property accessor expression that was meant to be the beginning of an array, that sort of thing.

Template literals add a new "ASI hazard:" if you start a line with a backtick to start a template literal, it can be seen as a tag call to a function referenced at the end of the previous line (just like an opening parenthesis).

So if you rely on ASI, add the backtick to your list of characters you put a semicolon in front of at the beginning of a line, just like (or [.

IMPROVED UNICODE SUPPORT

ES2015 markedly improved JavaScript's Unicode support, adding several features to strings and regular expressions to make working with the full Unicode character set simpler. This section covers the string improvements. The regular expression improvements are covered in Chapter 15.

First, a bit of terminology and review before we get to the new features.

Unicode, and What Is a JavaScript String?

If you already have a solid understanding of Unicode and Unicode transformation formats (UTFs), code points, code units, etc., then: a JavaScript string is a series of UTF-16 code units that tolerates invalid surrogate pairs. If you're one of the few people who comfortably understood that sentence, you can skip to the next section. If you're in the vast majority who didn't (because let's face it, those are some pretty arcane terms!), read on.

Human language is complicated; human language writing systems doubly so. English is one of the simplest: hand-waving away some details, each native English *grapheme* ("a minimally distinctive unit of writing in the context of a particular writing system"[2]) is one of 26 letters or 10 digits. But many languages don't work that way. Some, like French, have a base alphabet and a small number of diacritical marks used to modify some of those letters (such as the grave accent on the "a" in "voilà"); that "à" is perceived by native readers as a single grapheme, even though it's made up of parts. Devanagari, a writing system used in India and Nepal, uses a base alphabet for syllables with a given consonant and a default vowel sound (the "a" in "about"). For example, "na" is the "letter" न. For syllables with other vowel sounds (or no vowel sound), Devanagari uses diacriticals. To write "ni"

---

[2] https://unicode.org/faq/char_combmark.html

instead of "na," the base letter for "na" (न) is modified by a diacritical for the "i" sound (ि), creating "ni" (नि). "नि" is perceived as a single grapheme by native readers, even though (again) it's made up of parts. Chinese uses several thousand distinct graphemes, and (again waving away details) words are typically made up of one to three of them. So it's complicated even before we throw computers into the mix.

To handle all this complexity, Unicode defines *code points*, values in the range 0x000000 (0) to 0x10FFFF (1,114,111) with specific meanings and properties, typically written with "U+" followed by four to six hexadecimal digits. Code points are not "characters," although that's a common misunderstanding. A code point *may* be a "character" on its own (like the English letter "a"), or it may be a "base character" (like "न", the "na" syllable in Devanagari), or a "combining character" (such as the diacritical "ि" that turns "na" to "ni"), or a few other things. Unicode also has several code points for things that aren't graphemes at all, such as a zero-width space, and also for things that aren't parts of words at all, like emojis.

Unicode originally used the range 0x0000 to 0xFFFF, which fit in 16 bits (this was called "UCS-2"—2-byte Universal Character Set). A code point could be held in a single 16-bit value. Modern (at the time) systems used 16-bit "characters" to store strings. When Unicode had to be extended beyond 16 bits (0x000000 to 0x10FFFF requires 21 bits), it meant that not all code points would fit within 16-bit values anymore. To support those 16-bit systems, the concept of *surrogate pairs* was created: a value in the range 0xD800 to 0xDBFF is a "leading" (or "high") surrogate and is expected to be followed by a value in the range 0xDC00 to 0xDFFF, a "trailing" (or "low") surrogate. The pair, taken together, can be converted to a single code point using a fairly simple calculation. The 16-bit values are called *code units* to distinguish them from code points. This "transformation" of the 21-bit code point values to 16-bit code unit values is called UTF-16. In well-formed UTF-16, you never have a leading surrogate that isn't followed by a trailing surrogate or vice versa.

JavaScript is one of those modern-at-the-time systems. A JavaScript "string" is a series of UTF-16 code units, with the exception that JavaScript strings tolerate invalid surrogates (a leading surrogate without a trailing one or the other way around) and define semantics for them: if half of a surrogate pair is encountered without the other half, it must be treated as though it were a code point rather than a code unit. So for instance, if 0xD820 were found in isolation, it would be treated as code point U+D820, rather than a leading surrogate. (U+D820 is reserved and so has no assigned meaning, so the "unknown character" glyph would be rendered if the string were output.)

All of this means that a single grapheme from a human point of view may be one or more *code points*, and that a single *code point* may be one or two UTF-16 *code units* (JavaScript string "characters"). See the examples in Table 10-1.

TABLE 10-1: Code Points and Code Units Examples

"CHARACTER"	CODE POINT(S)	UTF-16 CODE UNIT(S)
English "a"	U+0061	0061
Devanagari "नि"	U+0928 U+093F	0928 093F
Smiley Face Emoji (☺)	U+1F60A	D83D DE0A

Although the English grapheme "a" is a single code point, and a single UTF-16 code unit, the Devanagari "ni" grapheme "नि" requires two code points, each of which (it happens) fits in in a single UTF-16 code unit. The Smiley Face emoji is a single code point, but requires two UTF-16 code units, and thus two JavaScript "characters":

```
console.log("a".length); // 1
console.log("नि".length); // 2
console.log("☺".length); // 2
```

UTF-16 is the relevant one for JavaScript, but it's worth noting that there are also UTF-8 and UTF-32. UTF-8 encodes code points into one to four 8-bit code units (with the ability to be extended to five or six code units if Unicode has to grow further). UTF-32 is just a one-for-one mapping of code points to code units using (you guessed it!) 32-bit code units.

Whew! What a lot of context. Now that we have it, let's see what's new.

Code Point Escape Sequence

In a JavaScript string literal, it used to be that if you wanted to use an escape sequence to write a code point that required two UTF-16 code units, you had to figure out the UTF-16 values and write them separately, like this:

```
console.log("\uD83D\uDE0A"); // ☺ (smiling face emoji)
```

ES2015 added *Unicode code point escape sequences*, which let you specify the actual code point value instead—no more fiddly UTF-16 calculations. You write it in curly braces in hex (in general, Unicode values are listed in hex). The smiling face with smiling eyes we've been using is U+1F60A, so:

```
console.log("\u{1F60A}"); // ☺ (smiling face emoji)
```

String.fromCodePoint

ES2015 also added the code point equivalent of `String.fromCharCode` (which works in code units): `String.fromCodePoint`. You can pass it one or more code points as numbers, and it provides the equivalent string:

```
console.log(String.fromCodePoint(0x1F60A)); // ☺ (smiling face emoji)
```

String.prototype.codePointAt

Continuing the theme of code point support, you can get the code point at a given position in the string via `String.prototype.codePointAt`:

```
console.log("☺".codePointAt(0).toString(16).toUpperCase()); // 1F60A
```

This one's a bit tricky, though: the index you pass it is in *code units* (JavaScript "characters"), not *code points*. So `s.codePointAt(1)` doesn't return the second code point in the string, it returns the code point that starts at index 1 of the string. If the first code point in the string requires two code units, `s.codePointAt(1)` will return the value of that code point's trailing surrogate code unit:

```
const charToHex = (str, i) =>
    "0x" + str.codePointAt(i).toString(16).toUpperCase().padStart(6, "0");
```

```
const str = "😊😊"; // Two identical smiling face emojis
for (let i = 0; i < str.length; ++i) {
    console.log(charToHex(str, i));
}
```

This outputs four values (0x01F60A, 0x00DE0A, 0x01F60A, 0x00DE0A) because each smiley face takes up two "characters" in the string, but the code only advances the counter by one on each iteration. The value that shows up in the second and fourth positions, 0x00DE0A, is the trailing surrogate of the pair that defines the smiley face. The code should probably skip those trailing surrogates and just list (or find) the actual code points in the string.

If you're looping from the beginning, the solution is simple: use `for-of` instead of a `for` loop. See the "Iteration" section later in this chapter for details.

If you're landing in the middle of a string and want to find the beginning of the nearest code point, that's not too hard either: get the "code point" where you are and check whether it's in the range 0xDC00 to 0xDFFF (inclusive). If so, that's the trailing surrogate of (presumably) a pair, so step back one to get to the beginning of the pair (repeating if necessary to allow for invalid surrogate pairs), or step forward to get to the beginning of the next code point (repeating as necessary). You might also check for isolated leading surrogates, the range 0xD800 through 0xDBFF. Those two ranges are next to each other, so you can use 0xD800 through 0xDFFF for a check that includes either a standalone leading or trailing surrogate.

String.prototype.normalize

Rounding out the improved support for Unicode, the `normalize` method of strings creates a new "normalized" string using one of the normalization forms defined by the Unicode consortium.

In Unicode, the same string can be written in more than one way. Normalization is the process of creating a new string written in a "normal" form (four of which are defined). This can be important for comparisons, or advanced processing, etc. Let's look at it more closely.

In French, the letter "c" is "hard" (pronounced like an English "k") if it's followed by the letter "a". In words where it's followed by an "a" but should be "soft" (pronounced like the letter "s"), it gets a diacritical mark called a *cédille* added under it. You can see this in the very name of the language: Français. It's pronounced "fransays," not "frankays," because of the cédille on the "c". When a "c" has that mark, it's creatively called a *c cédille*.

For mostly historic reasons, c cédille ("ç") has its own code point: U+00E7.[3] But it can also be written as a combination of the letter "c" (U+0063) and a combining mark for the cédille (U+0327):

```
console.log("Français");        // Français
console.log("Franc\u0327ais"); // Français
```

Depending on the font, they may look *slightly* different, but they're the same word—except a naïve comparison doesn't reflect that:

```
const f1 = "Français";
const f2 = "Franc\u0327ais";
console.log(f1 === f2);        // false
```

---

[3] Computer history, that is. French was one of the earliest languages supported by computers, and having separate characters in the character set for letters with diacriticals was the simple way to support it.

Normalization fixes it:

```
console.log(f1.normalize() === f2.normalize()); // true
```

This is just one way a string may vary but still encode the same text. Some languages can apply several diacritical marks to the same "letter." If the order of the marks is different in one string vs. another, the strings won't be equal in a naïve check, but will be equal in a normalized form.

Unicode has two primary types of normalization: Canonical and Compatibility. Within each, it has two forms: Decomposed and Composed. Without going into too much detail, here's what the Unicode standard has to say about the two types of normalization:

> *Canonical equivalence is a fundamental equivalency between characters or sequences of characters which represent the same abstract character, and which when correctly displayed should always have the same visual appearance and behavior . . .*

> *Compatibility equivalence is a weaker type of equivalence between characters or sequences of characters which represent the same abstract character (or sequence of abstract characters), but which may have distinct visual appearances or behaviors. The visual appearances of the compatibility equivalent forms typically constitute a subset of the expected range of visual appearances of the character (or sequence of characters) they are equivalent to. However, these variant forms may represent a visual distinction that is significant in some textual contexts, but not in others. As a result, greater care is required to determine when use of a compatibility equivalent is appropriate. If the visual distinction is stylistic, then markup or styling could be used to represent the formatting information. However, some characters with compatibility decompositions are used in mathematical notation to represent a distinction of a semantic nature; replacing the use of distinct character codes by formatting in such contexts may cause problems . . .*

Unicode Standard Annex #15: Unicode Normalization Forms

The standard provides a good example of when the "compatibility" type can cause problems: the string "i^9". In mathematics, that's "i to the 9th power." But if you normalize that string using compatibility normalization, you get the string "i9"; the superscript "⁹" (U+2079) was turned into just the digit "9" (U+0039). In a mathematical context, those two strings mean *very* different things. The canonical (rather than compatibiity) type of normalization preserves the superscript nature of the code point.

`normalize` accepts an optional argument allowing you to control which form is used:

➤ **"NFD"** (**Normalization Form D**): Canonical Decomposition. In this form, the string is decomposed in a canonical way into its most discrete pieces. For instance, with "Français" using the c cédille code point, NFD would separate the c cédille into the separate "c" code point and the combining cédille code point. In a string with multiple combining code points affecting a single base, they'd be put in a canonical order.

➤ **"NFC"** (**Normalization Form C**): Canonical Composition. In this form (which is the default), the string is first decomposed in a canonical way (NFD), and then recomposed in a canonical way, using single code points where appropriate. For instance, this form combines a "c" followed by the combining cédille into the single "c cédille" code point.

➤ **"NFKD"** (**Normalization Form KD**): Compatibility Decomposition. In this form, the string is decomposed into its most discrete pieces using the "compatibility" type of normalization (the one that changed the superscript "⁹" into a plain "9").

➤ **"NFKC"** (**Normalization Form KC**): Compatibility Composition. In this form, the string is decomposed with the compatibility type of normalization, then recomposed with canonical composition.

The default if you don't provide one is `"NFC"`.

Depending on your use case, you might choose any of the four forms, but for many use cases, the default canonical composed form is likely to be your best choice. It maintains the full information of the string, while using canonical code points for combined forms that have them, like c cédille.

That's it for the Unicode changes. Let's look at other ways strings have improved . . .

ITERATION

You learned about iterables and iterators in Chapter 6. In ES2015 onward, strings are iterable. The iteration visits each code point (rather than each code unit) in the string. Run Listing 10-6.

LISTING 10-6: Simple string iteration example—simple-string-iteration-example.js

```
for (const ch of ">☺<") {
    console.log(`${ch} (${ch.length})`);
}
```

The output is:

```
> (1)
☺ (2)
< (1)
```

Remember that the smiley is a single code point, but requires two UTF-16 code units (JavaScript "characters"). So since `length` represents the length in code units, the second iteration outputs "☺ (2)".

One by-product of this is that, depending on your use case, you may decide to change how you normally convert a string to an array of characters. The idiomatic way before ES2015 was `str.split("")`, which will split the string into an array of code units. As of ES2015, you might choose to use `Array.from(str)` instead, which results in an array of code points (not code units). You'll learn about `Array.from` in Chapter 11, but briefly, it creates an array by looping through the iterable you pass it and adding each iterated value to the array. So using `Array.from` on a string splits it into an array of code points via the string iterator:

```
const charToHex = ch =>
    "0x" + ch.codePointAt(0).toString(16).toUpperCase().padStart(6, "0");
const show = array => {
    console.log(array.map(charToHex));
};

const str = ">☺<";
show(str.split(""));   // ["0x00003E", "0x00D83D", "0x00DE0A", "0x00003C"]
show(Array.from(str)); // ["0x00003E", "0x01F60A", "0x00003C"]
```

That said, while `Array.from(str)` may be better (for some definitions of "better") than `str.split("")` depending on your use case, it will still break up code points that combine to form a single human-perceived grapheme. Remember that Devanagari syllable "ni" (नि)? The one that requires two code points (a base and a diacritical mark) but is perceived as a single grapheme? Even splitting into code points will separate those. The Devanagari word for Devanagari, देवनागरी, has five perceived graphemes (दे व ना ग री), but even the `Array.from` approach results in an array of eight code points. A more sophisticated algorithm could use the Unicode information about which code points "extend" a grapheme (which is available in the Unicode database), but string iteration doesn't attempt that level of sophistication.

NEW STRING METHODS

ES2015 added a few handy utility methods to strings.

String.prototype.repeat

No prize for guessing what this does from the name!

That's right, `repeat` simply repeats the string you call it on a given number of times:

```
console.log("n".repeat(3)); // nnn
```

If you pass it 0 or NaN, you'll get back an empty string. If you pass it a value less than 0, or Infinity (positive or negative), you'll get an error.

String.prototype.startsWith, endsWith

`startsWith` and `endsWith` provide a simple way of checking whether a string starts with or ends with a substring (with an optional starting or ending index):

```
console.log("testing".startsWith("test")); // true
console.log("testing".endsWith("ing"));    // true
console.log("testing".endsWith("foo"));    // false
```

Both `startsWith` and `endsWith` return `true` if you pass in a blank substring (`"foo".startsWith("")`).

If you pass `startsWith` a starting index, it treats the string as though it started at that index:

```
console.log("now testing".startsWith("test"));    // false
console.log("now testing".startsWith("test", 4)); // true
// Index 4 ------^
```

If the index is equal to or greater than the length of the string, the result of the call will be `false` (if you pass in a non-blank substring) since there's nothing in the string at that point that could match.

If you pass `endsWith` an ending index, it treats the string as though it ended at that index:

```
console.log("now testing".endsWith("test"));    // false
console.log("now testing".endsWith("test", 8)); // true
// Index 8 ----------^
```

In that example, using the index 8 makes `endsWith` act as though the string were just `"now test"` instead of being `"now testing"`.

Passing in 0 means the result will be `false` (if you pass in a non-blank substring), since effectively the string you're looking in is blank.

The checks `startsWith` and `endsWith` do are always case-sensitive.

In ES2015–ES2020 (so far), `startsWith` and `endsWith` are required to throw an error if you pass them a regular expression rather than a string. That's to prevent implementations from providing their own additional behavior for regular expressions, so that later editions of the JavaScript specification can define the behavior.

String.prototype.includes

This is another one where the name pretty much tells you what you need to know. `includes` checks the string you call it on to see whether it includes the substring you pass in, optionally starting at a given location in the string:

```
console.log("testing".includes("test"));    // true
console.log("testing".includes("test", 1)); // false
```

The second call in this example returns `false` because it starts checking at index 1 of the string, and so skips the leading letter "t", as though you were just checking `"esting"` rather than `"testing"`.

If you pass in a blank substring to look for, the result will be `true`.

Like `startsWith` and `endsWith`, you'll get errors if you pass in a negative or infinite index, or if you pass in a regular expression rather than a string (so that future editions of the specification can define behavior for that).

String.prototype.padStart, padEnd

ES2017 added string padding to the standard library via `padStart` and `padEnd`:

```
const s = "example";
console.log(`|${s.padStart(10)}|`);
// => "|   example|"
console.log(`|${s.padEnd(10)}|`);
// => "|example   |"
```

You specify the total length of the string you want and, optionally, the string to use for padding (the default is a space). `padStart` returns a new string with any necessary padding at the start of the string so that the result is of the length you specified; `padEnd` pads the end instead.

Note that you specify the total length of the resulting string, not just the amount of padding you want. In the preceding example, since `"example"` has seven characters and the length used in the code earlier is `10`, three spaces of padding get added.

This example uses dashes instead:

```
const s = "example";
console.log(`|${s.padStart(10, "-")}|`);
// => "|---example|"
console.log(`|${s.padEnd(10, "-")}|`);
// => "|example---|"
```

The pad string can be more than one character long. It's repeated and/or truncated as necessary:

```
const s = "example";
console.log(`|${s.padStart(10, "-*")}|`);
// => "|-*-example|"
console.log(`|${s.padEnd(10, "-*")}|`);
// => "|example-*-|"
console.log(`|${s.padStart(14, "...oooOOO")}|`);
// => "|...oooOexample|"
```

You may be used to seeing "left" and "right" in this context, rather than "start" and "end." TC39 decided to use "start" and "end" to avoid confusion when strings are used in a right-to-left (RTL) language context, such as modern Hebrew and Arabic.

String.prototype.trimStart, trimEnd

ES2019 added `trimStart` and `trimEnd` to strings. `trimStart` trims whitespace from the start of the string, `trimEnd` from the end:

```
const s = "    testing    ";
const startTrimmed = s.trimStart();
const endTrimmed = s.trimEnd();
console.log(`|${startTrimmed}|`);
// => |testing    |
console.log(`|${endTrimmed}|`);
// => |    testing|
```

The history behind this addition is somewhat interesting: when ES2015 added `trim` to strings, most JavaScript engines (eventually all major ones) also added `trimLeft` and `trimRight` although they weren't in the specification. When standardizing that, TC39 made the decision to use the names `trimStart` and `trimEnd` rather than `trimLeft` and `trimRight` in order to be consistent with ES2017's `padStart` and `padEnd`. However, `trimLeft` and `trimRight` are listed as aliases for `trimStart` and `trimEnd` in Annex B (Additional ECMAScript Features for Web Browsers).

UPDATES TO THE MATCH, SPLIT, SEARCH, AND REPLACE METHODS

The JavaScript string methods `match`, `split`, `search`, and `replace` were all made more general in ES2015. Prior to ES2015, they were tied quite closely to regular expressions: `match` and `search` required a regular expression, or a string they could turn into one; `split` and `replace` used a regular expression if they were given one or coerced their argument to string if not.

As of ES2015, you can create your own objects to use with `match`, `search`, `split`, and `replace` and have those methods hand off to your object if it has a particular feature the methods look for: a method with a specific name. The names they look for are well-known Symbols (you learned about well-known Symbols in Chapter 5):

➤ `match`: Looks for `Symbol.match`

➤ `split`: Looks for `Symbol.split`

➤ `search`: Looks for `Symbol.search`

➤ `replace`: Looks for `Symbol.replace`

If the object you pass in has the relevant method, the string method calls it, passing in the string, and returns the result. That is, it defers to the method on your object.

Let's use `split` as an example. As of ES2015, String's `split` method conceptually looks like this (glossing over some minor details):

```
// In String.prototype
split(separator) {
    if (separator !== undefined && separator !== null) {
        if (separator[Symbol.split] !== undefined) {
            return separator[Symbol.split](this);
        }
    }
    const s = String(separator);
    const a = [];
    // ...split the string on `s`, adding to `a`...
    return a;
}
```

As you can see, `String.prototype.split` hands off to its parameter's `Symbol.split` method if it has one. Otherwise, it does what it's always done with a non-regular expression separator in the past. It still supports using a regular expression as a separator because regular expressions have the `Symbol.split` method now, so String's `split` defers to that.

Let's look at using `replace` with a different kind of search mechanism: one that looks for tokens in the form `{{token}}` in the string and replaces them with matching properties from an object. See Listing 10-7.

LISTING 10-7: Non-regex replacer—non-regex-replacer.js

```javascript
// Defining the token replacer with configurable token matching
class Replacer {
    constructor(rexTokenMatcher = /\{\{(([^}]+)\}\}/g) {
        this.rexTokenMatcher = rexTokenMatcher;
    }

    [Symbol.replace](str, replaceValue) {
        str = String(str);
        return str.replace(
            this.rexTokenMatcher,
            (_, token) => replaceValue[token] || ""
        );
    }
}
Replacer.default = new Replacer();

// Using the default token replacer with `replace`
const str = "Hello, my name is {{name}} and I'm {{age}}.";
const replaced = str.replace(Replacer.default, {
    name: "María Gonzales",
    age: 32
});
console.log(replaced); // "Hello, my name is María Gonzales and I'm 32."

// Using a custom token
const str2 = "Hello, my name is <name> and I'm <age>.";
const replacer = new Replacer(/<([^>]+)>/g) ;
const replaced2 = str2.replace(replacer, {
    name: "Joe Bloggs",
    age: 45
});
console.log(replaced2); // "Hello, my name is Joe Bloggs and I'm 45."
```

The key thing to observe running Listing 10-7 is that String's `replace` calls `Replacer`'s `Symbol.replace` method; it no longer just accepts `RegExp` instances or strings.

You could do something similar with `match`, `split`, or `search`.

OLD HABITS TO NEW

Here are some old habits you might consider updating.

Use Template Literals Instead of String Concatenation (Where Appropriate)

Old habit: Using string concatenation to build strings from in-scope variables:

```javascript
const formatUserName = user => {
    return user.firstName + " " + user.lastName + " (" + user.handle + ")";
};
```

New habit: It's probably a matter of style, but you can use a template literal instead:

```
const formatUserName = user => {
    return `${user.firstName} ${user.lastName} (${user.handle})`;
};
```

In fact, some people are considering the idea of always using template literals instead of string literals. It's not quite possible to do that *everywhere*, though, there are still a couple of places where only string literals are allowed. The big ones are quoted property names in object initializers (you could use a computed property name instead), module specifiers for static import/export (Chapter 13), and "use strict". But you can use template literals nearly anywhere else you've normally used a string literal in the past.

Use Tag Functions and Template Literals for DSLs Instead of Custom Placeholder Mechanisms

Old habit: Creating your own placeholder mechanisms when creating DSLs.

New habit: In situations where it makes sense, use tag functions and template literals, taking advantage of the substitution evaluation provided by the templates.

Use String Iterators

Old habit: Accessing characters in strings by index:

```
const str = "testing";
for (let i = 0; i < str.length; ++i) {
    console.log(str[i]);
}
```

New habit: If you want to treat the string as a series of *code points* rather than *code units*, consider using codePointAt or for-of or other Unicode-aware features:

```
const str = "testing";
for (const ch of str) {
    console.log(ch);
}
```

11

New Array Features, Typed Arrays

WHAT'S IN THIS CHAPTER?

➤ New array features

➤ Typed arrays

➤ `DataView` objects

> **CODE DOWNLOADS FOR THIS CHAPTER**
>
> You can download the code for this chapter at `https://thenewtoys.dev/bookcode` or `https://www.wiley.com/go/javascript-newtoys`.

In this chapter, you'll learn about many new features of arrays in ES2015+, including new features for traditional arrays and the new typed arrays.

Before getting into the meat of the chapter, a brief note about terminology: There are a couple of words used to refer to the contents of arrays, the two most popular being "elements" and "entries." Although "elements" is probably used slightly more often than "entries," I use "entries" in this book to avoid confusion with DOM elements and because it's the name of the method on arrays, `entries`, that you use to get an iterator for the entries in the array. But you'll very often hear "elements" instead, including in most parts of the JavaScript specification. "Element" is also used in one place in the standard API for typed arrays.

NEW ARRAY METHODS

ES2015 (primarily), ES2016, and ES2019 added a host of new array methods, both for creating arrays and for accessing and modifying their contents.

Array.of

Signature:

```
arrayObject = Array.of(value0[, value1[, ... ]])
```

`Array.of` creates and returns an array containing the values you pass to it as discrete arguments. For instance:

```
const a = Array.of("one", "two", "three");
console.log(a); // ["one", "two", "three"]
```

At first glance, this may seem unnecessary, since you could just use an array initializer:

```
const a = ["one", "two", "three"];
console.log(a); // ["one", "two", "three"]
```

But `Array.of` is useful for array *subclasses*, since they don't have a literal form:

```
class MyArray extends Array {
    niftyMethod() {
        // ...do something nifty...
    }
}
const a = MyArray.of("one", "two", "three");
console.log(a instanceof MyArray); // true
console.log(a); // ["one", "two", "three"]
```

You learned in Chapter 4 that the prototype of the `MyArray` function is the `Array` function. That means `MyArray.of` is inherited from `Array`. `Array.of` is smart enough look at the `this` it was called with and, if it's a constructor, to use that constructor to create the new array (if `this` isn't a constructor, `Array.of` defaults to using `Array`). So without your having to override `of`, `MyArray.of` creates an instance of `MyArray`.

Array.from

Signature:

```
arrayObject = Array.from(items[, mapFn[, thisArg]])
```

Like `Array.of`, `Array.from` creates an array based on the arguments you pass it. But instead of taking discrete values, it accepts any iterable or array-like[1] object as its first argument and builds an array using the values from that object, optionally applying a mapping function to them. If you give `Array.from` `null` or `undefined`, it'll throw an error; for nearly anything else that isn't iterable or array-like, it returns an empty array.

---

[1] An array-like object is any object with a `length` property whose "entries" are properties with names in the canonical string form of the integers in the range 0 through `length - 1`.

As you know from Chapter 10, strings are iterable, and so `Array.from` can create an array from the "characters" (Unicode code points) in the string:

```
const str = "123";
const a = Array.from(str);
console.log(a); // ["1", "2", "3"]
```

Here's an example of building an array from an *array-like* object:

```
const a = Array.from({length: 2, "0": "one", "1": "two"});
console.log(a); // ["one", "two"]
```

(The property names `"0"` and `"1"` could be written with numeric literals, but they end up as strings, so I've used strings for emphasis here.)

`Array.from` accepts an optional second argument, `mapFn`: a mapping function to apply to each value as it's being added to the array. For instance, if you wanted to take a string containing digits and get an array of the digits as numbers, you could pass a conversion function in as `mapFn`:

```
const str = "0123456789";
const a = Array.from(str, Number);
console.log(a); // [0, 1, 2, 3, 4, 5, 6, 7, 8, 9]
```

The mapping function's signature is `mapFn(value, index)`, where *value* is the value being mapped and *index* is the index that the new value will have in the resulting array. This is similar to the arguments an `Array.prototype.map` callback receives, but there are two differences between `from` (when mapping entries) and `map`:

➤ The `Array.from` mapping callback does not receive the third argument that `map` callbacks do: the source object being mapped. There was talk of including it, but it's not very useful when it's an iterable rather than an array or array-like object, since indexing into it wouldn't work, so the team doing `from` decided it was best not to include the source object.

➤ While `map` only calls its callback for entries that exist in the source array (skipping "missing" entries in sparse arrays), when dealing with an array-like object, `from` calls its callback for every index in the range `0` through `length - 1` (inclusive), even if there is no corresponding entry at that index.

Since the mapping function receives the index as the second argument, you need to be sure to avoid the classic `map` pitfall of passing in a function that accepts multiple parameters and may get confused by the second argument it receives. The classic example is using `parseInt` with `map`; that issue applies to `Array.from`'s mapping function as well:

```
const str = "987654321";
const a = Array.from(str, parseInt);
console.log(a); // [9, NaN, NaN, NaN, NaN, 4, 3, 2, 1]
```

`parseInt` accepts two parameters, the second being the radix to use (the number base—2 for binary, 10 for decimal, etc.). So it gets confused when `map` passes it the index as though it were a radix. The `NaN`s in that example are because `parseInt` was called either with an invalid radix parameter or a radix that the digit it was trying to parse didn't fit in (the first worked because `parseInt` ignores it if you pass a radix of 0). For instance, the second call failed because 1 is an invalid radix. The third call failed because 2 is a valid radix (binary), but the digit "7" is not valid in binary. As with `map`, the answer is to use an arrow function or some other means of ensuring that the callback only receives appropriate arguments. With `parseInt`, you usually want to be explicit with the radix anyway, so:

```
const str = "987654321";
const a = Array.from(str, digit => parseInt(digit, 10));
console.log(a); // [9, 8, 7, 6, 5, 4, 3, 2, 1]
```

Aside from creating arrays from iterables and array-likes, another use case for `Array.from` is building *range arrays*: arrays filled with numbers in a given range. For instance, to create an array with 100 entries with the values 0 through 99, you can use:

```
const a = Array.from({length: 100}, (_, index) => index);
// Or: const a = Array.from(Array(100), (_, index) => index);
console.log(a); // [0, 1, 2, 3, ... 99]
```

`{length: 100}` and `Array(100)` both create objects with a `length` property with the value `100` (the first is a plain object, the second is a sparse array). `Array.from` calls its mapping callback for each index in the range `0` through `99` (inclusive), passing in the value `undefined` for the first argument[2] and the index as the second. Since the callback returns the index, the resulting array contains the index values in its entries. You could generalize that into a `rangeArray` function:

```
function rangeArray(start, end, step = 1) {
    return Array.from(
        {length: Math.floor(Math.abs(end - start) / Math.abs(step))},
        (_, i) => start + (i * step)
    );
}

console.log(rangeArray(0, 5));      // [0, 1, 2, 3, 4]
console.log(rangeArray(6, 11));     // [6, 7, 8, 9, 10]
console.log(rangeArray(10, 20, 2)); // [10, 12, 14, 16, 18]
console.log(rangeArray(4, -1, -1)); // [4, 3, 2, 1, 0]
```

Last but not least, `Array.from` accepts a third parameter, `thisArg`, which determines the value of `this` in calls to `mapFn`. So if you had an object (`example`) with a method (`method`) and wanted to use that method as the callback, you could use:

```
const array = Array.from(Array(100), example.method, example);
```

to ensure that `this` within the call to `method` referred to the `example` object.

Array.prototype.keys

Signature:

```
keysIterator = theArray.keys()
```

---

[2] The code in the example receives that `undefined` argument as an `_` parameter. A single underscore is a valid identifier in JavaScript. It's often chosen as the name for a parameter that isn't used by the function.

The `keys` method returns an iterator for the keys of the array. The keys of an array are the numbers 0 through `length` - 1. Example:

```
const a = ["one", "two", "three"];
for (const index of a.keys()) {
    console.log(index);
}
```

That outputs 0, then 1, then 2.

There are a few things worth noting about the `keys` method:

➤ It returns an iterator, not an array.

➤ Even though the names of array entries are technically strings (because traditional arrays aren't really arrays, as you learned in Chapter 5's "Property Order" section), the values returned by the `keys` method's iterator are numbers.

➤ All of the index values in the range 0 <= n < `length` are returned by the iterator, even if the array is sparse.

➤ It does not include the names of enumerable properties that aren't array indexes, if the array has any.

Contrast those points with `Object.keys(someArray)`, which would return an array, include the indexes as strings, omit the indexes of entries that aren't present in a sparse array, and include names of other own (non-inherited) enumerable properties if the array has any.

Here's an example of a sparse array, and how the `keys` iterator includes the indexes for the gaps:

```
const a = [, "x", , , "y"];
for (const index of a.keys()) {
    console.log(index, index in a ? "present" : "absent");
}
```

The array a has no entry at indexes 0, 2, or 3; it only has entries at indexes 1 and 4. That code outputs the following:

```
0 "absent"
1 "present"
2 "absent"
3 "absent"
4 "present"
```

Array.prototype.values

Signature:

```
valuesIterator = theArray.values()
```

The `values` method is just like `keys`, but returns an iterator for the values in the array rather than the keys. It's the exact same iterator you get from the array itself. Example:

```
const a = ["one", "two", "three"];
for (const index of a.values()) {
    console.log(index);
}
```

That outputs `"one"`, then `"two"`, then `"three"`.

As with `keys`, which includes indexes for missing entries in sparse arrays, `values` includes the value `undefined` for missing entries in the array:

```
const a = [, "x", , , "y"];
for (const value of a.values()) {
    console.log(value);
}
```

That code outputs:

```
undefined
"x"
undefined
undefined
"y"
```

As a result, when you get `undefined` as a value from the `values` iterator, you don't know whether it means there was an entry with the value `undefined` in the array or a gap in a sparse array. If you need to know, you probably don't want to use the `values` method (you might want `entries`, though; see the next section).

Array.prototype.entries

Signature:

```
entriesIterator = theArray.entries()
```

The `entries` method is effectively a combination of the `keys` and `values` methods: it returns an iterator for the entries in the array, where each entry it provides is an `[index, value]` array. Example:

```
const a = ["one", "two", "three"];
for (const entry of a.entries()) {
    console.log(entry);
}
```

That outputs:

```
[0, "one"]
[1, "two"]
[2, "three"]
```

When looping through the entries from `entries`, it's common to use destructuring assignment (see Chapter 7) to get the index and value as discrete variables or constants:

```
const a = ["one", "two", "three"];
for (const [index, value] of a.entries()) {
    console.log(index, value);
}
```

Output:

```
0 "one"
1 "two"
2 "three"
```

As with `keys` and `values`, the iteration includes an entry even when the entry doesn't exist in the array because it's sparse; unlike with `values`, you can differentiate whether you're getting an undefined value because of a gap or an actual entry by checking if the key (`index`) exists in the array:

```
const a = [, undefined, , , "y"];
for (const [index, value] of a.entries()) {
    console.log(index, value, index in a ? "present" : "absent");
}
```

Output:

```
0 undefined "absent"
1 undefined "present"
2 undefined "absent"
3 undefined "absent"
4 "y" "present"
```

Notice that the second `undefined` is for an entry that exists, while all the others are for gaps.

If the consumer of the iterator doesn't have access to the original array, though, it's impossible for that consumer to know whether an `undefined` value in the `[index, value]` array is from a gap or actually from `undefined`. The `[index, value]` arrays from the `entries` method always have both the index and value, even for the sparse entries.

Array.prototype.copyWithin

Signature:

```
obj = theArray.copyWithin(target, start[, end])
```

The `copyWithin` method copies entries from one part of the array to another part of the array, handling any potential overlap issues and without increasing the length of the array. You specify the `target` index (where to put the copied entries), the `start` index (where to start copying), and optionally the `end` index (where to stop, exclusive; the default is the length of the array). It returns the array it was called on (loosely speaking, see the "The copyWithin Return Value" inset for the details). If any of the arguments is negative, it's used as an offset from the end of the array. For instance, a `start` of -2 in an array of length 6 is used as a `start` of 4 because 6 - 2 is 4. The `start` parameter is not defined as optional, but if you leave it off, its effective value will be 0 because of the way the specification handles interpreting `start`'s value.

THE COPYWITHIN RETURN VALUE

When describing `copyWithin`, I said it ". . . returns the array it was called on." That's not true, strictly speaking. It takes the `this` value it was called with, converts that to an object if it isn't one already, does its work, and then returns that object. In the normal case, you call it on an array, so `this` refers to that array and that array is returned. But if you used `call` or `apply` or similar to call it with `this` set to an array-like object, it would return that array-like object, not an array. If you called it with `this` set to a primitive, it would convert that primitive to an object and return that object (if it didn't throw an error because it couldn't do the copying you'd requested).

Here's an example copying entries later in the array to an earlier place within it:

```
const a = ["a", "b", "c", "d", "e", "f", "g", "h", "i", "j", "k"];
console.log("before", a);
a.copyWithin(2, 8);
console.log("after ", a);
```

That outputs:

```
before ["a", "b", "c", "d", "e", "f", "g", "h", "i", "j", "k"]
after  ["a", "b", "i", "j", "k", "f", "g", "h", "i", "j", "k"]
```

The call copied the entries starting at index 8 through the end of the array (`"i"`, `"j"`, `"k"`) within the array, writing them starting at index 2. See Figure 11-1.

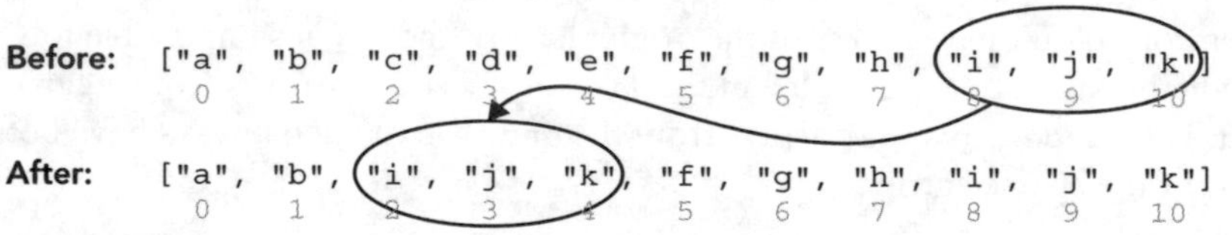

FIGURE 11-1

Note that it *overwrote* the previous entries at indexes 2-4 with the copies, it didn't *insert* the copies.

Here's an example copying earlier entries to a later location:

```
const a = ["a", "b", "c", "d", "e", "f", "g"];
console.log("before", a);
a.copyWithin(4, 2);
console.log("after ", a);
```

Output:

```
before ["a", "b", "c", "d", "e", "f", "g"]
after  ["a", "b", "c", "d", "c", "d", "e"]
```

See Figure 11-2.

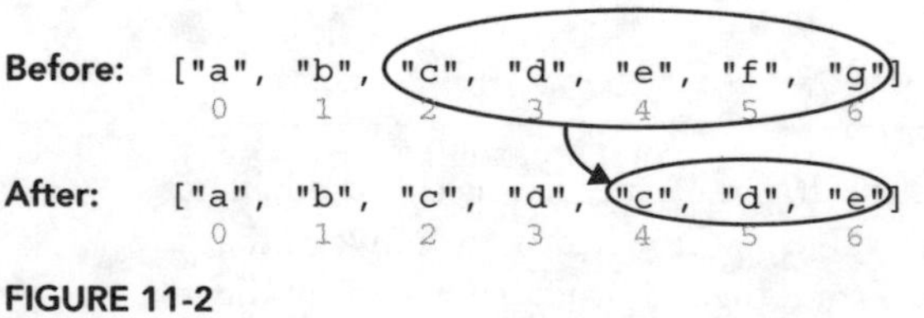

FIGURE 11-2

Two things to notice in that example:

➤ The copy isn't a naïve forward-moving `for` loop. If it were, the operation would have stepped on itself by copying `"c"` over `"e"` and later using that copied `"c"` for the last entry instead of (correctly) using `"e"`. Instead, `copyWithin` ensures that the entries being copied are as they were before the operation began.

➤ The copy stopped without extending the array. There's no end point (third argument) in the code, so the end point defaulted to the length of the array. The operation didn't copy `"f"` and `"g"` because doing so would have made the array longer. That's why in Figure 11-2, even though there are five source entries circled (because the call specified the entries at indexes 2 through 6), only three were copied before the method ran into the end of the array.

This may seem like a very specific operation—that's because it is. But it's a common operation in graphics applications. It's included in `Array` primarily because it's included in *typed arrays* (which you'll learn about later in this chapter), which are used for (among other things) graphics operations. TC39 made the decision to keep the API of arrays and typed arrays as similar as possible. Since typed arrays have a `copyWithin` method, arrays do too.

One interesting quirk of `copyWithin` that isn't down to typed arrays is how it handles sparse arrays (as you'll learn later, typed arrays are never sparse). `copyWithin` "copies" gaps, by deleting the entry at the location it would copy a missing entry to:

```
function arrayString(a) {
    return Array.from(a.keys(), key => {
        return key in a ? a[key] : "*gap*";
    }).join(", ");
}
const a = ["a", "b", "c", "d", , "f", "g"];
console.log("before", arrayString(a));
a.copyWithin(1, 3);
console.log("after ", arrayString(a));
```

Note the gap in that array, there's no entry at index 4 (`"e"` is missing). That outputs:

```
before a, b, c, d, *gap*, f, g
after  a, d, *gap*, f, g, f, g
```

The gap that existed at index 4 was copied to index 2 (and then the gap at index 4 was filled later when the value at index 6 was copied into it).

Array.prototype.find

Signature:

```
result = theArray.find(predicateFn[, thisArg])
```

The `find` method is for finding the value of the first matching entry in an array using a predicate function. It calls the predicate function for each entry in the array, optionally using the given `thisArg` as the `this` value for those calls, stopping and returning the value of the first entry for which the predicate returns a truthy value, or returning `undefined` if it runs out of entries. Example:

```
const a = [1, 2, 3, 4, 5, 6];
const firstEven = a.find(value => value % 2 == 0);
console.log(firstEven); // 2
```

The predicate function is called with three arguments (the same ones used with `forEach`, `map`, `some`, etc.): the value for that call, its index, and a reference to the object on which `find` was called (typically an array). `find` stops the first time the predicate returns a truthy value, not visiting subsequent entries in the array.

When you call `find` on an empty array it always returns `undefined`, since `find` runs out of entries before the predicate returns a truthy value (since the predicate is never called):

```
const x = [].find(value => true);
console.log(x);          // undefined
```

Modifying the array during the `find` operation is generally not best practice, but if you do so the results are well-defined: the range of entries that will be visited is determined before `find` starts its loop; the value that will be used for an entry is its value as of when the entry is visited (they aren't stored in advance). This means:

➤ If you add new entries at the end, they won't be visited.

➤ If you change an entry that's already been visited, it doesn't get visited again.

➤ If you change an entry that hasn't been visited yet, its *new* value is used when it's visited.

➤ If you remove entries from the array, reducing its length, the gaps at the end will be visited, with the usual value for gaps in arrays: `undefined`.

For instance, consider the following example:

```
const a = ["one", "two", "three"];
const x = a.find((value, index) => {
    console.log(`Visiting index ${index}: ${value}`);
    if (index === 0) {
        a[2] = a[2].toUpperCase();
    } else if (index === 1) {
        a.push("four");
    }
    return value === "four";
});
console.log(x);
```

That outputs:

```
Visiting index 0: one
Visiting index 1: two
Visiting index 2: THREE
undefined
```

You don't see the `"four"` entry get visited because it's outside the range of the entries that will be visited when `find` starts, but you do see `"THREE"` in uppercase, because it was changed before being visited. `find` returns `undefined` (as shown by the `console.log(x)` at the end) because the predicate never returned a truthy value, since the `"four"` entry was never visited.

Array.prototype.findIndex

Signature:

```
result = theArray.findIndex(predicateFn[, thisArg])
```

findIndex is exactly like find except that findIndex returns the *index* of the entry for which the predicate returned a truthy value, or -1 if it runs out of entries.

Example:

```
const a = [1, 2, 3, 4, 5, 6];
const firstEven = a.findIndex(value => value % 2 == 0);
console.log(firstEven); // 1 -- the first even value is the number 2 at index 1
```

Everything else is the same: the predicate function receives the same three arguments, the range of entries visited by findIndex is determined in advance, the values visited are as they are when they're visited (not stored in advance), if you reduce the length of the array gaps are visited at the end, and findIndex on an empty array always returns -1.

Array.prototype.fill

Signature:

```
obj = theArray.fill(value[, start[, end]])
```

The fill method fills the array (or array-like object) you call it on using the given value, optionally filling only the range defined by the start (default 0) and end (exclusive, default length) indexes. It returns the array it was called on (effectively; its return value is like copyWithin, see the inset earlier). If either start or end is negative, it's used as an offset from the end of the array.

Example:

```
const a = Array(5).fill(42);
console.log(a); // [42, 42, 42, 42, 42]
```

In that example, Array(5) returns a sparse array with length set to 5, but no entries; fill then fills the array with the given value (42).

Common Pitfall: Using an Object As the Fill Value

The value you provide is just that: a value. It ends up in the array very much as though you did this rather than calling Array.from:

```
const a = Array(5);
const value = 42;
for (let i = 0; i < a.length; ++i) {
    a[i] = value;
}
console.log(a); // [42, 42, 42, 42, 42]
```

Keeping that in mind, what do you think the following code outputs?

```
const a = Array(2).fill({});
a[0].name = "Joe";
a[1].name = "Bob";
console.log(a[0].name);
```

If you said `"Bob"`, nice one! `Array(2).fill({})` puts the *same* object in both entries in the array, it doesn't fill the array with a bunch of distinct objects. That means `a[0]` and `a[1]` both refer to the same object. `a[0].name = "Joe"` sets that object's name to `"Joe"`, but then `a[1].name = "Bob"` overwrites it with `"Bob"` instead.

If you want to put a distinct object in each array entry, `Array.fill` probably isn't the tool to pick; you'd use `Array.from`'s mapping callback:

```
const a = Array.from({length: 2}, () => ({}));
a[0].name = "Joe";
a[1].name = "Bob";
console.log(a[0].name); // Joe
```

But if you really wanted to use `Array.fill`, you'd fill the array first and then use `map`:

```
const a = Array(2).fill().map(() => ({}));
a[0].name = "Joe";
a[1].name = "Bob";
console.log(a[0].name); // Joe
```

You need the `fill` call there (which fills the array with `undefined`) because `map` doesn't visit entries that don't exist, and `Array(2)` creates an array with `length = 2` but with no entries in it.

Array.prototype.includes

Signature:

```
result = theArray.includes(value[, start])
```

The `includes` method (added in ES2016) returns `true` if the given value is present in the array according to the SameValueZero algorithm defined in the specification, or `false` if it isn't. Optionally, it starts the search at the provided `start` index if any; if `start` is negative, it's used as an offset from the end of the array.

Examples:

```
const a = ["one", "two", "three"];
console.log(a.includes("two"));      // true
console.log(a.includes("four"));     // false
console.log(a.includes("one", 2));   // false, "one" is before index 2
```

It's a common misconception that `includes(value)` is just a shorter way to write `indexOf(value) !== -1`, but that's not quite correct. `indexOf` uses the Strict Equality Comparison algorithm (like `===`) to check values, but SameValueZero (new in ES2015) differs from strict equality in how it treats NaN. With strict equality, NaN doesn't equal itself; with SameValueZero, it does:

```
const a = [NaN];
console.log(a.indexOf(NaN) !== -1); // false
console.log(a.includes(NaN));       // true
```

Other than NaN, SameValueZero is just like Strict Equality, which means that negative zero and positive zero are the same, so `[-0].includes(0)` returns `true`.

Array.prototype.flat

Added in ES2019, `flat` creates a new "flattened" array by taking each value from the original array and, if the value is an array, taking *its* values to put in the result rather than the array itself:

```
const original = [
    [1, 2, 3],
    4,
    5,
    [6, 7, 8]
];
const flattened = original.flat();
console.log(flattened);
// => [1, 2, 3, 4, 5, 6, 7, 8]
```

This mostly replaces a common idiom for flattening arrays using `concat`:

```
const flattened = [].concat.apply([], original);
// or
const flattened = Array.prototype.concat.apply([], original);
```

and is more efficient (though it usually doesn't matter), as it doesn't create and throw away temporary arrays. However, `flat` doesn't check `Symbol.isConcatSpreadable` (see Chapter 17), so if you have array-like objects with `Symbol.isConcatSpreadable` set to true, `concat` will spread them but `flat` won't; `flat` only spreads out actual arrays. (If you want that behavior, you can keep using concat, perhaps with spread notation: `const flattened = [].concat(...original);`.)

By default `flat` flattens only one level (like `concat`), so arrays nested beyond one level don't get flattened:

```
const original = [
    [1, 2, 3],
    [
        [4, 5, 6],
        [7, 8, 9]
    ]
];
const flattened = original.flat();
console.log(flattened);
// => [1, 2, 3, [4, 5, 6], [7, 8, 9]];
```

You can provide an optional *depth* argument to tell `flat` to do recursive flattening up to a given depth: 1 = just one level (the default), 2 = two levels, etc. You can use `Infinity` to completely flatten the structure regardless of how deep it is:

```
const original = [
    "a",
    [
        "b",
        "c",
        [
            "d",
```

```
            "e",
            [
                "f",
                "g",
                [
                    "h",
                    "i"
                ],
            ],
        ],
    ],
    "j"
];
const flattened = original.flat(Infinity);
console.log(flattened);
// => ["a", "b", "c", "d", "e", "f", "g", "h", "i", "j"]
```

Array.prototype.flatMap

Also added in ES2019, `flatMap` is just like `flat` except that it passes each value through a mapping function before flattening the result, and only flattens a single level:

```
const original = [1, 2, 3, 4];
const flattened = original.flatMap(e => e === 3 ? ["3a", "3b", "3c"] : e);
console.log(flattened);
// => [1, 2, "3a", "3b", "3c", 4]
```

The end result is exactly what you'd get by calling `map` and then calling `flat` on the result (with only one level of flattening, the default):

```
const original = [1, 2, 3, 4];
const flattened = original.map(e => e === 3 ? ["3a", "3b", "3c"] : e).flat();
console.log(flattened);
// => [1, 2, "3a", "3b", "3c", 4]
```

The only functional difference is that `flatMap` does it with just a single pass through the array rather than two.

ITERATION, SPREAD, DESTRUCTURING

In ES2015, arrays got some other features, which are covered elsewhere in the book:

➤ Arrays became iterable (see Chapter 6).

➤ Array literals can include spread notation (see Chapter 6).

➤ Arrays participate in destructuring (see Chapter 7.)

STABLE ARRAY SORT

Until ES2019, the sorting algorithm used by the `Array.prototype.sort` method was defined as "not necessarily stable," meaning that if two entries are considered equal, their relative positions in the resulting array might still get reversed. (This was also true of typed arrays like `Int32Array`.) As of ES2019, `sort` is required to implement a stable sort (both for normal and typed arrays).

For example, with the old definition, this code sorting an array ignoring case sensitivity:

```
const a = ["b", "B", "a", "A", "c", "C"];
a.sort((left, right) => left.toLowerCase().localeCompare(right.toLowerCase()));
console.log(a);
```

was allowed to produce any of several different possible results:

```
["a", "A", "b", "B", "c", "C"] - Equal entries weren't swapped (stable)
["A", "a", "B", "b", "C", "c"] - All equal entries were swapped (unstable)
["a", "A", "b", "B", "C", "c"] - Some equal entries were swapped (unstable)
["a", "A", "B", "b", "c", "C"] - "
["a", "A", "B", "b", "C", "c"] - "
["A", "a", "b", "B", "c", "C"] - "
["A", "a", "b", "B", "C", "c"] - "
["A", "a", "B", "b", "c", "C"] - "
```

As of ES2019, implementations are required to consistently produce only the first result: "a" must come before "A" (because it did before the sort), "b" before "B", and "c" before "C".

TYPED ARRAYS

In this section you'll learn about *typed arrays*: true arrays of primitive numeric values, added to JavaScript in ES2015.

Overview

JavaScript's traditional "arrays" famously aren't really arrays, in the usual computer science definition of a contiguous (all in a row) block of memory divided into fixed-size units. Instead, JavaScript's traditional arrays are just objects, like all other objects, with special handling around property names that fit the spec's definition of an "array index,"[3] a special length property, a literal notation using square brackets, and methods inherited from Array.prototype. That said, JavaScript engines are free to optimize where optimizing doesn't conflict with the spec (and they do).

JavaScript's traditional arrays are powerful and useful, but sometimes you need a real array (particularly when reading/writing files or interoperating with graphics or mathematics APIs). For that reason, ES2015 added true arrays to the language in the form of *typed arrays*.

Typed arrays are like traditional JavaScript arrays except:

➤ Their entry values are always primitive numeric values: 8-bit integers, 32-bit floats, etc.

➤ All of the values in a typed array are of the same type (which depends on the type of the array: Uint8Array, Float32Array, etc.).

➤ They're fixed-length: once you construct the array, you can't change its length.[4]

➤ Their values are stored in a contiguous memory buffer in a specified binary format.

---

[3] A string in canonical numeric form that converts to an integer in the range $0 <= n < 2^{32} - 1$.
[4] You'll learn about one *minor* caveat here in Chapter 16.

➤ Typed arrays cannot be *sparse* (they cannot have gaps in the middle), whereas traditional arrays can be. For instance, with a traditional array you can do this:

```
const a = [];
a[9] = "nine";
```

. . . and the array will have only *one* entry, at index 9, without having entries at indexes 0 through 8:

```
console.log(9 in a); // true
console.log(8 in a); // false
console.log(7 in a); // false (etc.)
```

That's not possible with a typed array.

➤ Typed arrays can share memory (their underlying data buffer) with other typed arrays, even of different types.

➤ The data buffer of a typed array can be *transferred* or even *shared* across threads (for instance, with web workers on a browser or worker threads in Node.js); you'll learn about this in Chapter 16.

➤ When getting or setting a typed array entry's value, there's always some form of conversion involved (other than when using numbers with a `Float64Array`, since JavaScript's numbers are `Float64s`).

Table 11-1 lists the eleven types of typed arrays (based on the table "The TypedArray Constructors" in the specification), giving the name of the type (which is also the global name of its constructor function), the conceptual name of its value type, how many bytes of memory an entry in that array takes, the abstract specification operation that converts values to the type, and a (brief) description.

TABLE 11-1: The Eleven Typed Arrays

NAME	VALUE TYPE	ENTRY SIZE	CONVERSION OPERATION	DESCRIPTION
`Int8Array`	Int8	1	ToInt8	8-bit two's complement signed integer
`Uint8Array`	Uint8	1	ToUint8	8-bit unsigned integer
`Uint8ClampedArray`	Uint8C	1	ToUint8Clamp	8-bit unsigned integer (clamped conversion)
`Int16Array`	Int16	2	ToInt16	16-bit two's complement signed integer
`Uint16Array`	Uint16	2	ToUint16	16-bit unsigned integer

NAME	VALUE TYPE	ENTRY SIZE	CONVERSION OPERATION	DESCRIPTION
Int32Array	Int32	4	ToInt32	32-bit two's complement signed integer
Uint32Array	Uint32	4	ToUint32	32-bit unsigned integer
Float32Array	Float32	4	See footnote[5]	32-bit IEEE-754 binary floating point
Float64Array	Float64/ "number"	8	(none needed)	64-bit IEEE-754 binary floating point
BigInt64Array	BigInt64	8	ToBigInt64	New in ES2020, see Chapter 17
BigUint64Array	BigUint64	8	ToBigUint64	New in ES2020, see Chapter 17

Typed arrays aren't just raw blocks of data with a pointer to them, though: as with traditional arrays, they're objects. All the usual object operations work with typed arrays. They have prototypes, methods, and a `length` property; you can put non-entry properties on them just like you can traditional JavaScript arrays; they're iterable; and so on.

Let's look at them in action.

Basic Use

Typed arrays don't have a literal form. You can create a typed array by calling its constructor or using its constructor's `of` or `from` methods.

The constructors for each kind of typed array (`Int8Array`, `Uint32Array`, etc.) all have the same available forms. Here's a list using `%TypedArray%` as a placeholder for the various specific types (`Int8Array`, etc.), like the specification does:

➤ *new %TypedArray%()*: Creates an array with `length` set to 0.

➤ *new %TypedArray%(length)*: Creates an array with `length` entries, each entry initially set to all-bits-off (zero).

➤ *new %TypedArray%(object)*: Creates an array by copying values from the given object by using the object's iterator, if it has one, or by treating it as *array-like* and using its `length` and array index properties to read its contents.

➤ *new %TypedArray%(typedArray)*: Creates an array by copying values from the given typed array. This doesn't go through the typed array's iterator; it works directly with the

---

[5] Numbers are converted to Float32 using the IEEE-754-2008 specification's rules for converting 64-bit binary values to 32-bit binary values using the "round to nearest, ties to even" rounding mode.

underlying buffers for efficiency. (When the types of the arrays are the same, this can be an extremely efficient memory copy.)

➤ `new %TypedArray%(buffer[, start[, length]])`: Creates an array using the given buffer (this is covered in a later section on `ArrayBuffer`).

If you construct an array by providing a length, the entry values are set to all-bits-off, which is the value 0 for all of the kinds of typed arrays:

```
const a1 = new Int8Array(3);
console.log(a1); // Int8Array(3): [0, 0, 0]
```

When you assign values to a typed array's entries (during construction by providing an object or other typed array, or afterward), the JavaScript engine passes them through the conversion function listed in Table 11-1. Here's an example of doing so after construction:

```
const a1 = new Int8Array(3);
a1[0] = 1;
a1[1] = "2"; // Note the string
a1[2] = 3;
console.log(a1); // Int8Array(3): [1, 2, 3] - note 2 is a number
```

In this example, all three values were converted, but it's most obvious with the value `"2"`, which was converted from a string to an 8-bit integer. (`1` and `3` were also converted, at least in theory, from the JavaScript standard number type—IEEE-754 double-precision binary floating point—to 8-bit integers.)

Similarly, here are examples using `of` and `from`:

```
// Using `of`:
const a2 = Int8Array.of(1, 2, "3");
console.log(a2); // Int8Array(3): [1, 2, 3] - "3" was converted to 3
// Using `from` with an array-like object:
const a3 = Int8Array.from({length: 3, 0: 1, 1: "2"});
console.log(a3); // Int8Array(3): [1, 2, 0] - undefined was converted to 0
// Using `from` with an array:
const a4 = Int8Array.from([1, 2, 3]);
console.log(a4); // Int8Array(3): [1, 2, 3]
```

In the example using `a3`, since there's no value for the `"2"` property in the array-like object even though the length of the array-like object is 3, the `from` method gets `undefined` when it gets the `"2"` property, then converts it to `0` using the conversion operation for `Int8Array`. (And again, all of those values were converted in theory, but it's most obvious with the string and `undefined`.)

In a moment you'll see a more complex example after learning about `ArrayBuffer`s; first, let's briefly look at value conversions in more detail.

Value Conversion Details

Let's look at value conversion in more detail.

The conversion operations performed when assigning values to array entries always result in a value, rather than throwing an exception if the value provided cannot be converted. For instance, assigning the string `"foo"` to an entry in an `Int8Array` sets that entry's value to `0` rather than throwing an error. In this section, you'll learn how the conversion gets done.

For floating-point arrays, it's fairly straightforward:

1. When assigning to a `Float64` entry, the value is first converted to a standard JavaScript number if necessary in the usual way, and then stored as-is, since standard JavaScript numbers are `Float64` values.

2. When assigning to a `Float32` entry, the value is first converted to a standard JavaScript number if necessary and then converted to `Float32` using the IEEE-754-2008 specification's "round to nearest, ties to even" rounding mode.

When assigning to integer-typed entries, it's more complicated:

1. The input value is converted to a standard JavaScript number if it isn't one already.

2. If the result of Step 1 is `NaN`, positive or negative `0`, or negative infinity, the value `0` is used and the following steps are skipped. If the result of Step 1 is positive infinity, the value `0` is used unless the array is a `Uint8ClampedArray` in which case the value `255` is used; in both cases, the following steps are skipped.

3. Fractional values are truncated toward zero.

4. If the array is a `Uint8ClampedArray`, a range check is used to determine the entry value:

    a) If the value from Step 3 is less than `0`, `0` is used; if it's greater than `255`, `255` is used.

    b) Otherwise, the value is used as-is.

5. Otherwise (the array is unclamped):

    a) A *modulo* operation (not *remainder*, see the "Modulo vs. Remainder" inset) using 2^n as the divisor is used to ensure the value is in the overall unsigned range for the size of the integer entry (where n is the number of bits, for example 2^8 with an `Int8Array`).

    b) For arrays with signed entries, if the value resulting from the *modulo* operation (which is always zero or positive, since 2^n is positive) is outside the positive range of the entry, 2^n is subtracted from it and the result is used.

MODULO VS. REMAINDER

Typed array integer value conversion uses a *modulo* operation at one stage. This is not the same operation as the *remainder operator* (`%`), despite the operator commonly—but incorrectly—being called the "modulo operator." Modulo and remainder are the same operation when both operands are positive, but they can differ otherwise, depending on which flavor of *modulo* you use.

The spec defines its abstract *modulo* operation like this:

> The notation "x modulo y" (y must be finite and nonzero) computes a value k of the same sign as y *(or zero)* such that `abs(k) < abs(y)` and `x - k = q × y` for some integer q.

> Since the modulo operations used in relation to typed array values always use a positive number for y (for instance, $y = 2^8$, which is 256, for a Uint8Array), the result of those operations will always be positive numbers within the full *unsigned* range of possible values for the size of the entry. For signed arrays, a subsequent operation converts values that are beyond the positive range of the type into negative numbers.

For example, assigning to an entry in an Int8Array, the number 25.4 becomes 25, -25.4 becomes -25:

```
const a = new Int8Array(1);
a[0] = 25.4;
console.log(a[0]); // 25
a[0] = -25.4;
console.log(a[0]); // -25
```

For the unsigned types (other than Uint8ClampedArray), conversion of negative values may seem surprising. Consider:

```
const a = new Uint8Array(1);
a[0] = -25.4;
console.log(a[0]); // 231
```

How did -25.4 become 231?!

The first parts are easy: -25.4 is already a number so you don't have to convert it to one, and when you truncate it toward zero, you get -25. Now it's time for that modulo operation (see the inset earlier). One way to compute that modulo is the following code snippet, where value is the value (-25) and max is 2^n (2^8, which is 256, in this 8-bit example):

```
const value = -25;
const max = 256;
const negative = value < 0;
const remainder = Math.abs(value) % max;
const result = negative ? max - remainder : remainder;
```

If you follow that through, you end up with 231. But there's another more direct way to get there: the *signed* 8-bit integer value -25, in the two's complement form used with signed values in typed arrays, has the same bit pattern as the *unsigned* 8-bit integer value 231. The pattern is 11100111 in both cases. The specification just uses mathematics rather than bit patterns to get there.

ArrayBuffer: The Storage Used by Typed Arrays

All typed arrays use an ArrayBuffer for the storage of their values. An ArrayBuffer is an object with an associated contiguous data block of a fixed size, given in bytes. Typed arrays read and write data in their ArrayBuffer's data block according to the type of data the array provides: an Int8Array accesses bytes in the buffer and uses the bits as signed (two's complement) 8-bit integers; a Uint16Array accesses pairs of bytes in the buffer, using them as unsigned 16-bit integers; etc. You can't directly access the data in the buffer, you can only access it through a typed array or a DataView (which you'll learn about in a bit).

The code in the earlier examples created typed arrays directly, without explicitly creating an `Array-Buffer`. When you do that, a buffer of the appropriate size is created for you. So, for instance, `new Int8Array(5)` creates a five-byte buffer; `new Uint32Array(5)` creates a 20-byte buffer (since each of the five entries takes four bytes of storage).

You can access the buffer attached to a typed array via the array's `buffer` property:

```
const a = new Int32Array(5);
console.log(a.buffer.byteLength); // 20 (bytes)
console.log(a.length);            // 5 (entries, each taking four bytes)
```

You can also create the `ArrayBuffer` explicitly, then pass it to the typed array constructor when creating the array:

```
const buf = new ArrayBuffer(20);
const a = new Int32Array(buf);
console.log(buf.byteLength);      // 20 (bytes)
console.log(a.length);            // 5 (entries, each taking four bytes)
```

The size you give the `ArrayBuffer` constructor is in bytes.

If you try to use a buffer that isn't the right size for the typed array you're creating, you get an error:

```
const buf = new ArrayBuffer(18);
const a = new Int32Array(buf); // RangeError: byte length of Int32Array
                               // should be a multiple of 4
```

(Later in this chapter you'll see how to use only part of a buffer.)

To help you create buffers of the right size, typed array constructors have a property you can use when creating the buffer: `BYTES_PER_ELEMENT`.[6] So to create a buffer for a five-entry `Int32Array`, you'd do this:

```
const buf = new ArrayBuffer(Int32Array.BYTES_PER_ELEMENT * 5);
```

You'd only do that if you had some reason for creating the buffer separately; otherwise you'd just call the typed array constructor and use the resulting array's `buffer` property if you needed access to the buffer.

Now that you've seen `ArrayBuffer`, let's look at a more real-world example of using typed arrays: reading a file in a web browser and checking to see if it's a Portable Network Graphics (PNG) file. See Listing 11-1. You can run that locally using the code from Listing 11-1 (`read-file-as-array-buffer.js`) along with `read-file-as-arraybuffer.html`, both available in the downloads for the chapter.

LISTING 11-1: Reading a local file and checking if it's a PNG—read-file-as-arraybuffer.js

```
const PNG_HEADER = Uint8Array.of(0x89, 0x50, 0x4E, 0x47, 0x0D, 0x0A, 0x1A, 0x0A);
function isPNG(byteData) {
    return byteData.length >= PNG_HEADER.length &&
           PNG_HEADER.every((b, i) => b === byteData[i]);
```

continues

---

[6] Remember I said at the beginning of this chapter that "element" is used in one place in the JavaScript standard library in relation to typed arrays? This is that place, the name of this property.

LISTING 11-1 *(continued)*

```
    }
    function show(msg) {
        const p = document.createElement("p");
        p.appendChild(document.createTextNode(msg));
        document.body.appendChild(p);
    }
    document.getElementById("file-input").addEventListener(
        "change",
        function(event) {
            const file = this.files[0];
            if (!file) {
                return;
            }
            const fr = new FileReader();
            fr.readAsArrayBuffer(file);
            fr.onload = () => {
                const byteData = new Uint8Array(fr.result);
                show(`${file.name} ${isPNG(byteData) ? "is" : "is not"} a PNG file.`);
            };
            fr.onerror = error => {
                show(`File read failed: ${error}`);
            };
        }
    );
```

PNG files start with a specific 8-byte header. The code in Listing 11-1 responds to a user choosing a file in the `type="file"` input by using the File API's `FileReader` object to read it as an `ArrayBuffer` (accessible via the `FileReader`'s `result` property), and then checking for that 8-byte header on the raw data received. Since the code in this example works with unsigned bytes, it uses a `Uint8Array` backed by the buffer from the `FileReader`.

Notice that `FileReader` is agnostic: it just provides the `ArrayBuffer`, leaving it to the code using the buffer to decide whether to access it byte-by-byte (as in the example in Listing 11-1) or in 16-bit words, or 32-bit words, or even a combination of those. (Later you'll see how a single `ArrayBuffer` can be used by multiple typed arrays so you can access one section using, say, `Uint8Array`, but another section using, say, `Uint32Array`.)

Endianness (Byte Order)

`ArrayBuffers` store bytes. Most typed arrays have entries that take multiple bytes of storage. For instance, each entry in a `Uint16Array` requires two bytes of storage: a *high-order byte* (or "high byte") containing multiples of 256 and a *low-order byte* (or "low byte") containing multiples of 1, kind of like the "tens column" and the "ones column" in the base 10 counting system most of us use. In the value 258 (0x0102 in hexadecimal), the high-order byte contains 0x01 and the low-order byte contains 0x02. To get the value, you take the high-order byte's value, multiply by 256, and add in the low-order byte's value: 1 * 256 + 2 is 258.

So far so good, but: what order should the bytes be in, in memory? Should the high byte come first, or the low byte? There's no one answer; both ways are used. If the value is stored in high byte/low byte order, it's in *big-endian* order (the big end—the high byte—is first). If the value is stored in low byte/high byte order, it's in *little-endian* order (the little end—the low byte—is first). See Figure 11-3.

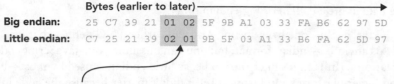

The value 0x0102 (258 in decimal) in context, in both big-endian and little-endian order

FIGURE 11-3

You're probably wondering: if both are used, what determines which is used when? There are two fundamental answers to that:

➤ The machine's computer architecture (in particular the CPU architecture) typically determines the endianness of values in memory on that system. If you tell the computer to store 0x0102 at a particular memory address, the CPU will write that value using its intrinsic endianness. The x86 architecture used by Intel's and AMD's mainstream CPUs is little-endian, and so the vast majority of desktop computers use little-endian order. The PowerPC architecture, used by older Macintosh computers before Apple switched to x86, is natively big-endian, though it has a mode switch that can make it little-endian instead.

➤ File formats, network protocols, etc., need to specify endianness to ensure they're correctly handled across different architectures. In some cases, the format dictates the endianness: the Portable Network Graphics (PNG) image format uses big-endian, as does the Transmission Control Protocol (the TCP in TCP/IP) for integers in headers, such as port numbers. (In fact, big-endian is sometimes called "network byte order.") In other cases, the format or protocol allows for specifying the endianness of the data within the data itself: the Tagged Image File Format (TIFF) starts with two bytes, which are either the characters II (for "Intel" byte order, little-endian) or MM (for "Motorola" byte order, big-endian) because when the format was being developed in the 1980s, Intel CPUs used little-endian and Motorola CPUs used big-endian. The multiple byte values stored in the file use the order defined by that initial tag.

Typed arrays use the endianness of the computer on which they're being used. The rationale for that is that typed arrays are used to work with native APIs (such as WebGL), and so the data sent to the native API should be in the machine's native endianness. Your code writing the data writes to your typed array (for example, a Uint16Array, Uint32Array, or similar), and the typed array writes to the ArrayBuffer in the endianness of the machine where the code is running; your code doesn't have to worry about it. When you pass that ArrayBuffer to the native API, it will use the native endianness of the platform on which the code is running.

That doesn't mean you never have to worry about endianness, though. When you read a file (like a PNG) or network data stream (like a TCP packet) that's defined as being in a specific order (big-endian or little-endian), you can't assume that order is the same as the platform your code is running on, which means you can't use a typed array to access it. You need another tool: DataView.

DataView: Raw Access to the Buffer

`DataView` objects provide raw access to the data in an `ArrayBuffer`, with methods to read that data in any of the numeric forms provided by typed arrays (Int8, Uint8, Int16, Uint16, etc.), with the option of reading multi-byte data in little-endian or big-endian order.

Suppose you're reading a PNG file, as the code from Listing 11-1 did earlier. PNG defines that its various multi-byte integer fields are in big-endian format, but you can't assume your JavaScript code is running on a big-endian platform. (In fact, it's likely not to be, as little-endian is used by most—but not all—desktop, mobile, and server platforms.) In Listing 11-1 it didn't matter because the code just checked to see if the file was a PNG by checking an eight-byte signature one byte at a time. It didn't involve any multi-byte numbers. But suppose you want to get the dimensions of the PNG image? That requires reading big-endian Uint32 values.

That's where `DataView` comes in. You can use it to read values from an `ArrayBuffer` while being explicit about endianness. You'll see some code in a moment, but first a very brief note about the PNG file format.

You saw in Listing 11-1 that a PNG file starts with an 8-byte signature that doesn't vary. After that, a PNG is a series of "chunks," where each chunk is in this format:

➤ *length*: The length of the data segment of the chunk (Uint32, big-endian)

➤ *type*: The chunk's type (four characters from a restricted character set,[7] one byte per character, although the specification encourages implementations to treat them as binary data, not characters)

➤ *data*: The chunk's data, if any (*length* bytes, format varies depending on the chunk type)

➤ *crc*: The chunk's CRC value (Uint32, big-endian)

The PNG specification also requires that the first chunk (immediately after the 8-byte header) must be an "image header" ("IHDR") chunk providing basic information about the image, such as its width and height in pixels, its color depth, etc. The width is the first Uint32 in the chunk's data area; the height is the second Uint32. Both, again, in big-endian order.

Suppose you wanted to get the width and height of the PNG from the `ArrayBuffer` provided by a `FileReader`. You might first check that the 8-byte PNG header is correct, and perhaps also that the first chunk's type is indeed IHDR; then provided those are both correct, you know that the width is the Uint32 at byte offset 16 in the data (the first 8 bytes are the PNG header, the next 4 are the length of the IHDR chunk, and the next 4 are the type of the IHDR chunk; 8 + 4 + 4 = 16) and that the height is the next Uint32 after that (at byte offset 20). You can read those Uint32 values in big-endian format, even on little-endian machines, using `DataView`'s `getUint32` method:

```
const PNG_HEADER_1 = 0x89504E47; // Big-endian first Uint32 of PNG header
const PNG_HEADER_2 = 0x0D0A1A0A; // Big-endian second Uint32 of PNG header
const TYPE_IHDR = 0x49484452;    // Big-endian type of IHDR chunk
// ...
```

---

[7] The allowed chunk name characters are a subset of ISO 646, specifically the letters A–Z and a–z. These are consistent across all variants of ISO 646 (and are the same as ASCII and Unicode).

```
        fr.onload = () => {
            const dv = new DataView(fr.result);
            if (dv.byteLength >= 24 &&
                dv.getUint32(0) === PNG_HEADER_1 &&
                dv.getUint32(4) === PNG_HEADER_2 &&
                dv.getUint32(12) === TYPE_IHDR) {
                const width = dv.getUint32(16);
                const height = dv.getUint32(20);
                show(`${file.name} is ${width} by ${height} pixels`);
            } else {
                show(`${file.name} is not a PNG file.`);
            }
        };
```

(The downloads contain a runnable version of this in `read-png-info.html` and `read-png-info.js`; there's a PNG called `sample.png`.)

`getUint32` accepts an optional second parameter, `littleEndian`, which you can set to `true` to read the value in little-endian format instead. The default if it's not supplied (as in this example) is big-endian.

If that code had used a `Uint32Array` instead, it would have used the endianness of the platform. If that didn't happen to be big-endian (and again, most systems are little-endian), the code checking the PNG header and IHDR chunk type would fail. (See the downloads for `read-png-info-incorrect.html` and `read-png-info-incorrect.js`.) Even if you updated the header and type checks to use bytes instead, and only used the `Uint32Array` for reading the width and height, on a little-endian platform you'd get wildly incorrect values for them (try `read-png-info-incorrect2.html` and `read-png-info-incorrect2.js`). For instance, with `sample.png`, you'd get "sample.png is 3355443200 by 1677721600 pixels" instead of "sample.png is 200 by 100 pixels."

Sharing an ArrayBuffer Between Arrays

An `ArrayBuffer` can be shared between multiple typed arrays, in two ways:

➤   Without overlap: Each array using only its own part of the buffer

➤   With overlap: Arrays sharing the same part of the buffer

Sharing Without Overlap

Listing 11-2 shows a `Uint8Array` using the first part of an `ArrayBuffer` while a `Uint16Array` uses the rest of it.

LISTING 11-2: Sharing ArrayBuffer without overlapping—sharing-arraybuffer-without-overlap.js

```
const buf = new ArrayBuffer(20);
const bytes = new Uint8Array(buf, 0, 8);
const words = new Uint16Array(buf, 8);
console.log(buf.byteLength); // 20 (20 bytes)
console.log(bytes.length);   // 8 (eight bytes)
console.log(words.length);   // 6 (six two-byte [16 bit] words = 12 bytes)
```

You might do something like this if you were given a buffer with data you needed to access, and you needed to access the first part as unsigned bytes, but the second part as unsigned 16-bit words (in the platform-specific endianness).

In order to use only part of the buffer, the code uses the final constructor signature mentioned (but not described) earlier:

```
new %TypedArray%(buffer[, start[, length]])
```

Those parameters are:

➤ *buffer*: The `ArrayBuffer` to use

➤ *start*: The offset (in bytes) from the beginning of the buffer at which to start using it; the default is 0 (start at the beginning)

➤ *length*: The length for the new typed array in entries (not bytes); the default is however many entries will fit in the remainder of the `ArrayBuffer`

When creating the `Uint8Array` with the code new `Uint8Array(buf, 0, 8)`, the 0 says to start at the beginning of the `ArrayBuffer`, and the 8 says to make the `Uint8Array` eight entries long. When creating the `Uint16Array` with new `Uint16Array(buf, 8)`, the 8 says to start at byte offset 8 and by leaving off the `length` argument, it says to use the rest of the `ArrayBuffer`. You can find out what part of the buffer the arrays are using by looking at their `byteOffset` and `byteLength` properties:

```
console.log(bytes.byteOffset); // 0
console.log(bytes.byteLength); // 8
console.log(words.byteOffset); // 8
console.log(words.byteLength); // 12
```

Keeping in mind that the third argument is a count of *entries*, not bytes, what would you use as the third argument to the `Uint16Array` constructor if you wanted to supply it explicitly without changing what the code does?

If you said 6, good job! The length is always in entries, not bytes. It's tempting to say 12 (the number of bytes to use) or (if it weren't for the name "length") 20 (the offset of the end of the part of the buffer you want to use), but `length` always being the number of *entries* is consistent with the `%TypedArray%(length)` constructor.

Sharing with Overlap

Listing 11-3 shows two arrays, a `Uint8Array` and a `Uint16Array` sharing the same `ArrayBuffer` (all of it).

LISTING 11-3: Sharing ArrayBuffer with overlap—sharing-arraybuffer-with-overlap.js

```
const buf = new ArrayBuffer(12);
const bytes = new Uint8Array(buf);
const words = new Uint16Array(buf);
console.log(words[0]); // 0
bytes[0] = 1;
bytes[1] = 1;
```

```
console.log(bytes[0]); // 1
console.log(bytes[1]); // 1
console.log(words[0]); // 257
```

Note that `words[0]` starts out being 0, but after we assign 1 to `bytes[0]` and also to `bytes[1]`, `words[0]` becomes 257 (0x0101 in hexadecimal). That's because the two arrays are using the same underlying storage (the `ArrayBuffer`). So by writing 1 to `byte[0]` and also to `byte[1]`, we wrote a 1 to *both* bytes that make up the single `words[0]` entry. As discussed earlier in the "Endianness (Byte Order)" section, one of those is a *high-order* byte and the other a *low-order* byte. By putting the value 1 in both of them, we get the 16-bit value `1 * 256 + 1`, which is 257 (0x0101). So that's the value you get from `words[0]`.

Suppose you changed the code so that instead of assigning 1 to `bytes[1]`, you assigned 2. What value would you get in `words[0]`?

If you said "It depends," nice one! You'd probably get 513 (0x0201) because you're probably running the code on a little-endian platform and so `bytes[1]` is the big end (the high byte), so the result is `2 * 256 + 1 = 513`. But if you're using a little-endian platform, you'd get 258 (0x0102) because `bytes[1]` is the low end (the low byte), so the result is `1 * 256 + 2 = 258`.

Subclassing Typed Arrays

You can subclass typed arrays (perhaps so you have your own custom methods) in the usual ways: `class` syntax or using a function with `Reflect.construct` (you'll learn about `Reflect` in Chapter 14). It's probably only really useful for adding further utility methods. In general, it's probably best to include a typed array in a class via aggregation (as a field the class uses behind the scenes) rather than via inheritance.

If you do subclass a typed array class, note the restrictions on `map` and `filter` discussed in the following "Standard Array Methods" section.

Typed Array Methods

Typed arrays have most of the usual array methods, though not all, and a couple of methods specific to typed arrays.

Standard Array Methods

Typed arrays implement most of the same methods as traditional arrays using the same algorithms, in some cases with some slight tweaking discussed in this section.

However, since typed arrays are fixed-length, they don't have any of the methods that would (potentially) involve changing the length of the array: `pop`, `push`, `shift`, `unshift`, or `splice`.

Typed arrays also don't have `flat`, `flatMap`, or `concat`. `flat` and `flatMap` don't make sense for typed arrays, since typed arrays cannot contain nested arrays. Similarly, the flattening behavior of `concat` doesn't apply to typed arrays, and `concat`'s other operations can be implemented using `of` and spread notation (since typed arrays are iterable):

```
const a1 = Uint8Array.from([1, 2, 3]);
const a2 = Uint8Array.from([4, 5, 6]);
```

```
const a3 = Uint8Array.from([7, 8, 9]);
const all = Uint8Array.of(...a1, ...a2, ...a3);
console.log(all); // Uint8Array [ 1, 2, 3, 4, 5, 6, 7, 8, 9 ]
```

Prototype methods that create new arrays (such as `filter`, `map`, and `slice`) create arrays of the same type as the typed array you call them on. For `filter` and `slice`, that's probably not going to lead to any surprises, but it can for `map`. For example:

```
const a1 = Uint8Array.of(50, 100, 150, 200);
const a2 = a1.map(v => v * 2);
console.log(a2); // Uint8Array [ 100, 200, 44, 144 ]
```

Notice what happened to the last two entries: their values wrapped, because the new array is also a `Uint8Array` and so it can't hold the values 300 (150 * 2) or 400 (200 * 2).

The implementations of `map`, `filter`, and `slice` on typed arrays have another restriction: if you subclass a typed array, you can't use `Symbol.species` (see Chapter 4) to make methods like `map` and `slice` create non-typed arrays. For instance, this won't work:

```
class ByteArray extends Uint8Array {
    static get [Symbol.species]() {
        return Array;
    }
}
const a = ByteArray.of(3, 2, 1);
console.log(a.map(v => v * 2));
// => TypeError: Method %TypedArray%.prototype.map called on
//    incompatible receiver [object Array]
```

You could have them create a different *kind* of typed array (odd though that would be), but not a non-typed array. If you wanted to have a subclass that did that, you'd need to override the methods in the subclass. For instance:

```
class ByteArray extends Uint8Array {
    static get [Symbol.species]() {
        return Array;
    }
    map(fn, thisArg) {
        const ctor = this.constructor[Symbol.species];
        return ctor.from(this).map(fn, thisArg);
    }
    // ...and similar for `filter`, `slice`, and `subarray`
}
const a = ByteArray.of(3, 2, 1);
console.log(a.map(v => v * 2)); // [ 6, 4, 2 ]
```

%TypedArray%.prototype.set

Signature:

```
theTypedArray.set(array[, offset])
```

`set` sets multiple values in the typed array from the "array" you provide (which can be either a typed array, a non-typed array, or an array-like object—though not just an iterable), optionally starting writing at a given offset (given in entries, not bytes) within the typed array. `set` always copies the entire array you provide (there aren't any parameters for selecting a range within the source array).

You could use `set` to combine multiple typed arrays:

```
const all = new Uint8Array(a1.length + a2.length + a3.length);
all.set(a1);
all.set(a2, a1.length);
all.set(a3, a1.length + a2.length);
```

Note how the second set starts writing just after the last entry written by the first, and the third just after the last entry written by the second.

Note that `set` specifically requires an array, typed array, or array-like object. It doesn't handle iterables. To use an iterable with `set`, spread it into an array first (or use the `from` method of an appropriate array or typed array constructor, etc.).

%TypedArray%.prototype.subarray

Signature:

```
newArray = theTypedArray.subarray(begin, end)
```

`subarray` creates a new typed array for a subset of the array you call it on that *shares* the original array's buffer (that is, the arrays share the same data).

➤   `begin` is the index of the first entry in the source array that should be shared with the subarray. If it's negative, it's used as an offset from the end of the array. If you leave it off, 0 will be used.

➤   `end` is the index of the first entry not to share; if it's negative, it's used as an offset from the end of the array. It's not technically specified as optional, but if you leave it off, the length of the array is used.

Both indexes are in entries, not bytes.

Here's an example:

```
const wholeArray = Uint8Array.of(0, 1, 2, 3, 4, 5, 6, 7, 8, 9);
const firstHalf = wholeArray.subarray(0, 5);
console.log(wholeArray); // Uint8Array [ 0, 1, 2, 3, 4, 5, 6, 7, 8, 9 ]
console.log(firstHalf);  // Uint8Array [ 0, 1, 2, 3, 4 ]
firstHalf[0] = 100;
console.log(wholeArray); // Uint8Array [ 100, 1, 2, 3, 4, 5, 6, 7, 8, 9 ]
console.log(firstHalf);  // Uint8Array [ 100, 1, 2, 3, 4 ]
const secondHalf = wholeArray.subarray(-5);
console.log(wholeArray); // Uint8Array [ 100, 1, 2, 3, 4, 5, 6, 7, 8, 9 ]
console.log(secondHalf); // Uint8Array [ 5, 6, 7, 8, 9 ]
secondHalf[1] = 60;
console.log(wholeArray); // Uint8Array [ 100, 1, 2, 3, 4, 5, 60, 7, 8, 9 ]
console.log(secondHalf); // Uint8Array [ 5, 60, 7, 8, 9 ]
```

Notice how assigning to `firstHalf[0]` changes the value at `wholeArray[0]` as well, since `firstHalf` and `wholeArray` share the same buffer, starting at the very beginning of it. Similarly, assigning to `secondHalf[1]` changes the value at `wholeArray[6]`, because `secondHalf` and `wholeArray` share the same buffer, but with `secondHalf` using only the second half of it.

OLD HABITS TO NEW

Most of what you've learned in this chapter has related to new things you couldn't do before, but there are still have a couple of habits you might tweak.

Use find and findIndex to Search Arrays Instead of Loops (Where Appropriate)

Old habit: Finding entries (or their indexes) in arrays using a `for` loop or the `some` method, etc.:

```
let found;
for (let n = 0; n < array.length; ++n) {
    if (array[n].id === desiredId) {
        found = array[n];
        break;
    }
}
```

New habit: Consider using `find` (or `findIndex`) instead:

```
let found = array.find(value => value.id === desiredId);
```

Use Array.fill to Fill Arrays Rather Than Loops

Old habit: Filling arrays of values with loops:

```
// Static value
const array = [];
while (array.length < desiredLength) {
    array[array.length] = value;
}

// Dynamic value
const array = [];
while (array.length < desiredLength) {
    array[array.length] = determineValue(array.length);
}
```

New habit: Use `Array.fill` or `Array.from` instead:

```
// Static value
const array = Array(desiredLength).fill(value);

// Dynamic value
const array = Array.from(
    Array(desiredLength),
    (_, index) => determineValue(index)
);
```

Use readAsArrayBuffer Instead of readAsBinaryString

Old habit: Using `readAsBinaryString` on `FileReader` instances, working with the result data via `charCodeAt`.

New habit: Use `readAsArrayBuffer` instead, working with the data via typed arrays.

12

Maps and Sets

> **WROX.COM CODE DOWNLOADS FOR THIS CHAPTER**
>
> You can download the code for this chapter at `https://thenewtoys.dev/bookcode` or `https://www.wiley.com/go/javascript-newtoys`.

In this chapter, you'll learn about ES2015+'s Maps, Sets, WeakMaps, and WeakSets. Maps store key/value pairs, where the key and value can be (almost) anything. Sets store unique values. WeakMaps are similar to Maps, but the keys are objects and those objects are held *weakly* (they can be garbage collected, which removes the entry from the map). WeakSets hold unique objects weakly.

MAPS

You often want to create a map of one thing to another, for instance a map of IDs to objects that have that ID. In JavaScript, we've often used (some say *ab*used) objects for that. But since it's not what objects are designed for, there are some pragmatic issues with using objects for generic maps:

➤ The keys can only be strings (or Symbols as of ES2015).

➤ Until ES2015, you couldn't count on the order if you needed to loop through the entries in the object; and as you learned in Chapter 5, even though ES2015 added order, relying on it isn't usually a good idea because the order depends on both the order the properties were added to the object and the form of the property key (strings in the canonical integer index form come first, numerically).

➤ Objects are optimized by JavaScript engines on the assumption that they mostly only have properties added to them and updated, not removed.

➤ Until ES5, you couldn't create an object without a prototype with properties like `toString` and `hasOwnProperty` on it. While unlikely to conflict with your own keys, it was still a mild concern.

Maps deal with all of those issues. In a Map:

➤ Both the keys and the values can be any value at all (including an object).[1]

➤ The order of entries is defined: it's the order in which the entries were added (updating an entry's value doesn't change its place in the order).

➤ JavaScript engines optimize Maps differently from objects, since their use cases are different.

➤ Maps are empty by default.

Basic Map Operations

The basics of Maps (creating, adding, accessing, and removing entries) are quite straightforward; let's run through them quickly. (You can run all of the code in this section using the `basic-map-operations.js` file from the downloads.)

To create a map, use the constructor (more on this later in the chapter):

```
const m = new Map();
```

To add entries to it, use the `set` method to associate a key with a value:

```
m.set(60, "sixty");
m.set(4, "four");
```

The keys in that example are the numbers 60 and 4 (the first argument to each `set` call); the values are the strings `"sixty"` and `"four"` (the second argument).

The `set` method returns the map, so you can chain multiple calls together if you like:

```
m.set(50, "fifty").set(3, "three");
```

To see how many entries are in the map, use its `size` property:

```
console.log(`Entries: ${m.size}`);        // Entries: 4
```

To get the value for a key, use the `get` method:

```
let value = m.get(60);
console.log(`60: ${value}`);              // 60: sixty
console.log(`3: ${m.get(3)}`);            // 3: three
```

---

[1] There's one minor caveat here; see details in the "Key Equality" section.

The `get` method returns `undefined` if there's no entry for the key:

```
console.log(`14: ${m.get(14)}`);            // 14: undefined
```

All of the keys in this example so far are numbers. If you were doing this with an object instead of a map, the keys would have been converted to strings, but that's not true with Map:

```
console.log('Look for key "4" instead of 4:');
console.log(`"4": ${m.get("4")}`);          // "4": undefined (the key is 4, not "4")
console.log('Look for key 4:');
console.log(`4: ${m.get(4)}`);              // 4: four
```

To update an entry's value, use `set` again; it will update the existing entry:

```
m.set(3, "THREE");
console.log(`3: ${m.get(3)}`);              // 3: THREE
console.log(`Entries: ${m.size}`);          // Entries: 4 (still)
```

To delete (remove) an entry, use the `delete` method:

```
m.delete(4);
```

`delete` returns `true` if an entry was deleted, `false` if there was no entry matching the key. Note that `delete` is a *method* of Maps; you don't use the `delete` operator. `delete m[2]` would try to delete a property called `"2"` from the map object, but entries in the map aren't *properties* of the map object, so it wouldn't have any effect.

To check whether an entry exists in the map, use the `has` method, which returns a boolean (`true` if the map has an entry for the key, `false` if not):

```
console.log(`Entry for 7? ${m.has(7)}`); // Entry for 7? false
console.log(`Entry for 3? ${m.has(3)}`); // Entry for 3? true
```

Note that, again, entries are not properties, so you don't use the `in` operator or the `hasOwnProperty` method.

So far, all of the keys in this example have been of the same type (number). That's often going to be true in real-world use, but there's nothing requiring it; keys in a map don't all have to be the same type. You can add an entry with a string key to this example map we've been building up that so far only has number keys in it, for instance:

```
m.set("testing", "one two three");
console.log(m.get("testing"));              // one two three
```

Keys can be objects:

```
const obj1 = {};
m.set(obj1, "value for obj1");
console.log(m.get(obj1));                    // value for obj1
```

Different objects are always different keys, even if they have the same properties. The `obj1` key is a plain object with no properties; if you add another entry using a plain object with no properties as the key, it's a different key:

```
const obj2 = {};
m.set(obj2, "value for obj2");
console.log(`obj1: ${m.get(obj1)}`);      // obj1: value for obj1
console.log(`obj2: ${m.get(obj2)}`);      // obj2: value for obj2
```

Since keys can be (almost) any JavaScript value, valid keys include `null`, `undefined`, and even `NaN` (which famously isn't equal to anything, not even itself):

```
m.set(null, "value for null");
m.set(undefined, "value for undefined");
m.set(NaN, "value for NaN");
console.log(`null: ${m.get(null)}`);           // null: value for null
console.log(`undefined: ${m.get(undefined)}`); // undefined: value for undefined
console.log(`NaN: ${m.get(NaN)}`);             // NaN: value for NaN
```

Notice that `get` returns `undefined` in two separate situations: if there was no matching entry for the key, or if there was and its value was `undefined`. (Just like object properties.) If you need to tell the difference between those situations, use `has`.

To clear all entries out of the map, use the `clear` method:

```
m.clear();
console.log(`Entries now: ${m.size}`);  // Entries now: 0
```

Key Equality

Keys in Maps can be almost any value (more on that in a moment). They're compared using the "SameValueZero" operation, which is the same as strict equality (`===`) except that `NaN` is equal to itself (which, famously, it otherwise isn't). This means that:

➤ There's no type coercion when trying to match keys; a key is always different from a key of another type (`"1"` and `1` are different keys).

➤ An object is always a different key from any other object, even if they have the same properties.

➤ `NaN` works as a key.

The "almost" in "Keys in Maps can be almost any value" is that you can't have a map key with the value `-0` (negative zero). If you try to add an entry with the key `-0`, the map will use `0` as the key instead; if you look up an entry using the key `-0`, `get` will look up the entry for `0` instead:

```
const key = -0;
console.log(key);              // -0
const m = new Map();
m.set(key, "value");
const [keyInMap] = m.keys(); // (`keys` returns an iterator for the map's keys)
console.log(keyInMap);        // 0
console.log(`${m.get(0)}`);  // value
console.log(`${m.get(-0)}`); // value
```

This is to avoid ambiguity, since `0` and `-0` are hard to distinguish from each other. They're different values (per the IEEE-754 specification JavaScript numbers adhere to), but strictly equal to each other (`0 === -0` is true). Number's `toString` returns `"0"` for both of them, and most (but not all) JavaScript operations treat them as being the same value. When `Map` and `Set` were being designed, there was a lot of discussion about the two zeros (including, briefly, a flag you could use to decide whether they were the same or different in a given `Map` or `Set`), but the value of that didn't justify the complexity. So to avoid making it easy to accidentally shoot yourself in the foot, `Map` converts `-0` to `0` when you try to use it as a key.

Creating Maps from Iterables

Earlier, you saw that the `Map` constructor creates an empty map if you don't pass it any argument. You can also provide entries for the map by passing in an iterable of objects, typically an array of arrays. Here's a simple example doing that, mapping English words to Italian:

```
const m = new Map([
    ["one", "uno"],
    ["two", "due"],
    ["three", "tre"]
]);
console.log(m.size);        // 3
console.log(m.get("two"));  // due
```

However, neither the iterable nor its entries *have* to be arrays: any iterable can be used, and any object with `"0"` and `"1"` properties can be used for its entries. In effect, `Map`'s constructor looks something like this (notionally, not exactly):

```
constructor(entries) {
    if (entries) {
        for (const entry of entries) {
            this.set(entry["0"], entry["1"]);
        }
    }
}
```

Note that the entries are created in the order they're provided by the iterable's iterator.

If you pass more than one argument to the `Map` constructor, subsequent arguments are currently ignored.

You can copy a map by just passing it into the `Map` constructor (more on how this works in the next section):

```
const m1 = new Map([
    [1, "one"],
    [2, "two"],
    [3, "three"]
]);
const m2 = new Map(m1);
console.log(m2.get(2)); // two
```

Iterating the Map Contents

Maps are iterable. Their default iterator produces a `[key, value]` array for each entry (which is why you can copy a map by passing it to the `Map` constructor). Maps also provide a `keys` method for iterating the keys, and a `values` method for iterating the values.

When you need both the key and value, you can use the default iterator. For instance, in a `for-of` loop with iterable destructuring:

```
const m = new Map([
    ["one", "uno"],
    ["two", "due"],
    ["three", "tre"]
]);
```

```
for (const [key, value] of m) {
    console.log(`${key} => ${value}`);
}
// one => uno
// two => due
// three => tre
```

Of course, you don't have to use destructuring, you could just use the array in the loop body:

```
for (const entry of m) {
    console.log(`${entry[0]} => ${entry[1]}`);
}
// one => uno
// two => due
// three => tre
```

The default iterator is also available via the `entries` method (in fact, `Map.prototype.entries` and `Map.prototype[Symbol.iterator]` refer to the same function).

Map entries have an order: the order in which the entries were created. That's why the two previous examples showed the entries in the same order they appear in the array in the `Map` constructor call. Updating an entry's value does not move it in the order. However, if you delete an entry, then add another entry with the same key, the new entry is put at the "end" of the map (since once you deleted the old entry, it didn't exist in the map anymore). Here are examples of those rules:

```
const m = new Map([
    ["one", "uno"],
    ["two", "due"],
    ["three", "tre"]
]);

// Modify existing entry
m.set("two", "due (updated)");
for (const [key, value] of m) {
    console.log(`${key} => ${value}`);
}
// one => uno
// two => due (updated)
// three => tre

// Remove entry, then add a new one with the same key
m.delete("one");
m.set("one", "uno (new)");
for (const [key, value] of m) {
    console.log(`${key} => ${value}`);
}
// two => due (updated)
// three => tre
// one => uno (new)
```

The order applies to all of the Map's iterables (`entries`, `keys`, and `values`):

```
const m = new Map([
    ["one", "uno"],
    ["two", "due"],
    ["three", "tre"]
]);
```

```
for (const key of m.keys()) {
    console.log(key);
}
// one
// two
// three

for (const value of m.values()) {
    console.log(value);
}
// uno
// due
// tre
```

You can also loop through the entries in a map using its `forEach` method, which is exactly like the one provided by arrays:

```
const m = new Map([
    ["one", "uno"],
    ["two", "due"],
    ["three", "tre"]
]);
m.forEach((value, key) => {
    console.log(`${key} => ${value}`);
});
// one => uno
// two => due
// three => tre
```

Like the one for arrays, you can pass a second argument if you want to control what `this` in the callback is, and the callback receives three arguments: the value being visited, its key, and the map you're looping through. (Only key and value are used in the example.)

Subclassing Map

Like other built-ins, `Map` can be subclassed. For instance, the built-in Map class doesn't have a `filter` function like array's `filter`. Suppose you have maps in your code that you commonly want to filter. While you could add your own `filter` to `Map.prototype`, extending built-in prototypes can be problematic (particularly in library code rather than application/page code). Instead, you can use a subclass. For instance, Listing 12-1 creates `MyMap` with a `filter` function.

LISTING 12-1: Subclassing Map—subclassing-map.js

```
class MyMap extends Map {
    filter(predicate, thisArg) {
        const newMap = new (this.constructor[Symbol.species] || MyMap)();
        for (const [key, value] of this) {
            if (predicate.call(thisArg, key, value, this)) {
                newMap.set(key, value);
            }
        }
        return newMap;
    }
}
```

```
// Usage:
const m1 = new MyMap([
    ["one", "uno"],
    ["two", "due"],
    ["three", "tre"]
]);
const m2 = m1.filter(key => key.includes("t"));
for (const [key, value] of m2) {
    console.log(`${key} => ${value}`);
}
// two => due
// three => tre
console.log(`m2 instanceof MyMap? ${m2 instanceof MyMap}`);
// m2 instanceof MyMap? true
```

Note the use of `Symbol.species` that you learned in Chapter 4. The `Map` constructor has a `Symbol.species` getter that returns `this`. `MyMap` doesn't override that default, so its `filter` creates a `MyMap` instance while allowing further subclasses (for instance, `MySpecialMap`) to control whether `filter` should create an instance of that subclass, a `MyMap`, or a `Map` (or something else, though that seems unlikely).

Performance

The implementation of Map is naturally up to the specific JavaScript engine, but the specification requires that they are implemented ". . . using either hash tables or other mechanisms that, on average, provide access times that are sublinear on the number of elements in the collection." This means that, for instance, adding an entry should be faster on average than searching through an array to see whether it contains the entry and then adding it if it doesn't. In code, that means this:

```
map.set(key, value);
```

is required to be faster, on average, than this:

```
const entry = array.find(e => e.key === key);
if (entry) {
    entry.value = value;
} else {
    array.push({key, value});
}
```

SETS

Sets are collections of unique values. Everything you learned about Map keys in the last section applies to the values in a Set. A Set can hold any value except `-0`, which is converted to `0` if you add it (just like Map keys). Values are compared using the SameValueZero operation (just like Map keys). The order of values in a Set is the order in which they were added to the set; adding the same value again doesn't change its position (removing a value, then adding it again later, does). When you add a value to a Set, the Set first checks to see whether it already holds the value, and only adds it if it doesn't.

Prior to Set, objects were sometimes used for this purpose (storing the values as property names converted to strings, with any value), but that has the same sorts of disadvantages that using objects for

Maps has. Alternatively, arrays or array-like objects have often been used in place of sets, searching the array before adding to it to see if it already contains the value being added. (jQuery, for instance, is normally set-based: a jQuery instance is array-like, but adding the same DOM element to a jQuery instance doesn't add it the second time.) If you were implementing a jQuery-like library in ES2015+, you might consider having it use a Set internally. You might even make it a Set subclass, as long as you're okay with it potentially containing things other than DOM elements, thanks to the Liskov Substitution Principle. (jQuery does allow that, though it's not well-known.)

Basic Set Operations

Let's quickly run through the basics of Sets: creating, adding, accessing, and removing entries. (You can run all of the code in this section using the `basic-set-operations.js` file from the downloads.)

To create a set, use the constructor (more on this later in this chapter):

```
const s = new Set();
```

To add entries, use the `add` method:

```
s.add("two");
s.add("four");
```

The `add` method only accepts a single value. Passing it more than one value won't add the subsequent ones. But it returns the Set, so multiple `add` calls can be chained together:

```
s.add("one").add("three");
```

To check if the Set has a given value in it, use the `has` method:

```
console.log(`Has "two"? ${s.has("two")}`);        // Has "two"? true
```

Set entries aren't properties, so you wouldn't use the `in` operator or `hasOwnProperty` method.

To get the number of entries in the Set, use the `size` property:

```
console.log(`Entries: ${s.size}`);                // Entries: 4
```

Sets, by their nature, never contain the same value twice. If you try to add a value that's already present, it isn't added again:

```
s.add("one").add("three");
console.log(`Entries: ${s.size}`);                // Entries: 4 (still)
```

To delete (remove) an entry from the Set, use the `delete` method:

```
s.delete("two");
console.log(`Has "two"? ${s.has("two")}`);        // Has "two"? false
```

To clear the Set entirely, use the `clear` method:

```
s.clear();
console.log(`Entries: ${s.size}`);                // Entries: 0
```

While the example values in this section were strings, again, the values in a Set can be almost any JavaScript value (just not negative zero, as with Map keys), and they don't need to all be of the same type.

Creating Sets from Iterables

The Set constructor accepts an iterable and fills the set with the values from the iterable (in order) if you provide one:

```
const s = new Set(["one", "two", "three"]);
console.log(s.has("two")); // true
```

Naturally, if the iterable returns the same value twice, the resulting Set has it only once:

```
const s = new Set(["one", "two", "three", "one", "two", "three"]);
console.log(s.size); // 3
```

Iterating the Set Contents

Sets are iterable; the order of iteration is the order in which the values were added to the set:

```
const s = new Set(["one", "two", "three"]);
for (const value of s) {
    console.log(value);
}
// one
// two
// three
```

Adding a value that's already in the set doesn't change its position in the set; removing it entirely and then adding it back later does (since by the time you add it back, it's not in the set anymore):

```
const s = new Set(["one", "two", "three"]);
for (const value of s) {
    console.log(value);
}
s.add("one"); // Again
for (const value of s) {
    console.log(value);
}
// one
// two
// three

s.delete("one");
s.add("one");
for (const value of s) {
    console.log(value);
}
// two
// three
// one
```

Since Sets can be constructed from iterables, and Sets are iterables, you can copy a Set by passing it into the Set constructor:

```
const s1 = new Set(["a", "b", "c"]);
const s2 = new Set(s1);
console.log(s2.has("b")); // true
s1.delete("b");
console.log(s2.has("b")); // true (still, removing from s1 doesn't remove from s2)
```

Using Set's iterability is also a handy way to copy an array while removing any duplicate entries in it (the classic `unique` function so many programmers have in their toolkits):

```
const a1 = [1, 2, 3, 4, 1, 2, 3, 4];
const a2 = Array.from(new Set(a1));
console.log(a2.length);      // 4
console.log(a2.join(", ")); // 1, 2, 3, 4
```

That said, if you want only unique values, you may have been able to use a Set in the first place rather than an array.

The default iterator of a Set iterates its values. That same iterator is also accessible via the `values` method. To make the Map and Set interfaces similar, that same iterator is *also* available via the `keys` method. In fact, `Set.prototype[Symbol.iterator]`, `Set.prototype.values`, and `Set.prototype.keys` all refer to the same function. Sets also provide an `entries` method that returns two-entry arrays (like Map's `entries`) where both of the entries contain the value from the Set, almost as though a Set were a Map where the keys map to themselves:

```
const s = new Set(["a", "b", "c"]);
for (const value of s) { // or `of s.values()`
    console.log(value);
}
// a
// b
// c
for (const key of s.keys()) {
    console.log(key);
}
// a
// b
// c
for (const [key, value] of s.entries()) {
    console.log(`${key} => ${value}`);
}
// a => a
// b => b
// c => c
```

Subclassing Set

`Set` is easy to subclass. For instance, suppose you wanted an `addAll` method that adds all the values from an iterable to the set, rather than having to call `add` repeatedly, but you didn't want to add it to `Set.prototype` since you were writing library code. Listing 12-2 has a simple Set subclass with the added method.

LISTING 12-2: Subclassing Set—subclassing-set.js

```
class MySet extends Set {
    addAll(iterable) {
        for (const value of iterable) {
            this.add(value);
        }
        return this;
```

```
        }
    }

    // Usage
    const s = new MySet();
    s.addAll(["a", "b", "c"]);
    s.addAll([1, 2, 3]);
    for (const value of s) {
        console.log(value);
    }
    // a
    // b
    // c
    // 1
    // 2
    // 3
```

As with Map, if you were going to add a method that produced a new set, you might want to use the species pattern to create the new instance.

Performance

As with Map, the implementation of Set is up to the specific JavaScript engine, but as with Map the specification requires that they are implemented ". . . using either hash tables or other mechanisms that, on average, provide access times that are sublinear on the number of elements in the collection." So this:

```
    set.add(value);
```

is required to be faster, on average, than this:

```
    if (!array.includes(value)) {
        array.push(value);
    }
```

WEAKMAPS

WeakMaps let you store a value related to an object (the key) without forcing the key to remain in memory; the key is *weakly held* by the map. If the map would be the only reason the object is kept in memory, its entry (key and value) is automatically removed from the map, leaving the key object eligible for garbage-collection. (The *value* of the entry, if it's an object, is held normally by the map as long as the entry exists. Only the *key* is held weakly.) This is true even if the same object is used as a key in more than one WeakMap (or if it's held in a WeakSet, as you'll learn in the next section). Once the only remaining references to the key object are in WeakMaps (or WeakSets), the JavaScript engine removes the entries for that object and makes the object available for garbage collection.

For instance, if you wanted to store information related to a DOM element without storing it in a property on the element itself, you could store it in a WeakMap using the DOM element as the key and the information you want to store as the value. If the DOM element is removed from the DOM and nothing else refers to it, the entry for that element is automatically removed from the map and the DOM element's memory can be reclaimed (along with any memory allocated for the map entry's value, provided nothing else refers to that value separately from the map).

WeakMaps Are Not Iterable

One significant aspect of WeakMaps is that if you don't already have a particular key, you can't get it from the map. This is because an implementation might have a delay between when the key isn't reachable by other means and when the entry is removed from the map; if you could get the key from the map during that time, it would introduce indeterminacy to the code doing it. So WeakMaps don't offer any way to get a key if you don't already have it.

That has a significant impact on WeakMap: it's not iterable. In fact, WeakMap provides very little information about its contents. Here's what it provides:

➤ `has`: If you give it a key, it will tell you whether it has an entry for that key.

➤ `get`: If you give it a key, it will give you the value for the key's entry in the WeakMap (or `undefined` if it doesn't have a matching entry, like Map does).

➤ `delete`: If you give it a key, it will delete that key's entry (if any) and return a flag: `true` if the entry was found and deleted, `false` if it wasn't found.

There's no `size`, no `forEach`, no `keys` iterator, no `values` iterator, etc. `WeakMap` is not a subclass of `Map`, although the common parts of their API intentionally mirror each other.

Use Cases and Examples

Let's explore a couple of use cases for WeakMaps.

Use Case: Private Information

One classic use case for WeakMaps is private information. Consider Listing 12-3.

LISTING 12-3: Using WeakMap for private information—private-info.js

```
const Example = (() => {
    const privateMap = new WeakMap();

    return class Example {
        constructor() {
            privateMap.set(this, 0);
        }

        incrementCounter() {
            const result = privateMap.get(this) + 1;
            privateMap.set(this, result);
            return result;
        }
    }
```

```
        showCounter() {
            console.log(`Counter is ${privateMap.get(this)}`);
        }
    };
})();

const e1 = new Example();
e1.incrementCounter();
console.log(e1);            // (some representation of the object)

const e2 = new Example();
e2.incrementCounter();
e2.incrementCounter();
e2.incrementCounter();

e1.showCounter();          // Counter is 1
e2.showCounter();          // Counter is 3
```

The implementation of `Example` is wrapped in an inline-invoked function expression (IIFE) so that `privateMap` is entirely private to just the class's implementation.

PRIVATE CLASS FIELDS

In Chapter 18 you'll learn about the proposed *private class fields*, which will be in ES2021 and provide a way for a class to have truly private information (both instance-specific and static). That could be used here in two ways: you could simply use a private field for the counter instead of using a WeakMap, or if you had reason for using the WeakMap (perhaps not all instances need private information), you could make the map itself a static private field (which would simplify the implementation by doing away with the IIFE wrapper).

When you create an instance via the `Example` constructor, it saves an entry in a WeakMap (`privateMap`) with the value `0`, keyed by the new object (`this`). When you call `incrementCounter`, it updates that entry by incrementing its value, and when you call `showCounter`, it shows the current value. To see it in action, it's probably best to run it in an environment with a debugger or an interactive console. Be sure to dig into the object logged on the "(some representation of the object)" line. If you do, you won't find the counter value anywhere, even though the object can access and even change the counter value. The counter value is truly private to the code within the scoping function wrapped around the `Example` class; no other code can access that information, because no other code has access to `privateMap`.

Question: what would happen if you used a Map for this instead of a WeakMap?

Right! Over time the Map would just get bigger and bigger and bigger as `Example` objects kept getting created and never cleaned up, even when all other code was done with them, because the Map would keep them in memory. But with a WeakMap, when all other code is done with an `Example` object and drops its reference to it, the JavaScript engine removes the WeakMap entry for that object.

Use Case: Storing Information for Objects Outside Your Control

Another major use case for WeakMaps is storing information for objects that are outside your control. Suppose you're dealing with an API that provides objects to you, and you need to keep track of your own information related to those objects. Adding properties to those objects is usually a bad idea (and the API may even make it impossible by giving you a proxy or a frozen object).

WeakMap to the rescue! Just store the information keyed by the object. Since the WeakMap holds the key weakly, it doesn't prevent the API object being garbage-collected.

Listings 12-4 and 12-5 show an example, tracking information about DOM elements by using the DOM elements as keys in a WeakMap.

LISTING 12-4: Storing data for DOM elements (HTML)—storing-data-for-dom.html

```
<!doctype html>
<html>
<head>
<meta charset="UTF-8">
<title>Storing Data for DOM Elements</title>
</head>
<style>
.person {
    cursor: pointer;
}
</style>
<body>
<label>
<div id="status"></div>
<div id="people"></div>
<div id="person"></div>
<script src="storing-data-for-dom.js"></script>
</body>
</html>
```

LISTING 12-5: Storing data for DOM elements (JavaScript)—storing-data-for-dom.js

```
(async() => {
    const statusDisplay = document.getElementById("status");
    const personDisplay = document.getElementById("person");
    try {
        // The WeakMap that will hold the information related to our DOM elements
        const personMap = new WeakMap();
        await init();

        async function init() {
            const peopleList = document.getElementById("people");
            const people = await getPeople();
            // In this loop, we store the person that relates to each div in the
            // WeakMap using the div as the key
            for (const person of people) {
                const personDiv = createPersonElement(person);
```

```
                    personMap.set(personDiv, person);
                    peopleList.appendChild(personDiv);
                }
            }

    async function getPeople() {
        // This is a stand-in for an operation that would fetch the person
        // data from the server or similar
        return [
            {name: "Joe Bloggs", position: "Front-End Developer"},
            {name: "Abha Patel", position: "Senior Software Architect"},
            {name: "Guo Wong",   position: "Database Analyst"}
          ];
    }

    function createPersonElement(person) {
        const div = document.createElement("div");
        div.className = "person";
        div.innerHTML =
            '<a href="#show" class="remove">X</a> <span class="name"></span>';
        div.querySelector("span").textContent = person.name;
        div.querySelector("a").addEventListener("click", removePerson);
        div.addEventListener("click", showPerson);
        return div;
    }

    function stopEvent(e) {
        e.preventDefault();
        e.stopPropagation();
    }

    function showPerson(e) {
        stopEvent(e);
        // Here, we get the person to show by looking up the clicked element
        // in the WeakMap
        const person = personMap.get(this);
        if (person) {
            const {name, position} = person;
            personDisplay.textContent = `${name}'s position is: ${position}`;
        }
    }

    function removePerson(e) {
        stopEvent(e);
        this.closest("div").remove();
    }
    } catch (error) {
        statusDisplay.innerHTML = `Error: ${error.message}`;
    }
})();
```

Values Referring Back to the Key

The DOM data example in the previous section (storing-data-for-dom.js) stored a value object (each person) in personMap for each person display div element. Suppose that person object had referred back to the DOM element? For instance, if the `for-of` loop in `init` replaced the `personDiv` constant with a property on the `person` object, like this:

```
for (const person of people) {
    const person.div = createPersonElement(person);
    personMap.set(person.div, person);
    peopleList.appendChild(person.div);
}
```

Now, the WeakMap's entry key is `person.div` and its value is `person`, meaning that the value (`person`) has a reference back to the key (`person.div`). Would the existence of the `person` object's reference to the key keep the key in memory, even if *only* the `person` object (and `personMap`) referred to the key?

You probably guessed: no, it wouldn't. The spec's language on this is one of its easier-to-read parts. It says:[2]

> *If an object that is being used as the key of a WeakMap key/value pair is only reachable by following a chain of references that start within that WeakMap, then that key/value pair is inaccessible and is automatically removed from the WeakMap.*

Let's prove that. See Listing 12-6.

LISTING 12-6: Value referring back to key—value-referring-to-key.js

```
function log(msg) {
    const p = document.createElement("pre");
    p.appendChild(document.createTextNode(msg));
    document.body.appendChild(p);
}

const AAAAExample = (() => {
    const privateMap = new WeakMap();

    return class AAAAExample {
        constructor(secret, limit) {
            privateMap.set(this, {counter: 0, owner: this});
        }

        get counter() {
            return privateMap.get(this).counter;
        }

        incrementCounter() {
            return ++privateMap.get(this).counter;
        }
    };
})();

const e = new AAAAExample();

let a = [];
document.getElementById("btn-create").addEventListener("click", function(e) {
    const count = +document.getElementById("objects").value || 100000;
    log(`Generating ${count} objects...`);
    for (let n = count; n > 0; --n) {
```

---

[2] https://tc39.github.io/ecma262/#sec-weakmap-objects

```
        a.push(new AAAAExample());
    }
    log(`Done, ${a.length} objects in the array`);
});
document.getElementById("btn-release").addEventListener("click", function(e) {
    a.length = 0;
    log("All objects released");
});
```

The code creates an `AAAAExample` object that it references in `e` and never releases. When you click a button, it creates a number of further `AAAAExample` objects that it remembers in the `a` array, and when you click another button it releases all of the objects from the `a` array.

Open a page using the following HTML and that `value-referring-to-key.js` file from the Listing 12-6 (you can use `value-referring-to-key.html` from the downloads):

```
<label>
    Objects to create:
    <input type="text" id="objects" value="100000">
</label>
<input type="button" id="btn-create" value="Create">
<input type="button" id="btn-release" value="Release">
<script src="value-referring-to-key.js"></script>
```

With that page freshly opened, follow these steps:

1. Open your browser's developer's tools and navigate to its Memory tab or similar. Figure 12-1 shows what it would look like in Chrome with devtools docked at the bottom.

2. Click the Create button in the web page. This creates 100,000 objects (or whatever number you may have changed it to) using the `AAAAExample` constructor and retains them in an array (a).

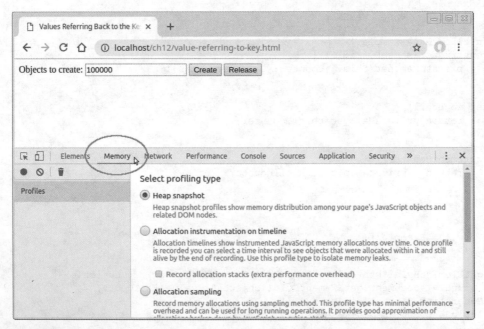

FIGURE 12-1

3. Using whatever mechanism your browser provides, look to see how many objects there are in memory that were created using the `AAAAExample` constructor (so named so that it will appear near the top of alphabetical lists). In Chrome, you'd do this by clicking the **Take Heap Snapshot** button (Figure 12-2, opposite) and then looking in the list of objects by Constructor (you may have to pull the panel called Retainers down to view the Constructor panel's contents). See Figure 12-3. In that figure, you can see there are 100,001 `AAAAExample` objects in memory (the initial one that never gets released, and the 100,000 created in response to clicking the button). You may find it useful to type **aaa** in the Class Filter box so only the `AAAAExample` row is shown (see Figure 12-4).

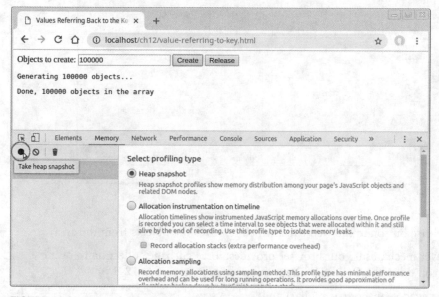

FIGURE 12-2

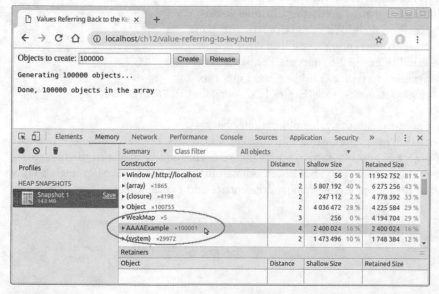

FIGURE 12-3

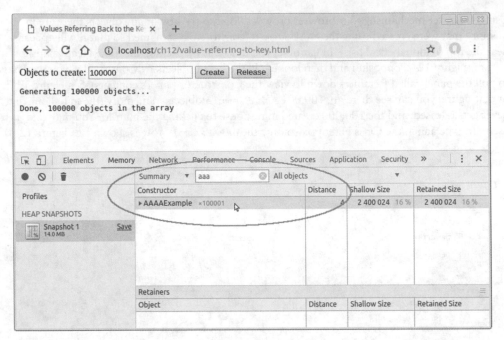

FIGURE 12-4

4. Click the Release button in the web page, which removes the objects from the array.

5. Using whatever mechanism your browser provides, force garbage collection to occur. In Chrome, you'd use the **Collect Garbage** button shown in Figure 12-5.

6. Take another heap snapshot (or similar) and look to see how many objects created using the `AAAAExample` constructor there are now. To do that in Chrome, you'd take another snapshot, then look in the Constructors pane again. If you scroll around enough, you'll find the one `AAAAExample` listed (Figure 12-6, opposite) or, again, you may find it convenient to type **aaa** in the Class Filter box to just show the `AAAAExample` row (Figure 12-7, opposite).

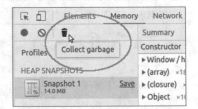

FIGURE 12-5

This demonstrates that even though the value objects refer back to their key objects, they don't prevent cleanup of those entries. In fact, the value object of one entry could refer to the key object of another entry whose value refers to the key object of the first entry (a circular reference), or some other entry; but once nothing outside of any WeakMap refers to those key objects anymore, the JavaScript engine removes the entries and makes the objects available for garbage collection.

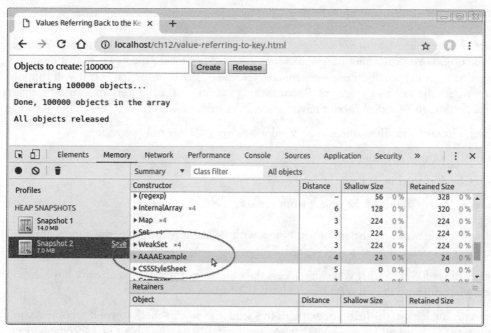

FIGURE 12-6

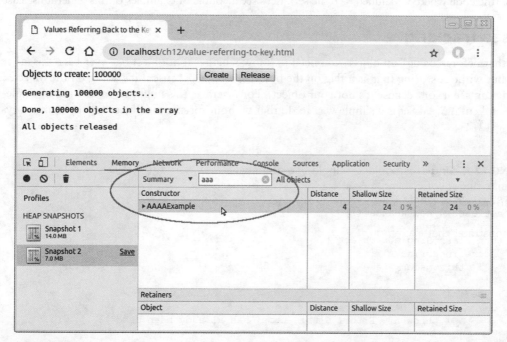

FIGURE 12-7

WEAKSETS

WeakSets are the Set equivalent of WeakMaps: sets of objects where being in the set doesn't prevent cleanup of the object. You can think of a WeakSet as a WeakMap where the key is the value in the set and the value is (conceptually) `true`—meaning, "yes, the object is in the set." Or if you think of Sets as Maps where the key and value are the same thing (as Set's `entries` iterator kind of suggests), that's fine too, although WeakSet doesn't have an `entries` iterator.

WeakSets aren't iterable, for the same reason WeakMaps aren't. They only provide:

➤ `add`: Add an object to the set.

➤ `has`: Check if the object is in the set.

➤ `delete`: Delete (remove) the object from the set.

Consequently, WeakSet isn't a subclass of Set, but as with WeakMap and Map, the common parts of their API are intentionally aligned.

So what's the point of WeakSet? If you can't access the objects in it unless you already have those objects, then what purpose does it serve?

The answer is the analogy in the first paragraph of this section: you can check to see if an object you have is in the set. This is useful for checking that you've previously seen an object in a specific part of your code (the code where you added it to the set). Let's see a couple of examples of this general use case.

Use Case: Tracking

Suppose that before "using" an object, you need to know whether that object has ever been "used" in the past, but without storing that as a flag on the object (perhaps because if it's a flag on the object, other code can see it; or because it's not your object). For instance, this might be some kind of single-use access token. A WeakSet is a simple way to do that without forcing the object to stay in memory. See Listing 12-7.

LISTING 12-7: Single-use object—single-use-object.js

```
const SingleUseObject = (() => {
    const used = new WeakSet();

    return class SingleUseObject {
        constructor(name) {
            this.name = name;
        }
        use() {
            if (used.has(this)) {
                throw new Error(`${this.name} has already been used`);
            }
            console.log(`Using ${this.name}`);
            used.add(this);
        }
    };
})();
```

```
const suo1 = new SingleUseObject("suo1");
const suo2 = new SingleUseObject("suo2");
suo1.use();                                  // Using suo1
try {
    suo1.use();
} catch (e) {
    console.error("Error: " + e.message); // Error: suo1 has already been used
}
suo2.use();                                  // Using suo2
```

Use Case: Branding

Branding is another form of tracking: suppose you're designing a library that provides objects, and later accepts those objects back to do something with them. If the library needs to be absolutely certain that the object it got back originated from the library code, that it hasn't been faked by the code using the library, it can use a WeakSet for that. See Listing 12-8.

LISTING 12-8: Only accept known objects—only-accept-known-objects.js

```
const Thingy = (() => {
    const known = new WeakSet();
    let nextId = 1;

    return class Thingy {
        constructor(name) {
            this.name = name;
            this.id = nextId++;
            Object.freeze(this);
            known.add(this);
        }

        action() {
            if (!known.has(this)) {
                throw new Error("Unknown Thingy");
            }
            // Code here knows that this object was created
            // by this class
            console.log(`Action on Thingy #${this.id} (${this.name})`);
        }
    }
})();

// In other code using it:

// Using real ones
const t1 = new Thingy("t1");
t1.action(); // Action on Thingy #1 (t1)
const t2 = new Thingy("t2");
t2.action(); // Action on Thingy #2 (t2)

// Trying to use a fake one
const faket2 = Object.create(Thingy.prototype);
```

```
faket2.name = "faket2";
faket2.id = 2;
Object.freeze(faket2);
faket2.action(); // Error: Unknown Thingy
```

The `Thingy` class creates objects with `id` and `name` properties, and then *freezes* those objects so they cannot be changed in any way: their properties are read-only and can't be reconfigured, properties can't be added or removed, and the prototype can't be changed.

Later, if code tries to use the `action` method on a `Thingy` object, `action` checks that the object it was called on is a genuine `Thingy` object by looking in the `known` set. If it wasn't, it refuses to perform its action. Since the set is a WeakSet, this doesn't prevent the `Thingy` objects from being garbage-collected.

OLD HABITS TO NEW

Here are some old habits you might consider updating to new ones.

Use Maps Instead of Objects for General-Purpose Maps

Old habit: Using objects as general-purpose maps:

```
const byId = Object.create(null); // So it has no prototype
for (const entry of entries) {
    byId[entry.id] = entry;
}
// Later
const entry = byId[someId];
```

New habit: Use a Map instead:

```
const byId = new Map();
for (const entry of entries) {
    byId.set(entry.id, entry);
}

// Later
const entry = byId.get(someId);
```

Maps are better suited to general purpose mapping, and don't force the keys to be strings if they aren't already strings.

Use Sets Instead of Objects for Sets

Old habit: Using objects as pseudo-sets:

```
const used = Object.create(null);
// Marking something as "used"
used[thing.id] = true;
// Check later if something was used
if (used[thing.id]) {
    // ...
}
```

New habit: Use a Set instead:

```
const used = new Set();
// Marking something as "used"
used.add(thing.id);         // Or possibly just use `thing` directly
// Check later if something was used
if (used.has(thing.id)) {   // Or possibly just use `thing` directly
    // ...
}
```

Or if appropriate, a WeakSet:

```
const used = new WeakSet();
// Marking something as "used"
used.add(thing);
// Check later if something was used
if (used.has(thing)) {
    // ...
}
```

Use WeakMaps for Storing Private Data Instead of Public Properties

Old habit: (See caveats in the "new habit" section.) Using a naming convention, such as an underscore (_) prefix, to indicate that a property on an object is private and shouldn't be used by "other" code:

```
class Example {
    constructor(name) {
        this.name = name;
        this._counter = 0;
    }
    get counter() {
        return this._counter;
    }
    incrementCounter() {
        return ++this._counter;
    }
}
```

New habit: (See caveats after the example.) Use a WeakMap instead, so the data is truly private (but see caveat following the code):

```
const Example = (() => {
    const counters = new WeakMap();

    return class Example {
        constructor(name) {
            this.name = name;
            counters.set(this, 0);
        }
        get counter() {
            return counters.get(this);
        }
        incrementCounter() {
            const result = counters.get(this) + 1;
```

```
            counters.set(this, result);
            return result;
        }
    }
})();
```

Two caveats on this new habit, though:

➤ Using a WeakMap for this increases the code complexity; in any given situation, the privacy gain may or may not be worth the complexity cost. Many languages have "private" properties but then make it possible to access those properties anyway; for instance, Java's private fields can be accessed via reflection. So just using a naming convention isn't really all that much worse than using Java's private properties (although accessing them is definitely easier than using Java's reflection to do so).

➤ Before too much longer, `class` syntax (at least) will provide a means of having private fields without using a WeakMap, as you'll learn in Chapter 18. Jumping on the habit of using a WeakMap for private data now may just set you up for refactoring later.

It'll be a case-by-case basis. Some information really needs to be properly private (from code; remember, nothing is private from debuggers). Other information is probably fine if you just mark it with a convention that says "Don't use this."

13

Modules

> **CODE DOWNLOADS FOR THIS CHAPTER**
>
> You can download the code for this chapter at `https://thenewtoys.dev/bookcode` or `https://www.wiley.com/go/javascript-newtoys`.

In this chapter, you'll learn about ES2015's modules, which make it easy to divide your code into small, maintainable pieces and bring them together as needed.

INTRODUCTION TO MODULES

For years, JavaScript programmers either just put their code into the global namespace, or (since the global namespace is crowded) wrapped their code in a wrapper function (a *scoping function*). Sometimes they'd have that scoping function return an object (sometimes called a *namespace object*) they assigned to a single global variable (the "revealing module pattern").

In projects of any size, programmers would run into issues with name conflicts, complex dependencies, and splitting the code into appropriately sized files. Those issues led to various different—and incompatible—solutions for defining and combining *modules* of code, such as CommonJS (CJS), Asynchronous Module Definition (AMD), and variations of them. Multiple incompatible standards make life difficult for programmers, tool builders, library authors, and anyone trying to use modules from different sources.

Thankfully, ES2015 standardized modules for JavaScript, providing *mostly* common syntax and semantics for tools and authors to use. (We'll get to that "mostly" in a moment.) Adding to the earlier list of acronyms, native modules are often called *ESM modules* (ESM = ECMAScript Module), differentiating them from CJS modules, AMD modules, or other types.

MODULE FUNDAMENTALS

This section provides a quick overview of modules, which later sections build on providing more details.

A *module* is a unit of code in its own "compilation unit" (loosely, "file"). It has its own scope (instead of running its code at global scope like scripts do). It can load other modules, including *importing* things (such as functions and variables) from those other modules. It can *export* things for other modules to import. A group of modules importing each other's exports form a graph, commonly called a *module tree*. See Figure 13-1.

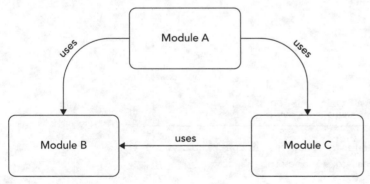

FIGURE 13-1

When importing, you say what module you're importing from using a *module specifier*, which is a string saying where to find the module. The JavaScript engine works with the host environment to load the module you specify. The JavaScript engine loads a module only once per realm;[1] if multiple other modules use it, they all use the same copy of it. A module can have *named exports* and/or a single *default export*.

---

[1] You may remember from Chapter 5 that a *realm* is the overall container in which a bit of code lives: its global environment, the intrinsic objects for that environment (`Array`, `Object`, `Date`, etc.), all the code loaded into that environment, and other bits of state and such. A browser window (whether it's a tab or full window or iframe) is a realm. A web worker is a realm, separate from the realm of the window that created it.

To export something from a module, you use an export declaration, which starts with the `export` keyword. Here are examples of two named exports:

```
export function example() {
    // ...
}
export let answer = 42;
```

To load a module and (optionally) import something from it, you use either an import declaration or a dynamic import. You'll learn about dynamic imports later in this chapter; for now, let's just look at import declarations (also called static imports). They use the `import` keyword followed by the thing(s) you want to import, then the word "from" followed by a module specifier string literal saying what module to import from, like this:

```
import { example } from "./mod.js";
import { answer } from "./mod.js";
// or
import { example, answer } from "./mod.js";
```

The curly braces in those declarations show that they import named exports. (You'll learn the details in a moment.)

Here's a default export (note the word `default`):

```
export default function example() {
    // ...
}
```

A module can only have one default export (or none). You can import it like this (note that there aren't any curly braces; again, you'll learn the details in a moment):

```
import example from "./mod.js";
```

You can also import a module just for its side effects, by simply not listing anything to import from it:

```
import "./mod.js";
```

That loads the module (and the modules it depends on) and runs its code, but doesn't import anything from it.

Those are the most common forms of `export` and `import`. You'll learn some further variations and details later in this chapter.

Only code in modules can use these declarative forms of `export` and `import`; non-module code can't. Non-module code *can* use the dynamic import you'll learn about later, but can't export anything.

`import` and `export` declarations can only appear in the top-level scope of a module; they cannot be inside any control-flow structure like a loop or `if` statement:

```
if (a < b) {
    import example from "./mod.js"; // SyntaxError: Unexpected identifier
    example();
}
```

A module can only export things it declares or re-export things it imports. A module can't export a global variable, for instance, because it didn't declare it. A module can't declare a global variable, because module code doesn't run at global scope. (It can add a property to the global object via assignment, for instance `window.varName = 42` on browsers, or using the `globalThis` you'll learn about in Chapter 17, but that's not a declaration.)

Winding up that whirlwind overview: importing an export creates a read-only "live" *indirect binding* to the exported item. That binding is read-only: a module can read the value of an item it imports, including seeing a new value if the original module changes the item's value, but cannot change the value directly.

Whew! Let's look at those various things more closely.

The Module Specifier

In the preceding examples, the `"./mod.js"` part is the module specifier:

```
import { example } from "./mod.js";
```

With an import declaration, the module specifier must be a string *literal*, not just an expression resulting in a string, since declarations are static forms (the JavaScript engine and the environment must be able to interpret them without *running* the code). Either single or double quotes may be used. Aside from that, the JavaScript specification says almost nothing about module specifiers. It leaves the form and semantics of module specifier strings to host environments. (This is the reason for the "mostly" in ". . . *mostly* common syntax and semantics . . ." in the introduction.) The form and semantics of module specifiers for the web are defined by the HTML specification; the ones for Node.js are defined by Node.js; and so on. That said, the teams handling specifiers for major environments like those are conscious that modules are being created for use across environments and are trying to avoid unnecessary differences. For now, don't worry about module specifiers, you'll learn more about them in "Using Modules in Browsers" and "Using Modules in Node.js" later in this chapter.

Basic Named Exports

You've already seen a couple of basic named exports. In this section you'll learn more about them.

You can use a named export to export anything declared within the module that has a name—variables, constants, functions, class constructors, and things imported from other modules. There are a couple of different ways to do it. One way is to simply put the `export` keyword in front of what you want to export when you declare or define it:

```
export let answer = 42;
export var question = "Life, the Universe, and Everything";
export const author = "Douglas Adams";
export function fn() {
    // ...
}
export class Example {
    // ...
}
```

That code creates five named exports: `answer`, `question`, `author`, `fn`, and `Example`. Notice how each of those statements/declarations is exactly the way it would have been without being exported, just with `export` tacked on the front. The function declaration and class declaration are both still declarations, not expressions (and so don't have semicolons after them).

Other modules use those names to say what they want to import from the module. For example:

```
import { answer, question } from "./mod.js";
```

In that example, the module only needs the `answer` and `question` exports, so it only asks for those and not `author`, `fn`, or `Example`.

You'll remember from the introduction that the curly braces are what indicate you're importing named exports, not the default export. Although those curly braces make that part of the `import` look a bit like object destructuring (Chapter 7), it *isn't* destructuring. Import syntax is entirely separate from destructuring. It doesn't allow nesting, handles renaming differently from destructuring, and doesn't allow default values. They're different things with superficially similar syntax.

You don't have to export something in the same place you create it; you can use a separate export declaration instead. Here's the same module as earlier, using a single export declaration (in this case, at the end):

```
let answer = 42;
var question = "Life, the Universe, and Everything";
const author = "Douglas Adams";
function fn() {
    // ...
}
class Example {
    // ...
}
export { answer, question, author, fn, Example };
```

You can have multiple separate declarations, like this:

```
export { answer };
export { question, author, fn, Example };
```

although the primary use case of a separate declaration is for coding styles that group all exports together in one place.

Export declarations can be at the end, at the beginning, or anywhere in between; here's an example of putting a single declaration at the beginning:

```
export { answer, question, author, fn, Example };
let answer = 42;
const question = "Life, the Universe, and Everything";
const author = "Douglas Adams";
function fn() {
    // ...
}
class Example {
    // ...
}
```

The styles can be intermixed, though it's probably not best practice:

```
export let answer = 42;
const question = "Life, the Universe, and Everything";
const author = "Douglas Adams";
```

```
export function fn() {
    // ...
}
class Example {
    // ...
}
export { question, author, Example };
```

The only real restriction is that the names of your exports must be unique; you can't export answer in the previous example twice using the name answer for both, or try to export a variable named answer and also a function named answer. That said, it *is* possible (if unusual) to export the same thing twice, either by renaming one of the exports (more on that in a later section) or exporting something both as a named export and the default export. For instance, you might export a function under its primary name and also under an alias.

Which you use—inline, declaration at the end, declaration at the beginning, or some combination—is entirely a matter of style. As usual, it's probably best to be consistent within a codebase.

Default Export

Aside from named exports, a module can also optionally have a single default export. A default export is just like a named export using the name default, but it has its own dedicated syntax (and doesn't create a local binding called default). You set the default export by adding the keyword default after export:

```
export default function example() {
    // ...
}
```

Another module imports it by using any name the author likes, without curly braces around it:

```
import x from "./mod.js";
```

If what you're exporting has a name, that name isn't used in the export, since this form exports the default. For instance, with the preceding export of a function called example, other code can import it this way:

```
import example from "./mod.js";
// or
import ex from "./mod.js"; // The name of the import doesn't have to be "example"
```

but not like this, because it's not a named export:

```
// WRONG (for importing a default export)
import { example } from "./mod.js";
```

More than one export default in a module is an error; a module can only have one default export.

You can declare something and then export it as the default separately:

```
function example() {
}
export default example;
```

There's a second form of default export that lets you export the result of any arbitrary expression:

```
export default 6 * 7;
```

EXPORTING AN ANONYMOUS FUNCTION OR CLASS DECLARATION

It's almost just a curiosity, but note that this:

```
export default function() { /*...*/ }
```

is an exported function *declaration*, not a function *expression*. A default export is the only place you can have a function declaration without a name; the resulting function will have the name `default`. Since it's a function declaration, it's hoisted like all other function declarations (the function is created before the step-by-step execution of the module begins), although that's rarely important.

You can also have an anonymous `class` declaration, again only when doing a default export:

```
export default class { /*...*/ }
```

But since it's a `class` declaration, the class isn't created until execution of the code reaches the declaration; it's in the TDZ until then. (More on how the TDZ applies to modules later in this chapter.)

This form of default export is exactly like a `let` export, just without an identifier that the module code could use to access it. If you could call a variable `*default*`, then

```
export default 6 * 7;
```

would be the same as

```
// Conceptual, not valid syntax
let *default* = 6 * 7;
export default *default*;
```

but with `*default*` not being accessible to the module's code. (You'll learn why I used `*default*` later when we talk about bindings.)

Even though technically the specification has this arbitrary expression export create the equivalent of a `let` variable (not a `const`), there's no way for code to change its value, so it's effectively constant.

Since this form evaluates an expression, just like a `let` export it doesn't have a value until the export declaration is reached in the step-by-step execution of the code. Until then, it's in the TDZ.

Using Modules in Browsers

In a web page application, you typically use a single entry point module to start loading the module tree (although it's possible to have more than one). The entry point module imports from other modules (which may in turn import from other modules, and so on). To tell the browser that a `script` element's code is a module, you use `type="module"`:

```
<script src="main.js" type="module"></script>
```

Let's look at a simple browser-based example; see Listings 13-1, 13-2, and 13-3. You can run this example using the files from the downloads in any modern browser.

LISTING 13-1: A simple module example (HTML)—simple.html

```html
<!doctype html>
<html>
<head>
<meta charset="UTF-8">
<title>Simple Module Example</title>
</head>
<body>
<script src="./simple.js" type="module"></script>
</body>
</html>
```

LISTING 13-2: A simple module example (entry point module)—simple.js

```js
import { log } from "./log.js";

log("Hello, modules!");
```

LISTING 13-3: A simple module example (log module)—log.js

```js
export function log(msg) {
    const p = document.createElement("pre");
    p.appendChild(document.createTextNode(msg));
    document.body.appendChild(p);
}
```

When you load `simple.html` in the browser, the browser and JavaScript engine work together to load the `simple.js` module, detect its dependency on `log.js`, load and run `log.js`, and then run `simple.js`'s code—which uses the `log` function from `log.js` to log a message.

Note that `log.js` isn't listed anywhere in the HTML. The fact that `simple.js` depends on it is indicated by the `import` statement. You *could* add a `script` tag for `log.js` before the one for `simple.js` if you liked, perhaps to start the process of loading it earlier, but normally there's no need. (If you did, `log.js` would still only be loaded once.)

Module Scripts Don't Delay Parsing

A `script` tag with `type="module"` doesn't hold up the parsing of the HTML while the script is fetched and executed like a non-module `script` tag does. Instead, the module and its dependencies are loaded in parallel with the parsing; then the module's code is run when the parsing is complete (or when it finishes loading, whichever happens last).

If that sounds familiar, it's because it's how a `script` tag with the `defer` attribute is handled. In effect, `script type="module"` tags implicitly have `defer` on them. (Specifying it explicitly has no effect.)

There is one difference though: the `defer` attribute only defers scripts that load their content from an external resource via the `src` attribute, not script tags with inline content. But `type="module"` defers scripts with inline content, too.

Notice that although the module's code isn't run until the HTML parsing is complete, the browser and JavaScript engine *do* work together to determine the module's dependencies (from its `import` declarations) and fetch any modules it depends on in parallel with the HTML parsing. The module's code doesn't have to run for its dependencies to be loaded, since modules are statically analyzable.

As with non-module `script` tags, you can include the `async` attribute to make the browser run the module's code as soon as it's ready to be run, even if the HTML parsing isn't complete yet. You can see how different `script` tags are processed in Figure 13-2, which is inspired by the diagram in the WHAT-WG HTML specification in the section describing the `async` and `defer` attributes.[2]

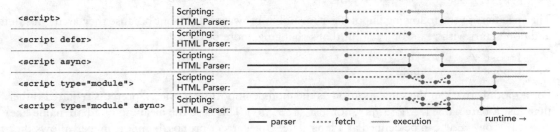

FIGURE 13-2

The nomodule Attribute

If you want to serve modules to browsers that support them but serve non-module scripts to browsers that don't (like Internet Explorer), you can use the `nomodule` attribute on the non-module scripts, like this:

```
<script type="module" src="./module.js"></script>
<script nomodule src="./script.js"></script>
```

Unfortunately, Internet Explorer will download *both* files, even though it will only run the `script.js` file. Safari did that for several versions as well, as did Edge (even once it added module support), but both are fixed now.

To work around that, you can identify the module/script to load using inline code instead:

```
<script type="module">
import "./module.js";
</script>
<script nomodule>
document.write('<script defer src="script.js"><\/script>');
</script>
```

(If you don't care for `document.write`—and many don't—you could always use `createElement` and `appendChild`.)

---

[2] `https://html.spec.whatwg.org/multipage/scripting.html#attr-script-defer`

Module Specifiers on the Web

As of this writing, the HTML specification defines module specifiers quite narrowly so that they can be enhanced over time: module specifiers are either absolute URLs, or relative URLs starting with / (a slash, or "solidus" as the spec calls it), ./ (dot slash), or ../ (dot dot slash). Like URLs in CSS files, relative URLs are resolved relative to the resource the import declaration is in, not the base document. The module is identified by its *resolved* URL (so different relative paths to the module all resolve to the same module).

The specifiers in the following imports are all valid:

```
import /*...*/ "http://example.com/a.js"; // Absolute URL
import /*...*/ "/a.js";                    // Starts with /
import /*...*/ './b.js';                   // Starts with ./
import /*...*/ "../c.js";                  // Starts with ../
import /*...*/ './modules/d.js';           // Starts with ./
```

The specifiers in the following imports are invalid in browsers at present because they aren't absolute and don't start with /, ./, or ../ (but that's changing, more below):

```
import /*...*/ "fs";
import /*...*/ "f.js";
```

For a module that's in the same location as the module importing it, the ./ prefix is required rather than just a bare name ("./mod.js", not just "mod.js"). This is so the meaning of a bare name like "mod.js" or "mod" can be defined at a later date. One current proposal, import maps,[3] allows the page to define a map of module specifiers to URLs, so that the contents of the modules could use bare names while allowing the containing page flexibility in terms of where those modules are actually located. That proposal is still in flux, but seems likely to progress.

The specifier must include the file extension if you use one on your files; there's no default extension or extensions. The extension you use is up to you, just as with non-module scripts. Many programmers stick with .js. However, some are choosing .mjs instead to flag up the fact that the file contains a module, not just a script. If you do that, be sure to configure your web server to serve the file with the correct MIME type, text/javascript, because modules don't have their own MIME type. For what it's worth, my view is that modules are the new normal, and so I'm sticking with .js.

Aside from the next section on Node.js, the specifiers shown in this chapter are all as defined for the web by the HTML specification.

Using Modules in Node.js

Node.js supports JavaScript's native modules (ESM), in addition to its original CommonJS-like (CJS) modules.[4] As of this writing, ESM support is still marked "experimental" but it's quite far along. In v12 (including the v12 long-term status release) it's behind an --experimental-modules flag, but it's no longer behind a flag in v13 and above.

> **CHANGES BETWEEN V8 THROUGH V11 AND V12 AND ABOVE**
>
> Node.js's ESM support in v8 through v11 was primarily based on file extensions; this section describes the newer behavior in v12 and above.

---

[3] https://wicg.github.io/import-maps/
[4] https://nodejs.org/api/esm.html

Because Node.js has long has its own CJS-based module system, you have to opt in when using ESM. You do that in one of three ways:

1. Have a `package.json` in your project with a `type` field with the value `"module"`:

```
{
    "name": "mypackage",
    "type": "module",
    ...other usual fields...
}
```

2. Use `.mjs` as the file extension on your ESM module files

3. When passing a string to `node` (as an argument to `--eval`, `--print`, or piping text into `node`), specify `--input-type=module`

This applies both to the entry point you provide the `node` command line and to any modules you `import` in your ESM code.

See Listings 13-4, 13-5, and 13-6 for an example with `package.json` with a `"type": "module"` field. You'd run the example like this with v12:

```
node --experimental-modules index.js
```

With v13 and above, the flag is no longer needed:

```
node index.js
```

LISTING 13-4: A simple Node.js module example (main entry point)—index.js

```
import { sum } from "./sum.js";

console.log(`1 + 2 = ${sum(1, 2)}`);
```

LISTING 13-5: A simple Node.js module example (sum module)—sum.js

```
export function sum(...numbers) {
    return numbers.reduce((a, b) => a + b);
}
```

LISTING 13-6: A simple Node.js module example (package)—package.json

```
{
    "name": "modexample",
    "type": "module"
}
```

Alternatively, if you removed the `type` field from `package.json` (or changed it to `"commonjs"`), you could use ESM by changing the names to `index.mjs` and `sum.mjs` instead (both in the names of the files and in the `import` statement in `index`).

By default, when you're importing a module from a file using ESM you must include the file extension in your `import` statement. (More later in the "Module Specifiers in Node.js" section.) Notice that it's `./sum.js` in Listing 13-4, not just `./sum`. You *don't* use an extension when importing built-in packages such as `"fs"` or packages in `node_modules`. You just use the module name:

```
import fs from "fs";

fs.writeFile("example.txt", "Example of using the fs module\n", "utf8", err => {
    // ...
});
```

The built-in modules all provide named exports as well, so the preceding code could be written like this:

```
import { writeFile } from "fs";

writeFile("example.txt", "Example of using the fs module\n", "utf8", err => {
    // ...
});
```

Regardless of whether you're using `"type": "module"` in `package.json`, if you import a file with the extension `.cjs`, Node.js will load it as a CJS module:

```
import example from "./example.cjs"; // example.cjs must be a CJS module
```

ESM modules can import from CJS modules: the `exports` value in the CJS module is treated like a default export. For instance, if `mod.cjs` has

```
exports.nifty = function() { };
```

an ESM module would import it like this:

```
import mod from "./mod.cjs";
```

and then either use `mod.nifty` or perhaps use a destructuring assignment after the import to get a standalone `nifty`:

```
import mod from "./mod.cjs";
const { nifty } = mod;
```

That code can't use the named export form `import { nifty }` because that's a static import declaration, which means it has to be statically analyzable. But CJS module exports are dynamic, not static: you specify CJS exports by assigning to an `exports` object with runtime code. Supporting named imports from CJS would require a change to the JavaScript specification to allow dynamic named exports. There are ongoing discussions of whether and how to address that, but for now (or possibly forever), the CJS `exports` value is supported as just the default export. (This is true even when using dynamic import, which you'll learn about in a later section.)

CJS modules cannot import from ESM modules except through dynamic import.

Module Specifiers in Node.js

When importing a module *file*, module specifiers in Node.js are very much like those defined for the web by default: absolute or relative filenames (rather than URLs), and the file extension is required. The file extension part of that is different from Node.js's CJS module loader, which lets you leave off the extension and then checks for a file with various extensions (`.js`, `.json`, etc.). However, you can enable that behavior using a command-line argument. In v12, you'd do it like this:

```
node --experimental-modules --es-module-specifier-resolution=node index.js
```

In v13, the flag is slightly different (and you don't need the modules flag):

```
node --experimental-specifier-resolution=node index.js
```

If you were using the flag, the `import` in Listing 13-4 earlier could leave off the `.js` extension:

```
import { sum } from "./sum"; // If node resolution mode is enabled via flag
```

As you saw earlier with the example using the `fs` module, you use bare names when importing built-in packages or ones installed in `node_modules`:

```
import { writeFile } from "fs";
```

Node.js is Adding More Module Features

Node.js isn't just sticking with the `type` property in `package.json` and the basic features described herein. There's lots of work going on—export maps, various package features, etc. Most of these are still at relatively early stages as of this writing, so I won't go into details here as the details are a moving target for now. You can learn about them on the Node.js website in the ECMAScript Modules section (`https://nodejs.org/api/esm.html`).

RENAMING EXPORTS

The identifier you export from a module doesn't have to be the same as the identifier you use for it within your module's code. You can rename the export by using an `as` clause within the export declaration:

```
let nameWithinModule = 42;
export { nameWithinModule as exportedName };
```

You'd import that in another module using the name `exportedName`:

```
import { exportedName } from "./mod.js";
```

The `nameWithinModule` is just for use *within* the module, not outside it.

You can only rename on export when exporting separately, not when exporting inline (so not when doing `export let nameWithinModule` or similar).

If you want to create an alias (for instance, for a situation like `trimLeft`/`trimStart` that you learned about in Chapter 10), you can both export inline with one name, and then use a renaming export as well:

```
export function expandStart() {        // expandStart is the primary name
    // ...
}
export { expandStart as expandLeft }; // expandLeft is an alias
```

That code creates two exports, `expandStart` and `expandLeft`, for the same function.

You can use renaming syntax to create a default export as well, although it's not best practice:

```
export { expandStart as default }; // Not best practice
```

As you learned earlier, the default export is just like a named export using the exported name `default`, so that's equivalent to the default-specific form you learned earlier:

```
export default expandStart;
```

RE-EXPORTING EXPORTS FROM ANOTHER MODULE

A module can re-export another module's exports:

```
export { example } from "./example.js";
```

These are called *indirect exports*.

One place this is useful is in "roll-up" modules. Suppose you were writing a DOM manipulation library like jQuery. While you could write it as a single massive module containing everything the library provides, that would mean any code using it has to reference that one module, which brings *all* of the module's code into memory even if it won't all be used. (Probably; more later when we talk about *tree shaking*.) Instead, you might break the library into smaller parts that consumers of the library could import from. For instance:

```
import { selectAll, selectFirst } from "./lib-select.js";
import { animate } from "./lib-animate.js";
// ...code using selectAll, selectFirst, and animate...
```

Then, for projects that are likely to use all of the library's features or that don't care about loading the entire lib into memory, the lib could provide a roll-up module with all of its parts gathered together, perhaps as `lib.js`:

```
export { selectAll, selectFirst, selectN } from "./lib-select.js";
export { animate, AnimationType, Animator } from "./lib-animate.js";
export { attr, hasAttr } from "./lib-manipulate.js";
// ...
```

Code can then just use `lib.js` when importing all of those functions:

```
import { selectAll, selectFirst, animate } from "./lib.js";
// ...code using selectAll, selectFirst, and animate...
```

Explicitly listing those exports introduces a maintenance issue, though: if you add a new export to `lib-select.js` (for instance), it's easy to forget to update `lib.js` to export the new item. To avoid that, there's a special form using an asterisk (*) that says "export all named exports from this other module":

```
export * from "./lib-select.js";
export * from "./lib-animate.js";
export * from "./lib-manipulate.js";
// ...
```

`export *` does not export the default export of the module, just the named ones.

Re-exporting only creates an export; it doesn't import the item into the scope of the module re-exporting it:

```
export { example } from "./mod.js";
console.log(example); // ReferenceError: example is not defined
```

If you need to import the item as well as exporting it, you do each part separately:

```
import { example } from "./mod.js";
```

```
export { example };
console.log(example);
```

When re-exporting, you can change the name of the export using an `as` clause:

```
export { example as mod1_example } from "./mod1.js";
export { example as mod2_example } from "./mod2.js";
```

As it almost literally says in the syntax, that re-exports `mod1.js`'s example as `mod1_example`, and `mod2.js`'s example as `mod2_example`.

There's another way a module can export another module's exports which you'll learn about in "Exporting Another Module's Namespace Object" later in this chapter.

RENAMING IMPORTS

Suppose you have two modules that both export an `example` function, and you want to use both of those functions in your module. Or the name the module used conflicts with something in your code. If you've read the earlier sections about renaming exports, you've probably guessed you can rename imports the same way—with an `as` clause:

```
import { example as aExample } from "./a.js";
import { example as bExample } from "./b.js";

// Using them
aExample();
bExample();
```

When importing the default export, as you've already learned you're always picking your own name, so an `as` clause isn't relevant:

```
import someName from "./mod.js";
import someOtherName from "./mod.js";
console.log(someName === someOtherName); // true
```

As with the renaming form of `export`, you can also use the renaming form of `import` to import the default export if you like, although it's not best practice:

```
import { default as someOtherName }; // Not best practice
```

IMPORTING A MODULE'S NAMESPACE OBJECT

Instead of (or in addition to) importing individual exports, you can import a *module namespace object* for an entire module. A module namespace object is an object with properties for all of the module's exports (if there's a default export, its property's name is, of course, `default`). So if you have this `module.js`:

```
export function example() {
    console.log("example called");
}
export let something = "something";
export default function() {
    console.log("default called");
}
```

you could import the module's namespace object using a form of import declaration you haven't seen beforet:

```
import * as mod from "./module.js";
mod.example();                 // example called
console.log(mod.something);   // something
mod.default();                 // default called
```

The `*` `as` `mod` means to import the module's namespace object and associate it with the local identifier (binding) `mod`.

The module namespace object is not the same thing as the module. It's a separate object that is constructed the first time it's requested (never constructed at all if nothing requests it) with properties for all of the module's exports. The properties' values are updated dynamically as the source module changes the values of its exports (if it does). Once the module namespace object has been constructed, it's reused if other modules also import the module's namespace object. The object is read-only: its properties can't be written to, and you can't add new properties to it.

EXPORTING ANOTHER MODULE'S NAMESPACE OBJECT

As of a normative change in ES2020 which fast-tracked a proposal,[5] a module can provide an export that resolves to another module's namespace object. Suppose you have this export in `module1.js`:

```
// In module1.js
export * as stuff from "./module2.js";
```

That creates a named export in `module1.js` called `stuff` that, when imported, imports the module namespace object for `module2.js`. That means that in, say, `module3.js`, this import:

```
// In module3.js
import { stuff } from "./module1.js";
```

and this import:

```
// In module3.js
import * as stuff from "./module2.js";
```

do the same thing: import the module namespace object from `module2.js`, creating it if necessary, and binding it to the local name `stuff` in `module3.js`.

As with the forms you learned in "Re-Exporting Exports from Another Module" earlier, this is sometimes useful when building rollup modules. It also improved the symmetry between the `import` forms and the `export...from` forms. Just like the import form

```
import { x } from "./mod.js";
```

has the corresponding `export...from` form

```
export { x } from "./mod.js";
```

and the `import` form

```
import { x as v } from "./mod.js";
```

has the corresponding `export...from` form

```
export { x as v } from "./mod.js";
```

---

[5] https://github.com/tc39/proposal-export-ns-from

the `import` form

```
import * as name from "./mod.js";
```

now has the corresponding `export...from` form

```
export * as name from "./mod.js";
```

IMPORTING A MODULE JUST FOR SIDE EFFECTS

You can import a module without importing anything from it, just to load and run it:

```
import "./mod.js";
```

Suppose that import is in the module `main.js`. This adds `mod.js` to the list of modules `main.js` needs, but doesn't import anything from it. Loading `mod.js` runs its top-level code (after loading any modules it depends on), so this is useful for when you only need to import the module for any side effects its top-level code may have.

In general, it's best if a module's top-level code doesn't have any side effects, but for the occasional use case where making an exception is appropriate, this provides a way of triggering the module's top-level code.

You briefly saw one possible use case earlier in the section on the `nomodule` attribute: providing a module entry point for browsers that support modules and a non-module entry point for browsers that don't, without making some browsers (Internet Explorer, some older versions of Safari and Edge, perhaps others) download *both* the module and non-module code even though they'll only execute one of them.

IMPORT AND EXPORT ENTRIES

When the JavaScript engine parses a module, it builds a list of the module's *import entries* (the things it imports) and a list of its *export entries* (the things it exports). The lists provide a way for the specification to describe how module loading and linking happens (which you'll learn more about later). Your code can't access these lists directly, but let's take a look at them, since they'll help you understand later sections.

Import Entries

A module's list of import entries describes what it imports. Each import entry has three fields:

➤   *[[ModuleRequest]]*: The module specifier string from the import declaration. This says what module the import comes from.

➤   *[[ImportName]]*: The name of the thing being imported. It's "*" if you're importing the module namespace object.

➤   *[[LocalName]]*: The name of the local identifier (binding) to use for the imported item. Often, this is the same as the [[ImportName]], but if you've used `as` in the import declaration to rename the import, they can differ.

To see how these fields relate to the different forms of import declarations, see Table 13-1 on the next page, which is strongly based on "Table 44 (Informative): Import Forms Mappings to ImportEntry Records" from the specification.

TABLE 13-1: Import Statements and Import Entries

IMPORT STATEMENT FORM	[[MODULEREQUEST]]	[[IMPORTNAME]]	[[LOCALNAME]]
`import v from "mod";`	`"mod"`	`"default"`	`"v"`
`import * as ns from "mod";`	`"mod"`	`"*"`	`"ns"`
`import {x} from "mod";`	`"mod"`	`"x"`	`"x"`
`import {x as v} from "mod";`	`"mod"`	`"x"`	`"v"`
`import "mod";`	An ImportEntry Record is not created.		

The reason there's no import entry created when you import a module just for its side effects (`import "mod";` at the end of the table) is that this list is specifically about what *things* (bindings) the module imports. The list of other modules a module requests is a separate list also created during parsing; modules imported just for their side effects are included on that other list.

This list of entries tells the JavaScript engine what this module needs in order to be loaded.

Export Entries

A module's list of export entries describes what it exports. Each export entry has four fields:

➤ *[[ExportName]]:* The name of the export. This is the name other modules use when importing. It's the string `"default"` for the default export. It's `null` for an `export * from` declaration that re-exports everything from another module (instead, the export list from that other module is used).

➤ *[[LocalName]]:* The name of the local identifier (binding) being exported. This is often the same as [[ExportName]], but if you've renamed an export, they can be different. This is `null` if this entry is for an `export ... from` declaration that re-exports another module's export(s), since there's no local name involved.

➤ *[[ModuleRequest]]:* For re-exports, it's the module specifier string from the `export ... from` declaration. This is `null` for a module's own exports.

➤ *[[ImportName]];* For re-exports, this is the name of the export in the other module to re-export. Often, this is the same as [[ExportName]], but if you've used an `as` clause in the re-export declaration, they can differ. This is `null` for a module's own exports.

To see how these fields relate to the different forms of export declarations, see Table 13-2, which is strongly based on "Table 46 (Informative): Export Forms Mappings to ExportEntry Records" from the specification.

This list of entries tells the JavaScript engine what this module provides when it's loaded.

TABLE 13-2:

EXPORT STATEMENT FORM	[[EXPORTNAME]]	[[MODULEREQUEST]]	[[IMPORTNAME]]	[[LOCALNAME]]
export var v;	"v"	null	null	"v"
export default function f() {}	"default"	null	null	"f"
export default function () {}	"default"	null	null	"*default*"
export default 42;	"default"	null	null	"*default*"
export {x};	"x"	null	null	"x"
export {v as x};	"x"	null	null	"v"
export {x} from "mod";	"x"	"mod"	"x"	null
export {v as x} from "mod";	"x"	"mod"	"v"	null
export * from "mod";	null	"mod"	"*"	null
export * as ns from "mod";	"ns"	"mod"	"*"	null

IMPORTS ARE LIVE AND READ-ONLY

When you import something from a module, you get a read-only live binding, called an *indirect binding*, to the original item. Since it's read-only, your code can't assign a new value to the binding; but since it's a live binding, your code does see any new values that the original module assigns to it. For instance, suppose you had the `mod.js` shown in Listing 13-7 and the `main.js` shown in Listing 13-8 (you can run these from the downloads using the provided `main.html` file).

LISTING 13-7: A simple module with counter—mod.js

```
const a = 1;
let c = 0;
export { c as counter };
export function increment() {
    ++c;
}
```

LISTING 13-8: A module using the counter module—main.js

```
import { counter, increment as inc } from "./mod.js";
console.log(counter); // 0
inc();
console.log(counter); // 1
counter = 42;          // TypeError: Assignment to constant variable.
```

As you can see, the code in `main.js` sees changes to `counter` that `mod.js` makes, but cannot directly set its value. The error message shown in the listing is V8's current message (in Chrome); SpiderMonkey (in Firefox) says `TypeError: "counter" is read-only`.

You'll recall from Chapter 2's "Bindings: How Variables, Constants, and Other Identifiers Work" section that variables, constants, and other identifiers are conceptually *bindings* in an *environment object* (very similar to properties in an object). Each binding has a name, a flag for whether it's mutable (mutable = you can change its value, immutable = you can't), and the current value of the binding. For instance, this code:

```
const a = 1;
```

creates a binding within the current environment object as in Figure 13-3.

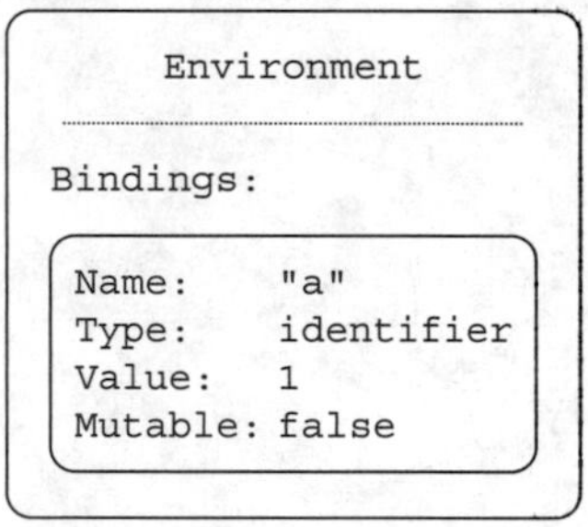

```
        Environment
..................................

Bindings:

  Name:     "a"
  Type:     identifier
  Value:    1
  Mutable:  false
```

FIGURE 13-3

Each module has a *module environment object*. (Don't confuse this with the similarly named "module namespace object;" they're different things.) The module environment object has bindings for all of the exports and imports of that module (but not its re-exports from other modules) as well as other top-level bindings that aren't either exported or imported (bindings just used within the module). In a module environment object, bindings can be either direct (for exports and non-exported bindings) or indirect (for imports). An indirect binding stores a link to the source module (which links to that module's environment object) and the name of the binding in that module's environment to use, rather than directly storing the value of the binding.

When `main.js` imports from `mod.js` as shown in the listings, `main.js`'s module environment has indirect bindings for `counter` and `inc` that refer to the `mod.js` module and its environment object's `c` and `increment` bindings, as in Figure 13-4. In the indirect bindings, `Module` is the link to the module, and `Binding Name` is the name of the binding in that module's environment to use.

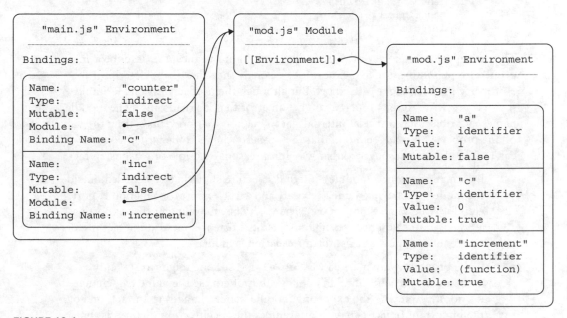

FIGURE 13-4

(You may be wondering how `main.js` knows that the binding for the `counter` export it imported from `mod.js` is `c`. The JavaScript engine got that information from the list of export entries for `mod.js` that you learned about in the last section. You'll learn more about this in a bit.)

When `main.js` reads the value of `counter`, the JavaScript engine sees that `main.js`'s environment object has an indirect binding for `counter`, gets the environment object for `mod.js`, then gets the value of the binding named `c` from that module's environment object and uses that as the resulting value.

This read-only-but-may-change nature of imported bindings is also evident in the properties of a module namespace object: you can only read the values of the properties, you can't set their values.

MODULE NAMESPACE OBJECT PROPERTY DESCRIPTIONS

If you use `Object.getOwnPropertyDescriptor` on the module namespace object property for an export, the descriptor you get back always looks like this:

```
{
    value: /*...the value...*/,
    writable: true,
    enumerable: true,
    configurable: false
}
```

The descriptor doesn't vary other than the `value`. For instance, the descriptor for a property representing a `const` export looks exactly the same as the descriptor for a property representing a `let` export. But although the property says its writable, if you try to write to the property, you get an error that it's read-only. (The module namespace object has a special internal [[Set]] method that prevents setting the value of any property.) It may seem odd that the property claims to be writable when you can't write to it, but it's marked that way for a reason. A couple of reasons, in fact:

➤ Information about a module's internal structure shouldn't be revealed outside the module, so having a `const` export and a `let` export (or function export, etc.) look the same is important. (There may be an argument that exporting a `const` means you're exporting not just its existence but also the fact it's a `const`, but for now at least the information is hidden.)

➤ If the property were marked `writable: false`, one might mistakenly assume that the value couldn't change, but of course the value *can* change if it's not a `const` and the exporting module's code changes it. In fact, one of the important object behavior guarantees the specification dictates is that if a non-configurable, non-writable *data property* (not accessor) has been observed to have a value, reading it again later must return that same value. (This is in the spec's "Invariants of the Essential Internal Methods" section.[6] You'll learn more about these invariant behavior guarantees in Chapter 14.) No object is allowed to break that rule. So these properties have to be defined as writable.

MODULE INSTANCES ARE REALM-SPECIFIC

Earlier you learned (in passing) that a module is loaded only once per realm (window, tab, worker, etc.). Specifically, the JavaScript engine keeps track of loaded modules within the realm and reuses ones that are requested more than once. That's realm-specific, though; different realms do not share module instances.

---

[6] https://tc39.github.io/ecma262/#sec-invariants-of-the-essential-internal-methods

For instance, if you have a window with an `iframe` in it, the main window and the `iframe`'s window have different realms. If code in both windows loads the module `mod.js`, it gets loaded twice: once in the main window's realm, and again in the `iframe` window's realm. Those two copies of the module are completely separate from one another, even more so than the two global environments in the windows (which have links between them via the main window's `frames` array and the `iframe` window's `parent` variable). Any modules loaded by `mod.js` are also loaded twice, as are their dependencies, etc. Modules are only shared within the realm, not between realms.

HOW MODULES ARE LOADED

The JavaScript module system is designed to keep simple use cases simple, but to handle complex use cases well. To do that, modules are loaded in three phases:

➤ *Fetching and Parsing*: Fetching the module's source text and parsing it, determining its imports and exports.

➤ *Instantiation*: Creating the module's environment and its bindings, including bindings for all of its imports and exports.

➤ *Evaluation*: Running the module's code.

To illustrate the process, we'll refer to the code in Listings 13-9 through 13-12.

LISTING 13-9: HTML page for module loading example—loading.html

```
<!doctype html>
<html>
<head>
<meta charset="UTF-8">
<title>Module Loading</title>
</head>
<body>
<script src="entry.js" type="module"></script>
</body>
</html>
```

LISTING 13-10: Module loading entry point—entry.js

```
import { fn1 } from "./mod1.js";
import def, { fn2 } from "./mod2.js";

fn1();
fn2();
def();
```

LISTING 13-11: Module loading mod1—mod1.js

```javascript
import def from "./mod2.js";

const indentString = "  ";

export function indent(nest = 0) {
    return indentString.repeat(nest);
}

export function fn1(nest = 0) {
    console.log(`${indent(nest)}mod1 - fn1`);
    def(nest + 1);
}
```

LISTING 13-12: Module loading mod2—mod2.js

```javascript
import { fn1, indent } from "./mod1.js";

export function fn2(nest = 0) {
    console.log(`${indent(nest)}mod2 - fn2`);
    fn1(nest + 1);
}

export default function(nest = 0) {
    console.log(`${indent(nest)}mod2 - default`);
}
```

As you can see from the listings, the `entry.js` module imports from two other modules, which are interdependent: `mod1.js` uses `mod2.js`'s default export, and `mod2.js` uses `mod1.js`'s named exports `fn1` and `indent`. The two modules are in a cyclic relationship. Most of your modules won't have cyclic relationships like that, but having that relationship lets the example show the basics of how that's handled.

When you run the listings' code from the downloads, this is the result you'll see in the console:

```
mod1 - fn1
  mod2 - default
mod2 - fn2
  mod1 - fn1
    mod2 - default
mod2 - default
```

Let's look at how the browser (the host for the JavaScript engine in this example) gets there.

Fetching and Parsing

When the host (the browser) sees the

```html
<script src="entry.js" type="module"></script>
```

tag, it fetches `entry.js` and passes the source text to the JavaScript engine to parse as a module. Unlike non-module scripts, module scripts don't hold up the HTML parser, so the HTML parser continues while the work to parse and load the module is done. Specifically, a module script is, by default, *deferred* (as though it had the `defer` attribute), which means that its code won't be evaluated until the HTML parser has finished parsing the page. (You can specify `async` instead if you want evaluation to happen as soon as possible, even before the HTML parser is done.)

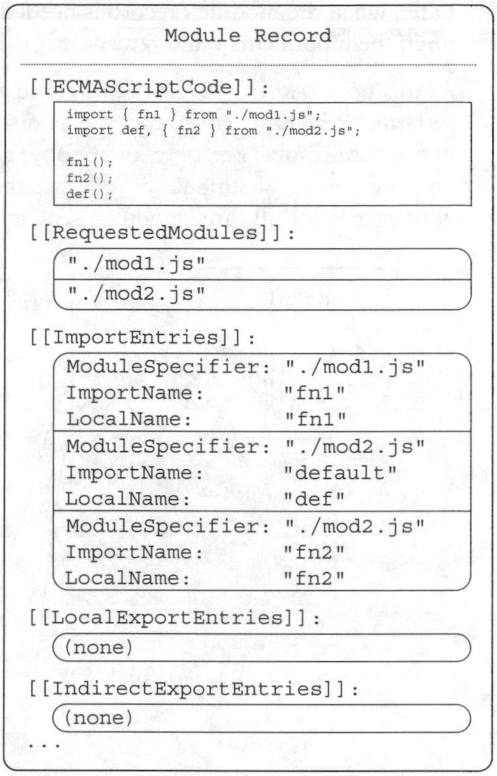

When the browser passes the contents of `entry.js` to the JavaScript engine, the engine parses it and creates a *module record* for it. The module record contains the parsed code, a list of the modules that this module requires, the module's lists of import entries and export entries that you learned about a couple of sections ago, and various other bookkeeping details such as the status of the module (where it is in the process of being loaded and evaluated). Note that all of that information was determined statically, just by *parsing* the module's code, not *executing* it. See Figure 13-5 for what the key parts of the module record for `entry.js` would look like. (The names in the figure are from the specification, which uses the convention `[[Name]]` — a name in double square brackets—for fields in conceptual objects.)

FIGURE 13-5

The JavaScript engine returns that module record to the host, which saves it in a map of resolved modules (the *module map*) under its fully resolved module specifier (for instance, `http://localhost/entry.js` if `loading.html` is from `http://localhost`). See Figure 13-6.

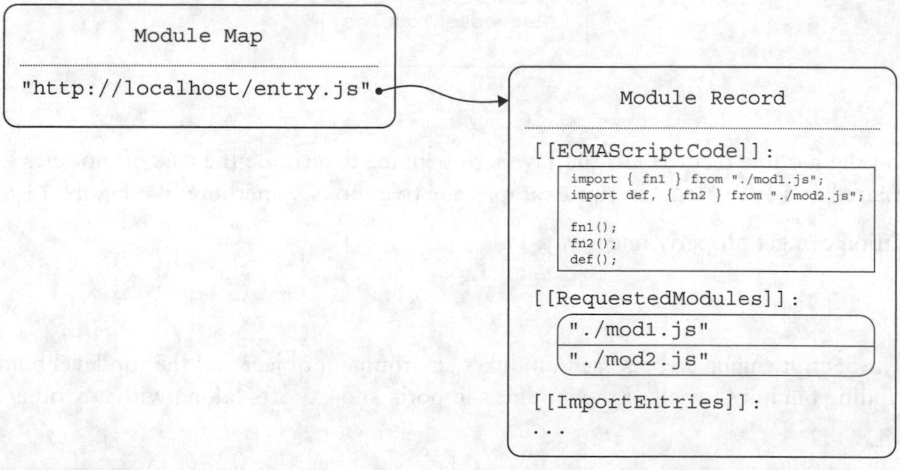

FIGURE 13-6

Later, when the module's record is needed, the JavaScript engine asks the host for it; the host looks it up in the module map and returns it if found.

At this point `entry.js` has been fetched and parsed, so the JavaScript engine starts `entry.js`'s *instantiation* phase (covered in the next section). Essentially the first thing that does is ask the browser to resolve `mod1.js` and `mod2.js`, which the browser and JavaScript engine interact to do just like they did with `entry.js`. Once they're fetched and parsed, the browser has a module map with entries for all three modules; see Figure 13-7.

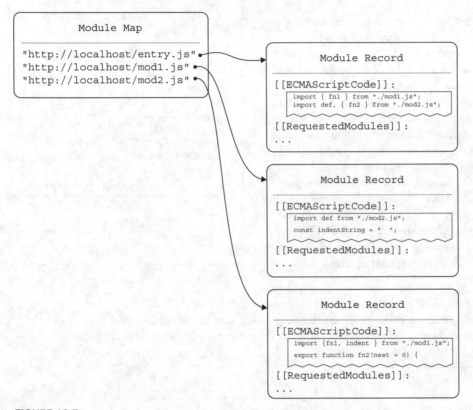

FIGURE 13-7

The information in the module records lets the JavaScript engine determine the tree of modules that need to be instantiated and evaluated.[7] In this example, the tree looks something like Figure 13-8.

Now, the instantiation can get properly underway.

Instantiation

In this phase, the JavaScript engine creates each module's environment object and the top-level bindings within it, including bindings for all of the module's imports and exports (along with any other

---

[7] Pedants like to point out that it's a *graph*, not a tree, since it can have cyclic relationships. But nearly everyone else calls it the module tree.

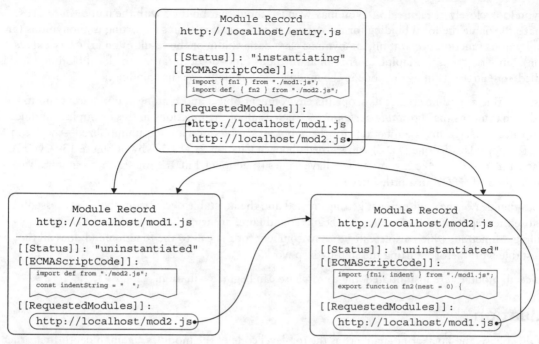

FIGURE 13-8

locals it may have, like `indentString` in `mod1.js`). For locals (including exported ones), these are direct bindings. For imports, these are indirect bindings that the engine wires up to the exporting module's binding for the export. Instantiation is done using depth-first traversal, so that the lowest-level modules are instantiated first. In the current example, the resulting environments look something like Figure 13-9.

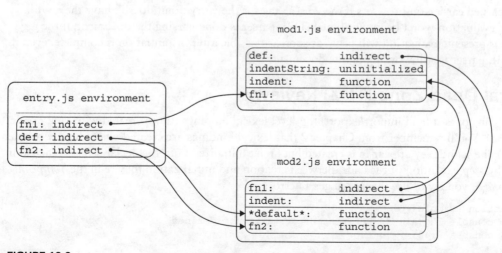

FIGURE 13-9

If you look closely at Figure 13-9, you may wonder about that binding with the name `*default*`. That's the name the local binding for the default export gets if what it's exporting is anonymous (an anonymous function declaration, anonymous class declaration, or the result of an arbitrary expression). Since `mod2.js`'s default export is an anonymous function declaration, the local binding for it is called `*default*`. (But again, code in the module can't actually use that binding.)

Instantiating a module creates its scope (its environment object and bindings), but doesn't run its code. That means that *hoistable declarations* (such as all of the functions in this example's modules) are processed, creating the functions for them, but lexical bindings are left uninitialized—they're in the Temporal Dead Zone (TDZ) you learned about in Chapter 2. That's why in Figure 13-9, you see that `indent` and `*default*` and others have values (functions), but `indentString` is uninitialized. More about the TDZ in a little bit.

Does the idea of the environment getting created and the hoistable declarations being processed before the step-by-step code execution begins sound familiar? Right! It's a lot like the first part of calling a function, which also creates the environment for the call to the function and does all the hoistable work before starting the step-by-step work.

Once all modules are instantiated, the third phase can begin: evaluation.

Evaluation

In this phase, the JavaScript engine runs the top-level code of the modules, again in depth-first order, marking each of them as "evaluated" as it goes. This is like the second part of a function call, the step-by-step execution of the code. As the code runs, any top-level uninitialized bindings (like `mod1.js`'s `indentString`) get initialized as they're reached in the code execution.

The JavaScript module system ensures that each module's top-level code is run just once. This is important, because modules may have side effects, although in the general case it's best if they don't (other than the main module of a page/application).

As you learned earlier, on browsers if the `script` tag for the entry point doesn't have the `async` attribute, evaluation won't begin until the HTML parser is done parsing the document. If the `async` attribute is present, evaluation will begin as soon as possible after instantiation is complete, even if the HTML parser is still working on the document.

Temporal Dead Zone (TDZ) Review

Modules can contain (and import/export) top-level lexical bindings (those created with `let`, `const`, and `class`). You'll remember from Chapter 2 that lexical bindings are created when the environment object for the scope they appear in is created but aren't initialized until the declaration is reached in the step-by-step execution of the code. Between creation and initialization they're in the *Temporal Dead Zone*; if you try to use them, you get an error:

```
function example() {
    console.log(a); // ReferenceError: a is not defined
    const a = 42;
}
example();
```

In that example, the environment object for the call to `example` is created upon entry to `example`, and so it has the a binding for its local `const`, but the binding is not yet initialized. When the code starts and the `console.log` gets run, since the binding for a is uninitialized, the attempt to use a fails.

You'll also recall that the Temporal Dead Zone is called *temporal* because it relates to the *time* between creation and initialization, not the relative location of the code "above" or "below" the declaration. The following works just fine:

```
function example() {
    const fn = () => {
        console.log(a); // 42
    };
    const a = 42;
    fn();
}
example();
```

It works because although the `console.log` line using a is above it in the code, that line isn't executed until *after* the declaration has been reached in the step-by-step execution of the code.

Finally, you'll remember that the TDZ only relates to lexical bindings, not to bindings created via hoistable declarations: `var`-declared variables or function declarations. A binding created with `var` is immediately initialized with the value `undefined`, and a binding created by a function declaration is immediately initialized with the function it declares.

How does this relate to modules? The TDZ applies to any time an environment object is created and gets its bindings—including the environment for a module. As you learned in the previous sections, the environment object for a module is created during module instantiation, and its code is run later during module evaluation. So any lexical bindings the module has in its top-level scope are in the TDZ from instantiation until the declaration is reached during evaluation.

This all means that if a module exports a lexical binding, in some situations that may make it possible for code to try to use the binding before it's initialized. For example, that's possible if module A imports from module B, and module B imports from module A (directly or indirectly)—a *cyclic dependency*. Let's look at that.

Cyclic Dependencies and the TDZ

In the module-loading example, `mod1.js` and `mod2.js` refer to one-another; they're in a cyclic dependency (a simple direct one). That's not a problem for the JavaScript module system, because of the three-phase process of loading and evaluating modules.

Notice how neither `mod1.js` nor `mod2.js` uses what it imports from the other in its top-level code; they only use what they imported in response to a function call. Suppose you changed that: modify your local copy of `mod2.js` to add a call to `console.log` at the top level as indicated in Listing 13-13.

LISTING 13-13: Module loading mod2 (updated)—mod2-updated.js

```
import { fn1, indent } from "./mod1.js";

console.log(`${indent(0)}hi there`);

export function fn2(nest = 0) {
    console.log(`${indent(nest)}mod2 - fn2`);
    fn1(nest + 1);
}

export default function(nest = 0) {
    console.log(`${indent(nest)}mod2 - default`);
}
```

Now reload `loading.html`. You get

```
ReferenceError: indentString is not defined
```

because `mod2.js` tries to use `indent` before `mod1.js` has been evaluated. The call to `indent` works, because `mod1.js` has been instantiated and so its hoistable declarations have been processed, but when `indent` tries to use `indentString`, it fails because `indentString` is still in the TDZ.

Now, try changing the declaration of `indentString` to a `var` instead of a `const`, and reload `loading.html`. You get a different error

```
TypeError: Cannot read property 'repeat' of undefined
```

because the binding was initialized with the value `undefined` during instantiation, since it's declared with `var`, and it hasn't been assigned the string with two spaces in it yet because the top-level code in `mod1.js` hasn't been evaluated yet.

Often, a cyclic dependency suggests that you may want to refactor. But when you can't avoid them, just remember that hoisted declarations will be fine (other than `var`-declared variables having the value `undefined`), and others will be fine if only used within functions (that aren't called directly from the top-level code), not in the top-level module code.

IMPORT/EXPORT SYNTAX REVIEW

You've learned about several different syntax options for import and export in this chapter. Let's do a quick roundup of them, showing you all of your options.

Export Varieties

Here's a rundown of the various export forms.

Each of the following declares a local binding (variable, constant, function, or class) and an export for it, using the binding's name for the export:

```
export var a;
export var b = /*...some value...*/;
```

```
export let c;
export let d = /*...some value...*/;
export const e = /*...some value...*/;
export function f() { // (and async and generator forms)
}
export class G() {
}
```

Each of the following declares exports for local bindings declared elsewhere in the module (they can be declared above or below the `export` declaration):

```
export { a };
export { b, c };
export { d as delta };      // The exported name is `delta`
export { e as epsilon, f }; // The local `e` is exported as `epsilon`
export { g, h as hotel, i}; // You can mix the various forms
```

For each binding, the binding's name is used for the export unless the as clause is included, in which case the name given after as is used for the export instead. The list of exports (the part within the curly braces) can have as many or as few exports in it as you like.

Each of the following declares an indirect export or exports, re-exporting one or more of mod.js's exports from the current module, optionally doing some renaming via the as clause:

```
export { a } from "./mod.js";
export { b, c } from "./mod.js";
export { d as delta } from "./mod.js";
export { e, f as foxtrot } from "./mod.js"; // You can do a mix of the above
```

This declares indirect exports for all named exports in mod.js:

```
export * from "./mod.js";
```

Each of the following declares a local binding (variable, constant, function, or class) and declares it as the default export:

```
// Only one of these can appear in any given module, since there can
// only be one default export in a module
export default function a() { /*...*/ }
export default class B { /*...*/ }
export default let c;
export default let d = "delta";
export default const e = "epsilon";
export default var f;
export default var g = "golf";
```

Each of the following declares a local binding called *default* (because each of these is anonymous), which your code cannot access since *default* is an invalid identifier. They export it as the default export:

```
export default function() { /*...*/ }
export default class { /*...*/ }
export default 6 * 7; // Any arbitrary expression
```

The function created by the anonymous function declaration will get "default" as its name, as will the class constructor created by the anonymous class declaration.

Import Varieties

Here's a rundown of the various import forms.

This imports the named export `example` from `mod.js`, using `example` as the local name as well:

```
import { example } from "./mod.js";
```

This imports the named export `example` from `mod.js`, using `e` as the local name instead of `example`:

```
import { example as e } from "./mod.js";
```

This imports the default export of `mod.js`, using `example` as the local name:

```
import example from "./mod.js";
```

This imports the module namespace object for `mod.js`, using the local name `mod`.

```
import * as mod from "./mod.js";
```

You can combine importing the default with *either* importing the module namespace object *or* named imports, but to avoid parsing complexity, you can't combine importing the namespace with named exports; you can't do all three together; and if importing the default, it has to come first, before the `*` for the namespace object or the `{` to start the list of named imports:

```
import def, * as ns from "./mod.js";          // Valid
import * as ns, def from "./mod.js";          // INVALID, default must be first
import def, { a, b as bee} from "./mod.js";   // Valid
import * as ns, { a, b as bee} from "./mod.js"; // INVALID, can't combine these
```

Finally, this imports `mod.js` just for its side effects, without importing any of its exports:

```
import "./mod.js";
```

DYNAMIC IMPORT

The import mechanism described so far in this chapter is a *static* mechanism:

➤   Module specifiers are string literals, not expressions resulting in strings.

➤   Imports and exports can only be declared at the top level of a module, not within control flow statements like `if` or `while`.

➤   A module's imports and exports can be determined by parsing the code without running it (they can be *statically analyzed*).

As a result, a module can't use information it gets at runtime to decide what to import or where it comes from.

In the vast majority of cases, this is what you want. It makes it possible for tools to do very powerful things, such as tree shaking (which you'll learn about later) and automatic bundling (figuring out what modules to include in a unified bundle without having a separate bundle manifest, which is a maintenance hassle), etc.

---

[8] https://github.com/tc39/proposal-dynamic-import

However, some use cases require that modules determine what to import, or from where, at runtime. For that reason, ES2020 adds dynamic import.[8] As of this writing it's widely supported, of the major browsers only the old non-Chromium-based version of Edge and, of course, Internet Explorer don't support it.

Importing a Module Dynamically

Dynamic import adds new syntax allowing `import` to be called as though it were a function. When called, `import` returns a promise of the module's namespace object:

```
import(/*...some runtime-determined name...*/)
.then(ns => {
    // ...use `ns`...
})
.catch(error => {
    // Handle/report error
});
```

Note that while it looks like a function call, `import(...)` is not a function call; it's new syntax called an *ImportCall*. As a result, you can't do this:

```
// DOESN'T WORK
const imp = import;
imp(/*...some runtime-determined name...*/)
.then(// ...
```

There are two reasons for this:

➤ The call needs to carry context information that normal function calls don't carry.

➤ Disallowing aliasing of it (the `imp` example earlier) makes it possible for static analysis to know whether dynamic import is used in a module (even if it can't determine what, specifically, that dynamic import does). You'll learn more about why this is important in the section later on tree shaking.

One obvious application for dynamic import is plugins: suppose you're writing a graphics editor in JavaScript as an Electron or Windows Universal Application or similar and want to allow extensions to provide transforms or custom pens or similar. Your code could look for plugins in some plugins location, and then load them with code similar to:

```
// Loads the plugins in parallel, returns object with `plugins` array
// of loaded plugins and `failed` array of failed loads (with `error`
// and `pluginFile` properties).
async function loadPlugins(editor, discoveredPluginFiles) {
    const plugins = [];
    const failed = [];
    await Promise.all(
        discoveredPluginFiles.map(async (pluginFile) => {
            try {
                const plugin = await import(pluginFile);
                plugin.init(editor);
                plugins.push(plugin);
```

```
        } catch (error) {
            failed.push({error, pluginFile});
        }
    })
)
return {plugins, failed};
}
```

Or perhaps you'd load a localizer for the app based on the locale:

```
async function loadLocalizer(editor, locale) {
    const localizer = await import(`./localizers/${locale}.js`);
    localizer.localize(editor);
}
```

Dynamically loaded modules are cached just like statically loaded modules.

Importing a module dynamically kicks off the process of loading any static dependencies it expresses, and their dependencies, etc., just like loading the entry point module does.

Let's look at an example.

Dynamic Module Example

Run the code from Listings 13-14 through 13-19 by running `dynamic-example.html`.

LISTING 13-14: Dynamic module loading example (HTML)—dynamic-example.html

```
<!doctype html>
<html>
<head>
<meta charset="UTF-8">
<title>Dynamic Module Loading Example</title>
</head>
<body>
<script src="dynamic-example.js" type="module"></script>
</body>
</html>
```

LISTING 13-15: Dynamic module loading example (static entry point)—dynamic-example.js

```
import { log } from "./dynamic-mod-log.js";

log("entry point module top-level evaluation begin");
(async () => {
    try {
        const modName = `./dynamic-mod${Math.random() < 0.5 ? 1 : 2}.js`;
        log(`entry point module requesting ${modName}`);
        const mod = await import(modName);
        log(`entry point module got module ${modName}, calling mod.example`);
        mod.example(log);
    } catch (error) {
        console.error(error);
    }
})();
log("entry point module top-level evaluation end");
```

LISTING 13-16: Dynamic module loading example (static import)—dynamic-mod-log.js

```
log("log module evaluated");
export function log(msg) {
    const p = document.createElement("pre");
    p.appendChild(document.createTextNode(msg));
    document.body.appendChild(p);
}
```

LISTING 13-17: Dynamic module loading example (dynamic import 1)—dynamic-mod1.js

```
import { log } from "./dynamic-mod-log.js";
import { showTime } from "./dynamic-mod-showtime.js";

log("dynamic module number 1 evaluated");
export function example(logFromEntry) {
    log("Number 1! Number 1! Number 1!");
    log(`log === logFromEntry? ${log === logFromEntry}`);
    showTime();
}
```

LISTING 13-18: Dynamic module loading example (dynamic import 2)—dynamic-mod2.js

```
import { log } from "./dynamic-mod-log.js";
import { showTime } from "./dynamic-mod-showtime.js";

log("dynamic module number 2 evaluated");
export function example(logFromEntry) {
    log("Meh, being Number 2 isn't that bad");
    log(`log === logFromEntry? ${log === logFromEntry}`);
    showTime();
}
```

LISTING 13-19: Dynamic module loading example (dynamic import dependency)—dynamic-mod-showtime.js

```
import { log } from "./dynamic-mod-log.js";

log("showtime module evaluated");
function nn(n) {
    return String(n).padStart(2, "0");
}
export function showTime() {
    const now = new Date();
    log(`Time is ${nn(now.getHours())}:${nn(now.getMinutes())}`);
}
```

In this example, the two dynamic modules have the same form, they just identify themselves as either Number 1 or Number 2.

When you load the `dynamic-example.html` page, you'll see output like this (on the page itself rather than the console):

```
log module evaluated
entry point module top-level evaluation begin
entry point module requesting ./dynamic-mod1.js
entry point module top-level evaluation end
showtime module evaluated
dynamic module number 1 evaluated
entry point module got module ./dynamic-mod1.js, calling mod.example
Number 1! Number 1! Number 1!
log === logFromEntry? true
Time is 12:44
```

In that example, dynamic module Number 1 was loaded, but it could just as easily have been Number 2.

Let's go through what happens there:

➤ The host (browser) and JavaScript engine go through the fetching and parsing, instantiation, and evaluation process on the entry point module and the `dynamic-mod-log.js` module it statically imports (I'll just call this the "log module"); that's the entire static tree, just those two modules. (See Figure 13-10.) Since evaluation is depth-first, the log module is evaluated first ("log module evaluated"), and then the entry point module is evaluated ("entry point module top-level evaluation begin", etc.).

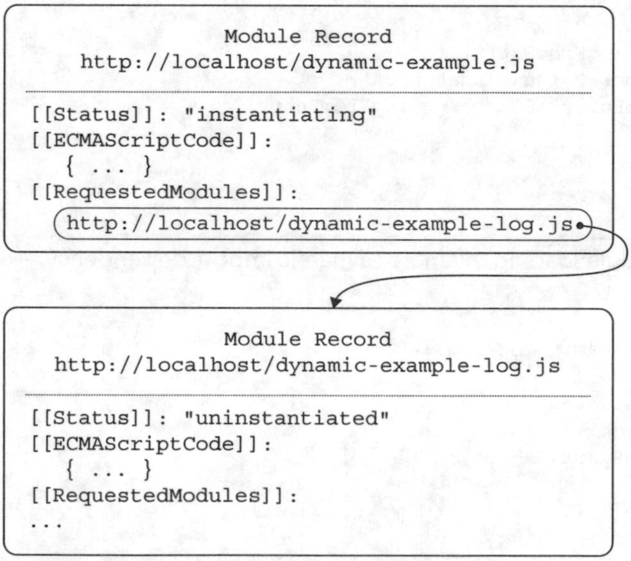

FIGURE 13-10

➤ During its evaluation, the entry point module randomly picks which dynamic module to use and calls `import()` to load it, using `await` to wait for the result. Its top-level evaluation is now complete; later, when the promise from import() is fulfilled, it will continue and use the module.

➤ The host and JavaScript engine start the process of fetching and parsing, instantiation, and evaluation again, starting with the dynamic module. The dynamic module has two static imports: log from the log module and showTime from the dynamic-mod-showtime.js module (I'll just call it the "showtime module"). The showtime module also imports log from the log module. When the parsing is complete, the tree of modules to process for this import call contains those three modules, but it connects to the existing tree (from the initial static import). See Figure 13-11. Note that the status ("[[Status]]") of the log module is "evaluated", so it's already been through all three parts of the loading process and isn't processed again. The showtime module hasn't been loaded yet, though, so it goes through the process with the dynamic module and, since it's deeper in the loading tree, it gets evaluated first ("showtime module evaluated"). Then the dynamic module is evaluated ("dynamic module number 1 evaluated"). (The only reason the example has the showtime module in this example is to demonstrate how it's different from the log module because the log module had already been evaluated, but the showtime module was loaded for the first time by the dynamic module.)

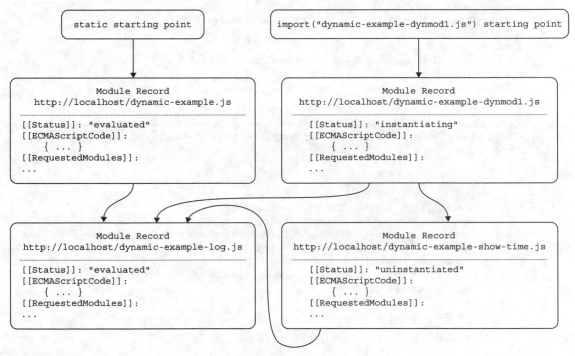

FIGURE 13-11

➤ The loading process for the import() call is complete, so its promise is fulfilled with the module namespace object for the dynamic module.

➤ The entry module's async function continues from the await ("entry point got module ./dynamic-mod1.js, calling mod.example") and calls mod.example, passing in its reference to the log function from the log module.

➤ The dynamic module's `example` function runs, outputting its module-specific message and then "log === logFromEntry? true". The `true` shows that the static and dynamic processes work with the same set of module records and associated environments; there is only one copy of the log module loaded, and so only one `log` function.

➤ Finally, the dynamic module calls `showTime`.

Dynamic Import in Non-Module Scripts

Unlike static import, dynamic import can also be used in scripts, not just in modules. Look at Listings 13-20 and 13-21, which are a different HTML page and entry point for the earlier dynamic example (reusing the remaining files).

LISTING 13-20: Dynamic module loading in script (HTML)—dynamic-example-2.html

```
<!doctype html>
<html>
<head>
<meta charset="UTF-8">
<title>Dynamic Module Loading in Script - Example</title>
</head>
<body>
<script src="dynamic-example-2.js"></script>
</body>
</html>
```

LISTING 13-21: Dynamic module loading in script example (entry point)—dynamic-example-2.js

```
(async() => {
    try {
        const {log} = await import("./dynamic-mod-log.js");
        log("entry point module got log");
        const modName = `./dynamic-mod${Math.random() < 0.5 ? 1 : 2}.js`;
        log(`entry point module requesting ${modName}`);
        const mod = await import(modName);
        log(`entry point module got module ${modName}, calling mod.example`);
        mod.example(log);
    } catch (error) {
        console.error(error);
    }
})();
```

As you can see, `dynamic-example-2.js` is being loaded as a script; there's no `type="module"` on its `script` tag. If you look at its code, it's similar in many ways to the `dynamic-example.js` code earlier, but it uses an `import()` call instead of a static `import` declaration. When you run it, the output is the same as before other than the fact the entry point code couldn't log the beginning and ending of the top-level evaluation because it had to wait for the log module, which arrives after top-level evaluation is complete:

```
log module evaluated
entry point module got log
entry point module requesting ./dynamic-mod1.js
showtime module evaluated
dynamic module number 1 evaluated
entry point module got module ./dynamic-mod1.js, calling mod.example
Number 1! Number 1! Number 1!
log === logFromEntry? true
Time is 12:44
```

Under the covers, it works largely the same as well, other than that the relationship between the entry point and the log module can no longer be determined through static analysis (although since the code uses a string literal to call import(), a clever tool can work it out).

One key difference, though, is that instead of just importing the named export, log, from the log module, the dynamic version imports the entire namespace object for the log module (but uses destructuring to pick out just the log function). In contrast, the module namespace object is never created in the static example, because nothing ever asks for it.

TREE SHAKING

Tree shaking is a form of *dead code elimination. Live code* is code that's potentially used by the page or application; *dead code* is code that definitely won't get used by the page or application (in its current form). Tree shaking is the process of analyzing the module tree to get rid of the dead code. (The term *tree shaking* comes from the image of shaking a tree vigorously to get the dead wood to fall out, while the living wood stays put.)

Let's revise the first example in this chapter by adding a function to the log module it uses; see Listings 13-22 to 13-24.

LISTING 13-22: An updated simple module example (HTML)—simple2.html

```
<!doctype html>
<html>
<head>
<meta charset="UTF-8">
<title>Revised Simple Module Example</title>
</head>
<body>
<script src="simple2.js" type="module"></script>
</body>
</html>
```

LISTING 13-23: An updated simple module example (entry point module)—simple2.js

```
import { log } from "./log2.js";

log("Hello, modules!");
```

LISTING 13-24: An updated simple module example (log module)—log2.js

```
export function log(msg) {
    const p = document.createElement("pre");
    p.appendChild(document.createTextNode(msg));
    document.body.appendChild(p);
}
export function stamplog(msg) {
    return log(`${new Date().toISOString()}: ${msg}`);
}
```

If you review the code in the listings, there are five things to make note of:

➤ Nothing ever requests the named export `stamplog`.

➤ Nothing ever requests the log module's module namespace object (if something did, a smart tree shaking tool might still be able to perform escape analysis on the resulting object to see if its `stamplog` property is ever used).

➤ Nothing in the log module's top-level code uses `stamplog`.

➤ Nothing in the log module's other exported functions, or functions they call, uses `stamplog`.

➤ Only static `import` declarations are used, no `import()` calls.

Additionally, all of that information can be determined with *static analysis* (just parsing and examining the code, without running it). That means that if you pointed a JavaScript bundler at `simple.html` and told it to bundle all the code together into an optimized file, it could determine—without running the code—that `stamplog` wasn't used anywhere and could be left out.

That's tree shaking. Tree shaking is one reason JavaScript bundlers aren't going away in the foreseeable future, despite native support for modules in browsers. Here's the result of using one bundler on this simple example, in this case, using Rollup.js and setting its output option to `iife` (immediately-invoked function expression), but you'll get similar results with any tree shaking bundler; more in the next section:

```
(function () {
    "use strict";

    function log(msg) {
        const p = document.createElement("pre");
        p.appendChild(document.createTextNode(msg));
        document.body.appendChild(p);
    }

    log("Hello, modules!");

}());
```

That one block of code is the optimized (but not minified) combination of `simple.js` plus `log.js`. The `stamplog` function is nowhere to be found.

Remember the last of the "five things to make note of" earlier?

➤ Only static `import` declarations are used, no `import()` calls.

In theory, even a single use of `import()` with anything but a string literal in any module in the tree means tools can't do tree shaking, since they can't prove that something really is unused. In practice, different bundlers will optimize the impact of dynamic imports in different ways and likely provide configuration options to give you control over whether and how aggressively they attempt to tree-shake them.

BUNDLING

Although modules are natively supported by modern browsers now, people have been using the syntax for a while by using JavaScript bundlers to convert the modules into optimized files that work on browsers without module support. Projects like Rollup.js (`https://rollupjs.org`) and Webpack (`https://webpack.js.org/`) are hugely popular and feature-rich.

On a project of any size, you're likely to want to use a bundler even if you're only targeting browsers with native module support. Tree shaking is one reason. Another is simply that transferring all of the individual module resources over HTTP (even HTTP/2) is still potentially slower than transferring a single resource. (Definitely slower if you're stuck with only HTTP/1.1.)

Google did an analysis[9] comparing native module loading with loading bundles, using two popular real-world libraries—Moment.js and Three.js—as well as many synthetically generated modules to determine whether bundling was still useful and where the bottlenecks were in Chrome's loading pipeline. The version of Moment.js[10] they tested used 104 modules, with a maximum tree depth of 6; the version of Three.js[11] they tested used 333 modules with a maximum depth of 5.

Based on the results of the analysis, Addy Osmani and Mathias Bynens, both at Google, recommend:[12]

➤ Using native support during development

➤ Using native support in production for small web apps with fewer than 100 modules and a shallow dependency tree (maximum depth less than 5) that target only modern browsers

➤ Using bundling for production for anything larger than that or projects targeting browsers without module support

There are tradeoffs either way, particularly if you're stuck with HTTP 1.1 for some reason. The full article is worth a read, and they'll likely add links to updated research over time.

---

[9] `https://docs.google.com/document/d/1ovo4PurT_1K4WFwN2MYmmgbLcr7v6DRQN67ESVA-wq0/pub`
[10] `https://momentjs.com/`
[11] `https://threejs.org/`
[12] `https://developers.google.com/web/fundamentals/primers/modules`

IMPORT METADATA

Occasionally, a module may need to know things about itself, such as what URL or path it was loaded from, whether it's the "main" module (in environments where there is a single main module, such as Node.js), etc. ES2015's modules don't currently provide any way for a module to get that information. ES2020 adds a way for a module to get information about itself: `import.meta`.[13]

`import.meta` is an object, specific to the module, that contains properties about the module. The properties themselves are host-specified and will vary by environment (for instance, browser vs. Node.js).

In the web environment, the properties of `import.meta` are defined by the HTML specification, in its `HostGetImportMetaProperties` section.[14] At the moment, only a single property is defined: `url`. It's a string giving the fully resolved URL of the module. For instance, `import.meta.url` in `mod.js` loaded from `http://localhost` would have the value `"http://localhost/mod.js"`. Node.js also supports `url`[15] by giving the absolute `file:` URL of the module. Over time, it's likely further properties will be added to either or both environments.

The `import.meta` object is created the first time it's accessed, through coordination between the JavaScript engine and the host. Because it's module-specific, it's largely owned by the module, and that's reflected in the fact that it's not locked down in any way: you can add properties to it for your own purposes (though it's not clear why you'd want to), or even change the default properties it comes with (unless the host prevents it, which it's allowed to do).

WORKER MODULES

By default, web workers are loaded as classic scripts, not modules. They can load other scripts via `importScripts`, but it's the old-fashioned way where communication with the loading script is through the worker's global environment. But web workers can be modules, so that they can use import and export declarations.

Similarly, Node.js's workers can now be ESM modules as well.

Let's look at each of those.

Loading a Web Worker as a Module

To load a worker as a module, so it gets all the usual benefits of being a module, you use the `type` option in the options object passed as a second argument to the `Worker` constructor:

```
const worker = new Worker("./worker.js", {type: "module"});
```

You can launch a worker this way from within a module or a classic script. Also, unlike classic script workers, you can launch module workers cross-origin provided they're served with Cross Origin Resource Sharing (CORS) information that allows the launching origin to use them.

---

[13] https://github.com/tc39/proposal-import-meta
[14] https://html.spec.whatwg.org/multipage/webappapis.html#hostgetimportmetaproperties
[15] https://nodejs.org/api/esm.html#esm_import_meta

If the browser supports workers as modules, the worker will be loaded as a module. As of this writing in early 2020, browser support for worker modules isn't widespread, though Chrome and other browsers based on the Chromium project (Chromium, newer versions of Edge) support them.

Listings 13-25 to 13-27 show an example of loading a worker as a module.

LISTING 13-25: Web worker as module (HTML)—worker-example.html

```html
<!doctype html>
<html>
<head>
<meta charset="UTF-8">
<title>Web Worker Module Example</title>
</head>
<body>
<script>
const worker = new Worker("./worker-example-worker.js", {type: "module"});
worker.addEventListener("message", e => {
    console.log(`Message from worker: ${e.data}`);
});
</script>
</body>
</html>
```

LISTING 13-26: Web worker as module (worker)—worker-example-worker.js

```js
import { example } from "./worker-example-mod.js";

postMessage(`example(4) = ${example(4)}`);
```

LISTING 13-27: Web worker as module (module)—worker-example-mod.js

```js
export const example = a => a * 2;
```

Loading a Node.js Worker as a Module

Node.js's support for ESM modules extends to worker threads. The same rules apply as for other ways of running code. You can launch a worker as a module by having a `type: "module"` setting in the nearest `package.json` file or by giving the worker the extension `.mjs`.

A Worker Is in Its Own Realm

When a worker is created, it's put in a new realm: it has its own global environment, its own intrinsic objects, etc. If the worker is a module, any modules it loads will be loaded within that realm, separately from modules loaded in other realms. For example, on a browser, if a module in the main window loads `mod1.js` and launches a worker that also loads `mod1.js`, `mod1.js` is loaded twice: once in the main window's realm, and again in the worker's realm. If the worker loads another module (say, `mod2.js`) that also imports from `mod1.js`, that other module and the worker module share a common copy of `mod1.js`; but they *don't* share the copy the main window loads. See Figure 13-12.

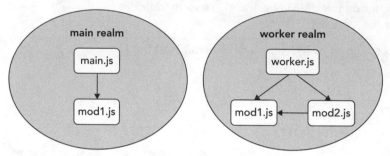

FIGURE 13-12

Worker realms are isolated not only from the main window's realm but from each other as well, so if you launch ten workers that all load `mod1.js`, it will be loaded ten times (once per worker). Since each worker is in its own realm, each has its own module tree.

This is true both on web browsers and Node.js.

OLD HABITS TO NEW

Here are a few old habits you might consider updating.

Use Modules Instead of Pseudo-Namespaces

Old habit: Using a "namespace" object to provide a single public symbol for your code (perhaps in a library, like jQuery's $ global):

```
var MyLib = (function(lib) {
    function privateFunction() {
        // ...
    }
    lib.publicFunction = function() {
        // ...
    };
    return lib;
})(MyLib || {});
```

New habit: Use modules:

```
function privateFunction() {
    // ...
}
export function publicFunction() {
    // ...
}
```

Note: don't export objects with properties/methods that are meant to be used individually. Use named exports instead.

Use Modules Instead of Wrapping Code in Scoping Functions

Old habit: Using a "scoping function" around your code to avoid creating globals:

```
(function() {
    var x = /* ... */;
    function doSomething() {
        // ...
    }
    // ...
})();
```

New habit: Use modules, since the top-level scope of a module is not the global scope:

```
let x = /* ... */;
function doSomething() {
    // ...
}
// ...
```

Use Modules to Avoid Creating Megalithic Code Files

Old habit: Having a single huge code file to avoid having to worry about combining smaller files for production. (But you didn't have this habit, right? Right?)

New habit: Use a variety of right-sized modules instead, with statically declared dependencies between them. The question of what size is the right size will be a matter of style and something to agree with your team. Putting each function in its own module is probably overkill, but then, a single massive module exporting this, that, and the other is probably not modular enough.

Convert CJS, AMD, and Other Modules to ESM

Old habit: Using CJS, AMD, and other modules (because there was no native JavaScript module format).

New habit: Use ESM, converting your old modules (either in one big leap, or more likely slowly over time).

Use a Well-Maintained Bundler Rather Than Going Homebrew

Old habit: Any of several ad-hoc mechanisms for combining your individual files used for development into a combined file (or small set of files) for production.

New habit: Use a well-maintained, community-supported bundler.

14

Reflection—Reflect and Proxy

WHAT'S IN THIS CHAPTER?

➤ The `Reflect` object

➤ `Proxy` objects

In this chapter, you'll learn about the `Reflect` object, which provides a host of useful utility features for constructing and interacting with objects, and `Proxy`, which provides the ultimate façade pattern for JavaScript—a pattern that can be important for providing APIs to client code.

`Reflect` and `Proxy` are designed to be used together, though each can be used without the other. This chapter will briefly introduce `Reflect`, but then mostly cover it in the context of covering `Proxy`.

REFLECT

`Reflect` was added in ES2015 with various methods corresponding to fundamental operations that are performed on objects: getting and setting a property's value, getting and setting the object's prototype, deleting a property from an object, etc.

Your first thought is probably: "Why do we need utility functions for that? We can already do those things just using operators on the object directly." That's partly true, and in cases where it isn't true, there's usually a function (or combination of functions) on `Object` that does the job; `Reflect` brings a few things to the table, though:

➤ It provides a thin wrapper function for all of the fundamental object operations, rather than having some of them be syntax and others be `Object` functions or combinations of `Object` functions. This means that you can pass fundamental object operations around, without having to write your own wrapper around things like the `in` or `delete` operators.

➤ Its functions provide return values for success/failure in some cases where the equivalent `Object` functions throw errors instead (more on that in a moment).

➤ As you'll learn in the section on proxies, it offers functions that perfectly match each "trap" that a proxy object can hook into, implementing the default behavior for the trap, making it simple to correctly implement traps that only modify behavior rather than replacing the behavior entirely.

➤ It provides an operation not available any other way outside of `class` syntax: `Reflect.construct` with the `newTarget` argument.

`Reflect` and `Object` have several functions with the same names and, largely, the same purposes:

➤ `defineProperty`

➤ `getOwnPropertyDescriptor`

➤ `getPrototypeOf`

➤ `setPrototypeOf`

➤ `preventExtensions`

They do fundamentally the same things, but there are slight differences between them:

➤ In general, the `Reflect` version will throw an error if you pass it a non-object where it expects an object, whereas the `Object` version will (in many but not all cases) either coerce a primitive to an object and operate on the result, or just ignore the call. (The exception is `Object.defineProperty`, which throws if you pass it a non-object, like `Reflect` functions do.)

➤ In general, the `Reflect` version of a modification function returns a flag for success/failure, whereas the `Object` version returns the object you passed it to modify (and if you pass it a primitive, either returns the object it coerced the primitive to, or just returns the primitive as-is if the call does nothing on primitives). The `Object` version usually throws an error on failure.

Separately, `Reflect` also has a function, `ownKeys`, which is superficially similar to `Object.keys`, but has two significant differences you'll learn about later.

While most of `Reflect`'s functions are primarily useful for implementing proxies, let's look at some that are useful on their own, too.

Reflect.apply

`Reflect.apply` is a utility function that does what the `apply` method on functions does. It calls a function with a specific `this` value and list of arguments, which is provided as an array (or array-like object):

```
function example(a, b, c) {
    console.log(`this.name = ${this.name}, a = ${a}, b = ${b}, c = ${c}`);
}

const thisArg = {name: "test"};
const args = [1, 2, 3];
Reflect.apply(example, thisArg, args); // this.name = test, a = 1, b, = 2, c = 3
```

In that example, you could replace the call to `Reflect.apply` with a call to `example.apply`:

```
example.apply(thisArg, args); // this.name = test, a = 1, b, = 2, c = 3
```

However, `Reflect.apply` has a couple of advantages:

➤ It works even if the `apply` property on `example` has been overridden or overwritten with something other than `Function.prototype.apply`.

➤ A slight variation on that: it works in the truly obscure case where the prototype of the function has been changed (for instance, with `Object.setPrototypeOf`) so that the function no longer inherits from `Function.prototype`, and so doesn't have `apply`.

➤ It works on anything *callable* (any object with a [[Call]] internal operation), even if it's not a genuine JavaScript function. There are fewer of these around than there used to be, but not all that long ago host-provided "functions" often weren't real JavaScript functions and didn't have `apply` and such. (There still are some.)

Reflect.construct

`Reflect.construct` creates a new instance via a constructor function, like the `new` operator does. However, `Reflect.construct` offers two features `new` doesn't:

➤ It accepts the arguments for the constructor as an array (or array-like object).

➤ It lets you set `new.target` to something other than the function you're calling.

Let's look at the arguments aspect first, since it's quite simple. Suppose you have the arguments you want to use with a constructor (`Thing`) in an array. In ES5, it was awkward to call the constructor with arguments from an array. The simplest way was to create the object yourself, and then call the constructor as a plain function via `apply`:

```
// In ES5
var o = Thing.apply(Object.create(Thing.prototype), theArguments);
```

That works in ES5 provided `Thing` uses the `this` it was called with (which is the normal thing to do) rather than creating its own object.

In ES2015+ you have two ways to do it, spread syntax and `Reflect.construct`:

```
// In ES2015+
let o = new Thing(...theArguments);
// or
let o = Reflect.construct(Thing, theArguments);
```

Since spread syntax goes through an iterator, it does more work than `Reflect.construct`, which accesses the `length`, `0`, `1`, etc. properties of the arguments "array" directly (not that that usually matters). That means spread works with non-array–like iterable objects, where `Reflect.construct` doesn't; and `Reflect.construct` works with array-like, non-iterable objects, where spread doesn't.

The second thing `Reflect.construct` provides that `new` doesn't, controlling `new.target`, is primarily useful when using `Reflect` with a proxy (more in a later section), but can also be used to create instances that are subtypes of built-ins like `Error` or `Array` (which notoriously can't be correctly subclassed using only ES5 features) without using `class` syntax. Some programmers don't like to use `class` or `new`, preferring to create objects in other ways. But they may still want to create their own instances of `Error` or `Array` or `HTMLElement` (for web components) that have a different prototype (with their own additional features). If you don't want to use `class` and `new` for that, `Reflect.construct` is the way you'd go:

```
// Defining the function that builds custom errors
function buildCustomError(...args) {
    return Reflect.construct(Error, args, buildCustomError);
}
buildCustomError.prototype = Object.assign(Object.create(Error.prototype), {
    constructor: buildCustomError,
    report() {
        console.log(`this.message = ${this.message}`);
    }
});

// Using it
const e = buildCustomError("error message here");
console.log("instanceof Error", e instanceof Error);
e.report();
console.log(e);
```

The highlighted line calls `Error` but passes in `buildCustomError` for the `new.target` parameter, which means that `buildCustomError.prototype` gets assigned to the newly created object, rather than `Error.prototype`. The resulting instance inherits the custom `report` method.

Reflect.ownKeys

The `Reflect.ownKeys` function is superficially similar to `Object.keys`, but returns an array of *all* of the object's own property keys, including non-enumerable ones and ones named with Symbols rather than strings. Despite the similarity of names, it's more like a combination of `Object.getOwnPropertyNames` and `Object.getOwnPropertySymbols` than it is like `Object.keys`.

Reflect.get, Reflect.set

These functions get and set properties on an object, but with a handy feature: if the property being accessed is an *accessor* property, you can control what this is within the call to the accessor. In effect, they're the accessor property version of Reflect.apply.

Setting this to a different object than the one you get the property accessor from may seem like an odd thing to do, but if you think about it, you've already seen something that does that, back in Chapter 4: super. Consider this base class that calculates the product of its construction parameters, and a subclass that takes that result and doubles it:

```
class Product {
    constructor(x, y) {
        this.x = x;
        this.y = y;
    }
    get result() {
        return this.x * this.y;
    }
}
class DoubleProduct extends Product {
    get result() {
        return super.result * 2;
    }
}

const d = new DoubleProduct(10, 2);
console.log(d.result);          // 40
```

DoubleProduct's result accessor needs to use super.result to run the result accessor from Product, not DoubleProduct, because if it used the version from DoubleProduct, it would call itself recursively and cause a stack overflow. But when calling the Product version of the result accessor, it has to make sure this is set to the instance (d1) so that the correct values for x and y get used. The object it gets the accessor from (Product.prototype, the prototype of the prototype of d1) and the object that should be this within the call to the accessor (d1) are different objects.

If you needed to do that without super, you'd use Reflect.get. Without Reflect.get, you'd have to get the property descriptor for result and call its get method via get.call/apply or Reflect.apply, which is awkward:

```
get result() {
    const proto = Object.getPrototypeOf(Object.getPrototypeOf(this));
    const descriptor = Object.getOwnPropertyDescriptor(proto, "result");
    const superResult = descriptor.get.call(this);
    return superResult * 2;
}
```

It's much simpler with Reflect.get:

```
get result() {
    const proto = Object.getPrototypeOf(Object.getPrototypeOf(this));
    return Reflect.get(proto, "result", this) * 2;
}
```

Of course, you don't have to do that in this specific case because you have `super`. `Reflect.get` lets you handle situations where you don't have `super` (for instance, in a Proxy handler as you'll learn later) or where `super` isn't applicable.

`Reflect.get` has this signature:

```
value = Reflect.get(target, propertyName[, receiver]);
```

➤ `target` is the object to get the property from.

➤ `propertyName` is the name of the property to get.

➤ `receiver` is the optional object to use as `this` during the accessor call, if the property is an accessor property.

It returns the property's value.

`Reflect.get` gets the property descriptor for `propertyName` from `target`, and, if the descriptor is for a data property, returns the value of that property. But if the descriptor is for an accessor, `Reflect.get` calls the accessor function using `receiver` as `this` (like the earlier "awkward" code did).

`Reflect.set` works the same way as `Reflect.get`, just setting the property rather than getting it. It has this signature:

```
result = Reflect.set(target, propertyName, value[, receiver]);
```

`target`, `propertyName`, and `receiver` are all the same; `value` is the value to set. The function returns `true` if the value was set, `false` if not.

Both are particularly handy with proxies, as you'll learn later in this chapter.

Other Reflect Functions

The remaining `Reflect` functions are listed in Table 14-1.

TABLE 14-1: Other Reflect Functions

defineProperty	Like `Object.defineProperty`, but returns `true` for success or `false` for failure instead of throwing an error.
deleteProperty	A function version of the `delete` operator, except it always returns `true` for success or `false` for failure, even in strict mode (whereas in strict mode, the `delete` operator throws an error on failure).
getOwnPropertyDescriptor	Like `Object.getOwnPropertyDescriptor`, except it throws an exception if you pass it a non-object (rather than coercing).
getPrototypeOf	Like `Object.getPrototypeOf`, except it throws an exception if you pass it a non-object (rather than coercing).

has	A function version of the in operator (*not* like hasOwnProperty; has checks prototypes as well).
isExtensible	Like Object.isExtensible, except it throws an exception if you pass it a non-object rather than just returning false.
preventExtensions	Like Object.preventExtensions, except 1) If you pass it a non-object, it throws an error rather than just doing nothing and returning that value to you; 2) It returns false if the operation fails (rather than throwing an error).
setPrototypeOf	Like Object.setPrototypeOf, except 1) If you pass it a non-object, it throws an error rather than just doing nothing and returning that value to you; 2) It returns false if the operation fails (rather than throwing an error).

PROXY

Proxy objects are objects you can use to intercept fundamental object operations en route to a target object. When creating the proxy, you can define handlers for one or more *traps* for the operation(s) to handle, such as getting a property's value or defining a new property.

There are a lot of use cases for proxies:

➤ Logging the operations that occur on an object

➤ Making reading/writing non-existent properties an error (rather than returning undefined or creating the property)

➤ Providing a boundary between two bits of code (such as an API and the consumer of it)

➤ Creating read-only views of mutable objects

➤ Hiding information in an object, or making it seem as though an object has more information than it actually does

. . . and many more. Since proxies let you hook into and (in most cases) modify the fundamental operations, there are very few limits on what you can do with them.

Let's look at a simple example; see Listing 14-1.

LISTING 14-1: Initial Proxy example—initial-proxy-example.js

```js
const obj = {
    testing: "abc"
};
const p = new Proxy(obj, {
    get(target, name, receiver) {
        console.log(`(getting property '${name}')`);
        return Reflect.get(target, name, receiver);
    }
});
```

continues

LISTING 14-1 *(continued)*

```
console.log("Getting 'testing' directly...");
console.log(`Got ${obj.testing}`);
console.log("Getting 'testing' via proxy...");
console.log(`Got ${p.testing}`);
console.log("Getting non-existent property 'foo' via proxy...");
console.log(`Got ${p.foo}`);
```

The code in Listing 14-1 creates a proxy, defining a handler for the get trap (getting a property's value). When you run that, you see

```
Getting 'testing' directly...
Got abc
Getting 'testing' via proxy...
(getting property 'testing')
Got abc
Getting non-existent property 'foo' via proxy...
(getting property 'foo')
Got undefined
```

There are a few things to notice there:

➤ To create the proxy, you pass the Proxy constructor the target object and an object with *trap handlers*. The example defines one trap handler: for the get operation.

➤ Operations performed directly on the target object do not trigger the proxy, only operations performed through the proxy do. Notice there's no "(getting property 'testing')" message between "Getting 'testing' directly..." and "Got abc."

➤ The get trap isn't specific to one single property: all property accesses on the proxy go through it, even for properties that don't exist, such as foo at the end of the example.

Even if proxies could do no more than just listen in on fundamental operations, they'd be hugely useful, but they can also change the result of the operation, or even suppress the operation entirely. In the previous example, the handler returned the underlying object's value from the handler unchanged, but it could have modified it. Run Listing 14-2 to see an example of doing that.

LISTING 14-2: Simple Proxy example with modification—simple-mod-proxy-example.js

```
const obj = {
    testing: "abc"
};
const p = new Proxy(obj, {
    get(target, name, receiver) {
        console.log(`(getting property '${name}')`);
        let value = Reflect.get(target, name, receiver);
        if (value && typeof value.toUpperCase === "function") {
            value = value.toUpperCase();
        }
        return value;
    }
});
```

```
console.log("Getting directly...");
console.log(`Got ${obj.testing}`);
console.log("Getting via proxy...");
console.log(`Got ${p.testing}`);
```

In the Listing 14-2 example, the handler modifies the value before returning it (if it has a toUpperCase method), resulting in this output:

```
Getting directly...
Got abc
Getting via proxy...
(getting property 'testing')
Got ABC
```

There's a proxy trap for every fundamental object operation; handlers for the traps can do almost anything (you'll learn about some limits in a bit). See Table 14-2 (overleaf) for a list of the trap names and the fundamental operation they trap (the names are the names of the fundamental operations in the specification). We'll look at the traps more closely once we get the basics out of the way.

ES2015 originally defined a 14th trap, enumerate, which was triggered by the initialization of a for-in loop on the proxy (and by a corresponding Reflect.enumerate function), but it was removed in ES2016 because of performance and observability issues raised by JavaScript engine implementers: when they got into the details of implementing it, it turned out it could be efficient and have observable side effects (e.g., you could tell whether you were dealing with a proxy or a non-proxy), or it could be inefficient. (This is an example of why the new enhancement process you learned about in Chapter 1 is a good idea; something doesn't make it into the specification until there are multiple implementations, to shake out this kind of problem before a feature lands in the spec.)

If you don't specify a handler for a trap, the proxy forwards the operation to its target object directly. That's why the code in Listing 14-2 only needed to define the get trap handler.

We'll go into the details of each trap later in the chapter, but let's start with an example of one proxy use case demonstrating all of the traps: a proxy that logs all of the fundamental operations on an object.

Example: Logging Proxy

In this section you'll see a logging proxy, logging all of the fundamental operations that occur on an object. The example says what trap was called and shows the parameter values it was called with. All the code in this example is in the downloads (logging-proxy.js), which you should run locally to see the results, but let's go through it in parts.

To make the output clearer, we'll keep track of names for objects and then when outputting a log message that says that object was the value of a parameter, we'll use its name rather than showing the object's contents. (There's another reason this example does that: when the object we need to log is the proxy object, logging its contents would trigger proxy traps, and in the case of some of those traps, it would cause recursion leading to a stack overflow.)

TABLE 14-2: Proxy Traps

TRAP NAME	OPERATION NAME	TRIGGERED WHEN ...
apply	[[Call]]	... the proxy is used as a function in a function call. (Only available when proxying functions.)
construct	[[Construct]]	... the proxy is used as a constructor. (Only available when proxying a constructor.)
defineProperty	[[DefineOwnProperty]]	... a property is being defined or redefined on the proxy (including when its value is being set, if it's a data property).
deleteProperty	[[Delete]]	... a property is being deleted from the proxy.
get	[[Get]]	... the value of a property is being retrieved from the proxy.
getOwnPropertyDescriptor	[[GetOwnProperty]]	... the descriptor of a property is being retrieved from the proxy (which happens much more often than you probably expect).
getPrototypeOf	[[GetPrototypeOf]]	... the prototype of the proxy is being retrieved.
has	[[HasProperty]]	... the existence of a property is being checked via the proxy (for example, using the in operator or similar).
isExtensible	[[IsExtensible]]	... the proxy is being checked to see if it's extensible (that is, it hasn't had extensions prevented).
ownKeys	[[OwnPropertyKeys]]	... the proxy's own property names are being retrieved.
preventExtensions	[[PreventExtensions]]	... extensions are being prevented on the proxy.
set	[[Set]]	... the value of a property is being set on the proxy.
setPrototypeOf	[[SetPrototypeOf]]	... the proxy's prototype is being set.

The code starts off with the `log` function that does the logging:

```
const names = new WeakMap();
function log(label, params) {
    console.log(label + ": " + Object.getOwnPropertyNames(params).map(key => {
        const value = params[key];
        const name = names.get(value);
        const display = name ? name : JSON.stringify(value);
        return `${key} = ${display}`;
    }).join(", "));
}
```

The `names` map is what the code uses to keep track of names for objects. So for instance, this code:

```
const example = {"answer": 42};
names.set(example, "example");
log("Testing 1 2 3", {value: example});
```

would output the name "example" rather than the contents of the object:

```
Testing 1 2 3: value = example
```

After the `log` function, the code continues by defining a `handlers` object with handler functions for all the traps:

```
const handlers = {
    apply(target, thisValue, args) {
        log("apply", {target, thisValue, args});
        return Reflect.apply(target, thisValue, args);
    },
    construct(target, args, newTarget) {
        log("construct", {target, args, newTarget});
        return Reflect.construct(target, args, newTarget);
    },
    defineProperty(target, propName, descriptor) {
        log("defineProperty", {target, propName, descriptor});
        return Reflect.defineProperty(target, propName, descriptor);
    },
    deleteProperty(target, propName) {
        log("deleteProperty", {target, propName});
        return Reflect.deleteProperty(target, propName);
    },
    get(target, propName, receiver) {
        log("get", {target, propName, receiver});
        return Reflect.get(target, propName, receiver);
    },
    getOwnPropertyDescriptor(target, propName) {
        log("getOwnPropertyDescriptor", {target, propName});
        return Reflect.getOwnPropertyDescriptor(target, propName);
    },
    getPrototypeOf(target) {
        log("getPrototypeOf", {target});
        return Reflect.getPrototypeOf(target);
    },
```

```
        has(target, propName) {
            log("has", {target, propName});
            return Reflect.has(target, propName);
        },
        isExtensible(target) {
            log("isExtensible", {target});
            return Reflect.isExtensible(target);
        },
        ownKeys(target) {
            log("ownKeys", {target});
            return Reflect.ownKeys(target);
        },
        preventExtensions(target) {
            log("preventExtensions", {target});
            return Reflect.preventExtensions(target);
        },
        set(target, propName, value, receiver) {
            log("set", {target, propName, value, receiver});
            return Reflect.set(target, propName, value, receiver);
        },
        setPrototypeOf(target, newProto) {
            log("setPrototypeOf", {target, newProto});
            return Reflect.setPrototypeOf(target, newProto);
        }
};
```

The definition is done in this verbose way in the example both for clarity and so that `log` can show names for the parameter values the trap handlers receive. (If we didn't want to do that, we could hook things up in a simple loop since `Reflect` has methods whose names are the same as proxy traps and that expect exactly the arguments the traps provide.)

Next, the code defines a simple counter class:

```
class Counter {
    constructor(name) {
        this.value = 0;
        this.name = name;
    }
    increment() {
        return ++this.value;
    }
}
```

Then it creates an instance of the class, wraps a proxy around it, and saves those two objects in the `names` map:

```
const c = new Counter("counter");
const cProxy = new Proxy(c, handlers);
names.set(c, "c");
names.set(cProxy, "cProxy");
```

Now the code starts doing operations on the proxy, triggering traps. First, it gets the initial `value` of the counter through the proxy:

```
console.log("---- Getting cProxy.value (before increment):");
console.log(`cProxy.value (before) = ${cProxy.value}`);
```

You've already seen a `get` proxy trap, so you won't be surprised by the output:

```
---- Getting cProxy.value (before increment):
get: target = c, propName = "value", receiver = cProxy
cProxy.value (before) = 0
```

The second line shows us that the `get` trap was triggered with `target` set to the target object `c`, `propName` set to `"value"`, and the *receiver object*, `receiver`, set to the proxy itself, `cProxy`. (You'll learn about the significance of the receiver object in a later section.) The third line shows us that the value returned was `0`, which makes sense as the counter starts out at `0`.

Next, the code calls the `increment` function on the proxy:

```
console.log("---- Calling cProxy.increment():");
cProxy.increment();
```

The output for this may seem a bit more surprising:

```
---- Calling cProxy.increment():
get: target = c, propName = "increment", receiver = cProxy
get: target = c, propName = "value", receiver = cProxy
set: target = c, propName = "value", value = 1, receiver = cProxy
getOwnPropertyDescriptor: target = c, propName = "value"
defineProperty: target = c, propName = "value", descriptor = {"value":1}
```

Four different types of traps were triggered, one of them twice!

The first part is simple enough: `cProxy.increment()` does a [[Get]] to look up the `increment` property on the proxy, so we see the `get` trap fired for that. Then, remember the implementation of `increment`:

```
increment() {
    return ++this.value;
}
```

In the expression `cProxy.increment()`, `this` within the call to `increment` is set to `cProxy`, so `this` in `++this.value` is the proxy: first the engine does a [[Get]] on `value` (getting `0`), then a [[Set]] on `value` (setting `1`).

You're probably thinking, "So far so good, but what's that `getOwnPropertyDescriptor` doing there? And why `defineProperty`?!"

The implementation of the default [[Set]] operation for ordinary objects[1] is designed this way specifically to allow for proxies. First it checks to see if the property is a data property or an accessor (this check is done directly, without going through the proxy.) If the property being set is an accessor, the setter function is called. But if it's a data property, the property's value is set by getting the property's descriptor through the proxy via [[GetOwnProperty]], setting its `value`, and then using [[DefineOwn-Property]] with the modified descriptor to update it. (If the property doesn't exist yet, [[Set]] defines a data property descriptor for the property and uses [[DefineOwnProperty]] to create it.)

---

[1] https://tc39.es/ecma262/#sec-ordinaryset

It may seem odd to use [[DefineOwnProperty]] to set the value, but doing so ensures that *all* operations that modify a property (its writability, configurability, extensibility, or indeed its value) go through a central operation: [[DefineOwnProperty]]. (You'll see the others as we continue through the example.)

The code continues with:

```
console.log("---- Getting cProxy.value (after increment):");
console.log(`cProxy.value (after) = ${cProxy.value}`);
```

which shows the updated value:

```
---- Getting cProxy.value (after increment):
get: target = c, propName = "value", receiver = cProxy
cProxy.value (after) = 1
```

So far, the example has triggered four of the thirteen traps: `get`, `set`, `getOwnPropertyDescriptor`, and `defineProperty`.

Next, the code uses `Object.keys` to get `cProxy`'s own, enumerable string-named property keys:

```
console.log("---- Getting cProxy's own enumerable string-named keys:");
console.log(Object.keys(cProxy));
```

This triggers the `ownKeys` trap, and then since `Object.keys` has to check whether the keys are enumerable before including them in the array, we see it get the property descriptors for both of the keys it returns:

```
---- Getting cProxy's own enumerable string-named keys:
ownKeys: target = c
getOwnPropertyDescriptor: target = c, propName = "value"
getOwnPropertyDescriptor: target = c, propName = "name"
["value", "name"]
```

Next, the code deletes the `value` property:

```
console.log("---- Deleting cProxy.value:");
delete cProxy.value;
```

The operation to delete a property is straightforward, so just the `deleteProperty` trap is triggered:

```
---- Deleting cProxy.value:
deleteProperty: target = c, propName = "value"
```

Then it checks to see if the `value` property still exists, using the `in` operator:

```
console.log("---- Checking whether cProxy has a 'value' property:");
console.log(`"value" in cProxy? ${"value" in cProxy}`);
```

That triggers the `has` trap. Since the proxy didn't prevent the deletion a moment ago, the object doesn't have the `value` property anymore:

```
---- Checking whether cProxy has a 'value' property:
has: target = c, propName = "value"
"value" in cProxy? false
```

Next, the code gets the prototype of the object:

```
console.log("---- Getting the prototype of cProxy:");
const sameProto = Object.getPrototypeOf(cProxy) === Counter.prototype;
console.log(`Object.getPrototypeOf(cProxy) === Counter.prototype? ${sameProto}`);
```

That triggers the `getPrototypeOf` trap:

```
---- Getting the prototype of cProxy:
getPrototypeOf: target = c
Object.getPrototypeOf(cProxy) === Counter.prototype? true
```

Remember, proxies pass through operations to their targets (unless a trap handler intervenes), so it's c's prototype, not the proxy's, that gets returned. (In fact, since proxies behave this way, they don't get a prototype assigned to them at all, and the `Proxy` constructor has no `prototype` property.)

To trigger the next trap, the code sets the object's prototype:

```
console.log("---- Setting the prototype of cProxy to Object.prototype:");
Object.setPrototypeOf(cProxy, Object.prototype);
```

And indeed, the `setPrototypeOf` trap handler is triggered:

```
---- Setting the prototype of cProxy to Object.prototype:
setPrototypeOf: target = c, newProto = {}
```

Then it checks to see if cProxy's prototype is still `Counter.prototype`:

```
console.log("---- Getting the prototype of cProxy again:");
const sameProto2 = Object.getPrototypeOf(cProxy) === Counter.prototype;
console.log(`Object.getPrototypeOf(cProxy) === Counter.prototype? ${sameProto2}`);
```

It isn't, because the code just changed it to `Object.prototype` a moment ago:

```
---- Getting the prototype of cProxy again:
getPrototypeOf: target = c
Object.getPrototypeOf(cProxy) === Counter.prototype? false
```

Next, the code checks for extensibility:

```
console.log("---- Is cProxy extensible?:");
console.log(`Object.isExtensible(cProxy) (before)? ${Object.isExtensible(cProxy)}`);
```

An extensibility check is a really straightforward operation; just a single call to the `isExtensible` trap handler is involved:

```
---- Is cProxy extensible?:
isExtensible: target = c
Object.isExtensible(cProxy) (before)? true
```

Next, the code prevents extensions:

```
console.log("---- Preventing extensions on cProxy:");
Object.preventExtensions(cProxy);
```

firing the `preventExtensions` trap:

```
---- Preventing extensions on cProxy:
preventExtensions: target = c
```

Then it checks to see if the object is still extensible:

```
console.log("---- Is cProxy still extensible?:");
console.log(`Object.isExtensible(cProxy) (after)? ${Object.isExtensible(cProxy)}`);
```

which it isn't anymore, since the trap didn't prevent the operation:

```
---- Is cProxy still extensible?:
isExtensible: target = c
Object.isExtensible(cProxy) (after)? false
```

So far, you've seen 11 of the 13 traps. The remaining two are traps that only make sense for proxies on function objects, so the example code creates a function and wraps a proxy around it (and registers those in names so it knows to log their names rather than contents):

```
const func = function() { console.log("func ran"); };
const funcProxy = new Proxy(func, handlers);
names.set(func, "func");
names.set(funcProxy, "funcProxy");
```

Then it calls the function:

```
console.log("---- Calling funcProxy as a function:");
funcProxy();
```

which triggers the `apply` trap handler:

```
---- Calling funcProxy as a function:
apply: target = func, thisValue = undefined, args = []
func ran
```

And then it demonstrates the last trap, `construct`, by calling the function as a constructor:

```
console.log("---- Calling funcProxy as a constructor:");
new funcProxy();
```

resulting in:

```
---- Calling funcProxy as a constructor:
construct: target = func, args = [], newTarget = funcProxy
get: target = func, propName = "prototype", receiver = funcProxy
func ran
```

That works, since traditional functions can all be used as constructors. But if you tried to call a non-constructor such as an arrow function or a method that way, the trap wouldn't be triggered because the proxy won't have a [[Construct]] internal function at all; instead, the attempt just fails. The example goes on to demonstrate that by creating an arrow function and a proxy for it:

```
const arrowFunc = () => { console.log("arrowFunc ran"); };
const arrowFuncProxy = new Proxy(arrowFunc, handlers);
names.set(arrowFunc, "arrowFunc");
names.set(arrowFuncProxy, "arrowFuncProxy");
```

and then trying to call it as a function and as a constructor:

```
console.log("---- Calling arrowFuncProxy as a function:");
arrowFuncProxy();
console.log("---- Calling arrowFuncProxy as a constructor:");
```

```
try {
    new arrowFuncProxy();
} catch (error) {
    console.error(`${error.name}: ${error.message}`);
}
```

which results in:

```
---- Calling arrowFuncProxy as a function:
apply: target = arrowFunc, thisValue = undefined, args = []
arrowFunc ran
---- Calling arrowFuncProxy as a constructor:
TypeError: arrowFuncProxy is not a constructor
```

Finally, just for emphasis, remember that functions are objects, so all of the other traps apply to them as well. The example ends by getting the arrow function's `name` property:

```
console.log("---- Getting name of arrowFuncProxy:");
console.log(`arrowFuncProxy.name = ${arrowFuncProxy.name}`);
```

which triggers the `get` trap:

```
---- Getting name of arrowFuncProxy:
get: target = arrowFunc, propName = "name", receiver = arrowFuncProxy
arrowFuncProxy.name = arrowFunc
```

Proxy Traps

You've seen all of the traps in action in the logging example. This section will go into detail on each trap, including any limitations on it.

Common Features

In general, the handler for a proxy trap can do nearly anything it likes, though some have *some* limits. In general, a trap handler can:

➤   Handle the operation itself, never touching the target object/function

➤   Adjust the operation (sometimes only within limits)

➤   Reject the operation, returning an error flag or throwing an error

➤   Perform any side effects you like (such as the logging statements in the logging example), since a trap handler is arbitrary code

Where trap handlers have limits, they're there to enforce the *essential invariant behavior*[2] that is expected of all objects, even exotic ones like proxies. Limits of specific traps are called out in the following sections.

The apply Trap

The `apply` trap is for the [[Call]] internal operation on callable objects (like functions). A proxy will only have a [[Call]] operation if the target object it's proxying has one (otherwise, trying to call the

---

[2] https://tc39.github.io/ecma262/#sec-invariants-of-the-essential-internal-methods

proxy will yield a type error because it's not callable), so the `apply` trap only applies to proxies whose target is callable.

The `apply` trap handler receives three arguments:

➤ `target`: The proxy's target

➤ `thisValue`: The value used as `this` when making the call

➤ `args`: An array of the arguments for the call

Its return value is used as the return value of the call operation (whether or not it actually did call the target function).

The trap handler can make the underlying call, or not, and can return any value you like (or throw an error). Unlike some other trap handlers, there are no limits on what the `apply` handler can do.

The construct Trap

The `construct` trap is for the [[Construct]] internal operation of constructors. A proxy will only have a [[Construct]] operation if the target object it's proxying has one (otherwise, trying to call the proxy as a constructor will yield a type error because it's not one), so the `construct` trap only applies to proxies whose target is a constructor (either a `class` constructor or a traditional function, which can be used as a constructor).

The `construct` trap receives three arguments:

➤ `target`: The proxy's target

➤ `args`: An array of the arguments for the call

➤ `newTarget`: The value for `new.target` (which you learned about in Chapter 4)

Its return value is used as the result of the construction operation (whether it actually did one or not).

It can do *almost* anything it likes. The one restriction on a `construct` trap handler is that if it returns something (rather than throwing an error), that something must be an object (not `null` or a primitive). If it returns `null` or a primitive, the proxy throws an error.

The defineProperty Trap

The `defineProperty` trap is for the [[DefineOwnProperty]] internal object operation. As you saw in the logging example, [[DefineOwnProperty]] isn't only used when something calls `Object.defineProperty` (or `Reflect.defineProperty`) on an object, it's also used when a data property's value is set, or when a property is created via assignment.

The `defineProperty` trap receives three arguments:

➤ `target`: The proxy's target

➤ `propName`: The name of the property to define/redefine

➤ `descriptor`: The descriptor to apply

It's expected to return `true` on success (the property definition was successful or already matched the existing property) or `false` on error. (Truthy and falsy values will be coerced as necessary.)

The trap handler can reject the change (either returning `false` or throwing an error), adjust the property descriptor before applying it, etc., or any of the other things all traps can do.

If the trap handler returns `true` (success), there are some limits on it. Fundamentally, it can't lie by saying the operation succeeded when it's observable that the operation wasn't done. Specifically, an error is thrown if it reports success and, when the handler returns, the property:

➤ . . . doesn't exist and the target isn't extensible.

➤ . . . doesn't exist and the descriptor was marking the property non-configurable.

➤ . . . exists and is configurable, but the descriptor was marking the property non-configurable.

➤ . . . exists and applying the descriptor to it would throw an error (for instance, if the property exists and is non-configurable, but the descriptor was changing its configuration).

Those rules are there because of the *essential invariant behavior* constraints on objects mentioned earlier. They still leave a lot of flexibility, though. For instance, the trap can say that a call to set the value of the property worked when the property's value isn't (now) the value that was supposedly set, even though it's a writable data property.

There are no limits on the trap handler when it returns `false` (failure), even if the property exists exactly as the descriptor describes it (which would normally mean it would return `true`).

As you learned earlier, the `defineProperty` trap is triggered when setting the value of a data property (as opposed to an accessor property), but that doesn't make the `set` trap redundant. The `set` trap is triggered when setting the value of accessor properties as well, whereas `defineProperty` is not.

Listing 14-3 shows a simple `defineProperty` trap that forbids making any existing property on the target non-writable.

LISTING 14-3: defineProperty trap example—defineProperty-trap-example.js

```js
const obj = {};
const p = new Proxy(obj, {
    defineProperty(target, propName, descriptor) {
        if ("writable" in descriptor && !descriptor.writable) {
            const currentDescriptor =
                Reflect.getOwnPropertyDescriptor(target, propName);
            if (currentDescriptor && currentDescriptor.writable) {
                return false;
            }
        }
        return Reflect.defineProperty(target, propName, descriptor);
    }
});
```

continues

LISTING 14-3 *(continued)*

```
p.a = 1;
console.log(`p.a = ${p.a}`);
console.log("Trying to make p.a non-writable...");
console.log(
    `Result of defineProperty: ${Reflect.defineProperty(p, "a", {writable: false})}`
);
console.log("Setting pa.a to 2...");
p.a = 2;
console.log(`p.a = ${p.a}`);
```

In Listing 14-3, note that when using the proxy, the code uses `Reflect.defineProperty` to try to mark a property non-writable rather than `Object.defineProperty`. Can you think why it's written that way? It's to do with one of the main differences between the `Object` and `Reflect` versions of functions that change things . . .

It's because I wanted to show you the `false` result, and the fact that the a property was still writable after the `defineProperty` call. If I'd used `Object.defineProperty`, it would have thrown an error rather than returning `false`, so I would have had to write a `try/catch` block. Which you use in this sort of situation depends on whether you want a return value or an error; there are uses for both calls.

One final note: if the trap was triggered by a call to `defineProperty` (either the version on `Object` or on `Reflect`), the trap does not receive a direct reference to the descriptor object passed into that function; instead, it receives an object created specifically for the trap, which has only valid property names on it. So even if extra, non-descriptor properties were included on the one passed to the function, the trap would not receive them.

The deleteProperty Trap

The `deleteProperty` trap is for the [[Delete]] internal object operation that removes a property from an object.

The `deleteProperty` trap handler receives two arguments:

➤ `target`: The proxy's target

➤ `propName`: The name of the property to delete

It's expected to return `true` on success and `false` on error, just like the `delete` operator does in loose mode (in strict mode, a failed `delete` throws an error). Truthy and falsy values will be coerced as necessary.

The handler can refuse to delete the property (returning `false` or throwing an error), or any of the other things all traps can do.

It can't return `true` if the property exists on the target and is non-configurable, as that would violate one of the essential invariants. Doing so causes an error to be thrown.

Listing 14-4 shows a `deleteProperty` trap that refuses to delete the `value` property.

LISTING 14-4: deleteProperty trap example—deleteProperty-trap-example.js

```javascript
const obj = {value: 42};
const p = new Proxy(obj, {
    deleteProperty(target, propName, descriptor) {
        if (propName === "value") {
            return false;
        }
        return Reflect.deleteProperty(target, propName, descriptor);
    }
});
console.log(`p.value = ${p.value}`);
console.log("deleting 'value' from p in loose mode:");
console.log(delete p.value); // false
(() => {
    "use strict";
    console.log("deleting 'value' from p in strict mode:");
    try {
        delete p.value;
    } catch (error) {
        // TypeError: 'deleteProperty' on proxy: trap returned
        // falsish for property 'value'
        console.error(error);
    }
})();
```

The get Trap

As you'll recall, the `get` trap is for the [[Get]] internal object operation: getting the value of a property.

The `get` trap handler receives three arguments:

➤ `target`: The proxy's target

➤ `propName`: The property name

➤ `receiver`: The object that received the [[Get]] call

Its return value is used as the result of the [[Get]] operation (the value the code accessing the property sees for its value).

The `receiver` property is significant when the property is an accessor property, not a data property: it's the value that would be `this` during the call to the accessor if there were no trap handler. Often, `receiver` is the proxy, but `receiver` could be an object using the proxy as a prototype—proxies are objects, after all, and nothing prevents using a proxy as a prototype. Depending on your use case, if passing the call on to `Reflect.get`, you might choose not to pass on the receiver, so `this` within the accessor is the target, or you might substitute a different target, etc.

A `get` trap can do *almost* anything it likes, modifying the value, etc., except that like other traps it can't violate certain essential invariants, which means an error is thrown if it:

➤ . . . returns a value that isn't the same as the value of the underlying target's property, if that property is a non-configurable, read-only data property.

➤ . . . returns a value other than `undefined` if the target's property is a non-configurable write-only accessor (has no getter, just a setter).

You've already seen several examples of `get`; there's no need to do another here. But `get` does show up again later in the "Example: Hiding Properties" section.

The getOwnPropertyDescriptor Trap

The `getOwnPropertyDescriptor` trap is for the [[GetOwnProperty]] internal object operation, which gets a descriptor object for the property from the object. As you learned during the logging example earlier, [[GetOwnProperty]] is called in a number of places during the processing of other internal object operations, not just when code uses `Object.getOwnPropertyDescriptor` or `Reflect.getOwnPropertyDescriptor`.

The `getOwnPropertyDescriptor` trap handler receives two arguments:

➤ `target`: The proxy's target

➤ `propName`: The name of the property

It's expected to return a property descriptor object, or `undefined` if the property doesn't exist; returning anything else (including `null`) will cause an error. Normally you'd get the descriptor object from `Reflect.getOwnPropertyDescriptor`, but you can also hand-craft the descriptor object or modify what you get back from that call (within limits). Here's a list of the properties of a property descriptor object, which are used in various combinations depending on the property:

➤ `writable`: `true` if the property is writable, `false` if not (data properties only, not accessor properties); default `false` if absent

➤ `enumerable`: `true` if the property is enumerable, `false` if not; default `false` if absent

➤ `configurable`: `true` if the property is configurable, `false` if not; default `false` if absent

➤ `value`: The value of the property, if it's a data property; absent otherwise

➤ `get`: The getter function for an accessor property (can't be combined with `value` or `writable`)

➤ `set`: The setter function for an accessor property (can't be combined with `value` or `writable`)

The descriptor object returned by the trap is not returned directly to the code requesting the descriptor; instead, a new descriptor object is created, taking only valid properties from the one provided. Any other properties are silently ignored.

This trap has some limits on what it can do in order to maintain essential invariants. An error is thrown if:

➤ ... the handler returns `undefined` and the target object has the property and the target is not extensible.

➤ ... the handler returns `undefined` and the target object has the property and the property is non-configurable.

➤ ... the handler returns a descriptor for a non-configurable property, but the property either doesn't exist or is configurable.

➤ ... the handler returns a descriptor for the property, but the property doesn't exist, and the target is non-extensible.

The primary use case of the `getOwnPropertyDescriptor` trap is probably hiding a property that the target has from code using the proxy. Doing so is non-trivial and involves handlers for several traps, however. See the "Example: Hiding Properties" section later in this chapter.

The getPrototypeOf Trap

The `getPrototypeOf` trap is for the [[GetPrototypeOf]] internal object operation. This is triggered when the `Object` or `Reflect` object's `getPrototypeOf` function is used (directly, or indirectly via the `Object.prototype.__proto__` getter on web browsers), or when any internal operation needs to get the prototype of the proxy. It is not called when [[Get]] is used on the proxy, even if the prototype chain is followed because the proxy doesn't have the property, because the [[Get]] call is forwarded to the target (in the normal case) and so the [[GetPrototypeOf]] operation used when following the prototype chain at that point is called on the target, not the proxy.

It receives just the one argument:

➤ `target`: The proxy's target

It's expected to return an object or `null`. It can return any object you want unless the target is non-extensible; in that case, you must return the target's prototype.

Listing 14-5 shows a proxy that hides the prototype of the target, even though the prototype is used for property resolution.

LISTING 14-5: getPrototypeOf trap example—getPrototypeOf-trap-example.js

```js
const proto = {
    testing: "one two three"
};
const obj = Object.create(proto);
const p = new Proxy(obj, {
    getPrototypeOf(target) {
        return null;
    }
});
console.log(p.testing);             // one two three
console.log(Object.getPrototypeOf(p)); // null
```

The has Trap

The `has` trap is for the [[HasProperty]] internal object operation, which determines if the object has the given property (itself, or via its prototype).

It receives two arguments:

➤   `target`: The proxy's target

➤   `propName`: The name of the property

It's expected to return `true` if it has it (directly, or via its prototype) or `false` if not (truthy and falsy values are coerced).

You can probably guess, based on the limits of previous traps, what the limits are for the `has` trap:

➤   Returning `false` for a property that exists and is non-configurable throws an error.

➤   Returning `false` for a property that exists on a target object that is non-extensible throws an error.

The handler *is* allowed to return `true` for a property that *doesn't* exist, even on a non-extensible target object.

The obvious things to do with `has` traps are hiding properties the object has or claiming the object has properties it doesn't. See the "Example: Hiding Properties" section later in this chapter for an example.

The isExtensible Trap

The `isExtensible` trap is for the [[IsExtensible]] internal object operation: checking if the object is extensible (that is, has not had the [[PreventExtensions]] operation performed on it).

The `isExtensible` trap handler receives just one argument:

➤   `target`: The proxy's target

It's expected to return `true` if the object is extensible or `false` if not (truthy and falsy values are coerced). This is one of the most restricted traps: it must return the same value that the target object itself would have returned. Consequently, this trap is only useful for side effects, such as logging, as you saw in the earlier example.

The ownKeys Trap

The `ownKeys` trap is for the [[OwnPropertyKeys]] internal object operation, which creates an array of the object's own property keys, including non-enumerable ones and ones named with Symbols rather than strings.

The `ownKeys` trap handler receives just one argument:

➤   `target`: The proxy's target

It's expected to return an array or array-like object (it can't just return an iterable, it must be array-like).

An error is thrown if the trap handler returns an array that:

➤   . . . has duplicates in it

➤   . . . has any non-string, non-Symbol entries

➤   . . . has any missing or extra entries, if the target object is non-extensible

➤   . . . is missing an entry for a non-configurable property that exists on the target

This means the handler can hide properties (as long as they're configurable and the target is extensible), or include extra properties (as long as the target is extensible).

One common use case for `ownKeys` is hiding properties, as you'll see in the "Example: Hiding Properties" example.

The preventExtensions Trap

The `preventExtensions` trap is for the [[PreventExtensions]] internal object operation, which marks the object non-extensible.

Its handler receives just one argument:

➤   `target`: The proxy's target

It's expected to return `true` on success or `false` on error (truthy and falsy values are coerced). It's an error if it returns `true` but the target object is extensible, but it is allowed to return `false` when the target is non-extensible.

The trap handler can prevent the target from becoming non-extensible, by returning `false` as in Listing 14-6.

LISTING 14-6: preventExtensions trap example—preventExtensions-trap-example.js

```
const obj = {};
const p = new Proxy(obj, {
    preventExtensions(target) {
        return false;
    }
});
console.log(Reflect.isExtensible(p));        // true
console.log(Reflect.preventExtensions(p));   // false
console.log(Reflect.isExtensible(p));        // true
```

The set Trap

The `set` trap is for the [[Set]] internal object operation: setting the value of a property. It's triggered when either a data property or accessor property's value is being set. As you learned earlier, if the trap handler allows the operation and the property being set is a data property, the `defineProperty` trap will also be triggered to set the data property's `value`.

The `set` trap handler receives four arguments:

➤   `target`: The proxy's target

➤   `propName`: The name of the property

➤   `value`: The value to set

➤   `receiver`: The object receiving the operation

It's expected to return `true` on success or `false` on error (truthy and falsy values are coerced). The essential invariant operations constraints mean it's an error if the handler returns `true` and:

➤   . . . the property exists on the target object, is a non-configurable, non-writable data property, and its value doesn't match the value being set.

➤   . . . the property exists on the target object, is a non-configurable accessor property, and has no setter function.

Note that `set` can prevent setting values, even on non-configurable properties and even on non-extensible target objects, by returning `false`. You'll see an example of that in the "Example: Hiding Properties" section later in this chapter.

The setPrototypeOf Trap

The `setPrototypeOf` trap is for the [[SetPrototypeOf]] internal object operation, which (and I know this will surprise you) sets the prototype of the object.

Its handler receives two arguments:

➤   `target`: The proxy's target

➤   `newProto`: The prototype to set

It's expected to return `true` on success or `false` on error (truthy and falsy values are coerced). To enforce the essential invariants, it can't return `true` if the target is non-extensible unless the prototype being set is already the prototype of the target. It can, however, refuse to set a new prototype, as in Listing 14-7.

LISTING 14-7: setPrototypeOf trap example—setPrototypeOf-trap-example.js

```
const obj = {foo: 42};
const p = new Proxy(obj, {
    setPrototypeOf(target, newProto) {
        // Return false unless `newProto` is already `target`'s prototype
        return Reflect.getPrototypeOf(target) === newProto;
    }
});
console.log(Reflect.getPrototypeOf(p) === Object.prototype); // true
console.log(Reflect.setPrototypeOf(p, Object.prototype));    // true
console.log(Reflect.setPrototypeOf(p, Array.prototype));     // false
```

Example: Hiding Properties

This section works through an example of hiding properties. Hiding properties in an immutable object is fairly easy; hiding properties when operations on the object can change a hidden property is rather more complicated.

Before we start, it's worth noting that hiding properties is rarely really necessary. Most languages with declaratively private properties have a back door (via reflection) that authors can use if they really want to get at the private information. (Although interestingly, JavaScript's own private fields, which you'll learn about in Chapter 18, don't.) So for most use cases, a simple naming convention or a bit of documentation saying "don't access this property" is usually good enough. For situations where that isn't good enough, you have four options (at least):

➤ Create your methods as closures in the constructor rather than putting them on the prototype, and store the "properties" in variables/parameters within the constructor call's scope.

➤ Use a WeakMap as shown in Chapter 12, so the properties you want to hide aren't on the object at all.

➤ Use private fields (which you'll learn about in Chapter 18) when they land in implementations (as of this writing, they're at Stage 3) or via transpilation.

➤ Use a proxy to hide the properties.

The fourth option, using a proxy, is useful if you can't—for whatever reason—use any of the other three, perhaps because you can't modify the implementation of the object you're proxying.

Let's see it in action. Assume you have a simple counter class like this:

```
class Counter {
    constructor(name) {
        this._value = 0;
        this.name = name;
    }
    increment() {
        return ++this._value;
    }
    get value() {
        return this._value;
    }
}
```

Code using this can directly observe and modify _value:

```
const c = new Counter("c");
console.log("c.value before increment:");
console.log(c.value);                    // 0
console.log("c._value before increment:");
console.log(c._value);                   // 0
c.increment();
console.log("c.value after increment:");
console.log(c.value);                    // 1
console.log("c._value after increment:");
console.log(c._value);                   // 1
```

```
console.log("'_value' in c:");
console.log('_value' in c);                  // true
console.log("Object.keys(c):");
console.log(Object.keys(c));                 // ["name", "_value"]
c._value = 42;
console.log("c.value after changing _value:");
console.log(c.value);                        // 42
```

(You can run that from the `not-hiding-properties.js` file in the downloads.)

Let's assume you want to hide the _value property so it can't be directly observed or changed by code using an instance of the counter, and you can't or don't want to use one of the other mechanisms for that. To do so, at a minimum you need to hook into several operations:

➤ `get` so you return `undefined` for the property instead of its value

➤ `getOwnPropertyDescriptor` so you return `undefined` instead of a property descriptor for it

➤ `has` so you don't report the existence of the property

➤ `ownKeys` for the same reason

➤ `defineProperty` so you don't allow setting the property (either directly or via `Object.defineProperty` or `Reflect.defineProperty`) and so you don't allow changing the property's enumerability, etc.

➤ `deleteProperty` so the property can't be deleted

There's no need to use the `set` trap, since as you learned earlier, all operations that modify a data property end up going through the `defineProperty` trap. (If you were hiding an accessor property, then you'd need to use the `set` trap since only data property changes go through `defineProperty`.)

Let's start there and see how we get on:

```
function getCounter(name) {
    const p = new Proxy(new Counter(name), {
        get(target, name, receiver) {
            if (name === "_value") {
                return undefined;
            }
            return Reflect.get(target, name, receiver);
        },
        getOwnPropertyDescriptor(target, propName) {
            if (name === "_value") {
                return undefined;
            }
            return Reflect.getOwnPropertyDescriptor(target, propName);
        },
        defineProperty(target, name, descriptor) {
            if (name === "_value") {
                return false;
            }
            return Reflect.defineProperty(target, name, descriptor);
        },
```

```
            has(target, name) {
                if (name === "_value") {
                    return false;
                }
                return Reflect.has(target, name);
            },
            ownKeys(target) {
                return Reflect.ownKeys(target).filter(key => key !== "_value");
            }
        });
        return p;
    }
```

That seems like it should do the trick, right? Let's do the same series of operations on it that we did before, but using `const p = getCounter("p")` instead of `const c = new Counter("c")`:

```
const p = getCounter("p");
console.log("p.value before increment:");
console.log(p.value);                    // 0
console.log("p._value before increment:");
console.log(p._value);                   // undefined
p.increment();                           // Throws an error!
```

It starts out okay, but then the call to `increment` fails (try it by running `hiding-properties-1.js` from the downloads), pointing to the `++this._value;` line:

```
TypeError: 'defineProperty' on proxy: trap returned falsish for property '_value'
```

Why was the proxy called for that line *within* Counter's code?

Let's look at what happens when `p.increment()` is executed:

➤   [[Get]] is called on the object to get the `increment` property; since that name isn't "_value", our `get` trap handler returns the function via `Reflect.get`.

➤   [[Call]] is called on `increment` with `this` set to . . . you see the problem, don't you? `this` is set to the proxy, not to the target. After all, the call was `p.increment()`, so within the call to `increment`, `this` is `p`.

So how do you make `increment` work with the target rather than the proxy? You have a couple of options: a function wrapper around `increment`, or . . . a *proxy* around it (this section is, after all, about proxies—and that way, the function's `name` and `length` and such are reflected by the wrapper). But that's fairly inefficient, creating a new proxy (or wrapper) for essentially every call to a function. In Chapter 12 you learned a convenient technique for keeping a map of things without forcing the key to stay in memory: a WeakMap. The code could use a WeakMap with the original function as the key and its proxy as the value. You might modify the `get` handler to proxy functions as and when required, remembering those proxies for reuse:

```
function getCounter(name) {
    const functionProxies = new WeakMap();
    const p = new Proxy(new Counter(name), {
        get(target, name) {
            if (name === "_value") {
                return undefined;
            }
```

```
                    let value = Reflect.get(target, name);
                    if (typeof value === "function") {
                        let funcProxy = functionProxies.get(value);
                        if (!funcProxy) {
                            funcProxy = new Proxy(value, {
                                apply(funcTarget, thisValue, args) {
                                    const t = thisValue === p ? target : thisValue;
                                    return Reflect.apply(funcTarget, t, args);
                                }
                            });
                            functionProxies.set(value, funcProxy);
                            value = funcProxy;
                        }
                    }
                    return value;
                },
                // ...no changes to the other trap handlers...
            });
            return p;
    }
```

Note how the proxy uses the original target object (the `Counter` instance, `target`) rather than the proxy when calling `increment`. That does the trick: try running `hiding-properties-2.js` from the downloads. You can see that `increment` still works, but `_value` is inaccessible from the outside.

It's still possible to make this proxied counter fail, by getting `increment` from the counter's prototype instead of from the proxy (`hiding-properties-fail.js` in the downloads):

```
const { increment } = Object.getPrototypeOf(p);
increment.call(p);
// => Throws TypeError: 'defineProperty' on proxy: trap returned falsish...
```

or by wrapping a proxy around the proxy or using the proxied counter as a prototype (since in both cases, the `thisValue === p` check in the `apply` trap wouldn't be true anymore), but the basic use case is handled correctly. It's possible to allow for the case of the proxy being used as a prototype (by looping the prototypes of `thisValue` to see if the proxy is one of them), but you probably can't work around the issue of a proxied proxy.

The takeaway here, other than "test your proxies very thoroughly," is that proxies are powerful, but also potentially complicated in real-world use.

Revocable Proxies

At the beginning of this chapter you learned that proxies are useful for providing a boundary between two bits of code, such as an API and its consumers. A *revocable proxy* is particularly useful for that, because you can *revoke* the object you provide (the proxy) when the time comes. Revoking a proxy does two important things:

➤ It makes all operations on the revoked proxy fail with an error. Gate-keeping at its finest!

➤ It releases the link the proxy had to its target object. The proxy releasing its link to the target means that although the consuming code may still reference the proxy, the target object can be garbage collected. This minimizes the memory impact of revoked proxies that are strongly held by the consumer code. For instance, a quick test suggests that a revoked proxy is only 32 bytes on Chrome's V8 engine (that could change, of course), where the target object is likely to be rather larger.

To create a revocable proxy, you call the `Proxy.revocable` method rather than using `new Proxy`. The `Proxy.revocable` method returns an object with a `proxy` property (the proxy) and a `revoke` method (to revoke the proxy). See Listing 14-8.

LISTING 14-8: Revocable proxy example—revocable-proxy-example.js

```
const obj = {answer: 42};
const { proxy, revoke } = Proxy.revocable(obj, {});
console.log(proxy.answer); // 42
revoke();
console.log(proxy.answer); // TypeError: Cannot perform 'get' on
                           // a proxy that has been revoked
```

Note that once the proxy was revoked, attempting to use it failed.

The example in Listing 14-8 doesn't specify any trap handlers, but that's just to keep the example short. It could have the same handlers with the same behaviors as the proxies you've seen throughout this chapter.

OLD HABITS TO NEW

The features provided by `Reflect` and `Proxy` are fundamentally new features to JavaScript and generally solve new problems rather than providing new solutions to old problems. But there are still a couple of practices you might consider changing.

Use Proxies Rather Than Relying on Consumer Code Not to Modify API Objects

Old habit: Providing API objects directly to consuming code.

New habit: Providing proxies—perhaps revocable ones—instead. This lets you control the access the consuming code has to the object, including (if you provide a revocable proxy) cancelling all access to the object when appropriate in your code.

Use Proxies to Separate Implementation Code from Instrumenting Code

Old habit: Intermixing instrumentation code (code designed to help determine patterns of object usage, performance, etc.) with implementation code (code that ensures the object does its job correctly).

New habit: Use a proxy to add the instrumentation layer, leaving the object's own code uncluttered.

15

Regular Expression Updates

WHAT'S IN THIS CHAPTER?

➤ The `flags` property

➤ The `y`, `u`, and `s` flags

➤ Named capture groups

➤ Lookbehind assertions

➤ Unicode code point escapes

➤ Unicode property escapes

In this chapter, you'll learn about the many new regular expression features added in ES015 and ES2018, including a `flags` property on instances reflecting all of the flags for the instance; named capture groups for more readable, maintainable regular expressions; lookbehind assertions; and Unicode property escapes providing access to powerful matching classes.

THE FLAGS PROPERTY

In ES2015, regular expressions got a `flags` accessor property that returns a string containing the flags for the expression. Prior to the `flags` property, the only way to know what flags the `RegExp` object had was to look at the individual properties reflecting its individual flags (`rex.global`, `rex.multiline`, etc.), or use its `toString` method and look at the end of the string. The `flags` property makes them available directly as a string:

```
const rex = /example/ig;
console.log(rex.flags); // "gi"
```

The specification defines that the flags are provided in alphabetical order, regardless of how they were specified when the expression was created: `gimsuy`. (You'll learn about those three new ones, `s`, `u`, and `y`, in the following sections.) You can see the order being applied in the example, which created the expression with the flags `ig` but then output `gi` when displaying the `flags` property's value.

NEW FLAGS

In ES2015 and ES2018, TC39 added new regular expression mode flags:

➤ y: The "sticky" flag (ES2015) means that a regular expression only matches starting at the regular expression object's `lastIndex` index in the string (it doesn't search for a match later in the string).

➤ u: The "Unicode" flag (ES2015) enables various Unicode features that are disabled by default.

➤ s: The "dot all" flag (ES2018) makes the "any character" token (.) match line terminators.

Let's look at each of those in more detail.

The Sticky Flag (y)

The `y` flag means that when evaluating the regular expression against a string, the JavaScript engine doesn't search through the string, it only checks for a match in the string starting at the regular expression object's `lastIndex` index. See Listing 15-1.

LISTING 15-1: Sticky flag example—sticky-example.js

```
function tryRex(rex, str) {
    console.log(`lastIndex: ${rex.lastIndex}`);
    const match = rex.exec(str);
    if (match) {
        console.log(`Match:     ${match[0]}`);
        console.log(`At:        ${match.index}`);
    } else {
        console.log("No match");
    }
}
```

```
const str = "this is a test";

// Non-sticky, searches string:
tryRex(/test/, str);
// lastIndex: 0
// Match:       test
// At:          10

// Sticky, doesn't search, matches only at `lastIndex`:
const rex1 = /test/y;   // `rex.lastIndex` defaults to 0
tryRex(rex1, str);
// lastIndex: 0
// No match

const rex2 = /test/y;
rex2.lastIndex = 10;    // Sets where in the string we want to match
tryRex(rex2, str);
// lastIndex: 10
// Match:       test
// At:          10
```

Running the code in Listing 15-1, you can see that a regular expression with no sticky flag (`/test/`) searches through the string to find a match: `lastIndex` is 0, but the regular expression finds the word "test" at index 10. With the sticky flag set (`/test/y`), it doesn't find "test" when `lastIndex` is 0 because "test" isn't in the string at index 0. But it does find it when `lastIndex` is 10, because the string "test" is in the string "this is a test" at index 10.

This is handy when moving through a string token by token and checking for matches against a set of possible token patterns (regular expressions), such as when parsing. To do this before the sticky flag was added, you had to use a ^ (start-of-input) anchor at the beginning of the expression and chop off characters you'd already processed from the string before doing matching, so the match would be at the beginning of the string. The sticky flag is simpler, and makes the process more efficient by allowing you to avoid creating those truncated strings.

You can check if the sticky flag is set by looking in `flags` or checking the expression's `sticky` property, which is `true` if the flag is set.

The Unicode Flag (u)

ES2015 improved JavaScript's support for Unicode in many areas (see Chapter 10 for improvements regarding strings), including in regular expressions. To avoid creating problems for existing code, though, the new Unicode features in regular expressions are disabled by default and enabled with the u flag. You'll learn about the features that require the u flag in the "Unicode Features" section later in this chapter.

You can check if the Unicode flag is set by looking in `flags` or checking the expression's `unicode` property, which is `true` if the flag is set.

The "Dot All" Flag (s)

ES2018 added the `s` flag ("dotAll") to JavaScript's regular expressions. With many flavors of regular expressions (including JavaScript's), it often trips people up that the "any character" token (`.`) doesn't match line terminator characters like `\r` and `\n` (and the two additional Unicode ones, `\u2028` and `\u2029`). "Dot all" is a common solution, modifying the behavior of `.` so it matches line terminators. Before ES2018, JavaScript didn't support it, forcing people to use workarounds like `[\s\S]` (anything that is or isn't whitespace), `[\w\W]` (anything that is or isn't a "word character"), or the highly JavaScript-specific `[^]` (an empty negated character class; "not nothing" equals "anything"), etc.

See Listing 15-3 for a "dot all" example.

LISTING 15-2: DotAll flag example—dotAll-example.js

```
const str = "Testing\nAlpha\nBravo\nCharlie\nJavaScript";
console.log(str.match(/.[A-Z]/g));   // ["aS"]
console.log(str.match(/.[A-Z]/gs));  // ["\nA", "\nB", "\nC", "aS"]
```

In the example, you can see that without the `s` flag, only the "aS" in "JavaScript" matched, because the letter "a" was matched by the `.` and the letter "S" was matched by `[A-Z]`. With the `s` flag, the line terminators before the "A" in "Alpha," the "B" in "Bravo," and the "C" in "Charlie" also matched.

You can check whether the "dot all" flag is set on an expression by looking in `flags` or checking the `dotAll` property, which is `true` when the flag is set.

NAMED CAPTURE GROUPS

ES2018 added *named capture groups* to JavaScript's regular expressions, joining the existing anonymous capture groups. A named capture group is written in this form:

```
(?<name>pattern)
```

You put the group's name in angle brackets just after a question mark (`?`) at the beginning of the group. A named capture group works exactly like an anonymous capture group, so it's accessible in the match result (`result[1]`, etc.), as a backreference later in the expression (`\1`, etc.), and in replacement tokens when used with `replace` (`$1`, etc.). But you can also refer to a named group using its name, as you'll learn in the following sections.

Basic Functionality

A named capture group appears in the usual place in the match result and also on a new `groups` object on the result as a property using the group's name.

For example, look at the result with this anonymous capture group:

```
const rex = /testing (\d+)/g;
const result = rex.exec("This is a test: testing 123 testing");
console.log(result[0]);     // testing 123
console.log(result[1]);     // 123
console.log(result.index);  // 16
console.log(result.input);  // This is a test: testing 123 testing
```

Since the match is successful, the result is an augmented array with the full matching text at index 0, the capture group at index 1, the index of the match in an `index` property, and the input to the matching operation as an `input` property.

Let's use a named capture group called `number` instead:

```
const rex = /testing (?<number>\d+)/g;
const result = rex.exec("This is a test: testing 123 testing");
console.log(result[0]);      // testing 123
console.log(result[1]);      // 123
console.log(result.index);   // 16
console.log(result.input);   // This is a test: testing 123 testing
console.log(result.groups);  // {"number": "123"}
```

The capture group's value still appears at index 1, but notice the new property, `groups`, which is an object with properties for each named capture group (in this case, just the one: `number`).

The new `groups` object has no prototype, as though it had been created with `Object.create(null)`. That's so it doesn't have any properties at all, not even the ones most objects inherit from `Object.prototype` like `toString` and `hasOwnProperty`. That way, you don't have to worry about possible conflicts between the names of your named capture groups and properties defined by `Object.prototype`. (When you ran the earlier example, depending on your environment you may have seen something in the output pointing out that `groups` has a `null` prototype.)

Having names for your capture groups is really useful. Suppose you're parsing a date in the U.S. mm/dd/yyyy format. With anonymous capture groups, you might do it as in Listing 15-3.

LISTING 15-3: Parsing U.S. date format with anonymous capture groups—anon-capture-groups1.js

```
const usDateRex =
    /^(\d{1,2})[-\/](\d{1,2})[-\/](\d{4})$/;
function parseDate(dateStr) {
    const parts = usDateRex.exec(dateStr);
    if (parts) {
        let year  = +parts[3];
        let month = +parts[1] - 1;
        let day   = +parts[2];
        if (!isNaN(year) && !isNaN(month) && !isNaN(day)) {
            if (year < 50) {
                year += 2000;
            } else if (year < 100) {
                year += 1900;
            }
            return new Date(year, month, day);
        }
    }
    return null;
}
function test(str) {
    let result = parseDate(str);
    console.log(result ? result.toISOString() : "invalid format");
}

test("12/25/2019"); // Parses; shows date
test("2019/25/12"); // Doesn't parse; shows "invalid format"
```

It's already slightly less than ideal that you have to remember that the year is at index 3 (`parts[3]`), the month is at index 1, and the day is at index 2. Suppose you decide to enhance the expression by having it try `yyyy-mm-dd` first and then fall back to the U.S. format if it doesn't match. It gets a bit painful, as you can see in Listing 15-4.

LISTING 15-4: Adding a second date format with anonymous capture groups—anon-capture-groups2.js

```
const usDateRex =
    /^(\d{1,2})[-\/](\d{1,2})[-\/](\d{4})$/;
const yearFirstDateRex =
    /^(\d{4})[-\/](\d{1,2})[-\/](\d{1,2})$/;
function parseDate(dateStr) {
    let year, month, day;
    let parts = yearFirstDateRex.exec(dateStr);
    if (parts) {
        year  = +parts[1];
        month = +parts[2] - 1;
        day   = +parts[3];
    } else {
        parts = usDateRex.exec(dateStr);
        if (parts) {
            year  = +parts[3];
            month = +parts[1] - 1;
            day   = +parts[2];
        }
    }
    if (parts && !isNaN(year) && !isNaN(month) && !isNaN(day)) {
        if (year < 50) {
            year += 2000;
        } else if (year < 100) {
            year += 1900;
        }
        return new Date(year, month, day);
    }
    return null;
}
function test(str) {
    let result = parseDate(str);
    console.log(result ? result.toISOString() : "invalid format");
}

test("12/25/2019"); // Parses; shows date
test("2019-12-25"); // Parses; shows date
test("12/25/19");   // Doesn't parse; shows "invalid format"
```

It works, but you have to pick out the values of different capture groups depending on which regular expression matched, based on their order in the expression, with indexes into the match array. It's awkward and hard to read, and awkward and error-prone to maintain.

Suppose the original version used named capture groups, as in Listing 15-5.

LISTING 15-5: Parsing U.S. date format with named capture groups—named-capture-groups1.js

```
const usDateRex =
    /^(?<month>\d{1,2})[-\/](?<day>\d{1,2})[-\/](?<year>\d{4})$/;
function parseDate(dateStr) {
    const parts = usDateRex.exec(dateStr);
    if (parts) {
        let year  = +parts.groups.year;
        let month = +parts.groups.month - 1;
        let day   = +parts.groups.day;
        if (!isNaN(year) && !isNaN(month) && !isNaN(day)) {
            if (year < 50) {
                year += 2000;
            } else if (year < 100) {
                year += 1900;
            }
            return new Date(year, month, day);
        }
    }
    return null;
}
function test(str) {
    let result = parseDate(str);
    console.log(result ? result.toISOString() : "invalid format");
}

test("12/25/2019"); // Parses; shows date
test("12/25/19");   // Doesn't parse; shows "invalid format"
```

It's already better since you don't have to remember the order of the groups, you can just refer to them by their names (`parts.groups.year` and such). But adding another format is dramatically simpler as well; see Listing 15-6 noting the highlighted parts, which are the only changes (other than the usage example) from Listing 15-5.

LISTING 15-6: Adding a second date format with named capture groups—named-capture-groups2.js

```
const usDateRex =
    /^(?<month>\d{1,2})[-\/](?<day>\d{1,2})[-\/](?<year>\d{4})$/;
const yearFirstDateRex =
    /^(?<year>\d{4})[-\/](?<month>\d{1,2})[-\/](?<day>\d{1,2})$/;
function parseDate(dateStr) {
    const parts = yearFirstDateRex.exec(dateStr) || usDateRex.exec(dateStr);
    if (parts) {
        let year  = +parts.groups.year;
        let month = +parts.groups.month - 1;
        let day   = +parts.groups.day;
        if (!isNaN(year) && !isNaN(month) && !isNaN(day)) {
            if (year < 50) {
                year += 2000;
```

```
            } else if (year < 100) {
                year += 1900;
            }
            return new Date(year, month, day);
        }
    }
    return null;
}
function test(str) {
    let result = parseDate(str);
    console.log(result ? result.toISOString() : "invalid format");
}

test("12/25/2019"); // Parses; shows date
test("2019-12-25"); // Parses; shows date
test("12/25/19");   // Doesn't parse; shows "invalid format"
```

Much simpler!

Backreferences

Named groups make *backreferences* clearer and easier to maintain.

You may know that you can include a backreference in order to match the value of a previous capture group later in the expression. For instance, the following expression matches text wrapped in either double quotes or single quotes, by using a capture group (`(["']`)) for the leading quote and a backreference (`\1`) for the trailing quote:

```
const rex = /(["']).+?\1/g;
const str = "testing 'a one', \"and'a two\", and'a three";
console.log(str.match(rex)); // ["'a one'", "\"and'a two\""]
```

Note how the backreference ensured that the first entry had single quotes on either side and the second entry had double quotes on either side.

A named capture group can make it clearer what you're referring back to. Named backreferences are in the form `\k<name>`:

```
const rex = /(?<quote>["']).+?\k<quote>/g;
const str = "testing 'a one', \"and'a two\", and'a three";
console.log(str.match(rex)); // ["'a one'", "\"and'a two\""]
```

Now you don't need to count capture groups to know what the backreference is referring to. The name makes it easy.

You might be thinking: "Hey, wait a minute, that `\k<name>` text for the backreference already meant something!" And you're right, it did: it's an unnecessarily-escaped k followed by the text <name>. Because such a thing may well exist in the wild (people often escape things unnecessarily, though k would be somewhat odd to escape), the `\k<name>` format only defines a named backreference if there are named capture groups in the expression. Otherwise, it falls back to its old meaning. Since there can only be named capture groups in new expressions written with named capture groups in mind (the sequence `(?<name>x)` was a syntax error before they were added), it's safe to interpret a named backreference as a named backreference in an expression that has named capture groups.

Finally: although it's best to use a named backreference with a named capture group for clarity, you *can* refer to a named capture group with the old anonymous form (\1, for example), because named capture groups are just like anonymous ones *plus* additional name-related features.

Replacement Tokens

When doing a replacement with a regular expression (usually via String.prototype.replace), in addition to the familiar way of referring to capture groups via tokens like $1, $2, etc., you can also use named tokens in the form $<name>. For instance, if you want to convert dates in a string from yyyy-mm-dd format to the common European dd/mm/yyyy format:

```
const rex = /^(?<year>\d{2}|\d{4})[-\/](?<month>\d{1,2})[-\/](?<day>\d{1,2})$/;
const str = "2019-02-14".replace(rex, "$<day>/$<month>/$<year>");
console.log(str); // "14/02/2019"
```

As with backreferences and match results, you can also use the anonymous form ($1 and such) with a named group if you like.

LOOKBEHIND ASSERTIONS

ES2018 adds *lookbehind assertions* to regular expressions, both *positive lookbehinds* (matching X only if it follows Y, without matching Y) and *negative lookbehinds* (matching X only if it *doesn't* follow Y, without matching whatever is where Y isn't). These balance the look*ahead* assertions JavaScript has had for years.

Unlike some other languages, JavaScript's lookbehind assertions are not limited to fixed-length constructs; you can use the full power of JavaScript's regular expressions in a lookbehind.

A key aspect of lookbehind assertions as implemented in JavaScript is that they are tested right-to-left instead of the usual left-to-right processing of regular expressions. We'll come back to this point in a couple of the following sections.

Let's look at lookbehind assertions in a bit more detail. You can find and run all of the examples in this section (in order) in lookbehind.js in the downloads.

Positive Lookbehind

Positive lookbehinds have the form (?<=Y), where Y is the thing to look for. For instance, to match a number following the Pound Sterling sign (£, the currency used in the United Kingdom) without matching the pound sign, you can use a positive lookbehind to assert that it must be there:

```
const str1 = "We sold 10 cases for £20 each, and 5 cases for £12.99 each";
const rex1 = /(?<=£)[\d.]+/g;
console.log(str1.match(rex1)); // ["20", "12.99"]
```

(To keep the example simple, this just uses [\d.]+ to match the numbers, which isn't rigorous.) Notice how 10 and 5 were not matched, because they didn't have the pound sign.

To do the match, conceptually the engine finds a match for the non-assertion part ([\d.]+) and then applies the lookbehind by taking each part of the expression in the lookbehind and testing it against the text in front of the match, part-by-part, moving right-to-left.[1] In this example, there's just one part in the lookbehind (£), but it could be more complicated:

```
const str2 = 'The codes are: 1E7 ("blue fidget"), 2G9 ("white flugel"),' +
             'and 17Y7 ("black diamond")';
const rex2 = /(?<=\d+[a-zA-Z]\d+ \(").+?(?="\))/g;
console.log(str2.match(rex2));
// => ["blue fidget", "white flugel", "black diamond"]
```

That expression has:

➤ A positive lookbehind that matches the code format (1E7, 2G9, etc.) and an opening parenthesis-quote combination: `(?<=\d+[a-zA-Z]\d+ \(")`

➤ The expression to match the description: `.+?`

➤ A positive lookahead to match a closing quote-parenthesis combination: `(?="\))`

The engine finds a match for `.+?`, then checks that the text just before the match matches the various parts of the lookbehind `(?<=\d+[a-zA-Z]\d+ \(")`, right-to-left, as in Figure 15-1. (Again, the engine may be able to optimize that, but it makes a good mental model for the operation.)

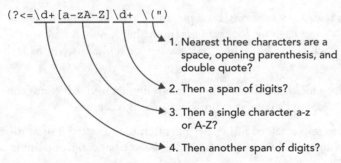

1. Nearest three characters are a space, opening parenthesis, and double quote?

2. Then a span of digits?

3. Then a single character a-z or A-Z?

4. Then another span of digits?

FIGURE 15-1

Negative Lookbehind

Negative lookbehinds have the form `(?<!Y)` where Y is what should *not* be present. So if you wanted to match the 10 and 5 from the previous example instead of matching figures after pound signs, your first thought is probably to just change `(?<=£)` to `(?<!£)`:

```
const str3 = "We sold 10 cases for £20 each, and 5 cases for £12.99 each";
const rex3 = /(?<!£)[\d.]+/g;
console.log(str3.match(rex3)); // ["10", "0", "5", "2.99"]
```

Huh? Why did it match extra numbers?

If you didn't already expect them, think for a moment why (for instance) the 0 in £20 matched.

---

[1] It's likely that an actual implementation does it more efficiently than that, but thinking of it this way helps understand some things we cover later on.

Right! Because the 0 in £20 doesn't have a £ right in front of it (the character right in front of it is a 2), nor does the 2.99 in £12.99 (the character right in front of 2.99 is 1). So you'll need to add digits and decimals to the negative lookbehind (again, this isn't as rigorous as you'd want in production code, in order to keep the example simple):

```
const str4 = "We sold 10 cases for £20 each, and 5 cases for £12.99 each";
const rex4 = /(?<![£\d.])[\d.]+/g;
console.log(str4.match(rex4)); // ["10", "5"]
```

As with positive lookbehind, negative lookbehind is also processed part-by-part, right-to-left.

Greediness Is Right-to-Left in Lookbehinds

Within a lookbehind that uses greedy quantifiers, the greediness is right-to-left, not left-to-right as it normally is. This naturally flows from the right-to-left processing of lookbehinds.

You can observe this if you have one or more capture groups within your lookbehind:

```
const behind = /(?<=(?<left>\w+)(?<right>\w+))\d$/;
const behindMatch = "ABCD1".match(behind);
console.log(behindMatch.groups.left);
// => "A"
console.log(behindMatch.groups.right);
// => "BCD"
```

Notice that the "left" \w+ only got one character, but the "right" \w+ got all the others—the greediness was right-to-left. Outside of a lookbehind (including in a look*ahead*), greediness is left-to-right:

```
const ahead  = /\d(?=(?<left>\w+)(?<right>\w+))/;
const aheadMatch = "1ABCD".match(ahead);
console.log(aheadMatch.groups.left);
// => "ABC"
console.log(aheadMatch.groups.right);
// => "D"
```

This is part and parcel of the right-to-left nature of lookbehinds in JavaScript.

Capture Group Numbering and References

Despite the right-to-left processing behavior of lookbehinds, the numbering of capture groups within them remains the same (the order in which they start in the regular expression, left-to-right). The earlier example of greediness used named capture groups and referred to them by name. Let's look at that same example with anonymous capture groups, referencing them by their position:

```
const behindAgain = /(?<=(\w+)(\w+))\d$/;
const behindMatchAgain = "ABCD1".match(behindAgain);
console.log(behindMatchAgain[1]);
// => "A"
console.log(behindMatchAgain[2]);
// => "BCD"
```

The greediness was right-to-left, but the group numbers were still assigned left-to-right. This is to keep the numbering simple. They're numbered according to where they are in the expression, not the order in which they're processed.

Even though they're ordered that way in the result, they're still *evaluated* right-to-left. You can see that with backreferences. Outside a lookbehind, you can't usefully refer to a group if the reference is to the left of the group:

```
const rex = /\1\w+(["']])/; // Doesn't make sense
```

It's not a syntax error, but the value of the reference (\1) won't match anything because when it's used by the expression the capture hasn't been evaluated yet.

For the exact same reason, in a lookbehind, the reference can't usefully be to the *right* of the capture:

```
const referring1 = /(?<=(["'])\w+\1)X/;      // Doesn't make sense
console.log(referring1.test("'testing'X"));
// => false
```

Instead, since the processing is right-to-left, you put the capture on the right and refer to it from the left:

```
const referring2 = /(?<=\1\w+(["']))X/;
console.log(referring2.test("'testing'X"));
// => true
```

That's true whether it's an anonymous capture group or a named one:

```
const referring3 = /(?<=\k<quote>\w+(?<quote>["']))X/;
console.log(referring3.test("'testing'X"));
// => true
```

The term "backreference" is still used. Think of the "back" in "backreference" as referring to looking back in the *processing* of the expression, rather than looking back in the expression's *definition*.

UNICODE FEATURES

In Chapter 10 you learned that JavaScript's handling of Unicode improved markedly in ES2015 and after. That improvement extends to regular expressions. To enable the new features, the regular expression must have the u flag, in order to preserve backward compatibility for existing regular expressions that may use the new syntax (possibly inadvertently or unnecessarily). For instance, one of the new syntax features assigns meaning to the sequences \p and \P, which previously were unnecessary escapes on the letters p and P, respectively. Simply changing the meaning would have broken any regular expression written with unnecessary escapes on p or P. But it's safe to give them new meanings in an expression created with the new u flag.

Code Point Escapes

The old Unicode escape sequence, \uNNNN, defines a single UTF-16 code *unit*. As you may recall from Chapter 10, though, a code unit may be only half of a surrogate pair. For instance, to match the "smiling face with smiling eyes" emoji (U+1F60A) using an escape sequence (rather than just using the emoji literally, ☺) you need two basic Unicode escape sequences representing the two UTF-16 code units for that emoji (0xD83D and 0xDE0A):

```
const rex = /\uD83D\uDE0A/;
const str = "Testing: ☺";
console.log(rex.test(str)); // true
```

Figuring out the UTF-16 code units for a Unicode code point (loosely, "character") is awkward.

As of ES2015, a regular expression using the u flag can use a *code point escape sequence* instead: a curly brace ({) after the \u followed by the code point value as hex followed by a closing curly brace (}):

```
const rex = /\u{1F60A}/u;
const str = "Testing: ☺";
console.log(rex.test(str)); // true
```

Code point escapes don't only work on their own; you can use them in character classes to match a *range* of code points. The following matches all of the code points in the "Emoticons" Unicode block:[2] /[\u{1F600}-\u{1F64F}]/.

Unicode Property Escapes

The Unicode standard doesn't just assign a numeric value to characters, it also provides a huge amount of information about the characters themselves. For instance, the Unicode standard can tell you (among other things) that the character "í" is Latin script, alphabetic, not numeric, and not punctuation; it can tell you that the character "¿" is punctuation common to multiple scripts; and so on. These various things are called *Unicode properties*. As of ES2018, a regular expression using the u flag can include *Unicode property escapes* to match characters by their Unicode properties. Since this is quite new, as always check support in your target environments.

There are several types of properties; the two relevant to JavaScript's regular expressions are *binary properties* that are (as the name indicates) either true or false, and *enumerated properties* that have a list of possible values. For example, the expression \p{Alphabetic} uses the binary property Alphabetic to match any character considered alphabetic by the Unicode standard:

```
const rex1 = /\p{Alphabetic}/gu;
const s1 = "Hello, I'm James.";
console.log(s1.match(rex1));
// => ["H", "e", "l", "l", "o", "I", "m", "J", "a", "m", "e", "s"]
```

As you can see, the escape starts with \p{ and ends with }, with the property to match inside the curly braces.

(You can find—and run—all of the examples in this section in the unicode-property-escapes.js file in the downloads.)

---

[2] https://en.wikipedia.org/wiki/Emoticons_(Unicode_block)

\p is for a *positive* Unicode property match. For a *negative* one (matching all *non*-alphabetic characters, for instance), you use a capital P instead of a lowercase one (this is in keeping with other escapes, such as \d for digits and \D for non-digits):

```
const rex2 = /\P{Alphabetic}/gu;
const s2 = "Hello, I'm James.";
console.log(s2.match(rex2));
// => [",", " ", "\"", " ", "."]
```

You can also use specified aliases (for instance, `Alpha` instead of `Alphabetic`). The boolean property values and aliases you can use are listed in the "Binary Unicode property aliases and their canonical property names" table[3] in the spec.

There are three enumerated properties you can use:

➤ `General_Category` (alias: `gc`): The most basic overall character property, a categorization of Unicode characters into Letters, Punctuation, Symbols, Marks, Numbers, Separators, and Other (with various subcategories). The `General_Category` values and aliases you can use are listed in the "Value aliases and canonical values for the Unicode property `General_Category`" table[4] in the spec. You can find more information about the `General_Category` property in Unicode Technical Standard #18.[5]

➤ `Script` (alias: `sc`): Assigns a single script category to a character, such as `Latin`, `Greek`, `Cyrillic`, etc.; `Common` for characters that are used across multiple scripts; `Inherited` for characters used across multiple scripts that inherit their script from a preceding base character; or `Unknown` for various code points that don't fit into script classification. The values and aliases you can use are listed in the spec in the "Value aliases and canonical values for the Unicode properties Script and Script_Extensions" table.[6] You can find more information about the `Script` property in "The Script Property" in Unicode Technical Standard #24.[7]

➤ `Script_Extensions` (alias: `scx`): Assigns a set of script categories to characters (rather than just `Common`) to more precisely specify the scripts in which a character occurs. The valid value names and aliases are the same as for `Script`. You can find more information about the `Script` property in "The Script_Extensions Property" in Unicode Technical Standard #24.[8]

For instance, to find all of the characters in Greek script in a string:

```
const rex3 = /\p{Script_Extensions=Greek}/gu;
const s3 = "The greek letters alpha (α), beta (β), and gamma (γ) are used...";
console.log(s3.match(rex3));
// => ["α", "β", "γ"]
```

---

[3] https://tc39.es/ecma262/#table-binary-unicode-properties
[4] https://tc39.es/ecma262/#table-unicode-general-category-values
[5] https://unicode.org/reports/tr18/#General_Category_Property
[6] https://tc39.es/ecma262/#table-unicode-script-values
[7] https://unicode.org/reports/tr24/#Script
[8] https://unicode.org/reports/tr24/#Script_Extensions

(You could use the alias scx instead: /\p{scx=Greek}/gu.)

The most useful enumerated property is General_Category, so there's a shorthand form you can use: you can leave off the General_Category= part. For instance, both \p{General_Category=Punctuation} and \p{Punctuation} find the punctuation in a string:

```
const rex4a = /\p{General_Category=Punctuation}/gu;
const rex4b = /\p{Punctuation}/gu;
const s4 = "Hello, my name is Pranay. It means \"romance\" in Hindi.";
console.log(s4.match(rex4a));
// => [",", "'", ".", "\"", "\"", "."]
console.log(s4.match(rex4b));
// => [",", "'", ".", "\"", "\"", "."]
```

You may be thinking "But isn't that how you specify a binary property like Alphabetic?" Yes, it is. Since there's no overlap between the valid General_Category values/aliases and the binary property names/aliases, it's not ambiguous to the regular expression parser, even though it may be a bit unclear to future readers of the code, if they don't happen to know the alias. Whether you use the shorthand form for General_Category properties is a matter of style.

Property names and values are case-sensitive; Script is a valid property name, script is not.

If you're used to similar features in other regular expression (regex) flavors, note that JavaScript's Unicode property escapes are quite strict and narrowly targeted (for the moment, anyway). The spec doesn't support various shorthand or alternative forms, or additional Unicode properties (and it doesn't allow engines to support them as an add-on). For instance:

➤   Leaving off the curly braces. In some regex flavors, \p{L} (using the alias for the Lower value in General_Category) can be written \pL. That is not supported in JavaScript.

➤   Using : instead of = when specifying the name and value. Some regex flavors allow \p{scx:Greek} in addition to \p{scx=Greek}. In JavaScript, it must be an equals sign (=).

➤   Allowing "is" in various places. Some regex flavors allow adding "is" on property names or values, for instance \p{Script=**Is**Greek}. This is not allowed in JavaScript.

➤   Properties other than the binary properties, General_Category, Script, and Script _ Extensions. Some regex flavors support other properties, such as Name. For now at least, JavaScript does not.

Adding the new property escapes feature with a small, clearly defined scope and strict rules makes it easier for engine implementers to add it and for people to use it. Additional features can always be added by subsequent proposals, if they gain enough support to progress through the process.

The examples so far have been a bit contrived; in terms of real-world usage, one of the examples from the Unicode escapes proposal[9] is useful: a Unicode-aware version of \w. Famously, \w is quite English-centric, being defined as [A-Za-z0-9_]. And it doesn't even match all characters found in many words commonly used in English having been borrowed from other languages (such as "résumé" or

---

[9] https://github.com/tc39/proposal-regexp-unicode-property-escapes

"naïve"), much less words written in other languages. The Unicode-aware version, as described in Unicode Technical Standard #18,[10] is:

    [\p{Alphabetic}\p{Mark}\p{Decimal_Number}\p{Connector_Punctuation}\p{Join_Control}]

or using shorthand aliases:

    [\p{Alpha}\p{M}\p{digit}\p{Pc}\p{Join_C}]

See Listing 15-7 for the proposal's full Unicode-aware \w example.

LISTING 15-7: Unicode-aware version of \w—unicode-aware-word.js

```
// From: https://github.com/tc39/proposal-regexp-unicode-property-escapes
// (Modified to use shorthand properties for page-formatting reasons)
const regex = /([\p{Alpha}\p{M}\p{digit}\p{Pc}\p{Join_C}]+)/gu;
const text = `
Amharic: የዪ ማንጓበሪያ ሚና በጓዣዎች ተጓዷቷል
Bengali: আমার হভারক্রাফ্ট কুঁচ মাছ-এ ভরা হয়ে গেছে
Georgian: ჩემი ხომალდი საჰაერო ბალიშზე სავსეა გველთევზებით
Macedonian: Моето летачко возило е полно со јагули
Vietnamese: Tàu cánh ngầm của tôi đầy lươn
`;

let match;
while (match = regex.exec(text)) {
    const word = match[1];
    console.log(`Matched word with length ${ word.length }: ${ word }`);
}

// Result:
// Matched word with length 7: Amharic
// Matched word with length 2: የዪ
// Matched word with length 6: ማንጓበሪያ
// Matched word with length 3: ሚና
// Matched word with length 5: በጓዣዎች
// Matched word with length 5: ተጓዷቷል
// Matched word with length 7: Bengali
// Matched word with length 4: আমার
// Matched word with length 11: হভারক্রাফ্ট
// Matched word with length 5: কুঁচ
// Matched word with length 3: মাছ
// Matched word with length 1: এ
// Matched word with length 3: ভরা
// Matched word with length 3: হয়ে
// Matched word with length 4: গেছে
// Matched word with length 8: Georgian
// Matched word with length 4: ჩემი
// Matched word with length 7: ხომალდი
// Matched word with length 7: საჰაერო
```

---

[10] http://unicode.org/reports/tr18/#word

```
// Matched word with length 7: ბალიშზე
// Matched word with length 6: საბანა
// Matched word with length 12: გველთევზებით
// Matched word with length 10: Macedonian
// Matched word with length 5: Моето
// Matched word with length 7: летачко
// Matched word with length 6: возило
// Matched word with length 1: е
// Matched word with length 5: полно
// Matched word with length 2: со
// Matched word with length 6: jагули
// Matched word with length 10: Vietnamese
// Matched word with length 3: Tàu
// Matched word with length 4: cánh
// Matched word with length 4: ngầm
// Matched word with length 3: của
// Matched word with length 3: tôi
// Matched word with length 3: đẩy
// Matched word with length 4: lươn
```

OLD HABITS TO NEW

There are various old habits you can switch to new ones if you like, provided your target environments support the new features (or they can be transpiled by your transpiler; as of this writing, Babel has plugins for most features in this chapter).

Use the Sticky Flag (y) Instead of Creating Substrings and Using ^ When Parsing

Old habit: When checking a regular expression against a string at a specified position, splitting the string at that position so you could use a start-of-input anchor (^):

```
const digits = /^\d+/;
// ...then somewhere you have `pos`...
let match = digits.exec(str.substring(pos));
if (match) {
    console.log(match[0]);
}
```

New habit: Use the sticky flag (y) without splitting the string and without ^ instead:

```
const digits = /\d+/y;
// ...then somewhere you have `pos`...
digits.lastIndex = pos;
let match = digits.exec(str);
if (match) {
    console.log(match[0]);
}
```

Use the Dot All Flag (s) Instead of Using Workarounds to Match All Characters (Including Line Breaks)

Old habit: Using various workarounds for matching all characters, such as `[\s\S]` or `[\d\D]` or the highly JavaScript-specific `[^]`:

```
const inParens = /\(((([\s\S]+)\)/;
const str =
`This is a test (of
line breaks inside
parens)`;
const match = inParens.exec(str);
console.log(match ? match[1] : "no match");
// => "of\nline breaks inside\nparens"
```

New habit: Use the "dot all" (s) flag and . instead:

```
const inParens = /\(((.+)\)/s;
const str =
`This is a test (of
line breaks inside
parens)`;
const match = inParens.exec(str);
console.log(match ? match[1] : "no match");
// => "of\nline breaks inside\nparens"
```

Use Named Capture Groups Instead of Anonymous Ones

Old habit: Using multiple anonymous capture groups (because you had no choice) and painstakingly ensuring you're using the right indexes—in the match result, in capture references in the regex itself, etc.:

```
// If you change this, be sure to change the destructuring assignment later!
const rexParseDate = /^(\d{2}|\d{4})-(\d{1,2})-(\d{1,2})$/;
const match = "2019-02-14".match(rexParseDate);
if (match) {
    // Depends on the regular expression's capture order!
    const [, year, month, day] = match;
    console.log(`day: ${day}, month: ${month}, year: ${year}`);
} else {
    console.log("no match");
}
// => "day: 14, month: 02, year: 2019"
```

New habit: Use named capture groups instead (`(?<captureName>content)`), and the named properties on the `groups` object (`match.groups.captureName`) or named references in the regex (`\k{captureName}`), etc.:

```
const rexParseDate = /^(?<year>\d{2}|\d{4})-(?<month>\d{1,2})-(?<day>\d{1,2})$/;
const match = "2019-02-14".match(rexParseDate);
if (match) {
    const {day, month, year} = match.groups;
    console.log(`day: ${day}, month: ${month}, year: ${year}`);
```

```
    } else {
        console.log("no match");
    }
    // => "day: 14, month: 02, year: 2019"
```

Use Lookbehinds Instead of Various Workarounds

Old habit: Various workarounds (unnecessary captures, etc.) because JavaScript didn't have lookbehind.

New habit: Use JavaScript's powerful lookbehind instead.

Use Code Point Escapes Instead of Surrogate Pairs in Regular Expressions

Old habit: Using surrogate pairs in regular expressions, sometimes complicating them markedly, instead of using code points (because you had no choice). For instance, to match both the "Emoticons" Unicode block (mentioned earlier) and the "Dingbats" block[11] in a regular expression:

```
    const rex = /(?:\uD83D[\uDE00-\uDE4F]|[\u2700-\u27BF])/;
```

Notice how that requires an alternation because it needs to handle a surrogate pair for Emoticons and then a separate range for Dingbats.

New habit: Use code point escapes instead:

```
    const rex = /[\u{1F600}-\u{1F64F}\u{1F680}-\u{1F6FF}]/u;
```

Note that now it's a single character class with a couple of ranges in it.

Use Unicode Patterns Instead of Workarounds

Old habit: Working around the lack of Unicode patterns with large hard-to-maintain character classes picking out the Unicode ranges to match.

New habit: Use Unicode property escapes instead (ensuring first that your target environment or transpiler supports them).

---

[11] https://en.wikipedia.org/wiki/Dingbat#Dingbats_Unicode_block

16

Shared Memory

WHAT'S IN THIS CHAPTER?

➤ Sharing memory across threads (`SharedArrayBuffer`)

➤ The `Atomics` object

> **CODE DOWNLOADS FOR THIS CHAPTER**
>
> You can download the code for this chapter at `https://thenewtoys.dev/bookcode` or `https://www.wiley.com/go/javascript-newtoys`.

In this chapter, you'll learn about JavaScript's *shared memory* feature (in ES2017+), allowing memory to be shared between threads, and the `Atomics` object you can use to perform low-level shared memory operations and to suspend and resume threads based on events in shared memory.

INTRODUCTION

For most of the decade or so that JavaScript on browsers hasn't been single-threaded (thanks to *web workers*), there was no way to share memory across threads in the browser. Initially, threads could post messages to each other with data in them, but the data was *copied*. When it's a lot of data, or it has to be sent back and forth a lot, that's a problem. A few years later when typed arrays (Chapter 11) were defined, originally outside JavaScript and then added to ES2015, in many cases it became possible to *transfer* data from one thread to another without copying it, but the sending thread had to give up access to the data being sent.

ES2017 changed that with `SharedArrayBuffer`. With a `SharedArrayBuffer`, JavaScript code running in one thread can *share* memory with JavaScript code running on another thread.

Before getting into how shared memory works in JavaScript, let's explore the question of whether you really need to use it at all.

HERE THERE BE DRAGONS!

Or: Do You Really Need Shared Memory?

Sharing memory across threads opens up a host of data synchronization issues that programmers working in typical JavaScript environments haven't had to deal with before. We could spend an entire book on the subtleties of shared memory—data races, reordered stores, hoisted reads, CPU thread caches, etc. In this chapter, we only have room to address the very basics of those issues, but in order to use shared memory in the real world, you need to thoroughly understand them or at least know and closely adhere to best practices and patterns for avoiding them. Otherwise, you'll spend hours or days tracking down subtle, often difficult-to-replicate bugs—or worse, you *won't*, and then you'll get nearly-impossible-to-replicate bug reports from the field. Developing that knowledge and/or mastering those best practices is a significant time investment. Dipping into shared memory is not something to do lightly.

For most use cases, you don't need shared memory, in part thanks to *transferables*: objects you can *transfer* between threads rather than copying between threads. Various objects are transferable (including some image types and canvases on browsers), including `ArrayBuffers`. So if you have data you need to pass back and forth between two threads, you can avoid the overhead of copying it by *transferring* it. For instance, the following code creates a `Uint8Array` and passes it to a worker thread, transferring its underlying data via its buffer rather than copying it:

```
const MB = 1024 * 1024;
let array = new Uint8Array(20 * MB);
// ...fill in 20MB of data...
worker.postMessage({array}, [array.buffer]);
```

The first argument is the data to send (the array); the second argument is an array of transferables to transfer rather than copying. The worker thread receives a clone of the array *object*, but its *data* is transferred: the clone reuses the *original* array's data because the array's `ArrayBuffer` is listed in the list of transferables. It's like handing off a baton in a relay race: the sending thread passes the buffer (the baton) to the worker thread, which takes it and runs with it. After the `postMessage` call, the sending thread's array no longer has access to the buffer: `array` in that example effectively becomes a zero-length array.

When the worker receives the array, it can use and operate on the data without worrying about other threads working on it, then if appropriate it can transfer it back to the original thread (or some other thread).

Transferring the data back and forth in this way is quite efficient and avoids entire classes of issues that can arise when literally sharing the underlying buffer between the threads. Before using shared memory, it's well worth asking yourself whether transferring would be sufficient. You may save yourself a *lot* of time and trouble.

BROWSER SUPPORT

One last thing before we get into the details of shared memory: in January 2018 browsers disabled shared memory in response to the Spectre and Meltdown vulnerabilities in CPUs. Chrome added support back for some use cases in July of that year on platforms where its site isolation feature was active, but a more general approach emerged toward the end of 2019 through the hard work of a large list of people, showing up in browsers from early 2020. Now it's possible to share memory again, but only between *secure contexts*.[1]

If you're not bothered about the "why" and are only interested in the "how," the short version is that to share memory, you need to do two things: A) serve your documents and scripts securely or locally (that is, via `https` or similar, or `localhost` or similar) and B) include these two HTTP headers with them:

```
Cross-Origin-Opener-Policy: same-origin
Cross-Origin-Embedder-Policy: require-corp
```

(The first header isn't needed on content intended for frames, or on scripts, but it's fine if it's there anyway.)

If you're not interested in the details, you can skip to the next section now.

(Brief pause . . .)

Still with me? Good!

Briefly, a *context* is a web specification concept for the container of a window/tab/frame or worker (such as a web/dedicated worker or a service worker). The context containing a window is reused as navigation is performed in the window, even when moving from one origin to another. The DOM and JavaScript realm are discarded and new ones created during navigation, but still within the same context—at least traditionally.

Browsers group related contexts together into *context groups*. For instance, if a window contains an `iframe`, the contexts for the window and `iframe` are traditionally in the same context group, because they can interact with each other (via `window.parent`, `window.frames`, and such). Similarly, contexts for a window and a popup it opens are traditionally in the same context group, again because they can interact. If the contexts are from different origins, their interaction is limited by default, but there is still some possible interaction.

Why do contexts and context groups matter? Because typically, all of the contexts in a context group use memory within the same operating system process. Modern browsers are multi-process applications, usually with at least one overall coordinating process and then a separate process for each context group. This architecture makes the browser more robust: a crash in one context group doesn't affect any of the others or the coordinating process, because they're in entirely different operating system processes. But everything in the same context group is typically in the same process.

Which is where Spectre and Meltdown come into the story.

Spectre and Meltdown are hardware vulnerabilities. They exploit branch-prediction in modern CPUs in such a way that code can access *all* memory in the current process, bypassing any in-process access checks. They aren't limited to browsers, but in browsers shared memory and high-precision timers made it possible to exploit those vulnerabilities from JavaScript code. That means that malicious code

---

[1] https://w3c.github.io/webappsec-secure-contexts/

can read *any* memory in the process, even the memory for another window or web worker. It can bypass any in-process access checks the browser may have in place, such as between contexts from different origins.

The solution is to ensure that the content of resources (scripts, documents) hasn't been tampered with (by requiring them to be delivered securely or locally) and to allow resources to restrict what context groups they can be loaded into (via the headers).

Let's look at those headers.

The first header, `Cross-Origin-Opener-Policy`,[2] lets a top-level window ensure that it is only in a context group with other top-level windows from the same origin that have the same header value it does (typically `same-origin`). When top-level navigation occurs, if the new content's origin and header don't match up with the previous one's, the browser creates a new context in a new context group to hold the new resource's content.

The second header, `Cross-Origin-Embedder-Policy`,[3] lets a resource specify that it can only be loaded by a same origin window or a window that the resource expressly authorizes via a Cross-Origin Resource Policy[4] (CORP) header or Cross-Origin Resource Sharing[5] (CORS). That ensures that the resource can't be embedded in a container it doesn't trust.

Taken together, those protect against using shared memory and high-precision timers to use Spectre or Meltdown to access data that the code shouldn't have access to. If you want to learn about it in more detail, I recommend "COOP and COEP explained"[6] by Artur Janc, Charlie Reis, and Anne van Kesteren.

SHARED MEMORY BASICS

In this section, you'll learn some of the basics of shared memory, such as what *critical sections* are; how to create, share, and use shared memory; and how to use locking to protect critical sections of code with *locks* and *condition variables*.

Critical Sections, Locks, and Condition Variables

A *critical section* is code running on a thread that needs to access (read and/or write) shared memory in a way that is *atomic* relative to any actions being performed by concurrent threads that share the memory. For example, in a critical section, reading the same memory twice must always result in the same value:

```
const v1 = shared[0];
const v2 = shared[0];
// In a critical section, `v1` and `v2` MUST contain the same value here
```

---

[2] https://docs.google.com/document/d/1Ey3MXcLzwR1T7aarkpBXEwP7jKdd2NvQdgYvF8_8scI/edit
[3] https://wicg.github.io/cross-origin-embedder-policy/
[4] https://fetch.spec.whatwg.org/#cross-origin-resource-policy-header
[5] https://fetch.spec.whatwg.org/#http-cors-protocol
[6] https://docs.google.com/document/d/1zDlfvfTJ_9e8Jdc8ehuV4zMEu9ySMCiTGMS9y0GU92k/edit

Similarly, in a critical section, if code reads from shared memory, updates the value, and writes back to shared memory, it must not be possible that it's overwriting a different value that has been written there by another thread in the meantime:

```
const v = shared[0] + 1;
shared[0] = v; // MUST NOT overwrite a value written by another thread after
               // the read above (in a critical section)
```

A *lock* is a means of protecting critical sections by providing exclusive access to the shared memory to a thread using the lock: the lock can only be acquired by a single thread at a time, and only that thread is allowed to access the shared memory. (A lock is sometimes called a *mutex*, which is sort for "mutual-exclusion.")

A *condition variable* provides a way for threads using a given lock to wait for a condition to become true, and to notify each other when it becomes true. Threads can wait on the condition and can notify waiting threads that the condition has become true. When a thread is notified that the condition is true, it can try to acquire the lock that condition variable relates to so it can do the work it needs to do now that the condition is true (or at least, now that it *was* true just a moment ago—as with time travel, verb tenses can be a bit tricky in concurrent programming).

In a simple situation, you need only one condition variable for a lock and the two things are sometimes combined: the condition is "the lock is available." That would be sufficient if, for example, you had multiple threads that all needed to do the same kind of work on a shared buffer.

But situations are often more complex than that, requiring more than one condition variable for the same lock and shared memory. One classic use of shared memory is distributing work to threads via a queue: a producer thread puts pieces of work in the queue, and consumer threads take work from the queue and do it. The queue is the shared memory. Putting work in the queue is a critical section of code: to do that without possibly breaking the queue, a thread needs temporary exclusive access to the queue. You can't have two threads changing the internal state of the queue at the same time, because they'll stomp on each other's changes. Taking work out of the queue is another critical section, for the same reason. The threads use a lock to protect those critical sections so the queue isn't modified by more than one thread at a time. So far so good.

If there's no work in the queue, the consumer threads have to wait until work gets added to it. Since the queue is of limited size (let's say it can hold 100 entries), if it's full the producer thread has to wait until it's not full anymore to add a piece of work to it. Those are two different conditions associated with the same lock: the condition "queue has work" that the consumers wait for, and the condition "queue has room" that the producer waits for.

Although it would be possible to implement this producer/consumer queue with just one condition ("the lock is available"), it would be inefficient, for a couple of reasons:

➤ If there were only one condition, both the producer thread and the consumer threads would need to wait on that one condition for their different reasons, even though when that condition becomes true it may or may not mean that they can do their work. For instance, if four workers are waiting for work and one piece of work is added, they all get notified and race to get the lock, and then the one that got the lock picks up the work while the other three go back to waiting. Once that consumer has taken the work from the queue, it releases the lock, notifying all of the other consumers, which makes them race to get the lock, even though no new work has been added to the queue—that second notification was for the *producer* thread, to let it know that there's room in the queue again, not for the *consumer* threads.

➤ If there were only one condition, *all* threads using the lock would have to be notified that the condition had become true (the producer and all consumers). In contrast, if there are two separate conditions ("queue has work" and "queue has room"), only *one* thread needs to be notified when each of those conditions becomes true. There's no need to wake up all of the consumer threads when "queue has work" becomes true, they'd all race for a lock when only one of them can win that race. And there's no point at all in waking up any consumer thread for the "queue has room" condition; only the producer thread cares about that one.

That's why locks and condition variables are separate concepts, but closely related ones. Later in this chapter, you'll see an example of exactly this kind of producer/consumer situation.

Creating Shared Memory

To create an array with shared memory, you first create the SharedArrayBuffer and then use it when creating the array. Since you specify the size of a SharedArrayBuffer in bytes, not *entries*, you often multiply the number of entries you want by the array constructor's BYTES_PER_ELEMENT property.[7] For instance, to create a shared Uint16Array with 5 entries:

```
const sharedBuf = new SharedArrayBuffer(5 * Uint16Array.BYTES_PER_ELEMENT);
const sharedArray = new Uint16Array(sharedBuf);
```

To share that array with a web worker in a browser, you can include it in a message via postMessage. For instance, assuming worker refers to a web worker, you can share the preceding sharedArray like this:

```
worker.postMessage(sharedArray);
```

The worker receives the shared array as the data property of the event object for the message event. Often, rather than just sending the array, it's useful to send an object with some kind of indication of what the message is about, making the array a property of that object:

```
worker.postMessage({type: "init", sharedArray});
```

That sends an object with the properties type ("init") and sharedArray (the shared array); the worker will receive that object as the data property on the event. (More on what's actually shared in a bit.)

Let's put those together into a basic example. Listing 16-1 shows the main thread code sharing a Uint16Array with a web worker thread.

LISTING 16-1: Basic SharedArrayBuffer usage (main thread)—basic-SharedArrayBuffer-main.js

```
const sharedBuf = new SharedArrayBuffer(5 * Uint16Array.BYTES_PER_ELEMENT);
const sharedArray = new Uint16Array(sharedBuf);
```

---

[7] *Entries* are often called *elements*, which explains why the property has the name BYTES_PER_ELEMENT. I use *entries* in this book to avoid confusion with DOM elements.

```
const worker = new Worker("./basic-SharedArrayBuffer-worker.js");
let counter = 0;
console.log("initial: " + formatArray(sharedArray));
worker.addEventListener("message", e => {
    if (e.data && e.data.type === "ping") {
        console.log("updated: " + formatArray(sharedArray));
        if (++counter < 10) {
            worker.postMessage({type: "pong"});
        } else {
            console.log("done");
        }
    }
});
worker.postMessage({type: "init", sharedArray});

function formatArray(array) {
    return Array.from(
        array,
        b => b.toString(16).toUpperCase().padStart(4, "0")
    ).join(" ");
}
```

Listing 16-2 shows the worker thread's code.

LISTING 16-2: Basic SharedArrayBuffer usage (worker)—basic-SharedArrayBuffer-worker.js

```
let shared;
let index;
const updateAndPing = () => {
    ++shared[index];
    index = (index + 1) % shared.length;
    this.postMessage({type: "ping"});
};
this.addEventListener("message", e => {
    if (e.data) {
        switch (e.data.type) {
            case "init":
                shared = e.data.sharedArray;
                index = 0;
                updateAndPing();
                break;
            case "pong":
                updateAndPing();
                break;
        }
    }
});
```

When the worker receives an "init" message, it remembers the shared array with its shared variable. At that point, the main thread and the worker are sharing the memory for that array; see Figure 16-1.

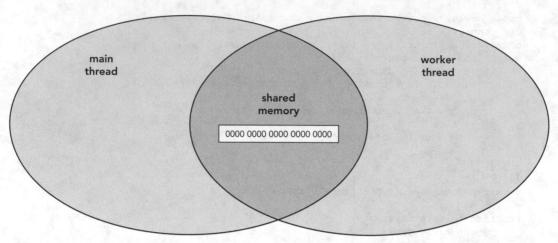

FIGURE 16-1

The worker then sets its `index` to 0 and calls its `updateAndPing` function. `updateAndPing` increments the entry at the `index` position in the array, increments `index` (wrapping around back to 0 at the end), and then sends a "ping" message to the main thread. Because the entry the worker updates is in shared memory, both the worker and the main thread see the update; see Figure 16-2.

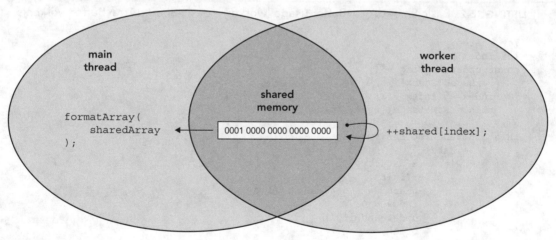

FIGURE 16-2

The main thread responds to the "ping" message by incrementing its counter and sending a "pong" message; the worker responds to a "pong" by calling `updateAndPing` again; and so on until the main thread's counter reaches 10 and it stops sending "pings." Each message to the worker makes it increment the next entry in the shared array, wrapping around when it reaches the end.

Run this code in your browser using the listing files and `basic-SharedArrayBuffer-example.html` from the downloads. Remember that you must serve the files from a web server (you can't just open the `.html` file from the file system), they must be served securely or locally, and they must be served with the headers you learned about in the "Browser Support" section earlier. If you prefer, you can use a version hosted on the book's website instead of running your own copy: `https://thenewtoys.dev/bookcode/live/16/basic-SharedArrayBuffer-example.html`. In the console, you should see output like this from the main thread (provided your browser has `SharedArrayBuffer` enabled):

```
initial: 0000 0000 0000 0000 0000
updated: 0001 0000 0000 0000 0000
updated: 0001 0001 0000 0000 0000
updated: 0001 0001 0001 0000 0000
updated: 0001 0001 0001 0001 0000
updated: 0001 0001 0001 0001 0001
updated: 0002 0001 0001 0001 0001
updated: 0002 0002 0001 0001 0001
updated: 0002 0002 0002 0001 0001
updated: 0002 0002 0002 0002 0001
updated: 0002 0002 0002 0002 0002
done
```

The output shows that the main thread sees the worker's updates to the shared memory.

If you've used shared memory and multiple threads in other environments, you might be wondering: how do we *know* that the updates are ready to be read by the main thread? What if the updates are in a thread-specific cache (in the JavaScript virtual machine, or even a per-thread CPU cache)?

The answer for this specific example is that `postMessage` is defined as a *synchronization edge* (that is, a boundary across which synchronization occurs). Since the worker thread notifies the main thread that it's done its work using `postMessage`, and the main thread only tries to read the result when it receives that message, it's guaranteed that the write is complete before the read occurs and any per-thread caches have had any stale contents invalidated (so that attempts to read them won't read old values; the fresh value will be retrieved instead). So the main thread can safely read the array knowing that any updates to it when the message was posted will be visible. This example also relies on the fact that the worker won't modify the array again until the main thread sends it a "ping," so the main thread doesn't have to worry about reading an in-progress write (more on that in a moment).

`postMessage` isn't the only synchronization edge; later in this chapter you'll learn about more synchronization edges (`Atomics.wait` and `Atomics.notify`).

In that example, the array used the entire `SharedArrayBuffer`, but it could have just used part of it, with perhaps another array using another part of the buffer for a different purpose. For instance, here's an example of a `Uint8Array` using the first half of a `SharedArrayBuffer` and a `Uint32Array` using the last half:

```
const sab = new SharedArrayBuffer(24);
const uint8array  = new Uint8Array(sab, 0, 12);
const uint32array = new Uint32Array(sab, 12, 3);
```

The buffer is 24 bytes long. The `Uint8Array` takes up the first 12 bytes for 12 one-byte-long entries, and the `Uint32Array` takes up the second 12 bytes for 3 four-byte-long entries.

Suppose we only needed 10 entries for the `Uint8Array`, though, rather than 12. You might think we could make the buffer two bytes smaller and just move the `Uint32Array` so that it starts with index 10 in the buffer. But that won't work:

```
const sab = new SharedArrayBuffer(22);
const uint8array  = new Uint8Array(sab, 0, 10);
const uint32array = new Uint32Array(sab, 10, 3);
// => RangeError: start offset of Uint32Array should be a multiple of 4
```

The issue is *memory alignment*. Modern computer CPUs can read and write memory in blocks of more than a single byte. Doing so is much more efficient when the block is *aligned* in memory; that is, when the block's location in memory is evenly divisible by the size of the block. See Figure 16-3, which shows a series of bytes. When reading a 16-bit value, for example, it's much more efficient to read it from location 0x0000 or 0x0002 than it is to read it from 0x0001, because of the way the CPU instructions are optimized. For this reason, `SharedArrayBuffer` instances always refer to blocks aligned at the CPU's largest granularity (that's handled by the JavaScript engine), and you can only create a multibyte typed array using an offset into the buffer that is aligned for the type of the array. So you can create a `Uint8Array` at any offset in a buffer, but a `Uint16Array` needs to be at offset 0, 2, 4, etc. Similarly, a `Uint32Array` must be at offset 0, 4, 8, etc.

Address	Value
0x0000	0x08
0x0001	0x10
0x0002	0x27
0x0003	0x16
. . .	

FIGURE 16-3

MEMORY IS SHARED, NOT OBJECTS

When using shared memory, it's just the *memory* that's shared. The wrapper objects (the `SharedArrayBuffer` and any typed arrays using it) are not shared. For instance, in the earlier example that passed a `Uint16Array` using a `SharedArrayBuffer` from a main thread to a worker, the `Uint16Array` and `SharedArrayBuffer` *objects* weren't shared; instead, new `Uint16Array` and `SharedArrayBuffer` objects were created at the receiving end and attached to the underlying memory block of the sending thread's `SharedArrayBuffer`. See Figure 16-4.

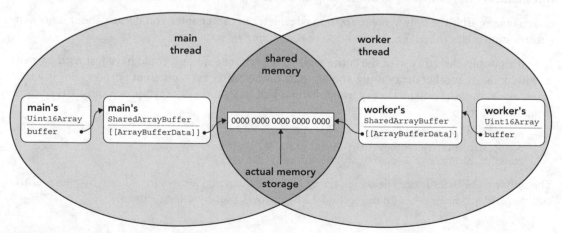

FIGURE 16-4

If you like, you can easily prove this to yourself by adding custom properties to the buffer and array objects, and then noting that you don't see those custom properties in the worker. See Listings 16-3 and 16-4, which you can run using `objects-not-shared.html` from the downloads (or on the book's website at `https://thenewtoys.dev/bookcode/live/16/objects-not-shared.html`, since again you need to serve it securely and with the right headers).

LISTING 16-3: Objects aren't shared (main)—objects-not-shared-main.js

```
const sharedBuf = new SharedArrayBuffer(5 * Uint16Array.BYTES_PER_ELEMENT);
const sharedArray = new Uint16Array(sharedBuf);
sharedArray[0] = 42;
sharedBuf.foo = "foo";
sharedArray.bar = "bar";
const worker = new Worker("./objects-not-shared-worker.js");
console.log("(main) sharedArray[0] = " + sharedArray[0]);
console.log("(main) sharedArray.buffer.foo = " + sharedArray.buffer.foo);
console.log("(main) sharedArray.bar = " + sharedArray.bar);
worker.postMessage({type: "init", sharedArray});
```

LISTING 16-4: Objects aren't shared (worker)—objects-not-shared-worker.js

```
this.addEventListener("message", e => {
    if (e.data && e.data.type === "init") {
        let {sharedArray} = e.data;
        console.log("(worker) sharedArray[0] = " + sharedArray[0]);
        console.log("(worker) sharedArray.buffer.foo = " + sharedArray.buffer.foo);
        console.log("(worker) sharedArray.bar = " + sharedArray.bar);
    }
});
```

The output when you run the example is:

```
(main) sharedArray[0] = 42
(main) sharedArray.buffer.foo = foo
(main) sharedArray.bar = bar
(worker) sharedArray[0] = 42
(worker) sharedArray.buffer.foo = undefined
(worker) sharedArray.bar = undefined
```

You can see that although the memory the buffer uses is shared, the buffer object and the array object using it are not.

RACE CONDITIONS, OUT-OF-ORDER STORES, STALE VALUES, TEARING, AND MORE

Again: Here There Be Dragons. We'll very lightly cover some of the dragons, but remember that entire books are written about correctly handling shared memory across threads.

Let's look at one scenario. Suppose you have a `Uint8Array` using a `SharedArrayBuffer` for its storage, and you've set the first couple of entries to specific values:

```
const sharedBuf = new SharedArrayBuffer(10);
const sharedArray = new Uint8Array(sharedBuf);
sharedArray[0] = 100;
sharedArray[1] = 200;
```

Having set it up, you've shared it with another thread. Now, both threads are running, and for the sake of this example, you've done no synchronization or coordination between them. At some point, the main thread writes to those two entries (first index 0, then index 1):

```
sharedArray[0] = 110;
sharedArray[1] = 220;
```

At that same time, the worker thread reads those two entries in the opposite order (first index 1, then index 0):

```
console.log(`1 is ${sharedArray[1]}`);
console.log(`0 is ${sharedArray[0]}`);
```

It's entirely possible that the worker thread might output:

```
1 is 220
0 is 110
```

Simple enough; the worker read the values after the main thread did its update, and the worker saw the updated values.

It's equally possible that it might output:

```
1 is 200
0 is 100
```

Perhaps the worker read the values just before the main thread did its update. But (this may be surprising) it's also possible that the worker read them *after* the main thread did its update, but still saw the old values. To maximize performance, the operating system, the CPU, and/or the JavaScript engine may keep a cached copy of a small part of memory for each thread for a brief time. (Or sometimes, a not-so-brief time.) So unless you do something to ensure that the memory is in sync, the seemingly unintuitive result of the worker seeing old values even after new values have been written can occur.

Here's the really tricky one, though—the worker might also output the following:

```
1 is 220
0 is 100
```

Take a look at that last output again. How can the worker see 220 (the updated value for `sharedArray[1]`) but *afterward* see 100 (the *original* value for `sharedArray[0]`)?! The main thread writes the new value to `sharedArray[0]` before writing the new value to `sharedArray[1]`, and the worker reads `sharedArray[1]` before reading `sharedArray[0]`!

The answer is that both reads and writes can be reordered by the JavaScript compiler or the CPU for optimization purposes. Within a thread, that sort of reordering is never apparent, but when you share memory between threads, it can become observable if you don't properly synchronize between threads.

Depending on the architecture of the platform your code is running on, in addition to complete values being stale or other similar issues, it's possible for a read operation to *tear*: read only *part* of an in-progress write. Suppose a thread is writing to an entry in a `Float32Array` (one entry = four bytes). It's possible for a thread reading that entry to read *part* of the old value (for instance, the first two bytes) and part of the new value (for instance, the second two bytes). Similarly, with a `Float64Array` (one entry = eight bytes), it could be that the first four bytes of the old value and the second four bytes of the new value get read. The problem can also happen when reading multibyte values via a `DataView`. It's *not* a problem for any of the integer typed arrays such as `Int32Array`; the specification requires those operations to be *tear-free*. When asked, one of the authors of the proposal, Lars T. Hansen, said this guarantee was present on all of the relevant hardware JavaScript engines were likely to be implemented on, so the proposal included the guarantee in the spec. (An engine implemented on hardware that doesn't provide the guarantee would need to handle guaranteeing it itself.)

These are just a few of the ways you can trip yourself up with seemingly logical code when shared memory and multiple threads are involved.

The solution (if you need to write in one thread and read in another) is to ensure some form of synchronization between threads operating on the same shared memory. You saw one form earlier that's specific to the browser environment: `postMessage`. There's also a way to do this that's defined by JavaScript itself: the `Atomics` object.

THE ATOMICS OBJECT

To deal with data races, stale reads, out-of-order writes, tearing, etc., JavaScript provides the `Atomics` object. It offers both high-level and low-level tools for dealing with shared memory in a consistent, sequential, synchronized way. The methods exposed by `Atomics` impose order on the operations, as well as ensuring that read-modify-write operations are uninterrupted, as you'll see later in this chapter. The `Atomics` object also provides signaling between threads that guarantees a synchronization edge (like the one browsers provide through `postMessage`).

"ATOMIC"?

You may be asking, "Why is it called `Atomics`? This is programming, not physics . . . ?" The `Atomics` object is so named because it supports *atomic operations*: operations that seem, from the outside, to happen in a single step, with no opportunity for other threads to interact with the data of the operation while it's in progress; the operation is *indivisible*. Although in physics it's long been known that atoms aren't indivisible, the word "atom" originally meant exactly that (from Greek *atomos* meaning "uncut, unhewn; indivisible"), which is why it was used (by John Dalton circa 1805) to refer to what he thought were the indivisible component parts of the natural elements like iron and oxygen.

In the previous section's example the main thread had a `sharedArray` with 100 at index 0 and 200 at index 1, like so:

```
sharedArray[0] = 100;
sharedArray[1] = 200;
```

and then did:

```
sharedArray[0] = 110;
sharedArray[1] = 220;
```

You learned in that section that other threads reading those entries may read stale values or even see the values get written out of order. To ensure that those writes were seen by other threads sharing the array, and seen in order, the main thread could use `Atomics.store` to store the new values. `Atomics.store` accepts the array, the index of the entry to write to, and the value to write:

```
Atomics.store(sharedArray, 0, 110);
Atomics.store(sharedArray, 1, 220);
```

Similarly, the worker thread would use `Atomics.load` to retrieve the values:

```
console.log(Atomics.load(sharedArray, 1));
console.log(Atomics.load(sharedArray, 0));
```

Now, if the main thread does its writes before the worker does its reads, the worker is guaranteed to see the updated values. The worker is also guaranteed not to see the update to index 1 before the update to index 0; using the `Atomics` methods ensures those operations aren't reordered by the JavaScript compiler or the CPU. (If the worker thread read the values in the other order, though, it would still be possible for it to see the updated value at index 0 and the original value at index 1, if the timing were just right and it did its reads after the main thread wrote to index 0 but before the main thread wrote to index 1.)

`Atomics` also offers methods for common operations. For instance, suppose you have several workers, all of whom are supposed to periodically increment a counter in shared memory. You might be tempted to write:

```
// INCORRECT
const old = Atomics.load(sharedArray, index);
Atomics.store(sharedArray, index, old + 1);
```

The problem with that code is that there's a gap between the `load` and the `store`. Within that gap, another thread can read and write that entry (even when you're using `Atomics`, because it happens *between* the two calls using `Atomics`). If this same code is running in two workers, you could have a race like the one shown in Figure 16-5 (opposite).

As you can see in the figure, Worker B's increment was overwritten by Worker A's, leaving the counter with the wrong value.

The answer? `Atomics.add`. It accepts the array, the entry index, and a value. It reads the value of the entry at that index, adds the given value to it, and stores the result back to the entry—all as an atomic operation—and returns the old value of the entry:

```
oldValue = Atomics.add(sharedArray, index, 1);
```

Another thread can't update the value at the given index after `add` reads the old value and before `add` writes the new value. The race between Thread A and Thread B described earlier can't occur.

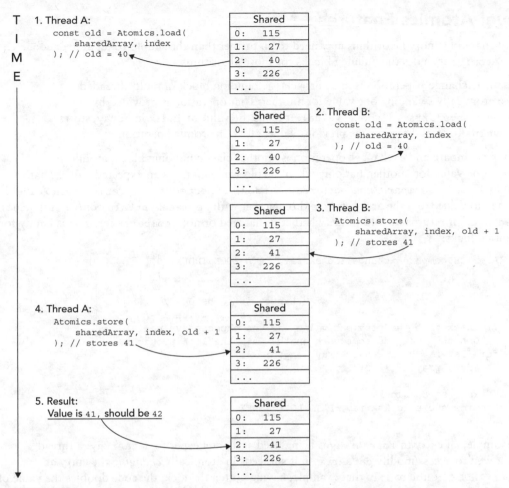

FIGURE 16-5

`Atomics` offers several operations that work exactly the same way `add` does other than the operation they perform on the entry's value: they accept a value; modify the entry's value according to the operation; store the result; and return the entry's old value. See Table 16-1.

TABLE 16-1

METHOD	OPERATION	ATOMIC VERSION OF:
`Atomics.add`	Addition	`array[index] = array[index] + newValue`
`Atomics.sub`	Subtraction	`array[index] = array[index] - newValue`
`Atomics.and`	Bitwise AND	`array[index] = array[index] & newValue`
`Atomics.or`	Bitwise OR	`array[index] = array[index]	newValue`
`Atomics.xor`	Bitwise XOR	`array[index] = array[index] ^ newValue`

Low-Level Atomics Features

Advanced shared memory algorithms may need to go further than the simple `load`, `store`, `add`, etc., methods. `Atomics` includes the building blocks for those algorithms.

The "atomic exchange" operation is one fairly classic building block of multi-threaded processes: atomically swapping one value for another. That operation is provided by `Atomics.exchange(array, index, value)`: it reads the value at `index` in `array`, stores the given `value` to it, and returns the previous value, all as an atomic operation.

The "atomic compare and exchange" operation is another classic building block: atomically exchanging one value for another, but only when the old value matches an expected value. That's provided by `Atomics.compareExchange(array, index, expectedValue, replacementValue)`: it reads the old value from the array entry and replaces it with `replacementValue` *only if* it matches `expectedValue`. It returns the old value (whether it matched or not). `compareExchange` is handy for implementing locks:

```
if (Atomics.compareExchange(locksArray, DATA_LOCK_INDEX, 0, 1) === 0) {
    //                                                    ↑  ↑      ↑
    //                                                    |  |      |
    //                            Expect it to be 0 --/   |      |
    //                                 If it is, write 1 -/      |
    // Check that the previous value was the expected value (0) --/
    // Got the lock, do some work on the data the lock protects
    for (let i = 0; i < dataArray.length; ++i) {
        dataArray[i] *= 2;
    }
    // Release the lock
    Atomics.store(locksArray, DATA_LOCK_INDEX, 0);
}
```

In that example, an entry in `locksArray` is being used as a gatekeeper to `dataArray`: a thread is only allowed to access/modify `dataArray` if it succeeds in atomically *changing* the entry at `DATA_LOCK_INDEX` from 0 to 1. In that example, having gotten the lock, the code doubles the value of each entry in the array; the programmer knows they can do that safely because of the lock. Having finished updating the array, the code atomically writes 0 back to the lock index to release the lock.

Important point: that lock only works if you make sure *all* code that may access `dataArray` uses the same lock. Using `compareExchange` in this way ensures that the current thread "owns" the shared array and that the array is up to date (no pending changes held in CPU per-thread caches, etc.).

Why would you want to write your own lock like that rather than using one of the `Atomics` features (like using `Atomics.load` and such in the `for` loop)? There are two reasons:

➤ *To ensure that you handle the entire array atomically*: `Atomics.load` and such only ensure that their individual operation is handled atomically; other parts of the array might be simultaneously accessed by other code, including even trying to operate on the same entry at nearly the same time.

➤ *For efficiency*: When you're accessing multiple entries, it's a lot more efficient to lock once for the entire operation than to make `Atomics` do the synchronization and locking on every individual operation.

Let's imagine the earlier code used just `Atomics` calls to modify `dataArray`:

```
for (let i = 0; i < dataArray.length; ++i) {
    let v;
    do {
        v = Atomics.load(dataArray[i]);
    } while (v !== Atomics.compareExchange(dataArray, i, v, v * 2));
}
```

That's slightly different from the earlier code: with the `locksArray` version, the entire `dataArray` is processed as a whole; with this second version, two threads could be operating on different parts of the array simultaneously. (Which may be useful, or not, depending on your use case—and unless you specifically intend allowing that concurrent access, it's likely a bug waiting to trip you up.)

This second version of the code is also more complicated. Note how each iteration has to have a `do-while` loop when updating its entry, since other code may change the entry value between getting the value and trying to save the updated value. (Think back to Figure 16-5—you can't just use `Atomics.load` and the `Atomics.store`, because threads could race.)

Finally, this second version also requires a *lot* of individual low-level locking/unlocking operations (no fewer than two per entry in `dataArray`, more if the `do-while` loop ever has to loop because another thread is also updating the array).

Using Atomics to Suspend and Resume Threads

As of ES2017, a thread can be suspended in the middle of a job, and then resumed to continue processing that job. Most environments don't allow suspending the main thread[8] but do allow suspending worker threads. The `Atomics` object provides the methods to do it.

To suspend a thread, you call `Atomics.wait` on an entry in a shared `Int32Array`:

```
result = Atomics.wait(theArray, index, expectedValue, timeout);
```

For example:

```
result = Atomics.wait(sharedArray, index, 42, 30000);
```

In that example, `Atomics.wait` reads the value from `sharedArray[index]` and, if the value is equal to 42, suspends the thread. The thread will remain suspended until something resumes it or the timeout occurs (the timeout in the example is 30000ms; 30 seconds). If you leave off the timeout, the default is `Number.Infinity`—that is, to wait forever to be resumed.

`Atomics.wait` returns a string saying what the result was:

➤ `"ok"` if the thread was suspended and subsequently resumed (rather than timing out)

➤ `"timed-out"` if the thread was suspended, and resumed because the timeout was reached

➤ `"not-equal"` if the thread wasn't suspended because the value in the array wasn't equal to the given value

To resume a thread waiting on that entry of the array, you call `Atomics.notify`:

```
result = Atomics.notify(theArray, index, numberToResume);
```

---

[8] Not via this mechanism, anyway. Antiquated functions like `alert`, `confirm`, and `prompt` on browsers suspend JavaScript on the UI thread until the modal dialog they show is dismissed, although browser makers are slowly eroding the absolute blocking they used to provide. (For example, Chrome no longer blocks on an `alert` in a background tab.)

For example:

```
result = Atomics.notify(sharedArray, index, 1);
```

The number you pass in (1 in the example) is how many waiting threads to resume; in that example, you're asking to resume just one thread even if multiple threads are waiting on that entry. `Atomics.notify` returns the number of threads that were actually resumed (0 if there weren't any waiting).

While it's suspended, a thread won't process any further jobs from its job queue. That's because of JavaScript's run-to-completion semantics; the thread can't pick up the next job from its queue until it finishes the one it's doing, and it can't do that if it's suspended in the middle of the job. This is why the main thread in most environments can't be suspended; it's usually critical that it keep processing jobs. (The main thread in browsers is the UI thread, for instance. Suspending the UI thread would make the UI unresponsive.)

In the next section, you'll see an example of suspending/resuming threads.

SHARED MEMORY EXAMPLE

The example in this section brings together the various things you've learned about shared memory and the `Atomics` methods throughout this chapter. It implements the producer/consumer queue mentioned earlier in "Shared Memory Basics" whose job (in this example) is to calculate the hash (MD5, SHA-1, etc.) of a block of memory. It shares memory between the main thread, a producer thread that fills in a block to be hashed and puts it into a queue, and several consumer threads that take blocks from the queue and hash their contents, posting the result to the main thread. (There are actually two queues, one for blocks waiting to be hashed and another for blocks that are available to be loaded with new data.) It uses critical sections protected by locks; condition variables to signal when conditions become true; `Atomics.wait` to suspend threads waiting for a condition to become true; and `Atomics.notify` to notify (resume) threads when the condition becomes true.

Let's start with reusable `Lock` and `Condition` classes; see Listing 16-5.

LISTING 16-5: Lock and Condition classes—lock-and-condition.js

```
// Lock and Condition are inspired by Lars T. Hansen's work in this github repo:
// https://github.com/lars-t-hansen/js-lock-and-condition
// The API of these is not the same as the ones there, but the inner workings are
// very similar. But if you find a bug, assume it's mine, not Hansen's.

/**
 * Utility function used by `Lock` and `Condition` to check arguments to their
 * constructors and certain methods that take the arguments this function takes.
 *
 * @param   {SharedArrayBuffer} sab        The buffer to check.
 * @param   {number}            byteOffset  The offset to validate.
 * @param   {number}            bytesNeeded The number of bytes needed at
 *                                          that offset.
 * @throws  {Error} If any of the requirements aren't met.
 */
function checkArguments(sab, byteOffset, bytesNeeded) {
    if (!(sab instanceof SharedArrayBuffer)) {
        throw new Error("`sab` must be a SharedArrayBuffer");
```

```
    }
    // Offset must be an integer identifying a position within the buffer,
    // divisible by four because we use an Int32Array so we can use
    // `Atomics.compareExchange`. It needs to have at least the given number of
    //  bytes available at that position.
    if ((byteOffset|0) !== byteOffset
        || byteOffset % 4 !== 0
        || byteOffset < 0
        || byteOffset + bytesNeeded > sab.byteLength
    ) {
        throw new Error(
            ```byteOffset`` must be an integer divisible by 4 and identify a ` +
            `buffer location with ${bytesNeeded} of room`
        );
    }
}

// State values used by `Lock` and `Condition`; these MUST be the values 0, 1,
// and 2 as below or the implementation of `unlock` will fail (the names are
// just for reading clarity):
const UNLOCKED = 0;        // The lock is unlocked, available to be acquired.
const LOCKED = 1;          // The lock is locked, and no threads are waiting.
const CONTENDED = 2;       // The lock is locked, and there may be at least one
                           // thread waiting to be notified that the lock was
                           // released.

/**
 * Class implementing a lock using a given region of a `SharedArrayBuffer`.
 *
 * You create a new lock within a SAB by using `new Lock` to initialize the SAB
 * and get a `Lock` instance for accessing it. To use an existing `Lock` in a
 * SAB, you must use `Lock.deserialize` to deserialize the object created by
 * `serialize`, **NOT** `new Lock`.
 */
export class Lock {
    // Implementation Notes:
    //
    // Lock state is a single 32-bit entry in a SharedArrayBuffer (via
    // Int32Array). That entry must be initialized to a known state before it
    // can be used for locking (`Lock.initialize`). Once initialized, the entry
    // may have the value `UNLOCKED`, `LOCKED`, or `CONTENDED`.
    //
    // This class makes no attempt to ensure that the code unlocking a lock
    // is the code that acquired the lock in the first place. This is for
    // simplicity and performance.

    /**
     * Creates a lock in the given `SharedArrayBuffer` and returns a `Lock`
     * instance that can use the lock or be serialized to be given to other code
     * to use (via `Lock.deserialize`).
     *
     * @param    {SharedArrayBuffer} sab        The buffer to use.
     * @param    {number}            byteOffset The offset of the region in the
     *                                          buffer to use. The `Lock` object
     *                                          will use `Lock.BYTES_NEEDED`
     *                                          bytes.
     */
```
```

```
constructor(sab, byteOffset) {
    checkArguments(sab, byteOffset, Lock.BYTES_NEEDED);
    this.sharedState = new Int32Array(sab);
    this.index = byteOffset / 4; // byte offset => Int32Array index
    Atomics.store(this.sharedState, this.index, UNLOCKED);
}

/**
 * Gets the `SharedArrayBuffer` this `Lock` instance uses.
 */
get buffer() {
    return this.sharedState.buffer;
}

/**
 * Gets the lock. Waits forever until it succeeds. Cannot be used by the main
 * thread of many environments (including browsers), because the thread may
 * need to enter a wait state, and the main thread isn't allowed to do that in
 * many environments.
 */
lock() {
    const {sharedState, index} = this;
    // Try to get the lock by replacing an existing `UNLOCKED` value with
    // `LOCKED`. `compareExchange` returns the value that was at the given
    // index before the exchange was made, whether the exchange was made
    // or not.
    let c = Atomics.compareExchange(
            sharedState,
            index,
            UNLOCKED,   // If the entry contains `UNLOCKED`,
            LOCKED      // replace it with `LOCKED`.
        );
    // If `c` is `UNLOCKED`, this thread got the lock. If not, loop until
    // it does.
    while (c !== UNLOCKED) {
        // Wait if `c` is already `CONTENDED` or if this thread's attempt
        // to replace `LOCKED` with `CONTENDED` didn't find that it has
        // been replaced with `UNLOCKED` in the meantime.
        const wait =
            c === CONTENDED
            ||
            Atomics.compareExchange(
                sharedState,
                index,
                LOCKED,      // If the entry contains `LOCKED`,
                CONTENDED    // replace it with `CONTENDED`.
            ) !== UNLOCKED;
        if (wait) {
            // Only enter a wait state if the value as of when this thread
            // starts waiting is `CONTENDED`.
            Atomics.wait(sharedState, index, CONTENDED);
        }
```

```
            // The thread gets here in one of three ways:
            // 1. It waited and got notified, or
            // 2. It tried to replace `LOCKED` with `CONTENDED` and found that
            // `UNLOCKED` was there now.
            // 3. It tried to wait, but the value that was there when it would
            // have started waiting wasn't `CONTENDED`.
            // Try to replace `UNLOCKED` with `CONTENDED`.
            c = Atomics.compareExchange(sharedState, index, UNLOCKED, CONTENDED);
        }
    }

    /**
     * Releases the lock.
     */
    unlock() {
        const {sharedState, index} = this;
        // Subtract one from the current value in the state and get the old value
        // that was there. This converts `LOCKED` to `UNLOCKED`, or converts
        // `CONTENDED` to `LOCKED` (or if erroneously called when the lock is not
        // locked) converts `UNLOCKED` to `-1`.
        const value = Atomics.sub(sharedState, index, 1);
        // If the old value was `LOCKED`, we're done; it's `UNLOCKED` now.
        if (value !== LOCKED) {
            // The old value wasn't `LOCKED`. Normally this means it was
            // `CONTENDED` and one or more threads may be waiting for the lock to
            // be released. Do so, and notify up to one thread.
            Atomics.store(sharedState, index, UNLOCKED);
            Atomics.notify(sharedState, index, 1);
            // max number of threads to notify ^
        }
    }

    /**
     * Serializes this `Lock` object into an object that can be used with
     * `postMessage`.
     *
     * @returns The object to use with `postMessage`.
     */
    serialize() {
        return {
            isLockObject: true,
            sharedState: this.sharedState,
            index: this.index
        };
    }

    /**
     * Deserializes the object from `serialize` back into a useable `Lock`.
     *
     * @param    {object} obj The serialized `Lock` object
     * @returns The `Lock` instance.
     */
```

```
        static deserialize(obj) {
            if (!obj || !obj.isLockObject ||
                !(obj.sharedState instanceof Int32Array) ||
                typeof obj.index !== "number"
                ) {
                throw new Error("`obj` is not a serialized `Lock` object");
            }
            const lock = Object.create(Lock.prototype);
            lock.sharedState = obj.sharedState;
            lock.index = obj.index;
            return lock;
        }
    }
}
Lock.BYTES_NEEDED = Int32Array.BYTES_PER_ELEMENT; // Lock uses just one entry

/**
 * Class implementing condition variables using a given lock and a given region of
 * a `SharedArrayBuffer` (a different region in the same buffer the `Lock` uses).
 *
 * A new condition variable is created in a SAB by using `new Condition`, which
 * sets the region of the SAB to initial values and returns a `Condition` object
 * that can be used to access the condition variable. Other code can use the
 * condition variable by using `Condition.deserialize` (**NOT** `new Condition`)
 * on the object created by `serialize` to gain access to the condition variable.
 */
export class Condition {
    /**
     * Creates a `Condition` object that uses the given `Lock` and state
     * information in the given region of the buffer the `Lock` uses. This region
     * must have been initialized at some point by `Condition.initialize` and
     * must not overlap regions used by the `Lock` or any other `Condition`.
     *
     * @param    {Lock}      lock      The lock to use.
     * @param    {number}    byteOffset The offset of the region in the `Lock`'s
     *                                  buffer to use. Will use
     *                                  `Condition.BYTES_NEEDED` bytes starting
     *                                  at that offset.
     */
    constructor(lock, byteOffset, noInit = false) {
        if (!(lock instanceof Lock)) {
            throw new Error("`lock` must be a `Lock` instance");
        }
        const sab = lock.buffer;
        checkArguments(sab, byteOffset, Condition.BYTES_NEEDED);
        this.sharedState = new Int32Array(sab);
        this.index = byteOffset / 4; // byte offset => Int32Array index
        this.lock = lock;
        Atomics.store(this.sharedState, this.index, 0);
    }

    /**
     * Unlocks this `Condition`'s `Lock` and waits to be notified of the condition.
     * The calling code must have the lock.
     */
```

```
wait() {
    const {sharedState, index, lock} = this;
    const sequence = Atomics.load(sharedState, index);
    lock.unlock();
    Atomics.wait(sharedState, index, sequence);
    lock.lock();
}

/**
 * Notify one waiting thread. Typically code does this when the condition has
 * become "true" (whatever meaning that has for a particular condition).
 * The calling code must have the lock.
 */
notifyOne() {
    const {sharedState, index} = this;
    Atomics.add(sharedState, index, 1);     // Move the sequence on by one
    Atomics.notify(sharedState, index, 1);  // 1 = notify one thread
}

/**
 * Notify all waiting threads. Typically code does this when the condition has
 * become "true" (whatever meaning that has for a particular condition).
 * The calling code must have the lock.
 */
notifyAll() {
    const {sharedState, index} = this;
    Atomics.add(sharedState, index, 1);     // Move the sequence on by one
    Atomics.notify(sharedState, index);     // No 3rd arg = notify all threads
}

/**
 * Serializes this `Condition` object into an object that can be used with
 * `postMessage`.
 *
 * @returns The object to use with `postMessage`.
 */
serialize() {
    return {
        isConditionObject: true,
        sharedState: this.sharedState,
        index: this.index,
        lock: this.lock.serialize()
    };
}

/**
 * Deserializes the object from `serialize` back into a useable `Condition`.
 *
 * @param   {object}   obj The serialized `Condition` object
 * @returns The `Lock` instance.
 */
static deserialize(obj) {
    if (!obj || !obj.isConditionObject ||
```

```
                        !(obj.sharedState instanceof Int32Array) ||
                        typeof obj.index !== "number"
                        ) {
                        throw new Error("`obj` is not a serialized `Condition` object");
                    }
                const condition = Object.create(Condition.prototype);
                condition.sharedState = obj.sharedState;
                condition.index = obj.index;
                condition.lock = Lock.deserialize(obj.lock);
                return condition;
            }
        }
        Condition.BYTES_NEEDED = Int32Array.BYTES_PER_ELEMENT;
```

`Lock` provides a basic, simple lock. You create a lock within a `SharedArrayBuffer` using the `Lock` constructor, passing it the `SharedArrayBuffer` and the offset at which to create the lock:

```
        const lock = new Lock(sab, offset);
```

The `Lock` constructor sets the initial state information for the lock in the `SharedArrayBuffer` and returns the `Lock` instance to use. Since locks use `Int32Array` instances, the offset must be evenly divisible by 4 to ensure that the array entries are aligned (you'll get a `RangeError` otherwise; see the discussion of alignment under "Creating Shared Memory" earlier in this chapter). The `Lock` class tells you how many bytes of the `SharedArrayBuffer` it needs via a property called `Lock.BYTES_NEEDED` (in case you're storing other things in the buffer, or need to make the buffer just big enough for the lock).

Since the point of locks is to be shared across threads, to share a `Lock` you call its `serialize` method to get a simple object you can post via `postMessage`:

```
        worker.postMessage({type: "init", lock: lock.serialize()});
```

In the receiving thread, you use `Lock.deserialize` to get the `Lock` instance for that thread to use:

```
        const lock = Lock.deserialize(message.lock);
```

The sending thread's `Lock` instance and the receiving thread's `Lock` instance will share the same underlying data, in the `SharedArrayBuffer`.

To *acquire* the lock (to *take ownership* of it) in order to prevent any other thread from having it, you call its `lock` method:

```
        lock.lock();
```

`lock` will wait indefinitely until it can acquire the lock. (A more complicated `Lock` class could provide a timeout mechanism.) Since it makes the current thread wait (via `Atomics.wait`), you can't call it on the main thread in most environments; you must use a worker thread. This example will use `lock` in the producer and consumer threads in code you'll see later.

Once the code owns the lock, it can proceed with its critical section code. When done, it releases the lock via `unlock`:

```
        lock.unlock();
```

`Condition` works in a similar way to `Lock`. You create a `Condition` using the `Condition` constructor, passing in the `Lock` instance it should use and the offset within the `SharedArrayBuffer` where it should keep the condition's state information:

```
const myCondition = new Condition(lock, conditionOffset);
```

Note that you provide the `Condition` constructor with a `Lock` instance. This is because the condition must use the same lock other conditions or code are using in relation to the same shared memory. For instance, in the producer/consumer thread example, the queue has a single lock used for fundamental queue operations like putting a value in and taking a value out, and for the conditions that those operations use such as "queue has room" and "queue has work."

As with `Lock`, `Condition` uses an `Int32Array` and so the offset you provide in the constructor call must be divisible by 4; it tells you how much room in the `SharedArrayBuffer` it needs via the `Condition.BYTES_NEEDED` property.

To make a thread wait for a condition, you call the condition's `wait` method. The thread must own the lock the condition uses when it calls `wait`, which may seem surprising, but it makes sense when you see how conditions are used. For instance, in a shared queue such as the one this example will use, the "put" operation (putting a value into the queue) is a critical section, because it needs to access and update the queue's data. So the thread doing the "put" must get ownership of the lock before it can do its work. But if the queue is full, it has to wait for the "queue has room" condition to become true. Doing that requires releasing the lock, waiting for notification the condition is true, and then re-acquiring the lock. `Condition`'s `wait` method handles doing that work in an appropriate way, so it has to be called only when the thread already has the lock. Here's a simplified example:

```
put(value) {
    this.lock.lock();
    try {
        while (/*...the queue is full...*/) {
            this.hasRoomCondition.wait();
        }
        // ...put the value in the queue...
    } finally {
        this.lock.unlock();
    }
}
```

(Note that, again, `this.lock` must be the same lock that `this.hasRoomCondition` uses, the lock protecting the queue as a whole.) Since there's inevitably a brief moment when the condition has become true but the waiting thread doesn't have the lock, it can't assume once it has the lock that the condition is *still* true; another thread may have snuck in before it! That's why the `wait` code in the `put` snippet earlier is in a `while` loop, not just an `if`.

So how does the condition become true? In the "queue has room" condition's case, another thread must perform an operation that removes an item from the queue, and then *notify* any waiting thread that the queue has room again. This would be in the queue's "take" method, which would look something like this:

```
take() {
    this.lock.lock();
    try {
```

```
            // ...ensure the queue isn't empty...
            const value = /* ...take the next value from the queue, making room... */;
            this.hasRoomCondition.notifyOne();
            return value;
        } finally {
            this.lock.unlock();
        }
    }
```

`Condition`'s `notifyOne` method resumes a single thread waiting for this condition, if any, using `Atomics.notify` (as you'll see in Listing 16-6).

Those preceding snippets gloss over the second condition the queue uses, "queue has work." That's also managed by the `put` and `take` methods, just in the reverse way (`take` waits, `put` notifies). Let's look at a complete locking shared memory queue implementation; see Listing 16-6.

LISTING 16-6: LockingInt32Queue implementation—locking-int32-queue.js

```javascript
// Ring buffer implementation drawn in part from
// https://www.snellman.net/blog/archive/2016-12-13-ring-buffers/
// Note that it relies on Uint32 wrap-around from 2**32-1 to 0
// on increment.

import {Lock, Condition} from "./lock-and-condition.js";

// Indexes of the head and tail indexes in the `indexes` array of
// `LockingInt32Queue`.
const HEAD = 0;
const TAIL = 1;

/**
 * Validates the given queue capacity, throws error if invalid.
 *
 * @param {number} capacity The size of the queue
 */
function validateCapacity(capacity) {
    const capLog2 = Math.log2(capacity);
    if (capLog2 !== (capLog2|0)) {
        throw new Error(
            "`capacity` must be a power of 2 (2, 4, 8, 16, 32, 64, etc.)"
        );
    }
}

/**
 * Converts the given number to Uint32 (and then back to number), applying
 * standard unsigned 32-bit integer wrap-around. For example, -4294967294 converts
 * to 2.
 *
 * @param   {number}    n   The number to convert.
 * @returns The result.
 */
```

```
function toUint32(n) {
    // The unsigned right-shift operator converts its operands to Uint32 values,
    // so shifting `n` by 0 places converts it to Uint32 (and then back to number)
    return n >>> 0;
}


// Utility functions for LockingInt32 Queue
// These will be useful private methods when private methods are further along.

/**
 * Gets the size of the given queue (the number of unconsumed entries in it).
 * **MUST** be called only from code holding the queue's lock.
 *
 * @param    {LockingInt32Queue} queue  The queue to get the size of.
 * @returns The number of unconsumed entries in the queue.
 */
function size(queue) {
    // Conversion to Uint32 (briefly) handles the necessary wrap-around so that
    // when the head index is (for instance) 1 and the tail index is (for
    // instance) 4294967295, the result is 2 (there's an entry at index
    // 4294967295 % capacity and also one at index 0), not -4294967294.
    return toUint32(queue.indexes[HEAD] - queue.indexes[TAIL]);
}


/**
 * Determines whether the given queue is full.
 * **MUST** be called only from code holding the queue's lock.
 *
 * @param    {LockingInt32Queue} queue  The queue to check.
 * @returns `true` if the queue is full, `false` if not.
 */
function full(queue) {
    return size(queue) === queue.data.length;
}


/**
 * Determines whether the given queue is empty.
 * **MUST** be called only from code holding the queue's lock.
 *
 * @param    {LockingInt32Queue} queue  The queue to check.
 * @returns `true` if the queue is full, `false` if not.
 */
function empty(queue) {
    return queue.indexes[HEAD] === queue.indexes[TAIL];
}


/**
 * Checks the value to see that it's valid for the queue.
 * Throws an error if the value is invalid.
 *
 * @param {number} v The value to check.
 */
```

```
function checkValue(v) {
    if (typeof v !== "number" || (v|0) !== v) {
        throw new Error(
            "Queue values must be integers between -(2**32) and 2**32-1, inclusive"
        );
    }
}

/**
 * Puts the given value into the given queue. Caller **MUST** check that there is
 * room in the queue before calling this method, while having the queue locked.
 * **MUST** be called only from code holding the queue's lock.
 *
 * @param   {LockingInt32Queue} queue   The queue to put the value in.
 * @param   {number}            value   The value to put.
 */
function internalPut(queue, value) {
    queue.data[queue.indexes[HEAD] % queue.data.length] = value;
    ++queue.indexes[HEAD];
}

/**
 * A queue of Int32 values with an associated `Lock` instance whose `put` method
 * blocks until there's room in the queue and whose `take` method blocks until
 * there's an entry in the queue to return.
 */
export class LockingInt32Queue {
    /**
     * Gets the number of bytes this queue implementation requires within a
     * `SharedArrayBuffer` to support a queue of the given capacity.
     *
     * @param   {number}    capacity    The desired queue capacity.
     */
    static getBytesNeeded(capacity) {
        validateCapacity(capacity);
        const bytesNeeded = Lock.BYTES_NEEDED +
                            (Condition.BYTES_NEEDED * 2) +
                            (Uint32Array.BYTES_PER_ELEMENT * 2) +
                            (Int32Array.BYTES_PER_ELEMENT * capacity);
        return bytesNeeded;
    }

    /**
     * Creates a new queue with the given capacity, optionally using the given
     * `SharedArrayBuffer` at the given byte offset (if not given, a new buffer
     * of the appropriate size is created). The constructor is **only** for
     * creating a new queue, not using an existing one; for that, use
     * `LockingInt32Queue.deserialize` on the object returned by the `serialize`
     * method of the queue instance.
     *
     * @param   {number}            capacity    The maximum number of entries
     *                                          the queue can contain.
     * @param   {SharedArrayBuffer} sab         The `SharedArrayBuffer` the
     *                                          queue should be maintained in.
     *                                          If you're supplying this arg,
```

```
 *                                        use the `getBytesNeeded` static
 *                                        method to get the number of
 *                                        bytes the queue will need.
 * @param   {number}          byteOffset  The byte offset within the SAB
 *                                        where the queue's state
 *                                        information should be stored.
 * @param   {number[]}        initialEntries  Optional entries to pre-seed
 *                                        the queue with.
 */
constructor(capacity, sab = null, byteOffset = 0, initialEntries = null) {
    const bytesNeeded = LockingInt32Queue.getBytesNeeded(capacity);
    if (sab === null) {
        if (byteOffset !== 0) {
            throw new Error(
                "`byteOffset` must be omitted or 0 when `sab` is " +
                "omitted or `null`"
            );
        }
        sab = new SharedArrayBuffer(byteOffset + bytesNeeded);
    }
    // Offset must be an integer identifying a position within the buffer,
    // divisible by four because we use an Int32Array so we can use
    // `Atomics.compareExchange`. It needs to have at least the given number of
    // bytes available at that position.
    if ((byteOffset|0) !== byteOffset
        || byteOffset % 4 !== 0
        || byteOffset < 0
        || byteOffset + bytesNeeded > sab.byteLength
    ) {
        throw new Error(
            `\`byteOffset\` must be an integer divisible by 4 and ` +
            `identify a buffer location with ${bytesNeeded} of room`
        );
    }

    // Create the lock and conditions
    this.byteOffset = byteOffset;
    let n = byteOffset;
    this.lock = new Lock(sab, n);
    n += Lock.BYTES_NEEDED;
    this.hasWorkCondition = new Condition(this.lock, n);
    n += Condition.BYTES_NEEDED;
    this.hasRoomCondition = new Condition(this.lock, n);
    n += Condition.BYTES_NEEDED;
    // Create the indexes and data arrays
    this.indexes = new Uint32Array(sab, n, 2);
    Atomics.store(this.indexes, HEAD, 0);
    Atomics.store(this.indexes, TAIL, 0);
    n += Uint32Array.BYTES_PER_ELEMENT * 2;
    this.data = new Int32Array(sab, n, capacity);
    if (initialEntries) {
        if (initialEntries.length > capacity) {
            throw new Error(
                `\`initialEntries\` has ${initialEntries.length} entries, ` +
```

```
                            `queue only supports ${capacity} entries`
                    );
                }
            for (const value of initialEntries) {
                checkValue(value);
                internalPut(this, value);
            }
        }
    }

    /**
     * The capacity of this queue.
     */
    get capacity() {
        return this.data.length;
    }

    /**
     * Locks the queue, puts the given value into it, and releases the lock.
     * Waits forever for the lock (no timeout) and for the queue to have room for
     * a new entry.
     *
     * @param   {number}    value   The value to put. Must be a number
     *                              representing a 32-bit unsigned integer.
     * @returns The size of the queue as of just after this value was put in (may
     *          be out of date the instant the caller receives it, though).
     */
    put(value) {
        checkValue(value);
        this.lock.lock();
        try {
            // If the queue is full, wait for the "queue has room" condition to
            // become true. Since waiting releases and reacquires the lock, after
            // waiting check again whether the queue is full in case another thread
            // snuck in and used up the space that became available before this
            // thread could use it.
            while (full(this)) {
                this.hasRoomCondition.wait();
            }
            internalPut(this, value);
            const rv = size(this);
            // Notify one thread waiting in `take`, if any, that the queue has work
            // available now
            this.hasWorkCondition.notifyOne();
            return rv;
        } finally {
            this.lock.unlock();
        }
    }

    /**
     * Locks the queue, takes the next value from it, unlocks the queue, and
```

```
 * returns the value. Waits forever for the lock and for the queue to have
 * at least one entry in it.
 */
take() {
    this.lock.lock();
    try {
        // If the queue is empty, wait for the "queue has work" condition to
        // become true. Since waiting releases and reacquires the lock, after
        // waiting check again whether the queue is empty in case another
        // thread snuck in and took the work that was just added before this
        // thread could use it.
        while (empty(this)) {
            this.hasWorkCondition.wait();
        }
        const value = this.data[this.indexes[TAIL] % this.data.length];
        ++this.indexes[TAIL];
        // Notify one thread waiting in `put`, if any, that there's room for
        // a new entry in the queue now
        this.hasRoomCondition.notifyOne();
        return value;
    } finally {
        this.lock.unlock();
    }
}

/**
 * Serializes this `LockingInt32Queue` object into an object that can be used
 * with `postMessage`.
 *
 * @returns The object to use with `postMessage`.
 */
serialize() {
    return {
        isLockingInt32Queue: true,
        lock: this.lock.serialize(),
        hasWorkCondition: this.hasWorkCondition.serialize(),
        hasRoomCondition: this.hasRoomCondition.serialize(),
        indexes: this.indexes,
        data: this.data,
        name: this.name
    };
}

/**
 * Deserializes the object from `serialize` back into a useable `Lock`.
 *
 * @param   {object} obj The serialized `Lock` object
 * @returns The `Lock` instance.
 */
static deserialize(obj) {
    if (!obj || !obj.isLockingInt32Queue ||
```

```
                      !(obj.indexes instanceof Uint32Array) ||
                      !(obj.data instanceof Int32Array)
                    ) {
                    throw new Error(
                        "`obj` is not a serialized `LockingInt32Queue` object"
                    );
                }
                const q = Object.create(LockingInt32Queue.prototype);
                q.lock = Lock.deserialize(obj.lock);
                q.hasWorkCondition = Condition.deserialize(obj.hasWorkCondition);
                q.hasRoomCondition = Condition.deserialize(obj.hasRoomCondition);
                q.indexes = obj.indexes;
                q.data = obj.data;
                q.name = obj.name;
                return q;
            }
    }
```

`LockingInt32Queue` is a simple ring-buffer queue implemented in shared memory using a single `Lock` and two `Condition`s: "queue has work" (`hasWorkCondition`) and "queue has room" (`hasRoomCondition`). For creation and sharing it follows the same approach `Lock` and `Condition` do, using the constructor to create the queue and sharing it via `serialize` and `deserialize`. Since the amount of memory it takes depends on how big the queue needs to be, it provides the `LockingInt32Queue.getBytesNeeded` method to tell you how many bytes it needs for the queue capacity you request.

Since a queue may be created by a main thread (which can't `wait`) and the main thread may need to pre-populate the queue with some values, the constructor optionally accepts the initial values for the queue. You'll see this later when the main thread in Listing 16-7 creates a queue of available buffers.

To put work into the queue, a thread simply calls `put`. The queue's code handles acquiring the lock, waiting for room in the queue if necessary, putting the value in the queue, and notifying any thread that may be waiting that there's work in the queue now (via `hasWorkCondition`). Similarly, to take a value from the queue, the code just calls `take` and the queue's code handles the locking and waiting necessary to take a value from the queue and to notify any possible waiting thread that the queue has room now (via `hasRoomCondition`).

Listings 16-7 and 16-8 have the main entry point for this example and a very small miscellaneous utilities module. The main entry point creates eight data buffers and two queues with capacity for the IDs of all eight buffers: one queue for the buffers that are ready to be filled with data to be hashed (`availableBuffersQueue`) and another queue for the buffers that are full and ready to have their contents hashed (`pendingBuffersQueue`). Then it creates a producer thread and four consumer threads and sends them the buffers and the serialized queues along with other initialization information. It adds a message listener to the consumer queues so it can receive the hashes they calculate. Finally, after a second it tells the producer to stop producing new values and to tell the consumers to stop as well.

Don't worry about the `fullspeed` flag for now, we'll come back to that in a bit.

```
// This example uses one producer worker and multiple consumer workers to calculate
// hashes of data buffers. The work is managed using two queues. The queues and the
// data buffers are all contained in a single `SharedArrayBuffer`. The producer
// gets an available buffer ID from the `availableBuffersQueue`, fills that buffer
// with random data, and then adds the buffer's ID to the `pendingBuffersQueue` to
// be processed by consumers. When a consumer takes a buffer ID from the pending
// queue, it calculates the hash, then puts the buffer ID back into the available
// queue and posts the hash to the main thread.

import {log, setLogging} from "./example-misc.js";
import {LockingInt32Queue} from "./locking-int32-queue.js";
const fullspeed = location.search.includes("fullspeed");
setLogging(!fullspeed);

// The capacity of the queues
const capacity = 8;

// The size of each data buffer
const dataBufferLength = 4096;

// The number of buffers, must be at least as many as queue capacity
const dataBufferCount = capacity;

// The size of the SAB we'll need; note that since the data buffers are byte
// arrays, there's no need to multiply by Uint8Array.BYTES_PER_ELEMENT.
const bufferSize = (LockingInt32Queue.getBytesNeeded(capacity) * 2) +
                   (dataBufferLength * dataBufferCount);

// The number of consumers we'll create
const consumerCount = 4;

// The number of hashes received from consumers
let hashesReceived = 0;

// Create the SAB, the data buffers, and the queues. Again, since the data buffers
// are byte arrays this code doesn't need to use `Uint8Array.BYTES_PER_ELEMENT`.
let byteOffset = 0;
const sab = new SharedArrayBuffer(bufferSize);
const buffers = [];
for (let n = 0; n < dataBufferCount; ++n) {
    buffers[n] = new Uint8Array(sab, byteOffset, dataBufferLength);
    byteOffset += dataBufferLength;
}
const availableBuffersQueue = new LockingInt32Queue(
    capacity, sab, byteOffset, [...buffers.keys()]
    //                         ^-- Initially, all the buffers are available
);
byteOffset += LockingInt32Queue.getBytesNeeded(capacity);
const pendingBuffersQueue = new LockingInt32Queue(
```

```javascript
        capacity, sab, byteOffset // Initially empty
);

// Handle a message posted from a consumer.
function handleConsumerMessage({data}) {
    const type = data && data.type;
    if (type === "hash") {
        const {consumerId, bufferId, hash} = data;
        ++hashesReceived;
        log(
            "main",
            `Hash for buffer ${bufferId} from consumer${consumerId}: ${hash}, ` +
            `${hashesReceived} total hashes received`
        );
    }
}

// Create the producer and the consumers, get them started
const initMessage = {
    type: "init",
    availableBuffersQueue: availableBuffersQueue.serialize(),
    pendingBuffersQueue: pendingBuffersQueue.serialize(),
    buffers,
    fullspeed
};
const producer = new Worker("./example-producer.js", {type: "module"});
producer.postMessage({...initMessage, consumerCount});
const consumers = [];
for (let n = 0; n < consumerCount; ++n) {
    const consumer = consumers[n] =
        new Worker("./example-consumer.js", {type: "module"});
    consumer.postMessage({...initMessage, consumerId: n});
    consumer.addEventListener("message", handleConsumerMessage);
}

// Tell the producer to stop producing new work after one second
setTimeout(() => {
    producer.postMessage({type: "stop"});
    setLogging(true);
    const spinner = document.querySelector(".spinner-border");
    spinner.classList.remove("spinning");
    spinner.role = "presentation";
    document.getElementById("message").textContent = "Done";
}, 1000);
// Show the main thread isn't blocked
let ticks = 0;
(function tick() {
    const ticker = document.getElementById("ticker");
    if (ticker) {
        ticker.textContent = ++ticks;
        setTimeout(tick, 10);
    }
})();
```

LISTING 16-8: Example miscellaneous module—example-misc.js

```
let logging = true;
export function log(id, message) {
    if (logging) {
        console.log(String(id).padEnd(10, " "), message);
    }
}
export function setLogging(flag) {
    logging = flag;
}
```

The producer thread is in Listing 16-9. It takes the buffers and queues from its initialization method and starts a loop, taking an available buffer ID from the availableBuffersQueue (possibly waiting, if the consumers are running behind), filling that buffer with random data (for this example), and then putting its ID in the pendingBuffersQueue. Once every 500ms or so it stops the loop and uses setTimeout to schedule it to start again almost immediately; this is so that it can receive any message posted to it via postMessage. When it receives a stop message, it fills the pendingBuffersQueue with flag values instead of buffer IDs to tell the consumers to stop.

LISTING 16-9: Example producer—example-producer.js

```
import {log, setLogging} from "./example-misc.js";
import {LockingInt32Queue} from "./locking-int32-queue.js";

// The basic flag for whether this producer should keep running. Set by
// `actions.init` (called by an `init` message from the main thread), cleared by
// the `stop` message or on receipt of a buffer ID of -1.
let running = false;

// The ID this producer uses when calling `log`, set by `actions.init`
let logId = "producer";

// The queues and buffers to use, and the number of consumers main has running (set
// by `actions.init`).
let availableBuffersQueue;
let pendingBuffersQueue;
let buffers;
let consumerCount;
let fullspeed;

// Fills buffers until either the `running` flag is no longer true or it's time
// to yield briefly to the event loop in order to receive any pending messages.
function fillBuffers() {
    const yieldAt = Date.now() + 500;
    while (running) {
        log(logId, "Taking available buffer from queue");
        const bufferId = availableBuffersQueue.take();
        const buffer = buffers[bufferId];
```

```
                log(logId, `Filling buffer ${bufferId}`);
                for (let n = 0; n < buffer.length; ++n) {
                    buffer[n] = Math.floor(Math.random() * 256);
                }
                log(logId, `Putting buffer ${bufferId} into queue`);
                const size = pendingBuffersQueue.put(bufferId);
                if (Date.now() >= yieldAt) {
                    log(logId, "Yielding to handle messages");
                    setTimeout(fillBuffers, 0);
                    break;
                }
            }
        }
    }

    // Handle messages, take appropriate action
    const actions = {
        // Initialize the producer from data in the message
        init(data) {
            ({consumerCount, buffers, fullspeed} = data);
            setLogging(!fullspeed);
            log(logId, "Running");
            running = true;
            availableBuffersQueue =
                LockingInt32Queue.deserialize(data.availableBuffersQueue);
            pendingBuffersQueue =
                LockingInt32Queue.deserialize(data.pendingBuffersQueue);
            fillBuffers(data);
        },
        // Stop this producer
        stop() {
            if (running) {
                running = false;
                log(logId, "Stopping, queuing stop messages for consumers");
                for (let n = 0; n < consumerCount; ++n) {
                    pendingBuffersQueue.put(-1);
                }
                log(logId, "Stopped");
            }
        }
    }
    self.addEventListener("message", ({ data }) => {
        const action = data && data.type && actions[data.type];
        if (action) {
            action(data);
        }
    });
```

The consumer code in Listing 16-10 is very similar to the producer code, just taking buffer IDs from the pendingBuffersQueue (possibly waiting for one to become available), calculating the "hash" (in this case a simple XOR with an arbitrary delay to simulate a more involved hashing function), putting that buffer's ID in the availableBuffersQueue, and posting the hash to the main thread. The consumer stops when it sees a buffer ID of –1.

LISTING 16-10: Example consumer—example-consumer.js

```javascript
import {log, setLogging} from "./example-misc.js";
import {LockingInt32Queue} from "./locking-int32-queue.js";

// The basic flag for whether this consumer should keep running.
// Set by the `init` message, cleared by the `stop` message or on receipt of a
// buffer ID of -1.
let running = false;

// The ID this consumer uses when calling `log`, set by `init`
let logId;

// This consumer's ID, and the queues and buffers to use (set by `init`)
let consumerId = null;
let availableBuffersQueue;
let pendingBuffersQueue;
let buffers;
let fullspeed;

// The "now" function we'll use to time waiting for queue operations
const now = typeof performance !== "undefined" && performance.now
                ? performance.now.bind(performance)
                : Date.now.bind(Date);

// An array we use to wait within `calculateHash`, see below
const a = new Int32Array(new SharedArrayBuffer(Int32Array.BYTES_PER_ELEMENT));

// Calculates the hash for the given buffer.
function calculateHash(buffer) {
    // A real hash calculation like SHA-256 or even MD5 would take much longer than
    // the below, so after doing the basic XOR hash (which isn't a reliable hash,
    // it's just to keep things simple), this code waits a few milliseconds to
    // avoid completely overloading the main thread with messages. Real code
    // probably wouldn't do that, since the point of offloading the work to a
    // worker is to move work that takes a fair bit of time off the main thread.
    const hash = buffer.reduce((acc, val) => acc ^ val, 0);
    if (!fullspeed) {
        Atomics.wait(a, 0, 0, 10);
    }
    return hash;
}

// Processes buffers until either the `running` flag is no longer true or it's time
// to yield briefly to the event loop in order to receive any pending messages.
function processBuffers() {
    const yieldAt = Date.now() + 500;
    while (running) {
        log(logId, "Getting buffer to process");
        let waitStart = now();
```

```
            const bufferId = pendingBuffersQueue.take();
            let elapsed = now() - waitStart;
            log(logId, `Got bufferId ${bufferId} (elapsed: ${elapsed})`);
            if (bufferId === -1) {
                // This is a flag from the producer that this consumer should stop
                actions.stop();
                break;
            }
            log(logId, `Hashing buffer ${bufferId}`);
            const hash = calculateHash(buffers[bufferId]);
            postMessage({type: "hash", consumerId, bufferId, hash});
            waitStart = now();
            availableBuffersQueue.put(bufferId);
            elapsed = now() - waitStart;
            log(logId, `Done with buffer ${bufferId} (elapsed: ${elapsed})`);
            if (Date.now() >= yieldAt) {
                log(logId, `Yielding to handle messages`);
                setTimeout(processBuffers, 0);
                break;
            }
        }
    }
}


// Handle messages, take appropriate action
const actions = {
    // Initialize this consumer with data from the message
    init(data) {
        ({consumerId, buffers, fullspeed} = data);
        setLogging(!fullspeed);
        logId = `consumer${consumerId}`;
        availableBuffersQueue =
            LockingInt32Queue.deserialize(data.availableBuffersQueue);
        pendingBuffersQueue =
            LockingInt32Queue.deserialize(data.pendingBuffersQueue);
        log(logId, "Running");
        running = true;
        processBuffers();
    },
    // Stop this consumer
    stop() {
        if (running) {
            running = false;
            log(logId, "Stopped");
        }
    }
}
self.addEventListener("message", ({data}) => {
    const action = data && data.type && actions[data.type];
    if (action) {
        action(data);
    }
});
```

Using the `example.html` file from the downloads, run the example with the console open using a recent version of Chrome. (You can also run it from `https://thenewtoys.dev/bookcode/live/16/example.html`, which handles serving it securely and with the right headers.) You'll see the example run for a little more than a second and calculate several hundred buffer hashes, scheduling the work between the various worker threads efficiently through JavaScript's shared memory, wait, and notification features. As you can see by the spinner and counter the main thread shows, it's all done without tying up the UI of the browser (thanks to the workers).

HERE THERE BE DRAGONS! (AGAIN)

Or: No, Seriously, Do You *Really* Need Shared Memory?

It bears repeating: sharing memory across threads opens up a host of data synchronization issues that programmers working in typical JavaScript environments haven't had to deal with before.

For most use cases, you don't need shared memory, in part thanks to transferables. Listings 16-11 through 16-13 have an alternate implementation of the same block hashing as the earlier example, using `postMessage` and transferable memory buffers rather than shared memory and `Atomics.wait`/`Atomics.notify`. No need for locks, condition variables, or the `LockingInt32Queue` (it doesn't use those files; it does reuse `example-misc.js`) and the code in the remaining files is much simpler and easier to understand.

LISTING 16-11: Example postMessage main—pm-example-main.js

```
// This is the `postMessage`+transferables version of example-main.js

import {log, setLogging} from "./example-misc.js";

const fullspeed = location.search.includes("fullspeed");
setLogging(!fullspeed);

// The capacity of the queues (which is also the number of data buffers we have,
// which is really how the queues in this example are limited)
const capacity = 8;

// The size of each data buffer
const dataBufferLength = 4096;

// The number of buffers, must be at least as many as queue capacity
const dataBufferCount = capacity;

// The number of consumers we'll create
const consumerCount = 4;

// The number of hashes received from consumers
let hashesReceived = 0;
```

```
// Flag for whether we're running (producer and consumers no longer need this flag,
// they just respond to what they're sent)
let running = false;

// Create the data buffers and the queues (which can be simple arrays, since
// only this thread accesses them)
const buffers = [];
const availableBuffersQueue = [];
for (let id = 0; id < dataBufferCount; ++id) {
    buffers[id] = new Uint8Array(dataBufferLength);
    availableBuffersQueue.push(id);
}
const pendingBuffersQueue = [];

// Handle messages, take appropriate action
const actions = {
    hash(data) {
        // Got a hash from a consumer
        const {consumerId, bufferId, buffer, hash} = data;
        buffers[bufferId] = buffer;
        availableBuffersQueue.push(bufferId);
        availableConsumersQueue.push(consumerId);
        ++hashesReceived;
        log(
            "main",
            `Hash for buffer ${bufferId} from consumer${consumerId}: ` +
            `${hash}, ${hashesReceived} total hashes received`
        );
        if (running) {
            sendBufferToProducer();
            sendBufferToConsumer();
        }
    },
    buffer(data) {
        // Got a buffer from the producer
        const {buffer, bufferId} = data;
        buffers[bufferId] = buffer;
        pendingBuffersQueue.push(bufferId);
        sendBufferToProducer();
        sendBufferToConsumer();
    }
};
function handleMessage({data}) {
    const action = data && data.type && actions[data.type];
    if (action) {
        action(data);
    }
}

// Create the producer and the consumers, get them started
const initMessage = { type: "init", fullspeed };
const producer = new Worker("./pm-example-producer.js", {type: "module"});
producer.addEventListener("message", handleMessage);
producer.postMessage(initMessage);
const availableConsumersQueue = [];
```

```
const consumers = [];
for (let consumerId = 0; consumerId < consumerCount; ++consumerId) {
    const consumer = consumers[consumerId] =
        new Worker("./pm-example-consumer.js", {type: "module"});
    consumer.postMessage({...initMessage, consumerId});
    consumer.addEventListener("message", handleMessage);
    availableConsumersQueue.push(consumerId);
}

// Send a buffer to the producer to be filled, if we're running and there are
// any buffers available
function sendBufferToProducer() {
    if (running && availableBuffersQueue.length) {
        const bufferId = availableBuffersQueue.shift();
        const buffer = buffers[bufferId];
        producer.postMessage(
            {type: "fill", buffer, bufferId},
            [buffer.buffer] // Transfer underlying `ArrayBuffer` to producer
        );
    }
}

// Send a buffer to a consumer to be hashed, if there are pending buffers and
// available consumers
function sendBufferToConsumer() {
    if (pendingBuffersQueue.length && availableConsumersQueue.length) {
        const bufferId = pendingBuffersQueue.shift();
        const buffer = buffers[bufferId];
        const consumerId = availableConsumersQueue.shift();
        consumers[consumerId].postMessage(
            {type: "hash", buffer, bufferId},
            [buffer.buffer] // Transfer underlying `ArrayBuffer` to consumer
        );
    }
}

// Start producing work
running = true;
while (availableBuffersQueue.length) {
    sendBufferToProducer();
}

// Stop producing new work after one second.
setTimeout(() => {
    running = false;
    setLogging(true);
    const spinner = document.querySelector(".spinner-border");
    spinner.classList.remove("spinning");
    spinner.role = "presentation";
    document.getElementById("message").textContent = "Done";
}, 1000);

// Show the main thread isn't blocked
let ticks = 0;
(function tick() {
    const ticker = document.getElementById("ticker");
```

```
        if (ticker) {
            ticker.textContent = ++ticks;
            setTimeout(tick, 10);
        }
    })();
```

LISTING 16-12: Example postMessage producer—pm-example-producer.js

```
// This is the `postMessage`+transferables version of example-producer.js

import {log, setLogging} from "./example-misc.js";

// The ID this producer uses when calling `log`, set by `actions.init`
let logId = "producer";

// Handle messages, take appropriate action
const actions = {
    // Initialize the producer from data in the message
    init(data) {
        const {fullspeed} = data;
        setLogging(!fullspeed);
        log(logId, "Running");
    },
    // Fill a buffer
    fill(data) {
        const {buffer, bufferId} = data;
        log(logId, `Filling buffer ${bufferId}`);
        for (let n = 0; n < buffer.length; ++n) {
            buffer[n] = Math.floor(Math.random() * 256);
        }
        self.postMessage(
            {type: "buffer", buffer, bufferId},
            [buffer.buffer] // Transfer the underlying `ArrayBuffer` back to main
        );
    }
}
self.addEventListener("message", ({ data }) => {
    const action = data && data.type && actions[data.type];
    if (action) {
        action(data);
    }
});
```

LISTING 16-13: Example postMessage consumer—pm-example-consumer.js

```
// This is the `postMessage`+transferables version of example-consumer.js

import {log, setLogging} from "./example-misc.js";

// The ID this consumer uses when calling `log`, set by `init`
let logId;
```

```
        // This consumer's ID and the fullspeed flag
        let consumerId = null;
        let fullspeed;

        // An array we use to wait within `calcluateHash`, see below
        const a = new Int32Array(new SharedArrayBuffer(Int32Array.BYTES_PER_ELEMENT));

        // Calculates the hash for the given buffer.
        function calculateHash(buffer) {
            // A real hash calculation like SHA-256 or even MD5 would take much longer than
            // the below, so after doing the basic XOR hash (which isn't a reliable hash,
            // it's just to keep things simple), this code waits a few milliseconds to
            // avoid completely overloading the main thread with messages. Real code
            // probably wouldn't do that, since the point of offloading the work to a
            // worker is to move work that takes a fair bit of time off the main thread.
            const hash = buffer.reduce((acc, val) => acc ^ val, 0);
            if (!fullspeed) {
                Atomics.wait(a, 0, 0, 10);
            }
            return hash;
        }

        // Handle messages, take appropriate action
        const actions = {
            // Initialize this consumer with data from the message
            init(data) {
                ({consumerId, fullspeed} = data);
                setLogging(!fullspeed);
                logId = `consumer${consumerId}`;
                log(logId, "Running");
            },
            // Hash the given buffer
            hash(data) {
                const {buffer, bufferId} = data;
                log(logId, `Hashing buffer ${bufferId}`);
                const hash = calculateHash(buffer);
                self.postMessage(
                    {type: "hash", hash, consumerId, buffer, bufferId},
                    [buffer.buffer] // Transfer the underlying `ArrayBuffer` back to main
                );
            }
        }
        self.addEventListener("message", ({data}) => {
            const action = data && data.type && actions[data.type];
            if (action) {
                action(data);
            }
        });
```

Put the files from those listings on your local server and run them via `pm-example.html` the
way you ran `example.html` earlier. (Or use `https://thenewtoys.dev/bookcode/live/16/`
`pm-example.html`.)

Just like `example.html`, running `pm-example.html` doesn't tie up the UI of the browser while it is running. It also gets almost the same number of hashes calculated (for instance, depending on your hardware, about 350 in total vs. about 380 for the shared memory version). Now try it by adding the query string `?fullspeed` to the URLs (for example, `http://localhost/example.html?fullspeed` and `http://localhost/pm-example.html?fullspeed`, or `https://thenewtoys.dev/bookcode/live/16/example.html?fullspeed` and `https://thenewtoys.dev/bookcode/live/16/pm-example.html?fullspeed`). This disables most of the logging and removes the artificial delay from the consumer's hash calculation. In this full-speed version, you'll probably see a bigger difference (the `postMessage+transferables` version doing roughly 10k hashes vs. the shared memory version doing roughly 18k, again depending on your hardware). So in that case, yes, the shared memory version is faster, though both versions could probably be optimized further. The take-away message is this: don't use shared memory until you know that you really need to use it, because the complexity and opportunity for subtle bugs it adds is very real. If you do really need it, though, hopefully this chapter has given you some basic tools to get to grips with it.

OLD HABITS TO NEW

Most of what you've learned in this chapter relates to new things you couldn't do before and probably won't need to do except in very specific situations. But in those situations, there are a couple of things you can do.

Use Shared Blocks Rather Than Exchanging Large Data Blocks Repeatedly

Old habit: Sending large blocks of data back and forth between threads.

New habit: Share a data block between threads with appropriate synchronization/coordination if you really need to (that is, if transferables aren't enough).

Use Atomics.wait and Atomics.notify Instead of Breaking Up Worker Jobs to Support the Event Loop (Where Appropriate)

Old habit: Artificially breaking up the work in a worker into jobs that it can complete so it can process the next message in the job queue.

New habit: Where appropriate (which it may be sometimes, and won't be other times), consider suspending/resuming the worker via `Atomics.wait` and `Atomics.notify` instead.

17

Miscellany

WHAT'S IN THIS CHAPTER?

- ➤ BigInt
- ➤ Binary integer literals
- ➤ Octal integer literals, take II
- ➤ Optional `catch` bindings
- ➤ New `Math` methods
- ➤ Exponentiation operator
- ➤ Tail call optimization
- ➤ Nullish coalescing
- ➤ Optional chaining
- ➤ Other syntax tweaks and standard library additions
- ➤ Annex B: Browser-only features

CODE DOWNLOADS FOR THIS CHAPTER

You can download the code for this chapter at https://thenewtoys.dev/bookcode or https://www.wiley.com/go/javascript-newtoys.

In this chapter, you'll learn about the various things that didn't really fit anywhere else in the book: BigInt, new forms of numeric literals; various new `Math` methods; the new exponentiation operator (and a "gotcha" about its precedence); tail call optimization (including why you can't rely on it, yet or possibly ever); some other minor changes; and finally, some browser-only features added to Annex B to document what's universally there anyway.

BIGINT

BigInt[1] is a new primitive type for working with large integers in JavaScript, added in ES2020.

BigInt can hold any size of integer, limited only by available memory and/or a reasonable limit imposed by the JavaScript engine's implementers. (Implementer limits are likely to be very, very high. V8 currently allows up to one *billion* bits.) Do you want to hold the number 1,234,567,890,123,456,789,012,345,678 (an integer with 28 significant digits) in a variable? JavaScript's normal number type (Number) can't begin to think about that, not precisely anyway; but BigInt's got you covered.

Because BigInt is a new primitive type, typeof identifies it as "bigint".

BigInts have a literal form (digits with an n suffix, more on that in a bit) and all the usual math operators (+, *, etc.) work with them. For example:

```
let a = 10000000000000000000n;
let b = a / 2n;
console.log(b); // 5000000000000000000n
let c = b * 3n;
console.log(c); // 15000000000000000000n
```

The standard Math *methods* like Math.min *don't* work with them; those methods are Number-specific. (There may well be a follow-on proposal providing some of those methods for BigInts, such as min, max, sign, and such; others like sin and cos probably don't make a lot of sense for an integer-only type.)

Why would you use BigInt? There are two primary use cases:

➤ The name kind of says it: you're dealing with big integers, ones that may be beyond the ability of the Number type to represent accurately (that is, ones greater than 2^{53}).

➤ You're dealing with financial information. The floating-point imprecision of the Number type (the famous 0.1 + 0.2 !== 0.3 problem) makes using it a poor choice for financial tasks, and yet, shopping carts powered by naïve JavaScript code often use them anyway. Instead, you can use BigInt: you work in whole numbers using your currency's smallest unit (or even smaller in some cases). For instance, in the U.S. you might use $1 = 100n—that is, work in cents rather than dollars. (Although for some purposes, $1 = 10000n—hundreds of cents— wouldn't be unusual, deferring any rounding to cents until the final result of the calculation.) Having said that, there's a Decimal type[2] starting out at Stage 1 which might be suitable for financial data. It's not clear whether the proposal will progress, but given the precedent of decimal types in databases and other languages like C# and Java, I wouldn't bet against it.

Let's look at BigInt in a bit more detail.

Creating a BigInt

The simple way to create a BigInt is to use its literal notation, which is like Number's literal notation for integers (almost) with the letter n after it:

```
let i = 12345678901234567890123456789012345678n;
console.log(i);      // 12345678901234567890123456789012345678n
```

---

[1] https://github.com/tc39/proposal-bigint
[2] https://github.com/tc39-transfer/proposal-decimal

Decimal, hexadecimal, and modern octal (not legacy!) are all supported:

```
console.log(10n);    // 10n
console.log(0x10n);  // 16n
console.log(0o10n);  // 8n
```

Scientific notation (specifically e-notation, like `1e3` for `1000`) is not supported; you can't write `1e9n` instead of `1000000000n`. This is primarily because other languages with similar notation don't support it, although those languages also don't have the `n` suffix so their reasons for not supporting it may not quite apply. Support for e-notation may be added by a follow-on proposal if use cases justify it.

You can also create a BigInt using the `BigInt` function, passing it either a string or a number:

```
let i;
// Calling BigInt with a string:
i = BigInt("12345678901234567890012345678");
console.log(i);          // 12345678901234567890012345678n
// Calling BigInt with a number:
i = BigInt(9007199254740992);
console.log(i);          // 9007199254740992n
```

You might be wondering why I used a 28-digit number in that example when calling `BigInt` with a string, but a much smaller number when calling `BigInt` with a number. Can you think of a reason I would do that?

Right! The whole point of BigInt is that it can reliably hold a much larger number than the Number type can. Although the Number type can hold numbers of the same magnitude as the massive number in the example, it can't do so with any precision. If you try to get that number in a Number, the value you actually get is more than 61 *billion* off:

```
// Don't do this
let i = BigInt(12345678901234567890012345678);
console.log(i);              // 1234567890123456850245451776n ?!??!!
```

The reason is that the numeric literal `12345678901234567890012345678` defines a Number; by the time it gets passed into the `BigInt` function, it's already lost precision—it's *already* the number 1,234,567,890,123,456,850,245,451,776 instead of 1,234,567,890,123,456,789,012,345,678 before the `BigInt` function even sees it. Which is why we have BigInt.

Explicit and Implicit Conversion

Neither BigInt nor Number is ever implicitly converted to the other; you can't mix them as operands to the math operators:

```
console.log(1n + 1);
// => TypeError: Cannot mix BigInt and other types, use explicit conversions
```

This is primarily because of the loss of precision: Number can't handle the big integers BigInt handles, and BigInt can't handle the fractional values Number handles. So rather than present programmers with a complex set of rules about what happens when you mix types in the same calculation, JavaScript simply doesn't let you mix them. It's also to leave the door open for adding generalized *value types* to JavaScript at some point in the future.

Explicit conversion *is* allowed. You explicitly convert from Number to BigInt using the `BigInt` function as you saw earlier. If the Number has a fractional portion, `BigInt` throws an error:

```
console.log(BigInt(1.7));
// => RangeError: The number 1.7 cannot be converted to a BigInt
//    because it is not an integer
```

You convert a BigInt to a Number using the `Number` function. If Number can't hold the value precisely because it's too big, then as usual with the Number type, the nearest value it can hold is selected, silently losing precision as the Number type often does. If you want a conversion that doesn't lose precision (throws or returns `NaN` instead), you can write a utility function for it:

```
function toNumber(b) {
    const n = Number(b);
    if (BigInt(n) !== b) {
        const msg = typeof b === "bigint"
            ? `Can't convert BigInt ${b}n to Number, loss of precision`
            : `toNumber expects a BigInt`;
        throw new Error(msg);
        // (or return NaN, depending on your needs)
    }
    return n;
}
```

Unlike strings, BigInts can't be converted to a Number using either unary minus or unary plus:

```
console.log(+"20");
// => 20
console.log(+20n);
// => TypeError: Cannot convert a BigInt value to a number
```

This might seem surprising at first, since until now +n and `Number(n)` have always been the same (assuming `Number` isn't shadowed, and other than the function call), but it turns out to be important for asm.js.[3] (asm.js is a strict subset of JavaScript designed to be extraordinarily optimizable.) Although you can write asm.js code by hand, its primary purpose is to be the output of compilers that take other languages such as C, C++, Java, Python, etc. as their input. Not breaking assumptions made by asm.js was an important design consideration for BigInt.

BigInt can be implicitly converted to string in the usual ways:

```
console.log("$" + 2n); // $2
```

BigInts also support `toString` and `toLocaleString`.

BigInts can be implicitly converted to booleans: `0n` is falsy, all other BigInts are truthy.

Finally, there's only one kind of zero with a BigInt (not zero and "negative zero" as with Number), BigInts are always finite (so there's no `Infinity` or `-Infinity` for BigInt), and they always have a numeric value (there's no `NaN` for BigInt).

Performance

Because BigInt isn't a fixed size like a 32-bit or 64-bit integer type (instead, it can be as large as it needs to be), BigInt performance isn't constant like Number performance is. In general, the larger the

---

[3] http://asmjs.org/

BigInt is, the longer operations on it will take, although of course that's subject to the vagaries of the implementation. Additionally, like most new features, BigInt performance will undoubtedly improve over time as JavaScript engine implementers collect real-world usage information and target their optimizations on the things that will provide real-world benefits.

BigInt64Array and BigUint64Array

A number of applications need integers that are bigger than Number can hold, but which could be held in a 64-bit integer type. For that reason, the BigInt proposal provides two additional typed arrays: `BigInt64Array` and `BigUint64Array`. These are arrays of 64-bit integers, whose values, when retrieved in JavaScript code, are BigInts (just like `Int32Array` and `Uint32Array` are arrays of 32-bit integers whose values, when retrieved in JavaScript code, are Numbers).

Utility Functions

The `BigInt` function has two methods on it, which provide a way to get the value of a BigInt wrapped to a given number of bits, either signed (`asIntN`) or unsigned (`asUintN`):

```
console.log(BigInt.asIntN(16, -20000n));
// => -20000n
console.log(BigInt.asUintN(16, 20000n));
// => 20000n
console.log(BigInt.asIntN(16, 100000n));
// => -31072n
console.log(BigInt.asUintN(16, 100000n));
// => 34464n
```

The first operand is the number of bits, and the second is the BigInt to (potentially) wrap. Notice that since 100,000 can't fit in a 16-bit integer, the value wraps in the usual two's complement way.

When wrapping the BigInt to a signed value, the BigInt is treated as though it were being written to a two's complement N-bit type. When wrapping to an unsigned value, it's like a remainder operation with 2^n, where n is the number of bits.

NEW INTEGER LITERALS

Moving on from BigInt ... ES2015 added two new forms of integer literals (numeric literals that don't have a fractional form): binary and octal.

Binary Integer Literals

A *binary integer literal* is a numeric literal written in binary (base 2; that is, with the digits 0 and 1). You start with 0b (a zero followed by the letter B, case-insensitive) and follow it with the binary digits for the number:

```
console.log(0b100); // 4 (in decimal)
```

As with hexadecimal literals, there is no decimal point in a binary literal. They're *integer* literals rather than *numeric* literals; you can only use them to write whole numbers. That said, just like hex literals, the resulting number is JavaScript's standard number type, which is floating point.

You can include any number of leading zeros after the b; they aren't significant, but they can be useful for aligning code or emphasizing the width of the field of bits you're working with. For instance, if you were defining flags that need to fit in eight bits (perhaps to go in a Uint8Array entry), you could do this:

```
const bitFlags = {
    something:          0b00000001,
    somethingElse:      0b00000010,
    anotherThing:       0b00000100,
    yetAnotherThing:    0b00001000
};
```

But those extra zeros after the 0b are entirely optional. The following code defines exactly the same flags, just (from a style perspective) less clearly:

```
const bitFlags = {
    something:          0b1,
    somethingElse:      0b10,
    anotherThing:       0b100,
    yetAnotherThing:    0b1000
};
```

Octal Integer Literals, Take II

ES2015 adds a new *octal integer literal* form (base 8). It uses the prefix 0o (a zero followed by the letter O, case-insensitive) followed by octal digits (0 through 7):

```
console.log(0o10); // 8 (in decimal)
```

Just as with hexadecimal and binary literals, these are integer literals, but they define standard floating-point numbers.

You might be thinking "Wait, didn't JavaScript already have an octal form?" Right you are! It used to be that just a leading zero followed by octal digits defined a number in octal. For example, 06 defined the number six and 011 defined the number nine. That format was problematic because it was so easily confused with decimal, and because if you included an 8 or 9 in the number, JavaScript engines parsed the number as decimal, leading to the confusing situation where both 011 and 09 defined the number nine:

```
// In loose mode only
console.log(011 === 09); // true
```

How confusing! In the third-edition specification (1999), this legacy octal form was removed as part of the language but left in a "compatibility" section as something implementations could choose to support or not. ES5 (2009) went further and said that in strict mode, a JavaScript implementation was no longer allowed to support legacy octal literals, and moved the "compatibility" information into the browser-only Annex B. (ES2015 further disallowed octal-like decimal literals like 09.) Disallowing the legacy format is one of the many reasons to use strict mode: 011 and 09 are both syntax errors in strict mode, avoiding confusion.

But that's all history. Now if you want to write octal, use the new 0o11 form; if you want to write decimal, leave off unnecessary leading zeros[4] (for instance, use 9, not 09, for the number nine).

---

[4] A leading zero followed by a decimal point, such as 0.1, is fine. It's only when the leading zero is followed by a digit that it's disallowed (for instance, 03 or 01.1).

NEW MATH METHODS

ES2015 added a whole range of new functions to the Math object. In general, they fall into these categories:

➤ General math functions often useful in a range of applications, particularly graphics, geometry, etc.

➤ Functions to support low-level code, such as digital signal processing (DSP) and code compiled to JavaScript from other languages

There's some overlap between the categories, of course, as they're a bit arbitrary. In this section, you'll find most of the ones that overlap in the low-level support category.

General Math Functions

ES2015 added a host of general math functions, primarily trigonometric and logarithmic ones. These functions are useful for graphics processing, 3D geometry, and such. Each of them returns "an implementation-dependent approximation of" its math operation. See Table 17-1, which lists them alphabetically, giving the operation each performs.

TABLE 17-1: General Math Functions

FUNCTION	OPERATION
Math.acosh(x)	The inverse hyperbolic cosine of x
Math.asinh(x)	The inverse hyperbolic sine of x
Math.atanh(x)	The inverse hyperbolic tangent of x
Math.cbrt(x)	The cube root of x
Math.cosh(x)	The hyperbolic cosine of x
Math.expm1(x)	Subtracting 1 from the exponential function of x (e raised to the power of x, where e is the base of the natural logarithms)
Math.hypot(v1, v1, ...)	The square root of the sum of squares of its arguments
Math.log10(x)	The base 10 logarithm of x
Math.log1p(x)	The natural logarithm of 1 + x
Math.log2(x)	The base 2 logarithm of x
Math.sinh(x)	The hyperbolic sine of x
Math.tanh(x)	The hyperbolic tangent of x

The majority of these new methods provide basic trigonometry and logarithm operations.

`Math.expm1` and `Math.log1p` may seem odd at first, since `Math.expm1(x)` is logically the same as `Math.exp(x) - 1` and `Math.log1p(x)` is logically the same as `Math.log(x + 1)`. But in both cases, when x is close to zero, `expm1` and `log1p` can provide a more accurate result than the equivalent code using `exp` or `log` would because of the limits of JavaScript's number type. An implementation can perform the `Math.expm1(x)` calculation using more precision than JavaScript's number type supports, and then convert the final result to a JavaScript number (losing some precision), rather than doing `Math.exp(x)`, converting the result to a JavaScript number (losing some precision), and then subtracting 1 from it within the bounds of the number type's precision. For these operations, when x is close to zero, it helps to delay the loss of precision until after doing the - 1 or 1 + part.

Low-Level Math Support Functions

In the last few years, there's been a lot of interest in and work on using JavaScript as a target for cross-compiling code from other languages, such as C and C++. Usually, the tools that do this compile to asm.js,[5] a highly-optimizable subset of JavaScript. (They also usually have the ability to output WebAssembly[6] instead of, or in addition to, JavaScript.) Two projects that do this, for instance, are Emscripten[7] (which is a back-end for LLVM compilers) and Cheerp[8] (formerly Duetto). To do what they do while targeting asm.js, these tools and others need to do some low-level operations in ways that are both fast and consistent with how they're done in languages with built-in 32-bit integers and floats. Low-level operations are often useful in compression and digital signal processing as well.

ES2015 added some functions to support these tools. By providing specific functions for them, among other things they provided an optimization target for JavaScript engines, sometimes making it possible to replace the function call with a single CPU instruction. The functions are listed alphabetically in Table 17-2 (opposite).

Like all other `Math` functions, if the input isn't a number, it's converted to a number before the operation is done.

EXPONENTIATION OPERATOR (**)

The exponentiation operator (`**`) is the operator equivalent of the `Math.pow` function: it raises a number to the power of another number. (In fact, `Math.pow`'s definition was updated to simply say it returns the result of using `**`.) Here's an example:

```
console.log(2**8); // 256
```

There's a "gotcha" to be aware of: using `x**y` in combination with a unary operator before the base (x), for example `-2**2`. In math, the equivalent expression -2^2 means $-(2^2)$, which is `-4`. But in JavaScript we're used to the unary - being very high precedence, and many of us (most?) would read `-2**2` as `(-2)**2` (which is `4`), despite how you'd read it in math.

---

[5] http://asmjs.org/
[6] https://webassembly.org/
[7] https://github.com/kripken/emscripten
[8] https://leaningtech.com/cheerp/

TABLE 17-2: Low-Level Math Support Functions

FUNCTION	DESCRIPTION

Math.clz32(x)	Converts x to a 32-bit integer, then counts the leading zero bits. For instance, if you call Math.clz32(0b1000), the result is 28 because when 0b1000 is converted to a 32-bit integer the result has 28 0s before the 1:
	
	`0b000000000000000000000000001000`
	`  ^^^^^^^^^^^^^^^^^^^^^^^^^^^^`
	
	This is useful for DSP, compression, encryption, etc. It has built-in support in many languages with an intrinsic 32-bit integer type (such as C and Java).

Math.fround(x)	Gets the value nearest to x that fits in a 32-bit binary floating-point number. Recall that JavaScript's numbers are 64-bit binary floating point ("binary64" in the IEEE-754 specification, commonly called a "double"). Many languages support the 32-bit version, "binary32" (commonly called "float"). This operation provides the (float) x operation of many of those languages that converts a double (x) to the nearest float. fround converts x to a binary32 using the "round ties to even" rounding method, then converts back to binary64, unless that step can be optimized out based on what's being done with the result. ("Round ties to even" means that if there is no exact match for the binary64 value—that is, there are two binary32 values, one numerically smaller and the other numerically larger—pick the one that's an even number.)
Math.imul(x, y)	Multiplies x and y using the rules for 32-bit two's complement integer multiplication with wraparound. This is the equivalent of an x * y operation where x and y are native 32-bit integers.
Math.sign(x)	Returns the sign of x. This is a common operation in many low-level algorithms. Since x is a JavaScript number, this has five possible results (though two of them are nearly always treated the same by code using the result): NaN if x is NaN, -0 if x is -0, +0 if x is +0, -1 if x is negative, and 1 if x is positive.
Math.trunc(x)	Truncates a number to its integer form, simply removing (without rounding) the fractional part. This is the equivalent of (int) x in a language with a 32-bit two's complement integer type (int), except of course that since x and the result are both JavaScript numbers, there are some complexities: NaN, positive infinity, negative infinity, +0, and -0 all result in themselves; a number greater than 0 but less than 1 results in +0; and a number less than 0 but greater than -1 results in -0. Unlike Math.floor and Math.ceil, the result is always the whole number part of the original number, whereas (for instance) Math.floor(-14.2) is -15 because Math.floor always rounds down, even with negative numbers. (You may have seen code along the lines of x = x < 0 ? Math.ceil(x) : Math.floor(x); now that could be just n = Math.trunc(x).) Likewise, you may have seen x = ~~x or x = x | 0 or similar, but those both involve converting x to a 32-bit integer; Math.trunc works with numbers larger than can fit in 32-bit integers.

After extensive discussion and debate,[9] TC39 made `-2**2` a syntax error, so you must write `(-2)**2` or `- (2**2)` instead to avoid the ambiguity. There were strong arguments for using the math convention, and there were strong arguments for keeping unary operators higher precedence than the exponentiation operator. In the end, rather than pick a runner in that race, TC39 went with "make it a syntax error, we can define it later if desirable."

Different implementations use different error messages in that situation, of varying levels of usefulness:

➤ "Unexpected token `**`"

➤ "Unparenthesized unary expression can't appear on the left-hand side of '`**`'"

➤ "Unary operator used immediately before exponentiation expression. Parenthesis (sic) must be used to disambiguate operator precedence"

So if you find yourself staring at an error pointing to what seems, on first glance, to be a perfectly reasonable use of the `**` operator, check to see if you have a unary minus or plus in front of it.

DATE.PROTOTYPE.TOSTRING CHANGE

In ES2018, `Date.prototype.toString` was standardized for the first time. Up through ES2017, the string returned was ". . . an implementation-dependent String value that represents (the date) as a date and time in the current time zone using a convenient, human-readable form." But all significant JavaScript engines had ended up being consistent with one another, so TC39 decided to document the consistency. Per specification it's now reliably:

➤ The three-letter day-of-week abbreviation in English (e.g., "Fri")

➤ The three-letter month abbreviation in English (e.g., "Jan")

➤ The day, zero-padded if necessary (e.g., "05")

➤ The year (e.g., "2019")

➤ The time in 24-hour format (e.g., "19:27:11")

➤ The time zone, in the form GMT followed by +/– and the offset

➤ Optionally, "an implementation-defined" string in parentheses giving the time zone name (such as "Pacific Standard Time")

each separated from its predecessor by a single space. For example:

```
console.log(new Date(2018, 11, 25, 8, 30, 15).toString());
// => Tue Dec 25 2018 08:30:15 GMT-0800 (Pacific Standard Time)
// or
// => Tue Dec 25 2018 08:30:15 GMT-0800
```

---

[9] `https://esdiscuss.org/topic/exponentiation-operator-precedence`

FUNCTION.PROTOTYPE.TOSTRING CHANGE

Recent JavaScript specifications have standardized `Function.prototype.toString`, and ES2019 continues that process[10] by increasing the fidelity of what's returned by using the actual source text that created the function when it's available, but without *requiring* that the host retain the source text (which it might throw away after parsing for memory consumption reasons). Bound functions and other functions provided by the JavaScript engine or environment return a function definition in the following "native function" form:

```
function name(parameters) { [native code] }
```

Functions defined directly by JavaScript source code return either the actual source text that defined them (if available), or a "native function" form as shown in the preceding example. This is a change from ES2018, which said that the JavaScript engine would provide ". . . an implementation-defined string . . ." matching certain criteria.

(There's also a Stage 2 proposal[11] that provides a way for authors to opt-in to a "censored" form, where the source text of the function is never stored, and so `toString` would always return the "native function" form.)

NUMBER ADDITIONS

ES2015 added some new properties and methods to the `Number` constructor.

"Safe" Integers

You probably know that the JavaScript number type[12] is not perfectly precise; it can't be and still be able to handle its huge range of values, including fractional values, while only using 64 bits. Often, instead of the exact number, the number type holds a very close approximation of the number. For instance, the number type can't hold `0.1` perfectly; instead it holds a number *very, very near* `0.1`. The same is true of `0.2` and `0.3`, leading to the famous example that `0.1 + 0.2 != 0.3`. We tend to think of this imprecision only in relation to fractional numbers, but if you have a number big enough, the imprecision occurs even in whole numbers. For example:

```
console.log(33333333333333333333); // 33333333333333330000
```

The number that's created by parsing the numeric literal `33333333333333333333` into a JavaScript number is markedly lower than it would be if numbers were precise at that magnitude. But the number type can't handle that number precisely; it had to round it to the nearest number it can handle precisely, which was several thousand lower.

To account for this, JavaScript has the concept of a *safe integer*. A number is a safe integer if it's an integer whose value is greater than -2^{53} and less than 2^{53}. (The 53 in that comes from the fact that the

---

[10] https://github.com/tc39/Function-prototype-toString-revision
[11] https://github.com/domenic/proposal-function-prototype-tostring-censorship
[12] Which is an implementation of the IEEE-754 double-precision binary floating-point standard.

number type effectively has 53 bits of binary precision; the remaining bits are an exponent.) Within that range, you can be sure that:

➤ The integer is represented exactly in the number type, and

➤ The integer is guaranteed not to be the result of another integer having been rounded to it thanks to floating-point imprecision.

The second rule is important. For instance, 2^{53} is represented exactly in the number type, but the number type can't represent $2^{53} + 1$. If you try, the result is 2^{53}:

```
const a = 2**53;
console.log(a);    // 9007199254740992 (2**53)
const b = a + 1;
console.log(b);    // 9007199254740992 (2**53) (again)
```

Since it might be the result of rounding, 2^{53} isn't "safe." But $2^{53} - 1$ *is* safe, because the number type won't round any imprecise integer to it:

```
const a = 2**53 - 1;
console.log(a);    // 9007199254740991
const b = a + 1;
console.log(b);    // 9007199254740992
const c = a + 2;
console.log(c);    // 9007199254740992
const d = a + 3;
console.log(d);    // 9007199254740994
```

To help you avoid having to write obscure magic numbers like `2**53` and `-(2**53)` in your code, the `Number` constructor has two properties and, probably more important a method to help. Let's look at them.

Number.MAX_SAFE_INTEGER, Number.MIN_SAFE_INTEGER

`Number.MAX_SAFE_INTEGER` is the number $2^{53} - 1$, the maximum safe integer.

`Number.MIN_SAFE_INTEGER` is the number $-2^{53} + 1$, the minimum safe integer.

Number.isSafeInteger

`Number.isSafeInteger` is a static method that accepts an argument and returns `true` if the argument is of the number type, is an integer, and is in the range of safe integers; if it's not a number, not an integer, or outside the range, `isSafeInteger` returns `false`:

```
console.log(Number.isSafeInteger(42));           // true
console.log(Number.isSafeInteger(2**53 - 1));    // true
console.log(Number.isSafeInteger(-(2**53) + 1)); // true
console.log(Number.isSafeInteger(2**53));        // false (not safe)
console.log(Number.isSafeInteger(-(2**53)));     // false (not safe)
console.log(Number.isSafeInteger(13.4));         // false (not an integer)
console.log(Number.isSafeInteger("1"));          // false (string, not number)
```

When dealing with integers of such magnitude that you may be pushing the limits of safe integers, two handy rules are that when performing the operation `c = a + b` or `c = a - b`, you can be certain of the result in `c` if `Number.isSafeInteger(a)`, `Number.isSafeInteger(b)`, and `Number.isSafeInteger(c)` are *all* `true`; otherwise, the result may not be correct. It's not sufficient to only test `c`.

Number.isInteger

`Number.isInteger` is a static method that accepts an argument and returns `true` if (you guessed it!) the argument is a number and also an integer. It doesn't attempt to coerce its argument to number, so `Number.isInteger("1")` is `false`.

Number.isFinite, Number.isNaN

`Number.isFinite` and `Number.isNaN` are just like their global counterparts `isFinite` and `isNaN`, except that they don't coerce their argument to number before doing their check. Instead, if you pass them a non-number, they return `false`.

`Number.isFinite` determines if its argument is a number and, if so, whether that number is finite. It returns `false` for `NaN`:

```
const s = "42";
console.log(Number.isFinite(s));       // false: it's a string, not a number
console.log(isFinite(s));              // true: the global function coerces
console.log(Number.isFinite(42));      // true
console.log(Number.isFinite(Infinity)); // false
console.log(Number.isFinite(1 / 0));   // false: in JavaScript x / 0 = Infinity
```

`Number.isNaN` determines if its argument is a number and, if so, whether it's one of the `NaN` values:

```
const s = "foo";
console.log(Number.isNaN(s));   // false: it's a string, not a number
console.log(isNaN(s));          // true: the global function coerces
const n1 = 42;
console.log(Number.isNaN(n1));  // false
console.log(isNaN(n1));         // false
const n2 = NaN;
console.log(Number.isNaN(n2));  // true
console.log(isNaN(n2));         // true
```

Number.parseInt, Number.parseFloat

These are the same functions as the global `parseInt` and `parseFloat`. (Literally the same, `Number.parseInt === parseInt` is `true`.) They're part of the ongoing move toward reducing reliance on default globals.

Number.EPSILON

`Number.EPSILON` is a data property whose value is the difference between 1 and the smallest value greater than 1 that can be represented as a JavaScript number value (it's approximately $2.220446049250313080847262633361816 \times 10^{-16}$). The term comes from *machine epsilon*, a measurement of floating-point rounding error in numerical analysis, which is denoted with the Greek letter epsilon (ϵ) or a bold Roman **u**.

SYMBOL.ISCONCATSPREADABLE

As you may know, the `concat` method on arrays accepts an arbitrary number of arguments and creates a new array with the entries from the original array plus the arguments you give it. If any of those arguments is an array, it "flattens" the array's entries (one level of them) into the resulting array:

```
const a = ["one", "two"];
const b = ["four", "five"];
console.log(a.concat("three", b));
// => ["one", "two", "three", "four", "five"]
```

Originally, `concat` only spread out the entries of standard arrays in this way. Famously, it didn't do that with the `arguments` pseudo-array, or other array-like objects such as the DOM's `NodeList`.

As of ES2015, `concat` was updated so that it will spread out any argument that's a standard array (according to `Array.isArray`), or that has the `Symbol.isConcatSpreadable` property with a truthy value.

For instance, in the following example, `obj` is array-like, but it doesn't get spread into the result by `concat`; instead, the object is put in the resulting array:

```
const a = ["one", "two"];
const obj = {
    0: "four",
    1: "five",
    length: 2
};
console.log(a.concat("three", obj));
// => ["one", "two", "three", {"0": "four", "1": "five", length: 2}]
```

But if you add `Symbol.isConcatSpreadable` to it with a truthy value, `concat` will spread its entries out as well:

```
const a = ["one", "two"];
const obj = {
    0: "four",
    1: "five",
    length: 2,
    [Symbol.isConcatSpreadable]: true
};
console.log(a.concat("three", obj));
// => ["one", "two", "three", "four", "five"]
```

Having it might be handy on the prototype of an array-like class that doesn't inherit from `Array`:

```
class Example {
    constructor(...entries) {
        this.length = 0;
        this.add(...entries);
    }
    add(...entries) {
        for (const entry of entries) {
            this[this.length++] = entry;
        }
    }
}
```

```
Example.prototype[Symbol.isConcatSpreadable] = true;

const a = ["one", "two"];
const e = new Example("four", "five");
console.log(a.concat("three", e));
// => ["one", "two", "three", "four", "five"]
```

When ES2015 was being defined, there was talk of the DOM's `NodeList` and similar possibly adding this property so they'd be `concat` spreadable, but it hasn't ended up happening (as yet).

No object in the JavaScript standard library has the `Symbol.isConcatSpreadable` property by default. (Not even arrays, but as described, `concat` checks for arrays explicitly.)

VARIOUS SYNTAX TWEAKS

In this section, you'll learn about some recent syntax tweaks—some of which are *really* useful.

Nullish Coalescing

When dealing with optional properties in an object, programmers often use the curiously powerful logical OR operator (||) to provide a default for the possibly missing property:

```
const delay = this.settings.delay || 300;
```

As you probably know, the || operator evaluates its left-hand operand and, if that value is truthy, takes that truthy value as its result; otherwise, it evaluates the right-hand operand and takes that value as its result. Because of that, the example sets the `delay` constant to the value of `this.settings.delay` if it's a truthy value, or to 300 if `this.settings.delay` is a falsy value. But there's a problem: the programmer probably meant to use 300 only if the property wasn't there or had the value `undefined`, but that code will also use 300 if `this.settings.delay` is 0, because 0 is falsy.

A new operator in ES2020[13] fixes that—the "nullish coalescing operator" (??):

```
const delay = this.settings.delay ?? 300;
```

That example sets `delay` to the value of `this.settings.delay` if that value isn't `null` or `undefined`, or to 300 if `this.settings.delay` is `null` or `undefined`. That statement using ?? is like this one using the conditional operator

```
// Recall that `== null` (loose equality) checks for both `null` and `undefined`
const delay = this.settings.delay == null ? 300 : this.settings.delay;
```

except that `this.settings.delay` is only evaluated once in the ?? expression.

---

[13] https://github.com/tc39/proposal-nullish-coalescing

Since the nullish coalescing operator short-circuits the same way || does, the right-hand operand isn't evaluated at all if the left-hand operand isn't `null` or `undefined`. That means any side effects in the right-hand operand aren't performed if it's not used. For instance:

```
obj.id = obj.id ?? nextId++;
```

In that code, `nextId` is only incremented if `obj.id` is `null` or `undefined`.

Optional Chaining

Have you ever had to write code like this?

```
x = some && some.deeply && some.deeply.nested && some.deeply.nested.value;
y = some && some[key] && some[key].prop;
```

Or like this?

```
if (x.callback) {
    x.callback();
}
```

With the optional chaining operator[14] in ES2020 you can write this

```
x = some?.deeply?.nested?.value;
y = some?.[key]?.prop;
```

and this

```
x.callback?.();
```

instead. The `?.` operator evaluates its left-hand operand and, if that value is `null` or `undefined`, results in `undefined` and short-circuits the rest of the chain; otherwise, it does a property access and allows the chain to continue. In the second form (`x.callback?.()`), if the left-hand operand is not `null` or `undefined`, it allows the call to continue.

This is handy when a property may or may not exist on an object (or may exist with the value `undefined` or `null`), or when you're getting an object from an API function that may return `null` and you want to get a property from that object:

```
const x = document.getElementById("#optional")?.value;
```

In that code, if the element doesn't exist, `getElementById` returns `null`, so the optional chaining operator's result is `undefined`, which is stored in x. But if the element exists, `getElementById` returns the element and x is set to the value of the element's `value` property.

Similarly, if an element may or may not exist and you want to call a method on it:

```
document.getElementById("optional")?.addEventListener("click", function() {
    // ...
});
```

---

[14] https://github.com/tc39/proposal-optional-chaining

the function call isn't made if the element doesn't exist. Here are some further examples:

```
const some = {
    deeply: {
        nested: {
            value: 42,
            func() {
                return "example";
            }
        },
        nullAtEnd: null
    },
    nullish1: null,
    nullish2: undefined
};
console.log(some?.deeply?.nested?.value);    // 42
console.log(some?.missing?.value);           // undefined, not an error
console.log(some?.nullish1?.value);          // undefined, not an error, not null
console.log(some?.nullish2?.value);          // undefined, not an error
let k = "nested";
console.log(some?.deeply?.[k]?.value);       // 42
k = "nullish1";
console.log(some?.deeply?.[k]?.value);       // undefined, not an error, not null
k = "nullish2";
console.log(some?.deeply?.[k]?.value);       // undefined, not an error
k = "oops";
console.log(some?.deeply?.[k]?.value);       // undefined, not an error
console.log(some?.deeply?.nested?.func?.()); // "example"
console.log(some?.missing?.stuff?.func?.()); // undefined, not an error
console.log(some?.deeply?.nullAtEnd?.());    // undefined, not an error
console.log(some?.nullish1?.func?.());       // undefined, not an error
k = "nullish2";
console.log(some?.[k]?.func?.());            // undefined, not an error
```

Note that even when the property being tested is null, the result of the optional chaining operator is undefined. In the previous example, you can see that on this line:

```
console.log(some?.nullish1?.value);                 // undefined, not an error, not null
```

Also note that using the optional chaining operator just once at the outset doesn't make the "optional-ness" carry over to subsequent property accessors or calls. For example:

```
const obj = {
    foo: {
        val: 42
    }
};
console.log(obj?.bar.val); // TypeError: Cannot read property 'val' of undefined
```

That would have output undefined if obj were null or undefined, because the optional chaining operator was used to defend against obj being null or undefined via obj?.bar. But obj is an object, so obj.bar is evaluated. Since there is no bar property on obj, that results in undefined.

Since optional chaining wasn't used to defend against that when accessing `val`, the code tries to get `val` from `undefined` and fails with an error.

To avoid that error, you'd use optional chaining when accessing `val`:

```
console.log(obj?.bar?.val);
```

Similarly, with that same object, this would fail:

```
obj?.bar(); // TypeError: obj.bar is not a function
```

Since there's no `?.` after `bar`, nothing checks it before trying to make the call. The rule is: the `?` is immediately after the thing that may be nullish.

Optional catch Bindings

Sometimes you don't care what error occurred, you just need to know whether something worked or failed. In that situation, it's common to see code like this:

```
try {
    theOperation();
} catch (e) {
    doSomethingElse();
}
```

Note that the code doesn't use the error (`e`) for anything.

As of ES2019, you can just leave the parentheses and binding (`e`) off entirely:

```
try {
    theOperation();
} catch {
    doSomethingElse();
}
```

It's almost universally supported in modern browsers, only Edge Legacy doesn't support it (but the Chromium version of Edge does). Obsolete browsers like Internet Explorer don't support it, of course.

Unicode Line Breaks in JSON

Okay, so this one is unlikely to have an impact on your day-to-day coding life.

Notionally, JSON is a strict subset of JavaScript, but that wasn't actually true until a change was made for ES2019 to allow two characters to appear unescaped in string literals that previously had to be escaped: Unicode's "line separator" (U+2028) and "paragraph separator" (U+2029) characters. JSON allowed them to be unescaped in strings, but JavaScript didn't, making for unnecessary complication in the specification.

As of ES2019,[15] they're both valid in JavaScript string literals without needing to be escaped.

---

[15] https://github.com/tc39/proposal-json-superset

Well-Formed JSON from JSON.stringify

This one probably won't show up on your radar either, but: technically, in some edge cases, JSON.stringify has been producing invalid JSON. You may remember from Chapter 10 that a JavaScript string is a series of UTF-16 code units that tolerates invalid (unpaired) surrogates. If a string value being stringified contains unpaired surrogates, the resulting JSON will contain the unpaired surrogates as literal characters, which makes it invalid JSON.

The change (in ES2019) is simply to have unpaired surrogates output as Unicode escapes.[16] So, for instance, instead of outputting the unpaired surrogate U+DEAD as a literal character, it outputs the Unicode escape sequence \uDEAD instead.

VARIOUS STANDARD LIBRARY / GLOBAL ADDITIONS

In this section you'll learn about various new methods becoming available in JavaScript's standard library, as well as some changes to existing methods.

Symbol.hasInstance

You can use the Symbol.hasInstance well-known symbol to customize the behavior of instanceof for a given function. Normally, x instanceof F checks to see if F.prototype is anywhere in the prototype chain of x. But if F[Symbol.hasInstance] is a function, that function gets called instead, and whatever it returns is converted to boolean and taken as the result of instanceof:

```
function FakeDate() { }
Object.defineProperty(FakeDate, Symbol.hasInstance, {
    value(value) { return value instanceof Date; }
});
console.log(new Date() instanceof FakeDate); // true
```

This is useful for some host-provided objects, and for codebases where prototypes and constructor functions largely aren't used in favor of builder functions that assign each object all of its properties and methods directly. They can use Symbol.hasInstance to return true for objects with the appropriate properties/methods, even though they don't have matching prototype.

Symbol.unscopables

This Symbol is to support legacy code; you're unlikely to need to use it in your code unless you're writing a library that A) may be added to a site with legacy code *and* B) adds methods to built-in prototypes.

Symbol.unscopables lets you specify which properties of an object should be left out when that object is used with the with statement. Modern JavaScript code doesn't usually use the with statement and it's disallowed in strict mode, but you may know that with adds *all* of an object's properties to the scope chain within the with block, even non-enumerable and/or inherited properties (like toString):

---

[16] https://github.com/gibson042/ecma262-proposal-well-formed-stringify

```
const obj = {
    a: 1,
    b: 2
};
with (obj) {
    console.log(a, b, typeof toString); // 1 2 "function"
}
```

You can tell `with` to leave out one or more properties by listing them with a truthy value in an object on the `Symbol.unscopables` property:

```
const obj = {
    a: 1,
    b: 2,
    [Symbol.unscopables]: {
        b: true      // Makes `b` unscopable, leaving it out of `with` blocks
    }
};
with (obj) {
    console.log(a, b, typeof toString); // ReferenceError: b is not defined
}
```

Why would you need such a thing? Perhaps for the reason TC39 did: TC39 needed it when adding methods to `Array.prototype`; the new methods conflicted with existing code using `with`. For instance, suppose some legacy code had this function:

```
function findKeys(arrayLikes) {
    var keys = [];
    with (Array.prototype) {
        forEach.call(arrayLikes, function(arrayLike) {
            push.apply(keys, filter.call(arrayLike, function(value) {
                return rexIsKey.test(value);
            }));
        });
    }
    return keys;
}
```

That code uses `with` to put `forEach`, `push`, and `filter` in scope within the block so they can easily be used on the array-like objects being passed in. It would have broken when the `keys` method was added in ES2015 because within the `with` block, the `keys` identifier would have resolved to the property instead of the `keys` variable the function is using.

Thanks to `Symbol.unscopables`, that code isn't broken by the `keys` method because `Array.prototype`'s `Symbol.unscopables` property lists all of string-named methods added to `Array.prototype` in ES2015 onward, including `keys`; so `keys` is skipped in the `with` block.

globalThis

JavaScript is getting a new default global: `globalThis`.[17] `globalThis` is the same value that `this` has at global scope, which is usually a reference to the global object although the host (for instance, browser) can define any value as `this` at global scope, and thus as `globalThis`. If you're used to writing code on

---

[17] https://github.com/tc39/proposal-global

browsers, you probably know that browsers already have a global variable for this: `window`. (Actually, they have at least three, but that's beside the point.) But until `globalThis`, there was no standard global for this outside of browsers, and it was quite awkward to access the global object in the (relatively rare) situation where you needed to in a cross-environment manner:

➤ Node.js provides `global` (which turned out couldn't be standardized on browsers as it would break some existing code on the web).

➤ At global scope, you can use `this` (which is how `globalThis` got its name), but a lot of code doesn't run at global scope (for instance, code in modules, as you learned in Chapter 13).

`globalThis` makes it easy to access the same value `this` has at global scope, which in almost all environments is a reference to the global object.

Symbol description Property

As you learned in Chapter 5, Symbols can have descriptions:

```
const s = Symbol("example");
console.log(s); // Symbol(example)
```

Initially, you could only access that description via `toString`. As of ES2019, Symbols have a description property you can get it from:[18]

```
const s = Symbol("example");
console.log(s.description); // example
```

String.prototype.matchAll

Often, if you have a regular expression with a global or sticky flag, you want to process all of the matches in a string. You can do that with the `exec` function of a RegExp object and a loop:

```
const s = "Testing 1 2 3";
const rex = /\d/g;
let m;
while ((m = rex.exec(s)) !== null) {
    console.log(`"${m[0]}" at ${m.index}, rex.lastIndex: ${rex.lastIndex}`);
}
// => "1" at 8, rex.lastIndex: 9
// => "2" at 10, rex.lastIndex: 11
// => "3" at 12, rex.lastIndex: 13
```

That's a bit verbose, though, and it involves modifications to the `lastIndex` property of the RegExp object (a well-documented issue with the RegExp object). Instead, a `String.prototype.matchAll` method was added to ES2020[19] that returns an iterator for the matches, and leaves the RegExp object's properties untouched:

```
const rex = /\d/g;
for (const m of "Testing 1 2 3".matchAll(rex)) {
    console.log(`"${m[0]}" at ${m.index}, rex.lastIndex: ${rex.lastIndex}`);
}
```

---

[18] https://github.com/tc39/proposal-Symbol-description
[19] https://github.com/tc39/proposal-string-matchall

```
// => "1" at 8, rex.lastIndex: 0
// => "2" at 10, rex.lastIndex: 0
// => "3" at 12, rex.lastIndex: 0
```

In addition to leaving `lastIndex` alone, it's more compact, providing a convenient iterator. It's especially powerful with destructuring, particularly with named capture groups:

```
const s = "Testing a-1, b-2, c-3";
for (const {index, groups: {type, num}} of s.matchAll(/(?<type>\w)-(?<num>\d)/g)) {
    console.log(`"${type}": "${num}" at ${index}`);
}
// => "a": "1" at 8
// => "b": "2" at 13
// => "c": "3" at 18
```

ANNEX B: BROWSER-ONLY FEATURES

Before getting into the meat of this section, just a quick note: you can't use some of what's here in strict mode, and you probably *shouldn't* use any of it at all.[20] Annex B is about defining legacy behavior for JavaScript engines running in web browsers. In new code, don't rely on legacy behavior.

Given that, two questions might come to your mind:

➤ What's the point of Annex B?

➤ Why include Annex B features, which are by definition legacy features, in a book about the *new* toys?

Annex B is in the spec both to document and constrain what JavaScript engines in web browsers do that is mostly outside the standard language, but which anyone building a JavaScript engine would need to know (and do) if they wanted to use that engine in a web browser dealing with real-world code. The legacy features that are newly documented in ES2015+ are included in this book (very minimally) for completeness.

What's in Annex B, then? Some early features of JavaScript were sufficiently problematic (such as the `getYear` and `setYear` methods of dates, as opposed to `getFullYear` and `setFullYear`) that ES2 documented them but with the note that they were "not part of this specification." ES3 relegated those things plus some others (like those legacy octal literals that were easily confused for decimal) to an "informational" compatibility section at the end: Annex B. Separately, almost since JavaScript's inception browsers have been extending JavaScript beyond what the specification describes, and some minor features (`escape`, `unescape`, etc.) defined by browsers were included in Annex B as a means of documenting and softly (at that time) specifying the common behavior they had. ES5 added one more method to the annex, but otherwise didn't change much.

It was ES2015 that aggressively documented the common behavior (where possible) of a large number of extensions common to web browsers, and also *required* for the first time that the features in Annex B must be provided by browser-hosted JavaScript engines. In theory, JavaScript engines *outside* of web browsers don't implement Annex B features, although in practice an engine built for use both inside and outside browsers is unlikely to increase complexity by disabling them in non-browser environments.

---

[20] With the one exception of HTML-like comments in a true, properly served XHTML page if the script really needs to be inline. True, properly served XHTML pages are rare.

This section covers the additions to Annex B in ES2015+: HTML-like comments, additions/changes to regular expressions, additional properties and methods on `Object.prototype`, `String.prototype`, and `RegExp.prototype`, an addition to object initializer syntax, various bits of loosened or obscure syntax for backward-compatibility, and some really special behavior for `document.all`.

But seriously: don't use them in new code.

HTML-Like Comments

JavaScript engines have long tolerated HTML comments wrapped around script code. This was primarily to support the practice of "commenting out" inline code in a `script` tag, either for *very* old browsers that didn't handle the `script` tag at all (and showed its contents in the document), or as part of a CDATA wrapper for XHTML browsers. That looks like this (or one of many variations, or indeed many incorrect attempts at doing this):

```
<script type="text/javascript"><!--//--><![CDATA[//><!--
// ...code...
//--><!]]></script>
```

Notice how the first thing inside what's supposed to be JavaScript code is an HTML-like comment. Annex B was updated in ES2015 to specify the behavior.

Regular Expression Tweaks

Annex B changes regular expressions in fairly small ways: a very small extension to control escapes in character classes, tolerating unmatched closing square brackets (`]`) and invalid quantifier groups (`{}`, `{foo}`), and adding a `compile` method.

Control Character Escape (\cX) Extension

Annex B allows digits (in addition to the usual letters) in control escapes (`\cX`), but only if the control escape is within a character class (`[]`). The same formula that applies to letters determines the control character to match: the code point of x `%` 32. For example, here's a valid control escape:

```
console.log(/\cC/.test("\u0003")); // true
```

That's true because `\cC` specifies control character #3 ("control c") because the code point of C is 67 and 67 `%` 32 is 3.

In standard (non-Annex B) regular expressions, `\c` can only be followed by an English letter (A–Z, case-insensitive), as in the previous example. Annex B allows digits after it as well, *but* only when it's in the character class (`[ ]`). For example:

```
console.log(/[\c4]/.test("\u0014")); // true
console.log(/\c4/.test("\u0014"));   // false
console.log(/\c4/.test("\\c4"));     // true
```

The first example matches `\u0014` because the `\c4` is in a character class, the code point of 4 is 52, and 52 `%` 32 is 20, which is 0x14 in hex. The second example doesn't match because it's not in a character class, so `\c4` isn't a control escape and falls back to defining a match for `\ c 4` as individual characters, as you can see from the third example.

Tolerating Invalid Sequences

A couple of invalid sequences are allowed in Annex B that aren't allowed by the main specification's grammar, such as an unescaped closing square bracket (`]`) with no opening one (with an opening one, it would form a character class, `[...]`), and an unescaped opening curly brace that doesn't define a quantifier. The following work in engines applying Annex B syntax, but would be errors in engines that didn't:

```
const mismatchedBracket = /]/;   // Should be /\]/
console.log(mismatchedBracket.test("testing ] one two three")); // true
console.log(mismatchedBracket.test("no brackets here"));         // false
const invalidQuanitfier = /{}/;  // Should be /\{\}/
console.log(invalidQuanitfier.test("use curly braces ({})"));    // true
console.log(invalidQuanitfier.test("nothing curly here"));       // false
```

RegExp.prototype.compile

Annex B adds a `compile` method to `RegExp` objects. It completely re-initializes the object on which it's called, changing it to a completely different regular expression:

```
const rex = /^test/;
console.log(rex.test("testing")); // true
rex.compile(/^ing/);
console.log(rex.test("testing")); // false
rex.compile("ing$");
console.log(rex.test("testing")); // true
```

`compile` accepts essentially the same parameters as the `RegExp` constructor, including a `RegExp` instance as the first parameter (in which case that instance's pattern and flags are used) or a string as the first parameter and flags as an optional second parameter. One small difference is that the `RegExp` constructor allows you to pass in a RegExp object as the first argument and new flags as a string in the second argument. `RegExp.compile` does not, you can't specify new flags if providing a RegExp instance as the first argument.

Annex B notes that using `compile` *could* be used as a signal to the JavaScript engine that the regular expression is intended to be reused and may be a good candidate for optimization. However, JavaScript engines generally optimize based on measuring live code performance and aggressively optimizing code that is used frequently, so that hint may not be of any value to a given engine.

Additional Built-In Properties

The built-in objects have some additional properties defined by Annex B.

Additional Object Properties

You learned about one of the Annex B additions to objects in Chapter 5: `__proto__`, both the accessor property defined on `Object.prototype` and the additional object initializer syntax for it.

Annex B also defines some other properties on `Object.prototype` for backward-compatibility with code that relied on extensions SpiderMonkey (Mozilla's JavaScript engine) added for accessor properties before the standard had them: `__defineGetter__`, `__defineSetter__`, `__lookupGetter__`, `__lookupSetter__`. They do exactly what they sound like they do—define and look up getter and setter functions for properties:

```
"use strict";
const obj = {x: 10};
obj.__defineGetter__("xDoubled", function() {
    return this.x * 2;
});
console.log(obj.x);
// => 10
console.log(obj.xDoubled);
// => 20
try {
    obj.xDoubled = 27;
} catch (e) {
    console.error(e.message);
    // => Cannot set property xDoubled of #<Object> which has only a getter
}
obj.__defineSetter__("xDoubled", function(value) {
    this.x = value / 2;
});
obj.xDoubled = 84;
console.log(obj.x);         // 42

console.log(obj.__lookupGetter__("xDoubled").toString());
// =>
// "function() {
//     return this.x * 2;
// }"
console.log(obj.__lookupSetter__("xDoubled").toString());
// =>
// "function(value) {
//     this.x = value / 2;
// }"
```

One non-obvious thing to note is that the "define" methods define the accessor on the object you call them on, but the "lookup" methods will follow the prototype chain if the object you call them on doesn't have the relevant accessor. (This is just like properties: setting a property assigns it to the object directly, but getting a property goes up the prototype chain.) If the "lookup" method returns a function, it may be defined on the object itself, its prototype, or its prototype's prototype, etc.

You wouldn't use these methods in new code. Instead, you'd use standard accessor property notation (`get foo()`, `set foo()`) when first creating the object, or if you wanted to add an accessor after the fact, you'd use `Object.defineProperty` or `Object.defineProperties`. To get the function for an accessor, you'd use `Object.getOwnPropertyDescriptor` (using `Object.getPrototypeOf` if you want to follow the prototype chain like the "lookup" methods do).

Additional String Methods

Annex B adds several string methods: `substr`, and a bunch of methods that wrap the string in HTML tags.

Just like `substring`, `substr` produces a substring of the string, but it accepts different arguments: the starting index and *length* of the substring, instead of `substring`'s starting and ending indexes. It also allows the starting index to be negative, in which case it's an offset from the end of the string:

```
const str = "testing one two three";
console.log(str.substr(8, 3)); // "one"
console.log(str.substr(-5));   // "three"
```

The HTML methods are `anchor`, `big`, `blink`, `bold`, `fixed`, `fontcolor`, `fontsize`, `italics`, `link`, `small`, `strike`, `sub`, and `sup`. They literally just put start and end tags on the string:

```
console.log("testing".sub()); "<sub>testing</sub>"
```

Don't use them in new code (not least because the majority of those HTML tags are deprecated anyway).

Various Bits of Loosened or Obscure Syntax

Annex B allows some syntax in loose mode that isn't in the main specification. None of the following is valid in strict mode; they all produce syntax errors. Since I strongly recommend using strict mode in all new code (and it's the default in modules and `class` constructs), this is, again, just information about things you may find in old code.

With Annex B's syntax, you can put a label in front of a function declaration (provided it's not a generator function):

```
label: function example() { }
```

There doesn't seem to be any point to the label, but (as with most Annex B "features") apparently it was allowed in an engine back in the day and so engines need to allow it in order to support obsolete code.

Similarly, you can have a function declaration attached to an `if` statement (without a block) or its `else` (again without a block), like this:

```
if (Math.random() < 0.5)
    function example() {
        console.log("1");
    }
else
    function example() {
        console.log("2");
    }
example();
```

Even now that function declarations are allowed in blocks (as you learned in Chapter 3), that example would be invalid without Annex B semantics because there aren't blocks around the function declarations. For compatibility with old code, they're allowed in loose mode only.

The loosened syntax also allows you to redeclare the `catch` binding with `var` in the `catch` block:

```
try {
    // ...
} catch (e) {
    var e;
    // ...
}
```

(That var could also be in a for or for-in loop initializer, but not a for-of loop initializer.) Without Annex B syntax, that would be a syntax error. With Annex B syntax, it declares a variable in the function (or global) scope where the code appears, but e within the catch block is still the catch binding, and assigning to it assigns to the catch binding, not to the variable:

```
"use strict";
function example() {
    e = 1;
    console.log(e);        // 1
    try {
        throw new Error("blah");
    } catch (e) {
        var e;             // Would be a SyntaxError if not for Annex B syntax
        e = 42;
        console.log(e);    // 42
    }
    console.log(e);        // 1
}
example();
```

Don't do that in new code. But there may be legacy code from 1996 on the web that still has it . . .

Finally (and this is a curious one), did you know that you could put an initializer on the variable in a for-in loop? You can with Annex B syntax:

```
const obj = {
    a: 1,
    b: 2
};
for (var name = 42 in obj) {
    console.log(name);
}
// =>
// "a"
// "b"
```

It only works with var, not let or const, and doesn't work in strict mode. The initializer is evaluated and assigned to the variable, and then immediately overwritten by the first property name in the object, so you never see it in the loop. But an initializer with side-effects is observable:

```
for (var name = console.log("hi") in {}) { // "hi"
}
let n = 1;
for (var name2 = n = 42 in {}) {
}
console.log(n);                            // => 42
```

You'll never write that, but if you see it in legacy code, at least now you know why it's not causing an error and what it does (so you can safely fix it, for instance).

When document.all Isn't There . . . or Is It?

This one's fun enough to take a moment to tell the story.

In the early days of the web, document.all was a Microsoft feature in Internet Explorer (IE): a collection of *all* of the elements in the document (with various properties for sub-collections of subsets of elements) that you could iterate over or look elements up in by their `id` or `name`. In contrast, Netscape Navigator (the other major browser at the time) used the fledging DOM standard (`getElementById` and such). Code written to work with both had to choose which to use. Sometimes programmers did that like this:

```
if (document.getElementById) { // or various variations
    // ...use getElementById and other DOM-isms...
} else {
    // ...use document.all and other Microsoft-isms...
}
```

Other times they did it the other way around, which is the problem:

```
if (document.all) {
    // ...use document.all and other Microsoft-isms...
} else {
    // ...use getElementById and other DOM-isms...
}
```

In place of `if (document.all)` they might use `if (typeof document.all !== "undefined")` or `if (document.all != undefined)`, but the intent was the same.

Of course, things moved on, and Microsoft implemented DOM standards, but not all web pages updated their script. Newer (at the time) browsers like Chrome, looking to support pages even if they were written for IE, included support for Microsoft-isms like `document.all` (and the global `event` variable and such).

Fast forward several years, and any page that checked for `document.all` instead of checking for `getElementById` would work just as well going along its DOM path rather than its Microsoft path, and browser makers wanted to make that happen. One way, of course, would be to drop `document.all`. But browser makers didn't want to drop support for `document.all` *entirely*, because they wanted to continue to support pages that used it without a check. What to do?

The solution was both ingenious and horrifying: they made `document.all` the only "falsy" object. More specifically, they gave it some very interesting features:

➤ It coerces to `false` instead of `true` when you coerce it to boolean.

➤ When you apply `typeof` to it, the result is `"undefined"`.

➤ When you use `==` to compare it to `null` or `undefined`, the result is `true` (and of course, `!=` comparisons are `false`).

That way, the `if (document.all)` and similar checks act as though `document.all` wasn't there, but code that doesn't do a check at all still works, because `document.all` *is* there and does still (for now) work.

Annex B defines this functionality for an object with an internal slot called [[IsHTMLDDA]]. `document.all` is the only such object, at least for now.

TAIL CALL OPTIMIZATION

In theory, ES2015+ requires that a JavaScript engine implement *tail call optimization* (TCO), which is primarily useful in situations involving recursion. In fact, only one JavaScript engine supports TCO and that seems unlikely to change any time soon. More on that in a moment.

First, a brief reminder about the stack and stack frames. Consider this code:

```
"use strict";
function first(n) {
    n = n - 1;
    return second(n);
}
function second(m) {
    return m * 2;
}
const result = first(22);
console.log(result); // 42
```

Without TCO, when the JavaScript engine handles the call to `first`, it pushes a *stack frame* on the stack with the address to return to, the arguments to pass to `first` (22), and perhaps some other book-keeping information, then jumps to the beginning of `first`'s code. When `first` calls `second`, the engine pushes another stack frame on the stack with the return address, etc., in it. When `second` returns, its frame is popped off the stack. When `first` returns, its frame is popped off the stack. See Figure 17-1.

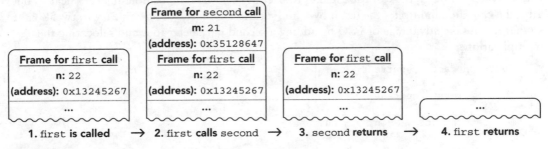

FIGURE 17-1

Since the stack isn't infinite, it can only hold so many stack frames before it runs out of room. You've probably accidentally written code that called itself endlessly (directly or indirectly) and seen a stack overflow error like this one:

```
RangeError: Maximum call stack size exceeded
```

If you look at `first`, though, you can see that calling `second` is the very last thing that `first` does before returning, and `first` returns the result of calling `second`. That means the call to `second` is a *tail call* (a call in the *tail position*).

With TCO, the engine can pop the stack frame for `first` off the stack before calling `second`; it just has to give `second`'s stack frame the return address `first` would have returned to. Other than that return address, `first`'s stack frame doesn't have much purpose, so TCO can eliminate it. See Figure 17-2.

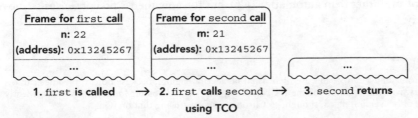

FIGURE 17-2

With this specific example, getting rid of `first`'s stack frame before calling `second` doesn't really make much difference. But particularly when you're dealing with recursion, avoiding having those frames on the stack can make a big difference. For instance, consider this classic factorial function:

```
function fact(v) {
    if (v <= 1n) {
        return v;
    }
    return v * fact(v - 1n);
}
console.log(fact(5n)); // 120
```

(I'm using BigInt in that code so that it's not limited by the capacity of the number type.) The size of the stack limits the factorials `fact` can calculate, because if it starts with a big enough number (say, 100000), all those stack frames from the recursive calls overflow the stack:

```
console.log(fact(100000n));
// => RangeError: Maximum call stack size exceeded
```

Unfortunately, though, the call `fact` makes to itself isn't in the tail position. It's very near it, but after the call `fact` multiplies the result by `v` and returns that instead. But it's easy to tweak `fact` so that it can take advantage of TCO by adding a second parameter to it and relocating the multiplication:

```
function fact(v, current = 1n) {
    if (v <= 1n) {
        return current;
    }
    return fact(v - 1n, v * current);
}
```

Now, `fact`'s call to itself is in the tail position. With TCO, each time `fact` calls itself, the stack frame for the new call replaces the stack frame for the previous call, just like `second`'s frame replaced `first`'s earlier, instead of all being pushed on the stack until the final result is found, and then all being popped off. So the stack no longer limits the size of the factorials that `fact` can calculate.

But as I mentioned at the beginning of this section, only one major JavaScript engine currently implements TCO: JavaScriptCore in Safari (and other browsers on iOS[21]). V8, SpiderMonkey, and Chakra don't support TCO, and at least the V8 and SpiderMonkey teams don't currently have any plans to. (V8 did have partial support for a while, but it was removed as the engine evolved.) The primary sticking point is the effect on stack traces. Think back to the `first`/`second` example at the beginning of this section. Suppose `second` threw an error. Since `first`'s stack frame was replaced by `second`'s thanks to TCO, the stack trace would look like `second` had been called where `first` was called, instead of from within `first`. There are various ways to solve this problem, and some suggested alternatives including opt-in (rather than automatic) TCO, but for now there's no consensus to move forward. Maybe someday.

---

[21] On iOS, browsers like Chrome and Firefox can't use their usual JavaScript engines, because non-Apple apps can't allocate executable memory, which is required for the JIT compiling that V8 and SpiderMonkey do. V8 has recently introduced an "interpreter only" version of V8, though, so Chrome may start using that on iOS.

OLD HABITS TO NEW

All of these miscellaneous additions give you a few habits you can update if you like.

Use Binary Literals

Old habit: Using hexadecimal numbers for bit flags and such where binary might be clearer:

```
const flags = {
    something:       0x01,
    somethingElse:   0x02,
    anotherThing:    0x04,
    yetAnotherThing: 0x08
};
```

New habit: Where it makes sense, use the new binary integer literal instead:

```
const flags = {
    something:       0b00000001,
    somethingElse:   0b00000010,
    anotherThing:    0b00000100,
    yetAnotherThing: 0b00001000
};
```

Use New Math Functions Instead of Various Math Workarounds

Old habit: Using various math workarounds, for instance to emulate 32-bit integer math, or truncating by doing `value = value < 0 ? Math.ceil(value) : Math.floor(value)`.

New habit: Where appropriate, use some of the new `Math` functions instead, like `Math.imul` or `Math.trunc`.

Use Nullish Coalescing for Defaults

Old habit: Using the logical OR operator (`||`) or an explicit `null`/`undefined` check when providing default values:

```
const delay = this.settings.delay || 300;
// or
const delay = this.settings.delay == null ? 300 : this.settings.delay;
```

New habit: Use nullish coalescing instead where appropriate so that not all falsy values (such as `0`) trigger the default:

```
const delay = this.settings.delay ?? 300;
```

Use Optional Chaining Instead of && Checks

Old habit: Using the logical AND operator (`&&`) or similar when accessing nested properties on objects that may or may not be there:

```
const element = document.getElementById("optional");
if (element) {
    element.addEventListener("click", function() {
        // ...
    });
}
```

New habit: Use optional chaining instead where appropriate:

```
document.getElementById("optional")?.addEventListener("click", function() {
    // ...
});
```

Leave the Error Binding (e) Off of "catch (e)" When Not Using It

Old habit: Writing `catch (e)` when not using e (because you had no choice):

```
try {
    theOperation();
} catch (e) {
    doSomethingElse();
}
```

New habit: Not writing the `(e)` part when using modern syntax (transpiling, or only targeting environments known to support the optional `catch` binding):

```
try {
    theOperation();
} catch {
    doSomethingElse();
}
```

Use the Exponentiation Operator (**) Rather Than Math.pow

Old habit: Using `Math.pow` for exponentiation, for instance:

```
x = Math.pow(y, 32);
```

New habit: Consider using the exponentiation operator instead, since `Math.pow` can be overwritten and using the exponentiation operator doesn't require the identifier lookup for `Math` or the property lookup for `pow`:

```
x = y**32;
```

18

Upcoming Class Features

WHAT'S IN THIS CHAPTER?

➤ Public class fields

➤ Private class fields, instance methods, and accessors

➤ Static class fields and private static methods

CODE DOWNLOADS FOR THIS CHAPTER

You can download the code for this chapter at `https://thenewtoys.dev/bookcode` or `https://www.wiley.com/go/javascript-newtoys`.

In this chapter, you'll learn about upcoming `class` features that are almost certain to be in ES2021, and which are stable enough (or nearly stable enough) to use with transpilation today (or even without, in some cases, in modern environments): class fields; private fields and methods/accessors; and static fields and private static methods/accessors.

PUBLIC AND PRIVATE CLASS FIELDS, METHODS, AND ACCESSORS

ES2015's `class` syntax was intentionally just a starting point. Multiple proposals that are likely to be adopted in ES2021 extend it with additional useful features:

➤ Public field (property) definitions

➤ Private fields

➤ Private instance methods and accessors

> ➤ Public static fields

> ➤ Private static fields

> ➤ Private static methods

These make the already-useful[1] `class` syntax markedly *more* useful, taking tasks that used to require hiding things in closures, assignments after-the-fact, behind-the-scenes use of `WeakMaps`, awkward syntax, etc., and making them simple syntax, and potentially improving the ways JavaScript engines can optimize the results as well.

The enhancements are spread across multiple proposals, which may advance at different rates, but which are all at Stage 3 in early 2020:

> ➤ *Class field declarations for JavaScript (often called the "class fields proposal")*: https://github.com/tc39/proposal-class-fields

> ➤ *Private methods and getter/setters for JavaScript classes*: https://github.com/tc39/proposal-private-methods

> ➤ *Static class features*: https://github.com/tc39/proposal-static-class-features/

This section goes through the various additions. They are supported by transpilers right now. Being Stage 3, these features are being implemented natively by JavaScript engines (for instance, private and public fields are available in V8, shipping without a flag in Chrome 74 and up).

Public Field (Property) Definitions

With ES2015's `class` syntax, only constructors, methods, and accessor properties were *declaratively* defined; data properties were created ad-hoc via assignment, often (but not always) in the constructor:

```
class Example {
    constructor() {
        this.answer = 42;
    }
}
```

The class fields proposal adds *public field definitions* to the language (essentially, *property definitions*). The following defines exactly the same class the previous example did:

```
class Example {
    answer = 42;
}
```

The definition is simply the name of the property, optionally followed by an equal sign (=) and an initializer expression, then terminated with a semicolon (;). (More on initializers in a moment.) Notice that there is no `this.` in front of the property name in the definition.

---

[1] Useful if you use constructor functions, that is; JavaScript also supports programming paradigms that don't use them and thus, don't use `class` syntax.

"PUBLIC FIELD" VS. "PROPERTY"

Since the class fields proposal adds private fields to the language, and private fields aren't properties (as you'll learn in the next section), it's increasingly common to refer to properties and private fields as simply *fields,* and by extension to refer to properties as *public fields.* Public fields are still properties; this is just another name for them.

If you have multiple properties to define, they must be defined separately; you can't chain definitions like you can with `var`, `let`, and `const`:

```
class Example {
    answer = 42, question = "...";
    //          ^--- SyntaxError: Unexpected token, expected ";"
}
```

Instead, write each definition standalone:

```
class Example {
    answer = 42;
    question = "...";
}
```

For properties whose initial values don't rely on constructor parameter values, the new syntax is more concise. If the initial value *does* rely on a constructor parameter, then adding the definition is slightly more verbose (at least for now):

```
class Example {
    answer;

    constructor(answer) {
        this.answer = answer;
    }
}
```

In that example the public field definition at the beginning of the class is redundant in terms of the properties that `new Example` creates on the newly created object; the object would have the `answer` property either way. But public property definitions have been added to the language for several reasons:

➤ Telling the JavaScript engine up front what properties the object will have reduces the number of *shape changes* the object goes through (changes to its set of properties and such), which improves the engine's ability to optimize the object quickly; see the inset.

➤ Defining the shape of the object up front is useful to human readers of your class as well and provides a convenient location for documentation comments describing the properties. Remember that you *read* code much more frequently than you *write* it, so a bit of extra effort to help readers is often useful.

➤ Having this syntax for public properties provides parity with the private field definitions you'll learn about in the next section.

➤ It provides a place to apply *decorators* to the property, if or when the decorators proposal[2] goes forward.

It will be down to your style and your team's style when (and whether) you define public properties declaratively rather than via assignment.

THE "SHAPE" OF AN OBJECT, AND SHAPE CHANGES

The *shape* of a JavaScript object is the set of fields and properties it has and what prototype it has. Modern JavaScript engines optimize objects aggressively; the shape of an object is an important part of that. Avoiding changing the object's shape over time helps the engine do its job more efficiently. For instance, look at the following class:

```
class Example {
    constructor(a) {
        this.a = a;
    }
    addB(b) {
        this.b = b;
    }
    addC(c) {
        this.c = c;
    }
}
```

A freshly constructed instance of Example has only one property: a. (Well, *very* briefly it has none at all, before a is assigned, but in many cases the JavaScript engine can avoid re-optimizing if the assignment is at the beginning of the constructor and unconditional.) But later, it may get a b property, a c property, or both. If that happens, the JavaScript engine has to adjust its optimization each time to allow for the change. But if you tell the engine up front what properties the object will have (by assigning to them in an unconditional early part of the constructor, or by defining them with property definition syntax), it can account for those properties just once at the outset.

If the property definition has an initializer, that initializer code runs exactly as though it were inside the constructor (other than that it doesn't have access to the constructor's parameters, if any). Among other things, that means that if you use this in the initializer, it has the same value it has in the constructor: a reference to the object being initialized. Instance properties created this way are configurable, writable, and enumerable, exactly as though they'd been created via assignment in the constructor.

---

[2] https://github.com/tc39/proposal-decorators

If the property doesn't have an initializer, it's created with the default value `undefined`:

```
class Example {
    field;
}
const e = new Example();
console.log("field" in e);   // true
console.log(typeof e.field); // "undefined"
```

While the class fields proposal is only at Stage 3, its basic features described in this section have long been used via transpilation. Until JavaScript engines are shipping with this feature in place (V8 and SpiderMonkey do, others will be soon), you'll need to transpile to use it, and of course depending on your target environment you may need to transpile to support older engines for a while.

ARROW FUNCTIONS IN INITIALIZERS

Since an initializer runs as though it were within the constructor, some programmers have taken to using a property referring to an arrow function as a convenient way to create a function that's bound to the instance. For example:

```
class Example {
    handler = event => {
        event.currentTarget.textContent = this.text;
    };

    constructor(text) {
        this.text = text;
    }

    attachTo(element) {
        element.addEventListener("click", this.handler);
    }
}
```

That works because the arrow function closes over `this`, and `this` where the arrow function is defined refers to the instance being initialized (just as though the initializer were inside the constructor).

While that seems convenient at first, there are some arguments against doing it. It puts `handler` on the instance itself, not `Example.prototype`, which means:

➤ It's hard to mock for testing. Often, testing frameworks work at the prototype level.

➤ It interferes with inheritance. Suppose you had `class BetterExample extends Example` and defined a new/better `handler`? It wouldn't have access to the `Example` version via `super`.

The alternative is to put the method on the prototype where it can be reused and (possibly) mocked for testing, and bind it to the instance when/where necessary. In this case, you could do that in the constructor, in the `attachTo` method, or . . . in a property initializer on a property definition! Like this:

```
class Example {
    handler = this.handler.bind(this);

    constructor(text) {
        this.text = text;
    }

    handler(event) {
        event.currentTarget.textContent = this.text;
    }

    attachTo(element) {
        element.addEventListener("click", this.handler);
    }
}
```

That takes the prototype's `handler`, binds it to `this`, and assigns the result as an instance property. Since the initializer runs before the property is created, `this.handler` in the initializer refers to the one on the prototype.

This pattern is sufficiently common that it's one of the example use cases for decorators (it's often called the `@bound` decorator).

The name of a public field can be computed; to do so, you use brackets around the expression defining the property key like you do in an object literal. It's particularly useful for when the property key is a Symbol:

```
const sharedUsefulProperty = Symbol.for("usefulProperty");
class Example {
    [sharedUsefulProperty] = "example";

    show() {
        console.log(this[sharedUsefulProperty]);
    }
}

const ex = new Example();
ex.show(); // "example"
```

Earlier you learned that if the public field definition has an initializer, it runs exactly as though it were in the constructor. Specifically, they're done in source code order, as though they were written right at the beginning of the constructor (in a base class) or just after the call to `super()` (in a subclass—remember that the new instance is created by the `super()` call, so `this` isn't accessible before then). The order means that a later property can rely on an earlier property, since the earlier property will be created and initialized first. See Listing 18-1 for an example showing both the order and the fact that the initialization is done just after the call to `super()`.

LISTING 18.1: Public property definition order—property-definition-order.js

```
function logAndReturn(str) {
    console.log(str);
    return str;
}
class BaseExample {
    baseProp = logAndReturn("baseProp");
    constructor() {
        console.log("BaseExample");
    }
}
class SubExample extends BaseExample {
    subProp1 = logAndReturn("example");
    subProp2 = logAndReturn(this.subProp1.toUpperCase());
    constructor() {
        console.log("SubExample before super()");
        super();
        console.log("SubExample after super()");
        console.log(`this.subProp1 = ${this.subProp1}`);
        console.log(`this.subProp2 = ${this.subProp2}`);
    }
}
new SubExample();
```

When you run Listing 18-1, it outputs:

```
SubExample before super()
baseProp
BaseExample
example
EXAMPLE
SubExample after super()
this.subProp1 = example
this.subProp2 = EXAMPLE
```

Private Fields

The class fields proposal also adds *private fields* to `class` syntax. Private fields are different from object properties (public fields) in several ways. The key difference is that, as the name implies, only code within the class can access a private field of the class. See Listing 18-2 for an example. Remember that you may need a transpiler (and appropriate plugin) to run the example, though depending on when you're reading this your browser's JavaScript engine may support private fields natively. (The plugin for Babel v7 is `@babel/plugin-proposal-class-properties`.)

LISTING 18-2: Simple private fields example—private-fields.js

```
class Counter {
    #value;

    constructor(start = 0) {
        this.#value = start;
    }

    increment() {
        return ++this.#value;
    }

    get value() {
        return this.#value;
    }
}
const c = new Counter();
console.log(c.value); // 0
c.increment();
console.log(c.value); // 1
// console.log(c.#value); // Would be a SyntaxError
```

Listing 18-2 defines a Counter class with a private instance field called #value. The class increments #value when its increment method is called and returns #value's value from its value accessor property, but doesn't let external code directly see or modify #value.

Some things to note from that example:

➤ You define a private field the same way you define a public field, marking it private by simply giving it a name starting with a hash sign (#). This (the #value part) is called a *private identifier.*

➤ To access the field, you use its private identifier (#value) in an accessor expression: this.#value.

➤ Code outside the Counter class's definition can't access the field, and it's a *syntax* error, not an *evaluation* error (in most cases; more on that in a moment). That is, it's the nice proactive kind of error that happens during the parsing of the code, not later when the code is run, so you catch it early.

Private fields have some key differences from object properties:

➤ Private fields can only be created via a private field definition; they cannot be created ad-hoc through assignment or defineProperty/defineProperties. Trying to use an undefined private field is a syntax error.

➤ The private identifier you write in the code (#value in the example) isn't the actual name of the field (though it's the name you use in your code). Instead, under the covers the JavaScript engine assigns the field a globally unique name (called a *Private Name*) that you, the programmer, never see. The private identifier is effectively a constant in the `class` definition's scope that has the Private Name as its value. When accessing the field (for instance, `this.#value`), the value of the private identifier `#value` is looked up in the current scope and the resulting Private Name is used to find the field in the object. (More on this in a moment.) In contrast, with a property name, the name you write in the code is that property's actual name.

➤ Private fields are stored separately from object properties, in an internal slot on the object called [[PrivateFieldValues]], which is (in the specification) a list of name/value pairs (though of course JavaScript engines are free to optimize, since you never see this list directly). The name is the Private Name, not the private identifier. The reason for this will become clear in a little bit.

➤ Private fields cannot be removed from an object. If you try to use the `delete` operator on a private field, it's a syntax error (after all, `delete` removes properties, and private fields aren't properties) and there's no equivalent to `delete` for private fields. This, combined with the fact you must define private fields using a field definition, means that the set of private fields available within the class is fixed; it never changes (which makes it highly optimizable).

➤ Private fields are not accessible through reflection. They aren't properties, so none of the property-oriented methods like `Object.getOwnPropertyNames` or `Reflect.ownKeys` applies to them, and there are no new methods on `Object` or `Reflect` that allow you to access them.

➤ Private fields cannot be accessed with brackets notation (`this["#value"]` doesn't work, for instance); in fact, there's no dynamic mechanism for accessing them at all. The names must be written using literal notation. (Follow-on proposals may change this.)

➤ Private fields are not accessible in subclasses. If class A defines a private field, *only* code in class A can access it. If class B subclasses A (`class B extends A`), code in B cannot access A's private field. This is a natural consequence of the private identifier being part of the `class` scope: it's not in scope in the subclass, so you can't use it. (There's a nuance here you'll learn about later, regarding *nested* classes.)

➤ Following on from that point, it's perfectly fine if class A and class B both have a private field with the same private identifier (`#value` or whatever). Those fields are completely separate, since each of them will get its own Private Name, and the private identifier is resolved to the Private Name using the class's scope. `#value` in code in class A refers to class A's private field, and `#value` in class B refers to class B's private field.

Let's look at how private identifiers are resolved to Private Names. You may recall the *environment object* from Chapter 2 that variables (and constants) are stored in. Private identifiers are stored in a similar object called the *private name environment*. See Figure 18-1 (overleaf) for how the private identifier, private name environment, Private Name, and class instance all relate to one another.

Because private identifiers are *lexically scoped* (the resolution of an identifier to its Private Name is scope-based), if you have a nested class (a class within a class), the inner class can access private fields of the outer class. See Listing 18-3.

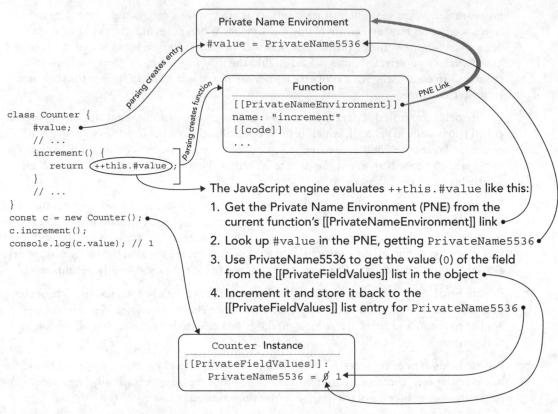

FIGURE 18-1

LISTING 18-3: Private fields in nested classes—private-fields-in-nested-classes.js

```
class Outer {
    #outerField;
    constructor(value) {
        this.#outerField = value;
    }
    static createInner() {
        return class Inner {
            #innerField;
            constructor(value) {
                this.#innerField = value;
            }
            access(o) {
                console.log(`this.#innerField = ${this.#innerField}`);
                // Works, because #outerField is in scope:
                console.log(`o.#outerField = ${o.#outerField}`);
            }
        };
    }
}
```

```
const Inner = Outer.createInner();
const o = new Outer(1);
const i = new Inner(2);
i.access(o);
// =>
// this.#innerField = 2
// o.#outerField = 1
```

Code in `Inner` can see the private fields in `Outer`, since `Inner` is defined *within* `Outer`. That is, normal scoping rules apply to the private identifier (`#outerField`).

This scope-based resolution of private identifiers ensures that they are intimately tied to the class in which they're defined. Even if you evaluate the same `class` definition more than once, resulting in two copies of the class, the private fields in one copy are *not* accessible to the other copy, because the private identifier in one class's scope has a different Private Name value than the same private identifier in the other class's scope. It's just like when you have a function that returns a function closing over a variable or constant:

```
let nextId = 0;
function outer() {
    const id = ++nextId;
    return function inner() {
        return id;
    };
}
const f1 = outer();
const f2 = outer();
```

Both `inner` functions created there (`f1` and `f2`) close over a constant called `id`, but those constants are separate from one another and have different values. It's exactly the same for the private identifiers in classes.

One way you might evaluate the `class` definition more than once is by loading the same class in multiple realms (for instance, in both a main window and an `iframe`) and then exchanging data between the two. But you could have multiple copies of the class within a single realm as well, just by evaluating the `class` definition more than once (just like the earlier example evaluated the `inner` function definition more than once). See Listing 18-4.

LISTING 18-4: Private fields in class copies—private-fields-in-class-copies.js

```
function makeCounterClass() {
    return class Counter {
        #value;

        constructor(start = 0) {
            this.#value = start;
        }

        increment() {
            return ++this.#value;
        }
```

```
        get value() {
            return this.#value;
        }

        static show(counter) {
            console.log(`counter.#value = ${counter.#value}`);
        }
    };
}

const Counter1 = makeCounterClass();
const Counter2 = makeCounterClass();

const c = new Counter1();
c.increment();
Counter1.show(c);    // "counter.#value = 1"
Counter2.show(c);    // TypeError: Cannot read private member #value from an
                     // object whose class did not declare it
```

(The specific error varies by JavaScript engine or by the transpiler you use. Another version is "TypeError: attempted to get private field on non-instance.")

Counter1 and Counter2 are two separate copies of the same class, so the #value in Counter1 isn't the same #value as in Counter2. They hold different Private Name values, so code in Counter1 can't access the #value field in an instance created by Counter2 and vice versa. This means code may fail to access a private field in two different ways:

1. If the private identifier is undefined in the scope where it's used. This is a nice early syntax error.

2. If the private identifier is defined in the scope where it's used, but its Private Name value is used on an object that doesn't have a private field with that Private Name.

Counter1 and Counter2 are in the second situation. The commented-out code in Listing 18-2 a few pages back, which tried to use #value when it wasn't in scope at all, was in the first situation.

That's all you need to know to use private fields in your classes. If you want to dive deeper into the two-step mechanism (resolving a private identifier to a Private Name, then using the Private Name to find the field), see Listing 18-5: it shows the code from Listing 18-4, but *emulating* the private fields using equivalents to the abstract operations described in the specification. (This emulation is purely meant to help you understand how private fields work; it's not a polyfill or anything close to one.)

LISTING 18-5: Private fields in class copies with emulation—private-fields-in-class-copies-emulated.js

```
// ==== Start: Code to emulate specification operations ====

// The names of the operations (NewPrivateName, PrivateFieldFind,
// PrivateFieldGet, and PrivateFieldFind) and their parameters
// (description, P, O, value) are from the spec.

// Creates a new Private Name with the given description.
// Private Names aren't described as objects in the spec, but it's
```

```javascript
// convenient to use an object in this emulation.
function NewPrivateName(description) {
    return {description};
}

// Finds the given private field in the given object.
// P = the private name, O = the object.
function PrivateFieldFind(P, O) {
    const privateFieldValues = O["[[PrivateFieldValues]]"];
    const field = privateFieldValues.find(entry => entry["[[PrivateName]]"] === P);
    return field;
}

// Adds a new private field to an object (only possible during initial
// construction). P = the private name, O = the object, value = the value.
function PrivateFieldAdd(P, O, value) {
    if (PrivateFieldFind(P, O)) {
        throw new TypeError(`Field ${P.description} already defined for object`);
    }
    const field = {
        "[[PrivateName]]": P,
        "[[PrivateFieldValue]]": value
    };
    O["[[PrivateFieldValues]]"].push(field);
    return value;
}

// Gets the value of the given private field of the given object.
// P = the private name, O = the object.
function PrivateFieldGet(P, O) {
    const field = PrivateFieldFind(P, O);
    if (!field) {
        throw new TypeError(
            `Cannot read private member ${P.description} from an object ` +
            `whose class did not declare it`
        );
    }
    return field["[[PrivateFieldValue]]"];
}

// Sets the value of the given private field of the given object.
// P = the private name, O = the object, value = the value.
function PrivateFieldSet(P, O, value) {
    const field = PrivateFieldFind(P, O);
    if (!field) {
        throw new TypeError(
            `Cannot write private member ${P.description} to an object ` +
            `whose class did not declare it`
        );
    }
    field["[[PrivateFieldValue]]"] = value;
    return value;
}

// ==== END: Code to emulate specification operations ====

// Here's the code from private-fields-in-class-copies.js, updated to use the
```

```javascript
// "spec" code above to emulate the private fields, to show approximately how
// they work under the covers.
function makeCounterClass() {
    // These next two lines emulate what the JavaScript engine does when it
    // starts processing the `class` definition:
    // 1. Creating the private name environment and linking it to the `class`
    //    definition (in this code, the "link" is that code in the class closes
    //    over the `privateNameEnvironment` constant).
    // 2. Doing the once-per-class part of the `#value;` definition: Creating
    //    the Private Name for the private name identifier and storing it in the
    //    private name environment.
    const privateNameEnvironment = new Map();
    privateNameEnvironment.set("#value", NewPrivateName("#value"));
    return class Counter {
        // Original code: #value;

        constructor(start = 0) {
            // Emulates the part of object construction that creates the
            // [[PrivateFieldValues]] internal slot.
            this["[[PrivateFieldValues]]"] = [];

            // Emulates the per-object part of the `#value;` definition
            PrivateFieldAdd(privateNameEnvironment.get("#value"), this, undefined);

            // Original code: this.#value = start;
            PrivateFieldSet(privateNameEnvironment.get("#value"), this, start);
        }

        increment() {
            // Original code: return ++this.#value;
            const privateName = privateNameEnvironment.get("#value");
            const temp = PrivateFieldGet(privateName, this);
            return PrivateFieldSet(privateName, this, temp + 1);
        }

        get value() {
            // Original code: return this.#value;
            return PrivateFieldGet(privateNameEnvironment.get("#value"), this);
        }

        static show(counter) {
            // Original code: console.log(`counter.#value = ${counter.#value}`);
            const value =
                PrivateFieldGet(privateNameEnvironment.get("#value"), counter);
            console.log(`counter.#value = ${value}`);
        }
    };
}

const Counter1 = makeCounterClass();
const Counter2 = makeCounterClass();

const c = new Counter1();
c.increment();
Counter1.show(c);    // "counter.#value = 1"
Counter2.show(c);    // TypeError: attempted to get private field on non-instance
```

Private Instance Methods and Accessors

The "Private methods and getter/setters for JavaScript classes" proposal builds on the class fields proposal's private mechanism to enhance `class` syntax with (as the name suggests) private methods and accessors.

Private Methods

You define a private method simply by putting a # in front of the method name. See Listing 18-6.

LISTING 18-6: Private methods—private-methods.js

```
class Example {
    #value;
    #x;
    #y;

    constructor(x, y) {
        this.#x = x;
        this.#y = y;
        this.#calculate();
    }

    #calculate() {
        // Imagine an expensive operation here...
        this.#value = this.#x * this.#y;
    }

    get x() {
        return this.#x;
    }
    set x(x) {
        this.#x = x;
        this.#calculate();
    }

    get y() {
        return this.#y;
    }
    set y(y) {
        this.#y = y;
        this.#calculate();
    }

    get value() {
        return this.#value;
    }
}

const ex = new Example(21, 2);
console.log(`ex.value = ${ex.value}`); // 42
// This would be a syntax error:
//ex.#calculate();
```

Like private fields, private methods must be defined in the `class` construct; you can't add them to the class afterward as you can with public prototype methods (for instance, via `MyClass.prototype.newMethod = function()...`). Also like private fields, the method identifier (`#calculate`) is lexically scoped.

But *unlike* private fields, private methods are not stored in the instance (object) itself; they're shared across objects (instances of the class). That means that the `#calculate` in the previous example is *not* the same as defining a private field and assigning a function to it. That would create a new function for every instance, instead of sharing the function across instances.

You might assume that private methods would be put on the prototype object for the class (`MyClass.prototype`), but that's not how they're shared across instances. The exact mechanism for sharing private methods across instances may change slightly between this writing and the time the proposal is adopted, so it's not useful to go too deeply into it here; see the inset if you're curious. The key takeaway is that they're tied to instances of the class but shared across instances.

HOW PRIVATE METHODS ARE LINKED TO OBJECTS

As with private fields, the private identifier for a private method is lexically scoped; its value is a Private Name. But the Private Name isn't just a key in a list as it is with private fields; instead, the Private Name holds the method *directly*. So the JavaScript engine looks up the private identifier in the private name environment to get the Private Name, and then gets the method directly from that Private Name. If that were all the engine did, you could get the private method "from" any object, doing `x.#privateMethod` where x is anything, even if it's not an instance of the class, since the method is part of the Private Name that `#privateMethod` resolves to. That would be confusing to say the least, and limiting for further enhancements to the language, so the specification has an explicit check to ensure that the instance you're getting the method "from" is in fact meant to have that method: every private method has an internal field (called [[Brand]]) which is the brand for the class they're a part of, and instances have a list of [[PrivateBrands]] for the classes they belong to. Before allowing code to get a private method from an instance, the JavaScript engine ensures that the method's [[Brand]] is on the instance's list of [[PrivateBrands]]. Of course, this is a specification mechanism; engines are free to optimize provided the external result is as defined by the spec.

This mechanism may change before the proposal is adopted, because several ways exist to get the same end result. But the fact that private methods are shared between instances is not going to change.

Private methods can be called with any `this` value, just like any other method. `this` does not have to refer to an instance of the class the method belongs to. For instance, you can use a private method as a DOM event handler:

```
class Example {
    constructor(element) {
        element.addEventListener("click", this.#clickHandler);
```

```
        }

        #clickHandler(event) {
            // Because of how it was hooked up, `this` here is the DOM element
            // this method was attached to as an event handler
            console.log(`Clicked, element's contents are: ${this.textContent}`);
        }
    }
```

That said, it's common to want to bind the method to the instance of the class so you can access the instance's properties, fields, and other methods. (Otherwise, you'd define a `static` private method, which you'll learn about later in this chapter.) With public methods, you may have used this pattern shown earlier to do that:

```
    class Example {
        clickHandler = this.clickHandler.bind(this);

        constructor(element) {
            element.addEventListener("click", this.clickHandler);
        }

        clickHandler(event) {
            // ...
        }
    }
```

Or perhaps you'd do it in the constructor:

```
    class Example {
        constructor(element) {
            this.clickHandler = this.clickHandler.bind(this);
            element.addEventListener("click", this.clickHandler);
        }

        clickHandler(event) {
            // ...
        }
    }
```

In both cases, those read `clickHandler` from the instance (which gets it from the instance's prototype, since the instance doesn't have an own property for it yet), creates a bound function for it, and assigns that back as an own property on the instance.

You can't do that using the same name with private methods (you can't have a private field and a private method with the same name—see inset on the next page—and you can't assign to a private method as though it were a field or property), but you can define a separate private field to assign the bound function to, and use that:

```
    class Example {
        #boundClickHandler = this.#clickHandler.bind(this);

        constructor(element) {
            element.addEventListener("click", this.#boundClickHandler);
        }
```

```
    #clickHandler(event) {
        // ...
    }
}
```

Or, again, you can do that in the constructor, although you still need the field definition, so having the initializer on it as in the last example is reasonable:

```
class Example {
    #boundClickHandler;

    constructor(element) {
        this.#boundClickHandler = this.#clickHandler.bind(this);
        element.addEventListener("click", this.#boundClickHandler);
    }

    #clickHandler(event) {
        // ...
    }
}
```

There's no need to bind in the definition (or constructor) if you're only going to use the bound function once as in that example (just `bind` in the call to `addEventListener`), but if you're going to use that bound function more than once, binding once and reusing the bound function is useful.

PRIVATE IDENTIFIERS MUST BE UNIQUE IN THE CLASS

A private method and a private field cannot have the same identifier. That is, this is invalid:

```
// INCORRECT
class Example {
    #a;

    #a() { // SyntaxError: Duplicate private element
        // ...
    }
}
```

While some languages let you do that, it's confusing if you actually do; JavaScript doesn't allow it. In fact, all of the private features you'll learn about in this chapter follow that same rule: you can't have two different class elements (for instance, a private field and a private method) with the same private identifier in the same class. Under the covers, this is because the private identifiers all share the same private name environment.

Private Accessors

Private accessors work just like private methods. You name them with a private identifier, and only code within the class can access them:

```
class Example {
    #cappedValue;

    constructor(value) {
        // Saving the value via the accessor's setter
        this.#value = value;
    }

    get #value() {
        return this.#cappedValue;
    }
    set #value(value) {
        this.#cappedValue = value.toUpperCase();
    }

    show() {
        console.log(`this.#value = ${this.#value}`);
    }

    update(value) {
        this.#value = value;
    }
}

const ex = new Example("a");
ex.show(); // "this.#value = A"
ex.update("b")
ex.show(); // "this.#value = B"
// ex.#value = "c"; // Would be a SyntaxError, `#value` is private
```

Private accessors can be useful for debugging, monitoring changes, etc. Just like private methods (and via the same mechanism), the accessor functions are shared across instances.

Public Static Fields, Private Static Fields, and Private Static Methods

ES2015's `class` syntax only had one `static` feature: public `static` methods (methods attached to the class constructor instead of the prototype given to instances). The "Static class features" proposal builds on the class fields and private methods proposals to round out the feature grid with `static` fields, private `static` fields, and private `static` methods.

Public Static Fields

Public `static` fields create properties on the class constructor. It's not uncommon to want to do that, but with ES2015's `class` syntax, you had to do it after-the-fact. For instance, if you were writing a class and there were a couple of "standard" instances of it that code might want to reuse, you could make those available as properties of the class by assigning those properties after the `class` construct:

```
class Thingy {
    constructor(label) {
        this.label = label;
    }
}
Thingy.standardThingy = new Thingy("A standard Thingy");
Thingy.anotherStandardThingy = new Thingy("Another standard Thingy");

console.log(Thingy.standardThingy.label);        // "A standard Thingy"
console.log(Thingy.anotherStandardThingy.label); // "Another standard Thingy"
```

With the new syntax from the "Static class features" proposal, you can do that declaratively instead, with the `static` keyword:

```
class Thingy {
    static standardThingy = new Thingy("A standard Thingy");
    static anotherStandardThingy = new Thingy("Another standard Thingy");

    constructor(label) {
        this.label = label;
    }
}

console.log(Thingy.standardThingy.label);        // "A standard Thingy"
console.log(Thingy.anotherStandardThingy.label); // "Another standard Thingy"
```

The public fields are initialized in source code order, so a later field's initializer can refer to an earlier field:

```
class Thingy {
    static standardThingy = new Thingy("A standard Thingy");
    static anotherStandardThingy = new Thingy(
        Thingy.standardThingy.label.replace("A", "Another")
    );

    constructor(label) {
        this.label = label;
    }
}

console.log(Thingy.standardThingy.label);        // "A standard Thingy"
console.log(Thingy.anotherStandardThingy.label); // "Another standard Thingy"
```

An *earlier* field's initializer can't refer to a *later* field, though; it'll get the value `undefined` because the property doesn't exist (yet).

With the new syntax, a static field's initializer has access to the private features of the class. If you added it to the class constructor after the fact, it wouldn't have that access, because the code for it wouldn't be within the class scope the private name environment is attached to.

Private Static Fields

The way you define a private static field is, shockingly, to define it like a public static field but name it with a private identifier. For instance, if you were writing a class that reused instances based on the parameter value the constructor receives, you might hold the cache of known instances on a private static field:

```
class Example {
    static #cache = new WeakMap();

    constructor(thingy) {
        const cache = Example.#cache;
        const previous = cache.get(thingy);
        if (previous) {
            return previous;
        }
        cache.set(thingy, this);
    }
}

const obj1 = {};
const e1 = new Example(obj1);
const e1again = new Example(obj1);
console.log(e1 === e1again); // true, the same instance was returned
const obj2 = {};
const e2 = new Example(obj2);
console.log(e1 === e2);      // false, a new instance was created
```

Private Static Methods

Finally, rounding things out, you can also define `static` private methods that are associated with the class constructor rather than an instance, for private utility methods that don't need to act on `this`:

```
class Example {
    static #log(...msgs) {
        console.log(`${new Date().toISOString()}:`, ...msgs);
    }
    constructor(a) {
        Example.#log("Initializing instance, a =", a);
    }
}

const e = new Example("one");
// => "2018-12-20T14:03:12.302Z: Initializing instance, a = one"
```

As with ES2015's public static methods, you do need to access them via the constructor (that is, `Example.#log` rather than just `#log`), since they're associated with the class constructor. (There may be a follow-on proposal that augments private methods with `class`-scoped standalone utility functions[3] you just call directly.)

---

[3] https://github.com/tc39/proposal-static-class-features/blob/
master/FOLLOWONS.md#lexical-declarations-in-class-bodies

OLD HABITS TO NEW

Here are some old habits you might consider switching for new ones using these features.

Use Property Definitions Instead of Creating Properties in the Constructor (Where Appropriate)

Old habit: Always creating your properties in the constructor, because you had no choice:

```
class Example {
    constructor() {
        this.created = new Date();
    }
}
```

New habit: Defining your class properties instead, to minimize changes to the shape of your class, for conciseness, and so you can apply decorators to them as necessary:

```
class Example {
    created = new Date();
}
```

Use Private Fields Instead of Prefixes (Where Appropriate)

Old habit: Using prefixes for pseudo-private fields:

```
let nextExampleId = 1;
class Example {
    constructor() {
        this._id = ++nextExampleId;
    }
    get id() {
        return this._id;
    }
}
```

New habit: Using true private fields:

```
let nextExampleId = 1;
class Example {
    #id = ++nextExampleId;
    get id() {
        return this.#id;
    }
}
```

Use Private Methods Instead of Functions Outside the Class for Private Operations

Old habit: Using functions defined outside the class for privacy even if you have to pass the instance into them:

```
// (The wrapper function isn't needed if this is module code; module
// privacy is usually sufficient)
const Example = (() => {
```

```
    // (Pretend it uses lots of stuff from Example, not just two things)
    function expensivePrivateCalculation(ex) {
        return ex._a + ex._b;
    }
    return class Example {
        constructor(a, b) {
            this._a = a;
            this._b = b;
            this._c = null;
        }
        get a() {
            return this._a;
        }
        set a(value) {
            this._a = value;
            this._c = null;
        }
        get b() {
            return this._b;
        }
        set b(value) {
            this._b = value;
            this._c = null;
        }
        get c() {
            if (this._c === null) {
                this._c = expensivePrivateCalculation(this);
            }
            return this._c;
        }
    };
})();
const ex = new Example(1, 2);
console.log(ex.c); // 3
```

New habit: Use private methods instead (this example could also use private fields, but I haven't used them here to avoid conflating things):

```
class Example {
    constructor(a, b) {
        this._a = a;
        this._b = b;
        this._c = null;
    }
    // (Pretend it uses lots of stuff from `this`, not just two things)
    #expensivePrivateCalculation() {
        return this._a + this._b;
    }
    get a() {
        return this._a;
    }
    set a(value) {
        this._a = value;
        this._c = null;
    }
}
```

```
        get b() {
            return this._b;
        }
        set b(value) {
            this._b = value;
            this._c = null;
        }
        get c() {
            if (this._c === null) {
                this._c = this.#expensivePrivateCalculation();
            }
            return this._c;
        }
    }
    const ex = new Example(1, 2);
    console.log(ex.c); // 3
```

That said, you'd probably want to go ahead and use private fields, too:

```
    class Example {
        #a;
        #b;
        #c = null;

        constructor(a, b) {
            this.#a = a;
            this.#b = b;
        }
        // (Pretend it uses lots of stuff from `this`, not just two things)
        #expensivePrivateCalculation() {
            return this.#a + this.#b;
        }
        get a() {
            return this.#a;
        }
        set a(value) {
            this.#a = value;
            this.#c = null;
        }
        get b() {
            return this.#b;
        }
        set b(value) {
            this.#b = value;
            this.#c = null;
        }
        get c() {
            if (this.#c === null) {
                this.#c = this.#expensivePrivateCalculation();
            }
            return this.#c;
        }
    }
    const ex = new Example(1, 2);
    console.log(ex.c); // 3
```

19

A Look Ahead . . .

> ## CODE DOWNLOADS FOR THIS CHAPTER
>
> You can download the code for this chapter at `https://thenewtoys.dev/bookcode` or `https://www.wiley.com/go/javascript-newtoys`.

This final chapter follows on from the preview of upcoming class features in Chapter 18 with a preview of what else is coming next (features at Stage 3 as of this writing). But what's coming next is ever-changing. You can keep up to date using the resources you learned about in Chapter 1, including of course this book's website, `https://thenewtoys.dev`.

The changes and additions run the gamut from relatively minor (but handy) syntax tweaks like numeric separators to significant additions like top-level `await`.

Most in-progress features are covered here, though some have already been covered:

➤ A couple of upcoming promise utility features were covered in Chapter 8.

➤ `import.meta` was covered in Chapter 13.

➤ You just learned about public and private class fields and private methods and accessors (including static ones) in Chapter 18.

Some readers may be surprised not to see Decorators[1] covered in this chapter. Decorators have been in the proposals process for some time, and one version or another of the proposal is in wide use via transpilers and TypeScript. But the proposal is still at Stage 2 and has gone through three major revisions, with the initial version of the third ("Static Decorators") still likely to change markedly before progressing, so unfortunately it's too much of a moving target to cover in this chapter.

> **STAGE 3 PROPOSALS MAY CHANGE**
>
> Remember that Stage 3 features may change before they're completed, and in rare cases may never be completed. In this chapter you'll learn about the proposals as they were in early 2020, but they can change afterward. Refer to each proposal's GitHub repo (and `https://thenewtoys.dev`) for up-to-date information.

TOP-LEVEL AWAIT

The Top-Level Await proposal,[2] at Stage 3 in early 2020, will make it possible to use `await` at the top level of a module. Let's take a look.

Overview and Use Cases

You may remember from Chapter 9 that in an `async` function you can use `await` to wait for a promise to settle before continuing with the logic of the function. The Top-Level Await proposal brings that to modules, allowing top-level module code to wait for a promise to settle before the top-level module logic continues.

Let's briefly recap how `await` works in an `async` function. Consider this `fetchJSON` function:

```
function fetchJSON(url, options) {
    const response = await fetch(url, options);
    if (!response.ok) {
        throw new Error("HTTP error " + response.status);
    }
    return response.json();
}
```

When you call `fetchJSON`, the code in the function runs synchronously up to and including the call to `fetch`, which returns a promise. `fetchJSON` awaits the promise, which suspends execution of

---

[1] `https://github.com/tc39/proposal-decorators`
[2] `https://github.com/tc39/proposal-top-level-await`

`fetchJSON`, returning a new promise. Once the promise from `fetch` is settled, the logic in `fetchJSON` continues, eventually settling the promise it returned.

It works essentially the same way with top-level `await` in modules: when the module body is evaluated, it runs until it `awaits` a promise. Then its execution is suspended, resuming later when that promise settles. Roughly, evaluating the module returns a promise of its exports, rather than returning them directly, just like an `async` function returns a promise of its return value rather than returning its value directly.

With `fetchJSON`, any code that wants to use the data it returns has to wait for the promise from `fetchJSON` to settle. Conceptually, that's exactly what happens with top-level `await` in modules as well: anything that wants to use the module's exports has to wait for the module's promise to settle. In the case of modules, the thing waiting for the module's promise isn't your code (not directly, anyway), it's the module loader in your host environment (for instance, the browser or Node.js). The module loader waits for a module's promise to settle before finishing loading any modules that depend on it.

When would you need top-level `await`?

The generic answer is: any time your module's exports aren't useful until something the module loads asynchronously is available. But let's look at a couple of specifics.

If your module imports from a dynamically loaded module (a module you load by "calling" `import()`, which you learned about in Chapter 13), and if you need the things you import from it before your exports can be used, you might `await` the promise from `import()`. The proposal gives a good example of this: loading localization information based on the current browser language. Here's that example (slightly modified):

```
const strings = await import(`./i18n/${navigator.language}.js`);
```

Assume for that example that this appears in a module that exports a translation function that is expected to do its work synchronously with the data in `strings`. That function can't be used until it has the strings, so it makes sense to prevent the module from being fully loaded until it has them.

The promise the module waits for doesn't have to be an `import()`, though; it can be any promise. For instance, if the strings came from a database in a Node.js module:

```
const strings = await getStringsFromDatabase(languageToUse);
```

Another use case is using `import()` with `await` to use a fallback module if the primary module isn't available. Continuing our previous example, the module importing the strings could fall back to a default language if a localization file for `navigator.language` isn't available:

```
const strings = await
    import(`./i18n/${navigator.language}.js`)
    .catch(() => import(`./i18n/${defaultLanguage}.js`));
```

or

```
let strings;
try {
    strings = await import(`./i18n/${navigator.language}.js`);
} catch {
    strings = await import(`./i18n/${defaultLanguage}.js`);
}
```

Using `await` at the top level of a module has two important ramifications:

➤ It delays the evaluation of any modules that depend on it until the promise it's awaiting is settled.

➤ If the promise it's awaiting rejects and your code doesn't handle that rejection, it's just like having an uncaught synchronous error in your module's top-level code—your module load fails, and so does the module load of any module depending on it.

For those reasons, it's important only to use top-level `await` when your module's exports can't be used until the promise you're awaiting settles.

Example

Let's look at an example of top-level `await`. Listing 19-1 has an entry point module (`main.js`) that imports from `mod1` (`mod1.js`, Listing 19-2), `mod2` (`mod2.js`, Listing 19-3) and `mod3` (`mod3.js`, Listing 19-4). `mod2` uses top-level `await`.

LISTING 19-1: Top-level await example—main.js

```
import { one   } from "./mod1.js";
import { two   } from "./mod2.js";
import { three } from "./mod3.js";

console.log("main evaluation - begin");

console.log(one, two, three);

console.log("main evaluation - end");
```

LISTING 19-2: Top-level await example—mod1.js

```
console.log("mod1 evaluation - begin");
export const one = "one";
console.log("mod1 evaluation - end");
```

LISTING 19-3: Top-level await example—mod2.js

```
console.log("mod2 evaluation - begin");

// Artificial delay function
function delay(ms, value) {
    return new Promise(resolve => setTimeout(() => {
        resolve(value);
    }, ms));
}
```

```
// export const two = "two";                         // Not using top-level `await`
export const two = await delay(10, "two"); // Using top-level `await`

console.log("mod2 evaluation - end");
```

LISTING 19-4: Top-level await example—mod3.js

```
console.log("mod3 evaluation - begin");
export const three = "three";
console.log("mod3 evaluation - end");
```

When I first wrote this chapter, neither Node.js nor any browser had top-level `await` support and to run this example you had to install the V8 engine on its own (see the inset). But as we were going to press, Node.js v14 came out with support behind a `--harmony-top-level-await` flag, so you can use that (it might not even be behind a flag anymore by the time you're reading this). Knowing how to install and use V8 directly is sometimes still useful, though, so if you're interested, see the inset.

INSTALLING V8

If you can't find a browser or version of Node.js that has a cutting-edge feature you want to try out that you know has just been supported in V8, you can install V8 and use it directly. One easy way to install V8 is to use the "JavaScript (engine) Version Updater" tool (`jsvu`).[3] To install `jsvu`, refer to the instructions on the project's page. As of early 2020 they are:

1. Open a shell (command prompt/terminal window).
2. Use `npm install jsvu -g` to install `jsvu`.
3. Update your PATH to include the directory where `jsvu` puts executables for the JavaScript engines:

   ➤ On Windows: the directory is `%USERPROFILE%\.jsvu`. Use the Windows UI to update the PATH to include that directory. On Windows 10 you do that by clicking the Search icon, typing "environment," and picking **Edit the system environment variables** from the local search results. In the resulting **System Properties** dialog box, click the **Environment Variables . . .** button. In the **System variables** box, double-click PATH. Click the **New** button to add a new entry to the list: `%USERPROFILE%\.jsvu`

   ➤ On *nix: the directory is `${HOME}/.jsvu`. Add it to your path by adding the following line to your shell's initialization script (for instance, `~/.bashrc`):
   `export PATH="${HOME}/.jsvu:${PATH}"`

4. If you have a shell open, close it and open a new one so it picks up the new PATH.

---
[3] https://github.com/GoogleChromeLabs/jsvu

Now you can install V8 via `jsvu`:

1. In a shell, run `jsvu --engines=v8`.
2. Since this is the first time you've run it, it will have you confirm your operating system; just press Enter (assuming it's auto-detected your system correctly).
3. If you're using Windows: Once V8 is installed, there should be a `v8.cmd` file in the `.jsvu` directory. Type `dir %USERPROFILE%\.jsvu\v8.cmd` to check; it should list `v8.cmd`. But as of early 2020, there's a Windows-specific issue with `jsvu` that prevents it creating the `v8.cmd` file. If it's not there, copy it from the chapter downloads or create it with these contents:

```
@echo off
"%USERPROFILE%\.jsvu\engines\v8\v8"
--snapshot_blob="%USERPROFILE%\.jsvu\engines\v8\snapshot_blob.bin" %*
```

4. Note that there are just two lines; the second line starting with `"%USERPROFILE%` is fairly long and word wraps in this inset's text.

Run the `main.js` file from the example. If you're using V8 directly (see the inset), run

```
v8 --module --harmony-top-level-await main.js
```

If you're using Node.js v14 or later, make sure you have a `package.json` with `"type": "module"` as you learned in Chapter 13 (there's one in the chapter downloads), and run

```
node main.js
```

or if your version needs the flag:

```
node --harmony-top-level-await main.js
```

If you're using a browser that has top-level `await` (perhaps behind a flag, or perhaps not), include `main.js` with a `script type="module"` tag in an HTML file and run it.

The console output is:

```
mod1 evaluation - begin
mod1 evaluation - end
mod2 evaluation - begin
mod3 evaluation - begin
mod3 evaluation - end
mod2 evaluation - end
main evaluation - begin
one two three
main evaluation - end
```

The module loader in the host environment fetches and parses the modules, instantiates them (see Chapter 13) and builds the dependency tree, then starts to evaluate them. If none of the modules used `await`, since the tree is just `main.js` importing from the three modules, they'd each be evaluated in the order they appear in `main.js`'s imports. But looking at the output, you can see that `mod2` *starts* being evaluated but then `mod3` is evaluated before `mod2` finishes. Here's what happens:

➤ The module loader evaluates the top-level code in `mod1` (the first module `main.js` imports from); since it doesn't use `await`, it runs all the way through:

```
mod1 evaluation - begin
mod1 evaluation - end
```

➤ The loader *starts* evaluating the top-level code for mod2:

```
mod2 evaluation - begin
```

➤ When the code reaches the await, it gets suspended, waiting for the promise to settle.

➤ In the meantime, since mod3 doesn't depend on mod2, the loader evaluates it; mod3 doesn't have any await, so it runs all the way through:

```
mod3 evaluation - begin
mod3 evaluation - end
```

➤ When the promise mod2 is awaiting settles, evaluation of mod2 continues; since that was its only await, it runs to the end:

```
mod2 evaluation - end
```

➤ Since all of its dependencies are now evaluated, the loader evaluates main.js, which uses the things it imported from the modules:

```
main evaluation - begin
one two three
main evaluation - end
```

Let's compare that with what would happen if mod2 didn't use top-level await. Open mod2.js in an editor and find these two lines:

```
// export const two = "two";                // Not using top-level `await`
export const two = await delay(10, "two"); // Using top-level `await`
```

Move the comment marker from the beginning of the first line to the beginning of the second, so you have:

```
export const two = "two";                  // Not using top-level `await`
// export const two = await delay(10, "two"); // Using top-level `await`
```

Now the module doesn't use top-level await. Run main.js again. This time, the console output is:

```
mod1 evaluation - begin
mod1 evaluation - end
mod2 evaluation - begin
mod2 evaluation - end
mod3 evaluation - begin
mod3 evaluation - end
main evaluation - begin
one two three
main evaluation - end
```

Note how mod2 was evaluated all the way through before mod3 started being evaluated, since mod2 no longer awaits a promise.

In the original code, note how mod1 was able to export a const that gets its value from something being awaited:

```
export const two = await delay(10, "two"); // Using top-level `await`
```

In that example, it does it all in one statement with an `export` declaration on it, but it doesn't have to be together like that. For instance, when using dynamic `import()`, the promise gets fulfilled with the module namespace object of the module that was loaded. Suppose your module needs to use the `example` function from the dynamic module locally, and also needs to re-export the `value` export of the dynamic module. It could do so like this:

```
const { example, value } = await import("./dynamic.js");
export { value };
example("some", "arguments");
```

Or of course, it could just keep a reference to the namespace object, although often it's best to pick out the parts you need to enable tree shaking (Chapter 13):

```
const dynamic = await import("./dynamic.js");
export const { value } = dynamic;
dynamic.example("some", "arguments");
```

Error Handling

In the "Overview and Use Cases" section earlier, you might have wondered about the fact that the code didn't handle rejection of all of the promises. For instance, one of the "fallback" examples was this:

```
let strings;
try {
    strings = await import(`./i18n/${navigator.language}.js`);
} catch {
    strings = await import(`./i18n/${defaultLanguage}.js`);
}
```

That example has code to handle rejection of the promise from the first `import()`, but nothing to handle rejection of the promise from the second. That might seem like a red flag, if you're remembering the fundamental promise rule from Chapter 8:

Either handle errors, or propagate the promise chain to your caller.

Does the example code break that rule?

No, but it was reasonable to wonder if it did. It doesn't for the same reason similar code in an `async` function doesn't break the rule: the module's promise is rejected if the promise being `await`ed is rejected, and the module's promise is returned to the "caller" (in this case, the module loader), so the "propagate the promise chain to your caller" rule is implicitly followed. Just like an `async` function always returns a promise and any uncaught errors in the function reject that promise, asynchronous modules always return a promise (to the module loader) and any uncaught errors reject that promise. The loader handles it by reporting the error through whatever host-defined mechanism there is for doing that (often a console message of some kind) and marking the module as failed (which makes all modules that depend on it fail to load).

With the earlier example, what if neither the module for the `navigator.language` nor the module for `defaultLanguage` loads? The module loader fails to load the module that code is in (and any modules depending on it), reporting that in the console (or similar).

Just like with `async` functions, you don't have to propagate the chain to the caller explicitly. It's implicit.

WEAKREFS AND CLEANUP CALLBACKS

In this section you'll learn about the WeakRefs proposal,[4] which brings *weak references* and *cleanup callbacks* (also called *finalizers*) to JavaScript. It's at Stage 3 as of early 2020 and is being actively added to JavaScript engines.

(A brief side note: If you read the developer documentation from the proposal or other documentation based on it, you might notice strong similarities between the examples and such in this section and the ones in that documentation. That's because I was very slightly involved in the proposal: I wrote the developer documentation for it.)

> ### WEAKREFS AND CLEANUP CALLBACKS ARE ADVANCED FEATURES
>
> As the proposal says, correct use of WeakRefs and cleanup callbacks takes careful thought, and they are best avoided if possible. Garbage collection is complicated and can seem to occur at odd times. Use them with care!

WeakRefs

Normally, when you have a reference to an object, that object will be retained in memory until and unless you release your reference to it (if there aren't any others). That's true whether you have a direct reference or an indirect one via some intermediary object or objects. That's a normal object reference, also called a *strong reference*.

Using a WeakRef, you can have a *weak reference* to an object instead. A weak reference doesn't prevent the object from being *garbage collected* (aka *reclaimed*) if the JavaScript engine's garbage collector decides to reclaim the object's memory.

You create a WeakRef with the `WeakRef` constructor, passing in the object you want a weak reference to (its *target*, also known as a *referent*):

```
const ref = new WeakRef({"some": "object"});
```

If you need to use the object, you can get a strong reference from the WeakRef using its `deref` ("dereference") method:

```
let obj = ref.deref();
if (obj) {
    // ...use `obj`...
}
```

(And then at some point you let `obj` go out of scope or you assign `undefined` or `null` to it, etc., so the strong reference is released.)

The `deref` method returns the target object held by the WeakRef, or `undefined` if the target has been reclaimed.

---

[4] https://github.com/tc39/proposal-weakrefs

Why would you want to have a reference to an object that might disappear if the garbage collector decides to reclaim its memory? One of the major use cases is caching. Suppose your page/app has some data resources that are expensive to retrieve from storage (and won't be cached by your host environment), and the specific resources it needs varies across the lifetime of the page/app. When you get a resource the first time, you could save it in a cache using a weak reference, so that if the page needs it again later, it may be able to avoid the expensive retrieval if the resource hasn't been reclaimed in the meantime. (A real-world cache would probably hold the most frequently or recent used entries strongly and use weak references for the rest.)

Another use case is detecting resource leaks through a combination of WeakRefs and cleanup callbacks; you'll learn about that in the next section.

Let's look at a basic example using WeakRef. See Listing 19-5. It creates an ArrayBuffer occupying 100 million bytes and keeps a weak reference to it. Then it periodically allocates other ArrayBuffer instances, keeping strong references to them, and checks to see if the *weakly held* ArrayBuffer (the one held via the WeakRef) has been reclaimed. Eventually, the JavaScript engine's garbage collector is likely to decide to reclaim the large initial ArrayBuffer that's only weakly held.

LISTING 19-5: WeakRef example—weakref-example.js

```javascript
const firstSize = 100000000;
console.log(`main:    Allocating ${firstSize} bytes of data to hold weakly...`);
let data = new ArrayBuffer(firstSize);
let ref = new WeakRef(data);
data = null; // Releases the strong reference, leaving us with only the weak ref
let moreData = [];
let counter = 0;
let size = 50000;

setTimeout(tick, 10);

function tick() {
    ++counter;
    if (size < 100000000) {
        size *= 10;
    }
    console.log();
    console.log(`tick(${counter}): Allocating ${size} bytes more data...`);
    moreData.push(new ArrayBuffer(size));
    console.log(`tick(${counter}): Getting the weakly held data...`);
    const data = ref.deref();
    if (data) {
        console.log(`tick(${counter}): weakly held data still in memory.`);
        // This `if` is just a sanity check to avoid looping forever if the weakly
        // held data is never reclaimed.
        if (counter < 100) {
            setTimeout(tick, 10);
        } else {
```

```
                     console.log(`tick(${counter}): Giving up`);
                }
          } else {
                console.log(`tick(${counter}): weakly held data was garbage collected.`);
          }
     }
}
```

Node.js v14 has support for WeakRefs behind a flag (it may not be behind a flag by the time you read this) and they're supported in the nightly version of Firefox as of early 2020. To run the example in Node.js v14:

```
node --harmony-weak-refs weakref-example.js
```

Or if you have V8 installed on its own (see the "Installing V8" inset in the "Top-Level await" section earlier in this chapter), you can run it in V8:

```
v8 --harmony-weak-refs weakref-example.js
```

The output will vary depending on your system, but it will look something like this:

```
main:    Allocating 100000000 bytes of data to hold weakly...

tick(1): Allocating 500000 bytes more data...
tick(1): Getting the weakly held data...
tick(1): weakly held data still in memory.

tick(2): Allocating 5000000 bytes more data...
tick(2): Getting the weakly held data...
tick(2): weakly held data still in memory.

tick(3): Allocating 50000000 bytes more data...
tick(3): Getting the weakly held data...
tick(3): weakly held data still in memory.

tick(4): Allocating 500000000 bytes more data...
tick(4): Getting the weakly held data...
tick(4): weakly held data still in memory.

tick(5): Allocating 500000000 bytes more data...
tick(5): Getting the weakly held data...
tick(5): weakly held data was garbage collected.
```

In that output, you can see that between the fourth and fifth calls to tick, V8 reclaimed the weakly held buffer. (It may run much longer than this example did; it varies a fair bit.)

Here are some closing notes on WeakRefs:

➤   If your code has just created a WeakRef for a target object, or has gotten a target object from a WeakRef's deref method, that target object will not be reclaimed until the end of the current JavaScript job[5] (including any promise reaction jobs that run at the end of a script job). That is, you can only "see" an object get reclaimed between turns of the event loop. This is primarily to avoid making the behavior of any given JavaScript engine's garbage collector apparent in code—because if it were, people would write code relying on that

---

[5] You may remember from Chapter 8 that a job is a unit of work that the thread will run from beginning to end without running anything else, and that there are script jobs (such as the initial execution of a script, a timer callback, an event callback) and promise jobs (callbacks to promise fulfillment, rejection, and finally handlers).

behavior, which would break when the garbage collector's behavior changed. (Garbage collection is a hard problem; JavaScript engine implementers are constantly refining and improving how it works.) If you were wondering why the earlier example used `setTimeout`, it's because of this aspect of WeakRefs. If the example just called `tick` in a loop, the weakly-held `ArrayBuffer` would never be reclaimed.

➤ If multiple WeakRefs have the same target, they're consistent with one another. The result of calling `deref` on one of them will match the result of calling `deref` on another of them (in the same job), you won't get the target object from one of them but `undefined` from another.

➤ If the target of a WeakRef is also in a `FinalizationRegistry` (which you'll learn about in a bit), the WeakRef's target is cleared *before* or at the same time any cleanup callback associated with the registry is called.

➤ You cannot change the target of a WeakRef. It will always only ever be the original target object, or `undefined` when that target has been reclaimed.

➤ A WeakRef might never return `undefined` from `deref`, even if nothing strongly holds the target, because the garbage collector may never decide to reclaim the object.

Cleanup Callbacks

The WeakRefs proposal also provides *cleanup callbacks*, also known as *finalizers*.

A cleanup callback is a function that the garbage collector may call when an object has been reclaimed. Unlike the finalizers, destructors, and similar in some other languages, in JavaScript the cleanup callback does not receive a reference to the object that is being or was reclaimed. In fact, as far as your code can tell, the object has *already* been reclaimed before your cleanup callback is called (and it's likely that it actually has been, but that's a detail for the garbage collector implementation). Designing it this way avoids the problem some other environments have had with complexities around what happens when an object that was unreachable (your code has no way to access it) becomes reachable again (because the finalizer receives a reference to the object and stores it somewhere). JavaScript's approach (not providing the object to cleanup callbacks) makes it easier to reason about cleanup callbacks, and makes things more flexible for engine implementers.

Why would you want a cleanup callback?

One use case is releasing other objects associated with the reclaimed object. For example, if you have a cache of WeakRefs weakly holding objects, and one of those objects is reclaimed, the cache still has its entry for that object in memory—the key and the WeakRef at a minimum, perhaps some other information. You can use a cleanup callback to release that cache entry when the target object related to it is reclaimed. This use case isn't limited to WeakRefs, though; there are other times you might have objects you don't need any more if another object is reclaimed, such as a Wasm object you could release if a corresponding JavaScript object is garbage collected, or a cross-worker proxy, where you have a proxy in one thread (typically the main one) for an object in a worker thread. If the proxy is garbage collected, the worker object can be released.

Another use case is detecting and reporting resource leaks. Suppose you have a class that represents an open file or a database connection or similar. Developers using the class are supposed to call its `close` method when done with it, which releases the file descriptor or closes the database connection, etc. If a user doesn't call `close` and just releases the object, your class won't release the file descriptor or the underlying database connection. In a long-running program, that could eventually cause a problem when the process runs out of file descriptors or the database reaches its limit of concurrent connections from the same client. You can use a cleanup callback to provide a warning message to the developer that they've failed to call `close`. The cleanup callback may *also* be able to release the file descriptor or database connection, but its primary purpose would be alerting the developer to their mistake so they can correct their code by making it call `close`.

We'll come back to both of those use cases in a moment, including why you wouldn't just use the cleanup callback to release the external resources in that second example. For now, let's look at how you actually use cleanup callbacks.

To request cleanup callbacks, you create a *finalization registry* via the `FinalizationRegistry` constructor, passing in the function you want called:

```
const registry = new FinalizationRegistry(heldValue => {
    // ....do your cleanup here...
});
```

Then you register objects with the registry to get callbacks for them, using its `register` method. For each target object, you pass in the object and a *held value* for it (`"some value"` in this example), like this:

```
registry.register(theObject, "some value");
```

The `register` method takes three arguments:

➤   `target`: The object you want a finalization callback for. The registry does not hold a strong reference to the object, as that would prevent it from being garbage collected.

➤   `heldValue`: A value the registry will hold in order to provide it to your cleanup callback if the target object is reclaimed. This can be a primitive or an object. If you don't supply any, `undefined` is used.

➤   `unregisterToken`: (Not shown in the preceding example.) An optional object to use later to unregister the target if you no longer need a cleanup callback for it. More on this in a bit.

Once you've registered the target object, if it's reclaimed, your cleanup callback may be called at some point in the future with the held value you provided for it. That's where you do your cleanup, perhaps using information from the held value. The held value (also called a "memo") can be any value you like, a primitive or an object, even `undefined`. If the held value is an object, the registry keeps a *strong* reference to it (so it can pass it to your cleanup callback later), meaning the held value will not be reclaimed unless the target object is reclaimed (which removes the entry for it from the registry) or you unregister the target object.

If you might want to unregister an object later, you pass a third argument to `register`, the *unregistration token* mentioned earlier. It's common to use the object itself as the unregister token, which is just fine. When you no longer need a cleanup callback for the object, call `unregister` with the unregistration token. Here's an example using the target object itself:

```
registry.register(theObject, "some value", theObject);
// ...some time later, if you don't care about `theObject` anymore...
registry.unregister(theObject);
```

It doesn't have to be the target object, though; it can be a different one:

```
registry.register(theObject, "some value", tokenObject);
// ...some time later, if you don't care about `theObject` anymore...
registry.unregister(tokenObject);
```

The registry keeps only a weak reference to the unregistration token, not least because it may be the target object itself.

Let's look at an example from the proposal (slightly modified), a hypothetical `FileStream` class:

```
class FileStream {
    static #cleanUp(fileName) {
        console.error(`File leaked: ${fileName}!`);
    }

    static #finalizationGroup = new FinalizationRegistry(FileStream.#cleanUp);

    #file;

    constructor(fileName) {
        const file = this.#file = File.open(fileName);
        FileStream.#finalizationGroup.register(this, fileName, this);
        // ...eagerly trigger async read of file contents...
    }

    close() {
        FileStream.#finalizationGroup.unregister(this);
        File.close(this.#file);
        // ...other cleanup...
    }

    async *[Symbol.iterator]() {
        // ...yield data from file...
    }
}
```

You can see all the parts at work there: creating the `FinalizationRegistry`, adding objects to it, responding to cleanup callbacks, and unregistering objects from the registry when they're explicitly closed.

This is an example of the second use case you learned about earlier. If the user of the `FileStream` class doesn't call `close`, the underlying `File` object is never closed, potentially resulting in a leaked file descriptor. So the cleanup callback logs the filename to warn the developer it was never closed, so they can fix their code.

Looking at that, you may be thinking "Why wouldn't you just always use the cleanup callback to release those resources? Why have a `close` method at all?"

The answer is: because you may never receive a cleanup call, and if you do, it may be much later than you expect. Earlier I said ". . . a function that the garbage collector *may* call when an object has been reclaimed . . ." not ". . . a function that the garbage collector *will* call when an object has been reclaimed . . ." There is no guarantee that the garbage collector will call a cleanup callback in any given implementation. From the proposal:

The proposed specification allows conforming implementations to skip calling finalization callbacks for any reason or no reason.

That means you can't use cleanup callbacks to manage external resources. In terms of that second use case (and the `FileStream` example), your file or database API needs that `close` method, and developers need to call it. The reason for having a cleanup callback in that API is so that if a developer is working on a platform with cleanup callbacks and releases an object from your API without calling `close`, your API can warn them they didn't call `close`. Their code may run later on a platform where cleanup callbacks aren't called.

However, signs are good that major JavaScript engines will call cleanup callbacks in normal circumstances. There are a couple of circumstances where they're unlikely to, though, even if they do normally:

➤ If the JavaScript environment is being torn down (for instance, closing a window or tab in a browser). In most cases this would make any cleanup your code did redundant.

➤ If the `FinalizationRegistry` object the callback is associated with is released by your code (you no longer have a reference to it). If you've released your reference to the registry, it makes little sense to keep it in memory and performing callbacks. If you want them, don't release the registry.

But if cleanup callbacks may not happen, what about caches using WeakRefs? If you can't rely on cleanup callbacks to remove entries for reclaimed objects, should you do some kind of incremental scan for entries whose `deref` returns `undefined`?

Guidance from the people behind the proposal is no, don't do that. It complicates the code unnecessarily for a relatively small gain (freeing up a bit more memory), and for an active cache you're likely to discover and replace those entries organically anyway (when the resource for them is requested again).

Let's see cleanup callbacks in action. See Listing 19-6.

LISTING 19-6: Cleanup callback example—cleanup-callback-example.js

```
let stop = false;
const registry = new FinalizationRegistry(heldValue => {
    console.log(`Object for '${heldValue}' has been reclaimed`);
    stop = true;
});
const firstSize = 100000000;
console.log(`main:    Allocating ${firstSize} bytes of data to hold weakly...`);
let data = new ArrayBuffer(firstSize);
registry.register(data, "data", data);
data = null; // Releases the reference
let moreData = [];
```

```
let counter = 0;
let size = 50000;

setTimeout(tick, 10);

function tick() {
    if (stop) {
        return;
    }
    ++counter;
    if (size < 100000000) {
        size *= 10;
    }
    console.log();
    console.log(`tick(${counter}): Allocating ${size} bytes more data...`);
    moreData.push(new ArrayBuffer(size));
    // This `if` is just a sanity check to avoid looping forever if the weakly held
    // data is never reclaimed or the host never calls the cleanup callback.
    if (counter < 100) {
        setTimeout(tick, 10);
    }
}
```

Node.js v14 and V8 itself both have WeakRefs behind a flag, but depending on which version of them you have, they may have the older semantics rather than the new ones, the proposal changed a bit late in the process. You can run the example like this:

```
# V8:
v8 --harmony-weak-refs cleanup-callback-example.js
# Node:
node --harmony-weak-refs cleanup-callback-example.js
```

If you get an error saying `FinalizationRegistry` is not defined, or if you see "Object for '[object FinalizationRegistry Cleanup Iterator]' has been reclaimed" instead of "Object for 'data' has been reclaimed" when the callback is called, run the code from `cleanup-callback-example-older-semantics.js` instead.

When you run the code, it outputs something similar to:

```
main:    Allocating 100000000 bytes of data to hold weakly...

tick(1): Allocating 500000 bytes more data...

tick(2): Allocating 5000000 bytes more data...

tick(3): Allocating 50000000 bytes more data...

tick(4): Allocating 500000000 bytes more data...
Finalizer called
Object for 'data' has been reclaimed
```

That output shows that the object was garbage collected after the fourth timer call.

Finally, `FinalizationRegistry` objects have an optional method, `cleanupSome`, that can be called to trigger callbacks for an implementation-chosen number of objects in the registry that have been reclaimed but whose callbacks have not yet been called:

```
registry.cleanupSome?.();
```

Normally, you don't call this function. Leave it to the JavaScript engine's garbage collector to do the cleanup as appropriate. This function primarily exists to support long-running code which doesn't yield to the event loop, which is more likely to come up in WebAssembly than ordinary JavaScript code.

You can give `cleanupSome` a different callback from the one registered on the registry object to override it just for these cleanup callbacks:

```
registry.cleanupSome?.(heldValue => {
    // ...
});
```

Even if there are pending callbacks, the number triggered by a call to `cleanupSome` is implementation-defined. An implementation might not do any of them, might do all pending ones, or somewhere in between.

Note that the preceding examples use the optional chaining syntax you learned about in Chapter 17, so that if an implementation doesn't define `cleanupSome`, the call is skipped without an error.

REGEXP MATCH INDICES

The match array returned by `RegExp.prototype.exec` has an `index` property giving the index in the string where the match occurred, but doesn't say where the capture groups occurred. The RegExp Match Indices proposal[6] changes that by adding an `indices` property. The `indices` property contains an array of `[start, end]` arrays. The first entry is for the overall match; the subsequent ones are for the capture groups.

Here's an example:

```
const rex = /(\w+) (\d+)/;
const str = "==> Testing 123";
const match = rex.exec(str);
for (const [start, end] of match.indices) {
    console.log(`[${start}, ${end}]: "${str.substring(start, end)}"`);
}
```

That regular expression searches for a series of "word" characters followed by a space and a series of digits. Both the word and the digits are captured. On an implementation with match indices, the output of that example is:

```
[4, 15]: "Testing 123"
[4, 11]: "Testing"
[12, 15]: "123"
```

---

[6] https://github.com/tc39/proposal-regexp-match-indices

The new feature supports named capture groups, too. You may remember from Chapter 15 that if you have named capture groups in the expression, the `match` array will have an object property called `groups` with the contents of the named groups. This proposal does the same by providing the indices of the group contents on `match.indices.groups`:

```
const rex = /(?<word>\w+) (?<num>\d+)/;
const str = "==> Testing 123";
const match = rex.exec(str);
for (const key of Object.keys(match.groups)) {
    const [start, end] = match.indices.groups[key];
    console.log(
        `Group "${key}" - [${start}, ${end}]: "${str.substring(start, end)}"`
    );
}
```

That example gives names to the two capture groups from the previous example, and uses `match.groups` and `match.indices.groups` to get information about those named groups. The output is:

```
Group "word" - [4, 11]: "Testing"
Group "num" - [12, 15]: "123"
```

With named capture groups and indices arrays, the match array has become quite a rich object. Here's the complete `match` array (including its non-array properties) for the preceding example in pseudo-JSON format ("pseudo" because it uses square brackets indicating arrays, but also has `name: value` pairs for the array's additional non-array properties):

```
[
    "Testing 123",
    "Testing",
    "123",
    index: 4,
    input: "==> Testing 123",
    "groups": {
        word: "Testing",
        num: "123"
    },
    "indices": [
        [4, 15],
        [4, 11],
        [12, 15],
        "groups": {
            "word": [4, 11],
            "num": [12, 15]
        }
    ]
]
```

STRING.PROTOTYPE.REPLACEALL

For years, people new to the JavaScript `String.prototype.replace` method have been making the same mistake: not realizing that it only replaces the *first* occurrence if you pass it a string or non-global regular expression. For example:

```
console.log("a a a".replace("a", "b")); // "b a a", not "b b b"
```

To replace all occurrences, you have to pass in a regular expression with the global flag:

```
console.log("a a a".replace(/a/g, "b")); // "b b b"
```

That's not too bad when the text you want to change is text you're typing literally, but if it's from user input or similar, you have to escape characters that have special meaning in regular expressions (and there's no built-in function for that, despite an effort some years back to add one).

The `replaceAll` proposal[7] makes it much easier, by replacing all occurrences:

```
console.log("a a a".replaceAll("a", "b")); // "b b b"
```

The `replaceAll` method behaves identically to `replace` except in two ways:

➤ If you pass a string to it as the search argument, it replaces all occurrences instead of just the first—which is the whole point of `replaceAll`!

➤ If you pass a regular expression *without* the global flag, it throws an error. This is to avoid confusion. Does the lack of a global flag mean "*don't* replace all?" Or is the flag just ignored? The answer as of this proposal is to throw an error.

The `replaceAll` and `replace` methods do exactly the same thing if you pass them a regular expression with the global flag.

ATOMICS ASYNCWAIT

In Chapter 16 you learned about shared memory and the `Atomics` object, including its `wait` method. Briefly recapping, it's possible to use `Atomics.wait` to synchronously wait on a location in a shared memory until "notified" (via `Atomics.notify`) by another thread. You can use `Atomics.wait` in worker threads, but typically not in the main thread (for instance, the main browser thread, or Node.js's main thread), since those must be non-blocking.

The Stage 3 `Atomics.asyncWait` proposal[8] makes it possible to wait for a notification on a shared memory location without blocking, by using a promise. When you call `Atomics.asyncWait`, instead of getting a string return value as with `Atomics.wait`, you get a promise that will be fulfilled with a string instead. The possible fulfillment strings are the same as the strings returned by `Atomics.wait`:

➤ `"ok"` if the thread was "suspended" and subsequently resumed (rather than timing out)

---

[7] https://github.com/tc39/proposal-string-replaceall
[8] https://github.com/tc39/proposal-atomics-wait-async

➤ `"timed-out"` if the thread was "suspended," and resumed because the timeout was reached

➤ `"not-equal"` if the thread wasn't "suspended" because the value in the array wasn't equal to the given value

"Suspended" is in quotes in that list because the main thread is never literally suspended as worker threads are by `Atomics.wait`, it's just that the promise remained unsettled for some period of time.

The promise from `asyncWait` is never rejected, it's always fulfilled with one of the three strings listed.

For example, if you had a `SharedArrayBuffer` called `sharedArray`, you could have the main thread wait for a notification at the index `index` like this:

```
Atomics.asyncWait(sharedArray, index, 42, 30000)
.then(result => {
    // ...here, `result` will be "ok", "timed-out", or "not-equal"...
});
```

If the value at `sharedMemory[index]` isn't `42` as of when the JavaScript engine checks it, the fulfillment callback will see the string `"not-equal"`. Otherwise, the engine will wait for a notification before fulfilling the promise. If there's no notification before the timeout (30000 milliseconds in this example), it will fulfill the promise with the string `"timed-out"`. If it gets a notification, it fulfills the promise with the string `"ok"`.

As usual with shared memory and threads, Here There Be Dragons. See Chapter 16 for details of the dangers and pitfalls.

VARIOUS SYNTAX TWEAKS

In this section, you'll learn about some minor syntax tweaks that are being done by various proposals.

Numeric Separators

Sometimes, a numeric literal can be a bit hard to read:

```
const x = 10000000;
```

Quick, is that 100 thousand? A million? 10 million? 100 million?

When writing numbers for people to read, we tend to group the digits in some way. For instance, in some cultures they're put in groups of three with commas in between: 10,000,000.

The numeric separators proposal[9] (currently at Stage 3) allows underscores as separators in numeric literals:

```
const x = 10_000_000;
```

That makes it much easier to see that the number is 10 million.

You can use numeric separators in decimal literals (both in the whole number part and the fractional part), binary literals, hexadecimal literals, and modern octal literals.

---

[9] `https://github.com/tc39/proposal-numeric-separator`

You're allowed to put separators anywhere you want *except*:

➤ Immediately after the number base prefix:

Invalid: `0x_AAAA_BBBB`

Valid: `0xAAAA_BBBB`

➤ Immediately next to a decimal point:

Invalid: `12_345_.733_444`

Invalid: `12_345._733_444`

Valid: `12_345.733_444`

➤ At the end of the number, after the last digit:

Invalid: `12_345_`

Valid: `12_345`

➤ Next to another separator:

Invalid: `10__123_456`

Valid: `10_123_456`

You also can't *start* a number with an underscore, like this: `_1234`. That's an identifier, not a number.

Hashbang Support

It's common for command-line interface hosts (like Node.js) to allow a JavaScript file to start with a "hashbang" like this:

```
#!/home/tjc/bin/node/bin/node
console.log("Hello from Node.js command line script");
```

Technically, that was invalid syntax per the specification. So the specification is being updated[10] to allow it (Stage 3 at present).

LEGACY DEPRECATED REGEXP FEATURES

A Stage 3 proposal[11] is standardizing, but officially deprecating, some long supported "features" of RegExp that are not in the specification. For instance, capture groups aren't only available in the match object you get from `exec`, but also as properties on the `RegExp` function itself (not the RegExp instance, the *function*) as `$1` for the first capture group, `$2` for the second, etc., through `$9`:

```
const s = "Testing a-1 b-2 c-3";
const rex = /(\w)-(\d)/g;
```

---

[10] https://github.com/tc39/proposal-hashbang
[11] https://github.com/tc39/proposal-regexp-legacy-features

```
    while (rex.exec(s)) {
        // NOT RECOMMENDED!
        console.log(`"${RegExp.$1}": "${RegExp.$2}"`);
    }
    // => "a": "1"
    // => "b": "2"
    // => "c": "3"
```

The proposal may codify another legacy feature as well, but as of early 2020 that wasn't certain.

Don't start using these static properties on `RegExp`. The reason they're being standardized is to ensure consistent behavior across implementations, in particular in relation to being able to remove them: the proposal makes it possible to remove these properties via `delete`. Consider that if your code uses capture groups, any code anywhere in the codebase can see the results of the last match done via these static properties `RegExp.$1`, etc. The proposal redefines them so security-conscious code can delete them after doing a match.

The proposal also ensures that these legacy features aren't supplied by subclasses of `RegExp`, since subclasses of `RegExp` may adjust the information they provide without considering the effect on the legacy features.

THANK YOU FOR READING!

Most of the proposals covered in this chapter are things you couldn't do before, so there isn't much in the way of new habits to call out, other than: use these new features where it seems appropriate to you, taking note of the warnings in a couple of places.

So instead of Old Habits to New, I'll say: Thank you for reading! I hope you've found this book useful. Don't forget to tune into the things that are coming down the pike as you learned in Chapter 1, and on the book's website at `https://thenewtoys.dev`. Happy coding!

APPENDIX

Fantastic Features and Where to Find Them

(With apologies to J.K. Rowling)

FEATURES IN ALPHABETICAL ORDER

NEW FUNDAMENTALS

NEW SYNTAX, KEYWORDS, OPERATORS, LOOPS, AND SIMILAR

`super`: Chapter 4

`super` outside classes: Chapter 5

template literals: Chapter 10

template tag functions / tagged template literals: Chapter 10

top-level `await`: Chapter 19

trailing commas in parameter list: Chapter 3

untagged template literals: Chapter 10

`yield`: Chapter 6

NEW LITERAL FORMS

BigInt: Chapter 17

binary integer literals: Chapter 17

numeric separators: Chapter 19

octal integer literals: Chapter 17

template literals: Chapter 10

STANDARD LIBRARY ADDITIONS AND CHANGES

`Array.from`: Chapter 11

`Array.of`: Chapter 11

`Array.prototype.copyWithin`: Chapter 11

`Array.prototype.entries`: Chapter 11

`Array.prototype.fill`: Chapter 11

`Array.prototype.find`: Chapter 11

`Array.prototype.findIndex`: Chapter 11

`Array.prototype.flat`: Chapter 11

`Array.prototype.flatMap`: Chapter 11

`Array.prototype.includes`: Chapter 11

`Array.prototype.keys`: Chapter 11

`Array.prototype.values`: Chapter 11

`ArrayBuffer`: Chapter 11

MISCELLANEOUS

INDEX

octal integer literals, 466
template literals, 5, 241–250
versus placeholders, 261
versus string concatenation, 260
Lock class, 434–455
locks, 420–422
logical OR (||) operator, 475–476, 491
lookbehind assertions, 405–408
loops
block scope, 26, 34–36
closures in, 26–28
destructuring in, 178–179
do-while, 33–34
for-in, 133
const, 36
for-of, 132–135, 142–143, 163
for-wait-of, 238
new, 548–550
while, 33–34, 134

M

map method, 88–89
concise arrow function and, 43
Maps, 5, 293–300
match method, 259
Math object, 467–468, 491
Meltdown, 419–420
memory. *See also* shared memory
shared, 5
memory alignment, 426
metadata, importing, 360
metaprogramming, dynamic, 5
methods
arrays, 264–276
catch, 192–194
class methods, 67
computed method names, 74–75
concat, 474
finally, 194–197
generator functions as, 149–150
instances
private, 507–511
returning new, 88–93
next, 136

private, 493–494, 507–510
prototype, inheriting, 83–86
prototype method, 67, 70–72
public, 493–494
sort, 41
static methods, 67, 72–73
inheriting, 86–88
private, 513
String.prototype.replace, 534
super and, 94–97
Symbol.iterator, 136, 138–140
syntax, 54, 71, 109–112, 130
then, 187, 199–201
typed arrays, 289–291
Microsoft Edge v79, 3
module scope, Node.js, 10
module specifiers, string literals, 322
module tree, 320
modules, 319–320
browsers and, 325–328
bundling, 359
default exports, 320, 324–325
exports, 320–321
anonymous functions, 325
class declarations, 325
entries, 336–337
forms, 348–349
re-exporting from another
module, 332–333
imports, 320–321
dynamic, 350–357
entries, 335–336
forms, 350
indirect binding, 338
metadata, 360
module environment object,
338–339
renaming imports, 333
side effects, 335
instances, realms and, 340–341
loading, 341–348
module environment object, 338–339
module records, 343
named exports, 320, 322–324
renaming, 331–332